Ann Carnahan
'99

IF WALLS COULD TALK

To our Friends at Edward Jones:

Thanks so much for sponsoring our 1999 Conference in St. Louis. Your support and presence has been appreciated by all.

Sincerely,

Bekki Cook

Missouri Secretary

on behalf of the National Association of Secretaries of State

6/29/99

IF WALLS COULD TALK

The Story of Missouri's First Families

by

Jean Carnahan
First Lady of the State of Missouri

MMPI, L.L.C.
Publisher
1998

Designer	Jean Carnahan
Assistant Designer	Scott Rule
Chief Researcher	Lisa Heffernan Weil
Historical Consultant	Dr. Kenneth H. Winn
Artist	Jim Dyke
Photographic Research	Mary Pat Abele
	Chris Carr
	Lisa Heffernan Weil
Architectural and Interior Photography	
	Alise O'Brien
Artwork and Historical Document Photographer	
	Roger Berg

Published 1998 by MMPI, L.L.C., a subsidiary of
Missouri Mansion Preservation, Inc., Post Office
Box 1133, Jefferson City, Missouri, 65102. All
rights reserved. No part of the contents of this
book may be reproduced without the written
permission of MMPI, L.L.C.

ISBN 0-9668992-0-2
Printed and bound in the USA
by
Walsworth Publishing Company

CONTENTS

Foreword Dr. Kenneth H. Winn   **Preface** Jean Carnahan

The First Families of the Mansion (1871-1998)

A Look Back (1803-1871)
The First Families of the Frontier and the Capital City

Time Line of Missouri Governors

Illustration Credits   **Bibliography**   **Notes**   **Index**

For my family,
Mel,
Randy,
Rusty, Debra, Austin, Andrew,
Robin, and
Tom

FOREWORD

Bricks and mortar are so much sand and stone, but when configured into our public buildings those elemental materials take on an almost sacred quality. Missouri's 1871 Governor's Mansion, with its brick Renaissance Revival design and Second Empire mansard roof, is one of America's most attractive executive homes but, as First Lady Jean Carnahan shows us in *If Walls Could Talk*, it is the life inside that gives it its special quality. Each governor and first lady wrestled with challenges unique to their own day—the bitter legacy of the Civil War, James Gang banditry, political bosses, prohibition, depressions, world wars, civil rights, and equal rights. Beneath these large events lay the small daily ones that link the first families' lives with the more mundane world that most of us inhabit: the night trains passing below the Mansion bedroom window that kept generations of governors from getting a good night's sleep; the family dog that barked a little too enthusiastically at arriving guests; the children who made a rushing governor wait his turn each morning for the family bathroom. Layer upon layer, these events—ranging from world-shaking catastrophe to harmless family anecdote—combine to form a tapestry that gives a rich texture to the Mansion's history.

In America, home and family are celebrated as the foundation upon which happy lives are built, creating a welcome haven from the stresses and strains of modern life. The Mansion, however, is hardly a natural family haven. While we like to think of our homes as a place of repose, there are precious few moments for inhabitants of the Mansion to remain free from the gaze of outsiders. Even in odd, irregular moments, workmen, security agents, stray politicians, and staff are likely to be present. During the most routine activities, the Mansion's occupants are scrutinized by others, as ordinary acts become proof of arrogance or nobility, kindness or pettiness, depending on the viewer's predilection. With extraordinary privilege comes extra-ordinary duty. This can be a tough way to live. Those who have attempted to lead private lives, especially in more recent times, have found it difficult indeed, while others who enjoy the limelight (not exactly a rarity in political families) have fared better. For every Governor Forrest Smith, who thought of himself as living in a "glorified jail," there were two Maggie Stephens who wanted to live in the Mansion forever. From a parent's point of view, such as that of First Lady Janet Ashcroft or Governor T. T. Crittenden, providing privacy or even protection for children was a never-ending task. Yet while some of the first parents found public life a threat to their children's wholesome upbringing, many of the first children, such as those of B. Gratz Brown and Herbert Hadley, regarded the large Mansion and its spacious grounds as no less than, in the words of one child, a huge "fairyland" to explore and enjoy.

If Walls Could Talk, then, is a social history of Mansion life written largely from the perspective of the governor's dinner table. The people at that table have been haughty and humble, generous and petty, witty and dull, bigoted and noble, and sophisticated and provincial—indeed, a lot like the people who chose them to govern. This book tells us a lot about the kind of people we select as our leaders. Most of the governors, in fact, have been remarkable men in their own way. If few have risen from dramatic events, such as the dash of war, most have risen by pluck and luck to surmount obscure origins. With the exception of an occasional Lloyd Stark or Christopher Bond, most of our governors were born into, at best, modest circumstances. That the governors have also tended to be white male lawyers from small towns who dislike spending money is only the beginning of the description.

Although the first lady's role is not prescribed by law or by any other formal rule, we, nonetheless, have certain expectations of her. She is to be a good helpmate to her husband: supportive, decorative, and gracious. She must engage in charitable works of a nonpartisan nature, such as helping disabled children. She is to pretend a disinterest in politics and deny, however implausibly, that she influences or shares her political opinions with her husband. She must be, above all, a good hostess at the Governor's Mansion. In this sense the Mansion is of crucial importance. It supplies the first lady with her field of action. The growth and development of the various customs we have come to expect first ladies to follow—teas, "at homes," balls, legislative dinners, and so on—are dependent on a physical space. Some of these customs have withered with time and technology while new ones have been added. The telephone has made obsolete the rituals associated with calling cards and "at homes." In more recent years, as a historical or "living" restoration, the Mansion has increasingly become a major tourist attraction with tours and regular public hours. Perhaps what first ladies know best is that the Mansion, like most old homes, is something to repair—and on occasion, something to improve. The Mansion has, in fact, survived many ghastly "improvements" over the years. Yet despite the misguided assistance a temporary resident may wish to inflict on the old building, most first ladies have served the Mansion well, frequently under trying circumstances. One of the consistent themes of Jean Carnahan's book is the first ladies' never-ending struggle to keep the Mansion in good repair in the face of inadequate funds supplied by husbands and legislators.

In *If Walls Could Talk*, we find governors busied with political triumphs and tragedies; first ladies hosting brilliant receptions and dealing with crumbling ceilings; the pageantry of inauguration days; children playing in fountains and climbing on the roofs; and pet dogs, cats, even goats, scampering after guests. Frail humans all, their stories sometimes descend to farce. At times, *If Walls Could Talk* is quite funny. At other times, the same frail humans inspire us with their self-sacrifice, desire to do good, and accomplishment in the face of great odds. In so doing, they make us a bit prouder of our common heritage as a people, a bit prouder of our state.

Kenneth H. Winn
Missouri State Archivist

PREFACE

Jean Carnahan

M y son climbs mountains; my husband climbs "ladders"—the political sort. I have asked both of them the "W" question many times. Their answer is simple enough, "It just seemed like the thing to do."

Perhaps that's as good an answer as any for why someone would take the risk of climbing an ice-covered hillside or the slippery slopes that lead to higher office. A sense of mission clearly divides those who aspire to reach the summit from those who actually achieve the goal.

Yet, I insist there must be something more inherent in those who seek such glory with its attendant difficulties. Like being blue-eyed or left-handed, maybe there's a gene that marks leaders, compelling them to jump out in front of their fellowman, pointing the way, leading the charge.

It is no surprise to me that our earliest governors were trailblazers. The explorers Meriwether Lewis and William Clark both served as territorial governors during the troublesome frontier era. Nor is it a coincidence that most of Missouri's governors have been lawyers—those who engage in finding answers and resolving conflict (although there are some who would dispute how well they do this).

Governors are hard to compare, but in one area they have a shared experience: most have survived the rigors of a political campaign—that unholy rite whereby the mantle of leadership is passed. Beyond that, they did not start on an equal footing in background, experience, or temperament; and as officeholders, each faced a unique set of political, social, and economic troubles, as well as personal problems. But once in office, each provided able, if not always dynamic, leadership.

Our state's leaders are best measured in the light of history as to how well each responded to the issues of the day—issues that ranged from slavery to abortion and from voting rights to women's rights. Some administrations were overcast by war, depression, and disaster; others were buoyed by optimism and economic prosperity. Faced with uncertain tides, some governors safely chose to tread water, while others moved full speed ahead. Except for occasional bursts of progressiveness, Missouri has been a "hold the course" state, not the first to try the new, nor the last to abandon the old.

While first ladies come in many varieties, they, too, show a thread of commonality. Whether in the White House or the Statehouse, there is a tendency for a first lady to do what is expected of her. Her role is made all the more difficult because there is no script. Thrust upon the stage, she must improvise before an audience eager for reasons to applaud and critics ready to fault her performance.

applaud and critics ready to fault her performance.

For the most part, she is left to rely on tradition and her own instincts. Surprisingly, the rules of first ladyhood have not changed all that much during the past century. Mrs. Calvin Coolidge said that a first lady requires three graces: strength, courage, and good health. Even with such endowments, she plays a delicate role, one with both a public and a private dimension. As wife and political partner, it is the first lady—more often than not—who must supply the encouragement and counsel her husband cannot find elsewhere.

On the public side, she is expected to be the ideal hostess, warm and congenial to visitors of all political persuasions, approachable and down-to-earth, yet possess the dignity befitting her husband's office. Her clothes should be fashionable, but not flamboyant; her children industrious, but not advantage-seeking; her entertainments modest, but not dull; her home well crafted, but not pretentious; her speech, though charming and sprinkled with wit, should be guarded against politically damaging opinions or revelations. No wonder Eleanor Roosevelt said, "The first requisite of a politician's wife is always to be able to manage anything."

Those who have evaluated Missouri's first ladies of yesteryear have occasionally used the word "queenly"—a term for the well-rounded governor's wife who measured up to the community's social expectations. "A credit to her husband. . . . not given to frivolity. . . . gracious hostess" were other accolades for those who didn't quite reach queenly status, but were nonetheless admirable. A few first ladies timidly carved out a role for themselves beyond that of adoring spouse, party-giver, and renovator. But most found it easier to function simply as a political appendage to her husband.

I have enjoyed meeting former first families, some in person and others through research. I am proud of what I found. Missourians have chosen wisely, for there is scarcely a scoundrel in the lot. In fact, the state's first couples have been, for the most part, men and women you would enjoy having as dinner guests in your home. Aside from their political aberrations, they are ordinary people faced with an extraordinary job.

Frequently I am asked which of the first ladies I like the best. I would love to have known the Civil War heroine Mary Phelps, the first lady who, by her own choice, never lived in the Mansion, but left a legacy of humanitarian service unmatched by any governor's wife.

In the twentieth century, I would have to pick Betty Hearnes for what Hollywood calls the "best performance in a supporting role." Her do-it-all, have-fun, never-give-up attitude served her well in the Mansion and in her "afterlife."

For my favorite governor—other than my husband, of course—my pick is Forrest Donnell. Interestingly, Donnell was also my husband's choice. The mild-mannered governor was a statesman and gentleman of the old school, a stickler for principle and right thinking, and undoubtedly Missouri's most intellectual CEO since B. Gratz Brown. From the nineteenth century, Governor Francis wins my vote, not so much for what he did as governor, but for his boundless energy and world-class accomplishments after leaving office.

Telling the story of those who lived in the 1871 Mansion and grappled with the problems of their day (as well as the frustrations of living in public housing) has been my intent. I can't recall how many times visitors to the Mansion have stepped through the massive front doors, scanned the rooms heavy with portraiture and ornate Victorian trimmings, and sighed wistfully, "Oh, if these walls could talk!" I thought the same myself, and so, the idea for this book was conceived.

Writing these essays has been one of the greatest pleasures of my life—the fulfillment of my childhood romance with words and storytelling. I began my odyssey shortly after the 1992 election that moved my husband and me into the Governor's Mansion in Jefferson City, the home of twenty-nine previous Missouri governors. At the time, I was convinced I could complete the work in six months; I was wrong. During the next five years, I bore this book anxiously, as I might an overdue child. I schlepped a burgeoning manuscript around the world, juggling words in an airplane high above the Andes, on the sandy beaches of the Dead Sea, and in the jungles of Costa Rica. Nonetheless, as a fledgling writer, I tread lightly into a world of professional historians, writers, and grammarians, hoping my intrusion will be forgiven in exchange for what I might offer as an insider living within the Mansion walls.

I have explored the lives of the thirty first families who resided in the current Mansion, giving them more thorough treatment than I did their twenty predecessors. Occasionally, a first lady received more coverage than her husband. The flamboyant Maggie Stephens, for instance, rated extra space because she was far more fascinating than the Governor. I have referred to some couples by their first names because it felt natural to do so. I might explain, too, that all chapters are not of equal length simply because images and information were scant for some families and abundant for others. When Mansion families were helpful in granting interviews and access to personal scrapbooks and photos—and nearly all were—the chapters were decidedly strengthened. I often quoted descriptive phrases and unusual expressions of governors, first ladies, contemporaries, and old newspapers in an attempt to preserve the word usage and flavor of a given time.

The earliest governors (1803-1871) are dealt with in an epilogue ("Looking Back") for those who want to delve farther into the state's history. A number of those early families bypassed the "honor" of living in the dowdy public housing provided for them at the time; some who did move in had their terms shortened by law or tragedy. Still, the troubles and triumphs of these frontier leaders are important threads in any tapestry of the state's heritage.

Designing this volume was as much fun as writing it. For the printed text, I chose an adaptation of Caslon, a typeface as old as the story this book tells. I selected Algerian for the headings because it has a Moorish feeling that reminded me of the early decorating influences on the house—and a design look that I repeated in the creation of a third-floor drawing room. The apsidal form of the house is reflected in the title bars and the dingbats dividing the text capture the shape of the ornamental grillwork crowning the roof. The addition of sidebars and photos is designed to enrich the text and to tease the reader with historical tidbits.

I want to warn the sensitive reader that some political bias might have slipped into the text. I sincerely tried, however, to cast each first couple in their best light without ignoring their human and political shortcomings. It pleased me that half the readers of this manuscript thought I was overly kind to the Republicans and about half thought I favored the Democrats. While I have inserted a few titillating stories regardless of political party, I resisted including undocumented reports, intriguing tales, and rumors, which might have earned the volume a more prominent location in bookstores.

There were many hands—and hearts—that went into this work. At the top of the list is Lisa Heffernan Weil, my chief researcher, who delayed starting her family and finishing her master's thesis in order to be a part of this project. She made the writing of this book less arduous—and occasionally joyous—and became a dear friend in the course of the venture. She did the hard work of scouring libraries, searching historical collections and microfilm, and tracking down photographs and the kin folk of governors-past, inundating me with wonderful discoveries from bygone years. She copied, collated, and assembled material in a valiant effort to keep me organized and checked the accuracy of citations and references.

I was also blessed by friends and kindred spirits who cheered me on: Sonia Pendergrass (now deceased), Ethel Burton, Wilma Turner, Jamie Anderson, Tom and Karole Green, and Betty Weldon. And, of course, there was my family, who endured as I ignored household chores, delayed meals, and bored them with historic trivia.

Of prime importance are the many underwriters of this project who made the research and printing of the first edition possible. I truly couldn't have done it without them.

Much praise is due Mary Pat Abele, the executive director of Missouri Mansion Preservation for the past twenty-four years. Her uncanny knack for keeping as many balls in the air as are thrown her way is legendary. She has a special talent for spotting and rehabilitating a troubled sentence and the tenacity to deal with printers, photographers, and deadlines.

Dr. Kenneth H. Winn, a most respected historian and director of the Missouri State Archives, read the manuscript with a critical eye toward accuracy. His patience with an amateur historian is a tribute to his good nature and determination to keep the record straight. Since I felt I could not make a fair and objective rendition of my husband's administration, we collaborated on the final chapter. His generosity further extended to writing the foreword.

Roger Berg, the affable photographer of Creative Photo, scanned many a brittle image, bringing it back to life using his skilled eye and state-of-the-art computer equipment. I found a rare treasure in the architectural and interior photographer Alise O'Brien, a precision artist at capturing color and form, and a thoroughly delightful lady. The talented and good-natured artist Jim Dyke enhanced the early chapters at those points where we had few illustrations and no color images. His care in researching each drawing adds greatly to the historical accuracy of the work.

Dr. Jim Goodrich, who heads The State Historical Society of Missouri, and his superb staff were extremely kind and accommodating of our many—and sometime unusual—requests for photos and resource materials. His staff, who helped in countless

Kubisch, Marie Concannon, Ara Kaye, and in the Western Historical Manuscript Collection, Cindy Stewart, Diane Ayotte, David Moore, and Randy Roberts.

I am also indebted to the Missouri State Archives and the assistance of Laura Jolly and Jenifer Burlis-Freilich; the State Capitol Museum director John Cunning; the Missouri Historical Society director, Dr. Robert Archibald, along with Duane Sneddeker and Tim Fox; the Cole County Historical Society, especially Elizabeth Rozier and Ann Gue; Charles Brown of the St. Louis Mercantile Library at the University of Missouri-St. Louis; the University of Missouri-Columbia Library; and, Julie March of the Springfield Museum.

Researchers included: Barb Hiatte, Amanda Johnson Willenberg, Gerald Hirsch, Dean Martin, and Amanda Lehenbauer. Newspapers kindly accommodating our requests included the *Jefferson City Post-Tribune, Kansas City Star,* and *St. Louis Post-Dispatch.* I am grateful, too, for the advice of Steve Turner, and the aid of James Corbett, Juli Price, Shelly Campbell, Debbie Minor, Columbia Photo and Video, and 50-Minute Photo.

Applause is due Walsworth Publishing Company, experts in quality book production, for accommodating the whimsy of a new writer. My sincere thanks to company president Don Walsworth, to Steve Mull and Scott Rule for their guidance and patience, and to all the artists and technicians who helped along the way. Scott's consistent good humor kept us going during the long hours we spent hunched over the computer as he skillfully brought this book to life on the screen.

My final comments are reserved for the Mansion staff. They are a "major league" team in every respect. Accolades are due all of them for making the old Victorian home work smoothly each day: the charming and indefatigable Mansion Manager Paula Earls, whose attention to detail makes each event a special treat for visitors; Chef Jerry Walsh, whose fine cuisine pleases both the eye and the palate; Chris Carr, who did the "detective work," tracking the most illusive photographs and cataloging the hundreds of images we turned up; and, Norma Jean Davidson, whose tender, loving care of the home adds to its rich luster. Rounding out the team is a corps of dedicated security personnel and docents.

As I have often told them, "You make me look good and you make guests feel good." What more could a first lady ask?

Left to right: Mary Pat Abele, Lisa Heffernan Weil, Norma Jean Davidson, Paula Earls, Jerry Walsh, and Chris Carr.

Jean Carnahan
Jefferson City, Missouri
1998

E ntrance into Missouri's stately Mansion is a handclasp with history. You can't live there long and not grow to love the building.

~ Mrs. John M. Dalton
First Lady 1961-1965

The First Families of the Mansion

CHAMPION OF FREEDOM

GOVERNOR BENJAMIN GRATZ BROWN
MARY HANSOME GUNN BROWN
1871-1873

"This is the age of transition. . . . It is a passage from the Old to the New. . . .
We are the Revolution." ~ B. Gratz Brown, September 17, 1862

M ary Gunn grew up across the street from a quaint two-story brick and wood building known to the residents of Jefferson City as the Governor's Mansion. It hardly qualified for so grand a title, but it was a vast improvement over the few rooms in the Statehouse set aside for the first governor who lived in the city.

From her fenced yard, Mary could watch the finely dressed ladies as they alighted from horse-drawn carriages, their hairdos decorated with flowers, feathers, and ribbons. She could hear their laughter and the swishing of crinoline skirts as they climbed the stairs to greet the Governor and his wife. At the time, Mary Gunn had no way of knowing that someday she would live on the other side of the street in a new, far more magnificent Mansion.

The romantic encounter that moved her onto the political scene happened one spring evening in 1858 when Mary was fifteen years old. According to a family legend, she was swinging on the garden gate of her parents' home when two legislators passed by, thirty-two-year-old Representative B. Gratz Brown of St. Louis and his friend, Senator John B. Henderson. As the gentlemen picked their way along the muddy street, Brown turned to the Senator, "Do you know that young lady?" he asked.

Henderson responded that he did—she was Miss Gunn, daughter of the state printer and former mayor. At Brown's request, the Senator agreed to go back and properly introduce the couple. The casual encounter led to a whirlwind courtship and, within three months, Gratz and Mary were married; she had just turned sixteen.

The newlywed couple moved to Brown's home in St. Louis. Having some of his relatives in the area eased the transition for Mary, but she was still unprepared for the rough-and-tumble political arena her husband so enjoyed.

Gratz, on the other hand, had grown up in a well-to-do Kentucky family steeped in the tradition of public service and acquainted with prominent people of the day. Both of his grandfathers served in the U.S. Senate. Senator John Brown, a close friend of Thomas Jefferson, called on the famous Virginian for architectural

Mary Gunn Brown, the sixteen-year-old bride of Representative B. Gratz Brown, was unprepared for the rough-and-tumble political arena her husband so enjoyed.

(Facing page)
B. Gratz Brown as a legislator.

3

advice in designing the family's spacious brick house—"Liberty Hill"—located in Frankfort. Having lost his mother, young Gratz lived with his father and grandparents at the ancestral home. As the son of a prominent lawyer and judge, he had every advantage of Southern aristocracy, including access to a fine home library and the best private schools.

Brown rounded out his formal education by earning degrees from Yale and Louisville Law School. He practiced law briefly in Kentucky before joining his cousins, Montgomery and Frank Blair, in their St. Louis law office. In 1849, when Gratz arrived to take up residence in a local boarding house, the city was recovering from a cholera epidemic that had killed thousands that year. Nonetheless, the thriving riverfront city still claimed nearly 55,000 residents, ranging from the old French elite to new German immigrants to rowdy traders, trappers, and miners.

Gratz quickly gained recognition in his new surroundings. He made such a powerful appearance during his first court case that he was employed by two other clients that same day. Frank Blair, an antislavery Democrat, became a political mentor to his twenty-three-year-old cousin and helped him to gain acceptance within the city's increasingly powerful German community. Under Frank's guidance, Brown soon shifted his allegiance from the disintegrating Whig Party and, in 1852, won election to the General Assembly as a Democrat.

B. Gratz Brown grew up in a well-to-do Kentucky family steeped in the tradition of public service and acquainted with prominent people of the day.

Though Brown was a new member of the legislature—and one of the youngest—he did not go unnoticed. The short, red-headed lawmaker showed boundless energy and a quickness to express his opinions. At the time, he favored maintaining slavery in the South, but opposed its extension into the western territories.

Apparently, many of Brown's constituents were against extending his legislative tenure. When he ran for reelection, he won by only twelve votes. Nor were some of the House members excited about his return. When a challenge to Brown's election reached the House, his colleagues came within one vote of refusing to seat him.

But Brown was not to be intimidated. He continued to wrestle with the changing social and economic problems of his day. During his three terms in the legislature, he found a vehicle for his views as editor of the *St. Louis Missouri Democrat*—a publication in which he and Frank Blair became part owners. The influential newspaper was well read, largely because of Brown's witty, but often times caustic, opinions.

Some of those opinions proved costly to the acid-penned editor. In 1855 a duel was set between Brown and pro-slavery Senator Robert M. Stewart—a man who would become governor two years later. Brown appeared on the field of honor at the

DUELING GOVERNORS

Gratz Brown turned out to be more skillful with his writing pen than his dueling pistol. In 1856, while serving as a legislator and editor of the *St. Louis Missouri Democrat,* Brown engaged in the last political duel fought in Missouri—a dispute with Thomas Chaute Reynolds, a U.S. district attorney, over a series of inflammatory editorials written by Brown.

At the time, both men were Democrats, but differed in that Reynolds favored slavery and Brown did not. But there were other, more personal animosities; Brown was apparently jealous of Reynolds' growing influence in the St. Louis German community. In his editorials, Brown found opportunities to attack Reynolds for prosecuting settlers cutting timber on government land and for his "scandalous" behavior as a foreign diplomat.

As the dispute escalated, the two men decided to settle the matter on the field of honor. However, several challenges were exchanged over a three-year period before they agreed on which weapons they should use and from what distance they should fire. Brown wanted a match with rifles at eighty yards. Though both were skilled marksmen, Reynolds, who was near-sighted, preferred pistols. They finally settled on English dueling pistols at twelve paces. According to the rules, the pistols carried a one-ounce ball of lead and were to be "dropped shot," that is, the muzzle held upward and lowered to fire on command.

On the fateful day just before dawn, Brown and Reynolds boarded skiffs, along with the two men designated as seconds, and pushed off the shore for a small sandbar in the Mississippi River. The thirty-five-year-old Reynolds had a wife who knew nothing about the venture; Brown, several years younger, was unmarried. By the time they faced each other, the eastern sky blazed a fiery red. Brown, in his black coat, made a good silhouette against the sunrise, whereas Reynolds, dressed in gray, blended with the sandbar.

At the order to fire, the shots rang out almost as one. Brown fired directly at Reynolds, but missed. Reynolds' shot sent a bullet deep into Brown's knee, splitting the bone and causing much bleeding and pain. Reynolds later said he never intended to shoot to kill; he wanted to fire first and spoil his opponent's aim. Brown demanded a second shot, but friends decided the matter had been settled and nothing more was necessary.

The two men shook hands and boarded a passing steamship—fittingly named the *Editor.* After placing Brown in a stateroom, those who assisted in the match used the money from Reynolds' wallet to strike up a lively poker game during the thirty-mile trip back to St. Louis. When the vessel docked, a large crowd gathered to learn the outcome of the duel. Among those interested were the mayor of St. Louis and police officials who boarded the boat, but made no arrests since technically the shoot-out had not taken place on Missouri soil.

The Brown-Reynolds duel was the last in the St. Louis area where there was bloodshed. Thomas C. Reynolds later became lieutenant governor. During the Civil War, he helped Governor Claiborne Fox Jackson set up Missouri's Confederate government in Arkansas and assumed the role of "governor-in-exile" following Jackson's death. A decade later, he served in the Missouri General Assembly. Brown fared better politically; he became a U.S. Senator, governor, and vice-presidential candidate. Although he walked with a limp for the rest of his life, the feisty politician never gave up his fondness for a spirited fight.

time and place designated for the match, but Stewart never showed up. The following year, Brown was not so lucky. His quarrel with fellow attorney Thomas Chaute Reynolds led to an illegal duel that left Brown with a limp for the rest of his life.

The encounter, however, did not cripple his spirit or dampen his enthusiasm for a vigorous political exchange. In 1857—at a time when three-quarters of Missouri legislators were pro-slavery—Brown delivered a fiery abolitionist address on the floor of the General Assembly. Although he had earlier promised to protect the property of slave owners, he now called for gradual, compensated emancipation. Brown's sentiments infuriated House members and they refused to let him finish speaking. According to historian Norma Peterson, Brown did not see slavery as morally wrong, only economically unsound. He felt that an unpaid labor force discouraged the immigration of white workers needed to develop the state's mining and agricultural areas.

With his defeat for a fourth term, Brown's political interests appeared to wane. He gave up editing the *St. Louis Missouri Democrat* after falling out with his partner, Frank Blair. In a letter to his brother, Blair explained the breakup, citing Brown's faulty management of the paper: "He assumes the dictator and makes everybody mad with him." Seeking a new business venture on his own, Brown organized a company to lay track and build the first "street railroad" in St. Louis.

The following year, however, Brown was back on the political scene. Having lined up with the new Republican Party, he went to the national convention that nominated Abraham Lincoln. When the Civil War broke out, he mustered a unit and served as a colonel for three months.

But Brown preferred ballots to bullets and returned to public life before the war ended. Although he was already viewed as an extremist on the slavery issue, he became even more militant. He called for the immediate freeing of slaves and for "eternal" punishment of those siding with the South. He lashed out at Governor Hamilton Gamble for being too easy on the rebels and too tolerant of slavery, and criticized President Lincoln for being soft on traitors.

As the Civil War raged, Brown set his sights on a U.S. Senate seat. In 1863 the General Assembly appointed him to fill one of the vacancies created by the ousting of Missouri's

The Jefferson City riverfront, circa 1853, when Brown served in the legislature.

6

two secessionist members. Despite Lincoln's efforts to undermine his selection, Brown won the seat and promptly wrote the President to express his displeasure over the intervention. Eager to assume his new duties, Brown left his wife in St. Louis to care for their fast-growing family and went to the nation's capital to fill the unexpired term.

O nce in Washington, Brown antagonized many by his support of voting rights for all, regardless of race, color, or sex. When his colleagues reasoned that women "did not bear arms" and, therefore, should not have the privilege of voting, he noted all the men who had never served in the military and yet sat in the U.S. Senate.

Although the glib-tongued Senator enjoyed taunting his opponents, the struggle for principle took its toll on him physically. After two years in Washington, Brown did not run for reelection. He and Mary, both in ill health, moved to their Iron County farm for a year of recuperation. During the interval, Brown could not resist the opportunity for an investment. He joined several businessmen in leasing a nearby granite quarry, rock from which would later be used to build the Eads Bridge across the Mississippi River.

Restless and unable to stay out of the political fray, Brown returned to St. Louis in 1869. He rallied the physical and political strength necessary for a gubernatorial campaign and became the nominee of the Liberal Republicans—a reform group that had just split with Radical Republicans on issues involving political patronage and voting rights.

At this stage in his political evolution, Brown was an ardent crusader for universal voting rights and amnesty for Southern sympathizers. In an attempt to spread his views, he traveled long distances by train, wagon, or horseback. He often got up before three o'clock in the morning in order to get to the next town to speak at a church meeting or on a courthouse square. Some communities greeted him warmly, but in others his handbills were ripped down and thrown in the streets before he arrived. The few who gathered to hear him responded with cold silence. President Ulysses S. Grant was actually behind much of the organized effort to oppose Brown. The Grant administration, which viewed Brown's rise as a threat, not only pressured supporters to defeat the reformists but also coerced government employees to fund the campaign of the old-line Republicans.

Despite the intense opposition, Brown won the governorship by more than 40,000 votes, largely because of the support of the politically weakened Democrats who chose not to nominate a candidate that year. The watershed election obliterated the Radical Republican coalition, returned voting rights to Confederates, and put the legislature in the hands of the newly formed alliance of Democrats and Liberal Republicans.

One New York journal referred to Missouri's election as "the most remarkable political revolution of the age." Brown was pleased with the spread of his revolution into other states as Liberal Republican groups sprung up across the nation. Ever alert to his next political move, Brown was eyeing the presidency, even as he took his oath as governor.

Political success brought a number of changes to the Brown family. In the flush of victory, past animosities were forgotten and cousin Frank Blair—himself a newly elected legislator—proudly escorted Gratz to the inaugural podium. For twenty-nine-year-old Mary Brown, her husband's victory meant returning to Jefferson City as First Lady of Missouri to live in the Mansion she had known as a child. But if Mary read the Jefferson City newspaper, she undoubtedly had second thoughts about moving her five children into the executive home. One Capital City reporter described the building as a "dilapidated old shell that has . . . many long years ago ceased to be worthy the name of Mansion . . . unsafe . . . horrible looking . . . colder than a barn."

The new Mansion was the masterpiece of St. Louis architect George Ingham Barnett.

Even incumbent Governor McClurg seemed eager to leave; he offered to vacate early or, at least, to provide Brown temporary housing. "[You are] welcome to a parlor and bedroom . . . an abundance of wood and a servant," McClurg wrote the Governor-elect who was awaiting the arrival of his family. When Mrs. Brown and the children showed up, they stayed only long enough for the inauguration. She returned a month later to hold a reception at the Mansion, but a number of invited guests refused to attend because of the shabby condition of the thirty-eight-year-old residence. Apparently embarrassed by the incident, lawmakers approved funding for a new Governor's Mansion on a lot behind the old one.

Mrs. Brown, pregnant with her sixth child, moved the family back to their Iron County farm to wait out the construction. It was hardly a restful stay in the country for the First Lady. In addition to seeing after her children, she cared for a number of ailing relatives, including her mother. When Mrs. Gunn died in September 1871 during a visit to the farm, Mary brought her body back to Jefferson City to lie in state in the old Mansion. The funeral marked the final public event held in the home before it was torn down a month later.

Muddy streets, roaming farm animals, ugly buildings, and a noisy train station engulfed the new showpiece of the Capital City.

The construction of the new residence was already underway on a site adjacent to the old home. Despite his executive duties and the distraction of his presidential aspirations, Brown took time to get involved with the fine points of the design, including the location of fireplaces and the size of rooms. The final product, the masterpiece of St. Louis architect George Ingham Barnett, cost $75,000 to build and partially furnish.

The new Mansion sat like a jewel in a pigsty.

On January 20, 1872, after seven months of construction, the Browns moved into the new, three-story Mansion. The Renaissance Revival-style home, sixty-six-feet square, was built of red brick, trimmed in stone, and gracefully topped with a mansard roof.

The interior of the house matched its impressive exterior. Massive walnut doors swung easily on their German silver hinges, revealing a Great Hall seventeen-feet high bordered by parlors, a library, and a divided dining room. The Double Parlor with its red upholstered chairs, gilded mirror, and window treatments of lace curtains and lambrequins further added to the home's Victorian charm.

On the second floor, seven spacious bedrooms opened into a large hall; six additional bedrooms flanked the third-floor supper room. (Later the third floor would be referred to as a billiard room or ballroom, which suggests that it might have been abandoned as a large dining area because of the difficulty in transporting food from the basement kitchen.) The dirt-floor basement also housed the servants' dining room, wine cellar, boiler, laundry, and storerooms. Despite its size and elegance, like most houses of the era, it contained no closets or bathrooms.

The massive front doors swung easily on their German silver hinges, revealing a Great Hall seventeen feet high bordered by parlors, a library, and a divided dining room.

Though the Mansion had thirteen bedrooms, like most houses of the era, it contained no closets or bathrooms.

Brown made his unique contribution to the house by donating four Missouri red granite columns for the portico, thus starting the tradition of each first family leaving a gift to the Mansion. The granite, cut from Brown's quarry in Iron County, arrived nine inches too short, causing one writer to label the occurrence an "unlucky mistake." The Governor refused to see it that way and corrected the problem by adding a piece of white stone to each base which remains there today.

In keeping with the fine interior decor, Brown ordered two brass chandeliers for the parlors.

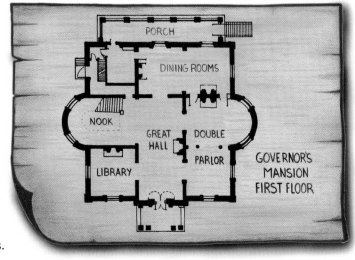

GOVERNOR'S MANSION FIRST FLOOR

PORCH

DINING ROOMS

NOOK

GREAT HALL

DOUBLE PARLOR

LIBRARY

But when he discovered that the lights cost $150 each, the irate Governor wrote the manufacturer threatening to return the items. The company replied gruffly, asking what Brown expected them to do with light fixtures so large that they could not be resold for an ordinary home. In the end, the Governor relented and the chandeliers remained at the Mansion.

Though Brown's chandeliers were elegant, the real highlight of the house was the walnut stairway with the hand-carved rail that spiraled gracefully between the first and second floors. Some thought the oversized house was far too pretentious for

Lawmakers quibbled for two weeks over whether they should entertain an "Imperial Highness."

Missouri's chief executive. But most felt the home should be "large enough to accommodate the members of the legislature and other citizens of the state." That it did, quite well.

Still, the stately Governor's Mansion sat like a jewel in a pigsty. Muddy streets, roaming farm animals, ugly buildings, and a noisy train station engulfed the new showpiece of the Capital City. One writer complained of being accosted "by filthy, wallowing porkers and . . . hungry cows" along the walkways to the Capitol and shopping district.

Nonetheless, commerce was brisk in the City of Jefferson in the 1870s. The bustling town of five thousand people was well known for its beer-making skills; two breweries in the sizable German community boasted an annual production of over ten thousand barrels. The townspeople were further encouraged that the Pacific Railway could transport passengers between St. Louis and Jefferson City in seven hours or less.

The first guests to enjoy the Mansion's hospitality arrived by train on January 23, 1872, just three days after the Governor and his family settled into their new home. Excited residents awaited the arrival of the Grand Duke Alexis, the twenty-two-year-old son of the Russian Czar, who was scheduled to stop in the Capital City

It was said that East Coast "society flung itself en masse at the Grand Duke's feet" when he arrived in America.

on his return from a buffalo hunt. The Duke's three-month tour of the United States demonstrated the cordial relations that had developed between the two nations after America's purchase of Alaska from Russia several years earlier.

It was said that "New York society flung itself en masse at the Grand Duke's feet" when he arrived in America and the rest of the nation followed suit. However, many Missouri lawmakers were not impressed with the titled visitor. The General Assembly spent two weeks quibbling over whether they should entertain an "Imperial Highness" and, if so, who should pay the expense of the visit, a cost predicted by opponents to reach $10,000 (an amount equal to $150,000 today).

While some resisted entertaining royalty, most lawmakers and residents were eager to have the distinguished traveler visit their town and see their new Mansion. Despite the cold, bitter wind, a large crowd turned out at the train station to greet the party. Curiosity ran high, not just to view the handsome Duke, but to see the fancy train car that he rented for $3,500 a day.

The young nobleman had been squired about the Nebraska plains by such notables as General George A. Custer and "Buffalo Bill" Cody, as well as a host of Sioux warriors. Not to be outdone in hospitality, the local welcoming committee sent seven of the town's best carriages to the depot. One of the carriages—on loan from the funeral parlor and pulled by four white horses—was designated for the guest of honor and his party, which included General Custer. In addition to the welcoming honors, a thunderous roar of cannons saluted the dignitaries as they arrived at the Capitol. Ladies dressed in plumed hats, silks, satins, and laces gathered in the rotunda hoping to catch a glimpse of

General George Custer and the Grand Duke Alexis of Russia, the first official visitors to the new Governor's Mansion, arrived three days after the Browns moved into their new home.

the young man. Customarily barred from the legislative halls, the women were permitted to enter only after a special resolution was passed.

Following the Duke's brief remarks to the General Assembly, Brown hosted an "unostentatious . . . but brilliant" lunch at the Mansion. After the meal, the men climbed the back stairs to the third floor where "a pleasant chat was had over a box of choice Havanas." Later the Duke greeted the public at the Madison House and, upon leaving, made several generous donations to beggars before reboarding his plush palace car. The cost of the six-hour visit came to $265, far less than reluctant legislators had feared.

Brown and the townspeople resumed their preparations for two simultaneous events the next day: a convention of the new Liberal Republican Party and the long-awaited public reception at the new Governor's Mansion. As one writer indicated, precedence was given to the reception: "There is assembled here a large number of people who have come to attend a ball tonight and a few of them will kill time by holding a convention this afternoon."

The grand ball, held on January 24, 1872, celebrated the official opening of the executive home. According to one newspaper, "The hairdressers had their hands so full that many ladies wore ball coiffures for days and slept at night in an upright position. . . . The ladies shone like a Louis XV salon, with high, light puffs of hair and nodding plumes." Not to be overlooked, the state guard ordered new uniforms, resplendent with polished brass buttons and gold epaulettes.

Had the Duke remained, he would have seen the Midwest version of a thoroughly democratic social affair. Though the Capital City's attempt at grandeur might have amused His Royal Highness, he surely would have marveled at the number in attendance. Exact estimates of the turnout varied. One St. Louis writer described the event as an "immense" gathering of fifteen hundred to two thousand persons—though local accounts suggested the attendance was closer to twelve hundred. He went on to describe the grand opening as "one of the most magnificent entertainments which ever occurred west of St. Louis. . . . [All] were received by His Excellency and Mrs. Brown . . . with a grace and elegance that would have done honor to the national capital."

Other descriptions of the occasion were less glowing. One journalist noted the jam on the staircase prevented him from seeing the upper floors and dancing could only be done with great difficulty. "Gracious, graceful guests of the first floor became a

Guests "rifled things like a flock of locust."

pushing crowd in the narrow stair and doorway, not so much to eat as to see the much talked of feast. . . . Everything caterers could supply was there, but the thing most mentioned was a pyramid of spitted snipe." Although it was reported that Governor Brown served no intoxicants, many who attended had already "whet their whistles" at the nearby Madison House.

Years later, one guest wrote disparagingly of the event, calling it a "fearful crush." Another recalled it as a "ghastly" evening, during which guests "jammed . . . into Mrs. Brown's beautiful rooms . . . particularly the supper room, and rifled things like a flock of locust."

The commotion at the Mansion did not end with its grand opening. The Brown children turned the house into a lively playground with their day-to-day antics. One of their escapades, however, greatly alarmed the Governor. One morning as he was walking to the Capitol with his friend, Senator Henderson, Brown took an intuitive glance back toward the house. He was horrified at what he saw: his children were running along the edge of the mansard roof! Only the low, filigreed-iron border screened them from the hard ground three stories below. The youngsters had apparently crawled into the attic and climbed through a hatch onto the roof. Greatly distressed, Brown turned to his friend and said, "Go on to the Senate, Henderson, while I go back and spank the children."

Brown's problems with the children did not compare with those he encountered at the Capitol. During his early months in office, he faced a growing menace in the Ku Klux Klan—a mob of marauders who, in those days, wore skull caps and long black-and-white striped gowns. At first reluctant to call out the militia, the Governor sent an investigator to south Missouri. When Brown learned that the Klan was, in fact, a gang of thieves and

The highlight of the open house was the presentation of a life-sized painting of the Governor, a gift to Mrs. Brown that hung on the library wall until early in the next century.

Using his tool kit, young Gratz K. Brown once shortened the legs of the Mansion's dining room chairs just before guests arrived for dinner.

murderers, he used the state militia to bring them under control. Because of his firm action in quelling the violence, the strength and influence of the Klan greatly declined in Missouri.

A filigreed-iron border outlined the mansard roof of the Renaissance Revival-style Mansion.

Other guerrilla bands, however, continued to stalk the countryside. Among them were the James gang and Younger brothers—groups made up of men who had fought in the Civil War and found looting easier than honest work. Even the prospect of a harsh prison term did little to discourage the outlaws; it would take another decade to rid Missouri of their plundering and violence.

Brown's political enemies not only accused him of failing to round up the criminal element but also charged him with condoning inhumane treatment of the inmates in the nine-hundred-man state penitentiary. Actually, the Governor advocated prison reform; he abhorred capital punishment and no criminals were executed during his tenure. He preferred jobs instead of jail for minor offenders and recommended reform school for juvenile lawbreakers rather than prison.

One story circulating at the time illustrated his concern for the humane treatment of prisoners. It was the practice to shave the heads and beards of convicts. But the remarkable beard worn by one of the new inmates fell to his ankles and spread across his body like a blanket and the inmate did not want it removed. Brown personally visited the prison to review the case and concluded that "it would be an act of vandalism to destroy such a natural curiosity." Upon leaving, he turned to the head of the penitentiary and said emphatically, "Warden, spare the whiskers."

Women also found a champion in the Governor. As an early advocate of education and voting rights, he told the legislature that the ladies of the state deserved "all the advantages that cultivated intellect and refined taste can throw around them."

Of course, Brown did have his enemies. While prisoners and women found him to their liking, the railroad barons had little use for the Governor. If left uncontrolled, Brown feared these men would become more powerful than the state. "For the public good" he recommended regulation of the railroads, insisting on fair rates, safety inspections, and the full payment of taxes due the state.

Through his controversial policies at home, Brown was attracting national attention. In 1872 when Liberal Republicans picked Horace Greeley for their presidential candidate, they chose Missouri's outspoken, red-bearded Governor as his running mate. Brown, then at the crest of his popularity, wanted the presidential nomination for himself, but settled for the second spot after his poor showing in the early convention balloting.

During the campaign, one historian noted that Brown was "an earnest candidate, but he was always under the influence of either a newly discovered theory or a newly found bottle." Opponents enjoyed telling of an incident that was said to have happened during Brown's class reunion at Yale. According to the story, the vice presidential candidate was so intoxicated that he "buttered his watermelon" instead of his bread—a claim that brought great amusement to his foes back home and earned him the nickname "Boozy Brown." Finally, one supporter publicly countered the tale, saying Brown had indeed buttered his water-

In 1872 when Liberal Republicans picked Horace Greeley for their presidential candidate, they chose Missouri's outspoken, red-bearded Governor as his running mate.

melon because "that is the only way in which fashionable and well-educated people ever eat a watermelon."

But there were other, deeper problems with the Liberal Republican ticket. Though Democratic leaders had also endorsed Greeley, the rank and file—whose support he needed to win—showed little enthusiasm for his candidacy. The Greeley-Brown ticket carried in Missouri and five southern states, but lost in the national election to General Ulysses S. Grant. Afflicted with severe depression, and having just lost his wife, Greeley died in an asylum three weeks following the election.

After that the Liberal Republicans vanished from the political scene. According to historian William Parrish, "the split in Republican ranks killed [the party] as an effective political agency in Missouri for the next quarter-century and paved the way for long-term Democratic ascendency."

Following his national defeat, Brown returned to the Capital City to finish his remaining months as governor. In his final speech to the legislature, the Governor spoke of the state's "abundant prosperity;" Missouri ranked fifth in population and fourth in the value of manufactured goods nationwide. He reflected on his major accomplishments, repeal of both the income tax and the poll tax. The Governor took particular pride in the improvements at the University of Missouri that included two new departments—one for law and another for medicine—and a new admissions policy permitting the enrollment of women in all areas of study.

Before stepping down, the Governor showed a last gracious gesture—one that initiated a tradition—when he

Despite the endorsement of the Democratic Party, the Liberal Republicans carried only six states in the presidential election of 1872.

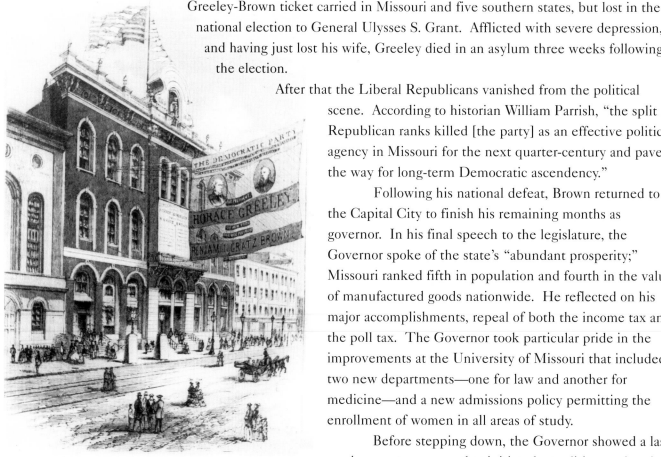

extended the hospitality of the Mansion to the next First Family. Brown invited the Woodsons to view their new home so he could visit with the incoming Governor and "induct him rightly into his new life." However, First Lady Mary Brown might have found it hard to recommend Mansion living to the Woodsons. Her two-year reign as First Lady had not been pleasant. Toward the end, she was nearly an invalid, relying heavily on her sister-in-law, a Kentucky socialite, to help with the duties at the Mansion.

Brown closed out his term and returned his family to St. Louis. He managed his street railway and granite quarry; Mary, in spite of frail health, gave birth to two more children bringing their family to six daughters and two sons. Though he had been in the political spotlight for twenty years as a newspaper editor, state legislator, U.S. Senator, and governor, Brown professed to an old friend that he found more enjoyment in family life.

Still, at age forty-seven, Brown was not ready to give up public life entirely. He returned to the Democratic Party and spoke occasionally at political events, often attacking Republicans for not doing enough for agriculture. In another apparent change, he took a strong stance in favor of prohibition and urged Missouri to become a "sober state." It was, he said, the purpose of government to suppress intoxicants. Writers ridiculed his new position, suggesting Brown must have, at last, abandoned the practice of "buttering his watermelon."

The former Governor had to suffer other indignities. Bad investments and speculation, coupled with the Panic of 1873, left him deeply in debt. In spite of failing health, he was forced to resume his law practice. During his final years, he devoted himself to civic affairs and scholarly writing, including a paper on mathematics and another on geometry. Nearly thirteen years after leaving office, Brown died of heart trouble at the age of fifty-nine. His wife, who had not been well for some time, died three years later at age forty-six.

During an era when the "political cauldron boiled," Brown had chosen to be a part of the heated debate that would shape his state and nation. In his search for solutions, he often shifted his political sails to catch the ever-changing winds. He had been a Whig, a Free-Soiler, an Emancipationist, a Unionist, a Radical Republican, a Liberal Republican, and a Democrat. One writer jested that Brown had "taken so many sides that he ought to suit everybody." While his positions sometimes seemed inconsistent, Peterson concluded that others attempting to lead during the troubled era showed a similar pattern.

B. Gratz Brown was a product of uncertain times, a political opportunist to some, an unsung hero to others. His battles gave purpose to his life and direction to his state during one of the most stressful periods in American history. "Perhaps I am not the right man to have taken the lead in such a conflict," he once said, "but there was no other that would do it, and the thing had to be done."

Margaret Wise Brown, apparently inherited her grandfather's interest in writing. Her award-winning book, *Goodnight Moon*, is a favorite of children nationwide.

MISSOURI'S THREE MANSIONS

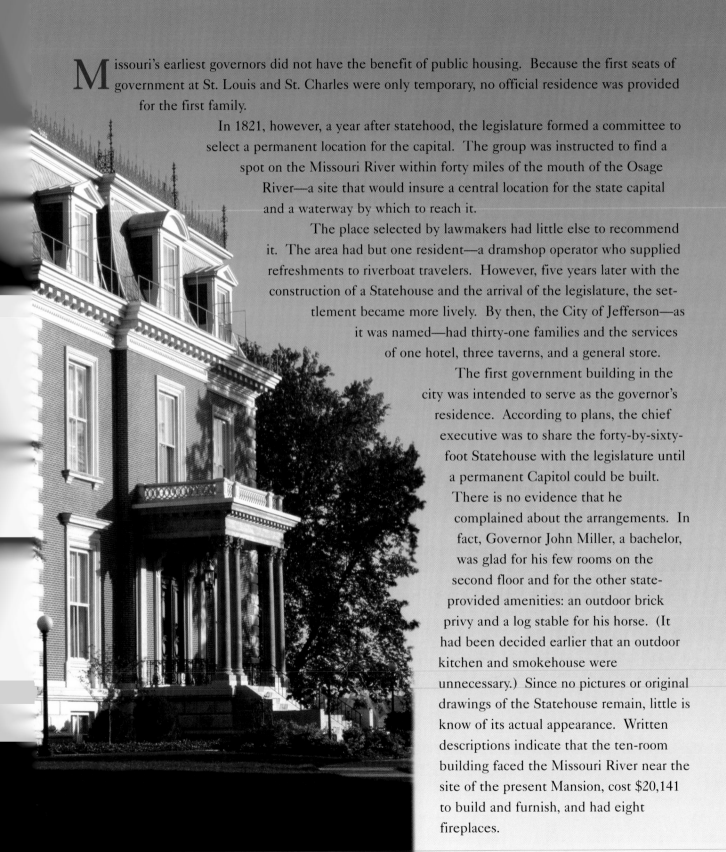

Missouri's earliest governors did not have the benefit of public housing. Because the first seats of government at St. Louis and St. Charles were only temporary, no official residence was provided for the first family.

In 1821, however, a year after statehood, the legislature formed a committee to select a permanent location for the capital. The group was instructed to find a spot on the Missouri River within forty miles of the mouth of the Osage River—a site that would insure a central location for the state capital and a waterway by which to reach it.

The place selected by lawmakers had little else to recommend it. The area had but one resident—a dramshop operator who supplied refreshments to riverboat travelers. However, five years later with the construction of a Statehouse and the arrival of the legislature, the settlement became more lively. By then, the City of Jefferson—as it was named—had thirty-one families and the services of one hotel, three taverns, and a general store.

The first government building in the city was intended to serve as the governor's residence. According to plans, the chief executive was to share the forty-by-sixty-foot Statehouse with the legislature until a permanent Capitol could be built. There is no evidence that he complained about the arrangements. In fact, Governor John Miller, a bachelor, was glad for his few rooms on the second floor and for the other state-provided amenities: an outdoor brick privy and a log stable for his horse. (It had been decided earlier that an outdoor kitchen and smokehouse were unnecessary.) Since no pictures or original drawings of the Statehouse remain, little is know of its actual appearance. Written descriptions indicate that the ten-room building faced the Missouri River near the site of the present Mansion, cost $20,141 to build and furnish, and had eight fireplaces.

By 1834 state government had outgrown its 5,000-square-foot accommodations. Furthermore, voters elected a governor with a family needing more than the allotted space in the combined legislative-executive building. Apparently content where they were, members of the General Assembly voted to retain the Statehouse and build the governor a new home. (Several years later, however, lawmakers began building themselves a more spacious Capitol even before the Statehouse burned.)

With an appropriation of five thousand dollars, a two-story, wood and brick Governor's Mansion was built in the yard behind the Statehouse. Poorly constructed, the residence

An artist's version of the Statehouse. The building, constructed in 1826, served as both the Capitol and the governor's residence.

began showing its age as early as the 1850s. Lawmakers ignored the disgraceful state of the home for as long as possible. When they finally agreed to replace the structure, the project was interrupted by the Civil War. In 1868 an editorial painted a bleak picture: "That old rookery, known as the Governor's Mansion, presents such a slushy appearance that a gentleman mistook it for a soap and candle manufactory a few days since."

A showdown occurred shortly after Governor Brown took office in 1871. A reception was held in the dilapidated house and many invited guests, fearing a disaster might result from overcrowding, refused to attend. The incident prompted the legislature to begin construction of a new home on a site next to the old residence.

With its completion in December 1871, Missourians, at last, had a Mansion worthy of the claim. The red brick structure, trimmed in stone, featured an imposing portico supported by four red granite columns. Designed for both public entertaining and private living space, the three-story structure perched on a bluff overlooking the Missouri River has served as home for thirty of Missouri's first families.

The poorly constructed executive residence portrayed in better times. Built in 1834, it was still standing a decade after the Civil War.

Within the walls of the Mansion have dined such notables as the Grand Duke Alexis of Russia, General George Custer, Jefferson Davis, William Jennings Bryan, Harry Truman, Henry Kissinger, Barbara Bush, Tipper Gore, and an array of entertainers and ambassadors from around the world.

Over the years, the stately home has withstood the ravages of neglect and the good intentions of its many decorators. Today the Mansion holds the distinction of being one of the oldest in the nation continuously used as a state executive residence. It is an outstanding example of Renaissance Revival architecture and one of the most beautiful and authentic restorations in America.

GREATNESS AND GRANDEUR

GOVERNOR SILAS WOODSON
VIRGINIA "JENNIE" JULIET LARD WOODSON
1873-1875

". . . huge rooms, magnificent furniture, magic carpets, chandeliers ablaze with rainbows gleaming through crystal pendants."

One Capital City newsman was so enchanted by the high-spirited First Lady, he could only pen superlatives: "When the party season is over [Jennie Woodson] will be the most universally popular lady" to ever grace the Executive Mansion. While her husband, Silas Woodson, led the state, the twenty-six-year-old First Lady reigned over the Mansion with a wonderful exuberance and hospitality, if not great experience. Jennie, a graduate of Christian College in Columbia, Missouri, was a perfect match for her new duties. A niece described her as "well-read, a brilliant conversationalist, always beautifully gowned."

Jennie's husband, twenty-seven years her senior, also brought a dash of natural charm to his new position—although he had little background in state government to recommend him. Silas had started his political pursuits in his native Kentucky. Like Abraham Lincoln, he rose from poverty to prominence by blending his law career with public service. With little formal schooling, he clerked in a store briefly, read the law, and gained local attention for his fine public speaking. His commanding presence and thunderous voice made him a powerful figure before juries and political gatherings.

While making his first bid for public office at the age of twenty-three, however, the young politician did not rely on oratory alone. In a campaign to oust an incumbent legislator, he visited every home in his area and successfully won a seat in the Kentucky legislature. Though Silas lost his reelection bid, he landed an appointment as circuit judge. In 1853 voters again returned him to the legislature, despite his position favoring the gradual emancipation of slaves—an unpopular stance in his home state.

But Woodson did not finish his term. Frustrated by the political climate in Kentucky and excited by the prospect of living in a thriving, fast-growing area, Woodson moved to St. Joseph, Missouri, the following year. In his new surroundings, he quickly earned a reputation as a dynamic lawyer and

Jennie Woodson's strict upbringing as a preacher's daughter did not deter her in the least from having frequent and lively parties at the Mansion.

magnetic orator. In 1860 he was again elevated to circuit judge, a position he kept throughout the Civil War in addition to his rank as colonel in the Union Army.

During the volatile Reconstruction Era, Woodson discovered the hard way how bitterly divided the state remained. Running as a Democrat in 1868, he lost his race for a legislative seat largely because a stringent loyalty oath barred many of his party from voting because of their Southern sympathies during the war. Temporarily discouraged by defeat, Woodson returned to his law practice.

Four years later, after voting barriers were dropped, he served as chairman of the State Democratic Convention when it met to select the party's nominees for state office. Frustrated delegates, searching for a gubernatorial candidate, balloted for days unable to break a tie. Without telling Woodson, a friend proposed that the vying candidates withdraw in favor of the St. Joseph judge. The idea caught on and Woodson won the nomination almost unanimously. With their new "dark horse" candidate, Democrats captured the governorship for the first time since the Civil War. The victory marked a revival of the Democratic Party in Missouri and the beginning of its control of the executive office for the next thirty-six years.

The sudden improvement in his political fortune surprised both Silas and his young wife. Eager to make a good first impression in the Capital City, Jennie imported a prominent St. Louis caterer to put on a splendid inaugural reception at the Mansion. The feat took a host of helpers working in the basement kitchen for a week before the event. On inaugural evening, "the huge banquet table, extending the full length of the double dining rooms, was a marvel of confectionery art and floral decoration." While the "elite of the state" devoured the inaugural spread, the new First Couple engaged in the traditional handshaking ritual—a task they endured "with unflagging warmth," it was reported.

Excited by the prospect of living in a thriving, fast-growing area, Woodson moved to St. Joseph, Missouri, in 1854.

One writer—not present for the occasion, but hopeful that the Mansion and its residents would serve as a model of Victorian propriety—declared the evening "an assemblage of ladies and gentlemen met for the purpose of rational,

The "elite of the state" devoured the inaugural spread.

intellectual enjoyment." However, those in attendance found the evening far more robust as sounds of music from a brass and string band filled the house. Inaugural guests delighted in such rollicking dances as the polka and schottische, which had replaced the minuet after the Civil War. It was reported that dancers swirled "all through the magnificent parlors, waltzing around, through doors, and from one room to another, galloping over people who came in the way, and schottisching recklessly about . . . until long after the noon of night."

In customary fashion, news stories gave greatly embellished accounts of what the hostess and ladies wore to the gathering. One writer praised Mrs. Woodson's gown, describing it as a "handsome brocade silk of beautiful color known as gaslight green, whose mingling and shimmering shades almost dazzled the eye." Her hair—also a subject of comment—lay "in puffs and curls, its only ornament being a pink plume."

Dancers swirled about "the magnificent parlors, waltzing around, through doors, and from one room to another."

After providing the Capital City with a grand inaugural display, the Woodsons settled into Mansion life. The former residents, Governor and Mrs. Brown, had no trouble filling the spacious new home with their six children and a score of visiting kinfolk. Now with only Silas, Jennie, and two-year-old Mary Alice comprising the First Family, it seemed there would be far fewer people in the house.

The Woodsons, however, soon began taking in relatives. Silas asked his brother-in-law, Dr. R. D. Shannon, to come to Jefferson City as his assistant. He offered to house the family of four that included Dr. Shannon, Jennie's sister, and their two daughters. One of the girls, Carey Shannon, would later write an account of the "greatness and grandeur" of her childhood home.

Assisting Mrs. Woodson (left) with her responsibilities as hostess was her sister, Mrs. R. D. Shannon.

The joint living arrangements were not new for the families. The Shannons had lived with the Woodsons in St. Joseph while R. D. studied medicine—a venture charitably financed by Silas. Dr. Shannon's orphaned sister, Cornelia, also joined the clan living at the Mansion and gained considerable attention about town for her fine attire and many social appearances.

Having live-in relatives was handy for the First Lady, who frequently called on her sister and Cornelia to help with the entertaining. Just a month after the inaugural reception, the ladies of the Mansion sent eight hundred invitations to another dance, which featured two bands—one in the Great Hall and another in the third-floor ballroom.

Jennie maintained an impressive schedule of weekly receptions, too, keeping the cooks at the Mansion and the socialites of the city busy preparing for upcoming events. One writer noted that Jennie's strict upbringing as the daughter of a prominent Campbellite minister did not deter her in the least from having frequent and lively gatherings at the Mansion. There were lawn parties, dinner parties, children's parties, and dance parties in profusion.

The talk of the town was her masquerade ball in February 1874. Mrs. Governor Woodson—as she came to be known in the society columns—greeted her guests costumed as the Queen of the Night, wearing a "dusky black silk robe and coronet of crescent moon and stars of brilliants" in her hair. Those attending wore outfits ranging from a Beggar Maid to the King of England. While Jennie enjoyed staging glittering parties, she drew the line at serving wine. Temperance was a popular cause in the 1870s and the First Lady had no intention of defying public sentiment.

THE NEWEL POST LADY

Some thought she was charming—just right for the Victorian Mansion. Others considered her garish and inappropriate. From the earliest period of the house, the five-foot-tall bronze Newel Post Lady—perched on the post at the foot of the stairs—greeted all those who climbed or slid down the Grand Stairway.

Jennie Woodson's niece, Carey Shannon, described her childhood fascination with the gaslit figure, which she used as a hiding place for watching the adults during Mansion parties. The glowing lamp in her "uplifted arms, flood[ed] the stairs with intriguing light," she recalled. "I felt wonderfully important, as I dangled my feet over the railing, to be noticed and spoken to by the 'Grandees' who passed me by."

However, by the late 1930s, decorating tastes had changed and the Newel Post Lady came down during a remodeling. For years thereafter, only pictures remained of the bronze figure that once guarded the stairway and amused small children.

Later, Missouri Mansion Preservation uncovered another Newel Post Lady nearly identical to the original and produced by the same manufacturer. During the Carnahan administration, the figure was refurbished and wired for electricity. Returned to her pedestal in 1995, the historic guardian of the Mansion (left) again watches silently over the passage of time.

Capital City reporters found more "shocking" things to report about the Mansion than Jennie's lively and lavish parties. According to one newspaper, the executive home had a strange problem: "The chandeliers, the door knobs, the railways for the doors, and the stair carpet rods emit flashes and give shocks." The perplexed reporter quizzed his readers: "What makes the Executive Mansion a grand electrical battery?"

The following week another writer explained the curiosity. Friction caused by feet rubbing across soft, thick carpets—like those in the Mansion—could generate enough electricity to give a mild shock to anyone touching a metal object. He also warned that the energy transmitted could "light the gas, if . . . the tip of the finger [was] held close to the burner."

"What makes the Executive Mansion a grand electrical battery?"

The real sparkle at the Mansion, however, came with the gathering of Mrs. Woodson's fascinating guests. The names of popular writers, as well as political and military leaders of the day, showed up on her guest lists. Such frequent entertainment was costly for the First Family at a time when the legislature made no appropriation for Mansion expenses. A relative estimated that Jennie's "extremely lavish" hospitality cost the Governor twice what he earned in salary. But Woodson did not seem to mind. In addition to sponsoring his wife's social extravaganzas, he hired a master gardener to landscape the grounds and to construct a breezy summerhouse on the southeast corner of the yard.

Though generous with the household budget, Woodson showed far more restraint when it came to state spending—and for good reason. The nationwide Panic of 1873 brought with it a loss of jobs and a dwindling money supply. The Governor reported to lawmakers that agriculture, manufacturing, mining, and other industries were greatly paralyzed by the economic downturn.

To make ends meet, Woodson tightened the reins on government, abolishing a number of state offices and cutting the mileage allowance for legislators. He attempted to make the state penitentiary self-supporting by leasing the facility to a private contractor for ten years. But when poor food and sanitation conditions resulted in two prison riots within two years, the state was forced to reclaim the deteriorating institution.

Woodson had a breezy summerhouse constructed on the south lawn of the Mansion.

Despite economic woes, the Governor reduced the state debt and lowered taxes. Education got shortchanged, however, when Woodson told legislators that an annual school term of four months adequately prepared children for the "ordinary duties of life." Higher education seemed to fare better. Credit is, nonetheless, due the Governor for his part in establishing the State Normal School at Cape Girardeau, later know as Southeast Missouri State University.

However, Woodson and the Democrats came in for severe criticism for failing to capture the notorious Younger and James gangs. Republicans accused the Democrats of being sympathetic "with their former comrades in arms" who had turned to robbery and crime after the Civil War. According to critics, Woodson and his cohorts could not be trusted to put down the outlaws who were disgracing the state. The Governor attempted to counter the charge. He proposed a twenty-five-man secret police to deal with violence in the state, but the legislature rejected the idea. As a result, the gangs ran unrestrained for the next eight years before Governor Thomas Crittenden finally brought them under control.

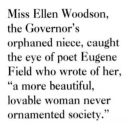

Miss Ellen Woodson, the Governor's orphaned niece, caught the eye of poet Eugene Field who wrote of her, "a more beautiful, lovable woman never ornamented society."

Woodson's personal hunting pursuits became another source of embarrassment when he and his friends were arrested in Kansas for shooting ducks out of season. But in the long run, his friends had something more than game birds in their sights for the Governor. They wanted him to make a mid-term race for the U.S. Senate. Woodson refused to consider it, saying Missourians who elected him were due a full term of service.

According to the Missouri Constitution then in effect, a full term for a governor lasted only two years. Still, it was time enough for the Woodson family to give the Mansion its first marriage and first births. In May 1873 Dr. Shannon's sister, Cornelia, "the beautiful . . . belle of [the] State Capital," was married in the Double Parlor of the new Mansion. A month later, Jennie's sister gave birth to twin daughters. (Jennie herself had twins a few years after leaving the Mansion.) With their expanding family and R. D.'s new job as state superintendent of schools, the Shannons decided the time had come for a home of their own.

The Shannons' departure made room for yet another young relative to join the household. Miss Ellen Woodson—a niece the Governor had adopted—moved in and assisted Jennie for several months before she, too, was married. Though the bride chose a church wedding, Jennie could not resist hosting a breakfast party for the newlyweds a few days before the Governor ended his term.

Departing the Mansion, the Woodsons headed back to St. Joseph where Silas resumed his law practice. In 1885 he returned to the bench when Governor

Crittenden appointed him to a judgeship. Woodson kept the office until his retirement following a cerebral hemorrhage; he died a year later in 1896.

The gay social whirl of the Woodson years—so enjoyed by the townspeople—vanished with the next administration. Although residents were accustomed to a shift in style with each new governor, the somber mood of the next First Family would diminish the social life of the city as well as the Mansion. The lively reign of Jennie and Silas Woodson, however, remained a fond memory in the state capital for many years thereafter.

A CHILD'S FAIRYLAND

One of the children living at the Mansion, eight-year-old Carey Shannon, wrote years later of the thrill of riding in the carriage up the steep hill to her new home.

"Arriving at the big iron gate, while the grown-ups looked after the baggage, in childish curiosity and wonder, I ran ahead, up the gas-lighted walk, which no great white way of modern times has ever been more brilliantly lighted; up the broad front steps, past the great granite pillars, to the 'BIG FRONT DOOR!' to be greeted by the ubiquitous butler. . . .

" 'Won't you please show me the way in?' was my awed request, and his amused answer was 'Certainly, Little Missus,'

as he lifted me bodily through the door and deposited me on one of the big divans facing the grand stairway; so 'Little Missus' became my title in my new world. 'What to my wondering eyes did appear?' Greatness and grandeur undreamed of before—a real fairyland, huge rooms, magnificent furniture, magic carpets, chandeliers ablaze with rainbows gleaming through crystal pendants."

Ten years later her childhood view of the great house had changed: "A visit to the place caused me to wonder what sort of reducing diet had been used on the very large Mansion of my early memories!"

RARE DEVOTION

Governor Charles Henry Hardin
Mary Barr Jenkins Hardin
1875-1877

"There is only one pledge that I will make to be fulfilled when I get to be governor. I pledge that there will be no masquerade balls at the Mansion." ~ Charles Hardin

The serious-minded Mary Hardin contrasted sharply with the former First Lady. Jennie Woodson's dances and parties had added a touch of gaiety to Mansion life that Capital City socialites greatly enjoyed. The town could still remember her masked ball—the highlight of the 1874 social season—when the youthful Mrs. Woodson had dressed as the Queen of the Night.

But the new First Lady, fifty-one-year-old Mary Hardin, was a devout Baptist who disapproved of such display. Still, she possessed qualities much admired in a Victorian lady. Charles Hardin once described his wife as "a lady of intelligence, refinement . . . a constant and close student of the Bible, and a lady of rare devotion and piety."

C. H. Hardin

"Will our next governor permit dancing at the Mansion is the question of the hour."

The strictness of the Hardins caused some dismay in the state capital even before they arrived. A Jefferson City reporter wrote, "Will our next governor permit dancing at the Mansion? is the question of the hour with metropolitan belles and beaux." For those who wondered, the new Governor made it very plain: no such frivolity would occur during his administration.

The new era of austerity began on inauguration day. In deference to the Hardins, all celebration was scaled back. A quiet swearing-in ceremony took place in the House chamber during a joint session of the General Assembly. The evening reception—though bountiful and tastefully presented by St. Louis caterers—was equally restrained.

True to his pledge, Hardin allowed no dancing, nor was a glass uplifted to toast the day. One writer bemoaned the lack of music, dancing, and alcohol, saying it "caused many a sigh to rise in the breasts of the young

Mary Hardin was "a lady of intelligence, refinement . . . a constant and close student of the Bible, and a lady of rare devotion and piety."

27

and the gay." Nonetheless, local newspapers—customarily generous to the first family—proclaimed the event "magnificent [and] attended by almost everyone in the city."

With their move into the Mansion, Charles and Mary could at last be together. As a legislator, her husband had lived in Jefferson City when the General Assembly met, but Mary had always stayed at home to tend the farm. The deeply devoted couple had known each other since their childhood days in Columbia, Missouri, though Charles, like Mary, had started life in Kentucky. During his college years, Hardin left Missouri to attend Miami University in Ohio where he was best remembered as one of the eight founders of the Greek fraternity Beta Theta Pi.

"I now declare freely my love for you— an ardent, an anxious, a growing love."

Having earlier lost his father, Charles looked to his uncle, Dr. William Jewell, for advice during his student days. Jewell, cofounder of the Liberty, Missouri, college that bears his name, recognized "the fires of an honorable ambition" in his nephew and urged him to begin laying the "foundation for future respectability and usefulness." Charles took the advice seriously and gained much admiration as a scholar and, later, as a lawyer and businessman in mid-Missouri.

Mary, too, was an adept student concerned about the future. As a pupil at Bonne Femme College in Columbia, she won special recognition for reading the Greek and Latin classics with "extraordinary ease [and] lucid diction." Following graduation, Mary put her learning to use as a teacher at Columbia Female Academy. In a letter to her brother, she described what a "Delightful task!" it was to "pour . . . fresh instruction o'er the mind." The eighteen-year-old schoolmistress also joked about her prolonged courtship with Mr. Hardin. She feared that the dress she had set aside for her wedding day would "be worn out or out of fashion" before she ever became a bride.

Handmade doll, a replica of Mary Hardin in her wedding dress.

Mary had no need for concern. Having established himself, Hardin soon turned his thoughts from law to love. After receiving the blessing of her father, her young suitor poured out his heart in a four-page letter: "I now declare freely my love for you—an ardent, an anxious, a growing love. . . . That love has already given rest and life to all the dormant affections of my soul—it has clambered up and lingers around every fiber and fold of my heart." Obviously impressed by such a poetic declaration, Mary accepted his proposal. They were married at her parents' home in 1844, only a year after she expressed concern over her unused wedding dress.

During the ensuing years, Hardin's political ambitions began to surface, much to Mary's dismay. He served first as circuit attorney and, in 1852, won a seat in the General Assembly on the Whig ticket. Mary stayed in their Mexico, Missouri, home for weeks at a time while Mr. Hardin—as she referred to her husband—served three legislative terms in the state capital. They both found the long separations difficult to bear. During one such time, Charles wrote his beloved that he was "miserable in his solitude." Apparently, Hardin viewed his scholarly young wife as an intellectual equal and missed her valuable advice. He once confessed, "If you were here, I would be under your guide and get along better."

Though bright and gifted, Mary—true to her upbringing—thought it inappropriate for a lady to advance herself publicly. With no children to care for and slaves to do much of the work, she filled her days with artistic, spiritual, and intellectual pursuits. Her creative nature came alive in oil painting and fancy handwork. Mary also enjoyed composing poetry and prose, though very little of it appeared in print. According to her diary, she also took an interest in more traditional household tasks—sewing, laundering, and candle molding. In the kitchen, she was a model Victorian housewife able to turn out such contemporary favorites as Sally Lunn cake, calf's foot jelly, and cornstarch cake.

Mary sought solace in reading the Scriptures in the original Greek and in pondering the Latin works of Cicero. Still, entries from her diary show that she suffered bouts of deep depression. She wrote of being "lonely . . . weary . . . sad," and of having a continuing dissatisfaction with her spiritual condition as well as that of her husband. At the end of the day, she would often fret at having spent too little time in prayer and Bible reading.

The fact that Mr.

Mary wrote of being "lonely . . . weary . . . sad."

Hardin had no religious affiliation and occasionally used tobacco also troubled his churchgoing wife. She extracted an annual pledge from him that he would abstain from using tobacco. According to his promise as recorded in her diary, Hardin agreed to pay Mary thirty dollars and to buy a silk dress for each of two relatives if he ever again indulged in such wickedness.

The devout First Lady extracted an annual pledge from her husband that he would abstain from the use of tobacco.

While Mary restricted herself to the details of homemaking and moral growth, Hardin advanced himself in politics and business. In 1860 after three terms in the House, he moved to the state Senate as a Conservative Unionist. Because of his skills in legal writing, he was placed on the judiciary committee where he became one of three men to revise the Missouri statutes.

"I shrink from strangers," Hardin once wrote his equally retiring wife.

As the Civil War approached, Senator Hardin opposed secession and argued for a neutral position for Missouri. Nonetheless, he attended the first session of the rebel legislature—the assemblage of Confederate lawmakers that had fled the Capital City at the onset of the war. However, Hardin was the only senator present at the Neosho, Missouri, meeting to vote against secession. Afterwards he returned home and spent the early years of the war at his small log cabin home, quietly tending the farm. According to friends, the couple was happier during this interlude in his political career than at any other time in their lives.

In spite of his attempt at neutrality and his vote against secession, Hardin was considered a Southern sympathizer. As such, he was disenfranchised, as was nearly one-third of Missouri's population. The so-called "Ironclad Oath" or "Loyalty Oath" stripped Confederates of their voting rights and fueled more hatred and fear in the severely divided state. One offensive portion of the new law required all lawyers, clergymen, school teachers, office holders, and jurors to swear to the eighty-six points of a loyalty provision.

Mrs. Hardin painted a portrait of herself and a matching portrait of her husband. Unfortunately, both were destroyed in a fire.

In 1862 Hardin took the oath of allegiance to the Union and, thereby, gained the right to resume his law practice. He also acquired an expanse of timberland that he converted into beautiful bluegrass fields. After the war, he built a new house on the tract known as "Forest Home." Much of the work on the 550-acre farm was done by others since Hardin, the country squire, had neither the inclination nor the physical stamina for hard labor. Each morning he rode several miles by horseback into the town of Mexico to tend his law business and to run the affairs of the Mexico Southern Bank, which he had helped organize.

Hardin returned to the state Senate in 1872. Not an outgoing man by nature, he resisted being pulled any further into politics. "I shrink from strangers," Hardin once wrote his equally retiring wife. Nonetheless, by the end of his term, when colleagues were eagerly promoting him for governor, Hardin reluctantly accepted.

Calling his race for governor a venture "upon a stormy sea," Mary gave her husband little encouragement. In a letter she cautioned him: "If, you, my husband, should not receive the nomination, yield not

THE GRASSHOPPER PROCLAMATION

First Lady Mary Hardin considered political life a venture "upon a stormy sea" and wanted no part of it. Even so, she influenced public affairs at least once when a horde of grasshoppers ravaged the state.

For two years, locusts had devastated crops, orchards, and trees in western Missouri, causing millions of dollars in damage. Reports told of "great clouds of the insects, dense enough to block the sun, hitting the roofs and sides of houses like hail stones. They swept the fields almost clean of vegetation, stripped trees of their leaves, and even relieved sheep of their wool." At one point, the swarm stretched three hundred miles long and one hundred miles wide. The invading pests were so thick that railroad trains stopped on their runs to allow crews to clean the insects from the tracks. One farmer quipped, "The hoppers ate everything I had but the mortgage."

Many solutions were offered to remedy the problem. The state entomologist, Professor Charles V. Riley, urged the state to offer a bounty on the grasshoppers, but the frugal Governor felt it was an unwise expenditure of revenue. As the plague persisted, Governor Hardin received an anonymous letter suggesting that a call to prayer might bring relief. The deeply spiritual First Lady agreed and pressed her husband to issue the famous "Grasshopper Proclamation" that set June 3, 1875, as a day of fasting and prayer.

A week after the proclamation, heavy rains broke the drought (some reports claimed the rains came as early as the next day) and within a month the grasshoppers abandoned Missouri. While some jokingly said the Hardins "prayed the grasshoppers clear out of Missouri and up into Iowa," most people praised the First Lady for her spiritual insight.

Perhaps unrecognized at the time, Mary's intervention marked the beginning of more involvement by a First Lady in public affairs. Mrs. Hardin, of course, did not see her participation as an invasion of her husband's political turf. Like Queen Esther, the biblical heroine, Mary felt she was an emissary of the Lord—one who had "come to the kingdom" (or in her case, the Mansion) for just such a time. Like Mary Hardin, future first ladies would continue to disavow their influence, "pretend[ing] to know less than they did and to be advising less than they were."

Unfortunately, Mary's intercession brought only temporary relief. The marauding hordes returned again for the next two years, leaving Missouri farmers and businessmen deeply in debt. Professor Riley offered another solution to the pestilence. He urged Missourians to use the locusts for food, saying they were edible, nutritious, and suitable for roasting. This "manna-like blessing from heaven" could be used for animal food or ground for flour like the Indians once did. "No different from shrimp," he said. Missourians, somehow, remained unconvinced.

yourself to gloomy regrets and 'bring not home the black and bitter frown that is stamped upon the forehead of ambition.' "

Hardin won the nomination by a "hairsbreadth." At a time when candidates were chosen by convention rather than popular vote, Democrats gave Hardin 159¹⁄₆ votes where 159 were required. (His fractional victory left General Francis Cockrell

Hardin was labeled "the driest speaker that ever took the stump in Missouri."

with the distinction of having lost the nomination for governor by the slimmest margin on record.) Hardin proved his worth as a candidate, in spite of being labeled "the driest speaker that ever took the stump in Missouri." Winning by a substantial margin over his Republican opponent, he carried the entire Democratic ticket to victory with him.

While Hardin may have been considered a dull public speaker, he was unusually sharp when it came to managing money. In spite of the distractions of public life, he had developed a lucrative law practice with enough income to become a wealthy money lender. These skills served him well as governor when he entered office and found Missouri greatly in debt from the war and the state's support of railroad construction. By frugal management and restructuring of debt, he cut the state's obligations by half without imposing new taxes. He further reduced the level of spending by limiting the legislature to biennial sessions.

Hardin was not only frugal with government spending but also with his par-

Jefferson Davis, former President of the Confederacy, was serenaded on the Mansion lawn during his visit with the Hardins.

don of prisoners. He felt that pardons had been issued "loosely and carelessly" and often for political purposes. Because he believed in the "wisdom and justice" of the courts, he pardoned far fewer criminals than other governors had; none were spared for capital offenses.

Though Hardin skillfully managed Missouri's postwar crises, he was having no luck in ridding the state of a destructive invasion of grasshoppers that ravaged farmlands. After the Governor received an anonymous letter suggesting that he seek divine intervention, Mary prodded her husband to issue the famed "Grasshopper Proclamation," calling for a day of prayer and fasting. When rain came shortly thereafter and the grasshoppers fled, the First Lady won plaudits for her wise counsel.

While Mary never drew acclaim for her social skills, her circumspect behavior continued to evoke comment. According to one journalist, there were "no receptions at which people dared speak above a whisper, no dances where flying feet might get the better of the glowing hours; no jollity, gaiety, nor social mirth; everything [was] gloomy and dull. . . ." Another writer cast his comments in a less negative vein; he declared that during Mary Hardin's reign as First Lady, nothing occurred "that could make her pastor bat his eye with the slightest disapproval."

Despite the Hardins' conservative bent, the Mansion was not without some social amenities. At least two notables visited the Capital City during the Governor's two years in office. Jefferson Davis, former President of the Confederacy, stayed overnight at the Mansion while on a Midwest tour of agricultural fairs. His visit, ten years after the Civil War, reflected the healing attitude that was slowly taking place in the nation. Davis was greeted by great crowds and ovations at every train stop along the way to Jefferson City. During his weekend stay, a large group assembled on the

King Kalakaua of Hawaii, the portly monarch, fascinated the townspeople, most of whom had never seen a Pacific islander, much less a king.

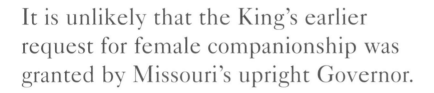

It is unlikely that the King's earlier request for female companionship was granted by Missouri's upright Governor.

Mansion lawn to serenade the Southern leader. On Sunday morning, Davis worshiped with the Hardins at Christ Church and later took a carriage ride about town.

The other distinguished visitor, King Kalakaua of Hawaii, was on a cross-country train trip when he stopped in Jefferson City for an appearance before the House and Senate. Earlier the King had dined at the White House where it was reported his cupbearers cautiously eyed every morsel of food set before him. There is no record, however, that the royal visitor risked dining at the Missouri Governor's Mansion. It is also unlikely that his earlier request of the St. Louis mayor to provide him female companionship was honored by Missouri's upright Governor. But there is no doubt that the portly monarch fascinated the townspeople, most of whom had never seen a Pacific islander, much less a king.

To ease the burden of entertaining visitors, the legislature began making a biennial appropriation of one thousand dollars for expenses at the governor's residence. But Mrs. Hardin used the new funds sparingly. Rather than sink public money into costly entertaining or

Earlier during his trip, the King had dined at the White House where it was reported his cupbearers cautiously eyed every morsel of food set before him.

At the close of his term, Hardin returned to his farm in Mexico, Missouri, and never again sought elective office.

decorations, she preferred to expend her own energy in charitable and religious work in Jefferson City.

The Governor, too, showed a generous nature. From his personal fortune, he gave freely to benevolent causes and gained recognition as one of the state's greatest philanthropists. His endowment of a defunct women's college in Mexico, Missouri, reactivated the school, which became known as Hardin College. The small town further benefited from his help in the creation of the Mexico Military Academy and by his provision for a park.

Hardin, one of the state's greatest philanthropists, reactivated a defunct women's college in Mexico, Missouri, which became known as Hardin College.

At the close of his term, Hardin returned to Mexico and never sought elective office again. He resumed farming and practicing law, became a curator of the University of Missouri, and—much to Mary's relief—joined the church. But his health began to diminish following a sunstroke and the onset of diabetes. In

search of a more healthful environment, the couple traveled extensively, staying for long periods in Colorado, New Mexico, Florida, and the mountains of Virginia. It was a futile quest, however, that ended with his death in 1892.

Mrs. Hardin had already lost a favorite niece. With her husband's death, followed closely by that of her sister, Mary was devastated. A relative noted that Mrs. Hardin always wore a black dress and black lace cap, and filled her days with handwork and Bible study. The grieving widow also authored a biography of her husband, outlining his accomplishments and including some of his writings.

Mary Hardin was nearly eighty years old when she died. Her portrait hanging in the Double Parlor at the Mansion captures the somber disposition

The grieving widow also authored a biography of her husband.

and the inner strength for which she was known. Though never proven, the painting was once thought to be the work of George Caleb Bingham, possibly because the artist served as adjutant general in Governor Hardin's cabinet.

Just as the Hardins had set a tone of sobriety at the Mansion, future first families would place their own unique, and often contrasting, style on the house. The people of Jefferson City had always been tolerant—even gracious—to those whom the whims of politics moved in and out of the Governor's Mansion. Nonetheless, by the close of the Hardin era, the Capital City was ready for more festive times.

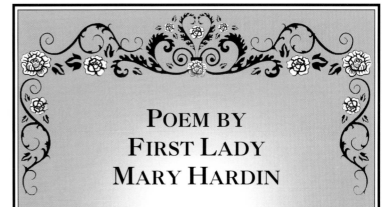

POEM BY FIRST LADY MARY HARDIN

The childless Mrs. Hardin formed a strong attachment to her sister's child, Mary Hardin Kennan. This poem was written in 1888 following the death of the sixteen-year-old niece and namesake.

The Land without a Graveyard

The Land without a Graveyard
How sweet to think, that while we weep
So sadly in the graveyard
Angelic hosts their vigils keep
Here in the silent graveyard.

Our eyes cannot now see them,
Our ears cannot now hear them,
But in our hearts we feel them,
Here in the silent graveyard.

While sitting by dear Mary's grave
So lonely in the graveyard,
We feel that He who died to save,
Is with us in the graveyard.

He never will forsake us,
But soon will come and take us,
Where Mary, glad will greet us,
In the land without a graveyard.

Our tears must cease, our tears must cease,
To die is not so hard.
Soon we shall meet where all is peace
In the land without a graveyard.

THE OLD SOLDIER AND THE NEW WOMAN

GOVERNOR JOHN SMITH PHELPS
MARY WHITNEY PHELPS
HOSTESS: MARY ANNE PHELPS MONTGOMERY
1877-1881

General John Phelps lost more of life's battles than he won. His family was frayed by discord and death and his career laden with political struggles.

John S. Phelps

One of Missouri's most exceptional first ladies never lived in the Governor's Mansion. Instead, Mary Whitney Phelps yielded her duties as hostess to her married daughter, Mary Anne Montgomery.

Mrs. Phelps—the orphaned daughter of a New England sea captain—had learned to chart her own course early in life. By the time she met the Connecticut lawyer John Phelps, she had already defied social convention by walking away from an "unfortunate marriage."

In 1837 John caused a rift in his own family when he declared his intention to marry the red-headed divorcee who was nearly three years his senior. Ignoring his father's threat to disinherit him, John and Mary were married that same year. The decision left John little choice but to leave the family law firm. Mary gave up her business as a seamstress (leaving behind several creditors) and the couple headed west in search of a new life on the frontier.

Phelps was just twenty-three years old when he and Mary arrived in Springfield, a rugged southwest Missouri village of about two hundred people. The area showed promise, however, and already boasted a half-dozen stores, two blacksmith shops, a tanyard, a tavern, and a post office.

It did not take long for Phelps to demonstrate his legal and political skills. As he unpacked his stash of law books from the bottom of his wagon, word spread about town that a new lawyer from the East had just arrived. Phelps was immediately summoned to the jail to meet his first client, an accused murderer for whom he subsequently won an acquittal. Several years later, when the townspeople needed a new legislator, they turned to John Phelps—"that little Yankee boy"—to represent them in the General Assembly.

In his dual role as circuit-riding attorney and lawmaker, John was sometimes gone for months, leaving Mary in a Springfield boarding house. Once upon returning,

(Facing page) An artist's version of Mrs. Phelps tending the wounded at the Battle of Pea Ridge. She is the only first lady of Missouri for whom there is no known photograph or portrait.

37

A Run for the Money

In 1858 Mary Phelps and her thirteen-year-old daughter, Mary Anne, accepted an invitation to take part in an exciting race. John Butterfield, owner of a stagecoach line and a friend of the Phelps family, had entered a $25,000 contest with a steamship company to see who could deliver mail the fastest from San Francisco to New York. Butterfield himself was to drive the last leg of the journey from Springfield to Tipton where the mail bags would be loaded onto an eastbound train. His oppo-nent's route was by steamship from California to Panama. From there the mail was moved by mules across the isthmus and reloaded onto boats.

Butterfield asked Mrs. Phelps and her daughter to join him for luck. After some pleading from Mary Anne, her mother agreed to make the journey. John Phelps did not object, for he knew there was little he could do to deter the headstrong women in his household.

All of Springfield turned out for the predawn send off. The warmly bundled women and driver hastily boarded the incoming stagecoach. Within minutes a fresh team was hitched to the coach and the horses dashed off into the darkness. Young Mary recalled that on the first leg of the trip she was wedged between her mother and the driver, fearful even to speak.

Fifteen hours later, after changing horses five times and being greeted by throngs of well-wishers at each stop, the mail coach thundered into Tipton "at breakneck speed, rounding the corners of the street on two wheels." Upon reaching the rail terminal, the mail pouches were hastily thrown aboard the waiting train as it pulled from the station to meet the New York Express in St. Louis.

Hungry and exhausted from their long journey, the stagecoach riders were, nonetheless, hopeful of victory. Two days later a telegraph message arrived: Butterfield had won the contest—a feat of luck that he attributed to Mrs. Phelps and Mary Anne who had the nerve to join him in the daring, cross-country race with the mail.

he was surprised to find she was no longer there. When Phelps inquired about his wife, he was told to look for her at the cabin. John was confused by the reply; although the couple had a parcel of land, they had not yet built a cabin. However, in a typical display of resourcefulness, Mary had taken it upon herself to have one built while he was gone and was busy decorating the interior. The couple later moved to their permanent residence on the edge of town, a one-thousand-acre farm, part of which was referred to as Phelps Grove.

While Mary's cabin building was a surprise to John, it was no surprise to Mary when her husband—who was not yet thirty years old—announced his candidacy for Congress in 1844. John won the race and prepared to move to Washington, but Mary did not go with him. She preferred to remain in Springfield where she managed the farm, operated a school, and cared for their family. (Five children were born to the couple, but only two survived to adulthood.)

Occasionally, Mary accompanied John to the nation's capital, leaving her young children in the care of a trusted slave woman. More often, John traveled alone, going overland across Missouri to Puducah, Kentucky. From the port city, he boarded a steamship, going by way of the Ohio River to Wheeling, West Virginia, where he could catch a train to Washington. Phelps made a lifelong friendship with a new congressman, Abraham Lincoln, while traveling from Springfield, Illinois, to the nation's capital. Though the two were of different political parties and disagreed about when emancipation should occur, they shared an unwavering loyalty to the Union.

On one of his journeys as a congressman, Phelps had a brush with death—an incident his daughter alluded to in her memoirs, but gave few details. Phelps was making speeches in the Territory of New Mexico to promote a bill for the

A Frontier "Bar" Exam

Before practicing law in Missouri, John Phelps—like countless lawyers before and after him—had to pass the bar exam. For the would-be attorney, this meant demonstrating his legal skills before Supreme Court Justice George Tompkins, a fine legal scholar and student of French literature. Phelps rode by horseback from Springfield to Jefferson City where the judge resided, but locating Tompkins proved to be difficult.

After a search, he finally found the judge clearing timber from a lot outside of the city. Tompkins invited the young man to sit with him on a nearby log and began to quiz him—mainly about literature and very little about the law.

Satisfied with the answers he received, Tompkins concluded by asking, " 'Now, just one more question, please; have you a bottle in your saddle-bags?' Whereupon young Phelps produced a bottle of very good liquor. The jurist took a drink, cleared his throat, and remarked: 'Young man, if you are as thoughtful of your clients' interests as you are of the comfort and convenience of the court, you will make a very good lawyer.' "

He then took out a pencil and, with no other paper available, wrote out the law license on a page torn from a printed leaflet. As Phelps rode away from the clearing, "his heart was full of gratitude, but his bottle was empty."

Springfield, Missouri, was a town of about 2,000 at the time of the Civil War.

southwestern extension of the railway and had even learned Spanish in preparation for the visit. On his return trip, however, he was captured by Indians and his life saved only through the rescue effort of a devoted slave.

By comparison, the remainder of his congressional service was far less exciting. During his eighteen years in Washington, Phelps headed the Ways and Means Committee for more than a decade. He was recognized most for his work in gaining the admission of Oregon to the Union, his part in reducing postage to three cents a letter, and his support for an overland mail route to California.

At the onset of the Civil War while John was still in Congress, Mary and their two children tended the farm with the help of their seventeen slaves. Among guests to the farm were Colonel Ulysses S. Grant and his officers who stopped for a leisurely meal during the early months of the war. Their presence, however, was a prelude to the harsh years ahead as the conflict escalated. In 1861, when the Union and Confederate armies engaged at Wilson's Creek, the Phelps family could hear the roar of cannons and see billowing smoke rising from the battlefield six miles away. In a fervor of patriotism, Mary's teenage son left home to join the fight. Badly outnumbered, the federal forces suffered a devastating defeat. By the end of the battle, the Union troops—including her son, John—were in retreat to Rolla.

Early the next day, Mary walked the few miles into Springfield to view the desolation. Reaching the abandoned city by dawn, she went immediately to the Union army headquarters which had been set up in a house owned by the Phelps family. There—stretched out on a table—she found the body of Union General Nathaniel Lyon who had been killed in the battle and left behind during the hasty evacuation of the city. Feeling it was improper to leave the fallen hero unattended, Mary remained at the headquarters throughout the day until a coffin could be made.

During her vigil, a Confederate soldier swaggered into the headquarters, brandishing a long knife. "I've come to cut out the heart of that damned Yankee," he declared contemptuously.

The Phelps family could hear the roar of cannons and see billowing smoke rising from the Battle of Wilson's Creek only six miles away.

Mrs. Phelps stood calmly beside the slain General and replied, "If you do, it will be over my dead body." Apparently, unwilling to take on such a strong-willed woman, the soldier relented and walked out.

When the coffin arrived, Mary had the corpse loaded onto a wagon and returned to her nearby farm. Upon arriving home, she found two Confederate regiments camped on her land and her house occupied by army officers. She placed

Mary's own losses during the Civil War strengthened her desire to relieve the suffering of others.

Lyon's body in an outdoor cellar temporarily, but soon grew fearful that his remains might yet be mutilated by pillaging soldiers. One night, accompanied by some family servants, she secretly buried the General on her farm until relatives arrived from the East to claim the body.

As the Southern army moved out, confiscating horses and wagons, Mary was left with only a two-wheel cart, a lame mule, and a house full of wounded soldiers. During the course of the war, the Confederates further ravaged the farm, burning forty acres of timber and taking silver, carpet, books, and furniture from the Phelps home. (Interestingly, some of the household goods were later recovered from an Arkansas cave by their son.)

By 1862 Congressman Phelps–defeated for reelection–returned to Missouri and mustered a Union regiment. That same year, Mary assembled a wagon train to carry food, clothes, and medical supplies to Pea Ridge, Arkansas, where both her husband and son were fighting the Confederates. She cared for the

Mrs. Phelps tended the slain Union General Nathaniel Lyon following the Battle of Wilson's Creek and secretly buried him on her farm to prevent his body from being mutilated by pillaging Confederates.

Mrs. Phelps placed herself on another "battlefield" during the postwar era. She turned her energy to a growing issue of the day—women's suffrage—and became a vice president of the National Women's Suffrage Association.

John Phelps won an acquittal for the notorious gun fighter Wild Bill Hickok (above) after he was accused of killing a man on the town square.

wounded soldiers on both sides of the conflict and—according to legend—tore pieces of her clothing into bandages when she ran out of supplies. One of those she tended was her husband, though his injuries were only minor. Shortly thereafter, President Lincoln called on his old friend Phelps to serve as the military governor of Arkansas. He lasted only two months in his new post before becoming ill and returning home.

Mary's own losses strengthened her desire to relieve the suffering of others. Despite personal hardships, she continued operating a hospital in her home throughout much of the war. "To the immense task of caring for all these wounded with only one or two doctors and no trained nurses of any kind, my mother gave herself," Mary Anne recalled. "There was no time for any personal or private life."

At the close of the war, Mary received an award of $20,000 from the U.S. Congress, making her the first woman to be honored this way for service to her country. Mrs. Phelps used the money to open a school for war orphans. As superintendent and teacher, she cared for as many as 250 children and supplemented her federal allotment by holding fund-raising fairs. When President Lincoln heard of Mary's compassionate efforts, he appointed her to care for other postwar needs in the area.

Mrs. Phelps placed herself on another "battlefield" following the war. She turned her energy to a growing issue of the day—women's suffrage—and became a vice president of the National Women's Suffrage Association. In 1869, when she and nine other suffrage leaders showed up at the Mansion, Governor Joseph McClurg received them graciously and signed a petition in support of their cause.

Later that day, Mrs. Phelps and women's activist Phoebe Couzins spoke to an informal session of the General Assembly, pleading forcefully for voting rights. But women's suffrage was not a popular cause. One disgruntled House member voiced his opposition, saying the women "unsexed themselves by coming here with their demands." Casting about for other reasons to deny the request, lawmakers tabled the suffrage proposal on the grounds that the petition was "premature" and not "formally presented." The suffragettes received no better treatment from the press. During a national meeting of the group, the *Washington Post* showed its contempt for their cause by labeling the reform-minded delegates "unwomenly women who wished to change their condition."

In many ways, Mary did embody the "New Woman" emerging after the Civil War—one searching for her own political and social identity. She achieved a degree of independence by managing her own business, a cheese-making venture she conducted on the family farm near Springfield.

While Mrs. Phelps saw to her dairy operation and the postwar problems of women and children, John returned to his Springfield law practice. One of his more notorious clients was Wild Bill Hickok, for whom he won an acquittal after the famed gunfighter killed a man on the town square.

Phelps, however, was less successful in the political arena. According to some accounts, in 1864 he came one vote short of being nominated by the Democratic caucus to be the presidential running mate for George McClellan. More disappointment was in store four years later when he made his first bid for governor. Defeat came primarily because so many Democrats—mostly Southern sympathizers—were not permitted to vote following the war.

Phelps waited another eight years before making a second try for high office. In 1876—a banner year for Democrats—he won the governorship by the largest majority vote cast for a Missouri governor from 1840 to 1920. The entire Democratic state ticket was swept into office on his coattails.

His victory came, in part, from a backlash brought about when opponents attempted to use rumors of improper conduct against him. During the campaign, the *St. Louis Globe-Democrat* and the *Chicago Tribune* accused the sixty-one-year-old Phelps of molesting a lady onboard a steamship. One report went so far as to dub him "Don Juan Phelps." The young lady involved denied the newspaper accounts, as did Phelps and several witnesses. Still, the ugly scandal made for spicy reading and his opponents

DON JUAN PHELPS.
A Democratic Paper's Version of his Peccadilloes.

[From the Chicago Times.]
St. Louis, August 6. The State campaign of Missouri opens under very peculiar circumstances. Old Gen. John S. Phelps, the Democratic nominee for Governor, finds himself confronted at the outset of his canvass with no aspersions upon his honesty or his abilities, but with an ugly scandal which grows worse with the stirring up. The circumstances only antedate the nomination by a few days, and all the details are so fresh as to give the affair the worst possible coloring. The scandal is known to the Radical managers, but has not been made public save through mysterious flings in the newspaper, the purpose being to DELAY SPRINGING IT until later in the canvass. The story is also known to Democratic leaders who are endeavoring to ferret out the truth. Some of them do not hesitate to say that if the first statement made is established the question of a withdrawal by Phelps from the ticket becomes a very serious one. Gen. Phelps

Whether it was because of illness or domestic discord, Mrs. Phelps did not come to the Capital City, not even for her husband's inauguration.

were quick to make use of it. By election time, most voters came to see the incident as politically inspired and gave their support to the esteemed leader.

Mrs. Phelps took no part in her husband's campaign. According to Mary Anne, her mother "disliked the glad-hand, glib-talk hurrah of political life." Moreover, her vigor had been greatly diminished by a travel accident. Months before the election, she had fallen twenty feet through the open hatch of a steamship, shattering her right arm.

But the fact that Mary had lived at various times with each of her children over an eight-year period caused many to suspect an estrangement between her and the Governor. Whether it was because of illness or domestic discord, Mrs. Phelps did not come to Jefferson City, not even for her husband's inauguration. It was the Governor's married daughter, Mary Anne Montgomery—not his wife—who accompanied him to the Capitol for the swearing-in ceremony.

Although eight inches of snow blanketed Jefferson City on inauguration day, the House chamber overflowed with spectators. The occasion—described as being "devoid of display"—was, nonetheless, a historic one. With his inauguration, Phelps became governor for the first four-year term allowed by law since before the Civil War.

Mary Anne Phelps Montgomery, the popular First Daughter, served as her father's hostess while caring for six of her own children.

"Scandalous" Behavior at the Mansion

It might have been the condition of the Mansion that caused the new hostess, Mary Anne Montgomery, to delay having a full-scale reception in the Capital City. Apparently, the five-year-old home had suffered from exposure to a great many children, relatives, and guests of former first families. "The executive mansion is sadly in need of renovation," one newsman wrote. "The furniture is worn out, the paint rubbed off, and the equipment all out of sorts."

It was rumored about town that Mrs. Montgomery, the Governor's daughter, would refurbish the Mansion before holding an official gathering. Instead, she prepared the house as best she could and held a modest public reception on inaugural evening.

The delay gave the new hostess the chance to issue one thousand invitations to a gala celebration held two weeks later. Mrs. Montgomery provided further details in a newspaper interview. Guests should arrive at eight o'clock in the evening and "be prompt in attendance." The home would not be decorated for the party, she declared, because of the expense of materials and the "vexation" of having to use convict labor—though the custom of using prison inmates at the Mansion was an accepted practice.

Mrs. Montgomery advised those attending to enter by the side door of the Mansion and proceed to the second floor, a course that wandered through a maze of corridors and up the narrow back stairs. Guests should then leave their wraps in the upper hall before making their entrance down the Grand Stairway. She also announced the performance of the Jefferson City string ensemble—"not a very expert organization," according to the town music critics, "but a vast improvement upon any local band of the past."

The news report continued: at midnight a buffet would be served to a limited number of guests at a time. This arrangement was designed to avoid any "rush . . . into the refreshment room" that might harm the ladies or damage their attire. Apparently, the rude behavior of Mansion guests had embarrassed

Guests "pocketed the cold roasted quails and other tidbits."

many of the townspeople as well as former Mansion residents. "The conduct of Jefferson City people at receptions of the past has been most scandalous," the writer noted. "On one of these occasions, they swarmed into the refreshment room, and in one fell swoop demolished all the delicacies upon the supper table, many of them so far forgetting themselves as to pocket the cold roasted quails and other tidbits."

Fearing the affair might become unruly, the mayor of Jefferson City and a delegation of local citizens asked the Governor not to serve refreshments. Phelps agreed to a compromise:

he would serve a fine buffet, but in keeping with the committee's concerns, he would limit the drink to lemonade. He also accepted an offer by the city fathers to assign uniformed police to the Mansion to preserve order, should that be necessary.

Fortunately, the event went without incident. The buffet, spread over a fifty-foot table, featured a center pyramid five foot high mounded with flowers. Horns of plenty overflowed with fruits. Twenty decorated cakes lined the table along with varieties of ice cream molded into swans, doves, and dolphins. The table fairly groaned with platters of "roast ham . . . buffalo tongue, roast turkey, oysters on the shell with citron, and fried oysters, stewed oysters, chicken salad . . . broiled quail, and all kinds of game."

A number of guests, reacting to the Governor's lemonade order, came prepared with their own refreshment. Throughout the evening, the pop of champagne corks could be heard in the far corners of a room and "mysterious black bottles" were passed among the guests. Undoubtedly, Mary Montgomery's sumptuous feast made up for the lack of display during the inauguration two weeks earlier and fulfilled the Capital City's expectations of a gala affair.

In a speech that followed his induction, Phelps told his audience that the world was governed too much. "But few laws are really necessary for the government and good order of a community." One observer noted that there was little interest in the Governor's high-sounding remarks, but a great deal of interest in who would fill the high-level positions available in the new administration.

That evening an informal gathering at the Mansion attracted a large crowd. But many were disappointed because Phelps and his daughter served no rum—a favored and expected refreshment of the day. However, those wanting a fuller celebration were pleased to hear that Mary Anne planned to have a more lavish party later in the month.

Having his daughter to oversee the social affairs at the Mansion greatly relieved Phelps, though it was a considerable sacrifice for Mary Anne. At the time, she lived in Oregon with her husband, James B. Montgomery, a railroad tycoon. Her return to Missouri meant a long separation for the couple. In addition to serving as hostess, she had to care for her six children, one of whom was born after she arrived in Jefferson City. Little Russell was the first grandchild of a chief executive to be born in the new Mansion and the Capital City welcomed the event with the sounding of bells and cannons. With five siblings to watch over him, Russell received more than enough attention, causing poet and family friend, Eugene Field, to dub the youngster "prince imperial."

Poet Eugene Field, among distinguished visitors to the Mansion during Phelps's term, is portrayed in a mural on the wall of the governor's office.

One writer described the popular hostess of the Mansion as "queenly," which she, indeed, appears to be even in this later photograph. She poses here in a gown worn at a reception given by the Kaiser of Germany in 1913.

Despite the size of her family, Mary Anne found time to be both mother and hostess. Having earlier attended a posh New York finishing school and mingled with East and West Coast society, the popular First Daughter charmed the Capital City. A metropolitan journal described the thirty-year-old hostess as "queenly," which she, indeed, appeared to be in photographs.

Mrs. Montgomery's frequent soirees invigorated the social life of the city. Mansion parties held every other week started at eight o'clock in the evening with visiting and dancing until ten o'clock, followed by refreshments. The gatherings brought members of the General Assembly, state officers, visiting strangers, and citizens of the city to the Mansion. Distinguished guests included journalists Eugene Field and Joseph Pulitzer, as well as Elihu Washburn, once a minister to France, and Elihu Root (later to be secretary of state and secretary of war). Root took a liking to the vivacious Mansion hostess and courted her with flowers and amorous notes. Mary Anne, however, wanted no part of a romantic affair and emphatically discouraged his advances.

While the Governor's daughter exhibited her social know-how, Phelps put his fighting skills to use attacking the problems of government. He came into office during the final years of a depression that followed the Panic of 1873. Missourians had endured five years of hardship and he wanted nothing to stand in the way of recovery. When the "Great Strike" of 1877—the first big labor revolt in the nation's history—reached Missouri, Phelps moved swiftly to lessen its effects in St. Louis. In a controversial move, he sided with the strike breakers and armed citizen volunteers who, along with the civil authorities, moved to restore order.

Despite such social and economic upheavals, Missouri continued to make headway. The Governor proudly announced that there were five hundred pupils attending the state university. Nationally, the state ranked fifth in population and second in support of permanent funding for public education. With a rapid economic recovery underway, Phelps erected a new asylum for the mentally ill, increased support of public schools, and accumulated a surplus in the state's treasury.

Even so, the Governor felt that more economy was needed to keep the state on course. One of his cost-saving measures was aimed at the penitentiary. By contracting with private industries to operate within the prison using convict labor, he hoped to make the institution self-sustaining. Phelps called his plan a "reasonable" solution, one that would pay for the upkeep of the prisoners as well as the salaries of the guards and administrators. As it turned out, Phelps was overly optimistic. By paying inmates at the rate of forty to fifty cents a day, it was the contractors, not the state, who profited most under the arrangement.

Though Phelps was generally successful in handling the problems of government, his political career was checkered with defeat and his family frayed by discord and death. He had failed in his first campaign for governor and lost a bid for the U.S. Senate after the war. During his tenure as governor, his wife suffered yet another injury to her arm, contracted pneumonia, and died before he could reach her bedside. The following year, Phelps faced more disappointment when he failed in his second try for a U.S. Senate seat.

At the end of his term, Phelps relinquished the governorship, but not his quest for public office. In 1884 the old soldier made a third run for governor. With his defeat for the nomination, he returned to managing his investments in Springfield. Bad health prevented him from taking President Grover Cleveland's offer to serve as a European ambassador, though he appeared to be in fair condition until shortly before he died in 1886. Newspapers attributed his death at the age of seventy-one to an illness brought on when he "partook of an oyster stew" three weeks earlier.

Mary Anne Phelps Montgomery, the widely acclaimed socialite, lived to be ninety-seven and kept up a lively correspondence in spite of failing eyesight.

Mrs. Montgomery endured her own hardships after leaving the Mansion. Faced with financial reverses, she and her husband decided the children should be educated abroad where it would be less costly. With her cousin serving as a diplomat in Europe, Mrs. Montgomery took the opportunity to spend three years in Germany along with six of her seven children. During her stay, the hearty pioneer woman, who once bounced about in a stagecoach race across Missouri, hobnobbed with the heads of state, including the Kaiser of Germany and the Queen of Holland.

But sorrow and misfortune continued to plague the adventuresome family. Mrs. Montgomery's husband developed diabetes and died in 1900, leaving her much in debt. Russell, her grown son who was born in the Mansion, vanished while aboard a whaling ship. Two of her grandsons were lost in hiking accidents—one in the Alps and the other in Labrador— and her daughter, grief stricken by the loss, died shortly thereafter.

But the intrepid Mrs. Montgomery refused to despair. In 1904, when St. Louis prepared to host guests for the World's Fair, she accepted the task of entertaining royal visitors to the city. Back in Oregon, she raised funds for earthquake victims and lobbied the legislature on behalf of Chinese laundry women. The widely acclaimed socialite lived to be nearly ninety-seven years old and kept up a lively correspondence in spite of failing eyesight.

Her father's administration had ended the first decade of life in the new Mansion—a time of gala parties, births, and marriages that brought many fanciful moments to the home and the city. But the hillside Mansion was no fortress against hardship; during the next decade, the stately home would be marred by death and tragedy. In that respect, the Mansion was beginning to mirror real life.

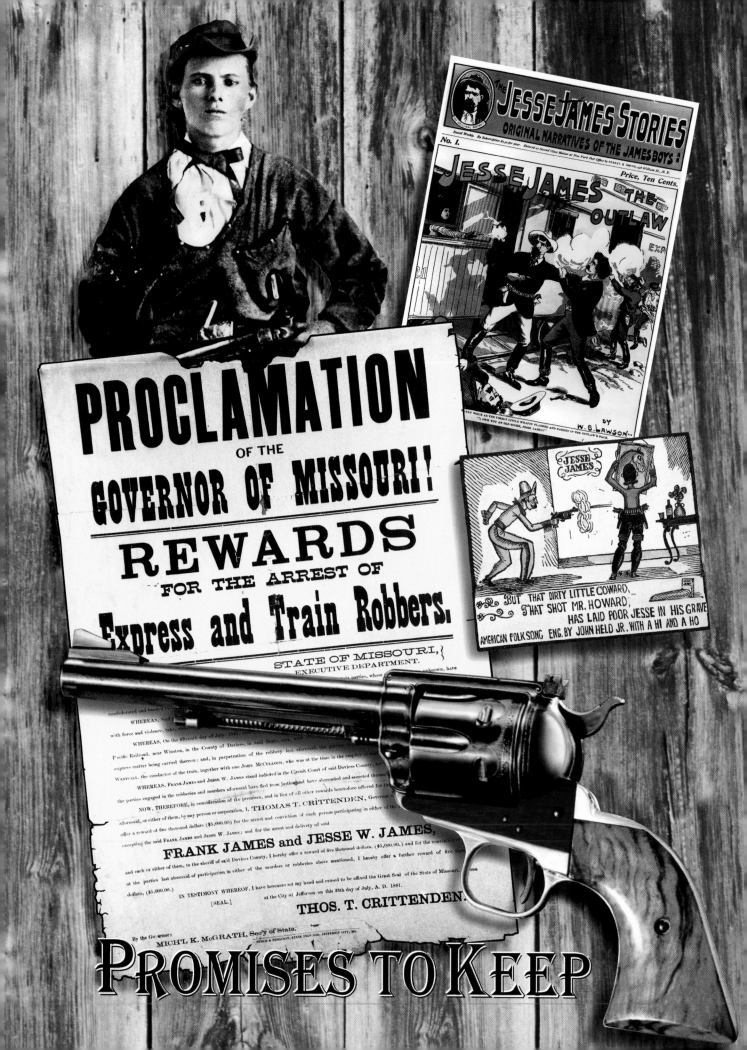

Governor Thomas Theodore Crittenden
Caroline Wheeler Jackson Crittenden
1881-1885

"Often the greatest trial to which a Governor can be subjected is to be called upon at a moment's notice to deal with events and conditions for which there is no precedent." ~ Thomas Crittenden

Thomas Crittenden made three promises to the people of Missouri while on the campaign trail for the state's highest office. The first two promises—strengthening the state's finances and increasing support for education—were easy to keep during the relatively prosperous postwar years. But keeping his third promise—capturing the infamous James gang—required a bold plan.

The wily bandits had outwitted the law for more than sixteen years. They had robbed at least fourteen banks and numerous trains, leaving detectives, local peace officers, and earlier governors in despair. Many felt that such violence harmed the economy by curtailing immigration and investment in the state. Crittenden agreed and told voters, if elected governor, he intended to rid Missouri of its reputation as "The Robber State."

His declaration was not an idle campaign promise. Crittenden had already exhibited remarkable courage and fortitude before he ever sought public office. He had grown up in Kentucky, the nephew of the prominent statesman John J. Crittenden who served as Governor, U.S. Senator, and presidential cabinet member. As a youngster having lost his father, young Thomas looked to his esteemed uncle for guidance and began studying law with him in 1855.

The following year, after being admitted to the bar, he married seventeen-year-old Caroline Jackson, the daughter of a well-to-do businessman and owner of the local iron works. Determined to be on their own, the young couple left Kentucky in 1857 and moved to Lexington, Missouri, an area recognized for its good lawyers. Leaving home with a new bride was, according to Crittenden, a "big move in those days, requiring much nerve . . . to go to a strange community unknown and unknowing, without a name, money or fame."

At first, all went well for the twenty-five-year-old attorney, but a few years later the threat of civil war began to divide the small community. Though a

Thomas Crittenden promised Missouri voters that if elected governor he would capture the infamous James gang that had outwitted the law for more than sixteen years.

According to one of Crittenden's sons, "Mother was never cut out for a political wife. It was hard for her to be diplomatic on occasion—she frequently spoke as she felt."

Southerner by birth, Crittenden was a strong Unionist—one of only twenty-seven other men in Lexington.

Fear and uncertainty about the future may have played a part in Caroline's return to Kentucky in 1859 for the birth of their first child. Not long afterwards, Crittenden, too, left Lexington, fleeing aboard a steamboat to St. Louis to escape a gang of men trying to kill him. While in St. Louis, he conferred with two of the city's strong Union leaders, General Nathaniel Lyon and Frank Blair Jr., and pledged his support for the Union cause.

After traveling to Kentucky to see after the needs of his wife and new son, Crittenden returned to Missouri and joined his college friend, John F. Philips, in mustering a cavalry regiment. Philips served as colonel and Crittenden as lieutenant colonel of the unit for three years. During that time, Mrs. Crittenden and Mrs. Philips took the opportunity to visit their husbands by traveling onboard ambulance wagons headed for the campsite.

Ironically, Crittenden captured his first political office while on the battlefield. Near the war's end, Governor Hall appointed him to fill the vacancy caused by the death of the attorney general. Under the circumstances, Crittenden felt his military duties were more important than his new ones and gave little attention to the state office.

The scrappy cavalry officer came close to death in one of the final encounters of the war. During the three-day Battle of Westport, a messenger reported that Crittenden had been shot. When Colonel Philips found him unconscious on the battlefield, he tore open the shirt of his fallen comrade and discovered a blue mark on his stomach, but no wounds. In an effort to revive him, Philips took out a canteen and poured brandy down Crittenden's throat.

In a few minutes, Crittenden opened his eyes and, upon seeing his old friend, asked, "Am I dead, Philips?" The Colonel's laughter dispelled all doubts. Crittenden's life had been spared by the thick pouch strapped around his waist that caught the bullet intended for him. Although knocked unconscious by the impact, Crittenden was otherwise unharmed. It was not long before he got up, mounted his horse, and announced, "Let's go on with the scrap."

At the close of the war, the Crittenden family moved to Warrensburg, Missouri, where he set up a law practice that later included the former Confederate General Frank Cockrell. Because of his Southern leanings, Cockrell was prevented from practicing law so Crittenden made the court appearances while his partner handled the office work.

It disturbed the young lawyer that there was no Democratic newspaper in Johnson County—an area where "a Democrat scarcely dared to live." In a bold and defiant move, he wrote to an editor in an adjoining county offering to help open a newspaper office in Warrensburg: "Come and let us plant the flag in the midst of the enemy's stronghold." In 1866 they raised the Democratic banner with the establishment of the *Warrensburg Journal*. Predictably, radicals in the area did not welcome the publication. A "howling mob" showed their disapproval by igniting an effigy of Crittenden and by threatening to burn the newspaper office. The crowd dispersed after Crittenden, standing bravely alongside the editor, vowed to "stand there, until he died."

A few months later, another clash occurred when Crittenden invited the famed orator General Frank P. Blair Jr. to address a Democratic rally in Warrensburg, the first such gathering in the area since before the war. The General was to speak in opposition to the loyalty oath, the onerous provision of the new state constitution that disenfranchised most Democrats because of their Southern sympathies. A great crowd poured into town for the outdoor assembly—many of them Confederate veterans daring to wear their tattered gray uniforms.

Ignoring assassination threats, Crittenden refused to cancel the meeting and vowed that the speech would be delivered. As Blair spoke, a mob mounted the platform, but Crittenden and others stood in front of the General and hurled back each man who tried to reach the podium. In the tussle, the speaker's stand was knocked down and a would-be assassin was stabbed and later died. Crittenden ignored the bloodshed, helped repair the podium, and Blair finished his speech.

In 1872, during less heated times, Crittenden rousted an incumbent to win a seat in Congress. His reelection bid pitted him against his old comrade, Colonel Philips. In the tight battle that followed, the Colonel captured the nomination at the state convention on the 691st ballot. Though Philips won the election, Crittenden reclaimed the seat two years later and served one more term before closing out his congressional career. He returned to Missouri and defeated General John Marmaduke, who was making his first try for a gubernatorial nomination. Crittenden won the office easily, but he confessed to being a bit embarrassed to follow the popular Governor, John Phelps.

Nonetheless, the people of Jefferson City—typically hospitable to the new residents of the Mansion—looked forward to the arrival of the Crittendens and their young daughter, Carrie. (The family's three grown sons were not living at home). The local gentry was especially eager to meet the Governor's wife. They felt the "Kentucky lady . . . reared up in the best society of that state" would invigorate the social climate of the Capital City.

In spite of the city's expectations, the Crittendens got off to a bad start. On the day of his inauguration, the Governor-elect and his exuberant supporters paraded to the Capitol led by a St. Louis military band, but there was no one present authorized to administer the oath of office. To relieve embarrassment, the lieutenant governor performed an unofficial ceremony. In true

In 1866 General Frank Blair Jr. faced a hostile mob when he spoke in Warrensburg just as he had earlier in the town of Louisiana shown below in this Capitol mural.

HOW TO TELL A REBEL:
A Civil War Tale

For a short while after the Civil War, a political party more interested in retribution than reconciliation dominated the political landscape in Missouri. Once in power, the so-called Radical Republicans designed a document known as the Drake Constitution, the brainchild of Charles D. Drake, a St. Louis lawyer.

Under its provisions, officeholders were replaced with members of the Radical Republican Party. Anyone wanting to practice a profession—lawyers, teachers, ministers—had to swear they had never engaged in any of eighty-six supposedly disloyal acts to the Union. Voting rights were also denied anyone "who had ever been in armed hostility to the United States (or) . . . ever given aid, comfort, countenance, or support to persons engaged in any such hostility (or) . . . ever disloyally held communication with such enemies."

The restriction on officeholders stayed in effect from 1865 until 1867 when it was overturned by the U.S. Supreme Court. The other loyalty provisions were gradually dropped until all were gone by the time Missouri adopted a new constitution in 1875.

Having to give proof of loyal citizenship was no longer required by the time Governor Crittenden served. Nonetheless, he enjoyed telling the story of a Pettis County farmer who came before his local registration board after the Civil War wanting to vote, but needing to prove he had always been a true Union man. He answered the questions correctly, but was still denied the vote. A neighbor serving on the "loyalty board" accused the farmer of Confederate sympathies. "When asked for his proof he said that he had noticed time and again after a great rebel victory in some battle that [his neighbor] always called his hogs a '*leetle*' louder and a '*leetle*' earlier.

gubernatorial fashion, Crittenden followed up with a long and exhaustive inaugural address.

Further embarrassment was in store when the Governor walked into his new office. Waiting to escort him to the inaugural ceremony was the outgoing Governor, John Phelps, and the secretary of state, their absence apparently undetected during the inaugural proceedings. Later that afternoon, at least one of the mishaps of the day was corrected when a judge was located and brought to the Governor's office to administer the oath officially.

The First Lady's inaugural reception at the Mansion also seemed awkward and got only ho-hum reviews. The informal gathering of some two thousand guests featured no dancing or refreshments. With terms of faint praise—and perhaps some disappointment—the local newspaper noted that "the first reception is always the trying occasion" and that a more magnificent event would be held within a month.

Living in the Mansion required more than just a social adjustment for the First Family. The ten-year-old home was beginning to look seedy and uninviting. Crittenden told the legislature that the place needed immediate repairs. Because of its soot-stained condition caused by trains passing nearby, the Mansion "should be painted inside and outside," he declared. Furthermore, the plumbing was in poor shape and if not fixed would "render the house unpleasant and even unhealthy." He went on to mention the roof, guttering, iron railing, lightning rods, laundry tubs, and cistern with equal concern.

Mrs. Crittenden, however, did not let the unseemly state of the Mansion deter her from entertaining. Her promised event a month after the inauguration received more enthusiastic acclaim than her first effort. In exaggerated terms typical of the time, the local press announced it was "one of the most brilliant gatherings that, perhaps, ever assembled under that historic roof," with guests dancing until one o'clock in the morning.

While the Crittendens enjoyed the social aspects of their new positions, the Governor found there were some unpleasant features to his job. Unrest among the prison's two hundred inmates had resulted in two attempts to burn the penitentiary located just several blocks from the Mansion. In response, Crittenden proposed some needed reforms. He wanted no jail sentences to run longer than twenty years and urged the adoption of the "three-fourths rule"—an incentive system that reduced a convict's term as a reward for good behavior. The Governor frowned on the idleness of prisoners and suggested to the legislature that inmates be put to work outside the prison walls, even though local laborers opposed the competition.

Crittenden also called on the legislators to separate hardened criminals from young offenders. He believed that a proper education along with religious instruction would be a deterrent to crime and encouraged the hiring of a full-time prison chaplain to teach reading, writing, and arithmetic, as well as Sunday school. In addition, he urged the warden to provide religious periodicals rather than newspapers for inmates.

But it was the criminals outside the prison walls that concerned him most. Noting that his predecessors had little luck apprehending outlaw gangs, Crittenden decided on a different, more extreme course. He felt that the right incentive—namely money—would ultimately lead to the collapse of the James gang. A large reward, however, was impossible under a Missouri law that prevented the Governor from offering more than three hundred dollars from state funds.

Refusing to be thwarted, Crittenden turned to the railroads for help. These companies had taken sizable losses from the robberies and agreed to put up the money to apprehend the outlaws. With the railroads behind him, Crittenden upped the reward to

The Governor received letters threatening his life and the kidnapping of his daughter.

five thousand dollars for the capture of each gang member and an additional five thousand dollars for the conviction of either Frank or Jesse James.

Following the reward offer, the Governor received anonymous letters threatening his life and the kidnaping of his nine-year-old daughter. Family members and concerned neighbors paid close attention to little Carrie Crittenden when she played about the Mansion yard and further security was provided by a trusted servant assigned as her bodyguard. The only attempted harm came when a demented farmer, brandishing pistols, pushed his way into the Mansion. Hearing the ruckus on the first floor, Mrs. Crittenden quickly summoned the town marshal to remove the intruder.

Fortunately, the extra precautions at the Mansion were not needed for long; the lure of the reward money worked quickly. Within months after the offer, several in the gang surrendered or were killed. In less than a year, two other gang members, Robert and Charles Ford, plotted and killed Jesse James; six months later, Frank James surrendered to the Governor.

Danger from the James gang did not prevent the Crittendens from hosting a grand silver wedding anniversary in November 1881. In addition to decorating the Mansion with fragrant flowers and exotic plants, the First Lady engaged a string band to set the background for the renewal of their marriage vows. It was a memorable evening for the Crittendens—as well as for some of their guests. During the party, a prisoner

A widely circulated photograph purported to be the James family – Frank, Jesse, and their mother, Zerelda.

working at the Mansion ransacked the guests' luggage, took what he wanted, and discarded the suitcases in the river.

Though married for twenty-five years, Mrs. Crittenden showed a tinge of jealousy when her husband made a public display of his regard for the popular soprano, Adelina Patti. During the singer's visit to St. Louis, the Governor was so overcome by her performance of "Home Sweet Home" that he went backstage and asked to kiss the beautiful young lady (some said he impulsively grabbed the kiss without permission). Miss Patti followed up the encounter by sending a large autographed picture to her admirer.

While the Governor was pleased to receive the memento, the First Lady was not and promptly banished it to the attic. One of Crittenden's sons later explained that his "mother was never cut out for a politician's wife—it was hard for her to be diplomatic on occasion—she was very outspoken."

In addition to his wife's displeasure, the Governor endured public ridicule because of the kissing incident. While appearing at the theater in Jefferson City, a famed burlesque queen parodied the Governor's stolen kiss in a melody, going so far as to point toward his theater box during her performance. Crittenden was incensed at being the brunt of her humor and immediately left the theater.

But no incident during Crittenden's term would compare with the tragedy that soon followed when death visited the Mansion for the first time. The golden-haired Carrie Crittenden, the "pet of her family," became ill with diphtheria and died on December 20, 1882. The colorful Christmas decorations put in place for the holidays became the setting for the little girl's funeral.

In the days that followed, a tomb-like silence shrouded the house. Not since Governor Dunklin lost an infant son in 1834 at the previous residence had such "desolation and great sorrow prevailed." The year following his daughter's death, Crittenden poured out his grief in the words of a song he wrote and published entitled "My Child."

While the Crittenden's were observing an appropriate period of mourning, Jefferson City had two distinguished visitors. In January 1883 Queen Victoria's daughter, Princess Louise, and her husband, the Marquis of Lorne, stopped in the Capital City during a cross-country train trip. Because of the recent death in the First Family, however, it is doubtful that they did more than greet the General Assembly and pay their respects to the Governor.

In time, the First Lady began to immerse herself in charitable and church work, as well as Mansion repairs. In one skillful act of fund-raising, Mrs. Crittenden acquired enough money to buy a bell for the Christian Church in Jefferson City. The money came from an unusual source—her husband's card-playing friends. Mrs. Crittenden called Supreme Court Judge John Henry, one of the card players, to the Mansion and said rather pointedly, "Judge Henry, I want you men in that poker game to buy a bell for our church." Henry, out of deference to the First Lady and perhaps some guilt for his gambling habit, agreed to see what he could do. He finally

When Adelina Patti, the popular soprano, visited St. Louis, Governor Crittenden was so overcome by her performance of "Home Sweet Home" that he went backstage and asked to kiss the beautiful young lady.

FRANK JAMES SURRENDERS TO THE GOVERNOR

In October 1882, six months after Jesse James was murdered, his older brother, Frank, came to Jefferson City late one evening and checked into the McCarty House under an assumed name. The notorious outlaw spent the next day strolling about town unrecognized by anyone. A relative of the hotel owner later declared that Frank actually went to the Mansion to make arrangements for his official surrender to Governor Crittenden. Through an intermediary, he had already laid some groundwork for the meeting. In a letter to Crittenden, he had pleaded for mercy, citing a "humbled, repentant and reformed" man would be a valuable example to society.

The day after arriving in the Capital City, Frank James—"armed to the teeth"—walked into the Governor's office. During the dramatic encounter that followed, he unstrapped his 44-caliber Remington revolver and told Crittenden, "I want to hand over to you that which no living man except myself has been permitted to touch since 1861, and to say that I am your prisoner." James requested that Crittenden keep the belt and pistol as a present.

That evening the hotel across the street from the Mansion became an open house for those wishing to meet the famous bandit before he was turned over to the Jackson County authorities. "A stream of people of all sizes, ages and color"—as many as five hundred visitors, it was reported—went in and out of Frank's hotel room. "Some . . . talked with the outlaw, while others were satisfied with simply looking at him a moment." The thirty-nine-year-old James was "pleasant and agreeable, and quite talkative" according to news accounts and told visitors he was "not guilty of half he [was] charged with." Among the callers were "Governor Crittenden and his wife, who in taking a walk, dropped in for a few moments and had a social chat."

Later when the Governor sent Frank James by train to Independence, Missouri, the outlaw's "triumphal ride"

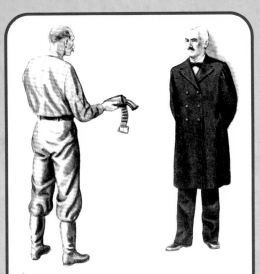

"GOVERNOR, I AM FRANK JAMES, I SURRENDER MY ARMS TO YOU. I HAVE REMOVED THE LOADS FROM THEM. THEY HAVE NOT BEEN OUT OF MY POSSESSION SINCE 1864. NO OTHER MAN HAS EVER HAD THEM. I NOW GIVE THEM TO YOU PERSONALLY. I DELIVER MYSELF TO YOU AND THE LAW."
Frank James
KANSAS CITY TIMES, OCT. 5, 1882

THE GOVERNOR ACCEPTED THE PISTOL AND BELT AND SAID, "YOU SHALL HAVE EVERY PROTECTION AFFORDED BY THE LAWS OF YOUR COUNTRY, AND AS FAIR A TRIAL AS THOUGH YOU WERE THE SON OF A PRESIDENT."
Thos. T. Crittenden
GOVERNOR OF MISSOURI
SEDALIA DISPATCH, JEFFERSON CITY MO, OCT 5, 1882

caused the *Kansas City Journal* to comment: "Had the train stopped long enough he would have been given an ovation at nearly every station." The *St. Louis Globe-Democrat* noted that "it was not entirely clear whether Frank James had surrendered to the State of Missouri or the state had surrendered to him."

In the end, Frank stood trial for the murder of a railroad employee, but the jury found him not guilty. The Ford brothers—responsible for the assassination of Jesse James—were sentenced to hang, but were pardoned by Crittenden the same day "upon the grounds of public policy." Crittenden paid twenty thousand dollars in rewards to various people—he did not say to whom. None of the money, he proudly announced to the General Assembly, came from the state treasury.

All too soon the violence and bloodshed were forgotten and the outlaws transformed into folk heroes. Frank James made the most of his notoriety by traveling with wild west shows around the country and lived an upright life until his death in 1915.

Ironically, the Crittenden family became one of the chief benefactors of the James family and kept up a relationship with the descendants. One of the Governor's sons became mayor of Kansas City and hired Jesse James Jr., son of the gang leader, as an office boy. Mayor Crittenden later backed young Jesse in opening a cigar store. Both the former Governor and his son came to the defense of the outlaw's son when he was charged with a train robbery.

Jesse Jr. apparently benefited from being nurtured by the Crittenden family and went on to become a practicing attorney in Kansas City. The relationship between the families continued: the younger Crittenden served as a pallbearer at Frank James's funeral and later acquired many of the family's keepsakes.

The young girl atop *The Missouri Children's Fountain* on the lawn of the Mansion represents nine-year-old Carrie Crittenden, the only child to die in the Mansion.

A bedroom on the third floor of the Mansion bears the Crittenden family name and contains the suite of ornately carved walnut furniture given in memory of their daughter.

convinced the card players— most of whom were state officials—to set aside all jack-pots for the purchase of the bell.

The congregation, not knowing the source of the fund-ing, eagerly thanked the "reli-giously inclined gentlemen" whose generosity made the church bells ring. Judge Henry later told the First Lady, "Every time I walk any-where on the streets of Jefferson City and hear the ding . . . dong, . . . ding . . . dong of that bell, it sounds exactly as though it was saying Jack . . . pot . . . Jack . . . pot! every time it rings."

In addition to being a successful fund-raiser for the church, Mrs. Crittenden earned accolades for her efforts on behalf of the Mansion. In his final remarks to lawmakers, the Governor paid tribute to his wife's stewardship, noting that the Mansion "has been as carefully managed and preserved by the better part of the executive office as if it had been her individual property." He applauded the excellent condition of the building, labeling it "one of the handsomest Executive Mansions in the United States."

Crittenden also pointed to the optimism and prosperity that prevailed in the state. His success in ridding Missouri of outlaws had increased the value of land by one-third, he claimed. In addition, crop production was up more than it had been in many years, restoring faith in the state's future.

As promised, the Governor had improved the finances of the state. He reduced the old debt and recovered more than three million dollars owed to the state from railroad bonds. In the process, the Governor also pushed to recover the full amount of interest due the state, going so far as to advertise the St. Joseph-Hannibal railroad for sale. Though the U.S. Supreme Court prevented the company from going on the auction block, the railroad was required to fulfill its legal obligation to the state. It had been troublesome collecting the investment, but the issuance of bonds had paid off; with the growth in railways came more jobs and better transportation.

Of all his accomplishments, Crittenden considered the capture of the James gang his greatest. But neither Missouri nor the nation voiced praise for the man who helped lay "poor Jesse in his grave." Even the *St. Louis Post-Dispatch* and the *New York Sun* denounced Crittenden for the contract killing of the gang leader—although it was never revealed who received the money. It was not just his handling of the outlaws that hurt Crittenden's popularity. Many faulted him for pardoning a leading St. Louis gambler and for enforcing the laws that required saloons to be closed on Sundays.

Crittenden ended his governorship on a sour note and never sought public office again. In his memoirs he wrote, "Having had long years of experience . . . [I] can knowingly say the governor of a state is often wickedly, cruelly, causelessly abused for doing, or not doing those things about which he is far more intelligently advised than his critics or libelers."

Upon leaving the Mansion, the couple spent the winter at the hotel across from the executive residence before moving to Kansas City. There was little else for him to do but practice law. President Cleveland refused to give him a diplomatic appointment because too many people believed the former Governor had bargained with the Fords to kill Jesse James.

In 1893, however, during Cleveland's second term, the President apparently thought it was politically safe to name Crittenden to the post of consul-general in Mexico City. Crittenden and his wife moved to Mexico along with their son, William, who became vice-consul. In his memoirs, Crittenden wrote fondly of his experiences, as well as the climate and scenery of the country. When the President offered him a similar position in Honolulu, he refused, saying he and Mrs. Crittenden preferred living in Mexico. Following his four-year assignment, the couple returned to Kansas City where, in 1909, he died following a stroke that occurred while he was attending a baseball game. He was seventy-seven.

Crittenden had known conflict all his life. He repeatedly defied death in the public arena as well as on the battlefield. As governor during the strife-ridden era, he stood up to notorious bandits and greedy railroad barons—a risky stance at the time, but one that would later cast him as a hero of the West.

Governor T. T. Crittenden

CRITTENDEN: "I'VE READ MY OBITUARY FOUR TIMES."

Crittenden enjoyed telling about the premature reporting of his death. "I read my obituary four times," he jokingly related to acquaintances. The first report of his death came after the Civil War Battle of Westport, when it was telegraphed throughout the state that Colonel Crittenden was fatally wounded during the encounter.

The second time, the press reported he had perished in a fire that happened shortly after he checked out of a St. Louis hotel.

Another false report came following the death of a relative bearing the same name as Crittenden.

This time the *St. Louis Globe-Democrat* published a long editorial eulogizing the former Governor.

The fourth time came when he suffered a stroke and lay unconscious. News of his death was again carried across the state.

His correct obituary came following a second stroke that occurred while he was attending a baseball game in Kansas City. Years later, Crittenden's son wrote, "I have often heard father amusedly remark about his strange experience of reading four times about his death and say 'he never heard of any one else who could say the same thing.'"

DUTY AND HONOR ABOVE ALL

"Gentlemen, you see that Capitol yonder? I will live to occupy it as governor of the state of Missouri." ~ Confederate General John S. Marmaduke, age 30, speaking to his military staff in the fall of 1864 from a hill overlooking Jefferson City as the Confederate army withdrew from the area.

GOVERNOR JOHN SAPPINGTON MARMADUKE
HOSTESSES: "LALLA" MARMADUKE NELSON AND IOLA HARWOOD
1885-1887

Despite his father's gloomy prediction for the Confederacy,
John Marmaduke cast his lot with the South.

The end of the Civil War left Confederate General John Sappington Marmaduke unemployed: "He was not a lawyer. He was not a merchant. He was not a farmer. He was not a business man. He was not a public speaker—at best a poor one. He was not a writer, nor a great editor," the *Kansas City Star* reported. "He was a military man out of a job."

As the son of a wealthy plantation owner, Marmaduke had grown up in the proper Southern tradition "with plenty of servants to do the heavy work, with fine horses to ride . . . the honor of his country and family to maintain." With access to the best schools, he attended Yale and Harvard before graduating from West Point. When the Civil War came, his father—the former governor Miles Marmaduke—was quick to advise the young military officer: "John, there can be but one result," he told his son. By going with the South, "you will sacrifice your profession. Secession will fail. Slavery will be abolished. But you must decide for yourself following your own convictions."

Lalla Marmaduke, a niece, served as hostess for the bachelor Governor. Her wedding at the Mansion was one of the few happy occasions during a term that was otherwise shrouded by death.

Despite his father's gloomy prediction, John cast his lot with the Confederacy. Serving as a colonel, he commanded troops during the Battle of Boonville, one of the earliest military engagements in Missouri. Temporarily discouraged by the outcome of the battle and the humiliating retreat of the Confederate army, Marmaduke gave up his commission. Later he joined the Southern forces in Virginia as a lieutenant, was wounded at Shiloh, and subsequently promoted to brigadier general. Marmaduke's regiment took part in a number of battles in Tennessee and Arkansas, as well as those in Missouri.

One incident during the war offered his men some comic relief at the expense of their distinguished general. After losing his horse in battle, Marmaduke appropriated a horse from a private under his command not knowing that the soldier had just stolen the animal. As the General charged off to lead his troops, items stuffed in the saddle bags—including ribbons and children's clothing—streamed in the air, giving him the ridiculous appearance of a flagship sailing into the wind. Further embarrassment came when the true owner of the horse showed up to claim his property.

More serious trouble occurred in 1863 when Marmaduke was arrested after a duel with Confederate General Lucius Marshall Walker. The two had been arguing over battle tactics and Walker, feeling his courage had been questioned, called for a gentlemen's resolution on the field of honor. The face-off at fifteen paces using Colt Navy revolvers took place on the lawn of an old plantation home near Little Rock. The men fired simultaneously and missed. Immediately, Marmaduke fired again,

SAVE YOUR CONFEDERATE MONEY

Though Governor John Marmaduke left behind a legacy of public service and good will, he died a poor man. The Governor's "extreme generosity" had left him destitute, according to his brother Darwin.

As if to prove the point, newspapers

recounted the story of the former general receiving a letter from an elderly widow that was accompanied by a Confederate twenty-dollar bill. She told the Governor that he had

paid her the twenty dollars for meals and for care of his horse during the war. The Confederate money, of course, had long been worthless to her, but now, being older and destitute, she needed cash for the bill.

Marmaduke promptly dictated a letter and included a new twenty-dollar bill. However, he cautioned reporters not to publish the story because, "I would be swamped with requests to redeem Confederate money I spent during the war."

striking his opponent in the side, paralyzing him from the waist down. Walker died the following day. Marmaduke was arrested, but the Confederacy was far too short on trained leadership to confine him for very long and he was soon released to head up a cavalry unit.

Following the Second Battle of Boonville in 1864, Marmaduke was imprisoned again—this time for nearly a year. After having two horses shot out from under him, he suffered the humiliation of being captured by a Union private and spent the remainder of the war in prison.

Upon his release, he toured Europe for eight months in an attempt to regain his health. Returning home, the out-of-work soldier tried his hand at a variety of enterprises, ranging from selling insurance to editing an agricultural journal. He also drew some favorable attention for his work as an appointee on the state board of agriculture and the railroad commission.

In 1880 Marmaduke tried to move from the business world into the political arena. But his military bearing caused him to appear "haughty and reticent" and he was unable to convince political leaders to cast him as the Democratic candidate for governor. Thomas Crittenden nabbed the nomination and the governorship, forcing Marmaduke to wait another four years to gain his party's nod.

During his second try for the office, Marmaduke again faced stern opposition. Republicans claimed it was the Confederate wing of the Democratic Party—those who

> Old-line politicians, railroad and business men, as well as religious leaders, opposed him.

had once upheld the James gang—that favored the former general. Old-line politicians, railroad and business men, as well as religious leaders of the day, opposed him. It was reported that Marmaduke, deeply hurt by tirades from the pulpit, never attended church again.

The Missouri Prohibitionist Alliance also made Marmaduke a target of their cause. Members pressured him for support, but he flatly refused to join forces with them. He went on to make the prophetic statement, "Legislation . . . can successfully and wholesomely regulate the liquor traffic, but never effectually suppress it." Nonetheless, Marmaduke promised the group that if elected governor he would enforce a prohibition law if one was passed. (Several years later, he would have the chance to make good on his promise after fifty Missouri counties voted to outlaw intoxicants.)

The harsh political attacks that Marmaduke endured undoubtedly cut into his margin of victory. He won the distinction of being the state's first postwar Confederate governor by less than 11,000 votes. Two of his relatives had preceded him as chief executive, causing some talk of a "political dynasty" ruling the state. His father, Meredith Miles Marmaduke, was the eighth governor and Claiborne Fox Jackson, his uncle, was the fifteenth to serve Missouri. Rather than flaunt his background or position, Marmaduke shunned fanfare and showed his preference for simplicity even on inauguration day.

Though the inaugural celebration was subdued, political tension in the Capital City was apparent. Outgoing Governor Crittenden and Marmaduke had not spoken since their bitter contest for the governorship in 1880. To make matters worse, the petty behavior of the presiding officer at the swearing-in ceremony deviated from tradition by refusing to allow Crittenden to introduce the Governor-elect and assumed the honor for himself.

Marmaduke delivered a short inaugural speech and finished the day without the usual social events. Because of the illness of his mother and sister, no formal reception or ball marked the occasion. "His first evening in office was celebrated only by a few friends and relatives," the *Jefferson City Daily Tribune* reported.

Joining the bachelor Governor at the Mansion was his thirty-year-old widowed niece, Lalla Nelson, and her seven-year-old son, Arthur. As hostess for the Governor, Lalla found the house "immaculately kept," but poorly furnished. The Crittendens had removed their personal belongings, leaving the large rooms stark in appearance and hollow-sounding. Although the Governor's room at the head of the Grand Stairway contained only a bed, nightstand, bookcase, and desk, he seemed content with his humble living quarters. Lalla recalled the first months: "We simply determined to make the best of what was there, and were very comfortable, if not luxuriously furnished."

Gloom lingered at the Mansion.

Though no major changes were made in the house, Marmaduke took the liberty of altering the front entrance to suit his taste. He wanted to have his sitting room in the Great Hall, but found the area too dark and cheerless. By adding a set of pine outer doors with glass panels and a transom, he gained more light as well as fresh air. Though functional, the doors were an ill match for the majestic walnut ones they covered and were later replaced during the Dockery administration.

No amount of light streaming through the new, glassed entrance could dispel the gloom that lingered at the Mansion. Death, again, brought a sense of foreboding to the home, just as it had during the Crittenden administration. The Governor's mother—once the First Lady of Missouri—died within a month after her son's inauguration; later that year, Marmaduke lost two sisters.

Though a period of mourning curtailed social activity, a touch of celebration came before year's end when his niece, Lalla, announced her plans to marry. Because of the recent period of mourning, however, the wedding was kept to a modest size with only relatives and state officials attending the parlor ceremony.

Forced to recruit another hostess for the Mansion, the Governor turned to Iola Harwood, daughter of his late sister. Following her own time of mourning, Iola threw open the Mansion for the traditional "at homes" and receptions. In keeping with the Governor's wishes, she kept the entertainment modest and the decorations simple. Still, guests felt at ease and Marmaduke encouraged them to roam freely about the house and grounds during social events.

One gathering honored thirty of the Governor's supporters known as Marmaduke's Guard. Arriving in full military regalia, they marched from the train station to the Mansion to dine with their old comrade and his invited guests. Afterwards the men gave an exhibition drill on the lawn that delighted the former General, as well as the local citizenry. From there, the troops marched to the nearby Madison House where they listened to speeches and refreshed themselves for the remainder of the evening.

Marmaduke not only enjoyed the camaraderie of his old army buddies, but also the challenge of competition with his fellow officeholders. His eagerness for a contest resulted in an incident that greatly amused Capitol employees. During a meeting in the treasurer's office one day, the Governor and Chief Justice Norton were teased by the group about the contrast in their physiques; Marmaduke, over six-foot tall, towered over the much shorter Chief Justice. Norton challenged the Governor to prove the value of his superior height in a wrestling match right then and there. One onlooker reported, "It was a surprising exhibition of strength and skill, but the little judge finally laid the chief executive of the great state of Missouri flat on his back on the floor."

Another niece, Iola Harwood, took her cousin Lalla's place as hostess. She opened the Mansion for the traditional parties and dances that had been displaced by long periods of mourning.

In time, the Governor took on the additional challenge of improving the looks of the Mansion. He had portraits of former chief executives, including one of his father, moved from the Capitol to decorate the dreary rooms. "The walls are no longer bare at the Mansion," the local press announced approvingly. Two other acquisitions—*Stump Speaking* and *The County Election*—were engravings made from the paintings of Missouri artist George Caleb Bingham. Marmaduke felt the pictures were

Faulty heating and ventilation in the Capitol made it "dangerous to the health of a man to serve a term in the General Assembly."

appropriate because they depicted election scenes in Saline County where his family had lived for many years. Guests were amused to find many familiar faces that Bingham cleverly tucked into his political paintings, including one of the Governor's father.

The Mansion was not the only state property to benefit from the Governor's watchful eye. After touring the public schools, state offices, asylums, and penitentiary, Marmaduke called for some immediate changes. For the first time, one-third of the state's revenue was earmarked for public schools, although only 25 percent was required by the state constitution.

The Governor noted that the Capitol also needed an additional appropriation for repairs and expansion. He told the General Assembly that the faulty heating and venting system made it "dangerous to the health of a man to undertake to serve a term in that House." Legislators heeded the warning and appropriated money for enlarging the Capitol and adding steam heat.

Like his predecessor, the Governor also pleaded for a branch prison to relieve overcrowding. Lawmakers again rejected the idea, but agreed to his proposal to separate juveniles from the prison system by setting up a boy's reform school and a girl's training school. However, Marmaduke's interest in the prison got him into some hot water. When he appointed his brother, Darwin, to the post of warden—one of the finer jobs in state government—accusations of nepotism followed. Finally, a newsman came to the Governor's rescue with a declaration that the new jailer was highly qualified and little more was made of the incident.

The Governor's sense of propriety often kept him from appointing staunch supporters and many of those selected for state positions were surprised to be chosen. No one was appointed to public office who drank excessively. Marmaduke made it clear "that if there was to be any drinking during his administration, he proposed to do it all himself."

County Election, a painting by Missouri artist George Caleb Bingham, shows the lively political atmosphere in the nineteenth century. Bingham, himself a politician, served as a legislator, state treasurer, and adjutant general.

In contrast to some Missouri governors, Marmaduke granted very few pardons. Often a governor could be swayed by the tender pleas of the first lady, urging leniency for prisoners. As a bachelor, Marmaduke generally found it easier to let justice take its course. Because he believed it was improper for the executive branch to reverse the findings of the courts, he issued pardons only when presented with convincing new evidence.

> "If there was to be any drinking during his administration, he proposed to do it all himself."

The Governor once made an exception to his policy when a woman with four children kept showing up each day at his Capitol office, begging for her husband's freedom. When she vowed to stay until the request was granted, Marmaduke issued the pardon just to get rid of her.

There were larger, even more pesky problems for the Governor: a cycle of economic depression and labor unrest overshadowed his term. In an effort to prevent riots and property destruction, Marmaduke tried to head off a serious railway strike in 1886. Although he had the authority to activate the state guard—and had done so the previous year—there was no means with which to pay the men or to enforce discipline. This time, instead of using state troops to quell protesters, Marmaduke found it more expedient to arm the local authorities and to let them handle the matter.

At one point, however, the Governor intervened directly. He took a boat to St. Louis to meet with those involved in the dispute. After several days of listening to both sides, he called the factions together and gave them forty-eight hours to settle their difference. "I will take charge of the railroad as governor of the state and operate it myself until the strike is settled," he declared to those gathered for negotiations. "I cannot operate it as well as you can, but I can get boys from the shops and farms to run the trains, and I can protect them, if need be, by the militia, and will do so." A collective gasp was heard about the conference room, but in less than forty-eight hours, the strike was settled.

In the wake of the labor disputes, Marmaduke pushed for broader regulation of the railroads. When legislators failed to act on the issue, he called them back for a special session and threatened to keep calling them back until they passed the necessary measures. Convinced of his intentions, lawmakers finally did their job by regulating common carriers.

The Governor also took aim at the Ozark Bald Knobbers—a group of vigilantes in southwest Missouri who had turned to stealing and killing. The group took their name from the site where they organized on a barren hilltop, locally referred to as a bald. The gang was brought under control with the indictment of eighty suspects, three of whom were later hanged.

Although the former General was a tough soldier and negotiator, he was soft-hearted when it came to children. Each year Marmaduke held a Christmas party for the youngsters of Jefferson City. It made no difference how rowdy they behaved. It

The ornately carved walnut clock and vases arrived from Italy after the Governor's death and serve today as a reminder of the only chief executive to die in the present-day Mansion.

was said that the Governor himself "entered into the spirit of the occasion with a zest and cordiality unlooked for in a confirmed bachelor."

However, Marmaduke showed less vigor during the legislative session of 1887. That summer, following a bout of poor health, he decided to take a trip to the East Coast and perhaps a brief Atlantic cruise for the fresh air benefits. Upon reaching New York, Marmaduke and his traveling companions changed their plans and set sail for Europe. For the next two months, they toured Ireland, England, Belgium, and France. But according to friends, the Governor's health seemed no better after he returned home.

Three days after Christmas Marmaduke lay gravely ill.

Several months later, Marmaduke came down with pneumonia. Three days after Christmas, he lay gravely ill in his southeast bedroom at the Mansion. On the date set for the traditional children's party, Marmaduke died at the age of fifty-four. The colorful decorations Miss Harwood had prepared for the holiday party remained in place as preparations were made for the funeral. However, the word "Welcome," spelled out in evergreens over the dining room door, was replaced with black crepe. Nearly every resident of Jefferson City, including children released from school for the day, filed through the Great Hall to view the remains of the stricken Governor.

Places of business closed, leaving windows and doors draped in black. Gun volleys fired every half hour from sunrise until the beginning of the funeral march that afternoon.

The funeral procession was the largest ever seen at the Capitol.

Newspapers reported that the funeral procession was the largest ever seen at the Capitol with more than three thousand people accompanying the body to the cemetery in spite of the damp, dreary weather.

With his death, the so-called Marmaduke "political dynasty" came to an end, although in 1924 one member of the family reemerged briefly on the state scene. Lalla Marmaduke's son, Arthur Nelson, who lived in the Mansion while his mother served as hostess, won the Democratic nomination for governor, but lost to Republican Sam A. Baker.

Several tributes remain to the beloved Governor. Some claim the old fiddle tune "Marmaduke's Hornpipe" honors the soldier-statesman for his exploits on the battlefield. Mansion visitors still admire the Marmaduke clock and vases displayed on the library mantel. The ornately carved walnut set arrived from Italy after the Governor's death and serves today as a reminders of the only chief executive to die in the present-day Mansion.

Perhaps the inscription written in pink roses across his grave honored him best. Atop the mound of floral wreaths was one that read, "John S. Marmaduke Loved God and the People." Those words expressed the feeling of all who knew him well and walked the last miles with him to the cemetery that day.

Governor Marmaduke's funeral procession was the largest in the city's history with over three thousand people accompanying the body to the cemetery in spite of the damp, dreary weather.

The appearance of utility poles
was a sign of . . .

CHANGING TIMES

. . . and more change was in store for the
sprawling river city as the state
approached a new century.

GOVERNOR ALBERT PICKETT MOREHOUSE
MARTHA "MATTIE" McFADDEN MOREHOUSE
1887-1889

Representative Morehouse complained to his constituents that the Capital City was "dull and gloomy," and the legislative process too slow and frivolous.

A. P. Morehouse

Change was in the air as Lieutenant Governor Albert Morehouse picked up the reins of office following the death of Governor John Marmaduke. The nation, spurred on by innovation, was racing toward a new century. New products and discoveries fascinated Missourians: a drink called Coca-Cola was being touted as a remedy for stomach problems and headaches; a simple, hand-held camera known as a Kodak turned its user into a photographer; and, a device of Thomas Edison's that showed "moving pictures" was hailed as a great educational tool for children.

In the Capital City other changes were noticeable. With the transition from gas to electrical power, new street lights brightened the city, as well as the Mansion yard. At the same time, the arrival of the Morehouse family at the executive home marked a change in political power.

The differences between the Mansion's previous governor and his replacement were striking: Marmaduke had been a bachelor; Morehouse and his wife, Mattie, headed a family that included two daughters and a son (they had lost four other children in infancy). And, unlike Marmaduke who spent years in military duty before holding public office, the new First Family was quite at home in Jefferson City, having lived there during Albert's two terms in the legislature and his three years as lieutenant governor.

Morehouse had started his career as a school teacher in his home state of Ohio when he was eighteen years old. In 1856 he accompanied his family to Missouri. Though he continued to teach, he also studied law in the evenings and had just been admitted to the bar at the outbreak of the Civil War. Over protests from his parents, he joined the Union army and served for six months with the militia. During much of that time, he wore a swallow-tailed coat and a tall

Young Mattie McFadden fell in love with the charming Lt. Morehouse during the Civil War.

(Facing page)
Jefferson City in the 1890s.

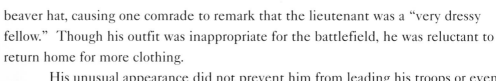

beaver hat, causing one comrade to remark that the lieutenant was a "very dressy fellow." Though his outfit was inappropriate for the battlefield, he was reluctant to return home for more clothing.

His unusual appearance did not prevent him from leading his troops or even attracting the eye of a young lady. When he and his band of men stopped one evening for food at the home of John McFadden near Springfield, they were served by Mattie, a daughter of the family. The love-struck Lieutenant began a correspondence with Miss McFadden that led to their marriage after the war.

Albert had spent most of the war years in Maryville and the couple settled in the northwest Missouri town where he continued to practice law, make loans, and trade in real estate. Later, he turned to journalism to express his political views and founded the *Nodaway County Democrat* newspaper. With his first try for political office in 1876, he captured a seat in the General Assembly by only 197 votes. Friends, elated by his narrow win, fired the town cannon in celebration.

Once in the office, Morehouse kept in touch with the voters through a regular newspaper column. He complained to his readers that the weather in the Capital City was "dull and gloomy" and the legislative process too slow and frivolous. As an example of his frustration, Morehouse cited the Grasshopper bill. Missouri had suffered from an infestation of grasshoppers that ravaged crop lands and caused the state huge economic loss for several years. Lawmakers responded with a makeshift proposal, offering a bounty of five dollars a bushel for the insect eggs, one dollar a bushel for young hoppers, and twenty-five cents a bushel for the mature ones. Morehouse joked with his readers, saying that in order to comply with the ludicrous state law the county courthouse would need to install a furnace to dispose of the insects. Reflecting further on the accomplishments of the General Assembly, he wrote a tongue-in-cheek commentary: "Some people are never satisfied—the grasshopper and rat bills have become law, and some people say this legislature has done nothing."

Morehouse did not limit his opinions to lawmaking; social affairs at the Mansion also drew comment. Crowding at the Mansion was "terrible," he wrote, largely because the legislature, as well as the townspeople, "always attended the governor's reception en masse."

> After observing a four-month period of official mourning, only five months remained in Morehouse's term.

In spite of his disdain for the social and political process in the Capital City, Morehouse permitted the Democrats to cast him as their candidate for lieutenant governor in 1884. With Confederate veteran Marmaduke at the top of the ticket, Morehouse, a Union man, gave his party the balance it needed for victory. His succession to office made him the fifth lieutenant governor in Missouri to be elevated because of the death or resignation of the governor.

WHAT DO YOU CALL THE GOVERNOR'S WIFE?

The job that devolves upon the wife of a governor (or the wife of a president) by virtue of marriage has no pay, no constitutional duties, not even an official title. For years, the public was left in the uncomfortable position of creating a title for the woman married to those they elected to lead the state and nation.

The first president's wife was addressed as "Lady Washington" in an attempt to copy the habits of European royalty. (Although it seemed a bit pompous to use such high-sounding titles on the frontier where most elected official boasted of their humble beginnings.) Still, Missouri's chief executive occasionally got majestic treatment along with his wife. Even today during the formal inaugural ceremony, the governor's entrance is heralded by the announcement, "His Excellency, the Governor of Missouri."

The early alternatives to the use of "Lady," when referring to the wife of a chief executive, showed some creativity. Abigail Adams, for instance, was dubbed "Mrs. President;" Julia Tyler was tagged with the tongue-twister "Lovely Lady Presidentress," and sometimes "Her Serene Loveliness." Dolley Madison was called "Madam Presidentress," or more often "Queen Dolley" by her adoring public.

In Missouri, Mary Brown, Jennie Woodson, Mary Phelps, Caroline Crittenden, Mattie Morehouse, and Jane Francis saw themselves designated in newsprint as "Mrs. Governor." But the term "Governess," though used to denote Maggie Stephens (1897-1901) and Gertrude Folk (1901-1905), appeared to define someone charged with the care of children. The flamboyant Maggie Stephens coined the expression "Mistress Supreme" in reference to herself, but prisoners she befriended dubbed her "Our Lady of the Kind Heart."

In time, the term "First Lady" was accepted in Washington as well as the state capitals. One of the first documented uses of the expression "first lady of the land" was in reference to President Grant's wife, Julia, but the title did not appear in the dictionary until 1930. In spite of its popular usage, many bearing the First Lady label have shown their displeasure. Jackie Kennedy, for instance, hated the term, claiming it made her sound like a saddle horse.

Modern espousers of political correctness suggest that the title "First Lady" be replaced by the non-gender specific "First Mate" or "First Spouse," but these alternatives have found few supporters.

The new First Family observed the customary period of state mourning for the former Governor before launching a round of entertainment. Four months after her arrival at the Mansion, Mattie Morehouse hosted a reception for members of the Imperial Club, a social group made up of the leading citizens of the community. In keeping with the Victorian fascination for theme parties planned around a color scheme, Mrs. Morehouse transformed the Mansion into a "palace of pink." Cascades of pink fabric draped the windows and pink roses adorned the first-floor rooms. The

Morehouse children did their share of entertaining, too. They often invited friends to play about the Mansion grounds or, on rainy days, to join them in the spacious third-floor ballroom.

The First Lady transformed the Mansion into a "palace of pink."

During her husband's brief time in office, Mrs. Morehouse had little opportunity to make any major changes to the Mansion—though she did renovate some old furniture. She took no part in public life or politics. She did, however, belong to a reading club in Jefferson City—a group commended by the local press for "filling [women's] minds with valuable thoughts." Writers of the day praised the quiet, unpretentious First Lady for her performance at the Mansion and cited her efforts as adding to her husband's political success.

While the press spoke highly of Mrs. Morehouse, the Governor did not speak highly of at least one member of the press. Morehouse lashed out at a reporter who published a speech before its delivery. The indignant Governor called the culprit a "scoundrelly liar" and, afterward, was undoubtedly more cautious in disclosing his remarks to newsmen.

Trouble with the press was not his only problem. When a labor dispute put six hundred miners out of work in the north Missouri town of Bevier, violence erupted. After several men were shot and the business district burned, Morehouse was forced to send the National Guard to the town to maintain order.

An inlaid wooden letter box given to Governor Morehouse by prisoners after he ended the practice of putting inmates in the "sweat box" as a disciplinary measure.

His abbreviated tenure prevented any major accomplishments.

The Governor found favor with at least one portion of the population—the penitentiary inmates. At the time, Missouri had the dubious distinction of housing more convicts than any other state. When Morehouse ended the practice of using the "sweat box" as a disciplinary tool, prisoners showed their appreciation by making the Governor a large letter box inlaid with over seven thousand pieces of wood.

Though the Governor made some advances in penal reform, his abbreviated tenure prevented any major accomplishments. Morehouse only addressed the General Assembly at the close of his term, telling the lawmakers that Missouri needed a penitentiary and two more colleges, one in the southwest and another in the northwest part of the state.

From the tone of his remarks, however, he did not seem to favor more revenue for elementary or secondary education. He argued against spending one-third of the state's revenue for public schools—a policy initiated by his predecessor. Morehouse felt the extra expenditure "depressed the finances of the state" and was not enough to be of any real benefit to students.

Needing time to implement his ideas, Morehouse hoped to gain the nomination for a full term as governor. Four years earlier, he had shown some political clout, racking up more votes for lieutenant governor than Marmaduke did for governor. As it turned out, he was little more than a place marker between the terms of two strong governors. Democrats, meeting at their 1888 state convention, preferred the flamboyant David Francis to the mild-mannered Governor and gave the nomination to the St. Louis businessman.

The First Family ended their stay at the Mansion with the traditional New Year's reception. In a final burst of hospitality, the First Lady "welcomed all who . . . gathered in the City of Jefferson," an invitation that brought five hundred friends, legislators, and strangers to the Mansion. In customary fashion, each guest placed a greeting card on to a salver, or tray, as they arrived. From the "great punch bowl" in the state dining room, the First Lady served eggnog, presumably without alcohol since Morehouse was once described as "an ardent Prohibitionist."

Upon leaving the Capital City, the First Family moved back to Nodaway County and away from the political spotlight. Morehouse traded in real estate, managed his farm, and showed little interest in making another bid for governor. When a friend wrote to him suggesting a return to office, Morehouse responded that he had too little money to finance a governor's race and would not consider it even "if I had a million [dollars]."

"I was offered money three years ago sufficient to have nominated me," he wrote, "but I would not accept it for the reason I would have been under too strong obligations to the parties who furnished it. . . . I would never have a nomination that way."

Sadly, he never had the chance to reconsider. In 1891, while herding cattle on his farm, he suffered a ruptured blood vessel in the brain, became delirious, and a week later took his own life.

NON-ELECTED GOVERNORS

Although Albert Morehouse was the last Missouri governor to ascend to office, he was not the only one. Six men have been elevated to the governorship because of the death or resignation of the chief executive:

Abraham J. Williams (1825-1826) president pro-tem of the Senate, following the death of Frederick Bates (There was no lieutenant governor in office.);

Lilburn W. Boggs (1836-1840) with the resignation of Daniel Dunklin;

Miles Meredith Marmaduke (1844) following the suicide of Thomas Reynolds;

Hancock Lee Jackson (1857) following the election of Trusten Polk to the U.S. Senate;

Willard Hall (1864-1865) upon the death of provisional Governor Hamilton Gamble; and,

Albert Morehouse (1887-1889) upon the death of John Marmaduke.

Only Lilburn Boggs was able to retain the office on his own behalf.

NOTHING IMPOSSIBLE

GOVERNOR DAVID ROWLAND FRANCIS
JANE PERRY FRANCIS
1889-1893

David Francis ushered Missouri into a robust new era—a time when anything seemed possible.

Friends said David Francis had little regard for time—"he puts off everything until the last moment," but then charges ahead at full speed. The risky habit brought him within minutes of missing trains. Living in the Governor's Mansion only made matters worse; he could wait until the last boarding whistle sounded before scrambling down the hill to the depot.

In addition to his cleverness in handling a train schedule, Francis was one of Missouri's best businessmen—though business was not his first career choice. Using the money he saved as a boy selling newspapers in Kentucky, Francis had entered Washington University at the age of sixteen with the thought of studying law. By 1870, when he finished his undergraduate degree, he had a $450 debt—a troublesome amount for such a conscientious young man. Debt-ridden and unemployed, Francis reluctantly returned to the family farm.

One evening after working in the fields until his feet were worn with blisters, Francis summoned his resolve and announced to his father that he would never again walk behind a plow. Soon after that his uncle, the owner of a commission firm, offered to hire him as a "mud clerk." It was yet another ground level job for the college graduate, one that involved tramping along the muddy riverfront to check and disperse cargo. But the attractive, sixty-dollars-a-month salary caused Francis to abandon his interest in law for a chance to learn the grain business.

Bright and ambitious, Francis caught on quickly and soon earned a raise. He constantly asked questions of those around him. "I was never satisfied until I understood everything everyone else was doing," he later recalled. "I don't remember having ever looked at the clock and wished that the hour of closing would come." Francis saved his money and within a year paid off his college debt.

Looking to the future, he began investing his income in the stock market and writing a newspaper column about the grain business. In 1876 the budding

(Facing page)
The St. Louis World's Fair was created by David Francis a decade after he left the governorship. Clockwise from top left: the Missouri Building; a new fad— the ice cream cone; the Ferris Wheel; the Pike; and, Francis welcoming President and Mrs. Theodore Roosevelt on dedication day.

Bright and ambitious, David Francis constantly asked questions of those around him.

Young David Francis worked as a "mud clerk," checking grain orders on the busy St. Louis levee—a job that started him on the road to being a millionaire businessman.

entrepreneur further enhanced his position in the St. Louis community with his marriage to Jane Perry, the daughter of a prominent banker. The following year, at age twenty-seven, Francis launched a company of his own. The D. R. Francis and Brother Commission Company, which started in a small one-room office, made him a wealthy man in less than a decade.

Business success also thrust him into the political limelight. The name of David Francis emerged in 1885 when St. Louis Democrats were deadlocked in their choice of a mayoral candidate. Weary delegates had balloted all night and, as a compromise, turned to Francis on the 182nd ballot.

Francis became a wealthy man in less than a decade.

Having left the meeting early, Francis was unaware of his selection until the next morning when an excited coworker rushed to tell him the news.

Though Francis was only thirty-four years old, he had been named president of the Merchants' Exchange the previous year. As head of the trade center for grain dealers, Francis was one of the most influential businessmen in St. Louis. His new standing gave him the edge he needed to oust the incumbent mayor by a 1,200 vote margin.

Francis put his business expertise to work, managing the city with the same attention to detail he gave his own company. He lowered the gaslight rates, collected a million-dollar debt owed by the railroad, and gave St. Louis the reputation for having the best-paved streets in the nation. Residents boasted of the "New St. Louis" that began to emerge under his progressive leadership.

All the while, Francis was making some friends in high places. In 1887 he opened his home to President and Mrs. Grover Cleveland when the First

Couple visited St. Louis. Mayor and Mrs. Francis had the honor of escorting the Clevelands to the Veiled Prophet Ball, the city's premier social event. In deference to the nation's First Lady, no "Queen of Love and Beauty" was crowned during the celebration that year. Apparently, the popular mayor made a good impression on the President for he was later asked to accompany Mrs. Cleveland to the opera during a visit to Washington.

In 1888 Francis captured the attention of Democratic

"The annoyances of official life tend to disgust a man of business."

politicians looking for a gubernatorial candidate and, with their urging, he agreed to enter the race. During the ensuing campaign, the former "mud clerk" discovered that the political arena could be as messy as the St. Louis docks on which he once worked. Opponents taunted the Mayor with a series of trivial charges during the mudslinging campaign. It was said that he enjoyed too much fine wine, engaged in "grain gambling" at the expense of farmers, and once voted Republican in a presidential election.

In spite of these "revelations," Francis won the contest for governor, although it was a narrow, bittersweet victory. In the four-way race, he was forced to accept 49.2 percent of the statewide vote, failing even to carry the City of St. Louis. His poor showing in his own area was caused, in part, by lack of support from workers who thought Francis did little for their cause during the 1885 streetcar strike.

Feeling unappreciated as a public servant, Francis wrote to a friend that "the annoyances of official life . . . tended to disgust a man of business." A further disappointment to Francis came with the defeat of his friend, Grover Cleveland, who would be forced to wait another four years to reclaim the presidency.

Though temporarily disheartened, Francis showed no reluctance in taking on his new executive duties when the time came. (No one seemed to mind that he was assuming the governorship with three months still left in his term as mayor.) At age thirty-eight, he was the nation's youngest governor and a new face in the state capital.

Even so, no parade or fanfare greeted his arrival in the Capital City. The fact that Francis would be Missouri's third governor in little more than a year might have dampened the town's enthusiasm for a celebration. Lieutenant Governor Albert Morehouse had ascended to office following the death of John Marmaduke, but had failed to win a nomination to a full term. Having served only twelve months, Morehouse had barely warmed the gubernatorial chair when Francis arrived. The incumbent Governor, who had earlier seemed a shoe-in for the Democratic nomination, was now in the awkward position of handing over the reins of government to his opponent.

Francis apparently felt uneasy, too. He and his party arrived in Jefferson City early on inaugural day and remained aboard their train car until nine o'clock when the family was escorted to the Governor's Mansion for breakfast. After the meal, they returned to the railway car to await the inaugural ceremony scheduled for noon. When the time came, Morehouse dutifully conducted his successor into the House chamber for the traditional swearing-in ritual. Following the ceremony, Francis—who suffered from a slight speech defect—delivered a prepared text with such skill that his remarks appeared to be impromptu.

That evening Mrs. Francis continued the restrained celebration, choosing to have an informal reception with dancing rather than a fancy inaugural ball. Later, in an attempt to get better acquainted in their new surroundings, the First Couple began hosting informal

The Governor amazed guests with his talent for remembering names and faces

gatherings for legislators and townspeople. As the Governor greeted guests, he often amazed them with his talent for remembering the names and faces of people, even those he had met only once.

Although the Governor was charming, the real social attraction was Mrs. Francis. All eyes were on the thirty-four-year-old First Lady described as "dainty and exquisite of stature with the bearing of a queen." According to friends, her natural poise and upbringing in St. Louis society put her at ease in any situation. Wearing an hourglass-figure gown and a large picture hat cocked over one eye, she had all the markings of a fashionable Victorian lady as she wheeled about town in her horse-drawn carriage.

Thirty-four-year-old Jane Francis, described as "dainty and exquisite of stature with the bearing of a queen."

But having to endure the discomforts of the run-down, eighteen-year-old executive home tested her fortitude. By contrast, her St. Louis residence, located on Vandeventer Place, featured a solid gold chandelier and was regarded as one of the finest homes in the city. Now, Mrs. Francis was forced to live in a so-called Mansion with threadbare carpet, sagging shutters, peeling paint, and partially-furnished rooms. Further adding to her annoyance was a sign posted on the Mansion porch that read, "The bell is broken. . . . Walk in and touch the bell on the table."

Two months after moving into the Mansion, she invited a special legislative committee to view the deplorable condition of the house. (A practice that future first ladies would follow when they became desperate for funds.) Following the inspection, sympathetic lawmakers came up with $11,000 for the first major renovation of the home.

Having studied architecture in France and Germany, Mrs. Francis was not at all intimidated at planning such a task, but caring for a family during the construction caused her some concern. Consequently, when the carpenters and painters moved in, Mrs. Francis moved out, taking her six sons—ranging from an infant to an

PET GRIPES AT THE MANSION

Most guests had learned to be wary of a pet goat that ran loose in the Mansion yard during the Francis administration. But the word did not get around to everyone. One dark evening St. Louis legislator Dennis Ryan had an unfortunate run-in with the animal. A St. Louis newspaper recounted the story in detail:

> After entering the grounds, [Ryan] encountered the goat and mistook it for a dog. [He] placed his hand on the goat's back and talked soothingly to it, but it quickly resented the familiarity of the St. Louis man and a vigorous bunt in the ribs revealed to Ryan that he was at the mercy of the billy goat. He started to run, closely pursued by the goat. After stumbling over various obstacles, Ryan reached the fence at the edge of the cliff and clambered on top, where he hung until the timely arrival of a friend who rescued him from his perilous position. He didn't attend the Mansion reception that night, and it isn't strange that he should have a grievance against Governor Francis' goat.

In retaliation, Ryan wrote a bill requiring the animal to be tied up in the interest of public safety. He failed in his effort, however, when a fellow lawmaker took the bill to the Mansion and fed it to the goat.

The goat was not the only animal on the Mansion lawn. Three dogs—Queenie, Bull, and Calamity—ran about the grounds and the city. A local newsman found Calamity especially offensive. In one of several articles, he suggested that the Governor's ownership of "the ugliest dog in existence anywhere in North America" showed poor judgment on the part of Missouri's leader. Calamity was described as "the color of the Missouri River," with missing chunks of hair, a sickly look, but a zealous appetite. Francis, hoping to improve his status as a pet owner, later purchased "a well-bred bird dog" that he sent off to be trained. The Governor was further embarrassed when the instructor found the animal unworthy of his efforts and returned him to the Mansion.

eight-year old—back to St. Louis while the work proceeded. Governor Francis evaded the decorators by spending much of his time at the Capitol where he usually arrived at eight in the morning and remained until seven at night.

U nfortunately, the Governor could not avoid all his difficulties as easily. The first problem he faced was one left on his doorstep by the previous administration—the fate of the Bald Knobbers, a group of vigilantes that had turned to terrorizing southwest Missouri. Four gang members were sentenced to hang, but former Governor Morehouse had delayed the execution, preferring to pass the politically sensitive case to the next governor. In spite of pleas for clemency from legislators and thousands of Missourians, Francis refused to override the decision of the court.

The Governor soon faced another conflict with the General Assembly. When Francis insisted that Missouri National Guardsmen go to New York for the George Washington centennial parade, tight-fisted lawmakers refused to provide the funds. Undeterred, Francis ordered the troops to the depot, wrote a personal check for $14,000 to cover their fare, and boarded the train to make the trip with the men. Arriving in New York with several hundred troops and a forty-piece band, Francis himself donned a uniform and marched in the parade at the head of his unit. On his return home, the legislature reluctantly reimbursed the Governor.

Though Francis encountered some vexing problems during his early months in office, at least the remodeling of the Mansion proceeded smoothly. Within several months, the First Family had a modernized home, one that was far more functional than it had ever been. A connection to Jefferson City's new water system made plumbing possible on the second floor and steam heat replaced outmoded furnaces. Rooms once lit by gasoliers now glowed with electric chandeliers and restored fireplaces gave a cozy feel to the house.

The front entrance was also more inviting. "Two finely polished French-glass doors, draped in the softest of silk and lace" greeted visitors as they stepped into the spacious entry. The hall, lined with portraits of earlier chief executives, was decorated in green with a four-foot dado of Lincrusta Walton and a stenciled frieze two feet wide.

Mrs. Francis designed two small, stained glass windows with bull's-eye mullion for the Nook beneath the Grand Stairway. This gave the First Lady a well-lighted, private area where she could sew, read, or gather with small groups of friends. Even the outside of the Mansion took on a fresh new look when the original pink-colored brick, long covered with soot from passing trains, got its first coat of dark red paint.

Mrs. Francis added more decorative touches. In the style of the time, she placed fox- and bear-skin rugs in the master bedroom at the top of the Grand Stairway. At the entrances of the parlor and music room, she hung portieres—ornate curtains popular for Victorian doorways—and replaced the twenty-year-old Steck

The new windows opened into the Nook from the original "dummy" windows located in the first floor bay area.

piano with a new Steinway grand. Servants' quarters on the third floor were turned into guest rooms and the refurbished billiard table again became "the mecca of all legislators."

Thrilled by her enhancement of the house, Mrs. Francis proudly displayed the improvements at a series of parties. To enliven these events, the First Lady invited attractive young ladies from St. Louis (all properly escorted, of course) to mingle with local guests. Charmed by the politicians of the Capital City, the young women often abandoned their escorts for a chance to dance with one of the distinguished lawmakers. At one gathering, guests competed to see who could waltz up the spiraling stairway and down again.

Guests competed to see who could waltz up the spiraling stairway and down again.

Legislators were not the only ones to enjoy the First Lady's gala parties. Her masquerade balls and old-fashioned country dances attracted scores of people from around the state. On one festive occasion, five hundred guests joined the Governor and his wife for their fifteenth wedding anniversary—a celebration that included the music of two orchestras, a multiple-course dinner, and flowers brought from St. Louis.

Mrs. Francis continued her rounds of entertaining, although an illness lasting more than six months slowed her pace. During that time, she managed her weekly receptions by being carried downstairs and remaining seated as she welcomed her visitors. Additional help came from her "Women's Cabinet." The group, composed of "the most outstanding ladies of Jefferson City," gathered regularly to plan Mansion events and to assist the First Lady at receptions.

Even the Francis children got their chance to entertain friends. One Christmas party featured a stage show at the end of the long ballroom and Santa

Claus with a bag of toys at the other. Having parties for his sons was one thing, but the Governor did not want the boys awarded any special privileges because of his position. During a bridge rededication, for example, Francis sat in a prominent location, while his sons were assigned to a section much farther away. An usher brought their appeal for different seating to the Governor. Francis agreed to the boys' request, transferring them to seats farther back than the first ones.

A far more serious appeal came to the Governor in 1892 after the main building of the University of Missouri burned. President Richard H. Jesse, fearing a mass exodus of students and teachers would mean disaster for the school, called on the Governor for help. Although the temperature was near zero, Francis took the first train to Columbia, assembled the six hundred university students in the local theater, and urged them to remain at the school.

Returning to Jefferson City, he promptly called a special session of the legislature to get the $250,000 needed to rebuild. The university curators later showed their appreciation to the Governor. They awarded him an honorary doctor of laws degree, hung his full-length portrait in the school library, and named the campus quadrangle in his honor.

While Missourians approved of Francis and his handling of such unfortunate incidents, they were even more pleased with the state's healthy economy—one that the Governor described as "throbbing with life." Under the circumstances, Francis happily lowered taxes twice, making reductions larger than any previous administration. He also

The columns on the University of Missouri-Columbia campus still stand as a reminder of the 1892 fire.

revitalized the National Guard, established a bureau of geology and mines to survey the state, and continued to distribute one-third of the state's revenue to schools.

One of the most noteworthy acts of his term was the introduction of a new voting procedure, referred to as the Australian ballot. Before 1889 votes were cast orally, or on tickets printed by the state's political parties. The new system, featuring the printed names of all the candidates, gave voters more confidence in the election process and also made ticket splitting possible.

Before 1889 ballots were cast orally or on tickets printed by the political parties, as depicted in this close-up of George Caleb Bingham's painting *County Election*.

✦

A s Francis's term came to a close, friends and supporters thought it was a shame to lose the services of such a fine governor. When a group of supporters gathered at the Mansion to urge him to run for the U.S. Senate, Francis called his wife to join them in the library and asked for her opinion. In no uncertain terms, she let the delegation know that the Francis boys needed the attention of their father and that she was much opposed to the idea of such a race. "I

Francis was "an engine in breeches." think it would be small compensation

to my husband and myself in our old age to know that he had represented Missouri in the U.S. Senate, if it had brought disastrous results to our sons."

In addition to forgoing the race, Francis pleased his wife by returning to St. Louis and building a magnificent mansion. The house, located on Newstead Avenue, looked much like the White House and was considered "the most beautiful" home in

the city. Eight marble pillars lined the central hall and supported two balconies overlooking the spacious entry.

David Francis had little time to enjoy his elegant new home. The former Governor, who was once described by William Howard Taft as "an engine in breeches," was just forty-two years old and still eager to participate in public life.

Francis poses for one of several sculptures he commissioned of himself.

Three years after leaving office, he agreed to serve as secretary of the interior toward the end of President Cleveland's last term. He stayed less than a year, but during that time he brought millions of acres of forest land under federal ownership.

Francis's next enterprise was decidedly his most ambitious. In 1898 he agreed to serve as chairman of the 1904 World's Fair in St. Louis—an event that was to give the nation a grand celebration of the one hundredth anniversary of the Louisiana Purchase. For years Francis had been an advocate of centennials and expositions that might promote St. Louis. He hoped to attract a fair to the city in 1893, but Missouri lost the competition to Illinois.

Nonetheless, Francis determined to learn all he could about conducting a world-class event and he spent three weeks in Chicago studying the exposition. Convinced of the worth of such a grand undertaking, Francis proclaimed, "Every exposition is a great international peace congress. . . . and brings the civilized races closer together."

For more than five years, Francis devoted his time and energy—without pay—toward a successful St. Louis fair. To promote the event abroad, he visited European heads of state, including the President of France, Emperor of Germany, and Kings of England and Belgium. Afterwards he wrote a book about his adventures entitled *Tour of Europe in Nineteen Days*. His preparation for the fair and his efforts to publicize it around the world paid off. Previous expositions in the United States had lost money, but Francis, the consummate businessman, made the fair a financial success, as well as an international showcase.

Returning to St. Louis, Francis pleased his wife by building a magnificent home on Newstead Avenue that was considered "the most beautiful" in the city.

There were those who thought Francis had something more in mind than running a fine exhibition. "We found tracks of Francis running for president wherever we went," one Republican announced after returning from the East Coast. Though tempted by the prospect of seeking higher office, Francis had the political disadvantage of being a "gold bug"—one who favored basing the monetary system on a gold standard. At a time when William Jennings Bryan and other silver advocates dominated the Democratic Party, Francis found too little support for a nationwide campaign.

In 1910 he reconsidered running for the U.S. Senate. By then Democrats had lost interest in his candidacy and gave the nomination to James A. Reed. Later

While serving as ambassador to Russia during the Bolshevik uprising, Francis (standing in sleigh) was forced to escape the country across Siberia.

Francis turned down an offer to serve as ambassador to Argentina. But in 1916, when President Wilson wanted a skilled businessman to serve as Ambassador to Russia, the sixty-five-year-old former Governor said he considered it a call to duty he could not refuse.

The appointment was to be one of the "most dangerous and undesirable" of diplomatic assignments. In January 1918, during the turmoil that would later lead to the Bolshevik Revolution, the Russians threatened Francis's life if authorities jailed a leading Communist in the United States. The fearless Ambassador remained at his post as long as he could, "moving from place to place, living on railroad trains, authorized to leave Russia whenever he thought best, deciding to stay, ignoring repeated threats of anarchists . . . [and] issuing appeal after appeal to the Russian people to repudiate the Bolshevik usurpation."

At one point it was reported that Francis "stood off a mob of crazy anarchists with a repeating rifle." Years later Francis said the incident was somewhat exaggerated; he was armed and prepared to do battle with an approaching mob, but they never reached the embassy gate. "Everyone seemed to prefer the more sensational story, so I suppose I shall have to resign myself to this heroic role," Francis declared.

His ambassadorship was one of the "most dangerous and undesirable."

Absence from his homeland, however, cost Francis the seat in the U.S. Senate he once wanted. In 1918, with the death of Senator William Stone, Governor Gardner tried to appoint Francis to fill the vacancy. But the Secretary of War refused, saying it would be a loss to the country to call the ambassador from his assignment during such critical times. Actually, Francis was quite intrigued by the Russians and until the hostilities broke out was pleased with his lifestyle in the country, which included a mistress.

As the political situation deteriorated, so did the Ambassador's health. He finally left his post in November 1918. Carried by stretcher on board an American warship, he was taken to a military hospital in London where he underwent prostate surgery. Following his recovery, he conferred with British monarch King George about conditions in Russia.

"Mr. Ambassador, what do you think we ought to do about Russia?" the English sovereign asked. "I think the Allies should overturn the Bolshevik government in that afflicted country," Francis replied. While King George agreed, he felt President Wilson would not want to get involved in the conflict.

In 1919, after attending the Paris Peace Conference, Francis returned to the United States and took his plan to the President. He explained his strategy that included sending a voluntary army of 200,000 Allied troops to Russia to give the people a chance to hold free elections. As King George had feared, Wilson saw the revolution as an internal matter for the Russians to settle themselves. American intervention was an unpopular course. Francis later wrote that if his plan had been carried out it would have saved Europe from Communism and relieved much unrest at home and abroad.

❦

Francis returned to St. Louis, but not to his stately mansion. The family moved to the suburbs, leaving his former home for use by civic organizations. During his retirement, he published a book entitled *Russia from the American Embassy*—an account of his experiences in the diplomatic corps. His name surfaced in 1920 as a possible nominee for vice president, an office some thought he would have pursued, except for the opposition of his family and physician.

Missouri's adventurous statesman died in St. Louis in 1927, several years after the loss of his wife. He was 76. His funeral was held in the palatial home he had built after leaving the Governor's Mansion. In his will, Francis remembered the state he had served so long. His estate, reportedly valued at $5.4 million, provided a scholarship fund for the University of Missouri, a bequest to the Missouri Historical Society, and a gift of one hundred acres of land for a park in St. Louis. All of his six sons grew up to be successful businessmen: five remained in St. Louis and the other moved to California after a much publicized divorce. Proud of the tall, young men, Francis referred to them as "thirty-six feet of Democrats."

Francis had often been reminded of what his uncle once said of him. When asked what he intended to do with the poor nephew he had taken under his wing, the uncle replied, "If there is anything in him, I may make him president of [the Merchant's Exchange. . . . If not,] I will run him for governor of Missouri."

Proud of his tall, handsome sons, Francis referred to them as "thirty-six feet of Democrats."

But there was no need to apologize for David Francis—ever. As a leader with a bent toward management, he proved his worth and lived up to every expectation of his state and nation.

His predecessors had been limited by the old animosities of the Civil War—a conflict that Francis could only remember as a youngster. All that had passed. He had ushered Missouri into a robust new era, a time when anything seemed possible. David Francis, able to see a new world, prepared his state for the twentieth century and, in his famed Louisiana Purchase Exposition, brought a piece of that world to Missouri's doorstep.

Washington University's
UGLY CLUB

One of Washington University's most unique organizations—the Ugly Club—was founded in 1869 by student David R. Francis. The organization was based on the premise that "diligent students gain their honors" and "meritorious ones their high marks," but other fine qualities went unrewarded. The Ugly Club was thus designed to acknowledge those "who excell[ed] in ugliness, beauty,

modesty, childishness, repugnance to labor, self-esteem [or] . . . love for the opposite sex." Members carried out their aims by hosting banquets and dances.

Remarks made during the groups "annual lampoon" of students and professors were often stinging enough to evoke comment at faculty meetings.

Despite his student shenanigans, Francis went on to become the city's mayor, governor of the state, president of the 1904 St. Louis World's Fair, and a U.S. ambassador. With the coming of financial and political success, apparently all was forgiven and the name of David R. Francis was given to the university's athletic field in honor of his world-class accomplishments.

"MEET ME IN ST. LOUIE, LOUIE"

St. Louis had three claims to fame at the turn of the twentieth century. According to a slogan of the day, the city was "First in shoes, first in booze, and last in the American League." Then came 1904 and the World's Fair. All across the country, the focus was on Missouri as people sang the catchy, little melody:

> Meet me in St. Louie, Louie
> Meet me at the Fair,
> Don't tell me the lights are shining
> Any place but there.
>
> We'll dance the hootchie-kootchie,
> I'll be your tootsie-wootsie,
> If you'll meet me in St. Louie, Louie,
> Meet me at the Fair.

Visitors traveled by horse, carriage, and train to the Louisiana Purchase Exposition, as the event was officially labeled. Nearly 20 million people attended the fair, designed by former Governor David R. Francis to commemorate the one hundredth anniversary of the great land purchase. On Dedication Day in 1903, Francis hosted two presidents at the fair—Theodore Roosevelt and former President Grover Cleveland.

With the grand opening the next year, fair-goers saw a life they had never seen before—a world on parade. Hundreds of buildings, some more like palaces, filled Forest Park with the displays of sixty-two countries. Visitors were told it would take two weeks to see it all—one building alone had nine miles of exhibits.

In addition, nearly every state was represented by a building copied after one of its famous structures. The 1,200-acre fairgrounds featured a Japanese garden, waterfalls, fountains, a canal of floating gondolas, six acres of roses, Arabs on camel back, a Swiss village complete with chalet and mountains, and even hootchie-kootchie dancers.

> "It has been a dear wish of mine to exhibit myself at the great Fair and get a prize." ~ Mark Twain

Marvelous new inventions intrigued young and old: the electric stove, the refrigerator, and a Victor "talking box." A gigantic Ferris wheel, the centerpiece of the fair, seated sixty people in each of its thirty-six cars. Even Geronimo, the notorious Indian chief, was on hand to sign autographs and pose for pictures.

Francis also asked Mark Twain to appear at the Fair. Twain replied from Italy: "It has been a dear wish of mine to exhibit myself at the great Fair and get a prize." Instead, the humorist sent his portrait with the comment that the likeness was "better than the original."

Among the most lasting features of the Fair were the ice cream cone and iced tea—treats that were widely popularized by vendors trying to fight the hot summer days in St. Louis. The historic exhibition also was a financial success with receipts of $32 million against a cost of $18 million.

On the last evening of the 184-day event, a band played "Auld Lang Syne" as Francis flipped the switch that plunged the park into darkness. Moments later, fireworks emblazoned the sky

and a wall of bright lights outlined a likeness of Francis and the words "Farewell—Goodnight." There were cheers and tears as thousands watched the final moments of America's grandest exposition—the St. Louis World's Fair, the masterpiece of Missouri's ingenious former Governor, David Francis, and, according to Mark Twain, "the most wonderful fair the planet has ever seen."

THE BURDEN OF CONSCIENCE

"The greater the storm the higher he rose above it. He was not willing when the crisis came to yield his convictions." ~ Spoken of William Stone by a Senate colleague.

When his brother joined the Confederate Army, thirteen-year-old William Stone felt disappointed at being too young to go off to war. Still determined to take part in the conflict, he hid aboard a supply wagon following the Battle of Richmond, hoping he would not be discovered until the army was well down the road. But his brother uncovered the stowaway and sent him back to his father and stepmother in Kentucky.

A few years later, still eager to get in the fight, Stone joined a supply unit delivering horses to the Southern army. Once again he was rejected because of his age. This time the teenaged adventurer did not return home. Bolstered by determination and a spirit of rugged individualism that would later mark his career, he chose to tramp westward to Columbia, Missouri, where his sister and her husband lived. His sister later declared she barely recognized the "tall, thin, ragged boy turning into her gate."

During the next several years, Stone attended the university and blossomed socially, becoming a popular beau of the local girls but not a particularly good student. A friend teasingly said it was "rumored in Columbia that Stone had placed the same engagement ring on the hand of three different young ladies."

Even so, Stone avoided marriage for several years longer. He rounded off his formal education at a commercial college in St. Louis before returning to Columbia to pursue his legal studies with his brother-in-law. In 1867, at the age of twenty, Stone was admitted to the bar and began practicing law in Indiana. Not long afterwards, he returned to Missouri and settled in the town of Nevada—a frontier community of three hundred people without a railway and with roads that were little more than trails. He opened his first office in a room behind a real estate office. To further economize, he took his meals in a nearby basement restaurant and slept at night on a lounge in his law office.

At the time, Stone was far more interested in politics than his living arrangements. He wanted to organize the Democrats in the area, but passions and

(Facing page)
Stone captivated his audiences with a blend of storytelling and Democratic ideas.

91

hatreds left over from the Civil War divided the little community. Southern sympathizers—most of them Democrats—were barred from voting because of a loyalty oath in force at the time.

When the measure was repealed in 1870, Stone became a militant spokesman for his party. To express his views more widely, he purchased an interest in a weekly newspaper, the *Vernon County Democrat*, and started speaking at area picnics and political gatherings. Nearly six feet tall with narrow, stooped shoulders and a drooping mustache, the young politician stirred his audiences with a blend of story-telling and Democratic ideals. Further adding to his charm was his platform habit of sweeping back a forelock of long hair that fell across his brow as he spoke.

Still it was dangerous to express Democratic Party principles in the area and most speakers were reluctant to do so. Once when he was scheduled to address a political rally in another county, Stone was intercepted before his arrival and warned of threats being made on his life. Stone told his greeting party that he had come some distance to give a Democratic speech and intended to do so if they still wanted to hear one. Assured that they were quite interested in what he had to say, the courageous young orator continued to the appointed place. He mounted the improvised platform and came face to face with his adversaries who lined the front row. Stone immediately launched an attack on the men for their cowardly acts, causing many in the audience to fear that violence might erupt from the direct encounter. Instead, "the men one by one got up and slunk away."

Such boldness paved the way for the later success of Stone and his reemerging party. When he ran for prosecuting attorney in 1872, the twenty-five-year-old politician rode to victory with the rest of the Democratic slate in the county. Stone did not seek reelection, but he continued to organize his party and speak throughout the area. By 1874 his enthusiasm earned him consideration as a congressional candidate. Though he lost the nomination that year, he won a conquest of another sort; one of his many romances culminated in his marriage to Miss Sarah Winston, daughter of a Cole County farmer.

Six years later, Stone made a dramatic change in his life. He abandoned his law practice, sold his newspaper interest, and took up cattle ranching. The so-called "Stone-Wall Cattle Company," in which he had a minor ownership interest, eventually expanded its operation to include four thousand acres of grazing land in the New Mexico Territory. Stone's new enterprise, however, did not dampen his political zeal. His association with farming and ranching enhanced his appeal among voters and led to a winning race for Congress in 1884.

Once in Washington, Stone grappled with the national issues of the day—tariffs, silver coinage, and western expansion. He also worked aggressively to reclaim unused land acquired by the railroad. After serving three terms, however, he returned home to seek the governorship. When asked what prompted his decision to run, he told the *Kansas City Star* it was not because of "any irresistible public pressure;" he simply wanted the honor of serving as governor and thought he could do the job well. Actually, Stone had earlier promised political leaders that he would not seek a fourth term in Congress if they gave him a third-term nomination without opposition.

Though his bargain spared him a primary fight in 1888, he later faced stern opposition within his party during his race for governor. At a time when nominations were made by an assembly of political leaders, Stone refused to pay the customary homage to the large block of St. Louis delegates whose backing usually assured victory. Instead, he focused his attention on the rural delegates and won the nomination for governor with their support.

As the Democratic standard bearer in 1892, Stone took his stump-speaking campaign to every corner of the state. According to historian Ruth Warner Towne, Stone engaged in "one of the last of the old-time campaigns in Missouri where torch light parades, brass bands and glee clubs, and rousing oratory were the chief means of attracting the voters." He also made use of another effective campaign tactic. By dressing in different clothing depending on where he was speaking, he literally tailored himself to the voters. When in south Missouri, "where a tailor-made suit was the sign of a 'dude' he wore attire which would have astonished a city audience." Attention to such details added to his strength at the polls and put him among the winners in an election that swept Democrats into office all across the nation.

The inaugural reception was "Trial Number One" for the new First Lady, Lula Stone.

Having landed the state's top political office, Stone, his wife, and three children packed up their belongings and headed for their new home in the Capital City. While Mrs. Stone was looking forward to living in her hometown, she was apprehensive about her debut as Mansion hostess. Her immediate concern was for the inaugural day reception—a public event set to happen just hours after the First Family moved into their new home.

Stone's older daughter, Mabel, called the situation "Trial Number One" for her mother. In her memoirs she wrote, "In the short intervening time that afternoon it was necessary for mother to make a hasty survey of the kitchen and pantries, interview the new cook and other servants, and order supplies for dinner that evening and breakfast the following morning."

Stone's home in Nevada, Missouri.

While servants at the Mansion prepared for the evening celebration, the townspeople and visitors paraded through the streets waving flags and beating drums. Politicians and office-seekers, eager to see and be seen, gathered in the lobby of the nearby Madison House hotel to fortify themselves for the brisk inaugural day. Apparently, most of them stayed around for the evening reception at the Mansion as well. The local newspaper reported that "all the visitors in the city, several thousand in number, and all of the citizens of Jefferson City called and paid their respects to the new governor and his wife."

Had William Stone known what was ahead, he might have given second thoughts to seeking high office. As it turned out, his administration coincided with the Panic of 1893—the worst depression in American history. Corn and wheat prices dropped as debt and unemployment rose. At the height of the depression, farmers were hit again with an unprecedented drought. A major railroad and mining union strike only made matters worse. Fortunately, Missouri escaped the violence that occurred in neighboring states, due to Stone's efforts at keeping the peace.

Stone's term coincided with an unprecedented economic depression.

Rather than call out the militia, he relied on city and county lawmen to suppress disorder. Even Coxey's Army—a group of angry, unemployed men on a protest march to Washington D.C.—passed through the state without incident.

The state treasury also felt the financial strain, partially due to the tax reductions initiated by former Governor Francis. Revenues plummeted after an automatic rollback of the tax rate took effect when assessed valuation hit the $900 million mark. With the loss of one-fourth of the state's income, Stone was forced to employ rigid economic measures.

The Stone family bore the burden of hard times along with other Missourians. It was not unusual to see the First Lady doing her own marketing. To further conserve funds, Mrs. Stone took on the daily management of the Mansion herself. Later she called on Alex Slater, the coachman, to do the marketing or any tasks she wanted to be well done.

The state customarily paid for five servants for the Governor's home—not an excessive number at a time when household help was common among middle-class families. Still, the Stones had to provide food for the staff, as well as for their own family and guests. Two of the Stone's children, however, were at school in Columbia much of the time: eighteen-year-old son, Kimbrough, studied at the university, and fourteen-year-old Mabel attended Christian College. Only Mildred, age ten, was at home regularly.

The garish elk horn costumer—of unknown origin—decorated the halls of the Mansion for many years before its fortuitous disappearance.

Mrs. Stone surveyed her sparsely furnished Mansion to see what could be done to make it more livable. Among the remaining items were the Prince of Wales bed, a grandfather's clock, a pier glass mirror, an elk horn coat rack, and the beautiful old sideboard left by antebellum Governor John Cummings Edwards. Although much of the furniture needed repair, Mrs. Stone felt the legislature would be "horrified" at the thought of improving the house. The Governor agreed. Even so, toward the end of his term, he admonished the General Assembly to replace the furnishings every seven or eight years because of the wear caused by large number of visitors to the home.

When it came to caring for the Mansion, the legislature responded to immediate problems more quickly than they did the threatened ones. A disaster that occurred in Mrs. Stone's dining room one evening left the lawmakers little choice. Just before a formal dinner, a ceiling pipe broke, spewing water onto the table and leaving "a dripping and disfigured ceiling" overhead. The First Lady, in her typically calm manner, directed the distressed servants to set up the table at the other end of the room and the dinner party took place as scheduled.

After assessing the damage, lawmakers dutifully appropriated four thousand dollars for improvements to the house. In an uncharacteristic display of generosity, they came up with another fifteen hundred dollars to demolish an old stable at the Mansion and enough funds to build a new one for the Stone's fine black riding horses.

Some of the repair money went for more artistic improvements. The Governor was aggravated by the bare walls at the Mansion and used part of the appropriation to purchase art work. Six portraits of former governors hung in the house and Stone acquired others. "The money," he said, "could not be spent more appropriately."

The new Mansion stable housed the Stones' fine riding horses, one of which his daughter is prepared to ride. The First Lady herself had once been a "fearless" horse-woman and enjoyed riding alone in the countryside.

While it was unusual for a Governor to inject his views on decorating at the Mansion, it was even more surprising for a First Lady to depart from her traditional role as silent helpmate. Mrs. Stone favored the "betterment of women" and improved education for children, and she let it be known. She also declared her belief, in print, that the poor should be encouraged to leave the crowded cities and move to the country where she felt they would have a better quality of life.

Mrs. Stone's good nature and quick wit often helped her to laugh at the tribulations that came with being a politician's wife. One day shortly after her husband's victory, she heard two men talking as they passed her Nevada home. "That is where Stone lives," one said to the other. Mrs. Stone said she had a strong urge to call out, "No, this is where the <u>Widow</u> Stone lives."

It was hard, however, for the Stones to find much humor in the burglary that occurred one night just a few months after they moved into the Mansion. While the First Family slept, robbers stole three rings along with a gold watch and five dollars they found in the Governor's trousers. The thieves rounded out their spree by raiding the executive wine cellar before escaping through an unlocked door. To prevent a reoccurrence, a friend gave the Governor a guard dog—a huge Danish mastiff that patrolled the grounds to ward off intruders.

A Danish mastiff—a new breed to the United States—was given to the Stones to patrol the Mansion grounds.

Though security at the Mansion was temporarily a concern, Mrs. Stone generally felt quite at ease in her home community. She found the people of Jefferson City friendly and cordial in spite of the "ever-changing official population." The town warmly welcomed each first family and expected the new Mansion residents to return the hospitality. According to Mrs. Stone's daughter, Mabel, the duties of the Governor's wife "tax the strength of the Lady of the Mansion. If she has a sense of humor and a cheerful spirit, she can go through the administration a bit worn perhaps, yet with the feeling of having done well. The people of the State usually meet her more than half way, and commend her efforts to be a hostess for the State."

It pleased Lula Stone to share the Mansion with visitors, friends, and relatives just as she would her own home. That same gracious spirit prevailed years later when Governor Dockery invited Stone's youngest daughter, Mildred, to be married in the Mansion where she had lived as a child. Mildred chose a church wedding, but had her reception at the Mansion.

The town warmly welcomed each first family and expected the new Mansion residents to return the hospitality.

In 1894 Mrs. Stone rekindled another tradition that continued for many years—the New Year's military reception attended by uniformed members of the Governor's staff. For the event, an orchestra performed in the Nook, the area young Mabel Stone remembered as "that cozy part of the large lower hall." Musicians, seated behind a screen of palms, played as guests danced the Virginia reel, waltzes, schottisches, polkas, and square dances popular during the nineties.

However, it was not the raucous evenings, but the quiet ones that the First Lady enjoyed most. When the children were home, the Stones often gathered before a warm fire in the library where the Governor would read aloud from a favorite book of poetry, much like he used to do in their Nevada home.

The Governor especially enjoyed the visit of friends during the Christmas season. On such occasions, he shared his keg of eighteen-year-old Kentucky whiskey in an eggnog concoction, which was much admired by the men who came to wish him season's greetings.

While family and friends provided some solace, it was a troublesome tenure for the Democratic Governor. The off-year election of 1894 was the worst year of the depression. Frustrated by the troubled economy, Missourians gave the Republicans a landslide victory—their first major triumph in twenty-two years.

Although disheartened by the failure of his party, Stone continued to push for his programs. As the economy improved, he built new facilities on several college campuses. His proposed reforms brought laws protecting mine workers and bank depositors, and tightened regulations on elections and candidate spending. During his tenure, the state met nearly all its obligations and kept on a sound financial footing in spite of the flagging economy.

Stone had to endure several disappointments at the hands of the legislature. He tried to restrain the power of lobbyists—especially the railroad lobby—but the lawmakers refused. General unrest caused a rise in crime and, with it, a 30 percent increase in the prison population. With over one thousand requests for pardons, the Governor urged that a board of pardons be established, but the legislature also rejected that idea.

THE VICTORIAN VISITORS

According to First Daughter Mabel Stone, the social custom known as "calling" was "one of the arduous duties of a governor's wife." When visiting their peers, the amiable, but very proper, Victorians adhered to a prescribed form. Part of the protocol required a caller to leave a name card on a silver tray, or salver, prominently displayed near the host's front door. Men usually carried cards tucked in vest pockets; ladies kept theirs in elegant cases made of silk, leather, or silver.

Etiquette books of the time offered a guide to the proper use of calling cards. For instance, folding the corner conveyed a message: the bottom right corner meant, "I came in person, but you were out;" a top right corner offered condolences; the bottom left corner, congratulations. Mark Twain, who always enjoyed poking fun at social rituals, insisted that it was "very necessary to get the corners right, else one may unintentionally condole with a friend on a wedding day or congratulate her upon a funeral."

First Lady Lula Stone, however, took the social formalities a lot more seriously than did the Missouri humorist. Callers at the Mansion on Sunday afternoon were graciously received and escorted to chairs in the Nook. Mrs. Stone undoubtedly complied with the practice of being busy with lace work, letter writing, or drawing so that she had something to lay aside as the guests entered.

Later when Stone became a U.S. Senator, his wife noted the difference in protocol between the state and the nation's capital. In Missouri, the First Lady returned her calls "personally and promptly," but in Washington a visitor could simply leave a card. In fact, the hostess had the option of receiving a guest or sending word that she was "engaged" or that she "begged to be excused." Mrs. Stone voiced her disapproval of such social shortcuts: "I thought everyone in Washington was in very much of a hurry; no one had time to be at home or finish a sentence."

Eventually, the quaint Victorian custom became obsolete. With the advent of the telephone, "calling" took on an entirely new meaning and the genteel pastime faded into history.

Other political brushfires tested the Governor's diplomacy. The boundary dispute that nearly caused a "war" between Iowa and Missouri in 1839 erupted again during Stone's term. This time, instead of amassing troops along the border, the governors of the two states negotiated a settlement. The "exasperating incident," as Stone called it, was settled when the Supreme Court once again fixed the boundary line. Yet another struggle ensued when an attempt was made to move the state capital to Sedalia. Voters temporarily resolved the matter by defeating the proposal in the 1896 election.

During that same election year, Stone and Richard "Silver Dick" Bland of Missouri were both mentioned as presidential contenders on a platform favoring the free coinage of silver. Avowing support for his friend, Stone decided to step aside. At the Democratic convention meeting in Chicago, when the tide turned to William Jennings Bryan, it was Stone's sad duty to withdraw Bland's name.

The forty-nine-year-old Governor closed out the remaining months of his term and resumed practicing law, this time in St. Louis. Even then, he refused to move off the political scene—much to the chagrin of his foes, including his successor,

Governor Lon Stephens. Stone took the position of vice chairman of the Democratic National Committee and continued to be embroiled in state and national affairs, all the while keeping an eye out for another political venture.

Although the governorship was often considered a political graveyard, Stone remained a viable candidate and by 1902 rallied enough support for a U.S. Senate race. Opponents, including political muckraker Lincoln Steffens, waged a fierce campaign against the former Governor, charging him with influence peddling. Though Stone had shown poor political judgment by representing corporations regulated by state government, he had done nothing unlawful. He survived the criticism, won the election, and returned to Washington. One observer labeled him "a match for any man in the Senate in subtle humor and keen sarcasm."

> The angry Senator reached into his pistol pocket and threatened to shoot the waiter "full of holes."

Senator William Stone was considered "a match for any man in the Senate in subtle humor and keen sarcasm."

Twice during his fifteen-year tenure in Washington, his actions brought him unfavorable national attention: once for his impulsiveness and another time for his reluctance. While aboard a Pullman car, Stone unleashed his temper on a waiter for his "impertinent" manner and poor service. After slapping the man several times, the angry Senator reached into his pistol pocket and threatened to shoot the fellow "full of holes." Stone was arrested and hauled off to jail in a patrol wagon.

During his day in court, Stone showed no remorse. Instead he declared that his action was completely appropriate under the circumstances. The judge admitted that he, too, had experienced similar difficulty in restraining himself on a train. He agreed that Stone "administered punishment justified by the circumstances" and dismissed the case. Stone's acquittal was greeted with cheers from the throng gathered in the Baltimore courtroom to observe the trial. Photographers and reporters followed the Senator to a nearby taxi to get his comment on the outcome. Stone reared back in his seat, took a long puff on his cigar, and mockingly told newsmen, "It is fine to breathe the free air of heaven again."

The Senator's other bit of notoriety had broader implications. In his third term, he became chairman of the Foreign Relations Committee, giving him the chance to work closely with his fellow Democrat, President Woodrow Wilson. But friction occurred between the two when the Senator firmly opposed America entering World War I.

Stone's antiwar sentiments were shared by one-fourth of Missouri's congressmen and much of the German population of the state. Nonetheless, the Missouri House adopted an unanimous resolution rebuking the Senator. Major newspapers called for his resignation as head of the Foreign Relations Committee and religious leaders in his area branded him a "pussy foot states[man]." Some eastern journalists questioned the patriotism of Missourians largely because of Stone's position. As one of six senators to oppose the declaration of war, he was labeled a traitor by prowar advocates and his effigy hung from a lamp post during a Washington demonstration.

Stone endured the attacks with a quiet confidence. He could still remember the hardships of the Civil War. Now, as an elder statesman, he struggled against the horror of a world war. Missouri Senator James Reed warned him: "War will be declared. A vote against it will mean your political ruin. You are old and you have no property."

In a voice choked with emotion, Stone replied: "I know that [war] is inevitable; but would you have me consider my personal welfare in a case that involves the lives of millions of men, the heartaches of countless mothers, the breaking up of homes? I cannot vote to send our boys into this conflict . . . the end of which we cannot see, and the results to our country and our civilization we cannot prophesy." Despite the furor, Stone stubbornly refused to give up his chairmanship and rallied enough support to keep his position. After Congress declared war, Stone—always a conciliator—threw his support behind the effort.

> Stone was labeled a "traitor" by prowar advocates and his effigy hung from a lamp post.

Looking back on Stone's lifetime in politics, a friend described him as a "poor man" who had a talent for public service. Some said he had passed up many opportunities for private gain that came his way as an officeholder associated with men of means. One such incident was described by a railroad owner who purchased speculative land in Stone's name in an attempt to help him financially. When the land value increased, the businessman wrote to Stone, telling the Senator that he needed only to sign the enclosed deed to make a ten thousand dollar profit.

But Stone refused to do so saying, "I had nothing to do with this. . . . I can't afford to jeopardize my reputation for honesty. . . . Nobody ever has accused me of using my influence as a senator or my personal friendship to make money for myself, and I'll not begin now." Though earlier charges of influence peddling had been hurled at him before he became senator, his ability to avoid the political scandals of the day was legendary. Some writers tagged him "Gumshoe Bill," a reference to seeing his political tracks, but no evidence of wrongdoing.

The sixty-nine-year-old Senator did not live to see the successful conclusion of the war or to complete his third term. In 1918, while riding a street car to his Washington office, he suffered a stroke and died four days later. His body was returned to Missouri to lie in state in the new Capitol.

It was noted by a contemporary that Stone had a "stormy political career" and an uphill battle for nearly every position he sought. As a congressman, governor, and U.S. Senator, he struggled with his conscience and his colleagues in making the tough decisions of public life. Whatever the battle, William Stone displayed a boldness that appealed to his contemporaries and distinguished him as one of the state's most colorful political figures.

THE GOVERNOR
AND THE
QUEEN OF MISSOURI

GOVERNOR LAWRENCE "LON" VEST STEPHENS
MARGARET "MAGGIE" NELSON STEPHENS
1897-1901

Maggie's reign at the Mansion was a "joyous social whirl."

"Oh, Lon, I wish you could be Governor forever!" Maggie Nelson Stephens exclaimed one day as she and her husband settled into the Mansion. "It is so good of the Democrats to let us live here."

The young couple had never expected to live anywhere but in Boonville, Missouri, where Lon worked in his father's bank and wrote for the family newspaper. Maggie, the daughter of a wealthy banker, had also grown up in the small central Missouri town.

Entries in her diary give a rare glimpse into the merry social life of a well-to-do young lady of the era. Maggie recorded her flirtation with Lon Stephens, the fourteen-year-old who caught her eye at a party with his offer of a plate of chicken salad and pickles. Although they had played together as children, this teenage encounter marked the budding of their youthful romance. She wrote, "Lon complimented me for being pretty and I got as red as a beet."

As time went on, Lon determined to marry the vivacious Maggie Nelson after he once established himself. He began by studying law at Washington and Lee University, but after one session, he quit school to become the editor of his father's newly acquired newspaper, the *Boonville Weekly Advertiser*. Several months later, he gave up his job to travel about Europe for a year.

Meanwhile, nineteen-year-old Maggie attended a swanky finishing school in New York. While there she studied music, French, Bible history, painting, needlework, and dancing—the curriculum for a well-bred Victorian lady.

Upon his return from abroad, Lon resumed working for the family newspaper. He showed a knack for writing and a strong desire to express his opinions. Any articles signed with Stephens's initials—L. V. S.—were read and respected throughout central Missouri.

(Facing page)
First Lady Maggie Stephens.

Young Lon Stephens showed a knack for writing and a strong desire to express his opinion.

A year later, Stephens left the newspaper again, this time for a position at the family bank. Still he continued to write and gained considerable recognition for a printed pamphlet entitled *Silver Nuggets* in which he advocated the free coinage of silver. Lon also undertook some new business ventures. Along with his brother, Speed Stephens, he acquired interests in the local utility and insurance companies and established the city's first telephone system.

By 1880 Lon felt confident enough about his future to propose marriage to his childhood sweetheart. The simplicity of their wedding ceremony—attended only by family members—gave little evidence of the gala atmosphere that would surround the couple in the years ahead. After a honeymoon in Montreal, the newlyweds moved into her parents' home and Lon resumed his work at the bank.

Stephens's first statewide recognition came at the age of twenty-nine when Governor Francis named him the receiver for a financially troubled bank in St. Louis. The Boonville banker earned much acclaim when, by astute management, he was able to return ninety-eight cents on the dollar to depositors. On the heels of his success, Stephens earned himself a position in state government. In 1890 Governor Francis called on him to finish out the term of the state treasurer who had absconded with public funds.

Unfortunately, his new appointment meant a move for Maggie from her beloved Boonville to the Capital City. Maggie was appeased by the construction of a new home located on Main Street, three blocks from the Governor's Mansion. The Victorian residence, which she called "Ivy Terrace," featured a turret, bays, and a wraparound porch. Built at a cost of $10,000, its ten rooms showcased Maggie's fine collections of art, tapestries, books, and porcelains. The third-floor ballroom was especially designed for entertaining on the grand scale she so enjoyed.

Maggie had the "royal gift" of remembering those she met.

Maggie was a bright new star on the social scene of the Capital City. The congenial hostess had, as one writer put it, the "royal gift" of remembering those she met and was quick to acquaint herself. With all the decorating and entertaining she found to do, there was little time to be homesick for

Ivy Terrace, the Stephenses' ten-room Victorian home, still stands at the corner of Jackson Street and Capitol Avenue in Jefferson City.

Maggie Stephens was a bright new star on the social scene of the Capital City. She entertains at a masquerade party in her ornately decorated home, Ivy Terrace. (Stephens is in the center on the floor.)

Boonville. She wrote excitedly in her diary: "Oh, the changes. . . . Think of me living in Jefferson City! We are happier here than I ever thought it possible. . . . Everyone is so kind." Maggie was fortunate to have Billie Hood, a trusted family servant who managed everything, caring for all the household affairs as well as the personal jewelry. Not having to worry with the day-to-day chores left the wealthy socialite free to plan and attend parties.

While Maggie was exhibiting her social skills, Lon quietly worked as treasurer, restoring the people's confidence in the state office. Because of his diligence, he earned a full term for himself at the next election.

❧

By 1896 Stephens was a well-known, highly respected officeholder ready to make a bid for governor. But Maggie publicly announced her distress with campaigning. "I wouldn't care if he could be appointed," she said, "but I dread political campaigns with their attending difficulties." Nonetheless, when it came time to pressure convention delegates to vote for her husband, Maggie was quick to do her part. She and her friends went to Lon's headquarters and pinned a Stephens campaign badge on the men as they assembled.

The extra attention from the ladies certainly did not hurt. When the delegates met in the House chamber to select the

Lon Stephens worked quietly as state treasurer to restore the people's confidence in the office.

103

Maggie and her friends went to Stephens's headquarters and pinned a campaign badge on the men as they assembled.

Democratic nominee for governor, Lon won by acclamation. To commemorate his selection, two bands struck up a spirited rendition of "Dixie" as cannons on the Capitol lawn boomed the announcement. Maggie was undoubtedly thrilled by her husband's response. Stephens told his fellow Democrats that it was the proudest moment of his life, unmatched since the day his childhood sweetheart looked him in the eye and declared her love.

During the ensuing campaign, Maggie voiced her opinion on one of the controversial issues of the day without much regard for the political consequences. On the question of moving the Capital City to Sedalia, she came down forcefully in favor of maintaining the Jefferson City site. Maggie obviously read the mood of the electorate correctly as the proposal to relocate failed by a two-to-one margin.

Stephens's outspoken wife was less of a hindrance to his political future than his own health. A reoccurring eye problem (likely a type of trachoma from the symptoms described) flared up during the campaign. He was confined to a darkened room in a St. Louis hotel for the last month of the campaign, fearful that the eye inflammation might blind him. During that time, Maggie stayed close by, seeing both to his care, as well as his political correspondence.

"I am opposed to Mr. Stephens for governor. I dislike politics and I dread political campaigns with their attending difficulties."

Though Maggie deplored what she called "the vexation of politics," she displayed a childlike exuberance on election night. "Such excitement! Bands playing and bunting flying and Democrats huddled together, awaiting election returns. I was nervous. . . . I just know Lon will win." (She had earlier been assured of victory by a fortune teller she visited in Arkansas.) "Think of me as First Lady!" she wrote. "It's more scary than having to say recitations for Mr. Haynes"—her logic teacher whom she once described as "determined to make me logical."

With Lon's victory and the improvement of his eye problem, Maggie turned her attention to planning a splendid inaugural ball— one that would give the city a taste of the grand style she would pursue during the next four years. "We'll not send formal invitations. We will invite all the people of Missouri to come celebrate with us," she declared in one of her flurries at being noticeably democratic.

In so doing, Maggie got her first exposure to Mansion-size entertaining when two thousand people showed up at the inaugural reception. Dressed in her fashionable brocade satin gown complemented by a diamond and pearl-studded tiara, Maggie displayed a regal air never before seen in the state's first lady. Even so, she suffered one of the maladies common to Mansion hostesses: in the course of shaking hands with so many well-wishers, Maggie was left with a swollen and painful hand for several days.

Governor Stephens about to take the oath of office.

But at least the dreaded political campaign was over. Maggie looked forward to her reign as first lady, although it dismayed her to leave beautiful Ivy Terrace for a mansion she described as being "scarcely habitable." The former First Family had replaced the furnace and cook stove, and made some emergency repairs, but they had done very little decorating. Much of the china was worn and broken and there was not enough tableware to serve a party of twelve.

Maggie solved the problem by packing up her own fine dishes and moving them to the Mansion until state funds were available to refurbish the house. She requested ten thousand dollars from the legislature; they gave her seven thousand (about

On the question of moving the Capital City to Sedalia, Maggie came down forcefully in favor of maintaining the Jefferson City site. This stylized view is from a poster opposing relocation.

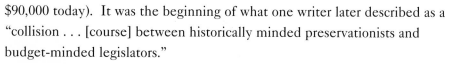

$90,000 today). It was the beginning of what one writer later described as a "collision . . . [course] between historically minded preservationists and budget-minded legislators."

Soon after moving into the executive residence, the First Lady had a crew of carpenters and painters working throughout the house. With the advice of a St. Louis decorator, she refinished the first floor in a Louis XVI style with brilliant colors and lavish ornamentation. The library dazzled in hues of purple and gold that matched the wall tapestry. In the dining room, a blue and gold color scheme complemented the foliage design in the French wallpaper. Shades of rose, coral, and ivory enlivened the parlor and engraved pictures of eighteen former governors lined the Grand Stairway leading to the second floor. At the top of the stairs, the traditional governor's bedroom featured a Marie Antoinette design in delicate blues and a brass bedstead draped in silk. Maggie turned the adjoining room into a boudoir—a sitting area—for entertaining her friends at tea.

Maggie often dressed her pets in ribbons matching those on her favorite hats.

Having been raised in a socially prominent family, the First Lady had developed a taste not only for lavish furnishings, but also for fine clothes and jewelry to match her lifestyle. The Mansion became a backdrop for flaunting her colorful, high-fashion gowns—many of which she imported from France. Author Nadine Coleman noted that "all shades of red from a rich maroon to an audibly brilliant poppy" high-lighted Maggie's extensive wardrobe. Writing of Mrs. Stephens's taste for quality

It dismayed Maggie to leave beautiful Ivy Terrace for a mansion she felt was "scarcely habitable."

jewelry, Coleman noted that the First Lady never selected gems from the stock displayed in a jewelry store. She preferred to order custom designs, specifying the number of diamonds she wanted in each.

Maggie also indulged her whim for stylish head wear. By the turn of the century, hats piled high with ostrich plumes, parrot feathers, and stuffed birds garnished the wardrobe of every well-to-do Victorian lady. Maggie once spent fifteen dollars (over $200 today) for an "exquisite" hat that featured the wings and head of an owl. When the new purchase was delivered, she carefully placed it in a band box. Later that day, as she started up the Grand Stairway, she found her husband standing on the steps with her new hat torn to bits. Her dog, Dot—whom she often referred to as "that mean fox terrier"—had also been attracted to the unusual hat and chewed it to shreds.

Maggie was greatly distressed. Determined to get rid of the pet, she directed a servant to send the dog to her sister's house at once. Lon felt sorry for the loss of his wife's new hat and gave her ten dollars to replace it, apparently unaware that it had cost more than that originally.

Still, Maggie loved small dogs and took them with her everywhere, carrying them in a pocket or purse or even draping one about her shoulder as a neckpiece. She noted in her diary, however, that traveling with a pet forced her to elude surly train conductors as much as possible. At home, she often dressed Fritz, a terrier pup, in ribbons that matched those on her favorite hats. At mealtime, Fritz would sit on his hind legs in a nearby chair and dine on quail, cake, and other delicacies from the Mansion table.

Maggie displayed a regal air never before seen in the state's first lady.

Fritz earned his keep and with it the title "Detective Dog" because of the skill he once displayed in spotting a thief. While prison inmates were working at the Mansion, the dog barked so furiously at one of them that he finally had to be penned up. Later it was discovered that $125 worth of silverware was missing. Searching the cells of the prisoners working at the Mansion revealed that "Detective" Fritz, with his unexplained barking, was trying to point out the crook earlier in the day. In addition to the silver heist, the inmate had also stolen two pounds of butter from the Mansion kitchen.

Fritz, and another dog named Nellie Bly, met with worse fates than the banished fox terrier: Fritz was mauled by a circus wolf and Nellie Bly apparently tangled with another one of Maggie's hats and "died after swallowing a seven-inch hat pin." With the loss of Fritz, friends of the First Family presented them with another pet, a dog named Prince. Much to the delight of Lon and Maggie, Prince took a liking to ragtime piano melodies and learned to dance on his hind legs in time with the music.

It took more than the loss of an expensive hat or even a favored pet to dishearten Maggie Stephens for very long. There were parties, showers, anniversary celebrations, masquerade balls, and picnics to arrange. Some of her events were simple gatherings, such as the one where she served "frappe . . . in the Turkish alcove under the imposing stairway," the area now known as the Nook. Larger receptions, like the one given

Governor and Mrs. Stephens request the pleasure of your company Friday evening, February the twenty fourth, eighteen hundred and ninety nine, at eight o'clock.

Executive Mansion,
Jefferson City,
Missouri.

Masquerade
R.s.v.p.

Tall and regal, Maggie dressed very convincingly as a queen at her 1899 masquerade party.

for the state teachers' convention, filled the house with fifteen hundred people and left the First Lady terrified by the excessive weight on the Grand Stairway.

Special guests or visiting dignitaries gave Maggie a chance to orchestrate a grand welcoming celebration. She hosted church bishops, famous musicians, and writers of the day, as well as prominent political figures. The great orator and presidential contender William Jennings Bryan was the most notable of those who enjoyed the Stephenses' hospitality. Bryan had visited the Mansion before, but this time he brought along his wife and young daughter, Ruth. An earlier trip to the nation's capital by Stephens had prompted a *Washington Times* gossip columnist to speculate on a Bryan-Stephens presidential ticket in 1900. The Mansion visit gave the two politicians a chance to talk and Maggie an excuse to hold a reception in honor of Mrs. Bryan.

At the hour appointed for the party, a receiving line formed and those invited waited anxiously for the guest of honor to arrive. But Mrs. Bryan sent word that Ruth wished to attend the festivities and was refusing to go to sleep. Maggie, who had no intention of having her party scuttled by the antics of a child, promptly dispatched a maid to entertain the youngster and the reception got underway—although somewhat later than planned.

Maggie seemed less annoyed by the awkwardness of living in a semiprivate home. In what was one of the earliest documented instances of a public tour, she opened the Mansion to small groups, leaving her servant, Billie, to act as a guide. Occasionally, Lon and Maggie themselves conducted a tour, such as the time Lon ushered a high school class through the home, insisting that the students see all the rooms.

Once when the Mansion was opened to tourists, Maggie and a friend returned home, climbed the steps to the second-floor private quarters, and found several women looking through the family wardrobes. Thinking Maggie and her friend were also tourists, one of the intruders exclaimed, "I'm seeing it all, you bet! There's enough silk waists and things in there to supply everybody here and they're mighty fine,

Maggie took up biking, but preferred to wait until after dark to pedal around the Mansion driveway with Lon.

WHAT GOV. LON V. STEPHENS CALLS HIS LATEST "DEVILMENT."

He is the First Chief Executive of Any State to Take to the Wheel and He Has Succeeded in Getting His Wife to Follow the Fad.

too!" With that, she hurried off to explore other rooms. Maggie's friend was aghast, but the incident only amused the First Lady, who had grown accustomed to people doing unconventional and unusual things at the Mansion.

Governor and Mrs. Stephens visit an encampment of Spanish-American War soldiers.

Maggie made the best of another minor intrusion into her life—the Spanish-American War of 1898. While the First Lady supported the war effort by forming a relief society to aid the troops and their families, the Governor did not rush to get involved. He refused to dispatch Missouri's ill-equipped guardsmen until Washington agreed to pay for their supplies and uniforms. By the time the state got around to sending troops—about eleven thousand men—the hostilities were nearly over and the only Missourians lost were those who died from disease or accidents. However, troop trains passing through town brought an air of excitement with crowds turning out to cheer the boys on to victory. One company of infantrymen disembarked at the railway station and marched to the Mansion to pay their respects to Governor and Mrs. Stephens.

Though Stephens drew criticism for his failure to outfit the Missouri units, as it turned out, the war brought some enduring benefits to the state and nation. Union and Confederate sympathizers laid aside their old animosities and united in a common, patriotic cause. The conflict lasted less than four months, but it spurred the economy, increased incomes and employment, and helped bring farmers out of the depression.

The playful Victorians found convivial competition more to their liking than warfare. An episode in Hot Springs, Arkansas, highlighted the friendly rivalry enjoyed in the Gay Nineties. When the bicycling craze swept the nation in the 1890s, Lon determined to master the art of wheeling. After two days of instruction and a few more days of practice, he felt confident enough to accept a challenge to race with his friend, General James Lewis.

On the day of the event, all of Hot Springs turned out to view the widely publicized contest. The participants looked much like twins when they each showed up in knickerbockers, a sweater, red shoes, and a natty bicycle cap. But there was a distinction: spectators agreed that the Governor's muscular legs were far more "pleasing to the eye than the General's."

The two cyclists took off amid the cheers of onlookers and remained neck and neck during the first half-mile until Lewis veered into the mud and fell behind.

With the help of a St. Louis decorator, Maggie furnished the parlor in a Louis XVI style in shades of rose, coral, and ivory.

The Governor went on to finish the eighteen-mile course and to win the huge victory wreath. Maggie also took up the sport, but preferred to wait until after dark to pedal around the Mansion driveway with Lon.

Unable to best the Governor when it came to cycling, his friends looked for other ways to outwit him. With Maggie's help, they managed to do so with a surprise party on his thirty-ninth birthday. Sixteen of his closest friends gathered in the Mansion library and announced to Stephens that they had come to celebrate his birthday and fully intended to do so with or without him. The Governor said he was much relieved to hear that, for his first thought when he saw the crowd was of office-seekers wanting his help.

Another milestone celebrated at the Mansion was Maggie and Lon's twentieth anniversary—a festive event compared to the simple gathering two decades earlier. For the occasion, private train cars shuttled friends from St. Louis and Kansas City to the capital. That evening four hundred guests watched the Governor and First Lady as they descended the Grand Stairway to the music of Lohengrin's "Wedding March." American Beauty roses, Spanish moss, and taffeta ribbons adorned the chandeliers, mantels, and doorways. Over the dining room entry the initials "N" (Nelson) and "S" (Stephens) were outlined in colored lights and carnations, while "1880" and "1900" were suspended over the parlor openings.

It took a half-column on the front page of the newspaper to describe Maggie's attire.

It took a half-column on the front page of the *Jefferson City Tribune* to describe Maggie's attire—a champagne-colored gown designed after one worn by Marie Antoinette at Versailles. Several more columns were needed to list all the Dresden, Wedgwood, and Limoge pieces they received to commemorate the china anniversary celebration. Friends, as well as newsmen, labeled the event her grandest achievement—"the complete eclipse of all former functions at the Mansion." Only one other compared—her splendidly decorated masquerade party of 1899 when Maggie, tall and regal, dressed very convincingly as a queen.

Maggie extended her "court" to include a number of protégées, or "ladies in waiting" as they were sometimes known. Mrs. Stephens coached her young admirers in the social graces and outfitted them with jewelry, gowns, and furs. In addition to teaching good grooming, Maggie schooled them in the womanly arts of entertaining and romance. After polishing their skills, she delighted in introducing her graduates to eligible legislators. Her fanciful parties offered a perfect setting for matchmaking and led to several weddings at the Mansion.

Around town the frequent party-goers became known as the "Mansion Set." Mrs. Stephens amused them with theme parties, often based around a flower or color. At a "violet" party, for instance, all table decorations, parlor games, flowers, and gifts revolved around the color. Some of the food was even tinted to reflect the theme. Guests answered questions using the letters in the word "violet" as a clue. Prizes included a Limoge compote with a violet design, an enameled violet scarf pin, and a violet paperweight.

Maggie's frequent guests were known about town as the "Mansion Set."

One of Maggie's many masquerade parties shows her guests assembled in the Nook and on the stairway of the Mansion. The Stephenses are seated in the lower left corner.

Whether at the Mansion or elsewhere, the Stephenses searched for new diversions to entertain themselves. Lon often took time from state business to spend a few hours at the local telegraph office. He had learned to operate the telegraph as a newspaper man and still found it amusing to contact friends by key.

The couple also delighted in attending the circus and church socials, or being confounded by the skills of a mind reader or hypnotist. Still, they never grew weary of simple pleasures such as their daily outing in a splendid victoria carriage. Each evening, Maggie rode to the Capitol where the Governor would join her for a ride to and from the fairgrounds before dinner.

The carefree, fun-loving First Lady had a more serious side, too. Those who knew Maggie Stephens described her as a devout Christian woman with high expectations of herself and those around her. She once wrote that she wanted to be "the best girl in the world" and that her idea of misery was "not to be as good as I want to be." She worried a great deal about Lon's disinterest in religion and showed great relief after he joined the church.

True to her Methodist upbringing, Maggie sternly believed in abstinence. In her mind, alcohol was for medicinal purposes and she indulged only to treat occasional bouts of

Maggie refused to serve intoxicants at the Mansion and often denounced those who partook.

"colic." Describing one of her sick spells in a diary entry, she wrote, "Lon ran down and brought me up ginger and whiskey—I was soon better."

However, in an era when the hatchet-wielding Carry Nation was splintering saloons around the nation, she refused to serve intoxicants at the Mansion and often denounced those who partook at social events. In one diary account she wrote,

"Whiskey is the cause of most of the broken hearts and troubles of this life!" She frequently quizzed Lon as to whether he drank when she was not around. The Governor enjoyed a gin fizz from time to time and Maggie showed her distress over this—when she knew of it—by calling drinking her "objection to politics."

Although Maggie opposed serving alcohol at the Mansion, she had no qualms about dancing. At the annual New Year's Day reception for the military, the Governor announced that the guests could amuse themselves in any way they wanted. They could "dance, waltz, pay court to the ladies, play billiards or chew tobacco." However, Coleman noted that anyone spending the night at the Mansion after a Saturday night party was expected "to rise early and attend Sunday School, preferably at the Methodist Church where Mrs. Stephens taught a class for young people."

Churches in Jefferson City and Boonville also benefited from her innovative fund-raising appeals. Maggie faithfully supported the church by organizing bazaars, writing solicitation letters to friends, and giving liberally of her own money. She even held fund-raisers at the Mansion, including a baby contest on the front lawn and a concert party. Once when Lon and Maggie visited President William McKinley at the

The blue and gold color scheme in the dining room complemented the foliage design in the French wallpaper.

White House, she met the wealthy businessman Jay Gould and convinced his daughter to make a $250 donation to the Methodist Church in Jefferson City.

Some thought Maggie's social whirl disguised her sadness at having suffered several miscarriages—referred to in her diary as "mishaps." Although the Stephenses never had children, they showed a great fondness for youngsters. Nieces and nephews, along with their playmates, were always welcome at the Governor's home.

Over four hundred children attended Maggie's rollicking Christmas party.

In 1899 Maggie and Lon invited every child in town, age ten and under, to a Christmas party at the Mansion. Over four hundred boys and girls attended the rollicking affair which featured refreshments and a brightly decorated tree reaching to the ceiling. During the event, their young guests ran up and down the Grand Stairway and "made a school yard out of the Mansion." The Governor also joined the festivities. Crawling under the sweeping branches of the Christmas tree, he gathered and distributed the gifts that included a toy, an orange, and some candy for each child.

Maggie's compassion also extended to the less fortunate wherever she came upon them. When she learned of the illness of friends or members of her church, she promptly sent a large pot of soup from the Mansion kitchen. The First Lady also visited the state prison and seemed greatly moved by what she saw. She took clothes to the "penitentiary babies"—those children born to the women inmates. She befriended one inmate who gave birth to triplets and the new mother asked Mrs. Stephens to name the three little girls. Maggie gladly complied, giving them the names of her three best friends, Ethel, Edna, and Katherine.

Each Fourth of July, Maggie accompanied the Governor to the prison where he would deliver a speech on the virtues of home and country before issuing his "holiday pardon" to several of the inmates. The highly emotional time sparked a great deal of adoration from the prisoners, one of whom referred to Mrs. Stephens as "Our Lady of the Kind Heart." The Governor once introduced his wife to the prisoners as the "Lieutenant Governor" and added, that if Mrs. Stephens had her way she "would turn [you] all loose."

Maggie once won a pardon for an imprisoned prostitute.

Her kindness encouraged more and more relatives of condemned prisoners to knock on the door of the Mansion with appeals for help. The tenderhearted First Lady wrote in her diary, "If I can lighten their burdened hearts it is a pleasure to me." But eventually the stress became unbearable. Unable to turn anyone away, she resorted to having a friend impersonate her and receive the callers. Finally, in desperation she instructed the butler not to admit those with personal requests.

Still, her compassion was criticized by newspaper editors who felt the First Lady urged her husband to grant pardons too freely. One widely publicized incident told of Mrs. Stephens coming to the aid of a prostitute. The woman, sentenced to fifteen years in prison for killing a St. Louis lawmaker, had been the victim of an abusive relationship. When Maggie convinced the Governor to pardon the battered woman, some members of the General Assembly were highly offended that one of their own could be murdered and the perpetrator set free largely through the efforts of the First Lady.

It was rumored that Maggie and her friends "mingled with the male lobbyists" in an attempt to influence legislation.

Earlier there had been annoying rumors about Maggie's political activities. It was said that she and her friends "mingled with the male lobbyists" in an attempt to influence legislation. The charge had some merit. The First Lady had sought recognition for homeopathic doctors—the practitioners of a branch of medicine she favored—and insisted that they be employed at state hospitals. In addition, she pressured her husband to veto a bill requiring all public hangings to occur in the Capital City rather than in the area where the crime was committed.

Legislators and newsmen felt that such intrusions by the First Lady were inappropriate. Calling Maggie a "strong-minded woman" and the Governor a victim of "petticoat rule," the *St. Louis Star* asked, "Is Missouri Run by a Governess?" The insinuation hurt Maggie deeply. Although women did not engage in public debate, she agreed to respond—but only if her husband was present.

Maggie's self-effacing remarks showed her occasional fear of appearing too forward. "I can truthfully say that I am timid about advising [the Governor] for he has the better judgment," she declared. Nor had

"Is Missouri run by a Governess?"

she interfered with legislation that favored execution for capital offenses, Mrs. Stephens claimed—though she admitted to having touched on the subject with legislators attending a Mansion party. She went on to explain that as a Christian woman, her happiest moments came when she could relieve distress, lighten hearts, and bring smiles to the faces of the unfortunate.

Mrs. Stephens also denied the accusation that she always required lawmakers attending Mansion receptions to be attired "in full dress." She did not, however, address rumors of extravagance at the Mansion, including a favorite story about a five-dollar toothpick (about $75 today) bought from state funds for the Governor's use. During the dispute, the *Hannibal Journal* came to her rescue. The newspaper noted that Mrs. Stephens was "a model woman and the state would not suffer should her splendid judgment prevail in matters of state."

Maggie did not deliberately set out to challenge the role of the Victorian woman; she was quite satisfied with her lifestyle. She felt her place was in the home, not in the voting booth, and denounced the idea of women having a "right to govern and direct public affairs," calling the thought "abhorrent." Once when a woman tried to get her signature on a suffrage petition to present to the legislature, she wrote in

MISSOURI'S MEDICINE MAN

Once while speaking to a gathering of druggists, Governor Stephens showed his sense of humor, even at his own expense. He confessed to feeling a kinship with the group because of his recent endorsement of a patent medicine called "Paine's Celery Compound"—an elixir he received through the mail.

"Characteristic of the average Missouri Democrat to drink anything which does not cost him anything, I indulged freely and disposed of it in about a month," the Governor explained.

GOVERNOR STEPHENS
His Family Joins Him in Sincere Praise of Paine's Celery Compound.

Later, Stephens said, a patent medicine salesman showed up in the executive office inquiring about his health and wanting to know if the compound had improved his physical condition. When the Governor responded that he had been feeling quite well—possibly due to the medicine— the salesman asked for a written testimonial.

Hoping the fellow would go away, Stephens busied himself with paperwork, refusing to say either "yes" or "no." The persistent young man returned each day for the following week, until Stephens "was worn to a frazzle" and agreed to sign a statement promoting the drug.

"I have used Paine's Celery Compound, keep it in my house for family use, and find it a splendid remedy," Stephens attested. When a large picture of the Governor and his endorsement appeared in the newspapers, he became the target of much ribbing.

"This testimonial has subjected me to many embarrassments," Stephens told the druggists, "and

I have regretted a thousand times that I did not have the stranger taken out and shot when he first appeared on the scene." Still, some good had come from the incident the Governor declared. Stephens told of receiving a letter from a man who said he had fallen into a threshing machine and been shredded

into small pieces. But upon receiving a dose of the miracle compound, he was wholly restored and immediately able to do handsprings. The writer urged Stephens to run for the Senate where he could continue to remedy mankind. The Governor encouraged the amused druggists to lay in a supply of the elixir for the upcoming harvest season and to be sure to forward him all commissions from any miracle cures.

Maggie kept a diary for over fifty years.

her diary: "Of course I did not sign it. We tried to make Lon think I did. He said he knew me too well to believe I did."

Even the diary Maggie had kept since she was eleven years old became a political item. After she gave portions of the journal to a society reporter, the writings later turned up in the *St. Louis Post-Dispatch*. "Oh, will I never hear the end of that affair!" Maggie moaned to reporters, all the while insisting that she and Lon took the matter in stride and "laughed about it many times." The *Post-Dispatch* took exception when others wrote of the silliness and lack of judgment displayed in the diary, calling the criticism "brutal" and "despicable." The writing simply "lays bare the heart of a sweet and gentle woman in maidenhood and wifehood," the newspaper declared.

Temporarily dismayed by politics, Maggie returned to her church work, entertaining, and, of course, the favorite pastime of first ladies—redecorating. On the outside of the Mansion, she added more electric lights and a new fountain, providing a splendid setting for her tent parties. During the hot summers in Jefferson City, she often served her guests cake and flavored ice in the summerhouse located on the north lawn—a site they shared with the Mansion's cow which grazed nearby. To escape the heat, Lon relaxed in a hammock on the river side of the Mansion where there was at least a prospect of a cool breeze.

But Maggie took to her bed when the heat became oppressive, calling for servants to bring wet cloths for her head and lemons to relieve heat prostration. For her more serious "nervous spells," she called on a local osteopath who used "quieting pills," morphine, or electrical therapy to aid her recovery. The Governor also relied heavily on pain relievers, including morphine, to treat his chronic eye condition.

Stephens might have wished for some such remedy for his political problems. Legislators and newsmen were frequently incensed by the Governor's belligerent, bullheaded disposition. One sensitive situation emerged when the Governor hired his brother-in-law as his private secretary. In spite of the nepotism wrangle that followed, the Governor did not remove the young man from his staff.

With equal determination, Stephens refused to quell one of the state's worst labor disputes. In 1900 several thousand striking streetcar workers in St. Louis marched in the streets, demanding recognition of their union, better wages, and fewer hours. Though violence erupted during the two-month-long strike, resulting in fifteen deaths and hundreds of injuries, Stephens rejected the city's plea for help from the state militia. Stephens declared (as he had during the Spanish-American War) that funds were unavailable and, furthermore, that the

Maggie returned to her church work, entertaining, and the favorite pastime of first ladies—redecorating.

situation was one for the local authorities. St. Louisans retaliated by hanging the Governor in effigy. Stephens's refusal to use his power to maintain order cast doubt on his effectiveness as governor that lingered throughout his term.

Though occasionally faulted for his poor judgment, the Governor achieved some progressive reforms. He won new laws regulating child labor and interest rates, set up employment bureaus in large cities, and provided compensation for injured workers. His inheritance tax for higher education gave a boost to the state's colleges.

Leaving the Mansion is "like being banished from heaven."

He also established the state fair, started the move for the 1904 World's Fair, created two mental institutions, and took over state ownership of both the Federal and the Confederate soldiers' homes. The penitentiary, typically a financial drain on the state, showed a surplus during his final two years in office. Though the institution held the reputation as "the most wretched prison in the country," Stephens apparently took pride in keeping the cost per inmate at twenty-five to twenty-eight cents a day.

The Governor determined to keep all the state institutions on a sound footing either by rigid economy or by arranging the funding himself. Previously, as state treasurer, he had loaned the state $100,000 to meets its obligations. Again, as governor, he came to the state's rescue. Rather than call a costly special session of the legislature when the state faced a $400,000 deficit, Stephens personally negotiated with a New York bank to borrow the needed money.

"I go out from the governorship with scarcely enough friends to bury me."

Toward the end of his term, the couple prepared to return to private life. Maggie made no pretense about how she felt. In her heart she knew Lon could not be governor forever, yet she greatly regretted leaving the Mansion. "It's like being banished from heaven," she wrote in her diary, "I now dislike to leave this home as I did Ivy Terrace when I came here." Even so, she reiterated her disdain for politics and the desire to have Lon free of the demands of public office.

Apparently, all was not well between the two from the tone of one diary entry: "I am so sad tonight. Lon has taken to sleeping on the back porch with our little dog, Trixie." If Lon had any regrets about Maggie, or about leaving the Mansion, he did not make it known. "I've had enough of politics," he declared, and vowed he would never seek public office again, even though his name was being circulated for the Senate and vice presidency at the time.

Provoked by harsh criticism of his administration, he called the abuse of officials a "crying evil of the times" and in his last speech to the General Assembly urged a new libel law to protect public servants. Aware of the strong feelings against him, Stephens declared, "I go out from the governorship with scarcely enough friends to bury me." (Years later, Stephens apparently took some consolation when

The Stephenses and their chauffeur-driven car.

The new home of Governor and Mrs. Stephens in St. Louis was located on Cabanne Avenue.

critics began to lambaste Governor Elliott Major. ("Thank God," Stephens declared, "they no longer can say I'm the worst governor Missouri ever had.")

But Lon's personal remorse and frustration did not prevent Maggie from performing her final responsibilities as First Lady: to sit for her portrait and to welcome the incoming residents. During the week she posed for the painting, she passed the time by reading the popular Victorian novel *When Knighthood was in Flower*, leaving the artist with the challenge of incorporating the styles from two of her favorite gowns. The five-hundred-dollar painting, paid for by donations mainly from women and children, became the first portrait of a governor's wife to be placed in the Mansion.

Before departing, Maggie invited the new First Lady to come view the Mansion. The executive residence would be home for Mary Dockery for less than a year before her death. Even during her visit, Maggie noted Mrs. Dockery's "shockingly delicate" appearance. In her diary she added, "[I told] her a thousand and one things—I liked her very much though—she seems so sincere." Maggie's assessment of the new Governor, however, was less generous. The mild-mannered Dockery, she feared, would be a "disappointment" because he would not "speak out."

The day finally came when Maggie and Lon closed the massive walnut doors of the Mansion for the last time, boarded a waiting carriage, and drove home to Ivy Terrace. Two years later they sold their fashionable home and prepared to

"I put on my inauguration dress and stood there thinking of all the ovations I have received."

move to St. Louis. Maggie, distraught at the thought of leaving the Capital City, became ill and was unable to supervise the packing. She remained in bed and required the visit of a doctor.

With their move to St. Louis, they continued the lifestyle of wealthy socialites. Lon served on bank, college, and corporate boards while managing his sizable fortune. Church and club activities, theater parties, and shopping occupied much of Maggie's time. A concerted effort to have President Woodrow Wilson appoint him comptroller of the currency failed, in spite of strenuous appeals from Stephens and friendly political leaders. When urged to be Missouri Democratic chairman, he refused, but agreed to write a statewide political paper. Even so, by the early 1920s, he was disgusted enough with his party to vote Republican.

Toward the end of his life, as Lon's eyesight failed, Maggie spent much of her time reading aloud to him. In an effort to prevent total blindness, he agreed to an operation. However, Stephens died in the night before he was scheduled for eye surgery the next morning. He was sixty-four.

Maggie continued writing in her diary, but less frequently than in her earlier years. During a moment of nostalgia, the former First Lady wrote, "[I] put on my inauguration dress and stood there thinking of all the ovations I have received. Lon seemed to be with me." In another entry she recorded sadly, "I hardly ever go to church anymore." Instead, Maggie sought fascinating new pursuits. She built a Spanish-style home in St. Petersburg, Florida, and traveled about Europe in her Packard limousine that she shipped ahead of her arrival.

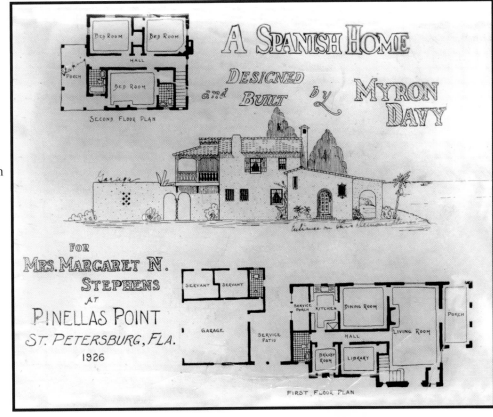

In 1928—five years after her husband's death—Margaret Nelson Stephens married Johnny Johnson, a clothing salesman and the suitor of one of her protégées. She was sixty-nine; he was twenty-nine and looked much like the handsome movie idol Rudolph Valentino. Maggie made every effort to deny her age. According to relatives, she chipped away the date from the tombstone of her twin brother who had died as an infant and erased Johnny's age from her diary and inserted forty.

In spite of early concerns over the age difference, relatives and neighbors agreed that Johnny treated Maggie well. Still, their marriage lasted only a year before she developed heart trouble and died. It was rumored that Maggie took to the Charleston and that the two of them danced the year away.

In a division of her estate—valued at $400,000—Johnny got over one-third of the money; friends, relatives, and churches divided the remainder. Johnny saw to it that Maggie was buried beside Governor Stephens in Boonville, where as teenagers she and Lon had fallen in love over a plate of chicken salad and pickles.

Looking back on Maggie's reign at the Mansion, one of her protégées described the four years as a "joyous social whirl." A newsman captured the essence of the First Lady when he wrote that by position, by culture, and even by nature, Maggie Nelson Stephens was entitled to be called the "Queen of Missouri." And, indeed, for a while she was.

The photo of Johnny Johnson and Maggie outside her Florida home was likely taken on their wedding day.

THE BEST OF TIMES

The optimism of a new century was shrouded by the loss of family and fortune.

When Alexander Dockery gave up his medical practice, his wife, Mary, was not surprised. Dr. Dockery had practiced for eight years in Chillicothe, Missouri, but Mary could tell he was becoming more and more interested in public life, first as president of the local board of education, then as curator of the University of Missouri.

In 1874, when Dockery had the opportunity to be part owner and cashier of a new bank in Gallatin, Missouri, the twenty-nine-year-old physician made the choice to change his career and his future. The townspeople took a liking to their new banker and elected him to serve as city councilman and then as mayor. His election as a Democratic congressman in 1882 sent the couple to Washington for sixteen years and, in time, gained him recognition as Speaker Pro Tempore of the House.

During most of Dockery's tenure in the nation's capital, the couple made their home at the now famous Willard Hotel. Mary, along with other congressional wives, hosted "brilliant receptions" for Washington society. She spent most of her time, however, helping with office correspondence and reading the newspapers from their home district to keep her husband informed about local concerns. One writer described her as "a very quiet, retiring lady. . . . of domestic taste;" another complimented her intelligence, saying she had the "mental processes . . . like those of a man."

Though the Dockerys enjoyed Washington, they eagerly headed back to Gallatin when Congress recessed each year. During his interlude

(Facing page) A 44-gun salute celebrated the final payment on the state's $44 million debt.
(Right) Mary Dockery, the only First Lady to die in the Mansion.

... THE WORST OF TIMES

DOCKERY'S SECRET WEAPON

A tide of Republican sentiment swept Missouri and the nation during the off-year election of 1894. The unprecedented depression that followed the Panic of 1893 caused voters to look for new leadership.

In a day before public opinion polls, Alexander Dockery, an incumbent Democratic congressman, sensed the mood as he campaigned in his district. He felt his only chance to survive depended on getting every Democrat to the polls.

It was the practice of candidates to write letters to local party leaders, encouraging them to produce a favorable vote. But under the circumstances, Dockery felt he needed to convey more urgency.

On the eve of the election, he sent three hundred telegrams to Democratic leaders asking for their help. In those days, telegrams were sent only to convey an urgent message and to receive one in a rural area was quite rare. As a result of the telegrams, local politicians spent the next day working harder than ever contacting voters.

When the ballots were totaled, Dockery had saved his congressional seat by fewer than three hundred votes. No doubt, his last minute appeal made the difference in the election that took from office Champ Clark and Richard Bland, two of his longtime House colleagues.

In this Capitol mural, artist Thomas Hart Benton depicts his father making a speech for Representative Champ Clark.

from lawmaking, Dockery enjoyed donning a large straw hat and boots to join the volunteer road crew working in his home area. He once confided to a friend, "I don't know what it is in my physical makeup, but I have always keenly enjoyed doing manual labor on the roads and nothing that I have ever done has given me more genuine pleasure."

His physical stamina, as well as his political doggedness, caused some writers to use the term "gritty" in referring to the Congressman. One described him as "aggressively economical." A biographer tagged him the "watchdog of the treasury" because of the close scrutiny he gave bills that came before him while serving on the appropriations committee.

His zeal at cost cutting made Dockery "one of the most unpopular members of Congress."

In a speech before the House, Dockery summed up his feelings about government spending: "Unnecessary taxation leads to surplus revenue, surplus revenue begets extravagance, and extravagance sooner or later is surely followed by corruption."

As chairman of the Dockery Commission, he devised a new accounting system for the Treasury Department that abolished red tape and antiquated methods. For a while his zeal at cost cutting made him one of the most unpopular men in Congress. Unhappy government clerks, determined to rid Washington of his meddling, began raising funds in an attempt to defeat him back home.

Despite their efforts, Dockery survived the election, returned to Congress, and continued to show his cautious bent. He not only opposed the annexation of the Philippine Island but also fought to keep Wyoming and Idaho from gaining statehood. Neither had the population or resources for admission to the Union, he declared. Furthermore, he objected to Wyoming permitting women to vote.

Though critical of westward expansion, Dockery was a strong supporter of the Spanish-American War. He felt that the conflict had the beneficial side effect of uniting Americans against a common foe after the many years of division that followed the Civil War. In addition, the Spanish-American War—though of brief duration—brought economic gain to the state. Missouri profited most by selling over one-half million dollars worth of its famous mules and horses for wartime use.

After eight terms in Congress, Dockery decided to take on a different battle. In 1899 he returned to Missouri with plans to spend the next eighteen months campaigning for governor. The groundwork proved successful when he won the nomination of the state Democratic convention by acclamation. In the campaign that followed, Dockery reached across party lines to solicit GOP support. But unlike many politicians of his day, he refused to promise jobs for votes. Instead, he told Republican facetiously that "the best he could do was to let them dance in the head set at the inaugural ball."

With Dockery heading the state ticket in 1900, Democrats captured all the statewide offices and control of the legislature. However, Missouri Republicans took heart from the reelection of President William McKinley and the statistical increase in their voting strength—a trend that would be reflected in subsequent elections.

For the moment, at least, Missouri Democrats were heady with victory and the optimism of a new century. Mrs. Dockery shared that enthusiasm as she and her sisters and nieces arrived in Jefferson City to prepare for the upcoming inauguration. It was their intent to move into the Mansion early and to begin decorating. But Mary

His personal trademarks: boots, a black felt hat, and a chewed cigar.

had second thoughts; it was Friday and, being superstitious, she did not want to begin her new life on such a fateful day.

The matter concerned her so much that she decided to stay overnight at the Madison Hotel while the others went ahead to prepare the house. York, the butler, met them at the door and, with "great deference" and pride, showed the women about the Mansion. Feeling better for her caution, Mary arrived the following morning to prepare for her new duties as First Lady—a role made easier by York's knowledge of the house and its traditions.

Apparently, the townspeople held few expectations for the new First Lady, whose strength was greatly reduced by a severe heart condition. Readers of the local newspaper were informed that the Governor's wife was "a delicate woman, not well able physically to enter upon a round of entertainment." The Mansion—usually the social hub of the Capital City—would be little more than a "homeplace," it was reported.

Upon becoming Governor, Dockery shaved the beard he had worn throughout his political life.

The serene composure of the First Lady masked not only her health problems but also the deep personal tragedy of having lost eight children—six in infancy and two in early childhood. Friends said she never spoke of her grief because she felt it would only sadden the lives of others. Rather than indulge in self-pity, Mary made new friends by getting involved with literary and church groups and the Daughters of the American Revolution.

The Governor also maintained a subdued manner and appearance. He is a "plain man and he likes plain things about him," a man who "still wears boots, and likes to take off his coat when it is warm," it was observed. In addition to the boots, he was easily recognized by his other personal trademarks: a black felt hat and chewed cigar. Missing, however, was his "bristling Van Dyke" beard. Soon after taking office, Dockery shaved the beard he had worn throughout his political life, explaining the clean-shaven look as his "contribution towards advancement."

One noticeable quirk that he maintained was the widely known "Dockery Wink." The Governor would often respond to a request with a wink—a gesture that freed him from an outright commitment and could be interpreted as either an agreement or a denial.

The new First Lady also showed a distinctive style. Unlike her predecessor—the flamboyant

124

Maggie Stephens—Mrs. Dockery shunned display, even preferring to have her official portrait painted in everyday attire rather than an extravagant ball gown. However, she showed great concern for the appearance of the Mansion. After the Stephenses removed their fine furnishings, the house looked all the more vacant and run-down. Fortunately, the legislature agreed and made an appropriation for improvements. Mary wasted no time before spending the money. She and her sister made several trips to St. Louis to purchase fabric, furniture, and artwork.

Defying earlier expectations, Mrs. Dockery seldom let a week pass without a small gathering at the Mansion. Her deep obligation to public duty remained even during her final hours. The frail First Lady had been ill for two weeks before the scheduled New Year's Day military reception. On the eve of the party, her conditioned worsened, but she refused to call off the event. Confined to her bed on the second floor, she urged the decorators to continue putting up the flags and bunting she had arranged for earlier.

On the morning of January 1, 1903, guests were notified of the death of First Lady Mary Dockery. That evening, her funeral was held in the parlor surrounded by

As hostess of the Mansion, Kate Morrow managed social events and the daily routine after Mrs. Dockery's death.

Mrs. Dockery was the only first lady to die in the Mansion.

the military decorations put in place for her party. Mrs. Dockery, the only first lady to die in the Mansion, was buried the following day in Chillicothe alongside her eight children. Death had come to the home on two previous occasions during the holiday season: Governor John Marmaduke died in 1887 just three days after Christmas and, in 1883, Carrie, the nine-year-old daughter of Governor and Mrs. Crittenden, died of diphtheria five days before Christmas.

With two years left in his term, Governor Dockery turned to his executive secretary, Al Morrow, and his wife for help. The couple moved into the Mansion where Kate Morrow assisted with social events and the daily routine. "I had only one rule laid down for my guidance when I took over the management of the Mansion," she recalled with good humor, "and that was that Governor Dockery wanted chicken in some form once every day. Needless to say, he had it." Al Morrow endured the same monotonous menu. Kate wrote of her husband, "Mr. Morrow once said he believed he could never eat chicken again; but he could and he did and enjoyed it, too."

For ten months following Mrs. Dockery's death, the Mansion residents remained in mourning and little entertainment took place. Even with reduced household expenses, Mrs. Morrow watched the budget closely. At that time, the Governor paid all of the Mansion food bills, both for his family and state guests. In addition, each First Family provided their own transportation, consisting of some form of horse-drawn equipment. As costs grew, the honor of living in the house was frequently outweighed by the financial burden. Unfortunately, it would be another decade before the legislature improved the situation.

There were other, more immediate, financial problems for the Governor and lawmakers to address. Dockery had made a campaign promise to free Missouri of debt by his second year in office. However, his attempts to bring the budget into line drew criticism when he slashed salaries of prison employees. Still, he came close to meeting his goal when he paid off all the state bonds except those issued for schools. Inspired by the Governor's efforts, both Democrats and Republicans celebrated his success. Along with speeches and music, a forty-four gun salute was fired in honor of the final payment on the $44 million debt remaining from the Civil War.

> "The Governor wanted chicken in some form once every day. Needless to say, he had it."

Later, the Governor irritated legislators with his caustic remarks about their accomplishments. Following one session, he credited the General Assembly with having done good work, but when asked what he meant, Dockery ridiculed the members, saying, "Whenever a legislature meets and doesn't make a fool of itself, it has been a good legislature."

Nonetheless, Dockery joined the unruly lawmakers in shaping some significant advances. He consolidated school districts, introduced new election laws, created a system of juvenile courts, and improved prison facilities.

The Governor also pushed to contain costs at the state penitentiary. Five shoe factories already operated within the prison walls, producing over ten thousand pairs of shoes daily using cheap convict labor. Inmates made saddle trees, men's clothing, and brooms, and the legislature approved a twine-making factory as well.

Dockery enforced the eight-hour day for mine workers and formed a mediation board to settle labor disputes. Another timely piece of legislation limited the speed of the horseless carriage to nine miles an hour. (As it turned out, automobile drivers had little trouble heeding the new requirement as they traveled the narrow, often muddy, roads built for horses and wagons.)

Under the leadership of the education-minded Governor, schools received more funding than they ever had previously. An "enthusiastic friend of education," Dockery took pride in recalling that the first ballot he cast was in favor of building a school.

> Dockery took pride in recalling that the first ballot he cast was in favor of building a school.

While schools fared well during Dockery's term, farmers did not. In 1901, when a severe drought devastated cropland, the Governor urged Missourians to pray for relief. Dockery had less success than former Governor Hardin, whose Grasshopper Proclamation in 1875 calling for prayer had produced almost immediate results. This time, Missourians were left to endure a below-average rainfall for the remainder of the summer.

In spite of its typically hot, dry summers, the state enjoyed a steady stream of visitors in 1904. Many guests, foreign and domestic, came to see the Capital City while visiting the World's Fair in St. Louis. One memorable occasion that fall, a dinner to honor former First Lady Lula Stone, ended with a tragic telegram telling of the loss of the Missouri Building at the fair. The state's showpiece—and one of the few buildings with a heating system—was destroyed by fire when a gas heater erupted in flames.

Kate Morrow recalled that Mrs. Stone, though regretting the loss, said she "would not be the least unhappy if the portrait of 'Mr. Stone' had been destroyed." His painting, along with those of other Missouri Governors, was on loan to the exposition. Fortunately, none were damaged and the works of art were returned to Jefferson City. Some years later, however, the Stone family replaced the offensive portrait with a more favorable likeness. Though many historical items were lost in

A 1904 view of Jefferson City and the Missouri River.

127

By entering the new porte cochere at the side of the house, guests could reach the second floor where they could make a grand entrance down the curved stairway.

the blaze, several pieces of furniture were retrieved and became a part of the Mansion collection at the close of the exposition.

Mrs. Morrow felt that there was more to be preserved at the Mansion than just the furnishings and building. When guests inquired about former first families and the traditions of the Mansion, Kate realized that no formal record had been kept. She pondered the idea of writing a history of the home, but thirty-three years passed before it came into being. In 1936 she and First Lady Eleanor Park published *Women of the Mansion*, a 435-page volume containing the biographies of former first ladies and a record of the furnishings and significant social events at the executive home.

In her own account, Kate tells of coming to the Mansion to act as hostess with an attitude of "awe and deepest responsibility." Her feelings on departing the house were much like those expressed by other residents, "One leaves it at the close of her stewardship with a love and veneration for this old building that is difficult to realize and certainly cannot be fully explained."

Mrs. Morrow's fondness for the Mansion prompted her to make its first major structural change. For years, gusts of wind and snow had blown through the Great Hall when doors were opened to visitors. To correct the problem, Mrs. Morrow added a porte cochere—a covered entrance that gave a protected driveway for vehicles and a door for guests on the south side of the house. The new entry also added an air of formality for those arriving at the Mansion for parties. Taking the backstairs, guests could go to the second floor, leave their coats, and freshen up a bit before making a grand entrance down the long, curved stairway.

Though the front entrance was used less often, Governor Dockery still insisted on improving the look of the area. Former Governor John Marmaduke, wanting more light in the hallway, had installed a set of pine outer doors inset with glass. Dockery upgraded the entry by substituting oak doors with beveled glass panels.

As work on the plumbing, floors, and walks got underway, the Governor kept a close eye on the projects. He paid so much attention to the details that Mr. Morrow, his clerk, gave the Governor a new title, "Superintendent of Public Works." Dockery also joined in the beautification of the grounds. Wielding a pair of pruning shears, he trimmed the trees along Capitol Street next to the house and gained favorable comments from those who stopped to admire his work.

Mrs. Morrow also drew accolades for keeping the tradition of hospitality at the Mansion. She graciously offered the home to former Governor Stone's daughter,

Mildred, giving her the opportunity to have her wedding reception in the stately surroundings where she once lived. Further credit is due Mrs. Morrow for formalizing the "change dinner"—the custom of the current governor entertaining the incoming family at dinner on inauguration eve.

Governor-elect and Mrs. Folk dined at the Mansion on Sunday, spent the night, and had breakfast the next morning before the inauguration. Other overnight guests included a well-known Democrat of the day, the presidential contender William Jennings Bryan, and his wife. The next day, sixty-year-old Alexander Dockery, the last of the old guard Democrats, handed over his office to political reformer Joseph Folk. At the time, the thirty-five-year-old St. Louis attorney was the youngest man ever to be elected governor of Missouri.

Dockery's term had reflected the "best of times . . . the worst of times." Treasury receipts were up and the tax rate was the lowest in the United States. The Louisiana Purchase Exposition in St. Louis had elevated Missouri in the eyes of the nation and the world. Yet, bribery scandals in St. Louis politics and in the legislature caused suspicion of public officeholders. During his term, Dockery had witnessed the resignation of his lieutenant governor and the indictment of several state senators.

None of these occurrances reflected on the Governor or dampened his interest in public service. In 1913 President Wilson brought the former congressman back to Washington where he served as third assistant postmaster general for the next eight years. In his position, Dockery organized the sale of more than a billion dollars worth of war savings stamps in support of American troops during World War I.

The Governor's take-charge hostess, Kate Morrow, became active in politics in her own right after leaving the Mansion. She organized Democratic women's clubs and attended the 1920 Democratic National Convention as one of the first four women delegates from Missouri. In 1924 she ran for secretary of state. By defeating two men in the primary election, she gained the distinction of being the first woman to run a statewide general election race in Missouri. But she could not overcome the Republican landslide that year and went down to defeat with the rest of the Democratic ticket.

There was more misfortune ahead for Dockery also. He returned home at the end of the Wilson administration to discover that the bank in Gallatin—the one he cofounded over fifty years earlier—had gone broke, wiping out most of his wealth. With no family to provide for, he had planned to leave his substantial fortune to his church, the local YMCA, and the park named in his honor. Now, all that had changed. Dockery downplayed his losses saying, "I am afraid my friends might try to send me money."

Less than a year after the bank failure, he died at the age of eighty-one. Though unable to bequeath the inheritance he had hoped, Alexander Dockery, nonetheless, left Missourians a legacy of honorable public service matched by few men.

THE FIRES OF REFORM

GOVERNOR JOSEPH WINGATE FOLK
GERTRUDE GLASS FOLK
1905-1909

The historic fire at the Mansion was destructive, but in the end,
it transformed the old house for the better.
The fires of reform ignited by the aggressive Governor did much the same for Missouri politics.

"No real lady would permit her picture to appear in a newspaper," Gertrude Folk announced as she denied the many requests for her photograph. Her husband tried to change her mind, saying that a picture "was due the public." But Gertrude stubbornly refused and came to regret her decision.

The paparazzi of the day, awaiting their chance, caught Mrs. Folk as she stepped awkwardly from a hansom cab at the St. Louis World's Fair. Facing a sea of cameramen, "there was nothing to do but submit," she recalled. "When this horrible creature bearing my name appeared in the Sunday paper the following day, I feared my husband's chance for election was jeopardized."

After that, Mrs. Folk came to accept publicity as a necessary part of her life as the wife of a public figure. Still, she shied away from politics as much as possible in her position. "My husband . . . knew the 'game,' but I was quite ignorant of the art of politics." Her upbringing by "conservative parents" in a small Tennessee town caused her to look "down on politicians because of the few we knew," she said.

The first photograph published of Mrs. Folk and one that greatly annoyed her.

Joseph Folk had grown up in Tennessee, too. His father practiced law, but later in life became a Baptist preacher. Joe's deeply devout parents required their eight children to attend Sunday school, church, and a prayer meeting each week. At home, family prayers, Bible reading, and grace at the table were daily rituals for

(Facing page)
The fireplace, shown as it looks today, was rebuilt of walnut after fire destroyed the original marble mantel.

131

Joe Folk, the young circuit attorney, prosecuted "Boss" Butler and other so-called "boodlers" in St. Louis.

the Folks. Such frivolity as dancing and card playing were sternly forbidden. Though two of his brothers became ministers, Joe persistently refused any religious affiliation and, for a while, was thought to be an atheist. However, he later joined the church, attended frequently, and sprinkled his speeches liberally with Bible references.

Joe was also slow in showing an interest in formal education. Upon completing high school, he worked a few years at various jobs as a shipping clerk, a bookkeeper, and a patent medicine salesman in the swamps of Arkansas. Yet he was always an avid reader, consuming anything in print from newspapers to classics. He remembered in detail everything he read and could repeat a list of numbers or words after only a brief review.

When Folk gave up his wanderings and resumed his education, he chose Vanderbilt Law School in his native state. After graduation, he practiced law with his father for a while before coming to St. Louis in 1894 to work in his uncle's law firm. According to one biographer, Folk's arrival went unnoticed; he was just "another country boy to be swallowed up in the herd."

Six years later, however, St. Louis hailed the young attorney when he settled one of the worst labor disputes in the city's history. The two-month-old streetcar strike that paralyzed the city in 1900 produced not only a disruption in service but also outbreaks of violence and arson. Thirty-one-year-old Joe Folk handled the negotiations with such skill and diplomacy that he earned himself the support of organized labor when he made a bid for public office later that year.

With his election as circuit attorney, Folk found he had landed the toughest job in one of the nation's largest and most corrupt cities. St. Louis, a river town of 160,000 during the Civil War, had jumped in population to nearly 600,000 by the beginning of the twentieth century, making it the fourth largest city in the nation. But according to Lincoln Steffens, the famed political muckraker, it was also one of the worst governed in America. Bribery of city and state officials

"I believe that honesty is the best politics, as well as the best policy."

was commonplace. Those wanting a contract, state license, low assessments, or special treatment paid "boodle" to political boss Edward R. Butler. The one-time blacksmith, who became a millionaire by selling political favors, had supported Folk for circuit attorney. But once in office, Folk would not respond to Butler's demands.

Instead, Folk began an investigation of crime and corruption in St. Louis. "I am neither a Democrat nor a Republican," he announced. "As circuit attorney, I am an official and I shall do my duty, regardless of what it may cost." While such bravado endeared him to the voters, it angered members of the political machine. Threats on his life forced him to use a bodyguard and to make fewer personal appearances.

Still Folk would not relent or be bought. He successfully prosecuted "Boss" Butler and twenty-three other so-called "boodlers." But corruption ran deep, reaching even to the Missouri Supreme Court, and some of Folk's convictions were reversed. Corruption tainted the Statehouse as well and ultimately resulted in the indictment of several lawmakers and the resignation of the lieutenant governor.

Following the convictions, Folk's political stock soared. "Folk for Governor" clubs sprung up across the state, a number of newspapers lined up behind him, and his name became known nationwide. Folk's more zealous supporters wanted him to bypass the governorship and run for president.

Folk insisted that he would rather be governor than president.

St. Louis, the site for the Democratic convention in 1904, certainly would have given the popular circuit attorney a home court advantage. But cooler heads felt it was too soon; he was not yet thirty-five years old and had no legislative or executive experience. In the end, Folk squelched the short-lived movement by insisting that he would rather be governor than president.

I n the gubernatorial race that followed, Folk's calm manner belied his intensity. Lincoln Steffens described him as "a thin-lipped, firm-mouthed, dark little man who never raises his voice" yet who "goes ahead doing, with a smiling eye and set jaw, the simple thing he said he would do." Immaculately dressed and wearing a pair of pince-nez glasses, Folk was the picture of propriety. On the campaign trail, he showed a reluctance to use humor because he felt it was inappropriate. One writer even commented on Folk's handshake, calling it a "limp and flabby thing." It was the strength of his ideas, not his personality, that endeared him to audiences. Folk based his campaign on what he

Had it not been for the young fire-brand, Missouri Democrats would have been completely ravaged by the tide of Republican sentiment.

called "the Missouri idea"—a moral crusade against corrupt officials, especially the boodlers. Clean government required the leadership of honest men fighting corruption even when it meant defying party loyalty, he declared.

It was the strength of his ideas, not his personality, that endeared Joe Folk to his audiences.

THE 'MYSTERIOUS STRANGER.

"The Mysterious Stranger," a famous cartoon by John McCutcheon, was published by the *Chicago Tribune* in 1904 after election returns showed Missouri had gone Republican.

Although old-line Democrats were cautious, reformers jumped on the bandwagon saying, "Folk is not running for Governor; the people are running him." The *Washington Post, New York Times*, and *Chicago Tribune*, as well as most national magazines, followed the race closely and hailed Folk's success as evidence of democracy at work.

Had it not been for the young firebrand, Missouri Democrats would have been completely ravaged by the tide of Republican sentiment that swept the state and the nation in 1904. The watershed election put an end to the continuous Democratic control of the state and ushered in a new era of more independent voting.

In what later would be labeled a new era in Missouri politics, voters began a trend toward splitting their ballots—voting for the person rather than the political party. For the first time in thirty-six years, Missourians cast a majority of their presidential ballots for a Republican—Theodore Roosevelt. Republicans also captured the Missouri House and all the statewide offices, except governor. For Folk, the Democratic survivor, it would be a lonely four years.

A s Joe Folk and his wife arrived in Jefferson City to take up their new duties, neither realized the impact these political shifts would have on their future. They focused on getting adjusted to the personal changes that came with living in the Capital City. Having never been to the Mansion before, Mrs. Folk was eager to learn all she could from Kate Morrow who had served as hostess for the widower Governor Dockery. It had long been a custom for the outgoing family to exchange cordialities and information with the new residents. But Mrs. Morrow formalized the event with the so-called "change dinner" on the eve of the inauguration. In addition, Mrs. Morrow offered to put the Folk's personal belongings in place before they moved in, to give them "a touch of the old home."

On inaugural morning, as she watched the ceremonial events, Mrs. Folk

Inaugurations are "a trying ordeal and a tax on the hands and feet."

noted the disparity in age between her husband and the outgoing Governor. White-haired and nearing sixty, Alexander Dockery was a striking contrast to Joseph Folk who, at age thirty-five, barely fulfilled the constitutional age requirement.

Following his swearing in, the new Governor launched a litany of reforms in a speech described as more of a "sermon on public morality" than an inaugural address. It is unlikely that his guest speaker for the day, the former presidential candidate William Jennings Bryan, objected to such an approach. Bryan, a monumental figure on the political scene for over three decades, was something of a political moralist himself and probably admired the crusading spirit of Missouri's new Governor.

With the day's official events and speeches behind them, the Folks and their guests gathered to celebrate that night at the Mansion. Like first ladies before her, Gertrude Folk found the traditional reception and ball "a trying ordeal. . . and a tax on the hands and feet." Still, she called the event "great fun" and an opportunity to meet people from all over the state. As the evening grew longer and the fun gave way to fatigue, Gertrude eased her weary feet by abandoning her "new high-heeled slippers . . . in one corner of the drawing room after the last hand had been shaken!" Despite the tortuous nature of the long receiving line, the new Republican officeholders were miffed at the Governor for asking them to participate and later retracting the invitation.

The First Lady abandoned her "new high-heeled slippers in one corner of the drawing room."

Gertrude showed no resentment toward those who rebuked her husband. She moved onto the social scene of the Capital City with an open and friendly attitude, appearing unconcerned about the Governor's many political enemies. Still, the transition was hard for her. She was fond of St. Louis and her friends there. With no children to care for and no close friends in the Capital City, the thirty-two-year-old First Lady—one of the youngest in Missouri history—felt alone in her new surroundings. At first, she worried if she could perform her "grave responsibility" as the Governor's wife. But, reassurance came to her, she said, from a "little voice that speaks within . . . 'of course you can do it—just be natural.'"

As many first ladies before and since, she soon discovered the people of Jefferson City to be "charming, cordial and gracious. . . . The governor's wife is usually the guest of honor and every consideration is shown her," Mrs. Folk declared. The Capital City's warm reception gave Gertrude new confidence. She determined to make her time at the Mansion "an adventure" rather than a difficult task. "I made up my mind that I would be a part of things and share the Mansion with the people to whom it really belonged," she later wrote. In addition to her dinner parties and receptions, Mrs. Folk set aside Mondays as a time when any and all could come enjoy the Mansion and its hospitality. Even convention-goers and tourists in Jefferson City were welcomed during her "at home" hours.

The First Lady's generosity, however, did not extend to members of the press who disrupted her privacy. She found it hard "to smile and be agreeable" when reporters showed up at the Mansion as uninvited guests on the evening of a scheduled dinner party. "How they timed their arrival exactly as we started for dinner, I shall never know," Mrs. Folk fumed. She concluded that to a hostess this was a disastrous time, but "to a Governor it [was] just as good a time as any."

With no children to care for and no close friends in the city, the thirty-two-year-old First Lady, Gertrude Folk, at first felt alone in her new surroundings.

TOTING PRIVILEGES

The Southern custom of "toting" grew out of the plantation system and continued in homes where there was a kitchen staff. If the employer offered toting privileges, food and perishables left over after an event or at the end of the week could be consumed by the servants. Though toting provided a use for leftovers, it was a costly practice that encouraged the kitchen help to overprepare. For years employees at the Mansion benefited from the arrangement.

However, Mrs. Folk found, to her chagrin, that toting sometimes occurred before it was intended. Traditionally, the outgoing first family retained possession of the Mansion until noon on inauguration day. Mrs. Folk planned for breakfast on Monday to be the last meal for the family at the Mansion. In preparation, she ordered a turkey dinner on Sunday, knowing there would be leftovers the next day.

On Monday morning, awakened by the sound of hammers and saws, she knew it meant workers were preparing the house for Governor Hadley's inaugural ball that evening. Still, she looked forward to enjoying a final breakfast of turkey hash and corn cakes. But to her amazement, as the family sat down to breakfast, the butler brought out a plate of bacon and eggs.

When Mrs. Folk gasped, "'Where is the turkey hash?' His reply was, 'We thought you were going away, so we just ate the turkey up.'" Her ebbing status as the lady of the house suddenly became apparent. She later wrote, "This was the last straw! I hadn't the strength or heart to remonstrate, but I understood better why [former] Governor Dockery dreaded the day of departure."

It is unlikely that Joe Folk was at home for many social gatherings. During his first year in office, he was busy testing the waters for a future presidential race. Hoping to generate publicity through numerous personal appearances, Folk—in a flurry of activity—presented thirty major addresses around the nation. In Philadelphia he gave his reform message twice: once to the overflow crowd waiting outside the hall where he was to speak and then to those jammed inside the building. Two thousand more people gathered in front of his hotel after midnight, shouting until the Missouri Governor came outside and delivered his speech again.

When Folk attempted to implement his ideas at home, he often found the going difficult. He recommended a host of reforms to the legislature, but had to wait until Democrats regained control of the House to win approval for most of his agenda. Among the proposals adopted was a new school law that established an eight-month term and mandated the attendance of children eight to fourteen years old. Workers benefited from child labor restrictions and an eight-hour day for some businesses.

Lobbyists, too, felt the sting of more regulation. Folk ruled that they could not stay in Jefferson City over thirty hours and must report their business to him personally. His tough stance apparently had some effect. The press reported that there was less lobbying activity during the legislative session than in past years.

In addition, Folk clamped down on the railroad's practice of giving free passes to elected officials because he felt it suggested undue influence. He won approval for the direct primary, a procedure that allowed voters to nominate their candidates rather than leave the selection solely to party leaders. The initiative and referendum processes designed to give voters more direct participation in lawmaking were also adopted.

The Governor found legislative support for his proposals by giving individual attention to key lawmakers. He invited one or two members at a time for private chats in his office or for a meal at the Mansion. Those visiting the office found the Governor seated in a chair wedged between two desks arranged in a "V" formation. Even with the extra space, his work area was still a "mountain of disorder."

> Folk's work area was a "mountain of disorder."

Folk had more on his mind than the condition of his office. Besides perfecting his reform strategies, he was plotting his way to the White House. By midterm, a Folk presidential bid seemed inevitable. When a reporter asked the Governor's mother how she felt about her son being "boomed for the presidency," she replied: "Well, he was raised to be a minister, but I always said if my boys didn't care to be ministers I would let one of them be President of the United States. So, if they want Joe to be President, he has his mother's consent."

If Folk's wife—the nonpolitician—cared one way or the other about her husband's ambitions, she did not make it public. Though she was intelligent and well educated, Folk did little to keep her informed. According to the First Lady, he "almost never" spoke of political or business affairs at home. At the time, she was content with her own pursuits, although years later she expressed regret at not being more of a political partner to her husband.

> He "almost never" spoke of political or business affairs at home.

Preferring music to politics, the First Lady gathered about her women of similar taste, organized the Jefferson City Music Club, and served as its first president. She tried to interest the Governor in opera, but he resisted. He found more pleasure, he said, in hearing her perform "Lorena" or "My Old Kentucky Home" on the piano at the Mansion.

Both, however, were early enthusiasts of motion pictures. Still, his evangelical conscience would never fully surrender to amusement. After attending a show, Folk felt compelled to make up for lost time by returning home and working late into the night.

T he First Couple also shared a common concern for needy families in the community. Each Christmas, Mrs. Folk opened the Mansion to youngsters for a party. She not only invited her friends to bring their children but also encouraged those attending to bring the children of prison inmates and poor families. Parents attending were asked to donate toys—from dolls and dishes to masks, fireworks, and wooden horses. The busy Governor also joined in the merriment, donning a Santa Claus outfit to distribute the toys to his young visitors.

The Folks' interaction with inmates and their families was not confined to Christmas; both the Governor and his wife made frequent trips to the prison. "My first visit to the penitentiary," recalled Mrs. Folk, "was a great shock, and I was consumed with a pity." Her reaction is not surprising. At the beginning of the twentieth century, Missouri's overcrowded penitentiary was noted for its harsh, and often cruel, treatment. Prisoners, hoping for a pardon, tried to curry favor with the Governor's wife by addressing her as "Governess" and presenting her with handcrafted gifts.

Prisoners addressed her as "Governess."

Like previous first ladies, Gertrude was sometimes approached at the Mansion with requests for pardons. Such pleas caused her much emotional distress, since she felt it was not her place to make such decisions. One desperate mother shoved passed the butler at the Mansion door and threw herself at the First Lady's feet, begging Mrs. Folk to save her son who was scheduled to hang the next morning. Another woman threatened to kill herself on the Mansion porch unless her son received a pardon from the Governor. Such threats were probably unnecessary. Folk gave executive clemency freely; 385 convicts were released during his term.

Gertrude Folk's most memorable episode occurred during her first year at the Mansion. She had spent much of that time redecorating and was eager to show off the home to friends. Gertrude invited seventy-five members of her St. Louis choral group to come for lunch and spend the day. She thought how cozy and welcome it would be to have a fire burning in the massive hall fireplace as her guests arrived. Feeling some concern because it had not been used for some time, she took the precaution of having the chimney inspected in advance.

On the day before her scheduled event, smoke was detected in the house, but no one could locate the source. Seeing no reason to distrust the recently approved fireplace, Mrs. Folk had a fire laid that she described as "fit for a king." Satisfied that the brightly burning logs would keep the

The Governor ran down the stairs in his nightshirt to fight the blaze.

chill from the house, she retired for the evening, as did seven overnight guests. But by three o'clock in the morning, all were awakened by smoke and flames that had spread to the first-floor ceiling. The Governor, still wearing his nightshirt, ran down the stairs to throw "one hundred tubes of fire dust" on the blaze.

Before the volunteer fire department could bring the flames under control, the interior walls were badly damaged. The oldest piece of furniture in the house, a rosewood secretary that once belonged to former Governor Austin King (1848-1853) was destroyed in addition to the marble fireplace and its overmantel mirror. Total damages—most of which were water inflicted—came to $15,000. The fire was thought to have started behind the marble mantel where the wooden facing apparently was smoldering a day earlier.

For the next several weeks, the Folks stayed at the Madison House, the hotel across the street from the Mansion. Using insurance money and funds appropriated

Mrs. Folk considered these tapestry-hung walls in the dining room "the best piece of work in the house." The next governor, Herbert Hadley, is seen enjoying the room at a formal dinner party. Below is an enlargement of the forestry scene on the tapestry.

by the legislature, the First Lady again took on the task of restoring the home. She replaced the white marble mantel with one carved from walnut featuring the state seal and green mosaic tiles. The Louis XIV-style furniture, salvaged from the fire at the Missouri Building during the St. Louis World's Fair, was reupholstered and added to the parlor.

Mrs. Folk's greatest satisfaction came from refashioning the dining room. She tore out the walnut arch that was left behind when the original dividing doors were removed. Above the ivory-colored wainscoting, she installed a tapestry of forest scenes. "I felt that nothing but tapestry on the walls was suitable for so handsome a room and it would never have to be replaced. I considered that the best piece of work in the house," she announced proudly. Having completed the renovation with money to spare, Mrs. Folk embellished the decor with the purchase of new china and a Steinway baby grand piano.

Just as the First Lady was winding down her work at the Mansion, her politically ambitious husband was gearing up for another campaign. His earlier desire to run for president was thwarted, however, by his friend, William Jennings Bryan. In a move that stymied Folk at the high point in his political career, Bryan chose—unwisely as it proved later—to make a third try for the White House.

This parlor in the Missouri Building at the World's Fair first displayed the Louis XIV-style furniture that was later moved to the Mansion after the fair building burned.

Folk turned instead to a race for the U.S. Senate in 1908. Flaunting his crusader image, he delivered three hundred speeches in an attempt to unseat incumbent Senator William Stone, a former governor. Folk reminded his audiences that he was the candidate who had brought reform and one of the few Democrats who could be trusted. While his political oratory had temporary appeal, Folk lacked the personal warmth needed to maintain the loyalty of his followers. As a result, he failed to build the organization needed to beat a well-entrenched officeholder.

Even so, the historic campaign had some unique sidelights. Missourians witnessed two new developments that greatly influenced future political activity in the state. With the adoption of the direct primary, the selection of nominees for the U.S. Senate was no longer in the hands of the legislature. Missourians, for the first time in history, made the choice themselves.

Another first—and more exciting for some—was the sight of senatorial hopeful Joseph Folk gallivanting around the state in a motorcade that occasionally included as many as twenty cars. It was the first time the automobile played an active role in a Missouri political campaign. Folk's forays through the countryside, where cars rarely traveled, attracted a lot of attention. Farm families would gather in their yards, waving flags, and cheering as his caravan passed. Rural Missourians hailed him as their "Folk" hero, "the man who cleaned up Missouri politics." Tales of his exploits, it was said, "displaced Jesse James in popular reading."

Urban voters, however, found Folk less appealing, identifying him with "repression rather than progress." As a hard-line reformer, he had stepped on too many toes, especially in St. Louis. He had closed the race tracks and insisted that the police in St. Louis and Kansas City get out of politics. Raids were made on the St. Louis beer gardens—the places where respectable German families traditionally gathered—and dance halls were closed in keeping with the "blue laws" prohibiting Sunday liquor sales. Nor did his support for closing livery stables and candy stores on Sunday—and even banning family picnics—endear him to city dwellers.

Folk closed the St. Louis beer gardens, the place where the city's respectable German families traditionally gathered to visit, dance, and drink.

While most people did not mind Folk going after the real crooks, they opposed his "fanatic zeal to moralize people by invading their personal liberty." As one writer concluded, "Pleasure must not be treated as a crime." The *St. Louis Post-Dispatch* concurred, calling Folk a "master busybody." Evangelicals and temperance groups, however,

Tales of Folk's exploits "displaced Jesse James in popular reading."

cheered him on in what the Governor labeled a struggle between "the Sunday saloon and the Sunday home."

In the end, "Holy Joe" Folk—or "Saint Joe"— antagonized enough of his party members to ruin his chance of unseating Senator Stone, a more traditional Democrat. Though Folk carried the rural areas, it was not enough to offset his loss of votes in St. Louis and Kansas City.

A few months after his senatorial defeat, Joe Folk's tenure as governor ended with him turning over the reins of office to the first Republican governor since Reconstruction. Distressed with Folk's heavy-handed administration, Republicans, aided by disgruntled Democrats, elected Missouri's trust-busting attorney general, Herbert Hadley, to lead the state.

As the Folks prepared to leave the Mansion, the First Lady thought of the lovely preinaugural hospitality extended by former Governor Dockery and Mrs. Morrow. She decided to show the same courtesy to Governor-elect Hadley—a man who, despite party differences, agreed with many of Governor Folk's reforms. As Mrs. Folk prepared to entertain her guests, she recalled how unhappy Governor Dockery had been at leaving office. At the time, she had been amazed at his attitude, thinking he would be pleased to part with his responsibilities after four years. "I found out how the place attached itself to one," the First Lady reflected.

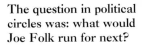

The question in political circles was: what would Joe Folk run for next?

Leaving the Mansion "is an indescribable feeling, as if one's home is being taken away."

According to Mrs. Folk, she and the Governor departed the Mansion "peacefully, but not joyfully. . . . It is an indescribable feeling, as if one's home is being taken away," she wrote years later. "I must confess I shed tears over this separation."

It is unlikely that Joe Folk's departure engendered any sadness among his many critics. Although the *St. Louis Post-Dispatch*—well known for its opposition to Folk's moralizing—editorialized favorably on his accomplishments, "Not even the Governor's enemies can deny that his administration has been marked by excellent work for the people and has raised the standard of government in this and other states."

T hose who thought the Governor would step quietly back into private life soon found out otherwise. Folk had no intention of getting out of politics; he was not yet forty years old and still quite ambitious. The question in political circles was: what would he run for next? Would he try again for the U.S. Senate or revive his campaign for the presidency? In a move designed to keep him from making another Senate race, old-line Democrats endorsed him in 1910 for the presidential race two years off.

At the urging of William Jennings Bryan, Folk toured the United States for the next few years on the Chautauqua lecture circuit and made more than $35,000 delivering speeches on "civic righteousness," the basis for his Missouri idea. Folk claimed to have visited the hometown of every congressman and to have spoken in every city in the United States with a population of 2,500 or more. Despite his marathon efforts, he ran no better than fourth in the *Chicago Tribune*'s poll of likely Democratic candidates for president.

With little hope of getting the nomination, Folk withdrew in favor of the more popular Missouri congressman and Speaker of the House, Champ Clark. At the 1912 Democratic National Convention, Clark held on to the lead until the thirtieth ballot before he was beaten by the dark horse candidate, Woodrow Wilson. Folk jumped on the Wilson bandwagon and campaigned all across the country for his party's nominee. When Wilson won the presidency, he called on Folk to help in his administration. The former Governor went to Washington and worked as solicitor general for the State Department and later as chief counsel for the Interstate Commerce Commission.

While Folk refused to consider a second-term bid for governor four years later, he made a last, but futile, try for the U.S. Senate after Stone's death in 1918. Though he gained the nomination by a substantial vote, he lost in the landslide Republican victory that repudiated President Wilson and his policies nationwide.

Mrs. Folk became one of Washington's most popular hostesses.

According to Mrs. Folk, her husband "reluctantly" put aside public life, finding it hard to accept his loss in popular appeal. He opened an office in the nation's capital and soon developed a highly successful law practice. His clients included the Hearst newspapers and some Hollywood movie companies, as well as the Peruvian government and Egyptian nationalists.

The Folks purchased a luxurious mansion in Washington where Gertrude, who had never lost her love of entertaining, became one of the city's most popular hostesses. The stately residence, previously the home of the Russian ambassador, was purchased by the couple for $140,000.

Folk's aggressive, hard-working style eventually caught up with him. In 1922, after only a few years of practicing law, he suffered a nervous breakdown, developed Bright's disease, and eventually lost his speech. He died the following year from a heart attack at the age of fifty-three and was buried in his native state of Tennessee.

According to historian Louis Geiger, Folk "made more history in the years 1900 to 1909 than most men make in a lifetime." Still, no Missourian of prominence attended his funeral. Long overdue honor was accorded him with the commissioning of the liberty ship *Joseph W. Folk* launched at the onset of World War II.

After her husband's death, Mrs. Folk revisited the Mansion in the thirties as the guest of Governor and Mrs. Park. While the former First Lady saw many changes, she found the house radiated the same friendly spirit. "Even the fireplace that had played such a trick on me seemed to bid me welcome," she said.

It had been twenty-five years since she served as First Lady of the Mansion. Then, as a young politician's wife, she avoided being photographed and shied away from public affairs. Years later, however, when President Franklin Roosevelt called on her to work in one of the recovery programs following the Great Depression, she gladly accepted. Catching the spirit of the time, she apparently wished to do something even more significant. She wrote to a friend, "Isn't this an era of rapid changes . . . I wish I were a real part of it."

Mrs. Folk outlived her husband by twenty-nine years. Shortly before her death in 1952, she saw another political reformer and crime fighter rise to prominence, U.S. Senator Estes Kefauver. The Tennessee Democrat was a second cousin of Joe Folk and shared similar aspirations for the presidency. Kefauver, who later became a vice presidential nominee, considered his crusading relative a "sort of hero" and copied his investigative style. After watching Kefauver's televised inquiries into crime and corruption, a tearful Mrs. Folk noted the Senator's many similarities to her husband.

During Joe and Gertrude's years on the political stage, both showed a talent for making the best of a bad situation. Her historic fire at the Mansion had seemed destructive, but in the end it transformed the old house for the better. The fires of reform ignited by the aggressive Joe Folk did much the same for Missouri politics.

HADLEY
FOR
PRESIDENT

A BREATH OF FRESH AIR

GOVERNOR HERBERT SPENCER HADLEY
AGNES LEE HADLEY
1909-1913

Hadley's moment of glory came in 1912 when the Republican delegates to the national convention erupted in a twenty-five-minute ovation, waving banners and shouting, "We want Hadley!"

A blizzard blanketed the Capital City. Still, ten thousand people flocked to Jefferson City for the inauguration of Missouri's first Republican governor in nearly forty years. Mrs. Hadley, the new First Lady, described it as "one of the coldest days I ever remember." Even so, Herbert Hadley joined the outgoing Governor for the traditional inaugural ride to the Capitol in an open victoria— a low carriage for two with an elevated driver's seat.

"I remember how I shuddered for possible consequences to my Governor's health," Mrs. Hadley later recalled. There was good reason for concern. The thirty-six-year-old former attorney general of the state suffered from pleurisy and lung problems, although the extent of his condition was never acknowledged.

What Hadley lacked in physical stamina, he made up for in mental fortitude. Growing up in Kansas of Quaker heritage, he had all the advantages of a well-to-do family; he kept a riding horse, played golf, and went fishing and hunting at his leisure. A severe speech impediment prevented him from starting school until he was eight years old, but he quickly caught up, overcame his handicap, and developed a flair for public speaking. He graduated from high school at age fifteen and further sharpened his speaking skills as an undergraduate at the University of Kansas and at Northwestern University Law School.

Bypassing his home state, Hadley hung out his shingle in nearby Kansas City, Missouri, where he soon gained the attention of GOP politicians long bereft of winning candidates. In 1900 he astounded party leaders when he scooped up the office of prosecuting attorney, making him the first Republican to hold the Jackson County position in thirty years. In his new role, Hadley put his early training to good use; he tried 225 felony cases and lost only 6. Despite his success, he was defeated for reelection two years later during a Democratic sweep in Missouri.

(Facing page)
Top: The 1912 Republican Convention. Bottom right: Hadley speaking in O'Fallon Park, St Louis.

145

His next political venture came quite by accident. During a meeting of the 1904 Republican State Convention, a delegate spotted Hadley entering the hall and was inspired to place the young man's name in nomination for attorney general. Hadley at first declined the unexpected recognition. In a state long accustomed to electing Democrats to high office, Hadley and the GOP delegates undoubtedly felt the nomination was of dubious value.

Nonetheless, he dutifully accepted the honor and, in a display of party loyalty, conducted an intense campaign that took him to every part of the state. Still, most people felt the likely winner would be Democrat Elliott Major—and Hadley probably did, too.

On election day, Hadley voted, but then left town to go quail hunting. Later he received a strange telegram from his wife in Kansas City, "Come home at once." Fearing one of the children was ill, Hadley jumped on his horse and rode into town to find a pay phone. While waiting for his connection, he overheard two men—apparently Democrats—discussing the election outcome.

"I never believed the Republicans would carry Missouri," one said.

Shocked by what he heard, Hadley left the phone and anxiously questioned the two men, "What's that about the Republicans carrying Missouri?"

"Joe Folk slipped in for Governor, but he was the only Democrat," the man answered, not knowing he was talking to one of the participants in the election.

"Look here, friend," Hadley responded sharply, "that's pretty serious for me."

"It's serious for the whole damned state," the man replied woefully.

Hadley immediately left for Kansas City where his wife was waiting to tell him the news: he had won the office of attorney general by 13,000 votes. In the landslide victory that put Republican Theodore Roosevelt in the White House, Hadley and the other GOP candidates picked off all the statewide offices except governor.

Hadley's antitrust lawsuits against the oil barons attracted national attention.

In his new position, Hadley immediately took on some tough adversaries. As the state's legal advocate, he began an attack on the corporate giants who were engaged in corrupt business practices. His antitrust suits against the oil barons attracted national attention and ultimately brought lower prices for consumers. According to historian Ralph E. Morrow, Hadley was "most famed for his prosecution of the Standard Oil Company, [but] he also sued farm implement, railroad, lumber, and insurance companies for illegal trade practices, indicted state legislators for misuse of their offices, and warred against organized gambling in St. Louis, a rich source of municipal

"LET THE CHILDREN PLAY ON THE GRASS."

One campaign leaflet circulated during Hadley's campaign for governor drew a lot of attention and greatly added to the appeal of the young politician. During the previous twelve years, there had been no youngsters playing about the Mansion grounds and Hadley's Democratic opponent had no children. "Let the children play on the grass" became a rallying cry of those advocating a family man in the Mansion.

When Hadley was elected, the children did, in fact, play on the lawn where they were frequently seen atop the old fountain or romping about the summerhouse.

Campaign leaflet,
front and back.

Wants Hadley's Children to Romp on Lawn at the Executive Mansion.

St. Louis Times, October 5, 1908.

4 REASONS WHY—

MRS. H. S. HADLEY AND CHILDREN.
The Children Are: John Lee Hadley, 6; Henrietta, 4;
and Herbert 2 Years Old.

Hadley children playing on the old fountain.

"Let the Children Play on the Grass."

Fond mothers and admirers of beautiful children—and who doesn't love them—will not object to the advice of David W. Hill, who urged voters in Southern Missouri to let the three Hadley children play on the grass surrounding the Executive Mansion at Jefferson City for the next four years.

It has been many years since the children of a Governor of Missouri have played on the green sward in the center of Jefferson City. It can be made possible, Hill points out, only through the election of Attorney General Hadley, the pride of whose life is a group of three little children.

"It would be a place where the children can romp to their hearts' content," Hill told the voters, to the cheers of the fathers and mothers.

As Cowherd has no children, Hill thinks it will be a shame to have the beautiful lawn go to waste without the shouts and hilarity of childish voices.

"Let the children play on the grass," urged the candidate for the United States Senate, in boosting the father of the children for the governorship.

The Executive Mansion is located near the center of one of the largest squares in Jefferson City, and during the summer there is no place in Missouri that affords a better spot for children's parties and other entertainments that are the joys of a child's heart.

Naturally, the children are the pride of the father and mother. Whenever the father can arrange his schedules during his stumping of Missouri he heads for his home at Jefferson City Saturday evening to spend Sunday with them. There are two boys and a girl, ranging in ages from 2 to 6 years.

Going backward through the administrations of Governors Folk, Dockery and Stephens, to the administration of Governor Stone, there have been no smiles of children to enliven the home of Missouri's governor. Even the daughters of Senator Stone, at the time of his administration, were almost grown. Before the Stone administration the sons of Gov. Francis made the welkin ring in the mansion yards. But since Stone was Governor there have been no children's parties gotten up and arranged for the little hostesses of the mansion.

"It's up to the Missouri voters," says Hill, "and the reasons are three good ones why Hadley should be elected."

corruption." But unlike Governor Folk, whose moralizing aggravated party leaders, Hadley was hailed for his assault on greed and corruption.

Although Hadley's political prospects looked bright, his health outlook did not. Intending to move to a better climate after completing his term, he had purchased a ranch in New Mexico. But Republicans, knowing they had a potential winner for the first time in years, pressured the popular attorney general to run for governor.

The call to carry his party's banner in 1908 posed a difficult decision for the popular politician. Five doctors told him that a campaign for the office would be fatal. But Hadley's family physician urged him to take the risk, saying he would be better off pursuing his dreams than sitting around waiting to die. Furthermore, presidential hopeful William Howard Taft needed Hadley's political coattails in Missouri and pressured him to enter the race. "You are the only man who can win and unless you run, I shall lose Missouri," Taft told Hadley.

Missouri Republicans lined up solidly behind Hadley, placing him unopposed on the state's first direct primary ballot for governor. The general campaign that followed was a dual success. The 1908 race catapulted Taft into the White House and made Herbert Hadley the first Republican to live in the Governor's Mansion since B. Gratz Brown's victory in 1870.

By inauguration day, Republicans were in high spirits. Flags and banners festooned the streets and stores of Jefferson City as a military regiment marched to Hadley's home to escort the Governor's carriage to the Capitol. Those lucky enough to have inaugural tickets jammed into the House chamber for the swearing-in ceremony and the raucous celebration that accompanied it. Members of a sixteen-piece military band from St. Joseph, eager to get on the program and advance the new Governor for the presidency, pushed their way into the chamber playing the national anthem. As everyone stood, Hadley supporters began to chant:

"Nineteen twelve, Oh, oh, oh,
Hadley to the White House, he will go,
Hadley, Hadley, watch him grow,
We are Republicans from old St. Joe."

For a full five minutes, the audience lavished its applause on the man who, at the time, had received more votes than any candidate in Missouri history. When Hadley stepped to the podium, smiled, and bowed in acknowledgment, the crowd went wild once again. More sound erupted from the Capitol grounds as cannons boomed a seventeen-gun salute announcing Missouri's new Governor.

As it turned out, Hadley proved more robust than anticipated simply by surviving the

Presidential hopeful William Howard Taft (right) needed Hadley's coattails in Missouri and pressured him to run for governor.

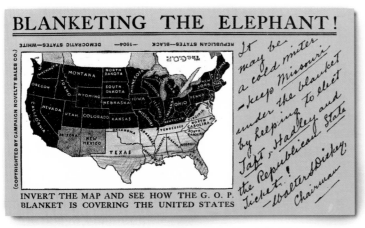

BLANKETING THE ELEPHANT!

INVERT THE MAP AND SEE HOW THE G. O. P.
BLANKET IS COVERING THE UNITED STATES

A campaign card touting the candidacy of Taft and Hadley.

rigors of his inauguration. During the reception at the Mansion, snow blew into the hall each time the doors opened. Men stood by with shovels to prevent it from piling up on the floor. One newsman who managed to edge his way into the Mansion declared that everyone in Jefferson City was there, "from the highest in station to the humblest citizen." The tongue-in-cheek report concluded that the press was so great that had the walls given way at the Mansion people "would have rushed pell-mell into the Missouri River."

Years later, Mrs. Hadley recalled her personal experiences of that evening: "My dress was white satin trimmed with pearls and Irish pointlace and I wore long sleeves and gloves. When my gloves got torn in the hand-shaking, I took them off, and after a while my hand bled and blood dripped down the front panel of my dress. I learned afterward that there is a trick in shaking hands: grip quickly, and first, the hand offered you. If you learn how, you can shake hands with any number of people."

President Taft's inauguration two months later again tested Hadley's vigor. The Hadleys made the trip to Washington along with the Governor's honorary colonels and their wives. According to Missouri's First Lady, it was "a grand affair that took place in another historic blizzard, second only to Governor Hadley's inauguration blizzard."

Agnes Hadley in her inaugural gown. The ordeal of shaking hands caused her hands to bleed and blood dripped down the front of her dress.

Returning from Washington, the First Family settled into the spacious Mansion along with their three children: ages two, four, and six. Mrs. Hadley chose the north bedroom with the bay windows overlooking the river—the Governor took the southeast room with the fire escape landing. Because of his lung condition, Mrs.

Get ready for "pink teas, card parties, and such frivolities," Hadley told his wife.

Hadley felt, "It was essential for him to have all the fresh air possible, [so] we arranged the platform of the fire

149

For the fresh air benefits, Hadley slept the first winter on a platform of the fire escape.

escape outside the south window and he slept there the first winter."

To Mrs. Hadley the Mansion looked "very handsome and comfortable, with red draperies and carpet, and much red in the wallpaper." The previous first lady, Mrs. Folk, had redecorated the dining room with tapestry and ivory-painted woodwork. The library, for some time, had been lined with maroon satin tapestry and bookcases. Pictures of former governors hung on the walls and up the staircase.

"Many a time those portraits helped me with shy visitors," Mrs. Hadley recalled. "After we had told each other about our towns, our husbands, and our babies with their diseases and ages, I would tell about the old governors: this one was the first governor of the territory of Missouri; that one, a Southern sympathizer who went away taking the state seal; this one, a one-legged shoemaker from Columbia . . . two governors took their own lives, one in the old first Mansion. . . . And so on. My little stories filled awkward pauses and never failed to interest my guests."

Mrs. Hadley took her role as Mansion hostess as seriously as the Governor did his new duties. The thirty-two-year-old First Lady, a former student at Vassar College and newspaper reporter for the *Kansas City Star*, would now be overseeing a household staff and the social requirements of the Governor's Mansion. Hadley warned his wife to get prepared for an array of "pink teas, card parties, and such frivolities" as would be expected of her as First Lady. Mrs. Hadley showed no reluctance in taking on her new duties. She illustrated her

The stairway lined with portraits of the governors. "Many a time those portraits helped me with shy visitors," Mrs. Hadley recalled.

hospitality with a newspaper announcement that she would be "at home" each Monday afternoon to receive any who wished to visit. Those who responded had the opportunity to talk with the First Lady and to enjoy the dainty sandwiches, wafers, and tea that she offered her guests.

According to Mrs. Hadley, her first open house was a "terrible affair." The event got off to a poor start even before guests arrived. Again, the culprit was the hall fireplace, the same one that had damaged the home four years earlier just before one of Mrs. Folk's parties. This time, there was no harm done, but smoke filled the first floor and the smoldering logs had to be quickly carried outdoors.

Mrs. Hadley literally "saw red" when she moved into the Mansion—former First Lady Gertrude Folk had redecorated the Mansion with vibrant red drapes, carpet, and wallpaper.

Though temporarily distraught by the incident, Mrs. Hadley composed herself before guests arrived. As it turned out, even more surprises were in store. The First Lady had prepared for a small gathering, but over three hundred people showed up, forcing the kitchen help to scramble to provide for them. (Today a Mansion hostess is unlikely to be surprised by large numbers of unexpected guests since security officers require the names beforehand of all those planning to attend a social event.)

As time went on, Mrs. Hadley became more comfortable as hostess of the Mansion. She invited members of the Order of the Eastern Star, Daughters of the American Revolution, and the local music club to meet at the Mansion. She also entertained the women's guild from the Episcopal Church and once held an antique exhibit where her guests could display their heirlooms.

Throughout the legislative session, the Hadleys hosted receptions, square dances, and small dinner parties of eight to twenty people at a time. On hand to help in the kitchen was "Aunt Hattie [Tolbert] . . . who couldn't either read or write, but who *could* cook," Mrs. Hadley recalled. "We always had the same menu, and I helped in the pantry. We had soup, a big chicken pie at each end of the table, vegetables, beaten biscuits, a salad, ice cream, cake, and small coffees."

The Governor looked forward to having friends or legislators join him for dinner. According to Mrs. Hadley, "he ate slowly and talked a great deal" in order to lengthen the pleasure of the evening. After dinner, the Governor would further extend the evening by inviting his guests to climb the stairs to the third floor where they could enjoy a game of billiards.

During one of the two occasions when William Jennings Bryan visited during Hadley's term, a rivalry broke out between the Republican governor and the

Democratic officeholders. Both wanted the honor of entertaining the Democratic orator and presidential contender. Hadley sent a delegation from his office to the train depot with orders to find Bryan and bring him to the Mansion before the Democrats got hold of him. While the Democrats searched the first-class Pullman cars for Bryan, Hadley's men correctly concluded that the "Great Commoner" would be traveling in the less pricey day coach. Before the Democrats knew it, the

"There was a constant flow of unexpected guests."

Republicans whisked Bryan from the train and headed him to the Mansion for an evening with the Governor.

On Bryan's next visit to the Mansion, he arrived late, missing the fried chicken dinner and the beaten biscuits prepared in his honor. Mrs. Hadley called for the meal to be set out again, but when Bryan sat down to eat, he turned to her and said, "May I ask you for what I would really like? A big bowl of bread and milk."

The Hadleys also welcomed other notables of the day, among them Mrs. George Pickett. The wife of the Confederate general enthralled Mansion guests by telling Civil War stories, including an account of Pickett's charge at the Battle of Gettysburg."

William Jennings Bryan, the famous orator and three-time presidential contender, was a frequent visitor to the Mansion.

In addition to Mrs. Hadley's scheduled events, "there was a constant flow of unexpected guests." Former Governor Francis once dropped by "to see if the Mansion still looked as big as it used to." Without warning, Hadley once brought fifteen men to lunch after they missed their train to Kansas City. The kitchen help was about to sit down to a lunch of bacon and greens when the First Lady commandeered the meal for the new arrivals. With the addition of ham and eggs to the menu, she was able to extend the traditional Mansion hospitality to the stranded travelers. Wanting to be prepared for such emergencies in the future, Mrs. Hadley set aside a storeroom, which she described as a "small grocery."

During the Christmas season, Mrs. Hadley and the ladies of Jefferson City kept busy baking traditional cookies and breads. Never was the German heritage of the city more obvious. "All the mothers were busy weeks before getting ready the *pfeffer kuchen*, the *nuss kuchen*, the *lebkuchen* and the *springerle*," she recalled. The First Lady got into the spirit of the season by delivering decorated Christmas trees to the needy. The Hadley children prepared for Santa by placing grains of corn on the bedroom windowsills for his reindeer. The children looked forward to a Christmas party during their second year at the Mansion, but an outbreak of contagious diseases caused local doctors to discourage public gatherings.

Having children live in the Mansion for the first time in twelve years brought a new energy to the staid, old Victorian home. The youngsters and their playmates not only romped about the grounds, they enjoyed playing in the cast-iron fountain and in the old pagoda-shaped summer-house.

The large open spaces inside the Mansion were also ideal for rowdy games. Once when the First Lady came downstairs to greet the Episcopal bishop, she found—much to her surprise—the churchman and the children kicking a football in the Great Hall. The spacious third floor also came in handy for

Hadley and friends enjoy the fresh air benefits of an open car decorated for a trip to a football game.

classes in dancing and party manners. During one cold winter, the area became a school room where the children were tutored at home for a while. Of all the benefits of Mansion living, the youngsters most enjoyed the many gifts they received. Visitors kept them provided with a variety of pets, including dogs, rabbits, a wolf, and two baby pigs.

Mrs. Hadley's duties were not confined to caring for her active family, the household, and social requirements of the Mansion. Like first ladies before her, she was also burdened by requests for executive clemency. Although she had promised herself not to meddle in the pardon of prisoners, she did so on several occasions.

"One morning I was called down to the library, where I found a woman with four little children clinging to her skirts and anybody could see that her fifth was

imminent. Her husband was in the penitentiary for repeated bootlegging. Some judge in a southern county had got tired of his promises and had sentenced him. She said her husband was good and kind to her, and I thought society would be better served if he was on hand to help her with number five. So I telephoned and asked Mr. Hadley if he would see my woman at once. He did, and she came away from his office with her husband's pardon. I never heard of her again."

In her memoirs, Mrs. Hadley mentioned two youngsters who came to the Mansion seeking her help. One was a little boy who continued to haunt the Mansion each week until "he got what he was

(Left)
The bronze figure on the fountain today portrays the African-American child who once lived in the Mansion barn.

153

GOVERNOR VS. ARTIST

While the Governor enjoyed his official duties and the time he spent on his farm, he begrudged the ten weeks he spent sitting for his official portrait and was not pleased with the results. He especially disliked the "gubernatorial lips" on his portrait and refused to pay the woman who painted him. According to the artist, the Governor's lower lip protruded more than he thought it should and he told her to fix it. Next, he complained that the expression was not "good-natured enough." He constantly argued about the eyes and forehead, she said, and once grabbed a brush himself to show how to bring out a certain feature in his face. Painting Hadley was "a nerve-racking job," the artist said, and one that caused her to need treatment by a physician.

The special committee, which had solicited the funds from five hundred Republicans, was not pleased either. Although the artist had improved the lips, now "the chin was too long" and the "collar too high." She obligingly agreed to put the collar wherever they wanted it, but took a ruler to the face to show the proportions were correct.

The widely acclaimed artist declared she had painted hundreds of other statesmen, but Hadley was "the toughest subject she ever handled." The general displeasure of all the parties involved made it necessary to commission another portrait. A year later, the new painter produced a more favorable likeness, one which a news writer described as "excellent."

Hadley's prison reforms included abolishing the requirement for prisoners to wear stripes.

after—a pardon for his father in the penitentiary." The other unidentified child seemed even more pathetic and was described by Mrs. Hadley only as "a little colored boy whom we found from time to time sleeping in the barn."

Governor Hadley's generosity toward the unfortunate was particularly evident in his prison reforms. He was appalled by conditions at the state penitentiary—the world's largest prison and one desperately in need of reform. When he discovered that a number of youth were imprisoned for nothing more serious than stealing a watermelon, chickens, or even candy, he initiated the idea of parole for first-time offenders. He encouraged the young men to find employment on farms in the belief that work, rather than prison, would turn them into productive citizens.

Inmates got a new wardrobe, too, when the Governor abolished the requirement for prisoners to wear stripes. On an even more humane level, he did away with flogging and marching in lockstep as punishment. He also ordered showers, better food, and job training at the prison. Hadley saw the results of his changes when disciplinary action dropped by one-half.

But his liberal use of the pardon drew harsh criticism. He averaged 161 pardons a year, while previous Governors averaged far fewer: Folk, 68; Dockery, 49; Stephens, 21; and, Stone, 14. Critics of his reforms pointed to an incident that happened right under the Governor's nose. One of the prisoners assigned to the Mansion—a forger with a prominent scar from ear to ear—escaped by climbing down the fire escape from the third floor. The only sign of him at the end of the day was the clothes he left behind. Later there were reports of a "suspicious looking woman" at the railroad yard, causing authorities to believe the inmate had escaped wearing women's clothing. In spite of the incident, Hadley maintained confidence in his prison reforms; only 10 of 175 violated the conditions of parole during a three-year period.

The Governor continued to urge his progressive agenda, but faced with a Democratic legislature, he had only partial success. He obtained new labor laws regulating working hours and conditions for women. However, his plans for reassessment, a public service commission, a simplified criminal procedure, and a bevy of new taxes, all failed. The frustrated Governor told lawmakers, "While economy in government is important, the issue shouldn't be how little might be spent, but what expenditures are needed." Though Hadley received only minimal acceptance of his programs, he succeeded in passing a $3.5 million bond issue to rebuild the Capitol after it was destroyed by fire in 1911.

The Governor felt that the state should face up to its growing responsibility in the areas of health, transportation, environment, education, and corrections. He even made an automobile tour across the state to highlight the need for more and better roads. But the Democratic Senate and Republican House refused to meet the costs of his proposals, making it difficult for him to complete much of his agenda. One writer called the session "the longest and one of the least productive of the progressive era."

While lawmakers rejected Hadley's major

Lawmakers rejected Hadley's reforms, but allowed him a new surrey and team of horses.

reforms, they provided $872 for a new surrey and team of horses, causing some Democrats to complain about the unprecedented allotment. They claimed that every other chief executive supplied his own transportation, but the "first Republican governor in forty years must have [his] furnished out of the pockets of the people."

The idea of the state providing more services for the Governor continued to irritate Democrats. Hadley charged the state sixty dollars a month for boarding five servants, one critic declared. Furthermore, when he traveled to a conference in another state, he asked to be reimbursed for expenses. One irate official said he would not be surprised to learn that the Governor purchased an automobile at state expense.

Others joined in heaping abuse on the Republican Governor. U.S. Senator William Stone, a Democrat and onetime governor of the state, called Hadley's expenses "wanton extravagance." The Democratic state auditor meticulously compared Hadley's spending to other administrations. He noted that over a twenty-month period Governor Folk had spent $746.25 on the Mansion grounds, while Hadley had spent $1,671.10. Even the Hadleys' selection of table linen came under attack. The First Couple obviously thought American-made goods were inferior, critics reasoned, because they imported linen for the Mansion table from Scotland.

"A Sudden Stroke of Lightning!"

Sunday evening, February 5, 1911. The Governor was dining with newsmen in the Mansion dining room. Mrs. Hadley had gone to her bedroom to catch up on some correspondence. "Shortly after sunset, flashes of lightning played across the sky," she recalled. "One of them reached down and touched the Capitol dome." At first, Mrs. Hadley thought the Mansion had been hit. Later when she looked from the bedroom window, she saw flames darting from the Capitol dome.

the three Hadley youngsters in blankets. Together they huddled in the northwest windowsills watching the red glare in the sky as the Capitol burned throughout the night.

"There was no sleep for anyone that night," Mrs. Hadley recalled. The evening repeated a scene in 1837 in the earlier Governor's Mansion when First Lady Panthea Boggs and her children watched the previous Capitol burn. That time, firefighters fearful of flames spreading to the nearby executive home had placed wet blankets over the Mansion roof for protection.

Soon, hundreds of people gathered to fight the blaze, including officials, the National Guard, inmates from the prison, residents of the city, and the Governor himself. As flames leaped a hundred feet into the air, people in small towns miles down river watched the glow from the Capital City. By 8:30 p.m. the dome toppled onto the north side of the building, setting fire to the roof over the House of Representatives.

When the lights went out at the Mansion, the First Lady and the family nursemaid swaddled

During the weeks following the 1911 fire, the work of government continued, but at new locations. The Missouri House first convened in the old Jefferson Theater and the Senate met in the county courthouse. Later the Senate met in the new Supreme Court building and the House convened in St. Peter's Catholic School until a temporary building was erected.

Although the fire was a hardship on the Capital City, it brought a happy outcome for some: Hadley gave pardons to several of the prisoners who fought the blaze.

Besides the tribulations of public office, the Governor had to contend with his persistent health problems. After doctors told him to spend more time outdoors, he took up farming for the fresh air benefit. When office-seekers and Democratic legislators became too annoying, he sought relief by heading for his 125-acre spread on the outskirts of town. "Weekends, vacations, holidays—whenever the Governor could get away—we spent at the farm," Mrs. Hadley recalled.

The Governor "knows almost as much about poultry as he does about politics."

In the process, Hadley became a big advocate of farming and a friend of the University of Missouri College of Agriculture, frequently testing their discoveries on his own land. One newsman wrote approvingly that the Governor "knows almost as much about poultry as he does about politics." Hadley took great pride in his newly acquired skills as a farmer. His land produced fruit, vegetables, and flowers in abundance and the Holstein cow kept fresh milk on the Mansion table. One year the Hadleys served over six hundred chickens brought in from the family farm.

In addition to the produce, the acreage provided a hunting grounds for the Governor and his friends. One of Mrs. Hadley's wild game dinners included roast quail, possum, 'coon, wild turkey, squirrel stew, fried rabbit, venison, and wild duck—all shot on the outskirts of town. When Hadley decided to build a woodland getaway, sixty men—many of them judges and elective officials—worked along with him in a one-day cabin raising.

The finished building had a bath and running water pumped from a well by a windmill. The only heat came from a large fireplace in the eighteen-by-twenty-foot living room and candles took the place of electric lights. The family spent all of one summer living at their primitive retreat. Getting up at five o'clock each morning, the Hadleys did the farm chores, drove back to the Capital City to see to their official duties, and returned to the farm in time for dinner.

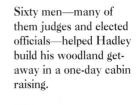

Sixty men—many of them judges and elected officials—helped Hadley build his woodland getaway in a one-day cabin raising.

Once when entertaining at the cabin, a heavy downpour washed out the roadways. With no way to get back to town, the First Family set out cots for their guests and all bedded down for the night. As time went on, the camaraderie of the sportsmen led to the formation of the Jefferson City Country Club on land south of Hadley's acreage.

But, his friendship with two presidential aspirants—William Howard Taft and Theodore Roosevelt—put the Governor in a political quandary. He had earlier supported Taft and attended his inauguration; Taft, in turn, came to Sedalia, Missouri, for breakfast at the state fair. But when Taft tried for a second term, the Governor viewed him as too conservative and chose to support Theodore Roosevelt instead.

At one point, however, both presidential candidates considered the Missouri Governor as a potential running mate. Hadley endorsed Roosevelt and acted as one of his floor leaders during the Republican National Convention of 1912. Hadley's moment of glory came when delegates erupted in a twenty-five-minute ovation, waving banners and shouting, "We Want Hadley." In view of his popularity, both Roosevelt and Taft leaders became frightened that the Missouri governor might become a compromise presidential candidate in a deadlocked convention.

Hadley feared that pursuing the presidency would kill him.

Historians have speculated that it was Hadley's health that kept him from pursuing the nomination for himself. According to his contemporary, William Allen White, Hadley was suffering from the early stages of tuberculosis and had a temperature of 103 degrees during most of the convention. The Governor feared that pursuing the presidency would kill him and told Roosevelt of his concern. Roosevelt, an advocate of the rigorous life, declared the pursuit "worth the sacrifice" and more important than any personal concern.

Ultimately, delegates disregarded Hadley and rejected Roosevelt in favor of Taft. The resulting rift split the GOP and led to the formation of a third party. Disgusted with the outcome of the convention, Hadley spurned Taft's offer to be his running mate and refused to join Roosevelt's new Progressive "Bull Moose" Party. The Governor reluctantly gave Taft a very tepid endorsement only one month before the election. The division within Republican ranks paved the way for the victory of Democrat Woodrow Wilson. For Hadley it also meant there would be no job offers coming from Washington.

When John Hadley, a prominent St. Louis lawyer, visited the Mansion years after his father served as Governor, he commented on his mother's portrait, "I wish I could put another dress on Mother. This looks like a nightgown." It was true. Formal gowns of a half-century earlier looked much like the night wear of the next generation.

At the end of his term, Hadley had little choice but to return to his law practice. On one of the last evenings for the family at the Mansion, friends dropped by to bid the First Couple farewell. As a token of remembrance, they presented Hadley with a large silver loving cup and a scroll signed by fifty-six officials, neighbors, and townspeople. "The Governor was deeply touched. The cup was filled with some of the nice Hermann wine, and the friends standing about the dining room drank, passing the cup from hand to hand," Mrs. Hadley wrote. In observance of the special moment, no one ever drank from the cup again.

Hadley practiced law in Kansas City for three years before retiring in ill health. In 1916 he moved out West, taught law at the University of Colorado, and gained enough attention to be urged to run for governor of that state. He also wrote a number of magazine articles on political and legal topics, as well as a book, *Rome and the World Today*, which won him a medal from the King of Italy.

In 1923, however, he returned to St. Louis to become chancellor of Washington University. Hadley's health was apparently stable enough to allow him to oversee his family's milling operation in Kansas and to be an active speaker and writer. He served as a member of the National Crime Commission and helped produce a crime survey report. In addition, he took part in a four-year project to develop a model code of criminal procedure that was later adopted.

In 1927, while still serving as chancellor, Hadley died of heart disease. He was fifty-five. Mrs. Hadley wrote of her husband, "[He] was the most industrious man I ever knew. He never had an idle moment. He worked hard and he played hard." Shortly before he died, Hadley had told his wife that their years in the Capital City "were the happiest of his life." For that reason, she had his body returned to Jefferson City and buried on a site in view of the Capitol, looking across to the Callaway bluffs—a scene he had enjoyed so often during his years in the Mansion.

Hadley was apparently in good enough health to oversee the family milling operation in Kansas.

Once thought too frail to seek public office, Herbert Hadley had broken the Democratic stronghold on the state by unexpectedly winning the governorship. Disproving the dire predictions of his doctors, he had completed his term and lived another fourteen years. During those years, he found strength and courage from bits of verse he carried with him. A favorite from William Henley's *Invictus* mirrors Hadley's indomitable spirit.

"Out of the night that covers me,
    Black as the pit, from pole to pole,
    I thank whatever gods may be
    For my unconquerable soul."

Refusing to be defeated by ill health, Herbert Hadley, the vigorous outdoorsman and public servant, brought the benefits of fresh air to himself, as well as to the operation of state government.

Four Missouri Governors gathered in St. Louis to pay tribute to Herbert Hadley, the new chancellor of Washington University. Left to right: Governor Hyde and former Governors Hadley, Francis, Gardner, and Major. Dockery was ill at the time and unable to attend.

"GOOD ROAD DAYS"

MISSOURI
STATE ROAD
MAP
LEGEND

STATE ROADS — — —
PROJECTS APPROVED ———
WORK STARTED ————
WORK COMPLETED ———

GOVERNOR ELLIOTT WOOLFOLK MAJOR
ELIZABETH TERRILL MYERS MAJOR
1913-1917

*Major seized the moment of high interest in road building
to establish a state highway department.*

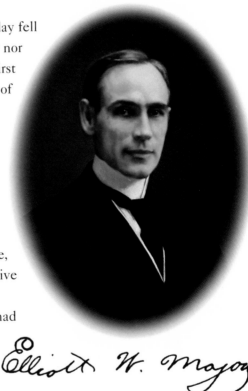

To those of a superstitious nature, Elliott Major's inaugural day fell on an unlucky date—January 13, 1913. Still, neither Major nor his wife, Elizabeth, showed any concern. Unlike former First Lady Mary Dockery, who refused to move into the Mansion because of her superstition about commencing a new venture on a Friday, Mrs. Major showed no fear. According to her daughter, also named Elizabeth, her mother "walked courageously into the Executive Mansion [without] even a charm or a rabbit's foot in her pocket."

The political strife that split Republicans nationwide in 1912 had already brought good fortune to many Democrats, including Missouri's attorney general, Elliott Major. His election as governor returned the state to the Democratic fold; while on the national scene, Woodrow Wilson defeated Republican Howard Taft and the Progressive Party's Theodore Roosevelt for the presidency.

But Elliott Major's success was not the product of luck. He had always made his own way, advancing himself to governor after a series of jobs. Starting as a teacher, he soon moved on to study law with Beauchamp "Champ" Clark at Bowling Green, Missouri. Clark, a Democratic state representative, took the twenty-four-year-old Major to Jefferson City as his legislative clerk. An aspiring young man like Major could not have found a more skillful political mentor than Clark who later went to Congress, became Speaker of the U.S. House, and aspired to the presidency.

By age thirty-two, Major felt confident enough to run for the state Senate. In 1904, after serving one term, he attempted to moved on to attorney general, but was caught in the Republican landslide that swooped up all the statewide offices that year, except governor. Four years later, Major captured the office when Attorney General Herbert Hadley became governor.

In his new position, Major became a vigorous prosecutor of Standard Oil and other trusts. While the former attorney general had started much of the legal

(Facing page)
A 1918 Missouri map showing the new roads under construction.

161

proceedings, Major pressed them to a successful conclusion. He took forty-nine cases to the U.S. Supreme Court—more than all the attorneys general combined in the history of Missouri. By the end of his term, Democrats proudly nominated him for governor without opposition.

Heralding his four-fold aim, Major offered Missourians a plan for "better schools, better roads, better agriculture, and better community life." He conveyed his message to the voters with a campaign budget, one that appeared lean by later standards. Records show his expenses included: $1,500.00 for postage, $716.00 for printing, $620.00 for campaign buttons and watch fobs, $254.05 for office management, and $75.40 for lithograph pictures—a total of $3,165.45.

Major called on lawmakers to "place their feet upon the middle path."

To celebrate Major's victory, Democrats swarmed to Jefferson City. With the Capitol devastated by the fire of 1911, the inaugural ceremony took place in a nearby temporary building. Though the site had changed, the festive atmosphere remained. Loud and prolonged cheering greeted Major's arrival. The band struck up a spirited rendition of "Dixie"—a tune that was traditionally played at Missouri inaugurations—and cannons on the Capitol lawn fired the customary seventeen-gun salute. In his inaugural address, the practical-minded chief executive told his audience not to expect him to be a reformer. His remark was undoubtedly aimed at the two previous governors whose progressive agendas had caused so much controversy. Major cautioned against extremism and urged the legislators to "place [their] feet upon the middle path . . . the path of safety."

While the new Governor was laying the groundwork for a safe administration, his wife was trying to cope with her duties as First Lady. Though she had been a guest at previous inaugurals, she was perplexed at being "one of the principals in the event." As the new Mansion hostess, she experienced some of the same feelings as had previous first ladies. Her account of the family's introduction to the Mansion showed the chaos of inaugural day from the First Lady's perspective: "With house guests and callers, the adjustment of the family, answering such questions of younger members as 'Where are you going to put me?' 'When do I eat?'. . . [it was] a bit bewildering, but withal the day passed rapidly."

That evening at the inaugural ball, guests crowded into the Mansion, once again pressing the old house far beyond its intended capacity. Throughout the house, dancers sashayed to old-time fiddle tunes, as well as the newer dances, the "Bunny Hug," the "Aeroplane Waltz," and the "Grizzly Bear." One woman said the space "she occupied could be covered by a ten cent piece." Some of the young people, in search of more room, left for a nearby meeting hall where a dance floor was available. However, those who endured the crush were rewarded by the music of world-famous vocalist Miss Felice Lyne with her rendition of "Comin' Thro' the Rye" and "The Last Rose of Summer."

Mrs. Major's next event at the Mansion—a tea for the ladies of Jefferson City—took place on a rare, springlike day in January. The massive front doors remained open as the throng of guests arrived, leaving the doorman with nothing to do but stand "like a statue" beside the entrance. Feeling he might be more helpful elsewhere, several of Mrs. Major's friends sent him to serve in the dining room and began greeting the guests themselves. The relaxed atmosphere pleased Mrs. Major. She later wrote, "From that occasion, I knew that the keynote for me to follow as near as possible for the next four years was informality."

Elizabeth Major had been a guest at previous inaugurals, but she was perplexed at being "one of the principals in the event."

Though Mrs. Major offered fewer fancy gatherings at the Mansion than the townspeople would have liked, she was careful to observe the traditional military ball in all of its formality. In announcing the upcoming ball, one newspaper declared that the uniformed gentlemen would "clank their swords and switch their gold braid" to the new sounds of a string orchestra.

For the past fifty years, guests had sashayed to fiddle music as they danced the Virginia reel, a cotillion, or the lancers; later the schottische, polka, and round waltz became popular. But changing times had introduced even more new dances and the Majors' children did not want their father to be out of step. Before the ball, they saw

"The keynote for me to follow was informality."

to it that he learned the "fox-trot," "one-step," and "the hesitation." Rumor had it that Major further polished his skills with dance instruction in St. Louis.

On the evening of the ball, guests gathered at the base of the spiraling stairway as officers of the National Guard paraded down the steps to the sounds of patriotic music. Confused by so many uniformed men wearing various insignias, Mrs. Major adopted a simple policy: when she was uncertain about military rank, she simply addressed an officer as "Colonel," happily elevating some before their time.

The First Lady's warm demeanor obviously impressed one newsman: "There is no silly froth about Mrs. Major—she does not assume the aristocratic role, or put on high-flown, haughty airs. Mrs. Major, who came from Pike County six years ago, is the same Mrs. Major in the Governor's Mansion today. She shakes hands in the same way, inquires after the folks in the same manner, makes you welcome in the same fashion, and entertains you in the same style."

Appreciation of the Governor came from his honorary colonels. The cadre of friends, supporters, and staff made their traditional presentation of the Governor's portrait at a Mansion reception. The event fell on a Friday—an inauspicious day, according to some. The Governor was among those superstitious of "hangings on Fridays" and asked that the installation of the portrait be delayed until the following day. When reminded that the next day was the thirteenth of the month, Major disclaimed any feeling of superstition about the number, saying several of his political achievements had occurred on the thirteenth.

The Mansion silverware on display in the parlor.

The Governor appeared to have no qualms about which day he played golf. He took up the game during his first year in office and spent enough time on the links of the Jefferson City Country Club to cause one writer to declare him the victim of "golf fever."

With only one child at home, Mrs. Major devoted her time almost entirely to her duties as Mansion hostess. Though there were three children in the family, one was married and another was in college much of the time. With room to spare in the old house, she often invited friends to spend the night. Overnight guests stayed in the bedroom at the top of the stairs—the President's Room—so named because it was thought that Theodore Roosevelt once occupied it, as had the three-time presidential hopeful William Jennings Bryan.

With room to spare in the old house, she often invited friends to spend the night.

164

The Majors continued to entertain visitors, all the while looking for ways to improve the comfort of the Mansion. Workers were brought in to install larger water pipes in the forty-two-year-old home and to add new electric lights in the yard. The Governor, feeling that no sitting room was comfortable without a rocking chair, requested that one be added to the parlor. Elizabeth Major gladly complied by placing a small cane rocker in the room.

More improvements came with the addition of a second-floor screened porch. The Majors could now enjoy a panoramic view of the new Capitol under construction, as well as a cool summer breeze from the river. "We never grew weary of the view of the Missouri River, the Callaway bluffs, the shifting scenes in the 'bottoms,' " Mrs. Major recalled.

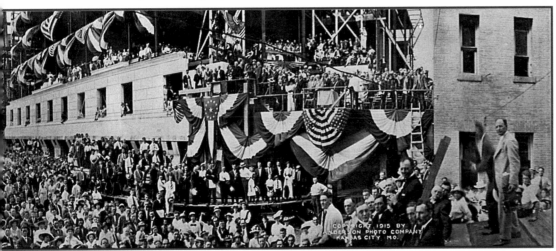

GOV. AND MRS. MAJOR AFTER THE CEREMONIES

Governor and Mrs. Major at the ground-breaking ceremonies for the State Capitol in 1913.

The Governor's love of Missouri's scenery might have influenced one of his vetoes. When the legislature offered Major an automobile, he rejected it in favor of his slower-moving team and surrey from which he could better enjoy the countryside. Although the local Ford dealer advertised a fine two-seater coupe fully equipped for $750, the Governor preferred the horse-drawn vehicle.

Curiously, improving Missouri's roads appeared to interest Major more than putting his car on one. Along with members of his staff and state officeholders, the Governor donned a brown fedora hat and his khaki work clothes to join volunteers in two "Good Road Days" in 1913 and 1914. Farmers and businessmen, wielding picks and shovels, worked side by side on the road building project. The hundred or more prisoners who joined the work force received a fifteen-day credit on their sentences for every two days of labor.

Even the Kansas Governor helped out, earning a handful of blisters along with the Missouri Governor. The First Lady of Kansas joined Mrs. Major and other ladies in providing meals for local work crews. Thousands of other women around the state also took part in helping to feed the one-quarter million men who worked

Cornerstone laying for the new State Capitol in 1915.

on creating nearly four hundred miles of roads. The Governor estimated the value of the improvements at $1.5 million.

Missouri's successful road days drew acclaim from around the globe. The Governor of Arkansas initiated a similar work program and hundreds of letters poured into Governor Major's office regarding the project. Many contained newspaper clippings, photos, and requests for more information on the cooperative venture. Major seized the moment of high interest in road building to establish a state highway department, an ongoing entity that would see to Missouri's future infrastructure needs.

While the Governor liked the idea of using prisoners for road work, he opposed the contract labor system used since the 1870s that permitted businesses to work inmates at the rate of fifty to seventy-five cents a day. But abolishing contract labor reduced state revenue at a time when Missouri could ill-afford the loss. The state was already suffering from lower tax receipts because some counties had voted to outlaw the sale of alcohol. The burden of replacing a building on the Warrensburg college campus and paying a pension both to the blind and to the Confederate veterans further crippled his budget. In addition, the Governor was faced with the cost of constructing a new State Capitol to replace the one destroyed by fire in 1911.

Farmers and businessmen, weilding picks and shovels, worked side by side to improve the roads.

The steel construction of the Missouri State Capitol in Jefferson City.

Rather than raise taxes as the demand for public services mounted, Major advocated thrift in government, starting in his own office. By leaving two clerk positions unfilled, he proudly announced a savings of $2,700. In another cost savings attempt, he suggested buying one thousand acres of land on which to grow food for the prison inmates. Despite his attempt at economy, Major had accumulated a sizable debt to pass on to his successor by the time he left office.

Though Major was faulted by some for his timidity in handling taxes, one of his decisions found approval, at least with his family. His success in forming a Pardon and Parole Board in 1913 not only pleased prison authorities but also protected Mrs. Major and subsequent first ladies from the heart-wrenching pleas that came when the relatives of an inmate brought their case to the Mansion door. At long last, a professional board would weigh the merits of each case and relieve the Governor and First Lady of this unwanted burden. Major's most significant contribution to state government, however, was the creation of the Public Service Commission—a five-person board appointed by the Governor to deal with public utility matters.

The addition of a second floor screened porch allowed the Majors a panoramic view of the new Capitol. A summerhouse can be seen near the back of the house and the stable in the foreground.

A further innovation was Major's mode of delivering his biennial message to the lawmakers. For the first time in history, a Missouri governor delivered his own text to the joint session of the legislature. Previously, a clerk read the governor's report, usually in a dry, monotonous tone. In 1915, however, Major chose to follow the lead of President Woodrow Wilson who had read his own speech to Congress. Although the address took Major an hour and a half to deliver, news reports commented on its brevity, perhaps compared to former biennial messages.

As Major prepared to leave office, he could not resist a last show of leniency—one, he said, "touching the human side of life." During his final week as governor, he granted a full pardon to ninety-two convicts between the ages of seventeen and twenty-one, all first-time offenders with good prison records. Assembling them as a body in the prison yard, the Governor spoke to the young men like a teacher instructing a class of delinquent boys.

"In an unguarded moment you missed the way—crossed the narrow line dividing good and evil," he said. "I want to help you and give you another chance in the great battle of life." Education had always been a priority with the former teacher turned politician. It is not surprising then, that his last official act was a lecture and a gift of opportunity.

At the end of his term, the Governor opened a law firm in St. Louis, leaving his successor with a $2.5 million debt and the task of raising taxes—a matter that Major had refused to face despite the increasing demand for public services. He apparently

Education had always been a priority with the former teacher turned politician.

continued to maintain an "active" legal practice for a newspaper article indicated that Major, at age seventy-five, suffered a broken ankle and lacerated hand while ejecting another attorney from his office.

The feisty Governor lived another decade. Looking back, friends observed that the Majors were not "swept off their feet by the fleeting favor of place and position" and left the Mansion unscathed by the spotlight of public office. Elliott Woolfolk Major, the good roads, good schools governor chose his own course, made his own luck, and cautiously directed Missouri along "the middle path" he had promised.

"A Dream Come True"

GOVERNOR FREDERICK DOZIER GARDNER
JEANNETTE VOSBURGH GARDNER
1917-1921

"A poor boy can rise by his own efforts to receive the highest position of public trust and honor that the people . . . can bestow upon a fellow citizen."
~ First Lady Jeannette Gardner

"A dream come true." That's what Jeannette Gardner called her husband's rise to the governorship. As a poor, motherless youngster growing up in rural Kentucky and Tennessee, success seemed unlikely for little Frederick Gardner. When he was only eight years old, his mother died while working as a nurse during a yellow fever epidemic.

In the difficult years that followed, he and his brothers and sisters were shuffled from one relative to the next. Forced to learn self-reliance early, Gardner earned his first income selling newspapers on the street. At seventeen, he borrowed money to go to St. Louis where he landed a job earning ten dollars a week as an office boy in a coffin factory. By age twenty-five, the talented, hard-working young man had become president of the company. A few years later, he was the sole owner of the business and on his way to being a millionaire.

Gardner's quest did not stop with financial success. Like another St. Louis businessman, former Governor Francis, Gardner wanted to apply his management skills to the problems of government. Like Francis, he had never held statewide office, although he had been elected to the Board of Freeholders in St. Louis—a bipartisan group picked to draw up a new city charter. Gardner turned his lack of political experience into an asset by telling voters that if elected governor he would be the business manager of the state.

The slogan had a certain appeal to Missourians. Farmers liked his idea of a land bank—a rural credit system that would provide them with low-interest loans over a long period. His plan for improving Missouri's roadways also interested voters. Prohibitionists, however, opposed him for his support of local option regulations rather than a statewide ban of alcohol. The heated contest ended with Gardner, a Democrat, winning the governorship by a scant 2,263-vote margin.

(Facing page) Frederick Gardner (right) takes the oath of office during the state's first outdoor inauguration.

169

Capital City politicians and socialites eagerly anticipated the arrival of the new First Family. Even before Mrs. Gardner took up her duties, rumors of her gala parties excited the community. "She has the money to entertain on any scale she pleases," one writer noted. There had been little social life at the Mansion since the days of Maggie Stephens at the turn of the century, no exclusive gatherings with lavish decorations, big city caterers, or musicians. In fact, most entertainment at the Mansion had been limited to ho-hum legislative receptions and the annual military ball.

Certainly no administration could have started on a happier, more optimistic note. Even the weather promised good times ahead for the Gardner administration as the traditional January weather gave way to a mild, sunny day in Jefferson City. Two thousand visitors were expected to attend the first inauguration to be held in the nearly completed Capitol. However, as trains kept bringing more and more passengers, it soon became obvious that there would not be space for everyone inside the rotunda.

"She has the money to entertain on any scale she pleases."

Noting the weather seemed unusually cooperative, the inaugural committee thought how pleasant it would be to hold the event outside. It had always been held indoors, yet something had to be done to accommodate the crowd. At the last minute, carpenters were called in to build a platform on the south side of the Capitol for what would go down in history as Missouri's first outdoor inaugural ceremony. Work was still going on as the crowd began to gather and it was nearly noon before the inaugural stand was ready.

Encircling the front of the platform were members of the legislature and thirty of the Governor's honorary colonels sporting their gold-festooned uniforms and shiny new swords. All were enjoying the balmy winter day. Missing the celebration, however, was incoming Lieutenant Governor Crossley and his wife. The couple was recovering from a bout of ptomaine poisoning and did not show up until later that afternoon. The Governor-elect arrived to the customary strains of "Dixie," a tune especially suited to Gardner's southern heritage.

Mrs. Gardner said her husband showed no emotion during the ceremony "except that his knuckles showed white" from his tight grasp of a small Bible, an award given him by his Sunday school teacher

The Governor-elect arrived to the strains of "Dixie," a customary tune at Missouri inaugurals.

when he was a child. The son of outgoing Governor Major sensed the impact of the moment on the new First Family. As they sat in the sun on the newly constructed platform overlooking the crowd of well-wishers, he hastily scribbled a note to Mrs. Gardner, "May all your days be like this one."

As the day unfolded, the Gardners may have wished otherwise. During the reception that followed the ceremony, Mrs. Gardner suffered from the same agonizing experience as former First Ladies Maggie Stephens and Agnes Hadley: her hand throbbed with pain from the crushing handshakes of friends and supporters. One seasoned politician advised her to "take hold first . . . or they will wring [your hand] off."

To the disappointment of many of his guests attending the reception, the Governor served sparkling grape juice rather than liquor. The cautious celebration might have stemmed from his chastisement by the Anti-Saloon League for not endorsing prohibition. During the gubernatorial campaign, the group charged that a decade earlier Gardner's St. Louis company had shipped whiskey in coffins to distributors in dry areas. While Gardner said the League was "making a mountain out of a molehill," he did not deny the accusation.

Disregarding Gardner's decision to have a dry inauguration, a friend sent bottles of champagne to observe the occasion. In the haste of filling glasses at the reception, waiters poured from every bottle in sight. "This caused little comedies to be enacted every time a fresh tray was brought into the room," Mrs. Gardner recalled. "The men waited their opportunities eagerly, their faces beaming with anticipation—a look that was soon confirmed by a happy smile or routed by a dour look of resignation." Years later Mrs. Gardner wrote, "The mistake—everyone was secretly glad it happened—made its own contribution to the success of the party."

Mrs. Gardner recalled that her hand throbbed with pain from the crushing handshakes of well-wishers.

The day after the inauguration, Mrs. Gardner, "in a spirit of adventure, explored every nook and cranny" of the Mansion. Everything seemed fine at the time, but during the months ahead the Gardners discovered a major inconvenience. One central bathroom and another small guest bath served the seven bedrooms on the second floor where visitors and classmates of their two teenage sons frequently spent the night. "Everyone would leave bedroom doors ajar, the better to hear the departing occupant of the bathroom. Often two or three persons would come tumbling at once into the hall on such a long-awaited signal," Mrs. Gardner recalled. Annoyed by these incidents, the Governor had another bathroom put in for his own use. For many years afterwards, the facility was referred to as "Governor Gardner's bathroom" because it was installed at his insistence.

The Governor was less enthusiastic when his wife asked to use state funds for other improvements at the Mansion. She wanted to restore the Grand Stairway to its original walnut finish and remodel the garage and kitchen. Gardner finally agreed, but paid for most of the improvements from his personal funds.

Gardner's restraint gave the appearance of economy at a time when Republicans were eager to denounce him as "a reckless spendthrift." Since the beginning of the century, legislators had overappropriated to finance the growing demands of Missourians and then passed the debt on to the next administration. In his inaugural address, Gardner faced the issue squarely. Having inherited more than a two million dollar deficit from the previous administration, he told the lawmakers that

ROMANCE AT THE MANSION

During the Gardner administration, life at the Mansion took on some aspects of a soap opera with the fostering of two love affairs. One day, Mrs. Gardner asked her nine-year-old daughter, Janet, if she had seen Essie, the housekeeper. "Oh," Janet replied, "she is in the cellar with Henry," one of the inmates working at the Mansion.

"They're going to be married," Janet announced excitedly.

"Why, Janet, what makes you think so?" her mother asked.

"Oh, I saw her kissing him in the coal bin good-bye."

The other housekeeper, Anna, was horrified to think of Essie's involvement with a convict. However, in a matter of months, Anna came to Mrs. Gardner to announce her own intention to marry one of the inmates. The Governor provided the needed paroles and both housekeepers left to be married. Essie's Mansion romance ultimately resulted in a divorce, but Anna and her husband remained a devoted couple for life.

Nine-year-old Janet Gardner and her backyard playhouse (right).

the state could not continue operating on its present revenue.

In response to the shortfall, he negotiated four-percent loans from St. Louis banks to pay off the indebtedness. He also pushed a series of tax increases through the legislature during his first two years in office. The conservative Governor got tough when the General Assembly wanted to overspend and told its members he would veto anything in excess of estimated revenue. His pledge forced him to turn down a pension for the blind and a children's home bill until funds became available. Even a $30,000 appropriation for Mansion improvements fell under the Governor's axe. In retaliation for Gardner's economies, legislators reduced the budget of the Governor's tax commission so drastically that its work of equalization was hampered.

While Gardner could deny legislators the money for a pet project, he could not say no to his nine-year-old daughter, Janet. Her request for a backyard playhouse easily won the Governor's support. The little girl conducted her own tea parties and once invited her mother to come join her. " 'Tea,' to my amazement, was fried potatoes and biscuits," Mrs. Gardner recalled.

Janet frequently played about town accompanied by her pony and Critt, the family Airedale. The dog was the namesake of Colonel H. H. Crittenden, son of

the former governor, who presented the puppy to the young lady of the Mansion. Janet and Critt became very attached. As time went on, the dog began escorting her to school each day and developed the uncanny ability to return at just the right time to walk the little girl home.

Although the Gardner's dog showed exceptional memory skills, the First Lady did not. People expected to be remembered by the Governor's wife, as one woman did after a casual introduction four years earlier. Mrs. Gardner wrote of "[a] little lady from Livingston County who, hopeful of being called by name as she passed along the receiving line at a reception during our last year at the Mansion, took my hand, saying, 'Oh, my dear Mrs. Gardner, I am sure you remember me; I met you when the Governor opened his campaign at Chillicothe.' "

The First Lady was more adept at protecting her husband from inquiring constituents. The Governor was unavailable most afternoons because of his golf game. Each day he would return to the Mansion during the lunch hour, slip up the back stairs, have a light lunch in his bedroom, and head for the country club. Luncheon guests, not knowing Gardner's schedule, would often remark, "It's too bad that the Governor has to work so hard that he cannot be here to enjoy this lovely luncheon." Mrs. Gardner recalled her response, "Deftly as possible, I would change the subject. 'My dear, won't you have another chop?' I would say."

As hostess of the Mansion, Mrs. Gardner also welcomed the visit of two former residents of the house. Once she was summoned from breakfast by a surprise visit of Governor Dockery. She found the old statesman standing in the parlor, gazing at the oil painting of his wife who had died in the Mansion nearly twenty years earlier. "I thought I detected tears in his eyes as he stood there so deep in reverie that he had not heard our approach," she recalled. "We withdrew quietly; and I think it was then that I knew for the first time how completely sad are a strong man's tears."

Another resident of the Mansion, William Stone, also enjoyed Mrs. Gardner's hospitality when she held a dinner party in his honor. Stone, who served as U.S. Senator and head of the Foreign Relations Committee, was interrupted during the meal by the receipt of a telegram from Washington. As Stone read the message, Mrs. Gardner noticed how weary he became. He excused himself and trudged slowly up the spiraling staircase to his bedroom. The news that disturbed the aging Senator told of the break in diplomatic relations with Germany—the first step to a global war that would change the life of the nation as well as the Gardner family.

The United States declared war just three months after Gardner took office. The new Governor wasted no time in preparing Missourians for their part in the effort or in condemning those with faint patriotism. With Senator Stone and most of the state's congressmen opposing the war, and with eastern journalists questioning the loyalty of Missourians, Gardner called for stern commitment. "There is no time for slackers . . . or soft pedalists," he told a St. Louis audience. "If there are any such among us, it is our duty to drive them out and brand them as traitors."

William, the oldest of Gardner's three children, was a college student at the

Food *is* Ammunition—
Don't waste it.

UNITED STATES FOOD ADMINISTRATION

University of Missouri-Columbia at the outbreak of the war. He and his friends were "alive to the high idealism of the times and the call of the hour," Mrs. Gardner recounted. "We were in the war; they wanted to go." Although William was too young to enlist, he convinced his father to help him and his friends form an ambulance unit. The young men purchased equipment for their twenty-five-man unit, bought their own uniforms, and paid their own expenses to join the troops abroad.

Mrs. Gardner gathered her son in her arms for "an aching farewell" at St. Louis's Union Station. Proud but fearful, she returned home, "flung herself across a bed and gave way to tears." During the months that followed, she reached out to other mothers and families. "From cantonments and naval bases, from ships on the high seas, and from 'somewhere in France,' letters poured into the Mansion." Showing a sincere concern, Mrs. Gardner tried to reply to each, occasionally enclosing a small gift or book. "Yes, war was real," she wrote, "and the service flag over the Mansion with its red star made life serious and my heart heavy."

On the home front, Mrs. Gardner put aside any thoughts she once had for an active social season. Instead, the First Lady helped with recruiting for the Navy, sold war savings stamps, and joined the Red Cross in making bandages. Teas and receptions at the Mansion gave way to weekly knitting sessions for the troops abroad.

The United States declared war just three months after Gardner took office.

The Gardners also set an example of self-sufficiency. They planted the first war garden in Missouri on the Mansion grounds where they grew onions, lettuce, peas, and other vegetables. A flock of chickens in the backyard provided an ample supply of eggs. At a time when families were accustomed to eating meat at each meal, the First Lady began serving it only four times a week, and then only at dinner. "Food conservation—

A large mural in the House chambers, depicting the "Glory of Missouri in War," was painted by French artist Charles Hoffbauer to honor Missouri soldiers who fought in France during World War I.

174

THE DEMOCRAT-TRIBUNE.

JEFFERSON CITY, MISSOURI · THURSDAY, JANUARY 16, 1919

VOL. 42 NO. 212

U.S. DRY

MISSOURI IS THE 37TH STATE TO RATIFY NATIONAL PROHIBITION

NATION IS DRY

The Senate Voted On Amendment First Thing
In Morning—House Sustained Senate
Amendment in Short Order.

'Hooverizing,' as we called it—was the order of the day," Mrs. Gardner recalled.

The sacrifices at home were small compared to those made by the nation's fighting men. The conflict took a heavy toll on the state: over 156,000 Missourians joined the battle in Europe and of those, 3,644 were killed and nearly 7,000 were wounded.

At the close of the war, Mrs. Gardner took on the more cheerful task of welcoming home the troops. Shortly before Christmas 1918, William Gardner and his friends returned from their ambulance duty in France and she went to New York to meet the ship. The Governor also had the pleasure of welcoming a distinguished military figure after the war. He presented General John J. Pershing, a Missouri native, with a medal in recognition of his leadership as commander of the American forces.

W ith the signing of the armistice, the nation focused its attention on two domestic issues—prohibition and women's suffrage. Passage of the Eighteenth Amendment not only turned the Mansion "dry" but also took $1.5 million in tax revenue from the state, forcing the Governor to raise a variety of taxes to make up the difference.

During the final weeks before the law became effective, party-goers around the state and nation drank a final farewell to alcohol. Even an inmate working at the Mansion wanted one final fling. He ran off taking with him a bottle of perfume and some hair tonic belonging to the Gardners. "[He] could not stand the thought of finishing his time and of being released in a bone-dry world, [and] went berserk," Mrs. Gardner explained. Not long afterwards, the prisoner was captured "several miles from town, very sick and very drunk, and quite willing to return to the confines of the cold, gray walls."

Jeanette Gardner showed only nominal interest in the other dominant issue following the war—women's suffrage. Nonetheless, she once attended a suffrage meeting along with the Governor and, after his speech, added a few words of support for the movement. The First Lady confessed that she had never made a speech before and added, in a humorous vein, that her silence might have gained her husband more votes.

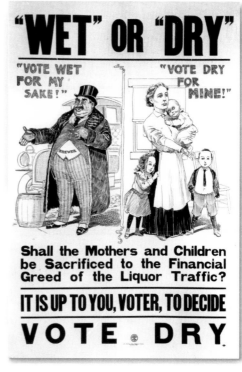

"WET" OR "DRY"

"VOTE WET FOR MY SAKE!"

"VOTE DRY FOR MINE!"

Shall the Mothers and Children be Sacrificed to the Financial Greed of the Liquor Traffic?

IT IS UP TO YOU, VOTER, TO DECIDE

VOTE ▪ DRY

Some women were already taking an active political role—one that laid the groundwork for passage of the Nineteenth Amendment granting women the vote. In 1914, by use of the initiative process, they had forced the question of suffrage onto the ballot, but male voters had rejected it. Two years later during the Democratic National Convention in St. Louis, 17,000 women staged a demonstration in favor of suffrage. But the way Mrs. Gardner saw it, the war did the most to promote women's rights: "Women were pressed into commercial and industrial service. This had a profound effect on political thought." In 1919—a year after the war ended—the women of Missouri had the right to vote.

The war did the most to promote women's rights.

Mrs. Gardner seemed relieved that the struggle for voting rights was over, saying that "it had grown to be a tiresome issue." In a final gesture, she invited the "jubilant" suffragette leaders to the Mansion for lunch. Young Janet Gardner was "elated" at the prospect of seeing the militant group of women who had won the much-publicized victory. However, she was somewhat disappointed when only one of them showed up wearing the severe black suit, high-collared white shirt, black bow tie, and sailor hat that she expected to see on a suffragette.

While prohibition and suffrage overshadowed many of Gardner's postwar programs, he promoted fiscal reforms, prison improvements, a state park system, and highway construction. Some of his reforms were short-lived: capital punishment, abandoned in 1917, was reinstituted two years later and his land bank idea lost out to a federal rural credit plan.

The Governor's road building program remained his greatest legacy. For two years, Gardner campaigned across the state to win approval for his $60 million bond issue. The passage of the Centennial Road Law in 1920 was a boon to road construction in Missouri. Until then, roads were built on a 50-50 cost basis with state and counties contributing equally. Because some counties could not raise their half of the funds, roads often were not connected.

Having put an end to local road building, a new system of statewide road planning and construction began in conjunction with the federal government. Using funds from auto license fees, Gardner constructed thousands of miles of paved roads throughout the state. Better highways, in turn, brought more tourists who created a demand for gas stations and restaurants and gave a new boost to the economy.

Gardner's strict money management also paid off, allowing him to eradicate the debt inherited from his predecessor and to leave a $5 million surplus in the state treasury. Part of the savings came by making the prison self-supporting and by consolidating its management. Just weeks before he became governor, the contract labor system at the prison had been abandoned. The policy that had been in effect for over four decades allowed local businesses to operate within the wall of the prison using inmate labor at the rate of seventy-five cents a day. Gardner found new employment for the inmates, putting them to work building roads and working on state-owned farmland and in state-run factories.

Though the governorship fulfilled a personal dream for Frederick Gardner, his term ended on a disappointing note. He had led Missouri during the austere and

A Ride with Royalty

In October 1919, when King Albert and Queen Elizabeth of Belgium visited St. Louis, residents turned out in great numbers to show their respects for the little European nation that had held on so bravely during World War I. Accompanied by Governor and Mrs. Gardner, the royal couple was paraded in an open car and showered with flowers during the warm welcome to the city. While standing on a corner watching the pomp and pageantry, a friend of Mrs. Gardner's was inspired to write the following poem about the stately first ladies and their plumed headwear.

Our own Jeannette wears feathers up,
The Belgian Queen's are down;
But gentle blood flows in each vein,
On each head is a crown.

Elizabeth may abdicate,
And with her kingdom part;
Jeannette will reign until the end
O'er every loving heart.

I drink this toast, 'long may both reign,'
From out a loving cup;
The Belgian Queen with feathers down,
Jeannette with feathers up.

troublesome war and postwar era, but voters, tired of conflict and longing for a return to "normalcy," looked to the GOP for new leadership. For the first time in fifty years, the entire state Democratic ticket lost. Republicans gained control of the General Assembly and Arthur Hyde became governor—the second Republican to lead the state since the Civil War era.

After leaving office, the Gardners returned to St. Louis and the following year took a three-month tour of Europe. Friends urged him to seek the 1924 presidential or vice presidential nominations as a favorite son candidate, but he preferred to continue running his coffin business. Twelve years after leaving office, Gardner died from a jaw infection that developed after having a tooth extracted. He was sixty-four.

In her memoirs written shortly after his death, Mrs. Gardner recalled how she felt on her final day as First Lady. "A new regime was coming in. The historic old house was to have a new mistress. The four years we had lived there were the happiest of my life. They were years filled with laughter and heartache, work and play . . . friendships, generous and warm. . . . That last day I stole away from the crowd and visited the Capitol and walked alone through the spacious corridors, and later drove with a friend from one end of Jefferson City to the other, deep in reveries as I passed the homes of my friends where I had spent so many delightful hours. I confess now that I was a little tired, but in another hour—it seemed incredible after the long absence—I was going home."

THE COMEBACK COUPLE

Governor and Mrs. Arthur Hyde (above) and their hometown supporters.

GOVERNOR ARTHUR MASTICK HYDE
HORTENSE CULLERS HYDE
1921-1925

From a faltering start, the Governor revived his programs and achieved an amazing political comeback.

It always amused people to learn that Republican Governor Arthur Hyde and his wife met at a Democratic political gathering. Hortense Cullers–a good Democrat at the time–never dreamed that seventeen years later she would be moving into the Governor's Mansion as the wife of a Republican governor.

In a state long known for electing Democrats, Arthur Hyde might have found it hard to envision himself winning public office, too. He had grown up in the small town of Princeton, Missouri, located near the Iowa border. Though gifted with a photographic memory, he was a clumsy youngster—so poorly coordinated that he avoided playing baseball. He preferred writing and often produced skits that he and his playmates performed in a barn for a few cents admission charge.

Hyde left home during his college years, but returned in 1900 with a law degree from Iowa State University and the intention of remaining in Princeton. His father—a former congressman and businessman—made room for his son in the family law firm.

Eight years later, voters elected Arthur to serve as the town's mayor. In his first public office, Hyde demonstrated the progressive tendencies that would mark his political career. He started a program of sidewalk paving, reduced the city's indebtedness, and purchased a site for a new town hall. Hyde also engaged in a number of businesses, ranging from banking to farming, but his primary activity was a Buick dealership that he eventually expanded into eight counties.

In addition to his civic and commercial pursuits, Hyde found time to teach the men's Bible class at the local Methodist church. His magnetic style and sense of humor undoubtedly contributed to the growth of the class. Attendance soared to over two hundred, forcing the group to find a larger meeting place at the courthouse. One member recalled that "Art Hyde gave a man more to think about in thirty minutes than most ministers would in a lifetime." Inspired by their teacher, the class sponsored revival meetings in nearby communities, causing a writer to compare Hyde's efforts to those of Dwight L. Moody, one of the nineteenth century's most prominent evangelists.

Hyde leaves the White House after conferring with President Warren Harding about congressional redistricting in Missouri.

But Hyde looked to a different role model as his interest in politics developed. He was especially drawn to the robust idealism of Theodore Roosevelt and eagerly campaigned on behalf of the presidential aspirant. In doing so, Hyde enhanced his own reputation, becoming one of the most dynamic speakers in northwest Missouri. In 1912, when Roosevelt renounced the GOP and formed the Progressive "Bullmoose" Party, Hyde followed suit, offering himself as the third party candidate for attorney general in Missouri.

"Art Hyde gave a man more to think about in thirty minutes than most ministers did in a lifetime."

Hyde injected an element of drama into the political oratory that year when he disavowed the Republican Party. During a stump speech, he brandished a knife, rolled up his sleeves, and declared, "If I had a drop of Republican blood in my veins, I would take this knife and let it out." In spite of such bravado, Hyde carried only 3 of the state's 114 counties as the entire Progressive ticket went down in defeat.

Several years later, Hyde left Princeton where he had done business for fifteen years and moved to Trenton, the adjoining county seat. With the demise of the Progressive Party, many in the community thought Hyde would not return to the Republican fold. Democrats, hoping the talented newcomer might line up with them, nominated him for prosecuting attorney, but Hyde declined. To allay any suspicion that he might be flirting with the Democratic Party, Hyde quickly declared his loyalty to the GOP and began speaking for Republican candidates around the state.

In 1917, with the outbreak of World War I, Hyde put aside his political aspiration and made several attempts to enlist in the armed forces. Though he was rejected for being color-blind, he worked on the home front, speaking in behalf of the Liberty Loan drive and the Red Cross.

With the end of the war two years later, Hyde again turned his thoughts to public office and became the president of the state's young Republican organization. But in 1920, when he tried to get on the Republican ticket for governor, party moguls wanted no part of him. They could still remember those blistering speeches he made in support of Teddy Roosevelt. While the GOP was glad to have the Progressives back in their ranks, they were not ready to hand over the party leadership to a political renegade.

"If I had a drop of Republican blood in my veins, I would take this knife and let it out."

In addition to his party disloyalty, many felt the former mayor of Princeton had too little experience in the political arena. Republican insiders preferred E. E. E. "Triple E" McJimsey, a Springfield editor who enjoyed the support of the GOP's political machine. One newsman commented that the forty-two-year-old Hyde had "more ambition than political judgment;" another dismissed his candidacy, saying he was "doomed for slaughter."

Being labeled a "dry" on the liquor issue did not help Hyde's popularity either. He did not want it to be a factor, but as a Bible-class teacher his attitude on prohibition was well known. Ultimately, he turned his position as a dry to political

"ARE YOU WET OR DRY?"

Arthur Hyde did not want prohibition to be an issue in his 1920 primary race for Governor—so he said. However, as a well-known Bible class teacher in northwest Missouri, Hyde was pegged as a "dry." His opponent, a man known as E.E.E. "Triple E" McJimsey, was an old-line Republican and clearly the choice of the "wets." Yet McJimsey refused to take a public position.

During a debate, Hyde found it to his advantage to force the issue. Having announced his dry position, he asked: "Does anybody know, certainly, Mr. McJimsey's attitude . . . . What, really, is Mr. McJimsey personally, wet or dry? Or does he maintain as he travels from wet territory to dry territory that varying degree of humidity that best suits the opinion of those with whom he is latest in contact."

Turning to his opponent, Hyde asked point blank, "Tell us, Mr. McJimsey, are you 'wet' or 'dry'? I pause here for you to explain your position."

McJimsey waited in silence for some moments before he spoke. Flustered by the confrontation, he declared that prohibition was a legal matter for the courts, not him, to decide. Hyde took the floor again, taunting his opponent further: "The only man on earth who knows whether Mr. McJimsey is wet or dry is Mr. McJimsey, and he won't tell." Again Hyde demanded, "Mr. McJimsey, you know how you voted in the last Springfield election on prohibition. How did you vote, wet or dry?"

His angry opponent shot back: "Upon that or no other question am I answerable to you."

With that Hyde responded, "When I was in school I once read of a toad which took its color from the leaves of the tree on which it perched. I take it that Mr. McJimsey is wet in St. Louis and dry in the country and of varying degrees of humidity in between."

The audience roared with laughter. Hyde, the consummate orator had made his point. One man who observed the exchange remarked: "I'm a wet, but there is one thing certain, I'm not going to vote for a man who does not know whether he's wet or dry."

The *St. Louis Post-Dispatch* apparently agreed, and urged voters to "strike down . . . the political chameleon . . . who tries to sneak into office by deceiving everybody." At the polls a week later, voters did just that as they trounced Hyde's wishy-washy opponent who refused to say whether he was "wet" or "dry."

A panel from Thomas Hart Benton's mural in the Missouri State Capitol depicts the Prohibition era with its speakeasies and dance clubs.

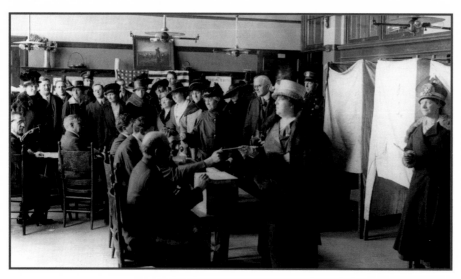

In November 1920, women "defied critics and hecklers and marched to the polls to vote in their first presidential election."

advantage during a debate. His opponent, who tried to hedge on the issue, lost credibility with voters on both sides while Hyde appeared honest and decisive.

Defying the odds, Hyde overcame his outsider status, won the primary, and went on to snatch the governorship from the hands of the Democrats. But as some historians are quick to point out, any Republican could have won in 1920, a year of unparalleled success for the GOP. The national disenchantment with the policies of President Woodrow Wilson—especially his support for the League of Nations—spilled over into Missouri politics, giving Republicans the advantage they needed for victory.

The GOP captured all the statewide offices and the General Assembly that year, a feat they had not accomplished since the post-Civil War era. Women, balloting for the first time in history, added to the high voter turnout that put Hyde in the Governor's Mansion and Republican Warren G. Harding in the White House.

Caroline Hyde peeps around the corner during a visit between her mother (left) and former First Lady Jeanette Gardner during the inaugural reception.

With his surprise victory, former car salesman Arthur Hyde moved from his Trenton showroom to the driver's seat in Jefferson City. Coming to the Capital City with him was his wife and their only child, nine-year-old Caroline. With the transition, Hortense Hyde—housewife and mother—became First Lady of Missouri and the state's official hostess. This rite of passage was marked by the traditional inaugural reception and ball hosted by the new First Lady. Because of the poor structural condition of the house, however, nothing more vigorous than eating and handshaking was planned at the Mansion; dancing was moved to the Capitol rotunda. The evening celebration lasted well past midnight, with St. Louis guests still dressed in their formal attire boarding the 2:30 a.m. train for the return trip.

Mrs. Hyde never forgot how exhausted she felt at the end of that day. Nor did she forget her first night in the splendid Victorian home with its seventeen-foot ceilings: "The crowds, the ceremonies, the reception tired me so that when I was awakened the next morning, my eyes were only half open. It was hard for me to understand just where I was. When I began looking for a ceiling, there was such a tremendous space above that I was somewhat dazed."

182

Hyde had something of a rude awakening, too, when he took up his new duties at the Capitol. As a progressive governor facing conservatives within his own party, it was not an easy task working with the General Assembly. Ignoring the handicap, the new Governor set a mind-boggling agenda for the legislators to consider. He called for election reforms, property reassessment, school and government reorganization, reduced taxes, workmen's compensation laws, and road improvements. But lawmakers were in little mood for change and dragged their feet for months before approving the Governor's proposals.

Democrats labeled his reforms "Hydeism."

Democrats labeled his reforms "Hydeism" and dismissed them as nothing more than an attempt "to legislate Democrats out of office." To defeat his agenda, opponents—some of them from his own party—pushed for a referendum on the newly passed laws. According to historian James L. Lowe, the ballot device had been around for over a decade, but this was the first systematic use of the referendum for political purposes in Missouri and perhaps in any state. With nineteen such proposals on the ballot in 1921, Missourians were thoroughly confused and they responded by rejecting all of them.

The Governor was furious that a ballot procedure designed to aid progressive legislation had become a means for its destruction. He called both the initiative and referendum "unmitigated evils" and "a vicious assault . . . upon representative government." Only the two constitutional amendments survived the balloting. One of those permitted women to hold public office and the other provided funding for the $60 million Centennial Road Program passed earlier.

Opponents continued to pound the Governor with bitter, and often personal, criticism. They accused him of nepotism when he hired his brother as state superintendent of insurance and again when he employed a brother-in-law at the state agricultural college. Some claimed that even the Governor's appointees placed their relatives on the state payroll. Hyde was faulted for spending too much time on the speaking circuit and for having his travel expenses paid from state funds. The First Lady also drew criticism because she used the prison band for Mansion concerts. The *St. Louis Censor*, a Republican newspaper, felt Hyde did not measure up to the party's standards and called for his resignation. "He is NOT a Republican. . . . Hyde is a party wrecker," the editor declared.

With all the bickering and stalemate, by midterm Missourians were ready for another change. In 1922 voters switched from the Republican column, putting Democrats back into control of the state legislature. The Governor went before the new General Assembly and

Horses frequently came to the aid of motorists mired in the mud. Hyde helped remedy the situation with the addition of more hard-surfaced roads.

MANSION CASSANOVA

Very few in Jefferson City knew that Governor Hyde's chauffeur was a convicted murderer. As a work-release inmate, he wore civilian clothes and ventured about town as he pleased in the Governor's car. His encounter with a local widow developed into a courtship when the inmate convinced her that he was a well-to-do detective and owner of the car he drove. He took his new-found love for excursions in the country, won her affection, and—with Hyde's permission—married the naive woman. The deception was exposed just as they were about to leave on their honeymoon in the Governor's car.

Local citizens, who did not like convicts working outside prison walls, criticized the Governor for turning criminals loose in town. They warned, if something wasn't done, "convicts would soon be swarming all over the town, posing as citizens, and marrying their daughters." Hyde took the heat for his negligence, but afterwards saw to it that restrictions were tightened and more guards added to supervise the work programs.

urged them to reenact the laws defeated by referendum the previous year and they did.

From a faltering start, the Governor revived his programs and achieved an amazing political comeback. Lawmakers funded a children's home, a pension for the blind, and more support for education. The repair and construction of state facilities, delayed by war, got underway with substantial support from the General Assembly. In addition, Hyde sped up the highway building program started by his predecessor, a project that brought 1,500 more miles of hard-surfaced roads to the state.

A number of first ladies posed for their portraits seated on the chairs given to the Mansion from the St. Louis World's Fair exhibit.

The First Lady was fighting a comeback of her own during much of her husband's term. A bout of poor health overshadowed her first two years and curtailed some of the social events at the Mansion. Mrs. Hyde's condition did not prevent her from undertaking an ambitious program of redecorating. Starting in the parlor, she added a new Steinway piano and a Victrola—an early model phonograph. Still, the room did not look right to her with its "colonial mahogany furniture in one end and . . . French gold leaf in the other." The chairs puzzled her, too; she was sure she had seen them somewhere before.

When the old upholstery was removed, she learned why the pieces seemed so familiar. Stamped on the white canvas were the words, "Bought for the Missouri Building, St. Louis Exposition, 1904." To her surprise, the chairs—salvaged from the fire that damaged the fair building—were the ones she had admired while visiting the exposition on her honeymoon seventeen years earlier.

The furniture now intrigued the First Lady more than ever. She decided to complete the set if she could find other matching pieces. For months, she hunted the antique stores and mailed photos to

184

manufacturers with no results. Finally, she found a St. Louis art dealer who ordered exact copies of the two arm chairs and four side chairs for $1,500.

Mrs. Hyde's next project—replacing the carpet in the drawing room—not only taxed her ingenuity but also put a crimp in the Mansion budget. The Governor, in a mood of fiscal thrift, refused any additional funding for the Mansion—a decision that did not please the determined First Lady. By "skimping and saving," however, Mrs. Hyde was able to replace the frayed, moth-eaten floor coverings. Her purchase of 170 square yards of carpeting nearly depleted her household account, leaving her a mere one hundred dollars at the end of the year. Legislators were pleased with the new look at the Mansion and offered the First Lady funds to

"People like to come to the Mansion— just the coming pleases them."

recarpet the entire house. Proud and protective of the completed work, she took the precaution of putting down tarpaulins over the new carpet when it came time for the annual military ball.

Restoration of the home's eight marble fireplaces brought more upheaval. An entire summer was devoted to rebuilding the toppling fireplaces. "When the marble mantels were torn apart, the Mansion looked like a mausoleum which had suffered an earthquake," Mrs. Hyde recalled.

A need for more repairs surfaced after a near tragedy occurred during an electrical storm. Nine-year-old Caroline Hyde was playing on the back porch when a big ball of fire struck the window. The impact of the lightning shattered the porch lights and threw the child across the room. Fortunately, Caroline was not injured, but the smell of frayed wires and scorched wood lingered as a reminder that the new wiring—already on order—was urgently needed.

As the Hydes' only child, Caroline held considerable sway with her father and was known to have influenced the Governor's decision making at least once. Hyde claimed his daughter pleaded "more eloquently than Missouri's most gifted lawyer" on behalf of a man scheduled for hanging.

Caroline recalled: "I did feel strongly on the matter and managed to lose my appetite for about a week prior to the scheduled hanging. . . . I did not want it on Dad's record that he had been given a chance to save a life, and had failed to do it." The child's concern did not go unnoticed by her father. On the morning of the hanging, she remembered her father calling down the stairs: "Kid, eat your breakfast before you go to school. I'm going straight to the office and commute that sentence."

The First Lady, on the other hand,

"When people meet socially, things political are forgot, and should be."

seemed content to exert her influence in the community rather than in state affairs. She found the townspeople friendly and receptive and "as eager to be pleased" as she was to please them. "Many of the legislators were of opposite political faith, and I had misgivings regarding them, but when people meet socially, things political are forgot, and should be. Perhaps it is unfair to tell a new hostess this, lest she miss the joy of the discovery for herself."

Mrs. Hyde soon made another discovery: there would be little privacy at the Mansion. Yet, she did not see the great parade of guests as an intrusion. Welcoming every occasion to share the charming old home, she opened the doors to a number of women's organizations, including the Morning Music Club, the P.E.O. state convention, and a state conference of the Daughters of the American Revolution. One historic event—the dedication of the new Capitol—brought members of five previous first families back to the Mansion: Mrs. Folk, Governor Dockery, and the Majors, Hadleys, and Gardners.

However, the hospitable Mrs. Hyde learned that her well-intended acts could be misinterpreted, especially by the press and her husband's political foes. A reporter accused her of removing the portraits of the Democratic governors from the Mansion because their presence disturbed her.

Although another newsman defended the First Lady against the wrongful accusation, Mrs. Hyde felt compelled to tell the whole story in her memoirs. When the portraits were displayed at the state fair, the disparity in the pictures drew attention. Besides being of various sizes, some were fine oil paintings, others merely etchings or pen-and-ink drawings. Instead of having the art returned to the Mansion, the First Lady followed the wishes of the legislature and had the portraits redone in oil and hung in the Capitol.

The new location provided a fireproof building with walls that could better support the weight and a place where more people could view the works, she explained. An incident at the Mansion proved at least one of her concerns to be valid: a large painting in the entry hall crashed to the floor one evening, bringing the Governor and the night guard, with gun in hand, to face the suspected intruder.

While Mrs. Hyde improved the state's art collection, the creation of her own portrait was stymied by two events, the death of her chosen artist and an auto accident that she suffered several months before leaving the Mansion. Bedridden for six weeks with a painful spinal injury, the First Lady gave up on the project until seven years after leaving the Capital City. She always regretted the delay. In her memoirs, she advised subsequent first ladies to move quickly to preserve "likenesses of oneself when younger." It was 1932 before Mrs. Hyde's painting was completed and presented to the Mansion.

While Hortense Hyde was always portrayed as a charming hostess, the picture that her husband left in history was one of a progressive, often thwarted by members of his own party. Even so, by the end of his term, the Governor enjoyed a burst of popularity

First Lady Hortense Hyde entertains four of her predecessors at the Capitol dedication. Left to right: Mrs. Elliott Major, Mrs. Joseph Folk, Mrs. Arthur Hyde, Mrs. Frederick Gardner and Mrs. Herbert Hadley.

evidenced by the persistent talk of a Coolidge-Hyde presidential ticket.

During that time, Hyde was a guest at a White House dinner. President Coolidge was undoubtedly aware of the rumor that the Governor might be picked as his running mate. In the middle of dinner Hyde spoke up: "By the way, Mr. President, I am going to be out of a job in a few months. I was looking around and have found exactly the job I want. You can give it to me if you will."

The new Capitol dedicated in 1924. In the back row are the colonels of the four governors—Hadley, Major, Gardner, and Hyde—whose terms extended through the construction. Hyde stands in the center; the other four Governors attending and members of the Capitol Decoration Commission are grouped around the small model of the Capitol. Each of the 114 counties is represented by one of the young women.

Somewhat startled by Hyde's boldness, Coolidge paused for a moment before asking, "What is it?"

"The job of lighthouse keeper on the coast of Florida in the months of February, March, and April," Hyde replied.

The tension melted into an uproar of laughter, with Coolidge agreeing to give Hyde the job in exchange for an invitation to visit the lighthouse.

In spite of his good humor at the White House, Hyde showed

"Hyde was advocating progressive measures during a conservative reaction."

some frustration with his term as he prepared to step back into private life. When asked what he considered to be his most outstanding accomplishment, he pointed to his staunch "refusal to surrender to the mercenary forces within the Republican Party." James Lowe summed up the Governor's problem: "Hyde was advocating progressive measures during a conservative reaction. 'The Progressive Era' from which Hyde had drawn some of his inspiration and ideals had gone into eclipse. Rapid changes were not desired; people wanted peace and quiet and 'normalcy.' "

Mrs. Hyde might have been looking forward to some of that peace and quiet as she prepared to leave the Mansion. However, before departing, the First Lady had two traditional tasks yet to perform: selecting a gift to leave behind as a memento of her tenure and meeting with the new hostess of the house. Wanting to leave something with "enduring practicality," she selected a silver punch bowl, ladle, water

First Daughter: "The Official Nuisance"

Caroline Hyde

In her memoirs, Caroline Hyde related many amusing events from her days as "First Daughter." Looking back on her childhood, Caroline dubbed herself the "Official Nuisance" of the Mansion. She remembered playing ball and roly-poly (a form of blindman's bluff) in the reception hall and hiding candy in the base of the grandfather's clock.

Her earliest trip to the Mansion was with her parents to dine with Governor and Mrs. Gardner at the traditional preinaugural meal. The high ceilings, immense rooms, and spiraling staircase fascinated the nine-year-old who had never before seen such splendor.

With preparation for the next day taking place in the dining room, Mrs. Gardner arranged to serve dinner on a card table in the upstairs hall. Because it was an unusual setup, the butler forgot the napkins.

Caroline announced that her family never used napkins at home.

Mrs. Gardner, greatly disturbed by the oversight, apologized profusely. Caroline, in her childlike way, attempted to ease the embarrassment by announcing that her family "had never used [napkins] at home anyway!"

Caroline's most vivid recollection of the inauguration was seeing a flash camera go off as she held the Bible for her father's oath of office. Never having witnessed a flashing camera "I thought certainly I had been shot." The sight of her father in his formal "stovepipe hat" was also a memorable experience for the little girl. "He carried it more than he wore it, and acted, even then, as if he were ashamed to be caught with such a thing. I was proud of him for that among many reasons."

During the inaugural ball, Caroline wanted to dance in the huge ballroom on the third floor. She later recalled looking at her orthopedic shoes and wondering if she would ever be able to move gracefully across the dance floor. "I would have tried even then if someone had asked me."

The young lady of the Mansion was immediately drawn to the long, curving rail of the staircase. She wanted desperately to slide down the "shiny, polished banister," but because of the mob on the stairs during the inaugural celebration, she had to wait until the next day. Caroline recalled it being a speedy descent. "Fortunately there was a substantial statue at the end of the banister or I might have been sliding yet!" The statue she referred to, the so-called "Newel Post Lady," was a favorite of another child of the Mansion, Carey Woodson, who frequently perched behind the figure to get a better view of the guests without being seen.

Like children of the Mansion before and after her, Caroline did not always meet adult expectations. "I was anything but an ideal child under the circumstances. When meeting people, I frequently ducked my head, much to Mother's embarrassment. This habit, I found, was my only defense against receiving lines."

Caroline hid her candy in the base of the old clock.

pitcher, and serving trays. Her visit with the incoming First Lady gave her the opportunity to give Nelle Baker some household tips. She proudly announced to her successor that the house had been "thoroughly gone over" except for the roof.

On their final day in Jefferson City, the Hydes drove down the hill to the railroad station below the Mansion, boarded the train, and headed back to Trenton. About seventy-five friends waved hats and handkerchiefs as the former Governor waved from the rear platform until the train rolled out of sight.

With his departure from the governorship, more challenges awaited Arthur Hyde. He resumed practicing law in Trenton and in Kansas City and became president of the Sentinel Life Insurance Company. In 1928 he gave some thought to running for the U.S. Senate, but by then his prohibitionist stance was even more of a political handicap.

> "I cannot change my views. . . . the senatorship is not worth the price."

Hyde announced, "I cannot change my views. . . . the senatorship is not worth the price." He went on to declare that "straddling [the prohibition issue] is equally abhorrent . . . in that it attempts to deceive." Instead of seeking elective office, Hyde accepted President Herbert Hoover's offer to serve as Secretary of Agriculture for the next four years.

In 1932 he hit the campaign trail for Hoover in what turned out to be a devastating defeat for the President as well as Republicans nationwide. Again in 1936 and 1938 he toured the nation on behalf of the GOP. Hyde bitterly attacked the New Deal and its proponents, especially Missouri's U.S. Senator James A. Reed and President Franklin D. Roosevelt. In 1940 he called Roosevelt the "Third Termite" and expressed alarm that Communists might infiltrate the federal government. He also claimed that FDR was using the threat of war in Europe "to cover up eight years of folly and failure."

Once out of the political limelight, Hyde retreated to the solace of his north Missouri home. In 1941 the couple suffered a personal tragedy when fire destroyed their nine-room residence in Trenton. The Hydes, scantily dressed, escaped by crawling through a window before the roof and floors collapsed. With the onset of World War II, they delayed rebuilding. Plans were underway for construction in 1947 when Hyde became ill and died following two operations for cancer. Though his wife completed the home just as the two of them had planned, she later moved to St. Croix, Virgin Islands, to live with their daughter, Caroline.

Like her parents, Caroline held fond memories of their years in the Capital City. When she heard that the "castle on the hill"—the home she revered as a child—was unfit to live in and might be torn down, it angered her. After all those years, she declared, "I love every brick in it. . . . scars and all."

Former Governor Hyde accepted President Hoover's offer to serve as Secretary of Agriculture.

PEACE AND PROSPERITY

Charles Lindbergh and
The Spirit of St. Louis

GOVERNOR SAMUEL AARON BAKER
NELLE TUCKLEY BAKER
1925-1929

It was the Roaring Twenties—an era that prompted new feats of daring and flamboyance in America.

Most Missourians felt quite happy and prosperous in 1924. It was the Roaring Twenties—an era that prompted new feats of daring and flamboyance in America. Even the new First Lady decided to be a bit bold at her husband's inauguration. In keeping with the trend toward rising hemlines, Nelle Baker wore a fashionable rhinestone-encrusted evening gown that exposed her ankles.

Republicans had every reason to feel confident as they gathered in Jefferson City to celebrate the governorship they had nearly lost. Incoming Governor Sam Baker had run far behind the other GOP candidates for state office, but he still defeated Democratic nominee Dr. Arthur W. Nelson by 5,872 votes. Though the margin was narrow, it was victory, nonetheless.

Improved transportation and greater personal affluence contributed to a record turnout for Baker's inauguration. One Capital City newspaper headlined the gathering as "the greatest throng in state history." Helping to swell the crowd were local students, freed from school that day to view the new Governor who once served as their superintendent.

At the Capitol, the House of Representatives was packed hours before the swearing-in ceremony. The band played "Hail to the Chief" as Baker's newly appointed and brightly uniformed colonels marched into the chamber and lined the back

(Left) At the inaugural ball, Mrs. Baker wore a fashionable, rhinestone-encrusted gown that exposed her ankles.

For the first time in history, Missourians heard the inaugural address across the airwaves.

walls. Following closely behind was the Governor-elect whose entrance drew excited cheers from the crowd. As he took the oath of office, Baker's only child, fourteen-year-old Mary Elizabeth, held the Bible—a gift from his mother when he had left home years earlier.

For the first time in the state's history, Missourians heard the inaugural address across the airwaves, with an estimated 75,000 people tuning in on home radios. Staunch supporters, however, wanted to savor the fruits of victory personally. Thousands lined up outside the Mansion, waiting an hour or more for the chance to greet the new First Family.

Nelle had hoped to have the inaugural ball at the Mansion that evening, but after examining the aging stairway, state architects cautioned against it. They convinced her—as they had the previous First Lady—to hold the gathering in the Capitol rotunda. Even in the more spacious area, crowding forced couples to move into the wings and the upper floors of the building to find room for dancing.

The Bakers found the transition to the Mansion less complicated than had most first families. Nelle was a native of Jefferson City and they lived there while Sam progressed from high school principal, to city school superintendent, to state superintendent. Both were already active in the community: Nelle participated in women's clubs and Sam served as an elder and president of the men's Bible class at the Presbyterian church. "We had the advantage, because of our long residence in the Capital City, of knowing something of the customs followed and, in slight measure, something of what was expected of us as occupants of the Executive Mansion," Nelle recalled.

Even in the Mansion, life would not be easy; it never had been for Sam Baker. He had come up the hard way, doing menial tasks as a hired hand around

The Bakers enjoyed a quiet life enriched by their love for books and music.

farms, lumber yards, and railways before moving on to jobs clerking in a drugstore and in a post office. From his earnings, he set aside one hundred dollars for a trip to Colorado, but Baker's mother insisted that he spend the money on his education.

Taking her advice, he enrolled in college with the intention of following in the footsteps of his father, a doctor who died before Sam was born. By using his savings and by working part-time, he paid his tuition and expenses while attending the State Teacher's College at Cape Girardeau. Later, an offer of thirty-five dollars a month lured him into teaching in a rural community, far away from his medical pursuits.

By the time Sam married Nelle, he was the high school principal in Jefferson City and she was a stenographer for the Missouri Supreme Court. After their marriage, the home-loving couple remained in the Capital City, living in a modest apartment where they enjoyed a quiet life enriched by their love for books and music.

Sam's first venture into politics came in 1918 when he won a statewide race for superintendent of schools—a position which, at the time, was elective. Four years later, he lost his reelection bid by 6,000 votes. It was close enough to entice Republicans in search of a gubernatorial candidate to pick him as their 1924 standard-bearer. As a bonus, they got Nelle, who was capable and willing to do some of the clerical jobs, involved in her husband's campaign. Party regulars were pleased with the demeanor of their new candidate. "Common as an old shoe," wrote the *Missouri Ruralist,* a farm newspaper that heartily endorsed Baker for the state's highest post.

With the surge in Sam's political fortunes, the Bakers sold their household goods at public auction and prepared for life on a grander scale. Nelle described her feelings as "mingled joy and reluctance." She did not expect her life at the Mansion to be entirely a "bed of roses," but it was more demanding than she anticipated. To make matters worse, she was left on her own after two months; Barbara Pohlman, the housekeeper who had served the last four governors, quit because of a family illness. Although the First Lady preferred not to use prison labor, except for yard work, she occasionally involved them in housecleaning out of necessity.

Sam soon found that state government was no bed of roses either. Six months into his term, he indicated some weariness with the demands of public office and let it be known that he planned to stay home for the Fourth of July—even though he had received a dozen invitations to speak. Having attended holiday celebrations for six consecutive

The Mansion is no "bed of roses."

years, he declared, "I'm thoroughly patriotic [but] . . . I would like to spend one Independence Day at home with my family and intend to this year."

Baker also learned to say no to other demands, particularly those coming from department heads or the Democratic-dominated Senate. When one of his cabinet members complained about not having enough funds to carry on the work of his department, Baker admonished him, "Fire half your employees, make the rest do the work formerly done by the whole staff and then you will keep within what your department should be run on."

Legislators showed the same toughness toward the Governor. They rejected his plan to abolish unnecessary boards and to end deficit spending. They turned down his proposal to consolidate school districts, which would have meant an expanded curriculum for rural students at less cost. Baker's call for a permanent school fund supported by inheritance, tobacco, and amusement taxes was likewise ignored. Though the state fell far below the national average in per-pupil support of education—and had since 1910—lawmakers continued reducing the percentage of school support during the next decade.

"Any Missouri homemaker, although delighted that she need not live in the Mansion, may envy the governor's wife this one thing only—the fact that living there means having all the blossoms a flower-loving woman could desire."

~Nelle Baker

Though the legislature thwarted much of his program, Baker chalked up a few victories. He secured new banking regulations and continued the road building program of his predecessor. His success in the passage of a workers' compensation law "climaxed a fifteen-year struggle between labor and employer groups."

While the Governor dealt with the state's problems, his wife faced her own troubles with the fifty-four-year-old Mansion. In 1926 when she wanted to hold the traditional military ball, state engineers again thwarted her plans. Cracking plaster and sagging supports under the elegant, spiraling stairway made it unsafe for large gatherings. According to inspectors, neither the main staircase nor the backstairs could withstand the overloading. Once again, Mrs. Baker was forced to move a traditional Mansion event to the Capitol rotunda and to settle for a small afternoon reception at the house.

The condition of the Mansion did not prevent the First Lady from hosting the usual legislative dinners and gatherings of the press corp. She also continued the "at home" teas for the ladies, meetings of the local music club, and the colonial tea for the Daughters of the American Revolution. Occasionally she capped off an evening at the Mansion with something as simple and pleasant as group singing.

Some of the Baker's close friends took the First Lady seriously when she lightly issued an invitation for them "to use the Mansion if any important social events should come their way." In spite of the rickety staircase, Mrs. Baker made good on her promise by hosting two weddings. The Bakers later celebrated their own nuptials. The local Knights of Pythias chapter helped commemorate the couple's twenty-second wedding anniversary by presenting them with a silver flower basket during a buffet dinner at the Mansion.

In 1926 Baker provided President Calvin Coolidge with a Missouri turkey for the White House Thanksgiving dinner.

A dutiful hostess, Nelle did her best to fulfill the many demands made of her, but she found it strange that dinner guests often treated the home like a restaurant. She recalled one man who asked to be served buttermilk, then became upset when the special order did not appear promptly.

In spite of such annoyances, Mrs. Baker often allowed organizations to use the Mansion for fund-raising events. She would not permit ticket selling at the door, though she compromised her policy at least once. When the War Mothers wanted to sell tickets for twenty-five cents each for their annual tea and bazaar, she could not refuse such a worthy cause.

The First Couple also entertained a variety of guests, including evangelist Charles R. Scoville and Sophie Loeb, a noted writer and social worker. In Kansas City, the Bakers welcomed two high-ranking visitors on the same day, President and Mrs. Coolidge and Queen Marie of Romania. Coolidge had spoken at an Armistice Day event just before the Queen arrived to attend the

THE MILITARY BALL
The Oldest and Most Colorful of State Functions

The gala event known as the Military Ball goes back to the early 1800s when territorial Governor Meriwether Lewis celebrated the formation of the state militia, a forerunner of the Missouri National Guard. For the occasion, Lewis invited officers of the guard and the U.S. Army to his St. Louis office where an improvised dance floor was set up. Though the event was dropped during the War of 1812, it was revived nine years later with the admission of Missouri to the Union. The ball continued each year thereafter, except when the guard was on duty outside the state.

With the construction of the current executive residence in 1871, the event became more elegant. The Mansion—festooned with patriotic bunting and flags—opened its doors to the finely dressed ladies and their military escorts. A fine stairway and spacious rooms provided a grand stage for the colorful event attended by state officials, supreme court judges, military personnel, and civilians. Stepping briskly to the military tunes, each couple was properly announced as they descended the graceful, curving stairs. In 1926, however, the event passed to the Capitol rotunda after engineers warned Nelle Baker that both the front and back stairs of the aging Mansion were unsafe.

In later years, the military gathering was held intermittently, but was most often observed on, or near, New Years' Day. First Lady Jean Carnahan reactivated the military observance in January 1994 to honor National Guard personnel who fought the devastating floods the previous summer.

American Royal horse show. In 1926 the President had another "taste" of Missouri when the Governor provided a twenty-four-pound Missouri turkey for the Thanksgiving Day table at the White House.

The next year Missouri had more to boast about than its poultry. In 1927 the pride of the state was the twenty-five-year-old Charles Lindbergh Jr. The young aviator thrilled the world with the first solo nonstop transatlantic flight from New York to Paris in thirty-three hours and twenty-nine minutes. Once called the "Flying Fool," Lindbergh was now romanticized as the "Lone Eagle," given the Medal of Honor, and further popularized by having a new dance, the Lindy Hop, named for him. In St. Louis he was paraded in an open car through the flag-draped streets of his adopted home city. The Baker family joined the celebration during which the Governor officially commissioned Lindbergh a colonel in the Missouri National Guard.

Charles Lindbergh, paraded in an open car through the flag-draped streets of St. Louis, was commissioned by Governor Baker.

While admiring the flying exploits of others, the Governor much preferred ground travel and made only one brief air trip himself. His adventuresome daughter, Mary Elizabeth, made several flights, one of which set a record time of fifty-five minutes between St. Louis and the Capital City. By midterm, however, Baker upgraded his transportation by trading in his blue Buick for a big brown Cadillac that cost nearly $5,000.

With little interest in either cars or planes, the First Lady worked on making the Mansion more livable. She completely renovated the third-floor ballroom—an area seldom used because the long, narrow back stairway limited its access. In the dining room, a window was replaced with French doors, allowing direct access to the back porch. A second-floor bedroom was also opened to the sleeping porch with the addition of doors. Mrs. Baker selected new china and crystal, and twice decorated the parlors. The exterior of the house was refreshed with another coat of red paint in an attempt to cover the original soot-stained brick.

In spite of her success as hostess and decorator, Nelle Baker regretted that she could not complete all she set out to do. "I had hoped to obtain portraits of all of the first ladies who had occupied the historic Mansion, but this task remains unfinished," she wrote regretfully.

Nor had Governor Baker done all he proposed for the state. Before the end of his term, he developed diabetes and his health began to decline, making it even less likely that he would reach his goals. Some said that Baker's conflicts with party leaders—much of it over his political appointments—took a toll on him physically. Nonetheless, in 1928 Missouri Republican leaders ignored their irritations and gave him a token endorsement for the vice presidency.

Baker's conflict with party leaders took a toll on him physically.

When it came time to leave the Mansion, Nelle extended the traditional courtesies to the incoming First Lady. In contrast to Nelle Baker who had grown up in the Capital City, Mrs. Caulfield had never been to the Mansion. To ease the transition, Mrs. Baker and Mary Elizabeth hosted a reception for Mrs. Caulfield, giving her a chance to meet the women of Jefferson City.

But there was no way to prepare the next family for what lay ahead. During Governor Caulfield's term, the nation would be plunged into the Great Depression, an era that would leave its mark on the nation and public policy for decades to come.

Tragedy would soon visit the outgoing Governor. Within a few months after leaving office, Baker suffered a stroke that left him an invalid. He died four years later in Jefferson City; his wife continued to live with their unmarried daughter and died in 1966.

Sam Baker's record of pubic service remains a tribute to the hired hand who rose to the governorship. In the countless commencement addresses that he delivered throughout his life, he encouraged young people to selflessness, "The world does not owe you a living, but you do owe the world a life." Reminders of the Governor's life of service are still evident in the names of several state facilities, including the six-thousand-acre Sam A. Baker State Park in Wayne County near his birthplace.

In this 1955 photo, the Bakers' daughter, Mary Elizabeth, unveils a plaque in the Sam A. Baker State Park commemorating her father.

The Sam A. Baker State Park in Wayne County near the Governor's birthplace.

197

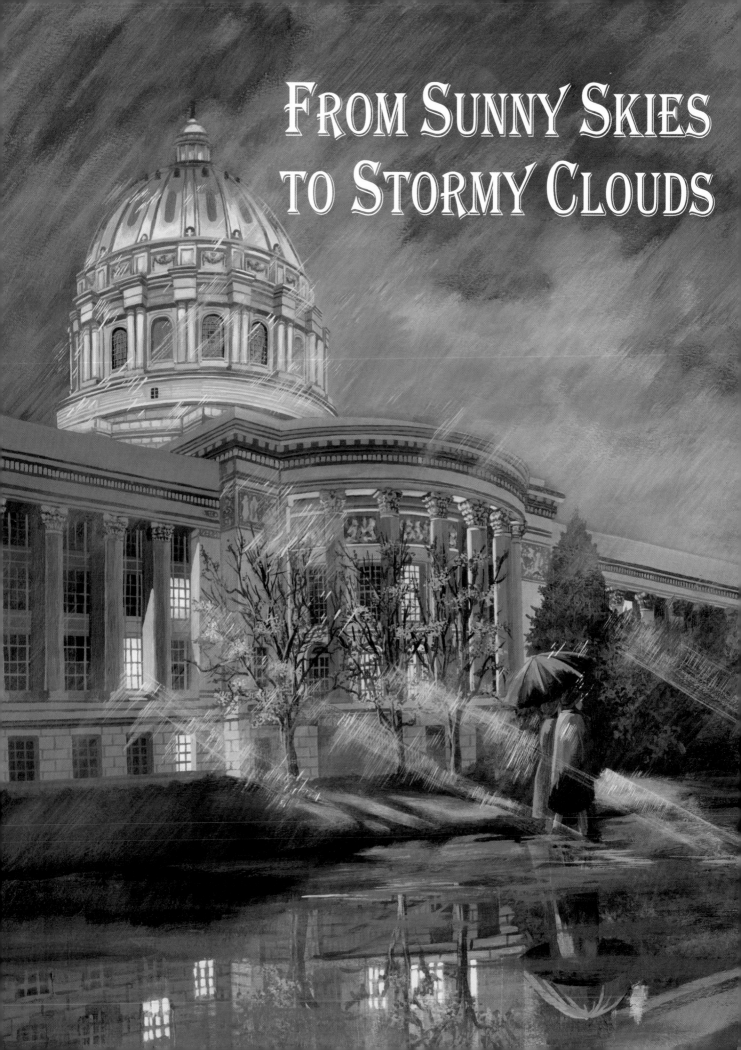

FROM SUNNY SKIES TO STORMY CLOUDS

GOVERNOR HENRY STEWART CAULFIELD
FRANCES "FANNIE" DELANO CAULFIELD
1929-1933

Caulfield lived to be ninety-two years old, long enough to see his optimism rewarded by the return of his party to state and national office.

As the wife of the Republican nominee for governor, Fannie Caulfield accompanied her husband around the state, taking a far more visible role in campaigning than had any previous Missouri first lady. She called the joint political venture a "very strenuous and grueling experience."

"We traveled incessantly," she wrote in her diary, "sometimes by train, but usually by automobile. My husband spoke several times a day, often in the county courthouse, but sometimes outside on a truck or an improvised platform; sometimes he stood on the sidewalk and addressed the people."

After months of such campaigning, family and friends gathered at the Caulfield home in St. Louis to await the outcome of the election. The family had a radio brought in for the evening so they could get the returns more quickly. The early numbers looked bad. About 3 a.m., the ladies decided to retire, but the men stayed up until morning, tabulating returns and taking phone messages from voting precincts around the state.

Despite early concerns, the final count put Caulfield over the top. The next day, when victory was assured, well-wishers inundated the house with flowers. "I feel like a debutante," Mrs. Caulfield wrote to her son, John, describing the day following the election. "Lovely roses and shaggy brilliant chrysanthemums are filling every vase."

On a somewhat sadder note, Henry Caulfield's victory meant that the couple would be leaving St. Louis where they had resided much of their married life. He had graduated from Washington University Law School in 1895 and married his first wife two years later. Following her death after a year of marriage, he had wed Fannie Delano—a school teacher, excellent swimmer, and horsewoman. She and Henry shared an unusual fondness for walking in the rain, a pastime they came to enjoy in the nation's capital during his one congressional term.

The Caulfields shared an unusual fondness for walking in the rain.

(Facing page)
The Missouri State
Capitol.

199

THE REPUBLICAN TIDE OF 1928

"Two chickens in every pot and a car in every garage."

Republicans had little to fear in 1928; their popular candidate, Herbert Hoover, led the ticket. Democrats, on the other hand, daringly nominated America's first Roman Catholic presidential candidate, Al Smith—a move that did not set well with heartland conservatives.

Not only were Democrats accused of advocating "Romanism," but one radio evangelist further denounced the party, saying it stood for "card playing, cocktail drinking, poodle dogs, divorces, novels, stuffy rooms, dancing, evolution, Clarence Darrow, overeating, nude art, prize-fighting, actors, greyhound racing, and modernism."

Humorist Will Rogers declared the Democrats had an additional liability—one that was far more damaging to their prospects—the economy was booming. "You can't lick this prosperity thing," Rogers told his audiences.

Hoover further boomed the good times, pledging "two chickens in every pot and a car in every garage."

Republican presidential candidate Herbert Hoover.

Humorist Will Rogers told his audiences, "You can't lick this prosperity thing."

Still, Missouri's GOP candidate for governor, Henry Caulfield, took no chances; he waged a vigorous stump-speaking campaign all across the state. It was fortunate for Caulfield that he did so, since Hoover backers gave little support to the state ticket. In an attempt to attract Democrats and independent voters, practical-minded Republicans urged people to "scratch" their ballot—that is, to vote for Herbert Hoover and then switch back to Democratic state and local candidates.

The strategy cut into Caulfield's margin of victory, giving Hoover 75,000 to 120,000 more votes than the other Republicans running statewide. As a result, Herbert Hoover carried the state by more votes than any previous presidential candidate. Those who savored the victory of 1928—the third in a row for Missouri's GOP—had no way of knowing how bleak the future would be for their party. During the next forty-five years, only one other Republican would lead the state.

However, in 1928 the skies appeared cloudless for Caulfield and the Republican Party. GOP nominees had won all the top races as well as the state House. With Herbert Hoover on his way to the White House and Henry Caulfield headed for the Governor's Mansion, sunny skies prevailed.

The new First Family arrived in Jefferson City filled with enthusiasm, but with little knowledge of the Capital City and its workings. Never having been to the Mansion, Mrs. Caulfield welcomed First Lady Nelle Baker's advice about living in the old house.

After conferring with Mrs. Baker and state engineers, Fannie Caulfield felt it was unsafe once again to hold the inaugural reception at the Mansion. Fearful that the winding stairway could not handle the stress of the expected crowd, she agreed to move the traditional event to the Capitol. (Apparently, the faulty stairway noted eight years earlier still had not been satisfactorily repaired.)

As plans got underway for the inauguration, Henry Caulfield made only one request: he wanted the pomp kept to a minimum, saying he preferred a display of "true Missouri simplicity" instead of the usual fanfare. The Governor got his wish for true Missouri simplicity and along with it some true Missouri weather. Though sleet and ice blanketed the state, three thousand people attended the inaugural ceremony, more than enough to fill the rotunda and corridors of the first and second floors of the Capitol. Just

The new Governor wanted all pomp kept to a minimum.

before noon, lawmakers assembled in their chambers and then marched as a body to the rotunda. Awaiting them were the Missouri colonels who lined the arched stairway leading to the executive office.

In accord with the Governor's call for simplicity, the blue uniforms of the colonels—devoid of the usual gold braiding—appeared less flamboyant than usual. Caulfield, however, kept the tradition of wearing a black morning coat and pin-striped pants.

A bugle sounded the beginning of the inaugural ceremony as the Governor-elect took his place on the second-floor landing overlooking the rotunda. With his hand upon a Bible held by his youngest daughter, fifteen-year-old Jane, Caulfield repeated the oath to uphold the Constitution of the state and nation, just as all governors before him had pledged. Amid flashing bulbs and grinding movie cameras, the Caulfields, along with the Bakers, marched off to the Mansion accompanied by the colonels and a military band.

That evening, friends and supporters dressed in gala attire filed through the executive reception room of the Capitol to congratulate the First Couple. Having formally greeted their new Governor, guests continued on to the rotunda to vie for a place on the crowded dance floor. Like most of the ladies, Mrs. Caulfield wore a fine, new ball gown for the occasion. But former First Lady Nelle Baker wore the gown from her husband's inauguration four years earlier—a custom started by Mrs. Gardner and continued by Mrs. Hyde.

That evening ice-slick roads kept many from returning home, among them Caulfield's oldest daughter, Elizabeth Barksdale, and her husband. The couple, expecting the birth of their first child, was eager to drive back to St. Louis. With no more tire chains to be found in Jefferson City, they waited for a set to arrive by train the next morning. The Barksdales arrived home with little time to spare. The following day, Elizabeth gave birth to Henry Caulfield Barksdale, the Governor's first grandchild and namesake.

Of the Caulfields' other three children, Frances was married, John was a student at Amherst College, and Jane was away at boarding school much of the time. Since there were no youngsters to play about the roomy old house each day, the Caulfields seemed all the more delighted with visits by their grandsons—first Henry, who was joined two years later by a baby brother, Clarence "Cedgie" Barksdale.

Even without children, the house was far from empty. Several servants lived on the third floor. Fannie's mother, Mrs. Maude Delano, moved in and stayed for a few months before her death at the Mansion. Another occupant not to be overlooked was Skippy, the wire-haired terrier whose bark frequently broke the stillness of the immense rooms.

As Mrs. Caulfield settled into the Mansion, she began exploring all the nooks and crannies of the old house. The mansard-roofed building was a sharp contrast to the family's small, unpretentious home in St. Louis. She marveled at the size of the seven bedrooms on the second floor. The gold-leaf parlor chairs with the rose-brocade covers reminded her of furnishings from a splendid French palace. As she looked from an east bedroom, she could see the old iron fountain and its goldfish pool in the front yard. Peering through the bare tree branches toward the Missouri River that first winter, she often caught a glimpse of huge chunks of ice drifting downstream.

"It is so easy here . . . I have only to see a thing needs mending and say I want it fixed and it is fixed. I hope I do not let it spoil me for regular life. ~ Fannie Caulfield

Mrs. Caulfield likened her new life at the Mansion to a "fairyland [where] things I want come so easily." After walking about the lawn one morning, she commented to one of the yardmen, "We ought to have a couple of stepping stones at the foot of the porch." That afternoon when she passed the porch, workers had already embedded stones in the grass, just as she suggested.

But managing the household expenses was more difficult for the First Lady.

Skippy, the wire-haired terrier, performs his tricks for the Governor.

Groceries often came to as much as sixty dollars a week—not including meat and milk. Her need for a more extensive wardrobe also made personal expenses high. Though she felt the costs of living in the Mansion were "pretty big," she was pleased with the prices at the local hairdresser where she could get a "fingerwave and a shampoo—all for $1.00."

Her new lifestyle also required some physical adjustments. Though she adored the "winding floating stairway" of the Mansion, she admitted, "the first few days I was there, I got very tired and stiff from going up and down those long, circular stairs." Adding an elevator seemed like the solution, "not just for myself, but for the many people who found the climb too strenuous," she said. Fannie eventually gave up the idea, saying it was simply "too high for the Governor's budget."

Although her husband had to climb the stairs at the Mansion, he fared better at the Capitol where it was customary for the chief executive to use the elevator whenever he wanted it. Previous governors had a special signal—two short and one long rings—that alerted the elevator operator to clear the car of passengers and proceed, without stops, to pick up the governor. Caulfield disliked the special privilege and abandoned the system, saying he preferred to "take his chances on the elevator the same as any other citizen."

The Ford Trimotor, or "Tin Goose," could fly the Governor from St. Louis to the Capitol in ninety minutes.

The Governor also shunned the idea of taking a pay raise. He told legislators that he did not favor a bill before the General Assembly to raise his annual salary from $5,000 to $8,000—plus another $3,000 for his service on boards and commissions. The Caulfields felt that they already had a number of extra benefits just by living at the Mansion: the state covered the cost of utilities, maintenance, servants, entertainment, and travel, including a car and chauffeur—although Caulfield paid the family's food bill.

The Governor indulged in one extravagance of the time, however. He enjoyed flying and once invited a group of newsmen and state officeholders to join him for a view of the Capitol from the Ford Company's giant trimotor plane. One of his trips from St. Louis was aboard the "Golden Shell," another trimotor plane owned by the Shell Oil Company. The ninety-minute trip must have excited the Governor for more air travel because, upon touching down in Jefferson City, he took off on another flight. This time he was joined by his wife, daughter, and former First Lady Agnes Hadley for a ride in a Goodyear blimp. Caulfield called flying the "ideal mode of transportation." However, when the Missouri National Guard offered to assign him a plane and pilot, he had second thoughts and declined.

Caulfield indulged in one extravagance of the time—air travel.

The Caulfields fared better in the air than they did motoring about the state. Twice the Governor was in minor auto accidents. Once his car went out of control and into a ditch, and another time he received cuts and bruises from being jostled about in his vehicle while traveling over a patch of rough pavement. The First Lady had car troubles of another sort. On her way to a Board of Charities meeting, her chauffeur was stopped for going fifty-eight miles an hour—thirty-eight miles an hour over the posted speed limit.

Mrs. Caulfield dutifully paid the $7.50 fine and, along with it, suffered the embarrassment of having the incident reported in the newspapers.

Fannie Caulfield kept a fast pace at the Mansion, too, filling her social calendar with garden parties, dinners, receptions, luncheons, and "at home" teas. The Governor entertained lawmakers at stag dinners for thirty to forty because it was a number that was easy to manage. To accommodate the guests, she used trestles and planks to create a long, formal table stretching the length of the dining room. On such occasions, the First Lady planned a menu of either chicken or steak. But with only twenty-three high-backed dining chairs on hand, she had to make do with the addition of folding chairs. While her husband entertained politicians in the main dining room, she invited several ladies to eat with her in the second-floor quarters. Fannie's charm as a hostess came in handy for the Governor during the final days of his first legislative session. When the Governor's programs started to falter, Caulfield feared he had been "neglecting the legislators" and called on Fannie to "do something quickly" at the Mansion to help him win support.

> Caulfield called on his wife to "do something quickly" at the Mansion to help him win legislative support.

The First Lady not only extended the Mansion's hospitality to lawmakers but also to newsmen, clubs, schools, and former first ladies—four of them on one day. After one reception in which the numbers unexpectedly ran to nearly four hundred guests, she recalled, "I spent my time shaking hands and saying 'how do you do' to seas of faces." Fortunately, she could pick up names easily and did well in receiving lines at recalling those she had met previously.

Even her grandest dinner parties could not rival the colonial ball sponsored by the Daughters of the American Revolution. The splendidly costumed ladies drifted gracefully up and down the Grand Stairway, flaunting their billowing skirts much like the guests of a bygone era. In spite of the many requests to use the Mansion for large affairs sponsored by outside groups, she permitted functions only when either she or the Governor could be present, but never let it be used for fund-raising.

Her most elegant—and demanding—social events were those given in honor of a high-ranking dignitary visiting the state. According to Mrs. Caulfield, entertaining foreign VIPs at the Mansion called for proper ceremony tempered with traditional Missouri hospitality. She and her staff spent considerable time fretting over the preparations for the visit of the Mexican and Japanese ambassadors—both participants in Journalism Week at the University of Missouri. Dining protocol was finally resolved by a call to the U.S. State Department. A seating chart for the event shows that the ambassadors sat on each side of the First Lady and the ambassadors' wives sat on either side of the Governor.

Mrs. Caulfield also worried over the pros and cons of offering a prayer before the meal, but the Governor argued that, as "a Christian people and state," it was appropriate and invited a local minister to provide a short blessing. The "talkative and jolly" Japanese ambassador noted that a prayer preceded every meal he attended in Missouri, but no such observance was made in Washington, Boston, or New York. Apparently approving the midwestern practice, he added graciously, "It is good."

Fannie took a liking to the Japanese ambassador's wife who appeared "so tiny and gentle and courteous." The First Lady treated her foreign guests to a formal American meal. The unusual breakfast menu—a treat to the American palate, but not likely to the Japanese—consisted of grapefruit supreme, chicken a la king on toast, fresh peas in carrot baskets, new potatoes with Hollandaise sauce, Parker House rolls, and strawberry ice cream and cake.

While the Japanese dignitary admired the dining room tapestry and compared the Mansion favorably to the White House, he showed little appreciation of Missouri's landscape. It was early May and the hillsides were not yet in bloom. Looking from a window, the ambassador commented on the bleakness of the countryside, telling the Governor, in all seriousness, that he should do something to correct the condition.

The "talkative and jolly" Japanese ambassador noted that a prayer preceded every meal he attended in Missouri, but none was offered at functions on the East Coast.

"The governor is like a little king."

When Caulfield explained the role of governor in the United States, the ambassador shook his head as if he understood. "Ah, yes," he said, "the governor is like a little king."

As residents of the Mansion, the Caulfields could direct some landscaping improvements—much of it performed by convict labor. Four or five prisoners came twice a week to clean, repair, and do any yard work or painting that was needed. "An armed guard was always with them. They were taken back to the prison for their meals and were not allowed to address me," Mrs. Caulfield recalled. "They were well-behaved as a rule. I remember, however, that one prisoner casually picked up our chauffeur's overcoat and ran down the hill, hopped a moving freight train and was soon out of town. He was eventually brought back, however."

The bulk of the housework was not done by inmates, but by live-in servants employed by the state. The First Lady herself managed the daily routine rather than hire a housekeeper to oversee the tasks. "The kitchen was in the basement, a floor below the dining and drawing rooms, and one of the duties I took upon

Inmate workers at the Mansion "were not allowed to address me."

myself was going each morning down the dark and uncomfortable stairs into the huge, low kitchen to discuss the menu with the calm black woman who cooked our meals," she explained. The cook made an especially tasty biscuit using the beaten biscuit machine—a device highly prized by the state's first ladies and often mentioned in their description of the kitchen.

It might have been the biscuits that precipitated the need for Mrs. Caulfield to put her husband on a strict diet. The Governor, who did not like having limits placed on his favorite foods, was not cooperative. Each evening around six o'clock, he would walk to a nearby drugstore and order an egg-malted milk at the soda fountain before going to the Mansion for his diet meal. Even so, Caulfield managed to shed twenty pounds.

In addition to "remodeling" her husband, the First Lady took on the task of shaping up the Mansion. In the basement kitchen, she replaced the old wood stove with

The old summerhouse was an ideal place to catch a breeze from the river in the days before air conditioning came to the Mansion.

an electric model, removed the icebox in favor of a refrigerator, and substituted a new washer for the one with the worn mangles. In the private quarters, she hung wallpaper, added curtains and slipcovers to the bedrooms, and transformed her closet into a small bathroom.

The Governor was especially pleased with his wife's improvements to the third floor. After she put a new felt cover on the old billiard table, the upper room became a favorite haunt for Henry and his friends. Even Fannie took up playing pool. The Governor wrote his daughter saying that her mother enjoyed the new game, but did not indicate the level of her skill.

Next on Mrs. Caulfield's list were exterior improvements. The old summerhouse with the Japanese-style roof had been moved from the south lawn some years earlier. Though it sat on a beautiful site overlooking the river, in recent years it had been used only as a chicken coop. With a coat of pea-green paint and some white wooden tables and chairs, it became the perfect place for eating breakfast while watching "the mist rise from the willows across the river." The First Lady also laid a rock patio under one of the trees on the lawn and placed stone steps along the river terraces. She grouped lawn furniture to form "cozy corners" where guests could enjoy tea, much as Mansion visitors had done a decade earlier. The lawn swing looked all the more inviting nestled beside colorful iris that Mrs. Caulfield had brought from her home in St. Louis and planted amid the larkspur and sweet william. Despite the many improvements she made to the Mansion, Mrs. Caulfield admitted that "there is always something more to do here."

Fannie combined her duties as First Lady with her fondness of writing. Several of her articles featured in the *Missouri Ruralist* magazine gave a glimpse of Mansion life. In one column, she described a typical schedule for her and the Governor. Their day began at seven o'clock with a wake-up bell, she wrote. The Governor got up first and performed his exercise routine before the two of them dressed for the day. Together they

"There is always something more to do here at the Mansion."

walked down the curving staircase to the Nook below the steps where they read the morning newspaper until breakfast was served between eight and nine o'clock. Afterwards Caulfield, an inveterate smoker, enjoyed his favorite pipe before heading to the office. During the noon hour, he returned to the Mansion where he had lunch and read more newspapers before returning to the Capitol.

The First Lady spent much of her time planning menus, marketing, and maintaining an active correspondence with family and friends. Occasionally her husband returned to the Mansion before the end of the workday. Mrs. Caulfield explained the routine to her readers: "When the Governor is trying to be very quiet and work on a speech without interruption, he comes over to the Mansion. There are so many big rooms that he can always find a quiet spot."

Fannie provided further protection to her husband by sorting through any critical or anonymous letters delivered to the Mansion. Disposing of the harsh complaints, she declared, "No one but the [waste]basket and I are the wiser." The First Lady also found time for her own pursuits, such as adding to her collection of old maps—a hobby she had acquired from her father. Among the items were many rare pieces, ranging from aviation charts to drawings of treasure islands.

Unfortunately, there were no maps to warn of the perils ahead for the state and nation in 1929. That summer, Caulfield was radiant with confidence. He eagerly anticipated the report of his survey commission that was charged with exploring the conditions and needs of state facilities. Using their recommendations, Caulfield hoped to lay the foundation for the next decade. At the state fair he spoke of Missouri's bright prospects, telling visitors that the coming years would bring great "commercialism, speed and industrialism." The Governor went on to describe the wonderful signs of advancement, drawing special attention to the shortwave radio, electricity, and air and sea travel.

However, several months after his speech, the soaring hopes of the 1920s suddenly vanished in the stock market crash of October 1929. Financial shock waves reverberated across the country, plunging the nation into a prolonged and unprecedented depression. People once fascinated by progress were now more concerned about jobs, drought relief, old-age assistance, and simple survival.

As the depression deepened, factories and banks closed their doors and families lost their savings, homes, and land. Long breadlines formed in St. Louis where 34 percent of the workers were without jobs. The Governor apparently failed to grasp the magnitude of the situation. He waited over a year before implementing the direct relief and old-age assistance urged by President Hoover. In the meanwhile, Caulfield—once described as "the least politically inclined governor" of the twentieth century—reduced appropriations and salaries, and undertook a limited public works program. But he offered no widespread relief, preferring to keep the responsibility for welfare at the local level.

In the fall of 1931, Caulfield made another rosy assessment of the economic situation. He announced to President Hoover that Missouri would be self-sustaining during the upcoming winter. To help make that goal possible,

The state and nation were plunged into a prolonged and unprecedented depression and soup lines became familiar scenes along city streets.

VARIETY

PRICE 25¢.

VOL. XCVII. No. 3

Published Weekly at 154 West 46th St., New York, N. Y., by Variety, Inc. Entered as second-class matter December 22, 1905, at the Post Office at New York, N. Y. under the act of March 3, 1879. Annual subscription, $10. Single copies, 25 cents.

NEW YORK, WEDNESDAY, OCTOBER 30, 1929

88 PAGES

WALL ST. LAYS AN EGG

Going Dumb Is Deadly to Hostess In Her Serious Dance Hall Profesh

DROP IN STOCKS ROPES SHOWMEN

Kidding Kissers in Talkers Burns Up Fans of Screen's

The first Missouri Highway Patrol car, a Ford Model-A.

he urged housewives to do more canning and to keep potatoes, turnips, and apples in their cellars.

Reluctant to apply for federal loans, the Governor continued his Band-Aid treatment of the state's gaping economic wounds. By early 1932, however, with over 115,000 Missourians unemployed, he had no choice but to seek aid from Washington. Even then, it was late that year before federal funds made the first general relief program available statewide. Frustrated by the inadequate response, Missourians turned control of the legislature back to the Democrats during the midterm election.

In addition to the woes inflicted on Missouri families, the crippled economy stymied Caulfield's long-range plans for the state. Though his survey report was temporarily shelved, its findings were, nonetheless, useful. The investigation of the state penitentiary revealed a deteriorating facility and 4,200 inmates housed in space designed for 2,500. Reform schools, sanitariums, and mental institutions were also in poor shape. Although Missouri ranked fifteenth in support of education nationwide, the commission uncovered gross inequalities in the school system. Because the commission's report coincided with the Wall Street panic, much of its impact was lost. Caulfield, however, was convinced of its value and pushed for the graduated state income tax recommended by the study.

Although the Governor secured only a small tax increase, it was enough to fashion some improvements in state services. He launched a statewide park system and accelerated the ten-year road building program to near completion. With the widespread use of the automobile came the need for more law enforcement and legislators responded by creating the Missouri Highway Patrol in 1931.

Caulfield's term marked the end of a Republican decade.

But all of Caulfield's attempts at election reforms failed. His proposal to elect only the governor and auditor did not appeal to lawmakers, even though he argued that appointing the other state officials would cause greater efficiency and reduce the number of separate agendas.

More difficulty with the legislature came in 1932 over the congressional redistricting bill. The new census showed that Missouri's growth had not kept pace with the nation. The slump in population cost the state three of its sixteen seats in Congress and forced new districts to be drawn. In response, the Democratic-controlled legislature presented Caulfield with a gerrymandered map favoring their party. When the bill reached his desk, the infuriated governor promptly vetoed the plan. In doing so, he made what one contemporary called "the blunder of his administration." His rejection of the map forced all congressional candidates to run statewide, a situation that proved even more adverse to

Republicans. In the at-large election, GOP candidates took a trouncing as Democrats scooped up all the state's congressional seats.

The financial crash dealt a devastating political blow to Republicans everywhere. New Deal Democrats led by Franklin Delano Roosevelt (a distant relative of Fannie Delano Caulfield) ushered in new programs and new faces across the country. In Missouri, Caulfield passed on the governorship to a little-known Democratic judge—Guy B. Park. Shortly after the election, the Caulfields invited the Parks to view their soon-to-be home. "We like the Parks immensely and got along fine," the Governor wrote to his daughter, Jane. Caulfield, a congenital optimist, concluded his letter with, "It was a colossal defeat for the Republicans, but we'll come back with a bang." But it did not turn out that way. Caulfield's election in 1928 had coincided with the presidential election of Herbert Hoover, climaxing the end of a Republican decade.

Concerned about the future of the Governor, supporters urged him to run for mayor of St. Louis, but he refused. Instead, he opened a law office in St. Louis the day after he left the governorship; his wife chose to take a Mediterranean cruise. During her visit to Egypt, Israel, France, and Turkey, she wrote articles for Missouri newspapers telling of her adventures.

Five years later, Henry Caulfield won the Republican nomination for the U.S. Senate, but Missourians still favored New Deal policies and would for years to come. However, the optimistic former Governor lived to be ninety-two years old—long enough to see his hopes rewarded by the return of his party to state and national office.

THE FIRST LADY'S HEMLINE

When it came time for Mrs. Caulfield to have her portrait painted to commemorate her time as hostess of the Mansion, she knew exactly how she wanted to be remembered. She wore her sleeveless, aquamarine dress with the scoop neck and a hemline just above the knees—a high fashion item for "Flappers" in the 1920s.

But time and styles changed. When the former First Lady visited the Mansion years later, she was embarrassed by her knees being so prominently displayed during a time when lower hemlines were in vogue. The thought of someone being offended by the exposure caused Mrs. Caulfield to call on the artist to "lengthen" her dress with a paint brush. Today, the touched-up painting hangs in the Mansion library where amused visitors often search for a faint view of the telltale hemline.

HAPPY DAYS ARE HERE AGAIN!

GOVERNOR GUY BRASFIELD PARK
ELEANORA GABBERT PARK
1933-1937

Led by the landslide election of Franklin D. Roosevelt, Democrats scored a smashing victory in the state and nation.

The Park's white farmhouse, surrounded by trees, had a friendly porch swing where neighbors often gathered to visit. Inside the house, easy chairs welcomed guests to pleasant rooms brightened with scatter rugs, crocheted afghans, and family pictures. Eleanora Park knew how much she would miss the old home as she locked the door behind her one chilly January morning. She and her husband, Guy, had boxed a few of their personal things to take with them: history books, photographs, bedspreads, and favorite pictures of Robert E. Lee and Andrew Jackson.

The truck loaded with their belongings had already left when the Parks climbed into their 1926 Buick and headed for Jefferson City. Just the day before, Guy Park had cleaned out his desk at the courthouse where he had served as circuit judge for the past ten years. He had not missed a day of court during that time and was proud to say so. Wearing a crumpled blue serge suit with mud-speckled trousers, he had then walked through the bank, drugstore, and pool hall, saying good-bye to his friends in Platte City, the place where he was born and had practiced law for thirty-five years.

The Parks' home in Platte City.

It was home for Eleanora, too, a talented drama coach who once aspired to be a professional actress. Those dreams had been stifled when her father objected to her leaving home for a "profession full of temptations and questionable associations." Eleanora continued performing, but in a local setting. She played the organ, taught a Sunday school class at the Baptist

(Facing page) Franklin D. Roosevelt, supported on his son's arm, accepts the presidential nomination at the 1932 Democratic Convention.

211

church, and worked with a little theater group. Her marriage to Guy Park, the county prosecutor, had raised a few eyebrows in the little community. "Audible weeping of older relatives dampened the [wedding] ceremony. They could not hide their disapproval of an alliance doomed because the groom was sixteen years older than the bride, and he did not own an acre of rich Platte County land."

D espite early concerns, the Parks had been happily married for nearly twenty-four years. Following the November 1932 election, however, their peaceful, predictable lives changed abruptly. Democrats—led by the landslide election of President Franklin D. Roosevelt—scored a smashing victory in the state as well as the nation. In Missouri, only ten Republicans seeking election to the state House survived the onslaught and all thirteen congressional seats went to Democrats running in the at-large election. Most astounding of all, Guy Park—the sixty-year-old political outsider—captured the governorship.

Less than a month before, Park had no thoughts of being governor. He had previously been elected city attorney, prosecutor, and circuit judge, but had no further aspiration for higher office. Like most Democrats, he anticipated the next governor would be the party nominee, Frances E. Wilson. Wilson had lost a bid for the state's top office four years earlier, but was considered the leading contender in 1932. Park once practiced law with Wilson and made speeches on behalf of his old friend, "France." But Wilson suffered a heart attack and died a month before the November election, forcing the Democratic State Committee, by law, to replace the nominee within twelve days.

According to historian Robert Ferrell, the selection of Park was the work of Kansas City political boss Tom Pendergast. In the heyday of machine politics, the chieftain of the Democratic party virtually controlled the entire state. As the dominant figure on the Democratic State Committee, Pendergast saw it as his responsibility to fill the ticket quickly and well. In accepting the Platte County judge, Pendergast honored the wishes of Wilson's widow, who felt that Park—in spite of his limited political career—embodied the ideals of her late husband.

"I'll have to admit I'm boss-ridden. I'm married."

Pendergast's backing earned Park unanimous approval, as well as some political baggage. Although the small town judge had never been a Pendergast follower, political foes began referring to the State Capitol as "Uncle Tom's Cabin." Park made a joke of the bossism claim saying, "I'll have to admit I'm boss-ridden. I'm married."

In Ferrell's estimation, Park "did not consider himself a machine candidate; he was an innocent man rather than a nefarious one." Pushed into the political spot-light, the modest and calm-mannered judge often seemed uncomfortable—some-times amused—as cameras started flashing all about him. "Boys, I'm not used to all this," he once told photographers. "Now you'll have to show me how to stand."

Park knew where he stood on the issues that were important to voters in

COLONELS AND CANNONS

No inauguration was complete without the traditional seventeen-gun salute to the incoming governor. Further adding to the pageantry was the entourage of newly appointed colonels—a group that varied depending on the number of supporters needing to be recognized. Military appointees had been around long before the turn of the twentieth century. But it was not until then that newsmen began poking fun at the brightly festooned civilians who looked very much like the "Captain of the Pinafore" with their gold braid, epaulettes, and lined capes.

According to Missouri's 1889 *Official Manual*—the oldest of the so-called "Blue Books"—Governor Francis named three aides-de-camp with the rank of lieutenant colonel. Dockery (1901-1905) designated eight men to serve on his personal staff— some as brigadier generals and others as colonels. Although the practice had its origin early in the state's history, it was 1909 before the group was given legal status by the legislature. Thus, each governor gained the privilege of appointing as many aides as he desired. By 1927-1928 the aides were listed in the *Official Manual* simply as colonels.

One news account declared a "great demand for the job of coloneling" in 1933. Park's designation of fifty-six men to hold the title was the largest group in memory. Each administration designed a new outfit. Colonels appointed by Governor Park wore double-breasted jackets of black flannel that extended to the knees. The high-collared uniform was emblazoned with a double row of shiny buttons bearing the state seal. The trousers, which featured a gold stripe down

the side, were further embellished by a gold belt and saber. In contrast to the uniforms worn by Governor Caulfield's colonels, there was no cape. The deliberately showy attire was one of the few ways a new governor could reward his faithful supporters. According to one reporter, the honorees could look forward to "a day of reflected glory, a night of aching feet, and a lifetime of being referred to as 'colonel.' "

Over the years, the group named to serve in this honorary capacity grew in number. Governor Hadley had designated 37 colonels, Caulfield 29, and Park 56, but Donnell named 69. Donnelly picked 138 his first term and 199 his second. Smith appointed 126, Blair 600, Dalton about 700, and Hearnes 750 his first term and 1,000 the next.

Though the statutory power to name honorary colonels remains, in 1973 Governor Christopher Bond made a point of abandoning the archaic custom. No subsequent governor has named colonels en masse to embellish his inauguration. However, Governor John Ashcroft—near the end of his term—appointed 350 honorary military aides as "a matter of appreciation," giving them the title of "commander" in the Missouri Naval Militia.

While colonels have faded into Missouri history, cannons continue to boom the announcement of a new chief executive. The first nineteen-gun salute for a Missouri governor was fired following Park's swearing-in ceremony to accord a governor the same honor given cabinet members. Humorist Will Rogers gave a more colorful explanation, "Governor's salutes used to be seventeen," he declared, "but Mr. Roosevelt, on account of being a governor himself, raised 'em two guns."

1932. With less than a month until the election, the new Democratic candidate took to the campaign trail, insisting that he be scheduled for six to eight speeches a day. At each stop, he pledged to trim state government, work for the repeal of prohibition, and reopen the breweries in St. Louis. He felt prohibition caused crime and put tax money due the state into the pockets of bootleggers.

Eleanora wanted little to do with the whirlwind campaign. She saw herself as a care giver for her husband rather than a political wife. "I consider it my duty to keep a cheerful, restful, happy home atmosphere for him," she announced. They each had their "own domain," she told reporters, although they were "mutually helpful when necessary. "I have helped him read [legal] briefs when he needed me in some press of duty and when some piece of furniture needs mending we do it together."

Henrietta Park campaigns for her father.

Despite her reluctance at being thrust onto the political stage, Mrs. Park was cast as the candidate's wife in a series of political teas that put her in touch with over two thousand ladies during the three-week road show. Also joining the effort was the Parks' only child, Henrietta, a twenty-year-old English teacher who worked around her classroom schedule in order to be a part of the campaign. Henrietta took her mother's place in welcoming Eleanor Roosevelt to St. Louis when Mrs. Park was detained in St. Joseph at a tea party and unwilling to take the risk of flying.

That November, led by the landslide victory of Franklin Roosevelt, Democrats were swept into office all across the state. Riding the presidential coattails, the unknown judge racked up the greatest plurality of votes in Missouri history. In an overwhelming show of hometown approval, Park received all but 26 of the 708 votes cast in Platte City.

❧

Still in his nightshirt and wrapped in an old bathrobe, the Governor-elect visited with newsmen from a comfortable rocker.

With a new face on the political scene, newsmen searched for homey anecdotes about the First Family and their transition to public life. They enjoyed reporting that Park was once a student at Gaylor Institute, a girls' school where his mother served as president. "Mr. Guy," as the young ladies called him, was the only man to

214

graduate from the all-female school. With Park's election, he gained the additional distinction of being the first University of Missouri graduate to become governor.

Park warmed the hearts of Missourians with his down-home demeanor. One neighbor described him as "the coolest cuss I've ever seen . . . never got excited about anything in his life." When reporters clamored for a statement early on the morning after his election, the Governor-elect—weary from only a few hours of sleep—pulled himself out of bed, wrapped an old bathrobe over his nightshirt, and visited with newsmen from a comfortable rocker.

Reporters continued to follow his trail from Platte City to the Mansion. On the eve of the inauguration, cameramen—eager to see the next Governor—crowded around the Parks' Buick as it pulled into the yard of the Mansion, followed closely by the Highway Patrol car that accompanied them. Governor Caulfield and his wife rescued the new residents, inviting them into the Mansion where dinner and an overnight stay were scheduled.

The Parks' pet, a German shepherd named Judge, had arrived earlier and caused quite a commotion when he leaped from the truck and ran off over the hill with West, the Mansion butler, in close pursuit. The chase and capture of the "First Pooch" two blocks beyond the Capitol gave reporters the human interest story they were looking for on inaugural eve.

The next day brought an unseasonable display of sunny weather to Jefferson City and with it, a feeling of optimism. Kansas City Democrats—encouraged by a two-dollar round-trip train ticket—poured into the Capital City to celebrate their party's first victory in twelve years. But hundreds who came from long distances missed seeing the new Governor sworn in to office. With the rotunda and halls filled to capacity, latecomers were forced to stand on the south step of the Capitol throughout the ceremony.

Among the visitors to the city were many of Park's longtime friends and neighbors. According to his hometown newspaper, Platte City "practically closed up shop and by train and motor cars swarmed into Jefferson City" to see their circuit judge become the state's governor. When Park spotted one group of Platte

The Parks' German shepherd, Judge, and West, the Mansion butler.

Park's formal attire for inaugural day included spats and a top hat. Standing is his wife, Eleanora (left), and daughter, Henrietta.

215

Countians wandering about the Mansion grounds, he rapped on the window to get their attention, then beckoned them inside just as he would have at home. The "slack-jawed butler" stood aside in surprise as the Governor greeted his friends at the door and invited them in to see the Mansion.

With all the excitement, the First Lady had little time to survey her new home. Her immediate concern was in preparing for the traditional reception and ball. For the evening event, she picked a long, shapely ball gown—a reversal of the shorter, loose-fitting styles worn during the Roaring Twenties. Earlier she let it be known that she did not intend to "bob" her hair in the fashion of the day for the inauguration or for any other occasion.

Still, she looked forward to the evening of gaiety that started with the First Couple dancing to the "Missouri Waltz," though dancing had been frowned upon in the Baptist home of her childhood. "[I am a] Baptist, all but my feet," Eleanora once declared as she and Guy twirled about the dance floor.

But with Democrats jammed into the Capitol rotunda, there was little space for twirling. The out-of-town guests had already filled the hotels for miles around and strained services to the point that many restaurants ran out of food. To make matters worse, the lights went out twice at the ball, causing some fear that the crowd might panic. Blame for the disruption in power was placed on pranksters—though some claimed it was caused by disgruntled employees angry at the prospect of losing their jobs.

※

After the ball, the Parks returned to the Mansion for their first night as Governor and First Lady. The family was not entirely unfamiliar with their new surroundings. Park could remember playing about the executive home forty-six years earlier when his father, the chief clerk for the secretary of state, came to the Mansion to visit his good friend, Governor John Marmaduke. Guy, thirteen years old at the time, recalled shuffling across the carpet so he could get a shock when he touched the metal newel post figure. During those visits, he had learned to play pool on the third floor of the Mansion with instruction from his father and Governor Marmaduke.

Mrs. Park was no stranger to the house either. During 1922 she often accompanied her husband to the Mansion when he visited there while serving on the Constitutional Commission. Young Henrietta sometimes came along, too, and played

Flaws unnoticed as a visitor seemed more apparent to her as a resident of the Mansion.

with Caroline Hyde, the daughter of Governor and Mrs. Hyde.

Now as the hostess of the house, rather than a guest, Mrs. Park viewed the oversized, sparsely filled rooms with a different perspective. The flaws, unnoticed as a visitor, seemed more apparent to her as a resident. She tried to warm up the decor by intermingling a few small furnishings from her farmhouse with the hand-me-downs from previous administrations. But the mismatched pieces differed in styles and time periods, frustrating any attempts at decorating. An interior decorator visiting the Parks observed the First Lady's predicament : An "Italian chest [sits] across the hall from a pair of Gothic pedestals, [each a] gift of different regimes." With no hope of changing the look of the home, the First Lady resigned herself to appreciating the "fine sentiment" reflected in the Mansion's eclectic furnishings.

Mrs. Park determined to focus on the more pleasant aspects of living in the old home, one of which was the spectacular view of the Missouri River. Each family member selected a second-floor bedroom overlooking the water. The servants gained more scenic accommodations, too, when Mrs. Park moved their bedrooms from the basement to the third floor. This was not a new arrangement; the servants' quarters had often been shifted about at the request of the new first family.

Still located on the third floor was the old billiard table—the one on which Park played as a youngster.

The Parks' view of the Capitol from the port cochere on inaugural day.

In the intervening years, pool had become his favorite pastime. Back in Platte City, he enjoyed a few games at the local pool hall each day after lunch. However, when Governor Park climbed the backstairs of the Mansion for a relaxed game, no pool balls or cue sticks were to be found anywhere. In frustration, he searched the house from top to bottom, going so far as to look inside the basement refrigerator. When newsmen reported the Governor's disappointment in being unable to use the historic billiard table, offers of pool accessories came in from all around the state. Although he received a good supply of equipment, the Governor found time for only one game during his first six months in office.

Park also enjoyed fishing and took every opportunity to drop a line into the Lake of the Ozarks. However, his prize catch—an eight-foot shark—was landed on a

THE BEATEN BISCUIT

Nowhere was Missouri's Southern heritage more evident than in the foods served at the Mansion. Well into the twentieth century, the ubiquitous beaten biscuit showed up on the Mansion tables, both for company and everyday fare. Each First Lady had her own version of the recipe, which included some combination of wheat flour, pure pork lard, flour, milk, baking powder, sugar, and salt.

Preparation of the biscuit took some skill and stamina, since the dry, crumbly dough had to be literally beaten into shape. Using a flat iron, the dough was pounded, then rolled with a wooden pin for an hour or so until it was as shiny as satin. It took less time and effort if the cook was fortunate enough to have a beaten biscuit machine to do the work for her.

A magazine illustration of a beaten biscuit machine in use.

Mrs. Park found one of these discarded devices in the Mansion basement, had it repaired, and put back to use in the kitchen. The machine was nothing more than a set of rollers with a hand crank. Though it looked much like the mangles of an old washing machine, it was just what Ada Boyd, the longtime family cook, needed to turn out the tasty biscuit.

The procedure took about forty-five minutes of rolling. When the dough reached a quarter-inch thickness, it began to make loud, popping noises and to take on a smooth, glossy look. After that it was turned out on a floured board, pricked with the tines of a fork, and cut into biscuits. The dough was then left to rise before being baked in a slow oven for over an hour. Filled with a slice of country ham, the dry, often crumbly biscuits were served hot or cold any time of the day.

With changing tastes and attitudes, however, the Southern delicacy disappeared from the Mansion tables about the same time the strains of "Dixie" ceased to be a regular part of inaugural day.

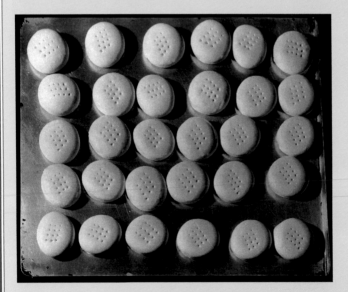

The ubiquitous beaten biscuit showed up on the Mansion table both for company and everyday fare.

GOV. PARK LANDS A MAN EATING SHARK OFF FLORIDA — IT WAS EITHER EIGHT OR EIGHTY FEET.

trip to Miami Beach. The Governor struggled with the fish (the weight of which varied in the telling from 135 to 185 pounds) for more than an hour before reeling it on board.

While Park enjoyed the fringe benefits that came with being the state's chief executive, it was not a pleasant time to hold public office. Hardships produced by the Great Depression were evident everywhere. When Park took office, the state treasury contained less than $300,000. Hundreds of banks were closed, thousands of farms and homes had sold at foreclosure, and the jobless jammed the corridors of the Capitol.

With the end of a twelve-year Republican reign in the state, thousands of Democrats flocked to the Capital City expecting employment. Even the First Lady received mail from job seekers. She did not object, but was frustrated that many of the letters came with postage due.

In an effort to prime the economic pump, the Roosevelt administration funded public works, direct relief, and a Civilian Conservation Corps for jobless youth. Park urged full cooperation with the new policies. In addition, he tightened the reins on spending by trimming state employment, salaries, and services. The Governor set an example by curbing his own expenses. In a show of thrift, Park had two of the five telephones in his office removed and he declined to use the state-provided Cadillac.

The old Buick with 100,000 miles on it—the one that had served him so well in the campaign—was adequate for his travels, Park declared. Besides, he preferred walking to and from the Capitol and visiting about town on foot. The Cadillac, however, was not totally abandoned. Along with her mother, Henrietta—who by now had quit teaching to help at the Mansion—claimed the unused vehicle. A few months later, Park acknowledged his need for more reliable transportation and traded in the seven-year-old Buick for a Dodge coupe.

ON WAY TO ST. LOUIS, GOV. PARK'S CAR BURNS. NO ONE INJURED.

The state-owned Cadillac had to be replaced as well, after an unfortunate incident that occurred twenty miles east of the Capitol while Raymond Carter, the chauffeur, was transporting the Parks to St. Louis. When Raymond discovered the floorboard was burning, he pulled off the road, evacuated the passengers, and rescued the luggage. Flames broke out, destroying the engine and leaving the Parks stranded along the highway. While the Governor hailed a passing car and resumed his schedule, Mrs. Park waited for their personal auto to be dispatched for her return to the Mansion. But her woes for the day were not over. Before reaching home, the second vehicle broke down, forcing her to change cars again.

Though the First Lady may have lost confidence in her vehicles, she had every reason to feel secure in running the Mansion. For needed support, there was Ada Boyd, the African-American woman who had worked for the Park family since Guy was a little boy and knew how to cook the country ham and desserts the Governor so enjoyed. Ada also kept the Governor's favorite butterscotch cookies stored in a yellow pottery jar within easy reach of his bed, just as she had in Platte City.

Shortly after moving into the Mansion, Eleanora—with Ada's help—hosted a tea for the wives of legislators and the ladies of Jefferson City. To enhance the day, she brought in an orchestra from St. Louis to entertain the five hundred women who responded to her invitation. Putting on a fine social event had always been a challenge for the Mansion hostess who frequently had to import flowers, caterers, and musicians from St. Louis. Though Mrs. Park had enough china and silver to serve sixty-five guests at a formal dinner, food service was awkward. Cooks working in the basement kitchen sent meals to the dining room on a dumb-waiter located in the butler's pantry. Because of the distance, food seldom arrived on the table at its intended temperature.

What food lacked in temperature, Mrs. Park made up for with her warmth and charm.

What food lacked in temperature, Mrs. Park made up for with her warmth and charm as a hostess. She continued to entertain in much the same way she had in her own home. The only difference, she said, is that "the people of Missouri are now my neighbors." After hours of gracious entertaining, she would bid her guests farewell with a cheery, "Good-bye, hurry back!"

The Parks' dog, Judge, was less hospitable toward some who came to the Mansion. Although the Governor once told reporters that Judge was so friendly "he wouldn't even bite a Republican," the Mansion postman found out otherwise. After having the seat of his pants removed by the German shepherd, he learned to make a hasty delivery of the mail each day.

The Parks at a lawn party being watched over by Arthur Hardiman, a long-time Mansion employee.

Mrs. Park saw to it that Judge was not about when she held her summer lawn parties. These informal suppers on Sunday evenings were enhanced by the charming old fountain, garden furniture, and summer-house that decorated the Mansion yard. "The lawn was a great source of pride to me," Mrs. Park recalled. To ensure its beauty, she kept the grounds fertilized, seeded, and mowed until it had the look of "a green velvet carpet."

During the Christmas season, Eleanora turned her attention to creating a festive holiday spirit indoors. In the kitchen, the aroma of plum pudding and fruit cake mingled with the smell of country ham, turkey, and beaten biscuits. A huge tree placed in front of the hall fireplace nearly reached the ceiling and smaller evergreens decorated the front porch. "Choosing colored lights and decorations delight me as much as a child," she once wrote.

Mrs. Park did not confine herself solely to Mansion decorating and party giving. She participated in the local music club, the Tuesday Club, and the Order of Eastern Star, but not as often as she would have liked. "When an hour or so could be spared, I slipped away and enjoyed it with my good friends and club members," she recalled. In 1935 when the state P.E.O. convention met in Jefferson City, Mrs. Park graciously opened the Mansion to the ladies from all across the state.

The First Lady made an attempt to reach beyond her role as homemaker and Mansion hostess. She once invited three hundred representatives from various women's organizations for a discussion of the unemployment problems in Missouri. Determined to do something on behalf of the state's ten thousand jobless females, the group began an effort to appoint someone in each county to encourage the hiring of women.

In 1936 Eleanora took on another challenge when she agreed to entertain the National Governors' Association in Missouri. During a previous conference, the Parks had enjoyed the hospitality of the California governor and the chance to hobnob with cinema stars Jean Harlow, Marie Dressler, Mary Pickford, and Will Rogers. The three-day conference gave the Parks an opportunity to showcase Missouri. The visiting governors and first ladies, traveling by train from St. Louis to Kansas City, stopped in Jefferson City where they were entertained at the Mansion. As an optional activity, some chose the adventure of a plane trip to the new Lake of the Ozarks for a view of the recently constructed dam.

Trimming the Mansion Christmas tree.

In addition to the governors, Missouri also attracted other political figures during the thirties. President Roosevelt and Mrs. Roosevelt visited the state on separate occasions. While they did not come to the Capital City, Postmaster General James Farley enjoyed the hospitality of the Mansion.

Preparing for guests pointed up the need for renovation of the sixty-four-year-old house. One near tragic incident forced immediate repairs. The First Lady occupied the middle bedroom on the north side of the house. One evening while she was gone, several huge chunks of plaster—some weighing fifty pounds or more—fell from the ceiling directly onto her bed. The loud sound and dust created so much "smoke" in the house that the night watchman, thinking a bomb had exploded, sent for the police. Mrs. Park was visiting her mother at the time and no one was injured, but the incident clearly pointed up the danger in delaying needed repairs.

Huge chunks of plaster fell from the ceiling directly onto her bed.

Traditionally, a First Lady did all she could to enhance the historic home, but Eleanora recognized that the times demanded restraint. Lawmakers had slashed the Governor's budget dramatically, reducing the biennial appropriation from $40,000 to

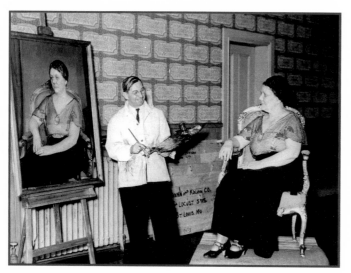

Mrs. Park poses for artist Richard E. Miller. According to Henrietta Park, her mother "never much cared for the painting."

$14,500—an amount that included repairs to the Mansion as well as the executive office. In view of the cuts, Mrs. Park felt uncomfortable suggesting any costly renovations or structural changes to the home. Instead, she repainted the house red and repaired the porch and woodwork. She also added to the crystal, linen, and silver, which included completing the set of Mount Vernon sterling flatware. Though it was inconvenient living in a big house with only two clothes closets, she made do by using wardrobes in each room for hanging garments.

Like other first ladies, Mrs. Park discovered that curtains had to be laundered every three or four weeks because of the soot that accumulated throughout the house from the coal-burning locomotives passing just below the bluff. Window, floor, and furniture coverings also needed frequent replacement.

When Eleanora once spent fifty dollars for ruffled curtains and accessories for a guest bedroom, her husband at first refused to authorize payment. But having been a judge for many years, the Governor was open to hearing his wife's side of the story. After she explained that it took as much material to curtain one room in the Mansion as it took for their entire home in Platte City, Park relented and ordered the bill paid.

In keeping with the Governor's call for economy, Ada, the housekeeper, proved she could match her boss in thriftiness. One day, in an uncharacteristic show of excitement, Ada called for the First Lady to come downstairs right away to see something. Eleanora rushed into the kitchen, where she found Ada, smiling broadly as she stood over two tubs filled with old-fashioned homemade soap rendered from the remains of hams served at the Mansion.

"Ada, why did you do this?" Mrs. Park asked, knowing how much work was involved in such a project.

"I wasn't going to let that fat go to waste," she replied proudly. "The state has got to economize."

But Mrs. Park had in mind something more enduring than practicing economy, giving teas, or decorating at the Mansion. When asked if she enjoyed cooking, she replied, "Yes, I really like to cook.

And I've done a good deal of it. But, there are lots of other things I'd rather do," she added quickly.

In fact, Eleanora had already determined what she wanted to do as First Lady before she ever arrived in Jefferson City. "I was appalled to find that no records had been kept, nor any history compiled of such an historic home." She always kept personal scrapbooks and had many of them filled with news items and family memorabilia. "It would have been such a great help for the wives of incoming governors if such records had been kept, for it would help them with their social duties," Mrs. Park declared.

She found a literary partner in Kate Morrow, a faithful supporter and friend who had been at the helm of the Park campaign office. At the turn of the century, Kate and her husband had lived at the Mansion. (He worked as Governor Dockery's secretary while Kate served as Mansion hostess following Mrs. Dockery's death.) Together, the ladies assembled the 435-page book, *Women of the Mansion*, offering a view of life in the executive home, as well as an accounting of its furnishings, traditions, and celebrations. At the time, seven former first ladies and five governors were still living and their recollections helped the two ladies preserve records that might otherwise have been lost. Still, Eleanora took little credit for her accomplishments. Like her predecessors, she played down her own skills and contribution, once telling reporters, "Don't make me look too literary."

Appalled that no records had been kept of the house, Mrs. Park compiled a 435-page book on the home and its first ladies.

The wedding of the Parks' daughter in 1933 made more Mansion history. Henrietta's marriage ceremony was the first performed in the 1871 Mansion for a governor's offspring. No one seemed to mind that the groom, St. Louis lawyer and former legislator J. Marvin Krause, was a Republican. "We never even mentioned politics," Henrietta Park declared forthrightly.

On their wedding day, three hundred guests gathered in the Double Parlor, then called the "Gold Room." Miss Park descended the Grand Stairway on her father's arm with her long, outstretched bridal train trailing gracefully behind her. Twelve young ladies holding ribbons formed an aisle for the bride as she crossed the hall to the Gold Room. Standing in front of the marble fireplace, Henrietta joined hands with the groom to recite their marriage vows.

For Guy and Eleanora, the day denoted yet another special occasion—their twenty-fourth wedding anniversary. In celebration of the dual events, guests were treated to a reception in the Mansion dining room that featured a four-and-one-half-foot-tall, 220-pound cake. After such a splendid observance, the Parks chose to ignore any formal recognition of their silver anniversary the following year and spent a quiet evening at the Mansion. Close friends recognized the occasion, however, by presenting the couple with a sixty-two-piece set of sterling silver.

While Park enjoyed these breaks from his duties, he was obliged to spend much of his time combating the state's economic woes. To benefit the indigent and to increase school funding, the Governor secured an additional one-cent sales tax. State colleges and institutions were refurbished with funds from the $13 million building program. Park's introduction of a new budgetary system and central purchasing procedures helped to streamline state government. Lawmakers passed an old-age assistance act, took over the counties' costs of caring for the mentally ill, and replaced prohibition laws with new liquor control regulations. With the legalization of beer, two cases of the brew were flown to the Mansion—more for symbolic reasons than anything else, since the Parks never served intoxicants. Nonetheless, the Governor touted the return of the breweries, claiming 20,000 new jobs as a result.

Hennrietta Park descended the elegant, spiraling stairway for her marriage ceremony, the first performed for a governor's offspring in the 1871 Mansion.

Guests at Hennrietta Park Krause's wedding were treated to a four-and-one-half-foot-tall, 220-pound cake.

Despite hard times, Missouri met all of its obligations and Park left office with a comfortable balance in the state treasury. Before his departure, employees and department heads gathered outside the Capitol to present the family with gifts of appreciation—an oriental rug and an automobile. It was a miserable, icy day, but workers came to show their esteem for the chief executive who had led the state during equally harsh times.

The Parks returned home to Platte County where he resumed practicing law, this time in nearby Kansas City. He wrote a friend that he looked forward to being "back in old Platte with my friends and taking an occasional fishing trip or playing a little poker." He revisited the Capital City as a delegate to the 1943-44 Constitutional Convention. Two years later he died of a heart attack in his Jefferson City hotel room while getting ready to argue a case before the Missouri Supreme Court. He was 74. Mrs. Park, left a widow for the next thirty-eight years, lived in Columbia near her daughter and died at the age of 95.

Guy Park had brought the traditions and virtues of a bygone era into modern times. He assumed the governorship as an obligation to his lifelong friend, Frances Wilson, but earned the esteem of Missourians with his own accomplishments in troubled times. Missourians liked Park for the same reason neighbors liked him in Platte City—"He was just himself," a man of fairness and decency who accepted public service as a sacred trust.

MEMORY LANE

In 1995 Henrietta Park Krause, accompanied by her daughter, returned to the Mansion for a visit at the invitation of First Lady Jean Carnahan. Henrietta, the first offspring of a governor to be married in the Mansion, was then in her eighties and walking with a cane.

As she moved slowly toward the long, spiraling stairway she had descended on her wedding day, Mrs. Carnahan offered her the services of the elevator. Mrs. Krause declined saying, "I want to climb this wonderful old stairway one more time." It was her last visit to the Mansion. She died two years later at the age of eighty-five.

THE APPLE MAN

STARK TREES BEAR FRUIT

Stark Nurseries–World's Largest Tree Growe
3,000 Acres–in Seven States and France.

GOVERNOR LLOYD CROW STARK
KATHERINE LEMOINE GUY PERKINS STARK
1937-1941

"I intend to spare no power at my command to make Missouri unsafe for the racketeer, the gangster, and the criminal." ~ Lloyd Stark

It was not easy being a member of the Stark family. Having so many illustrious forebearers can be demanding. Lloyd Stark's great-grandfather had come to Missouri on horseback in 1816, carrying a saddlebag full of sprouts from an apple tree grown on his farm in Kentucky. From these seedlings, a family-run nursery had sprung up in Louisiana, Missouri, that eventually blossomed into a multi-million-dollar operation. Credit for much of that success was due Lloyd Stark whose business, military, and political skills brought him state and national prominence.

Around the turn of the century, Stark—a teenager at the time—began planning his future. He wanted to attend Yale and asked an old family friend, Representative Champ Clark, for a personal recommendation. In addition to the endorsement, the Missouri congressman offered the young man an appointment to the U.S. Naval Academy. Stark chose the academy.

As a cadet, he was tagged with the nickname "Molly." The reference was to his Revolutionary War relative General John Stark's famous words to his troops before the Battle of Bennington, "There are the red coats and they are ours, or this night Molly Stark sleeps a widow." In the years ahead, Lloyd would show the same do-or-die spirit as his illustrious ancestor.

After graduating from the academy with honors, the newly commissioned officer spent four years at sea. But in 1912 he resigned his post and returned home to help run the nursery. The business was in the doldrums and desperately in need of management. Instead of cutting back on expenses, Stark followed the advice of his father,

Revolutionary War General John Stark is remembered for his do-or-die spirit before the Battle of Bennington.

227

Annapolis
midshipman
Lloyd Stark.

the man who introduced the Delicious apple to the world. "Boys, never stop advertising," he had told his sons. "Do this in good times and bad times and the business will grow and prosper."

Stark began an extensive advertising campaign and before long newspapers, magazines, barns, and buildings all over the country carried the slogan, "Stark Trees Bear Fruit." As one of the early businesses to advertise nationwide, Stark saw his profits soar. The nursery quadrupled in size, making him a renowned horticulturist and the country's largest apple producer. In addition to his orchards, Stark opperated three large farms. His northeast Missouri acreage was the site for breeding fine hunting dogs and prize-winning livestock, including Hampshire hogs, Hereford cattle, Percherons, and five-gaited saddle horses.

When the United States entered World War I, Stark left his farm and business enterprises to reenlist in the armed forces. This time he signed up as a captain in the army and led a field artillery unit in France, earning several battle citations and a major's leaf.

Returning home after the war, Stark ran the family business for a number of years before he decided to take on another conquest—a battle for the governorship. He had never held public office, but he had visited every Missouri county as chairman of the Citizens' Road Committee during the Baker administration. As the spokesman for road improvement, Stark had urged the approval of a $75 million bond issue for developing a highway system. The successful campaign caused some to refer to him as the "Father of the Farm to Market Road System" in Missouri.

Although Stark was not an orator who inflamed his audience, he met people easily and a number of them urged him to run for governor. At the time, a successful statewide race depended on the endorsement of Kansas City politician Tom

Stark inspects his
orchards on
horseback.

Pendergast, once dubbed by the *New York Times* "the most powerful boss in America." In an era of strong ward organization in the big cities, the Jackson County kingpin knew how to deliver the Democratic vote. Stark sought Pendergast's endorsement for a 1932 gubernatorial race, but was refused. State Senator Francis Wilson got the nod, but died several weeks before the election.

When the Democratic State Committee cast about for another candidate, Stark appeared to be an obvious choice. However, Pendergast went along with the Wilson family when they suggested that the replacement be Judge Guy B. Park—an old friend of Francis Wilson. At the time, Stark was considered by many to be a political novice, but he knew better than to challenge Pendergast, the wheelhorse of the Democratic Party.

In 1936 U.S. Senator Harry Truman and other Democratic politicians decided to help Stark become governor by appealing to Pendergast for support. The "Boss" was hard to convince. He did not like Stark, the former military officer who was once described as "a severe, humorless man with the eyes of a zealot and the mouth of a Puritan."

Stark chats with Kansas City political boss Tom Pendergast (left) whom he would later dethrone.

After much urging, Pendergast decided that it was better to back Stark than to fight him. Assured that all would go well in Kansas City, the fifty-year-old millionaire hit the campaign trail, telling voters he would be a "business manager" for the state and vowing to follow Governor Gardner's example for well-managed government.

That fall, Stark watched both his orchards and his political efforts bear fruit. Missourians voted in record numbers, giving Stark the largest plurality in the state's history up until then. All the Democratic statewide officeholders were swept into office as Franklin Delano Roosevelt won a landslide victory that kept him in the White House for a second term. During the election, the Pendergast machine performed at its best, racking up equally historic margins for the Democratic ticket.

Though the "Boss" delivered on his pledge, Stark must have been uneasy about his methods. A later investigation showed that the Kansas City political machine produced over fifty thousand illegal "ghost voters." According to historian Paul Nagel, some wards turned up more voters than residents by "exhuming names of [the] long-deceased." The city's first ward, for instance, with a population of 18,478, tallied 19,771 ballots for Stark and 835 for his opponent—a whopping 96 percent for Pendergast's candidate!

According to Truman biographer Robert Ferrell, there were workers whose election-day job was to alter the ballot of those defiant enough to vote Republican. "In one precinct a ballotsmith erased 113 Republican ballots. It was hard work he complained. 'I am all in. Some of these damned Republicans marked their ballots so hard it was all I could do to rub them out.'"

While Stark was the beneficiary of Pendergast's tactics, the new Governor had no intention of being another one of his henchmen. Nor did he show any gratitude to the

(Above) Stark takes the oath of office while his daughters, Molly and Katherine, hold the Bible.
(Right) Holding a large bouquet was an acceptable way for the First Lady to avoid the fatigue and pain of shaking hands with thousand of well-wishers.

political czar. Historian David McCullough concluded, "It was Stark's conviction that his loyalty belonged to the people, not to any machine or its boss." For the moment, however, the apple man from Louisiana chose to savor the sweet fruits of victory. There was the inauguration to plan, new duties to learn, and the move to the Mansion to consider.

On inaugural day, Stark and his wife, Katherine, prepared for their new political role with a communion service at the Mansion conducted by the local Episcopal priest. Next came the parade along the ice-covered streets, followed by a swearing-in ceremony in the Capitol rotunda. The Governor-elect stood under the archway at the top of the double staircase, taking his oath on a Bible he had carried when he served in the navy twenty-five years earlier.

As usual, the Missouri colonels added to the fanfare of the day, each sporting a new blue uniform replete with gold braid and flashing sword. All stood smartly along the stairway as Stark, in an hour-long address, outlined his agenda for the state, which included the adoption of a two-cent sales tax. That evening the chic, thirty-five-year-old First Lady chose—for sentimental reasons—to wear the gown she had worn on her wedding day nearly six years earlier.

In the months that followed, Mrs. Stark turned her energy toward making the house more livable for her family. Not since Governor Hyde's election sixteen years earlier had there been youngsters living in the home. Now the staid old Mansion radiated the warmth and cheer of children—Molly, three, and Katherine "Kaffie," two—playing about its spacious rooms. In addition, the Governor—whose first wife had died seven years earlier—had two grown sons and two grandchildren who occasionally visited the Mansion.

As the First Family settled into the sixty-six-year-old house, its deficiencies became apparent. They had to stuff rags around the windows to keep out the chilling drafts and set buckets in the ballroom to catch leaks from the roof. The Grand Stairway, temporarily braced with planks during the inaugural reception, needed permanent support. Even more disgusting, rats were beginning to infiltrate the dark, damp basement where the kitchen was located. Service, by way of a dumbwaiter, was far too slow, often causing food to be room temperature by the time it arrived at the table.

There were other annoyances. One newspaper graphically described the noise problem endured by first families, "Every time trains passed on the tracks at the foot of the bluff directly behind the Mansion, dozens of twelve-foot windows with loose glass and frames set up a mighty rattling, and the vibration throughout the great structure set the dignified oil likenesses of the former first ladies jiggling in their golden frames." Architects examining the aging structure declared that they could remedy the window rattling and curtail the smoke damage caused by passing trains, but their changes provided only limited relief. (The smoke would eventually be eliminated by modern engines, but noise and vibrations remained.)

Rags stuffed around the windows helped keep out the chilling drafts.

A decade earlier there had been talk of turning the house into a museum or tearing it down in favor of a more modern home in a better location. As usual, the venerable Victorian structure survived the abuse of its detractors and the good intentions of its decorators. This time, the Mansion was about to get a major overhaul, one of the most drastic ever.

It all began after a committee of legislators came to inspect the Mansion and found Mrs. Stark ill with the flu, bundled up in bed to protect herself from the drafty windows that chilled the house. Upon seeing the First Lady in such discomfort, the chairman immediately committed to asking his colleagues for $50,000 to make the needed repairs. The sympathetic lawmaker must have made a convincing argument because the legislature actually came up with $55,000–a sizeable sum in the postdepression era when a new Packard coupe could be purchased for less than one thousand dollars.

With the resources to get the job done, Katherine turned the house over to workmen for the next seven months. For part of that time, she took the girls on vacation to Massachusetts and later sent them for an extended stay with her parents in St. Louis. The Governor escaped the upheaval briefly by taking a two-week Alaskan cruise aboard a Navy flagship.

However, there was no escaping the power struggle that faced Stark when he returned. Since taking office, the Governor had distanced himself from Pendergast and refused to appoint some of his men to office. Stark waited until the end of his first legislative session before making any serious moves against the "Boss." With numerous Pendergast men sitting in the General Assembly, the Governor did not want to risk losing his legislative programs. After the session adjourned, however, he joined federal authorities in

The Starks celebrate a birthday at the Mansion.

Mrs. Stark inspects the food preparation in the kitchen.

stepping up efforts to topple the political boss who had held sway in Kansas City for nearly twenty-five years.

Fearing retaliation from Pendergast, armed highway patrolmen were assigned to the Mansion to protect the First Family. Mrs. Stark recalled that the "children never knew what it was to run and play freely on the lawn or in their playhouse out back." To be on the safe side, Stark himself often carried a gun and sometimes officed in a room on the third floor of the Mansion rather than go to the Capitol.

By 1938 the noose was beginning to tighten about Pendergast and his cohorts. During the year, one hundred of Pendergast's followers were indicted for election fraud; the next year the "Boss" himself was sentenced to prison for fifteen months for income tax evasion. Stark had earlier appointed an independent board of election commissioners in Kansas City—a feat he considered to be one of the major accomplishments of his administration. He further invaded Pendergast's turf by abolishing the corrupt police system and replacing it with a bipartisan board administered by the mayor and four commissioners appointed by the Governor.

Despite earlier concerns for the safety of the Starks, there were no incidents at the Mansion stemming from the clash with Pendergast. In fact, the greatest threat to the family's well-being came from within the walls of the deteriorating Mansion. While repairs were being made to the dining room, four-inch chunks of plaster—"hard as rocks"—had come crashing from the ceiling. Upon further inspection, workmen found more loose plaster in the house, some of it held in place only by the wallpaper.

Though the renovation was inconvenient and sometimes hazardous, the

Trees and shrubs donated by the Starks were added to the Mansion grounds along with a retaining wall banked with flowers of the season.

improvements made the home far more comfortable than it had been in years. Eager to show off her stylish decor, the First Lady hosted a series of parties. She revived the traditional military reception and ball—an event that had not been held since 1933. She invited the Daughters of the American Revolution to have their colonial ball at the Mansion because she felt it would be appropriate for the group to dance the minuet on the new walnut floors. Katherine also displayed the remodeled Mansion to one of Franklin Roosevelt's cabinet members, Postmaster General James A. Farley, when he came to dinner. Helen, the Mansion cook, took great pride in making each of these occasions a culinary delight. She once baked nine cakes on the day of an event because she wanted them to be as fresh as possible.

Whether she was entertaining or performing routine chores, the First Lady went methodically about her duties. From her desk in one corner of the library, she personally went through her mail each day and wrote the necessary replies. Each morning she called the five servants in for their daily instructions, but oversaw the grocery shopping herself. The Starks preferred paying for their own food and required all personal food items to be bought at a separate store to avoid confusion. Still, Katherine admitted there was some problem with breaking down costs when the family ate turkey hash made from the leftovers of a state dinner.

She likened her duties as First Lady to managing a big hotel and having "a slice of private life on the side." To keep up with the unusual requirements of living in the house, she devised a maintenance schedule. For example, the net curtains that covered the Mansion's thirty-some windows were systematically washed and put on stretching frames in the basement to dry. Working on a rotation basis, she explained, prevented window care from becoming such an overwhelming task.

Both Lloyd and Katherine were horticulturists. They had met when she was a college student visiting the nursery. Sharing such a common interest, it was just a matter of time before they turned their attention to the Mansion plantings. Thousand of trees and shrubs donated by the family were added to the grounds along with a rose garden and a retaining wall banked with the flowers of the season. The rugged stones brought to the Mansion from the Governor's home county were set in place by prison inmates. When Katherine stopped to admire the work being done by one of the prisoners, he informed her that "every man in his lifetime wants to do one masterpiece and this is mine."

Katherine Stark, pregnant with her third child at the time her portrait was painted, later lost the infant shortly after birth.

Perhaps Charles Galt, the St. Louis artist, had some of those same feelings when he unveiled his portrait of the First Lady in 1938. The painting, a gift of Stark's honorary colonels, was not produced under the most favorable conditions. Molly and Kaffie, sick and confined to their beds, required repeated trips by their mother to the second floor. Katherine, pregnant at the time with her third child, was pleased with the "remarkably serene results" produced by the painter. Later that year, Katherine gave birth to the first baby to be born to a governor's wife while serving in the Mansion, but the infant lived for just eleven days.

While Mrs. Stark could

Living at the Mansion is like managing a big hotel with "a slice of private life on the side."

portray a feeling of serenity under pressure, the Governor showed a more combative nature—a trait that he found useful in advancing his legislative agenda. He pushed an increase in the sales tax that generated more funding for old-age benefits, direct relief, mental health, and public education. In addition, the reform-minded Governor won a $10 million insurance refund for policy holders and led a nationwide campaign to remove interstate trade barriers.

Stark also worked aggressively to end the public hanging of criminals. Capital punishment was administered in the county seats, where the event often attracted curiosity seekers as well as ticket hawkers. Stark proposed abandoning the gallows for the gas chamber and carrying out the death sentence at the state penitentiary in Jefferson City with as little fanfare as possible.

A Facelift for the Mansion

The Mansion underwent one of its most extensive remodelings under the direction of First Lady Katherine Stark. Repairs began on the outside with the removal of the sagging porte cochere—a covered entrance built on the south side of the house during the Dockery years. In its place, workers erected a two-story addition, making room for a twenty-by-thirty-foot kitchen on the first floor and a three-car garage below. To harmonize the divergent-colored brick, the house was transformed from red to what some called "Stark White." With the construction of the new garage, the dilapidated stable that stored the Mansion vehicles came down and the summerhouse was removed.

Katherine extended her remodeling to every floor of the house. She had all the unsightly heat pipes insulated and sealed up in the walls. (As yet, there was no air conditioning, except for several portable units.) The spacious second-floor landing was reduced in size by five feet to make room for another bathroom and more closets—the house had originally been built without either. She updated three bedrooms and cut new doors from the second-floor hallway to give direct access to all the bedrooms. Communications within the spacious, four-level building improved, too, when the First Lady added a buzzer system that displayed the location of the caller.

Stark preferred the new "Sports Room" and often worked there instead of going to the Capitol.

The third-floor ballroom—often forsaken as being too difficult to reach—took on a patriotic flair with its new red, white, and blue color scheme. The old billiard table, a favorite gathering spot for political discussions, got a companion piece at the other end of the room with the addition of a Ping-Pong table. A doorway was cut into the northwest bedroom allowing direct access from the ballroom. The Governor chose the area for his "Sport's Room," redoing it in pine paneling with built-in cabinets to display his gun collection. Stark preferred the newly decorated room and often worked there instead of going to his Capitol office. (Some felt Stark chose the safety of the Mansion because of his fear of Kansas City political boss Tom Pendergast.)

The Starks also lined the ballroom walls with eight mounted deer heads and the formal dining room with two other horned trophies. Far from minding the display of her husband's hunting prowess, Katherine acknowledged that she had bagged some of the animals herself. Another antlered item decorated the upstairs hall even before the Starks arrived: a garish elk horn costumer, a piece that had been there for so long that no one knew its origin.

The "dancing chandeliers" add to the mystery and charm of the house.

Katherine continued her renovations with the addition of venetian blinds, a black walnut parquet floor in the front hall, carpet throughout the first floor rooms and stairway, and a second set of French doors off the dining room. Workers replaced the tin roof with a composition covering, installed an underground water system, and relocated the flagpole to the east side of the house. Steel supports embedded into the Grand Stairway eased Mrs. Stark's fears for its safety and the fears of those living in the house thereafter. The addition of a cross beam and pillars further stabilized the steps that had concerned first ladies and state engineers for the past sixteen years.

The addition of three imported French chandeliers, sparkling with prisms, brought a soft glow to the first floor. Katherine was so proud of the new fixtures that she would not let anyone but herself dust them. The chandeliers caused some concern one evening when Mrs. Stark heard the tinkling of glass and looked up to see the light fixtures trembling and swaying from the ceiling. Katherine soon discovered that the tremors came from the third floor where Stark's son, John, and his friends were practicing the "Big Apple," a popular dance of the time. Although the floor is well shored up today, the "dancing chandeliers" remain a phenomenon that adds to the mystery and charm of the old building.

The newly redecorated dining room.

The Governor's range of accomplishments did not help his popularity among Democrats, some of whom resented his methods. He failed to consult party leaders and refused to heed their advice in making appointments. Even his mannerisms came under attack; many disliked his military air, the presence of uniformed colonels at his side, and the chauffeur's snappy salute when he approached. State employees grumbled about the 5 percent "lug" on their paychecks that went into the Governor's campaign fund—a practice that was not forbidden at the time and one that Stark declared to be "voluntary."

Angry Democrats, attending the party's annual Jackson Day dinner in Springfield, took the opportunity to vent their frustrations. When a prepared speech was read on behalf of the Governor, some in the crowd booed and became disruptive. Several weeks later, Stark found a more respectful audience when he called his supporters together for a counter celebration in the city.

Ignoring his party troubles at home, Stark tried to move onto the national political scene in 1939, hoping for either the vice presidency, a cabinet post, or at least a Senate seat. He became very chummy with the President, whom he called "the Chief," kept FDR posted on developments in Missouri, and even played poker onboard the presidential yacht. In the long run, the association did little for Stark's ambitions; Roosevelt discounted him, according to McCullough, as a politician with "no sense of humor . . . [and] a large ego."

However, some opponents of a third term for Franklin Roosevelt mentioned Stark as a replacement for the President. For a while, the Missouri Governor seemed to be the man of

FIRST LADY TALK

Mrs. Stark had not been in the Mansion long before she started "conferring" with the former first ladies whose portraits lined the Mansion walls. The new First Lady took some solace in the presence of other women with whom she shared some common woes. Their portraits offered a silent challenge for her to continue the traditions, hospitality, and care of the old house.

Looking up at Mrs. Baker's picture, the new First Lady thought to herself, "I know exactly how exasperated you must have been that day you got all ready for a party and the ceiling plaster fell on your pretty flowers and broke some of your nice dishes. But wasn't it fortunate your guests hadn't arrived?"

Eyeing Mrs. Caulfield, she mused, "You . . . must have been surprised to learn that lovely stairway was unsafe if as many as fifty persons were allowed on it . . . [and] that the third floor ballroom simply couldn't stand up under another inaugural ball, even if only forty persons danced the most sedate steps."

Turning to Mrs. Park's portrait, she pondered aloud, "And that kitchen, Mrs. Park—you know good food. Tell me, how did you ever manage to have those delicious hot biscuits for luncheon when ours are stone cold by the time they are carried across the basement and pulled up on that dumbwaiter?"

"Ladies," she said determinedly, "something has to be done about it. Things can't go on this way much longer!" Soon after she "spoke" with the First Ladies, Mrs. Stark commenced one of the major renovations of the Mansion, remedying many of the problems long endured by the ladies of the house.

the hour—the Democratic Party's answer to Tom Dewey, the New York crime crusader who was expected to get the Republican nomination for president.

Mrs. Stark began acting like a candidate's wife, working with the women's division of the Democratic National Committee and speaking before Michigan's Democratic State Convention. In an attempt to advance his political quest, Stark mailed gift packages of apples to Democratic leaders around the nation. He also made what was called a nonpolitical trip to the World's Fair in California. But with an escort of fifty friends and a sixty-piece band, the tour had all the trappings of a campaign swing. When two thousand people jammed the Kansas City train depot to view the crime-fighting Governor, Stark's opponents labeled it nothing more than a publicity stunt.

The Starks' home in Louisiana, Missouri.

Ultimately, Stark launched a primary campaign against incumbent U.S. Senator Harry S. Truman, although Truman had earlier supported Stark for governor. Upon hearing of the challenge, Truman—in his usual outspoken fashion—invited the Governor into the race with the blunt declaration, "I'll beat the hell out of him."

Despite his earlier declaration for the Senate, Stark still hoped for a place on the national ticket. At the 1940 Chicago Democratic Convention, a "Roosevelt and Stark" banner flew prominently across the convention hall and the Governor distributed bushels of Delicious apples to key delegates in an attempt to woo votes. According to Ferrell, "the delegates ate them and then voted for Roosevelt's choice, Secretary of Agriculture [Henry A.] Wallace."

With his aspirations for national office crushed, Stark returned to Missouri and renewed his efforts to unseat Truman. It did not seem like too difficult a task. Stark had the backing of the major state newspapers and far more money than Truman. Stark's lavish spending on radio and newspaper advertising brought him within 7,396 votes of ending Truman's political career.

Animosities left over from the campaign ruined Stark politically and he never sought elective office again. A fighter by birth, he did not take defeat well and even refused to endorse his party's candidate for governor. Disgruntled Democrats felt that an endorsement by Stark would have made the difference in the narrow defeat of Lawrence V. McDaniel by Republican Forrest Donnell in the 1940 election.

Upon leaving Jefferson City, "the apple man from Louisiana" returned to his nursery operation. In 1952 when GOP candidate General Dwight D. Eisenhower ran for president, Stark found the former military leader more to his liking than the Democratic nominee, Adlai Stevenson. Stark continued to support Republican presidential candidates until his death in 1972 at the age of eighty-five.

In his lifetime, Lloyd Stark was both hailed and hated for his bravado and defiance—traits that had once marked his Revolutionary War ancestor. Regardless of the cost, Stark repeatedly took risks—it was part of his nature to do so. Whether on the battlefields of Argonne, in the orchards of northeast Missouri, or in the halls of the Capitol, the challenge to bear fruit impelled him to action and gave meaning to his life.

NO ORDINARY TIME

To Have and to Hold!

WAR BONDS

Governor Forrest C. Donnell
Hilda Hays Donnell
1941-1945

Donnell came to office after a shaky victory, during a time of fear and uncertainty at home and abroad.

Snow-covered streets and piercing winds from off the river made it seem like an ordinary inauguration day in Missouri, but it was not. A bitter election contest had caused a forty-four-day delay that kept the newly elected Republican, Forrest Donnell, from occupying the governor's chair. In the November 1940 general election, Donnell, the underdog, netted only 3,613 more votes than his opponent, Lawrence V. McDaniel—an outcome that caused an uproar in the traditionally Democratic state.

Democratic lawmakers, distraught at the thought of losing the governorship and the patronage jobs that went with it, alleged voting irregularities. In the reading of the official election winners, the House Speaker defiantly refused to announce Donnell's name. Instead, legislators called for a "general and sweeping investigation." GOP members were appalled by the maneuver, which they saw as an "attempt to steal the governorship."

Others felt the same way. Angry groups of Republican women converged on the State Capitol, chanting protests

Forrest Donnell (right) on inauguration day. (Facing page) A World War II poster encouraging the purchase of war bonds.

239

An Uncertain Victory

Forrest Donnell, a newcomer to state politics, had done all he could to wrap up the governor's race for himself and the Republican party. A superb orator, he had traveled twenty-five thousand miles, making more than three hundred speeches in the course of his campaign against six primary opponents and his general election challenger, Lawrence V. McDaniel.

On election night, family and friends gathered in the Donnells' frame bungalow in Webster Groves. At a time when ballots were hand counted, the results were not always known until the following day, particularly in a close race. By midnight, McDaniel was well ahead and the race, apparently over. Donnell's wife, son, and daughter retired for the night, but the candidate was not ready to give up yet. He continued his vigil by the radio until two o'clock in the morning before he was finally convinced of defeat.

The next morning, he read the newspaper, had a leisurely breakfast, and began to follow the news broadcasts again. Much to his surprise, by ten o'clock McDaniel's lead had shrunk. At noon, the two candidates were neck and neck and, by four o'clock, Donnell was ahead by one thousand votes with less than thirty precincts to count. An hour later, with only two precincts out, Donnell's margin of victory continued to grow.

Flowers of congratulation began to arrive, joining those sent earlier when defeat seemed evident. That evening, more than two thousand friends and well-wishers— including a high school band—showed up outside the home of the Governor-elect.

With only a several thousand vote margin, Donnell had to accept an uncertain victory and await a court decision affirming his right to office. A partial recount later affirmed his win, making him the only Missouri Republican to gain statewide office in 1940.

as they marched onto the House floor, forcing an adjournment for the day. Several prominent Democrats also saw the election inquiry as unmerited. Senate Majority Leader Phil Donnelly (later to be governor) would not join the fray. Incumbent Governor Lloyd Stark showed no tolerance for his fellow Democrats and refused to approve funds for the investigation—though that did not prevent the legislature from proceeding with a recount.

Until the question was settled, Donnell made no effort to assume the powers of office or to address the issue publicly. He waited patiently and showed no resentment. McDaniel was his opponent, but he was also a friend and fellow trustee at the Grace Methodist Church in St. Louis; Mrs. Donnell and Mrs. McDaniel had belonged to the same clubs for over twenty years.

During the impasse, the state was not without a chief executive. Stark remained in office for six weeks beyond his term—continuing to receive his thirteen-dollars-a-day state salary. The matter was finally resolved after the Missouri Supreme Court declared Donnell the winner and confirmed the refusal to seat him, unconstitutional. A week after the decision, Donnell was inaugurated. McDaniel, the loser, was still unsatisfied and demanded that the recount continue even after Donnell took office. Not until the ballot check began turning up more and more votes for Donnell did McDaniel withdraw his request and concede defeat.

Mrs. Donnell said she never doubted that her husband would be governor. Still, she was much relieved when the matter was finally decided and they could move into the Governor's Mansion. They would be alone, however, much of the time in their new home. Their son, John, was attending law school at Washington University and their daughter, Ruth Donnell Rogers, had recently married and lived in St. Louis. With just the two of them living in the Mansion, the rooms seemed empty compared to their homey, Webster Groves bungalow on the outskirts of St. Louis.

As a political outsider moving on to the state scene, the fifty-six-year-old attorney was unknown in the Capitol. Though he had gained considerable recognition—as well as respect—for his conduct during the election standoff, some in the Capital City were not sure just how to pronounce his name. The local newspaper announced the correct version: not "Don-nell," but "Donal," and the "C" in the middle of his name was only an initial.

Donnell was valedictorian of his high school, college, and law school classes. Classmates considered him a superb orator.

Most of the Governor's credentials came from his academic achievements. He graduated first in his high school class in Maryville, Missouri, when he was only fifteen years old. At the University of Missouri, he earned a Phi Beta Kappa key, was the class valedictorian in 1904, and the top student in the law school.

As a young man, he served as city attorney for Webster Groves and as president of the Young Republicans of Missouri. His brief experience in state politics came during the 1908 governor's race when he served as a campaign aide to Herbert Hadley. The Republican candidate that year suffered from a lung condition that sometimes troubled him during his speaking tours. After addressing an audience for thirty minutes, Hadley would turn over the podium to his aide and slip out of the meeting, his absence unnoticed once Donnell began charming the audience.

Later, when Donnell became governor, that same easy, straightforward manner made friends for him among legislators, newsmen, and even Democrats. "Pinpoint sharp to details, meticulous against false impressions. Still, he's informal as a tennis shirt," one reporter wrote of the new chief executive. Each morning before eight o'clock, he walked to the Capitol where he worked until after seven in the

The Donnells in their Webster Groves home. Left to right: their son, John, a lawyer; Mrs. Donnell; daughter Ruth Donnell Rogers; the Governor; and, son-in-law Boyd Rogers.

evening. The last hour of each work day was spent on Masonic business—an extra task for him as Grand Master of Missouri Masons.

Still, the Governor never seemed too busy for visitors. One observer noted that Donnell's office door always stood open with

people coming and going "like commuters in a suburban [train] station." If his secretary was busy, Donnell would handle the phone calls himself. Bypassing formality, he would place a call to St. Louis and identify himself simply as "Forrest Donnell—the governor down at Jefferson City."

Donnell's pleasant manner and casual appearance made him seem all the more accessible. Unlike the impeccably groomed Stark, his conservative suits were often rumpled and his bronze-colored hair tumbled about in unmanagable curls. Though he enjoyed driving a car—and called it a hobby—he often strolled the sidewalks of Jefferson City just to visit. Whenever possible he avoided using the telephone in favor of going directly to see a legislator or official in person.

The Donnells pose with their grandchild in front of the playhouse in the Mansion backyard.

His refreshing attitude drew comments from all those with whom he associated. "He's enthusiastic about everything," one writer observed. "If he makes a mistake, it'll just be because he tried so hard not to," a businessman declared after meeting with the new Governor. Ruth Donnell Rogers described her father in much the same way, "Father was a workaholic, adamant about being on time, a perfectionist, yet kind and sympathetic."

However, taking over the leadership of the debt-ridden state required some toughness on the part of the new Governor. The *St. Louis Post-Dispatch* painted a bleak picture: "Departments were penniless, employees were payless, and the governor's office was borrowing stamps." Facing a $3.5 million state debt and shrinking revenues, Donnell pushed his department heads to

> "Father was a workaholic, adamant about being on time, a perfectionist, yet kind and sympathetic."

practice economy. In the meanwhile, he was forced to make arrangements with local banks to carry on financial operations until state receipts increased.

The General Assembly reflected the sluggish economy in its lack of action. Although the Governor went before the body in the final weeks of the 1941 session with nineteen measures he wanted approved, his efforts had little effect. By then it was mid-July and the lawmakers, who had been in session longer than any previous legislature, were more interested in adjournment than passing bills and let most of the Governor's proposals die in the final hours. One measure lawmakers adopted was the secret ballot that required a black sticker to cover each ballot number. Even then, Missouri was ridiculed for being one of the last states to approve the system.

While the Governor struggled to make ends meet at the Capitol, Mrs. Donnell found the Mansion to be "homey" and in good order. Having Barbara Pohlman, the take-charge housekeeper, on hand added to the smooth management of the home. Mrs. Donnell and her staff conveyed the same warm, informal feeling at the Mansion that her husband did at the Capitol. Even the butler drew a smile from visitors with his quaint greeting: "Welcome to the Governor's Mansion. You can rest your wraps in the back hall."

Mrs. Donnell's wish to stay out of the limelight did not prevent her from doing what was expected of a politician's wife. She had traveled with her husband during the campaign and occasionally made brief remarks to women's groups. In her

It was the Governor's job to be political and her job "to welcome all who came to her door."

new role as first lady, she launched the usual teas, receptions, and legislative dinners. Her natural inclination to ignore party differences made her even more effective as a hostess. It was the Governor's job to handle the politics, she said, and her job "to welcome all who came to her door."

As the Donnells became more enmeshed in their new duties, they made a great effort not to lose touch with everyday life. They were frequently seen worshipping at the local Methodist church and shopping in the downtown stores. When it came his turn to serve the mid-week supper at the church, the Governor gladly put on an apron and hat to help with the kitchen chores.

Hilda got to know all the Jefferson City merchants, even the town shoe-shine boy. One newspaper told of her purchasing groceries at a local store. The clerk was shocked to learn that he was to make a delivery to the Mansion and that his customer—who had been waiting for some time—was the First Lady. Before leaving the store, however, she cautioned the clerk never to serve her out of turn or show her any special favors on future shopping trips.

But it was not to be an ordinary term, no matter how hard the Donnells tried. Before the end of their first year at the Mansion, America was at war in Asia and Europe and national defense became the main focus of the state and country. To show their support, the Donnells cut back on entertaining as the war progressed.

Mansion chauffeur, Arthur Hardiman, stands beside the Buick bearing the state's number one license plate.

Eventually, even the state fair and the New Year's open house were canceled, lights on the Capitol dome were turned off and motorists were urged to drive no more than forty miles an hour to save on gas and tires. A passenger traveling with Donnell during the war years said the Governor carefully heeded the restriction, insisting that the driver not exceed thirty-nine and one-half miles an hour. The reduced speed limit, however, did not prevent the Governor from visiting all 114 counties in the state during his term.

Donnell also promoted food conservation. Missourians responded by planting Victory Gardens to help provide the fruits and vegetables that were in short supply. The Governor asked people to eat no more than two and one-half pounds of meat weekly and to limit their coffee drinking to one cup a day. In addition to setting up conservation measures for a fair allotment of food, materials, and equipment, Donnell saw to the operation of the draft and the state's civilian defense system.

War rationing stamps and food conservation became commonplace in Missouri in the 1940s.

The First Lady did her part for the war effort, too. Her call for Red Cross volunteers brought six hundred women to the Mansion to sign up for duty on the home front. Soldiers and sailors—many away from home for the first time—found a warm reception at the Mansion. When shortages in gasoline and food forced Americans to adopt a rationing system, Mrs. Donnell endured the inconvenience, standing in line to receive her allowance of coupons along with the other women of the city. Once when she was unable to find a Thanksgiving turkey at the market, she said without hesitation, "so we'll have chicken."

But there were limits on what the Governor would permit in the name of civilian defense. When local authorities wanted to stage a mock attack on the Capitol using fake bombs, chemical smoke, and artificial flames, Donnell refused. He saw little benefit to the plan and too much chance of property damage or personal injury. Although a $5,000 bomb shelter was proposed to go on the Mansion lawn, it was never built.

When scrap metal became in short supply, the legislature disposed of the five German cannons on the Capitol lawn that the War Department had given to the state. In a fervor of patriotism, the legislature sold the thirty-five tons of artillery for $15.26 a ton, a good price they felt, in addition to the symbolic value of turning the cannons back on the Germans. Donnell managed to save three other cannons—relics of the Civil War and Mexican War—claiming it was unclear if the state owned them or not.

With the war still underway, Missourians voting in the 1942 mid-term election leaned toward the Republican candidates, giving the Governor a GOP-controlled House and an equally divided Senate. Even then, his legislative programs faltered and Donnell was forced to take his case to the people by speaking to clubs and on radio programs to win support. Still, both of his major proposals—one, a merit system for state employees, the other, a unified tax collection measure—failed to pass the General Assembly. Before adjourning, however, lawmakers mustered the votes for a bill to set the governor's salary at $10,000 a year and the other elected officials at $7,500 annually.

T hough preoccupied with finances and war-related problems, the Donnells had a chance to welcome some distinguished visitors. Missouri hosted royalty when the Grand Duchess Charlotte of Luxembourg came to St. Louis. Former first ladies, the mayor, and all elected officials attended. Donnell, however, thought the cost of printing formal invitations to the event was too high. In the interest of economy, he had them individually typed by the social secretary at the Mansion.

A former resident, Nannie Morehouse Neale, daughter of Governor Morehouse, also visited the Donnells. Having lived in the Mansion as a child fifty years earlier, Mrs. Neale was pleased to hear that the proposed park between the Capitol and the Mansion was finally underway. "It was discussed when we were here," she said. In addition to sharing the experience of living at the Mansion, the Donnells discovered that they and the Morehouse family had, at different times, occupied the same frame house in Maryville.

Another guest, Ruth Bryan Owen Rodhe, served as the U.S. Minister to Denmark. The daughter of three-time presidential aspirant, William Jennings Bryan, was on a speaking tour of the country describing her diplomatic role. As a little girl she had accompanied her parents to Jefferson City and caused quite a stir when she threw a tantrum because she could not attend the Mansion reception given by First Lady Maggie Stephens.

Although the Donnells entertained graciously, they never offered their guests intoxicants. The Governor's well-known distaste for alcohol prompted one humorous incident related by Mrs. Donnell's former secretary, Virginia Henwood Gottleib. It was the custom for the governors to send each other gifts from their respective states just before the annual meeting of the National Governors' Association. Mrs. Gottleib brought each item up to Mrs. Donnell's bedroom—an area that doubled as an office—in order to write thank-you letters. One box seemed to be unusually light. Upon inspection, it was found to be

"Mother could remember names, Father couldn't."

a full case of beer bottles—"Just the bottles, no beer in them," Mrs. Gottleib recalled. She later found that the inmates working at the Mansion had discovered the beer first. Knowing the Donnells wanted no intoxicants, they had taken care of the situation themselves, carefully replacing the bottle caps and resealing the box.

In addition to writing thank-you notes, Mrs. Donnell found other ways to be socially helpful to her husband. "Mother could remember names, Father couldn't," Ruth Donnell Rogers explained. When the Governor faced an awkward situation, the First Lady would prompt her husband by dropping the name somewhere in the conversation. Turning to the Governor she might say, "Isn't it nice to see Mary Jo again?" Donnell, in turn, would smile thankfully and agree that it was, indeed, "Nice to see Mary Jo again."

One problem that could not be smoothed developed between the Governor and the U.S. Navy. Because battleships bear the names of states, it was customary to ask the governor of the designated state to choose a lady for the honor of breaking a bottle of champagne across the vessel's bow. But when it came time to commission the battleship USS *Missouri*, the Navy bypassed the Governor and asked U.S. Senator Harry Truman to make the selection. Truman chose his daughter, Margaret, for the bottle-breaking ceremony. Donnell, justifiably miffed by this "rare deviation from an old . . . custom," refused to attend the event, saying he had work to do in Missouri.

Donnell installed his father's hitching post in the backyard of the Mansion where it still remains.

Furthermore, he told the Navy that he was unaware of the military tradition calling for a state to acknowledge its namesake vessel with a silver service for the officers' mess. The Navy resolved the embarrassing conflict by temporarily transferring a silver punch bowl set from the former battleship USS *Missouri*.

At Christmas, the Donnells put aside politics and receiving lines and headed back to their Webster Groves home. With family gathered around, the Governor and First Lady did a responsive reading of the Christmas story from the Bible just as they

As Hilda Donnell posed for her official portrait, she had only one bit of advice for the artist, "Make me lovely."

had in years past. For other family events such as the christening of their two grandchildren, the Donnells chose to have the ceremonies performed in the parlor, the site of previous weddings and christenings at the Mansion.

Before departing the Capital City, the Donnells arranged to leave behind a few remembrances of their term. As Hilda posed for her official portrait, she had only one bit of advice for Charles Galt, the artist. "Make me lovely," she said, expressing a sentiment no doubt held by other first ladies, but not always aired.

In addition to the First Lady's portrait, the Governor bequeathed a family memento to the Mansion: a four-foot-tall concrete hitching post that once stood in the yard of his boyhood home. The post, bearing the initials "J. C. D.," belonged to his father, John C. Donnell, who owned a grocery and dry goods store in Maryville, Missouri, and served as the mayor of the city. The elder Donnell died several months before the Governor left office. Forrest, an only child, found the sturdy post a fitting tribute to his father and had it permanently installed near the back driveway.

At the end of his term, the Donnells left the Mansion, but not politics. During his final year as Governor, he overcame six primary opponents to gain the Republican nomination for the U.S. Senate. His general election campaign resulted in another photo finish with a winning margin of only 3,558 votes. Still, it was an impressive win for a Republican during an avalanche of Democratic victories led by the fourth-term election of President Franklin D. Roosevelt.

Donnell campaigning for the U.S. Senate.

The Donnells left the Mansion for a modest apartment on Capital Hill, close enough for him to ride a bus to the senate office building. Within months after his arrival in Washington, Franklin Roosevelt died and Harry Truman was elevated to the presidency. But Donnell showed no fondness for the policies of his fellow Missourian and often challenged the new President on his choice of appointments. In addition to being "a needlier of Harry Truman," the freshman senator fashioned a reputation for himself as the ablest constitutional lawyer in the chamber.

In 1950, as Donnell faced reelection, his narrow margins of victory were a decided handicap in a state that had long shown a preference for Democrats. In an effort to help, Joseph McCarthy—the Communist-labeling senator from Wisconsin—campaigned in Missouri on behalf of the GOP ticket. The outspoken McCarthy labeled Democrats "Commiecrats" and called Truman a "red sympathizer." "McCarthyism"—as his tactics were called—did not set well in the President's home state and Donnell wound up being the only Republican senator in the United States to be defeated that year.

Leaving Washington after one term, Donnell returned to his St. Louis law practice, continuing to go to his downtown office even after he passed his ninetieth birthday. In 1980 he died in his sleep at the age of ninety-five; Hilda, at age ninety-one, had died a year earlier.

Forrest Donnell had come to public life after a shaky victory during a time of fear and uncertainty at home and abroad. Nonetheless, the man with the rumpled suit and the tousled hair gave Missouri the gentle, but firm, leadership the times demanded. For his efforts he earned the grateful respect of all who knew him.

Newly elected Senator Donnell (center) takes his oath of office from Vice President Henry Wallace (right) as President Truman looks on.

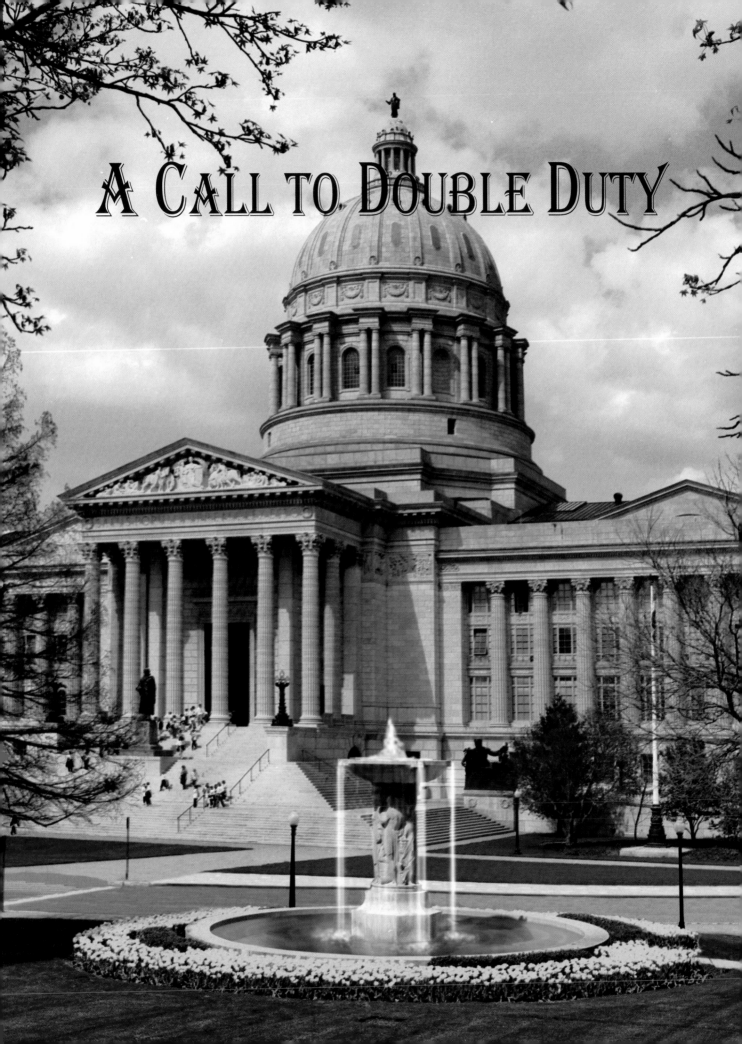

A Call to Double Duty

Governor Phil Matthew Donnelly
Juanita Flower McFadden Donnelly
1945-1949 and 1953-1957

Donnelly twice left the serenity of his hometown to shoulder the responsibilities that come to those living in the Governor's Mansion.

"Where's Lebanon, Missouri? I've never heard of the place." That was not an unusual comment among Missourians in 1944. But those who followed state politics knew that the quiet railroad town in south Missouri—population five thousand—was about to be thrust into prominence. Two of the town's favorite sons, fifty-three-year-old Phil Donnelly and thirty-eight-year-old Jean Paul Bradshaw, were facing-off in a political duel for the governorship.

When reporters rolled into town to cover the story, they found little evidence of the hotly contested race—no placards in the store windows, no posters decorating the trees and poles. The people of Lebanon had planned it that way. They wanted, at least outwardly, to be fair to their hometown boys and refused any visible taking of sides.

Under the surface, however, the conflict simmered, dividing families and friends in the little Ozark community. The local newspaper finally editorialized in support of Donnelly, but on election day the townspeople could not have been more evenly divided. They cast 1,731 votes for Republican Jean Paul Bradshaw and 1,731 votes for Democrat Phil Donnelly. (Laclede County, the traditionally Republican area in which they lived, went for Bradshaw and Tom Dewey, President Roosevelt's opponent.) Nonetheless, Phil Donnelly, the tall, silver-haired state senator, racked up winning numbers across the state to become

The Cedars of Lebanon . . . By Betty Love

LEBANON
5000 FRIENDLY PEOPLE
AND 2 CANDIDATES FOR GOVERNOR

JEAN PAUL BRADSHAW REPUBLICAN CANDIDATE FOR GOVERNOR

PHIL DONNELLY DEMOCRATIC CANDIDATE FOR GOVERNOR

(Facing page)
The Missouri State Capitol.

249

Phil and Juanita Donnelly at home in Lebanon, Missouri.

the first governor from southern Missouri in fifty years.

The victory caught Donnelly and his wife off guard. They had focused all their attention on election day and had made no plans beyond that point. When asked about their moving arrangements, Mrs. Donnelly told reporters, "It may seem strange, but we have not even talked about it."

Leaving the comfortable bungalow they had lived in for the last twenty-eight years was simply too painful to consider. The unpretentious cottage-style home, built by Donnelly's father, sat next door to the one where the new Governor was born. Juanita had put in many hours planting flower beds and tending a lovely lawn bordered with more than eighty varieties of irises. In addition to her gardening, she occasionally helped at her husband's nearby law office, taught a Bible class at the local Christian church, and cared for a chronically ill neighbor.

Juanita—often called "Neat" by her friends—showed little interest in fancy handwork or cooking—although her husband considered her quite a good cook. She enjoyed her service as a Gray Lady for the USO more than kitchen chores or political campaigning. As captain of the uniformed ladies corps, she radiated enthusiasm on her weekly trips to help wounded servicemen at the Fort Leonard Wood hospital. She explained, "The Gray Ladies do the big, little things for the soldiers. We shop for them, mail their packages, and send their telegrams, sometimes write letters for them."

In addition to her hospital routine, she served as hostess at the local USO center each Saturday evening. Phil sometimes joined her when his schedule permitted. With their only child, David, away at college, they often invited two to six servicemen into their home for the weekend.

Life would become a lot more complicated in the Governor's Mansion, but friends knew the Donnellys were well suited for their new roles in Jefferson City. Phil had always been a workhorse—a man who viewed the law as both his profession and his hobby. Even as a youngster, he was known as a serious, studious boy who seldom scuffled or fished or went swimming in the creek with the other boys. He found the activities at the county courthouse more intriguing. Attracted by the loud oratory coming from the open windows, he often slipped into a seat near the back of the courtroom to listen to the country lawyers argue the merits of a case. His competitive side later showed up in high school when he started playing baseball and football and eventually began umpiring sports events.

Upon graduation, Donnelly left his hometown to study at St. Louis University. After earning a law degree, he returned to Lebanon and engaged in a spirited, but unsuccessful, bid for prosecuting attorney. Even so, his quick smile and good humor served him well; he easily landed the office with a second try in 1916. Six years later at the age of thirty-one, Donnelly captured a seat in the General Assembly. In 1924, after serving only one term, voters advanced him to the state Senate.

During the next twenty years in the upper body, Donnelly served twice as president pro tem and twice as floor leader. His knowledge of state government—the players and the process—would later give him a clear advantage as chief executive.

Juanita Donnelly also benefited from knowing her way around the Capital City. As the wife of an influential senator, she often stood in receiving lines or served tea at the Governor's Mansion. She and Phil had once spent the night at the Mansion as the guests of Governor and Mrs. Stark. Yet she told reporters she felt "some fear" at the thought of becoming the state's first lady. To ease the transition, outgoing Governor and Mrs. Forrest Donnell entertained the new residents of the Mansion three times before the inauguration.

Moving some of her personal furnishings to the home also helped Mrs. Donnelly adjust to her new surroundings. She informed newsmen that her grand piano would be going to the Mansion for her own enjoyment, if not her husband's. "He has neither an ear or taste for music. Why, he wouldn't know Bach from boogie-woogie," she laughed. Mrs. Donnelly found her musical counterpart in their son, David, who often accompanied her by playing the horn.

If Phil Donnelly cared little for music, his wife cared even less for politics. She had taken no role in campaigning and attended political rallies or dinners only when specifically invited. However, the Donnellys shared one thing: a devotion to Chinkie, their chow dog. The couple agreed that a place must be made for him at the Mansion.

Moving to Jefferson City shifted Mrs. Donnelly's life from hospitals and USO centers to a stately Mansion. Still,

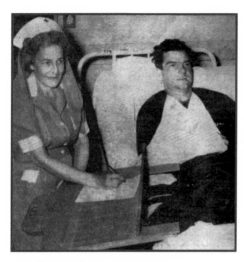

Mrs. Donnelly, a member of the Gray Lady Corps of the Red Cross, assists a wounded serviceman in writing a letter.

Friends and neighbors gather around the radio to hear the election returns in the Donnellys' home.

there was no getting away from the side effects of wartime—even during the inauguration. A shortage of fabric forced the honorary colonels to wear civilian clothes rather than the traditional gold-braided uniforms that had always added to the colorful celebration. In what was Missouri's only inauguration during wartime since the Civil War, the colonels—a cadre of 136 of the Governor's top supporters—

The Governor's cadre of 136 Colonels was designated only by white armbands.

were designated only by a white armband and badge.

The incoming First Lady showed restraint, too. She chose to have her inaugural gown made by a friend, but added the trim herself by sewing on hundreds of seed pearls in a floral pattern around the neckline of the dress. Wartime restrictions caused a scarcity of sugar and other food items she needed for the inaugural reception and the shortage of civilian men made it impossible to find waiters and butlers. Friends of the Donnellys came to the rescue by offering their household help to serve during the inaugural event.

(Lower left) Governor-elect Donnelly rides in an open limousine with his predecessor, Governor Forrest Donnell.
(Lower right) The Donnellys, their son David, and chow dog, Chinkie, pose on the Mansion steps.

THE "SECOND LADY" OF THE MANSION

When Juanita Donnelly first arrived at the Mansion, there to greet her was the small, gray-haired housekeeper. Primly attired in a light-blue uniform and crisp white apron, Barbara Pohlman ruled "like a benevolent and unobtrusive dictator." She had come to the Mansion in 1909 as housekeeper and nurse for Governor Hadley's three children and remained to serve subsequent families, except for a nine-year absence due to family illness.

Barbara saw to the day-to-day operations of the house, as well as the preparations for entertaining. It thrilled her to see people enjoying themselves at the Mansion. "I love parties," she declared with a broad smile as she

"I love parties."

readied the house for a special event. Though accustomed to unexpected guests, even Barbara was shocked once when she prepared for two hundred members of a church group and over one thousand showed up.

Barbara knew all the lore and legends of the old home by heart. Showing visitors through the spacious rooms, she could recount stories of former residents or point out such mysteries as a signature scratched on one of the bedroom window panes. Barbara made the house friendlier not only to visitors but also to each of the first families who moved in, most of whom were overwhelmed by the imposing Victorian home.

During World War II, she saw to it that all the Mansion finery, including the linen, was used only on special occasions. But she missed the fancy pre-war parties, the splendid military balls, and fancy receptions. "It use to be a big thrill for me to see all those people here," she declared. "What a sight those colonels were, all dressed up and marching down those front stairs with everything on but the kitchen stove!"

Barbara's role as guardian of the Mansion extended beyond preserving the traditions and furnishings. Her extraordinary memory was often tested when she was called upon to locate some item long removed or stored away. Just before the inauguration, for instance, when the Donnellys inquired about the three-piece clock and vase set left by Governor Marmaduke, Barbara quickly dug the old pieces out of storage and returned them to the library for display.

At the time of her retirement during Donnelly's second term, the indispensable housekeeper had served ten first families. In her more than forty years at the Mansion, she had made many contributions, ranging from reassuring distraught first ladies to caring for the children and pets of the Mansion. But most of all, she passed on a tradition of hospitality for those who followed in her footsteps. Mrs. Donnelly paid her the highest tribute when she said, "You feel as long as Barbara's in the house, everything will go all right."

Barbara Pohlman standing on the Mansion steps with former Governor and Mrs. Forrest Donnell's grandchildren.

The lack of artillery and ammunition nearly scuttled the nineteen-gun salute fired to honor a new Governor. The National Guard scoured the state's army bases in search of two cannons, but without success. In a show of neighborliness, Kansas offered two of its big guns for the day. When Donnelly discovered that delivery of the cannon would cost eight hundred dollars and require a squad of soldiers, he abandoned the idea and achieved the big boom effect with fifty-seven sticks of dynamite ignited at intervals from across the river.

"Every day some major problem presents itself" at the Mansion.

With the noise of the election and the inauguration behind them, the Donnellys anticipated quiet evenings at the Mansion. Having lived near the Frisco railroad tracks in their hometown, they adapted quickly to the rumbling of trains passing just below the bluff. It was not until the railroad started leaving cattle cars overnight on a siding that Donnelly started to take notice. The situation improved only after the Governor—drowsy from loss of sleep—complained to newsmen that something needed to be done about "those cows [that] keep me awake half the night."

During her first week at the Mansion, Juanita Donnelly intended to explore her spacious new home, meet the staff, and lay plans for upcoming social events. But news came that her mother had fallen, broken a hip, and was in a Springfield hospital. Juanita left immediately to be by her side, but there was little she could do. Her mother died five days after the accident. (A few years later, a similar tragedy occurred when Mrs. Donnelly's father fell at the Mansion, broke a hip, and died shortly thereafter.)

Faced with wartime shortages, Mrs. Donnelly had her inaugural gown made by a friend and added the trim herself by sewing on hundreds of seed pearls.

Following her mother's funeral, Mrs. Donnelly settled into her new surroundings where she soon discovered the unpredictable nature of life in the Mansion. "Every day some major problem presents itself," she declared. That being the case, she felt fortunate not to be entirely on her own. There to give her assurance was Barbara Pohlman, the housekeeper who had served eight previous first families.

Keeping good kitchen help, however, became a bigger problem than either Barbara or the First Lady anticipated. Author Jerena Giffin tells of the Governor being home alone one evening reading his newspaper in the Nook when he heard a strange noise coming from the dining room. He went to investigate and found the cook lying in front of the fireplace "sound asleep and snoring." After spending the afternoon at the local tavern, she was in no shape to prepare dinner for the Governor. The family continued to tolerate the frequent "sick spells" of the cook until the sheriff called one day to say she was in jail. The Governor—exasperated by her behavior—suggested that it might be a good idea to keep her there for a while.

In spite of cutbacks and shortages in household help, the First Lady tried to keep up appearances. She felt Missourians considered the Mansion their property and wanted it maintained "in tip-top shape at all times." They also wanted the opportunity to view the old house. Mrs. Donnelly complied by assigning her personal secretary to act as the tour guide. Groups were kept to no more than thirty-five and no children below high school age were allowed.

Although wartime restrictions caused the Donnellys to curtail many social events during their early months at the Mansion, the visit of Vice President Harry Truman called for a special celebration. The Mansion reception in February 1945 came just two months before he became commander-in-chief following the death of President Franklin D. Roosevelt.

With the conclusion of the war later that year, several military leaders visited the state. Among them were Missouri's own General Omar Bradley and European commander General Dwight D. Eisenhower. In 1946 Winston Churchill made a historic visit to Westminster College in Fulton where he delivered his famous speech declaring that an "iron curtain" of communism had fallen, dividing Europe. Later, the British prime minister waved from his open limousine to those who lined the streets during a parade in his honor.

The postwar era brought an end to rationing and the skimping endured by the First Family, along with other Missourians. Meat was served at formal dinners once again; trips were planned without the worry of gasoline and tire rationing; and, work resumed at the Mansion that had been delayed for lack of men and material. The exterior of the house got a new coat of white paint, worn appliances were

British Prime Minister Winston Churchill is paraded through the streets of Fulton in 1946 on his way to make his famed Iron Curtain speech. Next to Churchill is President Harry Truman; Donnelly is seated in front of them. Several Secret Service agents are hanging onto the side of the car.

On deck of the USS *Missouri*, President Harry Truman (left) looks over part of the $10,000 silver service presented to the battleship in 1948 by Governor Donnelly (far right).

When Sally Rand, the popular fan dancer, performed at the state fair, Donnelly was disturbed by the image she might portray.

replaced, and a second-floor bedroom became a private living room for the first time.

Mrs. Donnelly replaced the worn tapestry on the dining room walls with a large-patterned paper above the paneled wainscoting. She enhanced other walls on the first floor, too, adding her own oil portrait and photos of earlier first ladies not yet featured. Fifteen pictures from the book *Women of the Mansion* were put in oval frames made by prison inmates and placed in two neat rows along the back wall of the Nook.

Although the Donnellys made some minor repairs to the Mansion, the Governor refused to be lured into any unnecessary expenditures. When the legislature appropriated four thousand dollars to replace the prewar Buick he was driving, the Governor refused to spend it. In the hope of making a sale, a persistent car salesman left a shiny, new Cadillac sitting next to the Governor's parking space in the Capitol basement. But the ploy backfired. After a week the Governor requested that the car be moved. He did not need a new vehicle, he said, and if he did, he would pick it out himself.

Though the war abroad was over, the Governor had a few battles of his own yet to fight. He clashed with the federal bureaucracy, insisting that the state be permitted to run its own employment service. After hearing complaints about the School for Boys at Boonville, he conducted his own investigation which ended with firing the board and appointing a new administration.

In another confrontation, the Governor faced 250 veterans who had marched to the Capitol rotunda, each demanding a four-hundred-dollar bonus. Donnelly defused the situation, speaking reasonably—but firmly—to the men, he urged them to take up the issue with their legislators and not disrupt the democratic process they had fought to preserve and protect.

The Governor, however, did not always get his way when dealing with legislators. During such times, he was quick to use his veto pen to curtail special interest legislation. When the lawmakers attempted to increase their own salary by five dollars a day and to give the judiciary a pay hike, Donnelly refused to sign the bill. He rejected a total of twenty-six bills, more than any other governor, and none of his vetoes were overridden, not even by the Republican-controlled legislature.

The Governor turned down more than unfavorable legislation; he once spurned a performer at the state fair. When Sally Rand, the popular fan dancer, performed at the annual event in Sedalia, Donnelly was disturbed by the image she might portray. Rand, a native of Weaubleau, Missouri, owned a farm in Hickory County and was plainly the grand attraction at the fair. However, the Governor made it clear to the press that Sally was only a part of the carnival and did not represent the state of Missouri.

It saddened Mrs. Donnelly to look out the window and see the unfinished garden just below the house. The area was transformed by the addition of a sunken garden, shelter house, a goldfish pool, pergola, terraces, and walkways.

Although Juanita Donnelly's work greatly enhanced the Governor's Garden, she would not permit the area to be named for her. Years later this granite marker was added to commemorate her devotion to the project.

In Honor of
JUANITA McFADDEN
DONNELLY
First Lady of Missouri
1945-1949   1953-1957
Whose love and care was instrumental
in completing the Governor's Garden
in 1948

The Donnellys enjoy breakfast for two seated in front of one of the Mansion's marble fireplaces.

While the Governor was doing his best to preserve the morals and the money of the state, the First Lady ignored political issues. She delighted in blooming plants and went on with her landscaping and gardening, just as she would have done at home. It saddened her, however, to look out her window and see the unfinished garden just below the Mansion. The public eyesore was nothing more than "piles of rubble and unsightly excavations"—the remains of a depression-era project that ran out of funds.

The First Lady extracted fifteen thousand dollars from the legislature to make improvements on the abandoned site. Not content to oversee the project from the back porch of the Mansion, Juanita became the on-site supervisor. Once when a group of ladies arrived from her hometown, they found the First Lady in the garden, down on her hands and knees, digging alongside the prison work crew. Through her persistent efforts, the area was transformed by the addition of a sunken garden, shelter house, a goldfish pool, pergola, terraces, and walkways. Her plantings blossomed, as did the lily pads in the pool, but the goldfish—not as hearty as the plants—died by the scores.

In spite of her hard work, Mrs. Donnelly refused to permit the garden to be named for her. David Donnelly later explained that his mother was a "very private person and did not seek, nor would she allow, acclaim for anything she did." Nonetheless, one newspaper wrote, "Whether or not the small restful spot in the center of the city is ever given a name, Juanita Donnelly has left there the quiet reflection of a serene and gentle personality." Today, the area is simply called the "Governor's Garden," a place where children can play about the pool area and where weddings and outdoor performances are held throughout the year.

Toward the end of his term, Donnelly was asked to give the nomination speech for President Harry Truman at the 1948 Democratic National Convention in Philadelphia. He agreed and, out of courtesy, submitted his text beforehand. Convention managers felt that the Governor's remarks would not get enough applause without references to former President Roosevelt and rewrote the copy. Angered by the alterations, Donnelly let it be known that he was not delivering a tribute to President Roosevelt, but a speech about the record and accomplishments of Harry Truman.

In the end, the Governor delivered his own text and won a thirty-eight-minute ovation from the convention. Truman supporters wearing red, white, and blue hats led the lively demonstration with the sounds of horns, cowbells, whistle, drums, and washboards reverberating across the

THE MYSTERY OF THE MANSION MOTHS

During the upheaval of construction at the Mansion, Mrs. Donnelly unexpectedly solved the forty-year-old "Mystery of the Mansion Moths" when workers removed the old dining room wall-covering. First Lady Gertrude Folk had added tapestry to the dining room walls after a fire in 1905. She declared that her splendid art work would

"never have to be replaced." Since that time the Mansion had been overrun by moths. No one suspected that Mrs. Folk's much revered tapestry had anything do with the problem. When the wall covering came down, it was revealed that the pesky insects had been breeding in the paste used to attach the fabric to the walls.

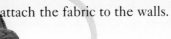

convention hall. The President, obviously pleased with the speech and its reception, later repaid the generous remarks by telling members of the Missouri legislature that Donnelly was Missouri's greatest governor.

More accolades came to the Ozark Irishman. By the end of his term, editorial writers were comparing Donnelly to such popular governors as Hadley and Gardner.

Juanita was not interested in her sixty-one-year-old husband resuming the heavy duties of the governorship.

"Few men have walked to bat as governor of the state of Missouri and have smacked out as many home runs," one editor proclaimed. Still, the Missouri Constitution prohibited the chief executive from serving two consecutive terms. Donnelly had no choice; it was time to return home.

Back in Lebanon, Donnelly joined his son, David, in a law partnership that signaled the end to the Governor's long career in state government—or so it appeared. But four years later, in another epoch-making election, Missourians clamored for the return of the former Governor. Juanita was not at all interested in her sixty-one-year-old husband resuming the heavy duties of the governorship. But Phil Donnelly, the consummate politician, could not resist the lure of another term. His reelection in 1952 made him the first chief executive in Missouri history to win two four-year terms.

A large banner beneath the inaugural podium hailed the Governor's return for a second term. Honorary colonels, designated by white arm bands, line the stairway.

When General Dwight D. Eisenhower, the popular war hero and Republican presidential candidate, carried the state by 20,000 votes, Donnelly's margin soared over 90,000.

The Capital City welcomed the Lebanon couple once

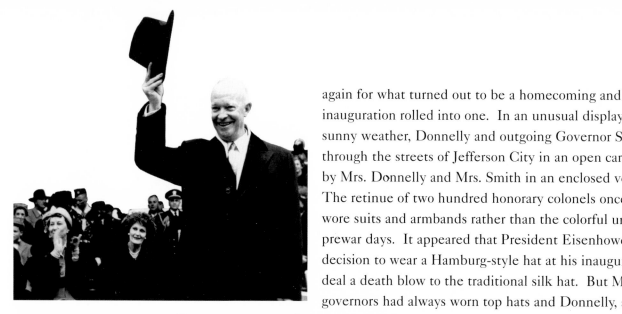

In 1952 President Eisenhower chose to wear a Hamburg hat at his inauguration, but in Missouri Donnelly stayed with the traditional top hat.

again for what turned out to be a homecoming and inauguration rolled into one. In an unusual display of mild, sunny weather, Donnelly and outgoing Governor Smith rode through the streets of Jefferson City in an open car, followed by Mrs. Donnelly and Mrs. Smith in an enclosed vehicle. The retinue of two hundred honorary colonels once again wore suits and armbands rather than the colorful uniforms of prewar days. It appeared that President Eisenhower's decision to wear a Hamburg-style hat at his inaugural would deal a death blow to the traditional silk hat. But Missouri's governors had always worn top hats and Donnelly, a Democrat, was not about to take his fashion cues from a Republican. One noticeable absence was that of his son, David, who sent congratulations from Verdun, France, where he was on military duty.

Fortunately, there was no evidence of the ill-feeling that had developed between the Forrest Smith and the Phil Donnelly camps during the primary. Publicly, Smith had taken no sides, but many of his supporters did not back Donnelly for a second term. Nonetheless, the Smiths invited the incoming First Family to a turkey and ham dinner at the Mansion on the night before the inauguration. Smith even left his successor a new car—a $6,700 Cadillac that he had ordered earlier.

Though excited by their return to the Capital City, living at the Mansion would not be the same for Mrs. Donnelly. Longtime housekeeper Barbara Pohlman, feeling the house was in good hands, took the opportunity to retire after having served ten first families.

The Donnellys not only lost the "Second Lady of the Mansion" but also nearly lost the eighty-three-year-old executive home itself. In 1954 legislators eyed the historic site for a parking lot. Tired of repairing the "architectural monstrosity," they appropriated $250,000 to replace it with a more modern residence located elsewhere. But the Governor had grown fond of the old home and did not have the heart to let it be destroyed. His veto of the bill spared the Mansion until funds and sentiment would make a complete restoration possible.

Donnelly made judicial history with his appointment of Theodore McMillian of St. Louis to the circuit court—the state's first African-American to serve in the position.

At the Capitol, the Governor found a number of pesky problems awaiting his attention. Upon returning to office, he immediately launched an investigation of the alleged shortages in the Department of Revenue. He advocated several measures to control organized labor and opposed efforts to unionize the St. Louis police department—a position that cost him political support in the metropolitan areas.

The Governor took on monetary issues with equal tenacity. He told teachers that Missouri ranked among the top seven states in school funding and that no further money was available without new taxes. Although he declared a $9 million appropriation for education illegal, he went on to establish a school foundation program and to add a two-cent cigarette tax for education. He also secured a $75 million bond issue to upgrade the state's hospitals, prisons, and universities. Not since the road building program twenty years earlier had Missourians been asked to approve such a large capital improvements expenditure.

Governor Donnelly (center) told rioting inmates at the state penitentiary to return to their cells or be shot.

In 1954 Donnelly faced another test of his leadership. When a major prison riot broke out in the state penitentiary, the Governor quickly summoned all the resources at his command, including highway patrolmen and national guardsmen. Rampaging convicts in the one-hundred-year-old facility cited overcrowding, poor food, and unfair administration as reasons for the outbreak.

Donnelly, the former prosecuting attorney, proved to be a tough negotiator. Standing in the prison yard, he told inmates there would be no concessions until they released the guards and returned to their cells.

"Anybody who's not in their cell will be shot," he declared firmly. And added, "If you harm the hair on the head of one of those guards, we will kill the whole bunch [of you]." Within twenty-four hours, order was restored, but not before four inmates died and nearly $5 million in damages occurred at the institution. In the end, prison reform sprung from the incident with the construction of new inmate facilities and better training programs for personnel.

The harsh encounters of public life were offset by at least one joyous occasion during Donnelly's second term—the marriage of his son, David. But it was not a Mansion wedding; the young couple preferred a church ceremony and chose to be wed in Lebanon.

Upon retiring from public office for the last time, the sixty-five-year-old Governor returned home and again joined his son in the law practice. Five years later, however, Donnelly suffered a paralytic stroke and died a month afterwards.

His thirty years of unblemished public service remain a tribute to the Governor who twice left the serenity of his hometown to shoulder the responsibilities that come to those living in the Missouri Governor's Mansion. Each time Phil Donnelly, the silver-haired lawyer from Lebanon, gave Missourians the clean, conservative government they expected and knew that he would deliver.

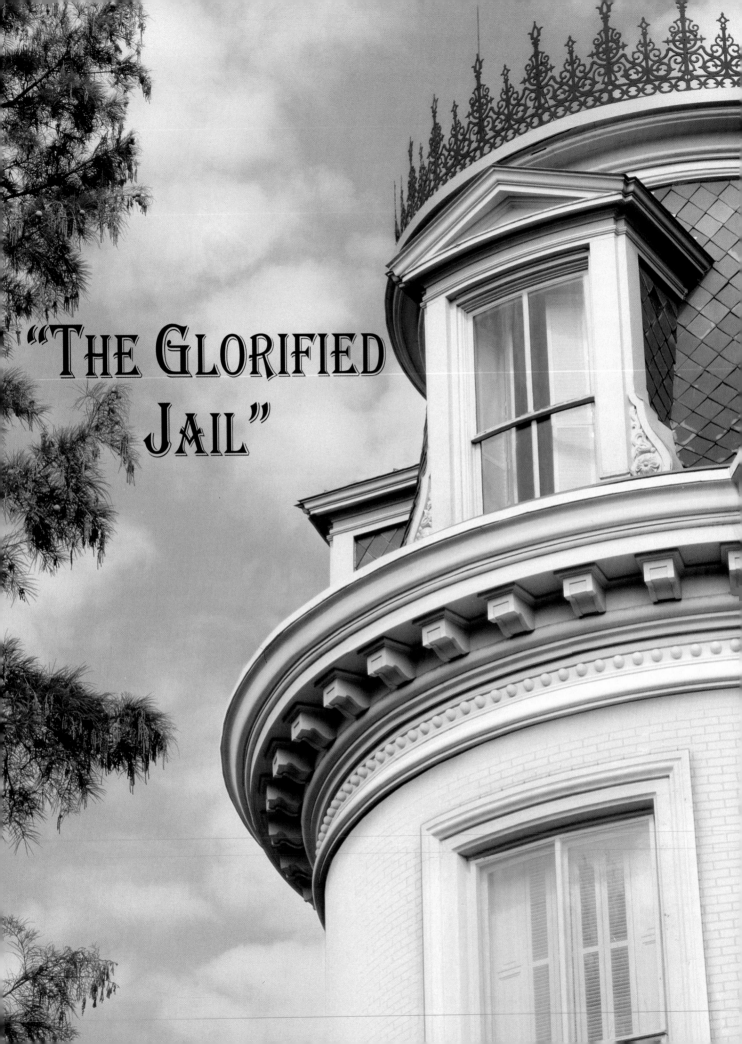

"The Glorified Jail"

GOVERNOR FORREST SMITH
MILDRED WILLIAMS SMITH
1949-1953

"Sometimes I feel like I am confined in a glorified jail. More than anything else I miss seeing and visiting with my many friends." ~ Governor Forrest Smith

One newspaper writer called Forrest Smith "the most visitin' man in Missouri." During the sixteen years he served as state auditor, the door to his private office on the second floor of the Capitol always stood open. His easy manner became a trademark of the onetime farm boy and educator who took a liking to politics.

Smith started his public service career as a deputy assessor. He later served eight years as county clerk before opening a jewelry store in Richmond, Missouri. With his appointment to the State Tax Commission, he traveled to every county in the state and greeted people in courthouses and on city streets, developing a wide range of friendships. His reduction in the assessed value of farmland made him highly regarded in rural Missouri.

Despite his popularity, when he ran for state auditor in 1928 on the Democratic ticket, he got caught in the GOP landslide and had to wait another four years to claim the office. By the time Smith ran for governor in 1948, he had been on the statewide ballot for auditor in five successive elections—four of which he won. As an established politician with high name recognition, it was little wonder that he carried 102 of the state's 114 counties, winning by the greatest majority ever given a candidate for governor in Missouri before him.

With Forrest Smith headed for the Governor's Mansion and Harry Truman back in the White House, Missouri Democrats had a lot to celebrate. But on inauguration day, a freezing drizzle and slippery roadways greatly reduced the number attending the Capitol ceremony. The weather also forced the cancellation of the flyover of bomber and fighter planes scheduled to highlight the event.

Even so, a number of rosy-cheeked spectators lined the streets to view the traditional parade that included 179 newly appointed Missouri colonels. The long-

(Facing page)
The south bay of the Mansion.

263

standing practice of outfitting the elite corps had been abandoned during World War II because of the shortage of fabric for uniforms. In the first inaugural celebration since peace was declared, the colonels marched briskly along the one-mile parade route, wearing their new uniforms topped with flowing, red-lined capes. Smith and outgoing Governor Donnelly wisely chose the warmth of an enclosed sedan rather than a ride in the traditional open vehicle.

Before the new First Couple had time to settle into the Mansion, they headed to Washington for another inaugural celebration. Along with five hundred Missourians, the Smiths traveled to the nation's capital aboard a thirty-five-car inaugural train in a show of support for President Harry S. Truman—the state's first resident to live in the White House. On the evening before the national event, the Smiths hosted a reception for the Trumans, at a Washington hotel with seventeen hundred guests attending.

One of Smith's honorary colonels smartly attired in a red-lined cape.

U pon returning home, the Governor packed up his personal belongings from the auditor's office and moved a few doors down the Capitol corridor to the executive suite. The "most visitin' man in Missouri" found the transition difficult; he felt isolated and restricted in his new job. "More than anything else, I miss seeing and visiting with my many friends," the new Governor lamented.

Forrest and Mildred also missed their family. They eagerly anticipated the visits of their two married daughters, Forrestine and Mary Jo, and their two grand-children. Three other grandchildren were born during Smith's term in office, one of whom was nicknamed "little Guv." To please the youngsters when they came on holiday visits, the Smiths added a sandbox and a slide to the Mansion grounds. During the early hours of Easter morning, the Governor could be seen sneaking about the house, hiding colored eggs for the children to find. The Smiths' two-year-old granddaughter, Jody, made the presentation of the First Lady's official portrait a more memorable event for the honorary colonels and their wives assembled for the unveiling. When Forrestine pulled the cord to loosen the heavy tapestry concealing the portrait of her mother, the covering fell on Jody, completely blanketing the little girl. Moments later Jody was unveiled, reappearing with the glee of a child delighted with a new game.

The visits of the grandchildren continued to enliven the old home. One youngster had to be rescued from a locked bathroom by the fire department and another released a squirrel in the Mansion that took some time to retrieve.

When the grandchildren returned home, the stillness of the Mansion was all the more apparent. Once when Mrs. Smith made a trip to visit family, the Governor commented on the emptiness of the old house and how big the rooms seemed when he was there alone. "Sometimes I feel like I'm confined to a glorified jail," he wrote in a constituent report.

The Smiths filled the void by frequently inviting guests to the Mansion. Among the steady stream of visitors were governors and Washington dignitaries, including Vice President Alben W. Barkley. Five hundred Democratic women who were meeting in Jefferson City also enjoyed the breadth of Mrs. Smith's hospitality, as did seven hundred ladies gathered for the state P.E.O. convention.

For the annual New Year's open house, the First Lady served punch and cookies to all her visitors.

Smith called himself a "flower lover" and wore a rose in his lapel most of the time.

One such celebration brought over four hundred guests to the Mansion, including the Governor's colonels who welcomed another opportunity to wear their expensive inaugural uniforms. Several Christmas trees still decorated the spacious rooms and the stairway was hung with greenery and greeting cards, many from governors of the forty-eight states and the territories.

Even uninvited guests received a cordial welcome at the Mansion. One night three traveling salesmen, who had spent too much time at the local tavern, wandered

Smith is sworn into office as his daughter juggles the grandchildren.

The Smiths hosted seventeen hundred guests at a Washington party for newly elected President Harry Truman.

into the Mansion thinking it was their hotel. A legislative dinner was just concluding and the doorman mistook the intruders for late arrivals. The Governor made no fuss over the incident. After visiting with the men, he sat them down to the same turkey dinner he had served his guests. Of all their guests, however, the Smiths found legislators the most difficult to entertain. Because of their schedules, the lawmakers often came late to social events, eating hurriedly in order to return to evening committee meetings.

Even uninvited guests received a cordial welcome at the Mansion.

Though the Governor happily fulfilled the social requirements of Mansion life, he welcomed every opportunity to take part in his two favorite pastimes: hunting and football. After bird season ended, he attended football games no matter what the weather. When duck season once overlapped with the Missouri vs. Nebraska football game, the Governor stopped hunting just long enough to take in the event. As a bird watcher, he was also fascinated by the sea gulls that took over a sandbar on the river opposite the Mansion, but once fussed about a flock of starlings on the Mansion grounds that kept waking him in the early morning hours.

At Christmas the First Lady decorated the stairway with greenery and greeting cards.

The Governor and First Lady shared a common fondness for gardens. He called himself a "flower lover" and wore a rose in his lapel most of the time. Mrs. Smith, eager to please the Governor, had a thousand crocuses planted at the Mansion in the shape of an "M," but only a few came up the following year. She later discovered the reason: prison inmates who had been instructed to place the bulbs below the frost line buried them too deep and the flowers never bloomed.

The First Lady had more success with her renovation of the Mansion. She rebuilt the front porch and painted the interior walls, including those in the ballroom. The kitchen got its first automatic dishwasher and the library was dressed down to become a small, less formal living room.

Her attempt at having the layers of accumulated paint sandblasted from the exterior walls was a disappointment, however. The eighty-year-old brick was too soft to withstand the stripping process then available. (Not until the Hearnes administration would new paint-removing techniques make it safe to restore the brick to its natural pinkish color.) Reluctantly, Mrs. Smith permitted the Mansion to get its customary face-lift—a task that took two weeks and one hundred gallons of white paint.

The Mansion is "just like a hotel" where guests are rough on the tea cups and linens.

Whether it was painting or planting, the First Lady quickly addressed the problems of the old house as soon as they came to her attention. Instead of trying to make do with the limited serving pieces, she completed the set of Castleton china and added to the set of Mount Vernon sterling silver flatware. Even the Governor got involved in the new purchases. Noting that the home was "just like a hotel" where guests were rough on the tea cups and linens, the Governor took time from the affairs of state to accompany his wife to St. Louis for a day of shopping.

As usual, other deficiencies at the Mansion came to light when least expected. The need for furniture repairs became obvious when the Governor fell through the seat of a dining room chair one evening just as he was pouring a glass of milk. Smith, who had just lost twenty-two pounds, quipped, "I thought my diet was going well until this happened."

Before long the Governor learned that things were not going well elsewhere. The suspicion of voting irregularities and syndicated crime in Kansas City and St. Louis brought U. S. Senator Kefauver's National Crime Commission to Missouri, casting an unfavorable light on the state. The Governor denied the report that he had received campaign money from gambling interests. Nor had he made any promises, he testified before the committee, although he suspected others may have made promises he knew nothing about. Smith proudly pointed to his law enforcement record and the performance of those he appointed. In defense of the metropolitan areas, he reported that Missouri's cities were "freer of rackets and commercial gambling than they have been for many years."

The state was not without political conflict, however. Harsh feelings developed between Smith and Truman over the candidates in the 1950 U.S. Senate race. The two had agreed to make a public announcement of their support for a mutual friend, State Senator Emory Allison. In addition, Smith was to ask another potential candidate for the office, Thomas Hennings, to step aside to avoid a primary battle. Smith apparently had second thoughts about his pact with the President and never made the request or the announcement.

As the two senatorial candidates went head-to-head in one of the state's most bitter political battles, Truman wrote a letter to the Governor sternly rebuking him for not carrying out his part of the agreement. When Hennings won the Senate seat, Truman was even more irritated, feeling that Smith's inaction had caused the election outcome.

First Lady
Mildred Smith.

While Smith may have moved too slowly to suit Truman, he moved quickly to work on one of the state's biggest needs—road construction. An outbreak of war in Korea in 1950 did not prevent the Governor from turning his attention to improving Missouri's roadways. The major highways of the state, built over twenty years earlier for model-T cars, were inadequate for transporting heavy-duty trucks. In addition, half of the state's farmers were still using dirt roads—a situation that the Governor felt hindered school consolidation and the development of regional hospitals.

Even before he took office, Smith was thinking of how to fix the problem. He had set up a bipartisan committee to recommend ways to "lift Missouri farmers out of the mud"—a slogan adopted from previous governors who urged road building. Based on the study, he proposed building forty thousand miles of all-weather roads that would run within two miles of every farm house in the state.

In support of the project, Smith called for an increase in the gasoline tax from two cents to four cents. While his proposal gained the backing of farm organizations, it drew stern opposition from the heavy truck operators—a group that Smith accused of damaging the roads without paying sufficiently for their maintenance.

During the ensuing debate, he reminded Missourians that they had one of the lowest gasoline levies in the nation and that national defense demanded the best possible road system. In a direct reference to the bus/truck lobby and the oil companies, the Governor declared, "I do not intend to let these selfish interests, some of which are tearing up our highways, block this effort to give Missouri the best highway system possible at a gas tax rate that will continue to be one of the lowest in the nation."

> Smith's vision for the future included a form of toll roads.

Opponents beat the measure on the first try, but a second attempt to raise the gas tax passed. Although Smith gained only a one-cent increase, it was enough to begin work on the ten-year road building project. Over the next decade, twelve thousand miles of farm-to-market roads would be built and repairs would be made on many of the main highways. Smith told citizens that the new tax measures represented "the most beneficial legislation that has been enacted in Missouri in the past twenty-five years." His vision for the future included more highway improvements in the form of toll roads, but he could never get legislative support for the plan.

Smith used his news column entitled *Your Governor Reports* to keep in touch with Missouri citizens about road building and other happenings in the Capital City. In the weekly feature that appeared in 233 state newspapers, he would sometimes digress from the affair of state to write about improvements to the Mansion and its gardens, the condition of his hay fever, or the adventures of his grandchildren.

STRANGE REQUESTS

Governors get strange requests all of the time, but Governor Smith was dumbfounded by one that came from a man wanting to be assigned to a cell in the state penitentiary where he could write a book without being disturbed. "I have had many, now confined in prison, ask me to help get them out, but it is the first time I have had a man on the outside ask me to try to get him put inside," the Governor declared.

One prisoner—also a writer—offered to help. He contacted the Governor and offered to exchange his cell and rejection slips for the other man's freedom. In addition, the generous inmate agreed to throw in his "faithful, battered and worn out typewriter." Still, the Governor refused to honor the request.

But he did respond to another unusual letter—this one from the producers of the quiz show *People Are Funny*. They wanted the seat from a pair of his pajamas for a patchwork quilt made up of gubernatorial night wear. Since it was for a charity auction, the Governor had no qualms about the contribution.

In 1952 "the wildest and most destructive" panty raids occurred on the University of Missouri–Columbia campus.

Student shenanigans known as "panty raids" caused a ruckus on college campuses.

He also kept Missourians informed of other, less pleasant, diversions he encountered as Governor. Severe flooding in 1951—and another round of record-breaking water levels the next year—destroyed or damaged more than three thousand Missouri homes. With no money in the state budget to cover an emergency call up of the National Guard, Smith was forced to go to Washington to seek federal help.

A controversy over Smith's handling of the floods developed between him and Lieutenant Governor James Blair. Both were Democrats and, at one time, next door neighbors, although they had never been close. As acting Governor, Blair faulted Smith for doing too little, too late, and took it upon himself to call out the National Guard after Smith left the state. (In the aftermath of the spat, Blair accused Smith of getting a primary candidate to oppose his renomination for lieutenant governor.)

Smith called the devastating floods the "greatest catastrophe in the state's history." The tragedy prompted Pope Pius XII to send a letter of sympathy and to offer prayers for Missouri flood victims. After flying over the flood-ravaged areas, President Truman called the destruction "the worst thing I have ever seen" and later criticized the Governor for moving too slowly in aiding recovery. The following year, the state faced more disaster. Ironically, that year a drought led to forest fires that ravaged nearly thirty thousand acres of land.

It was not enough that Smith had to contend with fires, floods, and upstart officeholders. In 1952, all across the nation, student shenanigans known as "panty raids" caused a ruckus on college campuses. Roving bands of male university students invaded women's dormitories to steal their undergarments. Smith attacked the "lawless uprising of a mob of University of Missouri students" more quickly than he did the floods, saying he would bring the "full force" of his office to restore order to the campuses.

I n spite of the difficulties that kept coming his way, the Governor saw much of his legislative package passed into law. He secured a state sales tax to carry forth his reforms for the elderly, sick, and unemployed; extended social security benefits to all state employees; and, started educational programs for prisoners. Smith boasted that he gave more aid to public schools than any governor before him. He also noted that Missouri's unemployment rate was the lowest of the forty-eight states and happily reported fewer crimes at a time when violence was escalating in adjoining states.

In the midst of a booming economy, the state treasury amassed a tidy surplus. Smith called for a reduction in state income taxes to occur whenever revenues rose above $20 million. But lawmakers rejected the idea, many feeling the proposal was only a gimmick to promote Smith's political aspirations. Though capital observers speculated about his future, Smith refused to make any declaration of his intent. As election year rolled around, many thought he would file on his birthday, February 14, the date on which he traditionally filed for office.

> "If I had spent that much time and energy with a popcorn stand, I'd be better off financially.

Though for a time, he acted like a contender for the U.S. Senate, he changed direction after prominent Democratic leaders came out in favor of another candidate. When asked if he would consider going to Congress, he replied with a brusque, "No, sir. . . . I have never had much desire to go to Washington." Besides, at sixty-six years of age, Smith said he and his family needed a vacation after his quarter-century as an officeholder. At one point, he remarked that his years as a public servant had not paid off too well. "If I had spent that much time and energy with a popcorn stand," he declared, "I'd be better off financially."

Having declined any further political involvement, Smith prepared to turn the office back to former Governor Donnelly, who four years earlier had passed the mantle of leadership to him. In preparation for retirement, the Smiths bought a home in their old neighborhood in Jefferson City. Having sold most of their furnishings when they moved into the Mansion, Mrs. Smith noted—with some surprise—that it would take "more money to outfit our new kitchen than we spent to furnish five rooms when we started housekeeping over thirty years ago."

The Governor was also amazed when people urged him to continue writing his weekly column. Although Smith abandoned his political writing, he applied for a permit to enter the television broadcast business after leaving office. He remained active in civic affairs over the next ten years until he suffered a fatal heart attack in 1962 while returning from a Florida vacation.

His forty years of pubic service cast him as one of the state's most dedicated officeholders, a leader who refused to be stifled by a glorified jail or by opponents of progress. As a promoter of an expanded highway system, Forrest Smith not only helped to lift Missouri out of the mud, he paved the way for a modern transportation system and the economic growth that came with it.

The Smiths turn over the Mansion keys to the next First Couple, Governor and Mrs. Phil Donnelly who were returning to the Mansion for a second term.

The Steep Climb To High Places

Governor James Thomas Blair
Emilie Garnett Chorn Blair
1957-1961

As a youngster playing about the Mansion yard, Blair determined that he would someday become governor and live in the hilltop house with the winding stairway.

Sixty-seven-year-old Grace Blair was stopped by a state patrolman in Kansas City while visiting her daughter. Her son, James T. Blair, was serving as lieutenant governor at the time, but she made no mention of it.

"Please let me see your driver's license," the officer asked politely. "You went pretty fast around that last curve."

Mrs. Blair rummaged through her purse. She could find everything but her license.

The officer grew impatient. "Madam," he said, "I've got other work to do."

"Just give me time," pleaded Mrs. Blair, "and I'll find it."

When she eventually produced the license, the patrolman looked at it and said, "Are you any kin to Sam and Jim and Bill Blair?"

"I'm their mother," she replied proudly.

The officer replied, "Drive on. Drive on. I know better than to try to stop a Blair from trying to go anywhere."

Those who knew Jim Blair would agree: there was no stopping him once he made up his mind. For years he had wanted to be governor and live in the old executive home overlooking the Missouri River. He had determined that when he was a youngster playing about the Mansion yard with Governor Hadley's and Governor Major's children.

Although Jim was born in Maysville, Missouri, he grew up in Jefferson City. He and his two brothers had a role model in their father, Judge James T. Blair Sr. a former legislator, assistant attorney general, and Missouri Supreme Court justice. Jim could remember the

Blair appeared to be on the quick road to political success.

fascinating political talk he heard from the many governmental leaders who visited his childhood home. Based on these early influences, it is not surprising that each of

(Facing page)
The stairway the Governor named "Cardiac Hill" is pictured after the Blair renovation of the Mansion.

Blair returned home after World War II with the rank of lieutenant colonel and a chest covered with battle ribbons.

Circuit Judge Sam C. Blair, Governor James T. Blair, and Probate Judge William C. Blair with "Mother" Blair.

the Blair boys followed in his father's footsteps, graduating from Cumberland College Law School before launching a career in public service.

At first, Jim Blair appeared to be on the fast track to political success. He returned to Jefferson City in 1924 after receiving his law degree, hung out his shingle, and, at age twenty-three, won a race for city attorney. He also found time for romance, taking as his bride Miss Emilie Chorn, an attractive young lady from Kansas City.

In 1928 he further advanced his political career by winning a seat in the Missouri House. During his second term, colleagues picked Blair for majority floor leader, making him, at age twenty-eight, the youngest member ever to hold the post. The next year, Blair gained the distinction of being the youngest attorney to serve as president of the Missouri Bar Association.

Even with his early start, Blair's journey to the Governor's Mansion would be long, arduous, and occasionally interrupted. One such interruption came with the onset of World War II when military duty took precedence over political ambition. Blair joined the Air Force and served three and one-half years in Europe and Africa, returning home with the rank of lieutenant colonel and his chest covered with battle ribbons.

In 1947 a winning race for mayor of Jefferson City put him back on course for higher office. The following year, Jim Blair spotted an opening on the state political stage. When no other Democrats seemed interested in running for lieutenant governor, he entered the race and captured his first statewide office. He assumed the part-time duties of the lieutenant governor and continued his Jefferson City law practice.

Sometimes it was awkward for the Blairs to have so many family members practicing law in the same area—though apparently no one objected to Jim trying more than one hundred cases in his brother's courtroom. Mostly it was Jim who felt handicapped at having his brother, William Blair, on the judicial bench. When Judge Blair overruled an objection, Jim would often turn to the jury with an expression on his face calculated to extract sympathy for his position.

Before the end of his term, Blair was looking forward to moving up the political ladder. But instead of seeking the governorship in 1952, he bowed out in favor of former Governor Phil Donnelly—the choice of the Democratic leadership—and settled for the number two spot again. His return to office gave Blair's mother the opportunity to administer the oath of office to all three of her sons who were elected that year: Lieutenant Governor

James T. Blair Jr., Circuit Judge Sam C. Blair, and Cole County Probate Judge William C. Blair. To make the event official, Governor Forrest Smith—once Jim's next door neighbor—commissioned Grace Blair a notary public. The sprightly little woman with bright gray eyes, known affectionately as "Mother Blair," enjoyed the privilege and once told reporters, "I am not interested in the glory my sons may bring to the family, I'm interest in the good that they do."

In keeping with custom, the Donnellys hosted the new First Family to a preinaugural dinner.

By the time Blair had his chance at the top office, he was fifty-four years old, had developed a four-pack-a-day cigarette habit, and was troubled with heart disease. Still he showed remarkable stamina throughout his victorious campaign for governor in 1956 and during the celebrations that preceded his inauguration. Jefferson Citians reveled in the selection of one of their townsmen to high office and hailed the occasion with a whirlwind of parties on the weekend before he took office. One gala at the local country club was hosted by Cardinal baseball star Stan "The Man" Musial, a close friend of the Blairs.

On inauguration day, Blair's swearing-in ceremony centered on the family. His brother Sam administered the oath of office; his son, Jim Tom, and married daughter, Mary Margaret Cook, held the Bible. Earlier during the parade, the new

Blair is sworn in on a Bible held by his son, Jim Tom, and daughter, Mary Margaret Cook.

An arm injury prevented Mrs. Blair from taking part in the customary handshaking ritual.

275

Governor had endured the frigid temperature along with thousands of onlookers. Once Blair and the official party arrived at the reviewing stand, gas heaters warmed their feet, but offered little protection from the bone-chilling winds.

Six hundred colonels named by the Governor—ranging from his barber to Stan Musial—shared in what was termed the "biggest and flashiest" inaugural celebration in memory. However, Thomas Hart Benton, Missouri's free-spirited artist, declined the military appointment that required an outlay of $107.50 for a uniform. Benton later wrote a letter of explanation to the Governor, noting that an apology for not taking part was "a lot cheaper . . . than the uniform and the feathered hat."

In addition to coping with the bitter weather, the new First Lady endured a burden that became evident when she greeted the colonels and their wives at the Mansion. An earlier arm injury prevented her from taking part in the customary handshaking ordeal. Still intent on doing her duty as best she could, Mrs. Blair stood in the reception line holding a bouquet of flowers to avoid the pain that came from shaking hands. That evening, two inaugural balls—one in the Capitol rotunda and the other at a local hotel—capped the day's events. With hotels full for miles around, some guests bedded down in Pullman train cars parked in the Missouri Pacific rail yard.

Blair Won't Use Ancient Mansion

One Night Enough in Rat Infested Mansion

BLAIR FINDS MANSION UNCOMFORTABLE AND GOES HOME

"There is no incentive to become a governor if one has to live in such a barn especially having to look at all those portraits of the former governors' wives." ~Letter to Governor Blair from a sympathetic constituent.

The transition of leadership appeared to be going smoothly in the Capital City—a town used to changing faces every four years. However, a few days after the inauguration, a casual remark by the new Governor dropped like a bombshell on the people of Missouri. Disregarding his childhood ambition to live in the Victorian Mansion, Blair announced that he and his wife, Emilie, planned to remain in their own home. They had spent inaugural night at the eighty-five-year-old Mansion out of convenience, he said, but one night was all they could take. Declaring the new quarters "uncomfortable" and the beds as "hard as rocks," the Governor sent their clothing back to the brick bungalow in Jefferson City where they had lived for twenty-six years.

Missouri Mansion A National Disgrace

Blair shows the tire iron used to prop the window open in the master bedroom.

The plumbing throughout the house was antiquated and in need of repair.

Blair said he was unaccustomed to "castles," but he thought the Mansion was "unreasonably lacking in normal comforts." The new Governor ticked off a list of shortcomings he found in the old house: rats roamed freely about the basement, vermin infested the woodwork, and peeling wallpaper and cracked plaster marred the walls. In the master bedroom, the window was propped up with a rusty tire iron. The carpet was threadbare, the fireplaces boarded up, and the bathrooms on the second floor still had old-fashioned pull chains operating the toilets. Worn-out furniture—most of it made at the nearby prison—needed replacing.

" This old house is full of spiders, this old house is full of rats. This old house ain't fit for entertaining good old Democrats."
~Words sung to the tune *This Old House* at a roast of Governor Blair during a Missouri Press Club Gridiron dinner.

Furthermore, the china was inadequate for entertaining. Even if he and his wife wanted to give a large state dinner, it would be impossible because there were only fifteen place settings of china, Blair announced.

To the incoming Governor, "the Grand Stairway was anything but grand." Blair called the elegant, winding staircase "Cardiac Hill." There was no elevator and the Governor claimed that the trip from the garage to the third floor called for a climb of 140 steps. (That was a slight exaggeration; perhaps 140 paces are needed to reach the top floor, but only 85 of those are stair steps.)

Some thought that Blair's reluctance to move came from his wife not wanting to participate in the large social and political events that Mansion life required. Actually, the First Couple's unwillingness to live in the old house did not stem as much from Emilie's reluctance as from his health concerns. Unknown to most, Blair's

The backstairs were steep and creeky, and the carpet tattered.

doctor had urged him to avoid physical exertion because of the heart damage caused by two previous coronaries. For the Governor, an elevator was not a luxury; it was an essential.

Blair announced to the press that "no further statements or discussion" would take place on the subject of where he lived. As far as he was concerned, the matter of the Mansion was in the hands of the legislature. He wanted to discuss the real problems of the state—the poor living conditions in state institutions and the matter of school financing. Blair assured the public that all customary events would continue at the Mansion and visitors would be allowed on tours. Visitors did come, and in great numbers, to see what the excitement was all about.

When word of his refusal to move into the Mansion spread throughout the nation, the reaction was mixed. Some were amused, like the fellow from Iowa who sent the Governor a congratulatory note and enclosed a mouse trap. Traditionalists, on the other hand, thought that Blair was being picky. But the chairman of the Senate Appropriations Committee agreed with the Governor. Calling the executive home "a rat-infested fire trap," he urged the state to provide a modern residence and to turn the Mansion into a museum.

"Here is an opportunity to resist the American inclination to tear down every building that is old and erect orange brick structures with picture windows."

Spotlighting the Mansion's failings gave the General Assembly another opportunity to talk about tearing it down. Noting the acute need for more parking space near the Capitol, lawmakers felt that demolishing the decrepit landmark would relieve maintenance costs and solve the parking problem at the same time.

Architects and editorial writers also pondered what to do. One writer called the old residence a "national disgrace. . . . The Mansion has no historic associations that would entice us to want to preserve it as a museum," he continued. Another thought differently, "Here is an opportunity to resist the American inclination to tear down every building that is old and erect orange brick structures with picture windows."

A committee presented several options. One called for complete demolition and the building of a modern home on the same site or on the bluffs across the river: estimated cost, $350,000. Another plan proposed a total restoration of the property at a cost of one-half million dollars. Estimates for patching up the house for state functions and attaching new living quarters for the First Family ran $600,000. Presented with such costly alternatives, lawmakers opted to keep the house and appropriated $40,000 to begin work on the worst of its problems.

B lair not only found fault with his housing, he was also displeased with the state-provided transportation. Soon after becoming governor, he announced that the official car, a 1953 Cadillac, was "uncomfortable and sluggish to drive." Blair told friends that the state limousine, while in the hands of former

Governor Phil Donnelly, had "gotten into [the] bad habit of going only 55 [miles per hour]." In his search for sleeker, speedier transportation, Blair fancied a white Cadillac limousine, but thought the color unsuitable for someone in his position. Instead, he settled for one in black that was equipped with power steering, power brakes, and seating for eight passengers.

Mansion chauffeur, Arthur Hardiman, who had served eight previous governors, stood ready to drive the car that displayed the state's number one license plate. Starting with Governor Gardner in 1917, he had, except for one term, served continuously on the Mansion staff. The highly regarded African-American chauffeur maintained a strict confidentiality when it came to the first families. One Capital City resident remarked, "You can't get him to even express himself on how the governor is feeling!"

Blair, however, often bypassed the chauffeur in favor of driving himself, though one such excursion proved injurious to him. The new auto was less than a month old when the Governor swerved off the road to avoid an oncoming car and ended up with a head injury requiring five stitches.

One editorial writer commenting on the accident reasoned that anyone making $25,000 a year—as the Governor did at that time—rated a *full-time* chauffeur. A driver, he concluded, would give the Governor more freedom to ponder the affairs of state. Some newsmen used the incident to push for a state speed limit that was long overdue. Blair agreed. By the end of his term, the Governor secured both a speed limit law and an increase in the number of highway patrolmen.

As much as he enjoyed driving, Blair preferred flying whenever possible. He had flown with paratroopers during World War II and held the rank of colonel in the Missouri Air National Guard while serving as governor. He traveled as much as a thousand miles a week—usually by air—and often took control of the Highway Patrol plane that was transporting him.

Though the Governor maintained an intense travel and work schedule, he was occasionally forced to take time out for health reasons. On one such occasion, he underwent prostate surgery at the Mayo Clinic in Rochester, Minnesota, followed by a three-week recuperation in Colorado Springs. Mild heart attacks put seventy-five-year-old Mother Blair in the hospital twice during his term. Even so, the robust mother of five lived well into her nineties, outlasting her husband and two of her children.

The Blairs greet British Queen Elizabeth and Prince Philip during a visit by the royal couple to Chicago.

Comedian Bob Hope jests with Governor Blair and son, Jim Tom, during a charity golf match in St. Louis.

Health problems did not prevent the Governor from enjoying a few special visitors. The First Couple hosted the British ambassador when he stopped for lunch at the Mansion during a goodwill tour of the United States. Later when Britain's Queen Elizabeth II and Prince Philip came to Chicago aboard the royal yacht *Britannia*, the Blairs were among the dignitaries on hand to greet them. Emilie observed that the Prince looked a lot like their friend, Stan Musial.

While the Blairs sometimes entertained dignitaries at formal gatherings, they preferred more intimate occasions with friends. "We serve lots of game—quail, ducks, geese—whatever is in season," the First Lady told a reporter who inquired about the Mansion menus. Her small dinner parties, casual barbecues on the Mansion lawn, and pregame brunches during football season gave the Governor a chance to favor his supporters with special attention. Mrs. Blair found ways to show her gratitude, too. Each Thanksgiving and Christmas she saw to it that the prisoners working at the house year-round were treated to a turkey dinner with all the trimmings.

In a break from his official duties, the Governor often enjoyed a game of golf and once took part in a tournament with Bob Hope to raise money for St. Louis Children's Hospital. While playing on the golf course of the Warson Country Club in St. Louis, one of Blair's drives went into the crowd and

"The people have no lobbyist and that's what I'm going to do."

Hope cautioned him to "watch out for the voters." Hope scored an eighty-eight, besting the Governor by one stroke.

Back at the Capitol, Blair was, indeed, watching out for the voters, especially those unable to care for themselves. Reporters tagging after the Governor called him "Missouri's number one lobbyist." Blair agreed without apology saying, "The people elected me to represent them because they have no lobbyist and that's what I'm going to do."

The Governor later proved his point. He set up centers for handicapped children and a Mental Health Commission with a professional director. Under Blair's program, monthly benefits to the elderly, disabled, and blind increased and medical care was offered to welfare recipients. He took a firm hand after a tragic nursing home fire in Warrenton, replacing the state health director and strengthening nursing home laws and inspection requirements.

Blair's compassion also extended to an inmate on death row. The Governor commuted the sentence of a twenty-three-year-old convicted killer found to have the mental capacity of a seven-year-old child. He explained his intervention saying, "I'm not in the business of sending children to the gas chamber."

Much of his attention was directed towards improving the state's fiscal policy. He projected a budget for one year rather than two, centralized a budgeting office under his direct control, and saw that the idle funds in the treasury were invested to best advantage. His pay-as-you-go financing policy avoided the extra cost of issuing bonds for capital improvements.

Blair was a "two-footed whirlwind."

Several items on Blair's legislative agenda made significant, long-lasting changes in the state. Looking to the future, he established a Governor's Council on Higher Education to formulate uniform policies for the state's colleges and university. In response to the civil rights movement, he created a Human Rights Commission to promote equal opportunity for all Missourians. However, his proposal to permit the governor two successive term failed—though the measure would not have applied to him.

As he monitored the legislative process, the colorful Governor frequently drew comments from the press. He moved about the Capitol halls like a "two-footed whirlwind," one writer noted as he observed the Governor rushing from one legislative committee meeting to the next. Another newsman, watching the gum-chomping antics of the Governor during a committee hearing, reported that Blair was "chewing furiously [as] he went to the defense of his record $534 million budget." His habit of speaking straight from the shoulder, using hardy language to emphasize his points, infuriated some and amused others.

The red star sapphire on Mrs. Blair's hand was the creation of the artist and added to accent the pink pastel gown.

While the Governor moved quickly in pursuit of his legislative goals, the First Lady was literally sitting still. Waiting for the restoration work to begin at the Mansion, she took the opportunity to have her portrait painted. The two-thousand-dollar artwork was the gift of the Governor's colonels. Still, it took a three-month commitment on Mrs. Blair's part, requiring her to travel to Kansas City to pose as often as once a week. She called "sitting still for two and one-half hours at a time . . . hard work" and expressed sympathy for the first ladies who chose to stand for their portraits.

For the painting, Emilie donned her favorite pink gown, the one she had worn at her husband's second inauguration as lieu-tenant governor and many times thereafter.

Complementing the dress was her diamond sapphire necklace, but her ring—a red star sapphire—was the creation of the artist added to accent the pink pastel gown. The Governor later gave substance to the fantasy ring by having one custom-made for his wife to match the artist's drawing.

With the official portrait behind her, Mrs. Blair turned her full attention to repairing the Mansion. She and her sister worked together redecorating the rooms to relieve the dark, somber feel of the house. They selected a soft beige color scheme for the first and second floors with lime and mauve accents in the window and furniture fabrics. The front door, previously covered with a dark, reddish paint, was stripped to its natural walnut color. Upholstery, refinishing, and repairs of furniture were done by inmates at the nearby penitentiary. One prison craftsman, using a penknife, carved an elaborate grape design to replace a broken section of the old Governor Reynold's sideboard. Local workers replaced faulty plumbing, updated electrical wiring, and removed the thirty-eight rats' nests found in the basement. Nonetheless, for added protection, the Governor acquired Sylvester, a cat who helped keep the rodents under control.

Despite the repairs, the Blairs found the old Mansion uncomfortable. During one cold spell in 1959, Emilie had to wear a coat indoors to keep warm.

In the fall of 1958, the Blairs, along with Tiger Lily their German shepherd, moved into the refurbished home. The twenty-one-month renovation project had cost more than $129,000; the elevator alone totaled $20,000 and took a year to install. But, at least, the First Family could reach the second floor easily and enjoy the air-conditioned comfort of three newly decorated rooms as well as the convenience of a small kitchen.

Still, much remained to be done. In main the kitchen, the Governor found only one usable skillet and a short supply of utensils. Blair solved the problem with a trip to the hardware store where he purchased the needed equipment, including a commercial stove to replace the two home-type cooking ranges.

However, some problems at the Mansion defied solution; the house was still drafty and uncomfortable in the winter. Cold air swirled around the rotted window and door frames, with the steam radiator unable to bring the temperature above 65 degrees during one wintry blast. For protection against the bitter winds, the Blairs stuffed newspapers between the window cracks and wore wool coats indoors.

To publicize the condition of the house, Blair led reporters on a tour, pointing

A newsman wrote of the Governor "shivering in the state Mansion."

out the cold radiators and the gaps around the windows. Afterwards one newsman ran a story telling of the Governor "shivering in the state Mansion." Unfortunately, heating the spacious house was a problem that neither Blair nor subsequent governors could solve completely.

To his credit, Blair never gave up his struggle to make the house more livable. He asked the General Assembly for an additional $100,000 to continue renovation, telling the lawmakers, "You will have to make up your minds whether you want to make only an historic shrine out of the Mansion, or whether you want to make it a livable place for your governors."

Although shortcomings remained obvious in the house, the Blairs were eager to show off the improvements. Shortly after moving in, Emilie entertained over 2,100 people at a public reception given in behalf of the March of Dimes. Ordinarily the Mansion was not used for fund-raising events, but because of the widespread support of the charity, Mrs. Blair made an exception. The First Lady poured coffee for her guests symbolically starting the chain of fund-raising coffees around the state.

A month later, the Blairs had another celebration when their son, Jim Tom, a noted golfer, married Myrna Alpern Rothchild, a widow with two children. The ceremony, performed in the Great Hall, marked the first wedding on record of a governor's son in any of Missouri's executive mansions.

By the end of his term, Blair had every reason to be pleased with his accomplishments. Not only had he modernized state government, he had refurbished the Mansion and saved it from possible destruction. Although the Blairs had spent only half of their term living in the Mansion, the First Lady confessed that she learned to "love that old building." In recognition of those years, she had a tea cloth especially designed for the dining room table as their official gift to the home.

With the inauguration of a new governor, the Blairs left the Mansion, but not Jefferson City. Unfortunately, within eighteen months a tragic accident took their lives. Jim and Emilie Blair were victims of carbon monoxide fumes pulled into their home from an attached garage. The lethal gas entered the living area through the air conditioning system after Blair neglected to turn off the ignition of his parked car.

Although his life was cut short at age sixty, Blair left an enduring legacy. His determination to leave things better than he found them had improved the Mansion, as well as state government and with it, bettered the lives of all Missourians.

MISSOURI ACADEMY OF SQUIRES

During his final year in office, Governor Blair established the Academy of Missouri Squires—a group formed to honor Missouri men and women who make "lasting contributions to their communities, the state and/or the nation."

Among the first ten named by Blair for this honor were former President Harry S. Truman, artist Thomas Hart Benton, and baseball star Stan Musial. Since then, nominations to the academy have come from the public and the Squires, with approval by the membership. The incumbent governor and former governors are members automatically.

The one-hundred-member body still meets once a year, usually for lunch at the Governor's Mansion, where they pose for the annual group photo and replenish their number by inducting new honorees. Each Squire is presented with a certificate and cane to commemorate selection to the prestigious academy.

To mark the group's long association with the Mansion, First Lady Jean Carnahan invited members to underwrite a restoration project on the third floor. The Squires' Room, completed in 1997, commemorated the Mansion's 125th year.

More Tranquil Pastures

GOVERNOR JOHN MONTGOMERY DALTON
GERALDINE "JERRY" HALL DALTON
1961-1965

Needing to get away from the stress of practicing law, Dalton thought politics would offer "more tranquil pastures."

The old clock in the hall had already struck midnight when the new First Couple arrived at the Governor's Mansion. Weary from the events of the day, they took the elevator to the private living quarters on the second floor. The inaugural celebration had started early that morning with a prayer service followed by the traditional parade and swearing-in ceremony. With his hand on a Bible held by his son and daughter, John Dalton had stood facing his brother, Supreme Court Justice S. P. Dalton, who administered the historic oath of office in the Capitol rotunda.

During the flurry of events that followed, the Governor and his wife shook hands with thousands of well-wishers at the Missouri colonels' luncheon, a reception, and two glittering balls—each with a grand march. Alone at last, they could slip off their shoes, relax, and review the events of the day. In contrast to most inaugurals, the weather had been nearly ideal. Further adding to the grandeur of the occasion was the surprise appearance of former President Harry Truman who drove from his home in Independence to attend the swearing-in ceremony.

Pleased and tired from the day's events—yet still too exhilarated for sleep—John and Jerry Dalton realized that neither had eaten since early that afternoon. Both were famished. Intent on raiding the refrigerator, the new Governor traipsed downstairs only to find everything securely locked for the

(Left) The unexpected appearance of former President Harry Truman added to the grandeur—and the humor—of the inaugural day. (Facing page) The Daltons enjoy breakfast on the back porch of the Mansion in view of the Capitol.

The Blairs welcome the Daltons to the Mansion with a preinaugural dinner.

night. Just the night before, the Daltons had feasted at a splendid black-tie event at the Mansion. The traditional "change dinner," hosted by outgoing Governor and Mrs. Blair, was to introduce the incoming First Family to their new surroundings but, apparently, kitchen security was not discussed.

"Let's go out to eat," Mrs. Dalton suggested after giving up hope of uncovering anything in the kitchen.

"We can't go out at this hour," the Governor declared, already assuming the decorum of his new position. Instead, they ordered food to be delivered and in the quiet hours of the morning, John and Jerry dined on sandwiches and drank tepid water because the ice cubes were also padlocked.

Unlike his predecessor who had played about the Mansion as a youngster, John Dalton had no early association with the old home or the state's political figures—although he remembered that as a child he once rode in a buggy on the lap of Governor Folk. At the time, the chief executive was on an inspection tour of the state asylum in Nevada, Missouri, where John's father served as steward.

Later the Dalton family moved to Columbia where John finished high school and attended college. His father, the owner of a retail coal operation, boasted that his seven children had received thirteen degrees between them from the University of Missouri. To earn spending money during his student years, John held various jobs: he sold brushes door-to-door, rented typewriters, swept floors, and clerked in a clothing store. After finishing law school, he moved to southeast Missouri and hung out his shingle in Senath, a small Bootheel town.

"I eloped with Johnnie Dalton."

One day while in nearby Kennett, he met Jerry Hall, "a pretty dark-haired girl—a fetching spit curl in the middle of her forehead—riding in a model-T Ford." The sixteen-year-old daughter of a cotton planter and ginner was seeking a two-year degree at Stephens College and planned to continue her education at the University of Missouri. But her budding romance with the young lawyer changed all that. Years later when Jerry was asked why she did not finish college, she said with a twinkle in her eye, "I eloped with Johnnie Dalton" instead.

The newlyweds set up housekeeping in Kennett where John began practicing law. In 1930, while a fledgling attorney, he ran an unsuccessful race for prosecuting attorney. The following year, the Daltons left the Bootheel area so John could become a marshal of the Missouri Supreme Court, a job that brought him to the Capital City and introduced him to state government.

Returning to south Missouri six years later, Dalton turned his energy to legal and civic pursuits. While Jerry cared for their two children—John Hall and Judy—he established himself as a cotton farmer, as well as a successful attorney, a school board member, a college curator, and an elder in the Presbyterian church. Jerry, however, sometimes mocked his agricultural pursuits, calling her husband a "windshield farmer" because he acted as an overseer of his cotton fields from the front seat of his car.

Dalton began thinking seriously about political office after taking part in Forrest Smith's race for governor. When Smith was hospitalized during the 1948 campaign, Dalton was asked to help keep the candidate's speaking schedule. "Delivering twenty-eight speeches on behalf of Smith whetted my appetite [for politics] and I never got over it," he recalled.

Dalton's decision to seek public office came after a bout with coronary disease. He needed to get away from the stress of practicing law and somehow thought politics would offer "more tranquil pastures." But when John announced his plans to run for attorney general, Jerry recalled that she was "very much put out with him." Her husband's new venture dashed all hopes for the early retirement they once considered.

In his new role as political candidate, Dalton started on a tour across the state, visiting town squares, courthouses, church picnics, and Democratic shindigs. Despite her early disapproval, Jerry became a part of the traveling team, too. She made no speeches, but her warm smile and generous manner won favor for her husband. "People don't vote for me, they vote for my wife," Dalton often declared.

Though opposed by urban politicians, the Kennett cotton farmer won the 1952 Democratic nomination for attorney general without carrying either Kansas City or St. Louis—a feat that had not been accomplished in forty years. His subsequent victory in the general election gave him a four-year term as the state's top lawyer and a springboard to the governorship.

Gubernatorial candidate John Dalton poses with the grand champion mule at the state fair.

However, when he showed an interest in running for governor, Dalton was thwarted by the Democratic power brokers who kept an orderly lineup of political candidates. The blessing of this group of influential businessmen and politicians insured the backing of the party faithful and averted a costly and divisive primary. Though Dalton did not want to wait, he knew that jumping out of line to run for office would mean a vicious primary fight.

It was James Blair, not Dalton, who got the nod of Democratic chieftains in 1956. John stepped back into his role as attorney general—a delay that meant he would be nearly sixty years old before his turn rolled around. Dalton, however,

Supporters celebrate
Dalton's primary
victory.

showed his political muscle that year when he racked up 110,000 more votes for attorney general than Blair did for governor.

While waiting his turn, Dalton put the time to good use, giving two hundred speeches a year, an average of four a week. According to the attorney general, he shook so many hands that the muscles in his right arm became larger than those in his left arm. By the next election, his popularity had soared, leaving party leaders with no choice but to grant him the nomination.

The "pudgy face" politician with the "half-moon smile" put in long hours on the campaign trail, giving as many as thirty speeches in one week. The extra work paid off at the polls. In 1960 when John F. Kennedy carried the state by about 10,000 votes, Dalton racked up 300,000 more votes than his opponent, Ed Farmer. In the process he became the first governor to receive more than a million votes.

T he political know-how of the new Governor was matched by his wife's impressive social graces. The Speaker of the Missouri House presented the silver-haired First Lady to the General Assembly, dubbing her the "Governor's Secret Weapon." John acknowledged his helpmate and hostess as his "better nine-tenths." As a proper political wife of her time, Jerry scoffed at such accolades saying, "A woman lives in her husband's accomplishments." But Jerry stepped out of the mold to make some outstanding contributions of her own. She immediately "made friends with the old house" and became one of its strongest

288

advocates. "This house makes me want to stand tall and be a little bit better," she declared.

The Governor was more forthright in his comments. The old place was still drafty, he told the House Appropriations Committee, and furthermore, the linen was in short supply. Because there was only a dozen towels at the Mansion, laundry had to be done every day, he testified. The newly elected governor of Kansas said he had found an abundance of towels at his executive residence and would gladly share with his less fortunate neighbor. Dalton declined the offer, but accepted a batch of towels from the Muehlebach Hotel in Kansas City with their logo affixed.

Overseeing the Mansion called for more than freshening the linen. It took management

> "Running the Mansion is like running any other house, only there is so much more of it."

ability on the part of the First Lady to direct a staff of twenty that included a personal secretary, cook, chauffeur, housekeeper, butler, and upstairs maid. Fourteen of the workers were prison inmates who did the repairs and yard maintenance. "Running the Mansion is like running any other house, only there is so much more of it," the First Lady explained. "So many more pipes to burst, drapery yardage to buy, finger marks to wash off the wall beside the staircase."

Mrs. Dalton felt a kinship with former ladies of the house whose pictures lined the walls of the Nook beneath the stairs. She explained to visitors that the "dour-faced women"—most of whom looked "much older and unhappier than their average age of forty-three years"—were the product of "bad dentistry and poor photography. Just look at this poor little lady," she told a reporter, "she doesn't have a tooth in her head."

COLONELS GALORE

Governor Dalton appointed over six hundred honorary colonels to embellish his inauguration. His predecessor, Governor James T. Blair, had designated nearly seven hundred political supporters to dress in blue, red, and gold uniforms for a one-day inaugural appearance in Jefferson City.

Besides marching in the traditional parade, the colonels performed a decorative function by lining the double staircase in the Capitol rotunda during the swearing-in ceremony. But their numbers had grown over the past fifteen years to the point that some legislators tried—without success—to restrict the governor's entourage to no more than two hundred.

In defense of the elite corps one lawmaker argued that the colonels were harmless, with a long tradition of uselessness. In addition, they performed at no cost to the state, he noted: "They pay for their own uniforms, pay their own expenses to the inauguration . . . and pay for a painting of the First Lady." The battle over the Governor's cadre did nothing to diminish the size of the group. Dalton's army paled in comparison to that of his successor Warren E. Hearnes, who designated over a thousand to hold the military honor.

Jerry's southern heritage showed up best in the kitchen. According to Mrs. Dalton, in the Bootheel area of Missouri "a day's eating wasn't complete without hot biscuits or fresh cornbread." John enjoyed country ham and green beans or cornfield peas seasoned with pork and simmered in an iron pot. Guests complimented Jerry's baked grits, shrimp creole, and amber pie—all made from family recipes she brought to the Mansion. Remembering her experience of finding a locked refrigerator on inaugural evening, she kept a well-stocked kitchen in their private quarters for those times when the Governor wanted a snack or a home-cooked meal.

Mrs. Dalton felt a kinship with the former first ladies whose pictures lined the walls of the Nook.

But serving finely prepared dishes to a large number of guests presented a problem for the First Lady; there were not enough matching pieces of china to set a table for eighteen. Former First Lady Emilie Blair had mentioned this inconvenience to the wife of an honorary colonel, Mrs. John Powers of St. Louis. Intent on remedying the situation for the Daltons, Mrs. Powers solicited twenty-five dollar contributions from the colonels to purchase seventy-five place settings of new china for the Mansion. With a total of $4,440 in hand, Mrs. Powers selected the Lenox pattern "Tuxedo," a bone-colored plate with a thin gold band and the state seal affixed. Miffed at being left out of the process, the chairman of the state Democratic Party—who also served as the unofficial leader of the colonels—urged her to return the money.

Although Governor Dalton had agreed to the china purchase months earlier, the state party chairman said the First Couple now preferred for the colonels to set up a scholarship fund. However, Mrs. Powers had

(Right) The official china, featuring a gold band and the state seal, was acquired during the Dalton era and remains in use today.

290

already placed the order for the dinnerware and was not inclined to turn back. Some thought the First Family might refuse the gift, but when the press publicized the incident, the Daltons graciously accepted the dinnerware and put it to use.

The next gift tendered by the colonels was better received. The group unveiled the official portraits of the Governor and the First Lady during a day-long celebration. In an atmosphere of glitter and revelry on the scale of a small inauguration, three hundred honorary colonels and their wives gathered at the Mansion for brunch. That afternoon they attended a football game in Columbia followed by a buffet dinner for seven hundred and a public dance in the Capitol rotunda.

While the Daltons continued to receive gifts of furniture and accessories for the Mansion, the First Lady also did some searching on her own, rummaging through old shops and bidding on antiques at farm auctions. Some treasures were uncovered stored away at the Mansion, such as the Dresden china plates hidden on a high shelf and a fine painting found in the attic. A tattered lounge chair and a Victorian footstool—also spotted in the attic—were reupholstered for the Governor.

"To live in this house is to have a handclasp with history. You can't live there long and not grow to love the building," Jerry Dalton declared.

Nestling into his new easy chair, Dalton would read his mail at home, making notes to his secretary on how to respond. On some letters, he jotted "yes" across the top, on others "no" or "sweet talk." He even read the crank mail just to keep informed about what was irritating Missourians. Jerry usually sat near the Governor, answering her own correspondence, knitting a sweater, or working on a handmade item for one of their five grandchildren.

Jerry "made friends with the old house," and became one of its strongest advocates.

The extra furniture gave the Mansion a facelift, but it did not address the problems of the aging house. Every First Lady had encountered an unexpected situation of one kind or another. The previous First Family had made many improvements in plumbing and wiring, but that did not prevent a leaky third-floor pipe from soaking the Governor's clothes closet on the floor below.

Other more embarrassing problems kept coming up. One warm day when the windows were open, a wasp began to buzz about the dining room. As one of the dignified guests took a swing at the insect, the legs of his chair collapsed. Later, the First Lady sank through the seat of a chair as she inspected a guest bedroom in preparation for the visit of U.S. Secretary of State Dean Rusk.

Besides having faulty furniture, she noted that the room had not been wallpapered in sixteen years. Jerry could not conceal her distress at having a presidential cabinet member stay in such shabby quarters and complained to the

Governor. "Do you mean to tell me the State of Missouri is so poor that we can't have a better room than that for a ranking government official of the United States," she argued.

The Governor knew when to give in. "Go ahead," he said, "and do anything you want." With the Governor's backing, the First Lady repaired the chair and refurbished the entire room, including the wall-coverings—a project that took forty-three rolls of paper. She chose a cotton fabric for the chairs and

THE GOVERNOR'S KIN FOLK

The Governor had trouble with people claiming to be his relative. One fellow picked up for driving while intoxicated claimed to be Dalton's nephew, but he was not. A would-be relative by the name of Bennie Dalton wrote from the Indiana state prison asking "Cousin John" to intercede for him with the Indiana Governor. He signed the letter, "As always, Bennie."

Another supposed "nephew" of the Governor, after getting in trouble with the St. Louis police, claimed he had a Capitol office directly across the hall from "Uncle John." The Governor found the story particularly amusing since the "office" across the hall was the ladies' restroom.

Dalton hosts the annual meeting of the Missouri Academy of Squires. Each new inductee holds a ceremonial cane.

drapes in the bedroom and throughout the house. Having grown up in the cotton-growing area of the state, the First Lady explained, "I want our friends in southeast Missouri to know we are loyal."

When it came to selecting colors, the First Lady loved pastels and preferred to decorate with them. When she did, the soft colors "faded to nothing" in the seventeen-foot-high rooms of the Mansion. Jerry also found it awkward dealing with designers and a state system that required bidding on any project over fifty dollars. Decorators had their own brands and fabrics, making it nearly impossible to compare bids.

For those concerned about the cost of repairs, Mrs. Dalton pointed out that all the work was done at the prison by a master craftsman whom the state paid a mere ten cents an hour. Jerry was pleased with the outcome of the room and eager to do more. "I'd love to do as they did at the White House, take everything apart and put it together again," she said.

As it turned out, the secretary of state postponed his visit, but the room was

Mrs. Dalton redecorated the guest bedroom that featured the old "Prince of Wales" bed.

ready when he came the following year. During his stay in 1962, Rusk slept in the "Prince of Wales" bed, once thought to have been occupied by its namesake. Secretary Rusk, a southerner by birth, enjoyed the comfort of the historic bedroom, as well as the breakfast of country ham and grits Jerry served the next morning.

Another visitor, Senator Edward "Ted" Kennedy enjoyed Mrs. Dalton's southern hospitality when he visited the Mansion, as did nine governors who came to the Capital City.

Jerry continued to juggle hospitality with house repairs.

"I'd love to do as they did at the White House, take everything apart and put it together."

She refinished the front doors and the gold leaf parlor set, gave the exterior a fresh coat of white paint, and brightened the library with a new red and white decor, renaming it the Victorian Room. When she started decorating in the dining room, she accepted the offer of a group of St. Louis ladies to needlepoint twenty-four seat covers featuring a sprig of dogwood on a red background.

Hoping to avoid the crisis and correction approach to maintaining the Mansion up until then, Mrs. Dalton went before a legislative committee to make a plea for a historical overseer of the house—a foundation that could receive tax-deductible gifts and provide continuity between administrations. The Mansion had been repaired by some first families, Mrs. Dalton said, but neglected by other residents. "A future First Lady could—if her budget permitted—throw out everything in the house and furnish it with Danish modern," she warned. Furthermore, she added "the people of Missouri love this house and want it kept in good condition."

The committee was not convinced. "They turned me down flat," she recalled sadly. According to news reports, her plan was rejected because of the estimated two-thousand-dollar annual cost of administering the commission. Legislators had long thought it was just "pouring money down a rat hole" to keep repairing the old building. Once again there

Seats for the dining room chairs were needlepointed by a group of St. Louis women who stitched their initials in the work (see leaf on right).

293

"Everyone feels they have to dress up and put on white gloves when they come to the Governor's Mansion," Mrs. Dalton noted.

was talk of turning the Mansion into a museum and building the Governor a nice ranch-style house overlooking the Missouri River.

Though disappointed, Mrs. Dalton was not surprised by the reluctance of the legislators to act on her proposal. "The Mansion has always been a stepchild caught right in the middle of a tug-of-war between the executive and legislative branches," she said. "But you can't live in that house without loving it, if you have any feelings for history at all."

While Jerry found few preservationists in the General Assembly, she did find admirers of the historic home among those who came to visit. There were no regular tours for the general public during the Dalton years, but Jerry and her secretary frequently escorted groups of women through the home, amusing them with stories of the people who once lived there. Convention-goers also received a warm welcome at the Mansion, among them five hundred Daughters of the American Revolution and several hundred state P.E.O. delegates.

Jerry was not content to entertain the usual dignitaries and women's clubs. She initiated an annual Easter Egg Roll for children with disabilities. Unperturbed by the rain the first year, she refused to cancel the long-awaited event and instead moved the children inside the three-car garage beneath the kitchen.

The increased openness of the Mansion had some drawbacks, however. Curious visitors often treated the home like a museum where they felt free to roam through any unlocked door. Reminiscent of First Lady Maggie Stephens finding women looking through her wardrobe, Jerry once discovered four ladies strolling through her bedroom. Guests were also curious about the Mansion-size kitchen. She did not mind showing it off occasionally, but she found it intrusive when a meal was being prepared.

In spite of all the Mansion guests, Jerry missed the casual visits of

(Right) Mrs. Dalton began the annual Easter Egg Roll for physically disabled children.

old friends. "Everyone feels they have to dress up and put on white gloves when they come to the Governor's Mansion," she said regretfully.

Even the "Beverly Hillbillies" dressed up for a visit to the State Capitol on their way to perform at the J-Bar-H Rodeo in Camdenton. Television characters "Granny," "Elly May," and "Jethro" were met at the airport by two thousand fans and later given an enthusiastic welcome in the House chamber. The Governor marked the occasion by proclaiming "Missouri Hillbilly Week" and was rewarded by a "peck on the cheek" from filmstar Donna Douglas who played Elly May. When she asked if the Governor needed a secretary, he replied, "Shore do." "Even a one-fingered one?" she replied.

Even the "Beverly Hillbillies" dressed up for a visit to the State Capitol.

Not all days were as relaxed and enjoyable for the Governor. The pace of traffic in the executive office forced him to limit his appointments to no more than fifteen minutes each. Even then, the arduous ten-hour days put a strain on the Governor that occasionally showed in his shortness of temper. "He does nothing but work," his secretary once told newsmen. "I'm glad there aren't thirty-six hours in a day." Dalton agreed lightheartedly, "Four to five interviews per hour all day long can get to be more tiring than picking potato bugs with a crick in your back." Fortunately, the Governor knew how to relax in the moments available to him and could nap easily in a chair or car.

GOVERNORS PLAY HARDBALL

Governor Dalton had the habit of keeping a tally of the legislators who voted for and against his proposals. He tucked the sheet in his desk for ready reference during those times when a lawmaker walked into his office wanting a favor that only the governor could grant.

His method of dealing with errant legislators is reminiscent of a story told by former Governor Ned McWhorter of Tennessee. When faced with a freshman representative who had just voted against one of the governor's pet projects, McWhorter reached into his desk and pulled out a picture of one of the state's road graders used to build county roads.

Eyeing the young fellow, he said, "Son, do you know what this is?"

"Yes, sir," the legislator answered, "that's a road grader."

McWhorter replied, " Well, take a good long look at it, 'cause it's the last damn one you're going to see for a while."

Dalton faced several major problems—or challenges as he preferred to call them: a deteriorating highway system, an empty treasury, and the educational needs of the space age. President John F. Kennedy's call to put a man on the moon before the end of the decade and to win the Cold War rivalry with Soviet Russia rallied Americans to educational excellence. Dalton led the charge in Missouri by fully financing the school foundation plan and by creating a four-campus university system from institutions located at Columbia, Rolla, St. Louis, and Kansas City.

The First Lady provided generous portions of her southern-style cooking while the Governor dished up "sweet talk."

The Governor used every resource at his command to promote his record $1.2 billion budget. To sell his tax proposals to the legislature, he enlisted the aid of his honorary colonels, most of whom were highly influential men in their communities. The colonels, in turn, pressured their state legislators to support the Governor's bills. The grassroots persuasion worked, giving Dalton the edge he needed to move his agenda in the General Assembly.

To get his way, the Governor alternated between gentleness and toughness. Calling a legislator shortly before noon, he would say: "This is John Dalton. I'd like for you to have lunch with me." The honored legislator would then be transported the few blocks from the Capitol to the Mansion in the Governor's chauffeur-driven car. At lunch the First Lady would provide generous portions of her southern-style cooking while the Governor dished up "sweet talk." The Daltons also used the breakfast hour to political advantage, often inviting several lawmakers to share the early morning meal at the Mansion.

Although Dalton knew how to exert pressure when necessary, he also relied on public opinion to move his agenda. Twice a day he held news conferences to keep the media informed. He stayed in touch with Missourians through his weekly radio talks and with a newspaper feature entitled "The Governor's Column." Dalton also used television to his advantage during a series of press interviews known as the "Governor's Report to the People."

Hard work and attention to detail paid off for John Dalton. Lawmakers, in an uncommonly progressive mood, supported the Governor's new tax measures. A two-cent gasoline tax increase came in 1962 and another penny of sales tax was dedicated to education in 1963. New liquor and cigarette taxes brought improvement in mental health with gains of a thousand dollars more per patient each year. State income tax collecting became more efficient with the adoption of the Governor's new payroll

A visit to Copenhagen.

withholding plan. Even with the added taxes, however, Missouri's per capita tax burden was still among the lowest in the nation.

The favorable economic climate during the Dalton era made other improvements possible. Lawmakers bettered their lot when the Governor signed a bill boosting their pay from $1,500 to $4,800 a year. He also approved a measure requiring equal pay for women employed in the same work as men. Missourians benefited from a dramatic increase in road building that brought 294 miles of new interstate highway into use. Of all his accomplishments, Dalton took the most satisfaction in fully funding the school foundation program that raised the annual state aid from $185 to $321 per pupil.

The Governor's veto power was his strongest weapon and he used it liberally, striking down a record thirty-five bills sent for his signature during his first term. However, by his second legislative session, the lame duck Governor had lost some of his clout. Many Democratic politicians and lawmakers were unhappy because he refused their patronage demands. His insistence on strict conflict of interest regulations and his purge of unnecessary political appointees in the Department of Revenue all earned him enemies in the General Assembly.

Not all of the Governor's contests were with legislators; Dalton welcomed the chance for some friendly competition with his staff and fellow governors. When it was time to harvest the exhibition row of cotton planted on the Capitol grounds, he put on an old pair of jeans and a plaid shirt to show off his farming skills. During the Capitol Cotton Picking Contest, which lasted no more than five minutes, the Governor out-picked the state commissioner of agriculture to win the prize, a set of cotton long johns.

A few months later he entered another contest, this time with the Governor of Kentucky, to see who could find the biggest Thanksgiving turkey. Missouri had more turkeys than people—close to five million birds—and the Governor felt confident he could find a winner. Writing to the Kentucky Governor, Dalton boasted that he had "a bird being

During his final year in office, Governor and Mrs. Dalton had the honor of spending the night in the White House at the invitation of the new President, Lyndon B. Johnson.

The sixty-minute filmed tour of the Mansion was patterned after the one done by Jackie Kennedy in the White House.

groomed for the show and would like to enter it if the problem of transportation can be worked out. The bird is so huge that our normal truck, rail, or barge lines are not equipped to handle it," he declared.

In a more serious economic competition, Dalton became the first Missouri governor to actively pursue markets abroad. Along with eight other governors, John and Jerry toured Japan for more than two weeks as participants in the Japan-U.S. Governors' Conference.

During the visit, Dalton became adept at eating with chopsticks and tolerant of the Japanese breakfast of rice wrapped in seaweed. The silver-haired First Lady attracted a lot of attention from the Japanese, several of whom asked if they could feel her unusual-colored hair. The highlight of the trip was their forty-minute visit with the Emperor and Empress. While the governors met with His Majesty, the first ladies chatted with the Empress about their respective children and grandchildren. In reports to the people back in Missouri, the Daltons hailed the Japanese as tremendously energetic and courteous. Pleased with his venture abroad, the Governor and his wife made another trade trip before leaving office, this time to seven European countries.

Dalton's term spanned an historic era that encompassed one of the nation's greatest triumphs and one of its worst tragedies: the launch of a space capsule in 1963 followed by the death of President John F. Kennedy the next year. The new chief executive, Lyndon B. Johnson, presided over a time of national mourning and uncertainty that prevailed in the country during the final years of Dalton's term.

In addition to witnessing such historic happenings, First Lady Jerry Dalton made some history on her own. Records show that while she served as the state's official hostess, 13,876 people dined at the executive residence—an average of 9 a day. She also conducted the first televised tour of the Victorian home. The sixty-minute show, filmed by KMOX-TV St. Louis, disrupted the Mansion for three days when a CBS camera crew moved in and began stringing lights and wires throughout the place. The tour—patterned after the one Jackie Kennedy had given of the White House a year earlier—displayed parts of the executive home that had not been open to the general public.

Whether Jerry was conducting a tour, hosting a state dinner, or responding to a constituent's request for a button off the Governor's jacket, a bottle of dirt from the yard, or a favorite recipe, the First Lady exuded a warmth that Missourians admired. She described herself simply as the housewife from Howard's Bluff (the name used by some for the hilltop site of the Mansion). But the *St. Louis Globe-Democrat* designated her one of the ten "Women of Achievement" in 1963. One editor even suggested that the First Lady should run to succeed her husband.

The Kennett cotton farmer and attorney, who had gone into public service to relieve the stress of practicing law, declared his tenure in office a success. Politics was harder than practicing law, he noted, but more fun. "Somehow, the public's business wasn't nearly as nerve wracking as attending to private clients," he said.

Reflecting on his four years, Dalton summed up his feelings, "I like to think of the things we have accomplished not in the cold terms of so many millions of dollars, but in what they may mean in the everyday living of Missourians." Indeed, the Dalton years had produced a progressive agenda and the new revenue needed to support it. One *Kansas City Star* analyst complimented the Governor saying, "Missouri has probably come farther in the last four years than at any equivalent period in the history of the state."

At the end of his term, John and Jerry departed the Mansion, but not the city. He opened an office and practiced law for another seven years before his death from spinal cancer in 1972. Jerry lived another seventeen years and died at the age of eighty.

Dalton once acknowledged that he had been a "controversial Governor," but added, "I don't think I would have been worth my salt if I had not been. Progress is not won by pleasing everybody. Yet it is idle to pretend harsh words do not hurt." Shortly before leaving office, the Governor expressed his feelings about public service in a letter written to a friend who had just won a seat on a city council. "Be prepared for criticism, whatever you do and however you go about doing it, but don't let it turn you aside," he cautioned. "I have found as attorney general and as governor that the only way to handle public office is to research every problem, get all the facts together, make the decision required by the circumstances—and never look back."

"The house makes me want to stand tall and be a little bit better." ~ First Lady Jerry Dalton

THE DYNAMIC DUO

"I wanted to be a help to my husband both politically and socially and yet keep his feet on the ground. [I told] him the facts whether he wanted to hear them or not." ~ First Lady Betty Hearnes

Warren Hearnes was not supposed to run for governor—at least not in 1964. He was still secretary of state and it was not his turn. For more than two decades, "a small, powerful coalition of bankers, lawyers, and professional politicians" had maintained an orderly lineup of statewide Democratic office-seekers. The arrangement had worked well for the party; it prevented divisive primary fights and repeatedly produced a winning slate of Democrats.

But forty-one-year-old Warren Hearnes did not like the selection system. Young and impetuous, he galloped into the political arena at full tilt and, like a knight bent on slaying the "dragon," took on the so-called "Establishment." Political insiders urged him to forget the race. "You can't beat the regular organization with all its money. You're just heading for a big heartache," one said.

Feeling he needed less advice and more hard-core support, Hearnes hit the campaign trail to promote his own candidacy. During the hot summer months of 1964, Warren and his thirty-seven-year-old wife, Betty, crisscrossed Missouri in search of receptive Democrats. No town was too small or day too long for the energetic couple. Sometimes they traveled in a small, borrowed airplane. Most often they rode in an unair-conditioned car with Hearnes' red, white, and blue campaign logo painted on the side. In speech after speech, he lambasted his lackluster primary opponent, Lieutenant Governor Hillary Bush who—with the support of the Establishment—was scheduled to move up the political ladder.

(Left) During the rigorous campaign, the Hearneses sometimes traveled in a small, borrowed airplane.
(Facing page) Warren and Betty Hearnes with their dog, Sonny.

While Bush hobnobbed with prominent Democrats and big contributors, Hearnes spent long days pumping hands outside factories, schools, and railroad yards—wherever there was a vote.

"Are [you] going to allow the establishment in Jefferson City to handpick [a] . . . puppet governor who will serve their special interest rather than the public interest?" he taunted his audiences. "I can afford to wait my turn," Hearnes told his listeners, "but can the people of Missouri afford to wait?"

In spite of the energy shown by the young politician, capital watchers gave the edge to Bush. One writer dismissed Hearnes as a "Mississippi County lawyer—whose voice often squeaked with a southern drawl and who looked like he could use another fifty pounds." The news media on the west side of the state blatantly ignored his campaign.

One night in a Kansas City hotel room, Warren bemoaned his lack of publicity, "Betty, how am I going to get my name in the paper so people will know I'm a candidate?"

"All a candidate's wife needs is two good feet."

His wife replied in her usual light-hearted tone, "Well, maybe you could push me out this hotel window."

Warren thought for a moment. "No," he said. "That won't do. They would print, 'An unidentified woman fell out a window.'"

During their months of campaigning, Betty turned out to be as good at garnering votes as her husband. On the stump, she delighted audiences with her homespun humor and easy manner. Although she frequently declared, "All a candidate's wife needs is two good feet," Betty brought considerably more than that to her husband's campaign.

The daughter of a Baptist minister, she had grown up in Charleston, Missouri, in a family of eight children, all of whom were musically talented. During her college years, she earned a teaching degree in public school music and further developed her fine soprano voice. With her marriage to Warren in 1948, she discovered that the skills she acquired as a preacher's daughter came in handy for a politician's wife, keeping her much in demand as both a singer and a speaker.

Hearnes, the youngest of five children, was also raised in Charleston where his father ran a general store before going broke and

No day was too long or town too small for Warren Hearnes in his quest for the governorship.

302

losing the family home during the Great Depression. His mother helped during those lean years by selling cakes, pies, and chips to local stores. Growing up in the troubled era, Warren developed a strong sense of duty and an urge to excel. At age sixteen, he joined the National Guard, though he was released a year later when his actual age became known. Hearnes was drafted while in college, but landed a congressional appointment to West Point, which led to a three-year stint as an infantry officer.

"A secretary of state in Missouri has so few duties it is difficult to neglect them."

In 1950, a month after his military duty ended, Hearnes returned home and filed for state representative from Mississippi County—a region near the Bootheel where politics is traditionally "played at top speed, full force, and with few rules." Warren won the seat, making him the youngest man ever to represent his county in the Statehouse. That same year, he enrolled in law school at the University of Missouri and commuted from the Capital City to Columbia, dividing his time between studying law and making it.

During his eight years in the General Assembly, Hearnes served as majority floor leader for two terms. "I made up my mind then what I was going to shoot for," he said, already eyeing the governorship. He moved a notch closer in 1960 after winning the post of secretary of state. That office had long been considered a "closed hunting grounds, reserved for out-state members of the Missouri Press Association." Hearnes ignored the practice and pulled off a winning campaign against the affable news editor James Kirkpatrick of Windsor.

Some said Hearnes did not work very hard at his new job. One writer agreed, but added, "A secretary of state in Missouri has so few duties it is difficult to neglect them." Hearnes surrounded himself with a dedicated core of supporters and used the next four years to lay the groundwork for what he really wanted—the governorship.

His early efforts and campaign strategy came together in August 1964 when he won the gubernatorial nomination by a 51,000-vote margin. At a time when winning the Democratic primary was akin to election, Hearnes was a virtual shoe-in for governor. In the November election, he made the outcome official after scoring 400,000 more votes than his opponent, Republican Ethan A. H. Shepley, a St. Louis attorney and former chancellor of Washington University. The victory was made all the sweeter for Democrats with the triumph of President Lyndon Johnson over conservative U.S. Senator Barry Goldwater.

Hearnes' political coup put him firmly in charge of Missouri's Democratic Party, as well as state government. In preparation for

In the inaugural parade Governor-elect Warren Hearnes rode in an open car with Governor Dalton.

Hearnes appointed the largest number of honorary colonels in Missouri history.

his new job, Warren, Betty, and a three-member transition team spent the next two months developing a budget, a legislative agenda, and a grand inaugural celebration.

On the appointed day, thousands of Democrats poured into the Capital City to savor the victory along with the new leader of their party. The Hearnes family started the celebration by attending the traditional inaugural eve dinner hosted by Governor and Mrs. John Dalton. The two families enjoyed a meal of clam bisque, chicken breasts, country ham, hot biscuits, and a popular recipe of the day, Bess Truman's Ozark pudding. The southern-style menu was not new to the Hearneses who lived in the same Bootheel region as the Daltons.

The next morning, Hearnes and his family attended a preinaugural church service, thus following the precedent set by the Daltons four years earlier. After worshipping at the First Baptist Church, Hearnes donned the usual formal morning attire in preparation for the parade and swearing-in ceremony. His youngest daughter, six-year-old Julie B., unaccustomed to seeing her father in such finery, called after him excitedly, "Daddy, come back here, your coat is split all the way up the back."

Hearnes observed another tradition by riding the parade route in a car with the outgoing Governor, while Mrs. Hearnes and Mrs. Dalton rode in the following vehicle. Close behind was an unusually large cadre of honorary colonels. Hearnes had appointed 750 of his supporters to hold the military title—the greatest number ever appointed by a governor. (Four years later, he would exceed his own record by naming more than one thousand colonels for his second inauguration). Bedecked in their "$164-gold-and-blue uniforms," the men marched sprightly— if not quite in step— along the downtown parade route.

Flanked by his family, Hearnes takes the traditional oath at noon on inauguration day.

Though most of the inaugural traditions were observed by the Governor-elect, the theme of the day was "change." In his nine-minute address, Hearnes said his administration would usher in "a new day," one with "fresh ideas, fresh faces, fresh attitudes, and fresh dreams." Several differences were already apparent to those gathered on the Capitol lawn for the swearing-in ceremony. For the first time since Governor Gardner's inauguration in 1917, the event was held outside on the south steps of the Capitol.

In another break with the past, the Governor's oath was placed at the climax of the program rather than the beginning. More deviation from custom came that evening in anticipation of the exceptionally large inaugural crowd. Rather than one dance to cap off the day, three simultaneous balls were scheduled: one at the Capitol rotunda, one at the Governor Hotel, and another at the Ramada Inn.

> Though the inaugural traditions were observed, the theme of the day was "change."

T he new First Family put a more youthful face on the old Mansion. Warren Hearnes was the youngest governor to live in the home in fifty-six years and Betty, the youngest first lady in thirty years. Having children playing about the place for the first time in twenty-four years brought a new energy to the staid Victorian residence.

For the Governor's three daughters—Lynn, 15; Leigh, 12; and, Julie B., 6—the thought of living in the "castle" on the hill had all the makings of a fairy tale. The house with its oversized rooms and curved stair rail had always been a wonderland for youngsters and the modern-day addition of eight telephones made it even more appealing for the Hearnes girls. Having a butler, housekeeper, maid, secretary, and chauffeur seemed like a dream come true. With so much extra help, the girls thought there would be no more housework for them, that is, until Betty explained that they would be caring for their rooms just as they had always done.

In spite of the initial excitement, the Hearnes family had mixed emotions about leaving their nine-room home in Jefferson City for the twenty-nine rooms in the Governor's Mansion. Julie worried about not having playmates nearby and disliked the eerie sounds made by wind blowing against the loose window frames.

Betty also had some misgivings about living in such a spacious house. Managing a full-time staff was a big adjustment for her after having a once-a-week housekeeper. The new sleeping arrangements were also awkward for the family. Betty and Warren—with their bedroom on the second floor—disliked being so far removed from the girls' bedrooms on the third floor.

Despite the distance, the third-floor rooms—once used for servants' quarters and storage—offered an escape from the more formal areas of the house. In addition to the old billiard table, the sixty-foot ballroom now sported a

The Governor and Colonel, the family poodle.

The girls brought a homey atmosphere to the staid, old Mansion.

Julie B. lounges on the floor while playing checkers.

trampoline, a Ping-Pong table, and a small bowling alley. Stacks of records by the Beatles and Ricky Nelson found a place alongside the antique accessories. When the music got too loud, the girls too rambunctious, or the first floor chandeliers began to shake, Betty would disappear from whatever social gathering she was hosting, quiet the girls, and return to her guests.

The Mansion was made all the more lively by the children's pets. The menagerie included at various times: Sonny, "a dog of mixed ancestry" that Warren had purchased from the pound for ninety-seven cents; Yertle, the turtle; Tweedie, the parakeet; Colonel, a toy poodle; a cat; and, a bowl of guppies.

Though the girls enjoyed the benefits that came with being the First Daughters of the state, they were sometimes embarrassed in their new roles. Leigh shied away from being delivered to school in a black limousine with the conspicuous number "1" license plate and sometimes asked the chauffeur to let her out a block away.

Julie B. tried to avert attention when her first-grade class planned a tour of the Mansion. Although the teacher required permission slips from all the parents, Betty saw no reason to send one for her daughter. However, on the day of the event, Julie made a last-minute call home, urging her mother to bring the note to school quickly. Betty complied with her daughter's wishes even though it amused the teachers and principal. Later that day, Julie, in an effort to maintain her anonymity, rode the bus, toured the Mansion, and never once let on that she lived there. As she left the Mansion with her classmates, she turned to her mother and said politely, "Thank you very much."

Indeed, the dual role of the Mansion as a private home and public building was always difficult to reconcile. But the social unrest in the sixties, along with the political assassination of John and Robert Kennedy, and Martin Luther King Jr., highlighted the need for extra protection of public figures. After several sightseers entered the Mansion and went undetected to the private living area on the second floor, greater security was instituted. In addition to the usual watchmen, Highway Patrol officers were posted at the Mansion for a while. Though the house was still a long way from having a full-scale security system, the officers' presence marked an increased interest in the safekeeping of the First Family, as well as the house.

While Betty and the girls settled into the Mansion, Warren was spending long hours at the Capitol promoting his legislative agenda. He proposed the adoption of an urban affairs department, civil rights legislation, four-year state universities at St. Joseph and Joplin, and mandatory breath

THE HEARNES RESTORATION . . .

Betty Hearnes found a big difference in her comfortable Jefferson City ranch-style home and the run-down Governor's Mansion. Upon moving to the Mansion in 1965, she commented on the worn, gray carpet in the downstairs area: "It looks like a funeral parlor. With a few flowers, they could lay you out in any room."

It was not the carpet, however, but a leaky roof that got Mrs. Hearnes started on making the place more livable. Betty and Warren discovered that the roof had to be fixed when one of their daughters was awakened during a storm by water dripping on her nose.

Buckets placed about the house temporarily contained the leaks, but engineers examining the aging house uncovered more problems. The floors were so unlevel that they feared the heavy Victorian wardrobes might topple over on someone. Engineers warned the family not to use the second-floor porch because of its deteriorating condition. Betty knew she could not do everything at once. But with an appropriation of $116,000 from a sympathetic legislature, she got started by repairing the ornamental ironwork and by replacing the slate

roof, the wooden cornices, and window casements.

Having a fine new roof, however, only pointed up the need for more exterior work—a task the First Lady tackled with gusto. Before the end of her husband's first term, Betty was into serious renovation work meant to restore the original look of the Mansion. The house was encrusted with thirty-some coats of paint that covered the soot-stained exterior, masking the original, handmade "pink" brick.

Periodically since the time of Governor Francis (1889-1893), the Mansion had received a fresh coat of red paint until Governor Stark transformed its color to what some referred to as "Stark White." He had also added a kitchen wing using the bricks from the demolished porte cochere on the side of the house. However, the porte cochere—which had been built in 1904 with bricks from the old stable—did not match the house and, thus, neither did the kitchen addition. Stark harmonized the building by painting it white.

When Betty found that the newer bricks used for the addition could be tinted to match the original, she determined to return the Mansion to its original look. During the transformation, chunks of paint

. . . A New Look For The Old House

several inches thick fell from the walls as workers used a chemical wash, high pressure water, and fine sand to clean the fragile brick without disintegrating it.

Determined to protect the plantings from the chemical, Betty worked with two men to wash the shrubbery each day and to run the water from around the house into trenches. The spray of sand used to remove the final flecks of paint filtered inside the Mansion, leaving a fine residue on the furnishings. "We cleaned the house about three times a day on the inside. Our last two months at the Mansion were the only ones we had free of dust and repairmen," Betty recalled.

The First Lady uncovered a well-hidden secret.

When she extended the stripping work to the interior wood, the First Lady uncovered a well-hidden secret. After a workman noticed a nail in a window casement, Mrs. Hearnes took a closer look and discovered a hinge. "If there's a hinge, there must be shutters," she shouted, and soon joined the carpenter in pulling nails and breaking through the paint seal. "The shutters unfolded like a butterfly from a cocoon," Betty recalled excitedly in telling of the discovery." More window and door shutters uncovered on both the first and second floors were released from their enclosures, stripped, and stained to match the woodwork.

The original shutters, which had been enclosed in the window casement for years (left), "unfolded like a butterfly from a cocoon" (right).

Moving methodically from one project to the next, Betty refurbished the brass chandeliers, acquired a number of antique lamps, cleaned the portraits of the first ladies, planted a rose garden, and added sliding doors from the hall to the dining room.

The back porches were repaired and enclosed with glass and the old, wooden floors finished with a clay brick tile. She rewired faulty electricity, ran new water lines, and replaced crumbling baseboards to match the originals. A heavy buildup of paint hid the design around the cap of the columns in the parlor until workmen chipped through the layers to reveal the original Corinthian styling.

Refusing to accept the story that the bricked-up fireplaces were beyond repair, Betty had the bricks removed and flues cleaned and relined. The addition of gas logs added cheer to the old house on chilly, winter days. But floor repairs literally proved to be her downfall. When the old flooring was pulled up, the family was forced to "hop around on boards" for nearly three months—an awkward arrangement that resulted in Mrs. Hearnes tripping over a miter saw and breaking her right elbow.

During the renovation, she did not ignore the third floor as had some previous first ladies. Needing the extra living area, she turned the "junk room" into a bedroom and added a bathroom. Still, the only way to the third floor was by a long, narrow staircase. By extending the second-floor elevator shaft, she lost a bedroom, but gained the third floor access that other first families had longed for. Their youngest daughter, Julie B., usually ignored the lift, however, saying she could go up and down faster on the stairs.

By dealing with the home's many structural problems, Mrs. Hearnes paved the way for extensive interior restoration by the next First Lady Carolyn Bond. Their combined efforts, spanning two decades, re-created a home of Victorian splendor that still marks the Missouri Governor's Mansion as one of the finest and most authentic restorations in America.

Clockwise from upper left: dining room; sideboard; Great Hall; Gold Room or parlor; and, library.

Hearnes signs the 1965 Missouri Civil Rights law. House sponsor of the bill, Majority Floor Leader Mel Carnahan, stands next to the Governor.

(Left to right) Committeeman Bennie Goins, Representative John Conley, Committeeman Leroy Tyus, Representative Deverne L. Calloway, Senator T. D. McNeal, Governor Warren E. Hearnes, and Representatives Mel Carnahan, Harold Holliday, Henry Ross, Leon Jordan, and James Troupe.

testing of those suspected of drinking and driving. When all of these first-year proposals passed into law, the Governor won plaudits for his outstanding leadership.

One controversial measure that gained approval gave the urban areas more representation in the legislature. Historically, every county—regardless of its size—had been represented in the General Assembly, but a new court ruling marked a growing sentiment for the reapportionment of legislative bodies based on population alone. Adoption of the so-called "one-man, one-vote" plan urged by Hearnes changed the face of the legislature and greatly reduced the influence of rural lawmakers.

Hearnes' "honeymoon" relationship with the General Assembly during his first year in office produced another extraordinary change in state government, as well as his own political future. By law he could only run for two nonconsecutive terms, but Hearnes got constitutional approval for two back-to-back terms for a governor, including himself. Some feared that an eight-year reign would allow the chief executive to create a political machine. Hearnes disagreed and declared, "I am a firm believer that a person who does not make a good governor would be defeated in a try for a second term."

The thought of spending eight years in a shabby Capitol office possibly influenced the Governor's decision to do some early remodeling of his work area. Hearnes revamped the large oval waiting room to serve as his office. Upgrading the carpet, draperies, and upholstery, he transformed the thirty-five-by-fifty-foot room into an executive office that rivaled its White House counterpart.

While Warren was renovating his Capitol office and "romancing" the legislature, Betty was also winning friends and influencing people. She became much in demand as a speaker, her topics ranging from "Missouri women in history" to "how the state budget works." One month she spoke at twenty-seven different events, including talks to servicemen's wives, journalism students, high school teachers, a mental health group, and several church and political gatherings. "I even talked to the Fulton football team," she recalled.

Betty also took on a legislative cause. In 1965 she lobbied the General Assembly to pass a bill funding the Missouri Council on the Arts. But the practical-minded lawmakers had little interest in what they felt was a whimsical expenditure of state funds. During the previous session, when the issue came before the General Assembly, legislators had demonstrated the extent of their musical appreciation by standing as a body to sing "Home on the Range."

Though Missouri's lawmakers did not take the arts seriously, Mrs. Hearnes did. Her lobbying efforts began with her husband. "I had the Governor in my bedroom, and that's a pretty good place to lobby," she declared. Undoubtedly, other Missouri first ladies had maneuvered to influence gubernatorial decision making, but Betty's confession of engaging in pillow talk was probably the first such public admission.

As her crusade became known, Betty was asked to speak at a meeting of the National Council on the Arts to tell how to win support in the legislature. She was

Hearnes shows off his newly renovated office that included new drapes, carpet, and upholstery.

Shotgun Slaughter on the Mansion Lawn

It wasn't enough that the nearly one-hundred-year-old Mansion housed a family of five, an array of pets, and visiting relatives. In 1967 a flock of ten thousand birds moved onto the lawn.

"Something needs to be done about those starlings," Governor Hearnes noted one day to a state trooper. "They're getting to be a real nuisance."

No one seemed to recognize that many of the "starlings" were actually purple martins, acclaimed for eating their weight in insects each day and a species protected by state and federal law. Intent on pleasing the Governor, three government workers and a few friends armed with shotguns, fired away at the pesky flock, killing eighteen hundred to two thousand birds with shots that were literally "heard 'round the world." Political pundits, environmentalists, and bird lovers joined in condemning the purple martin caper. To others, it was just a "Tempest in the Tree Top," but still one that left the Governor red-faced at having state employees charged in court with the shotgun slaughter of a much-revered species.

The matter ended when the judge decided there was no malicious intent and fined the assassins fifty dollars each. The massacre affected neither the Governor's reelection bid nor the political fortunes of one of the culprits who was later elected county clerk.

apprehensive about making the appearance because Missouri lawmakers still had not acted. Shortly before she went to the podium, the Governor called with the good news. "Make the speech," he said, "the bill just passed."

"Betty's Bill," as it was dubbed, cleared the General Assembly largely because of her efforts, making Missouri the second state in the nation to fund a state arts council. Later, when Warren appointed his wife to chair the Governor's Committee on Hunger, she took the task with equal seriousness, traveling the state and reporting back to the Governor on the plight of the needy.

In addition to lobbying, speaking, and parenting, Betty continued her usual pursuits about town. She sang in the First Baptist Church choir and attended meetings of local music and social clubs. She also found time for the traditional chores of a first lady—restoration and entertaining. As hostess of the Mansion, she welcomed an array of governors, congressmen, and cabinet members who came to visit. With equal cordiality, Mrs. Hearnes entertained the Mizzou basketball and

(Top) Lynn, Betty, Warren, Leigh, and Julie B. Hearnes. (Bottom) The Hearnes girls meet the Beatles.

football teams, her fellow choir members from the Baptist church, and Japanese visitors from Missouri's sister state of Nagana.

With help from her secretary and some close friends, Betty also organized and conducted public tours that attracted as many as fifteen hundred visitors during a peak month. The First Lady lost her patience on one occasion, however. After personally greeting three hundred students, she was surprised to hear one of the sponsors comment, "It looks like Mrs. Hearnes would have come downstairs to speak to us." Betty responded abruptly, "Lady, I am Mrs. Hearnes and I've been here all day."

One annual event enjoyed by friends and supporters of the Hearneses was their annual birthday. The couple shared a July 24th birth date, which they celebrated with a fund-raising dinner for the Democratic Party. In 1965 more than sixteen hundred guests showed up for the festive evening that raised $35,000 for the Democrats.

In 1967 Warren and Betty hosted an even more splendid gathering—the Midwestern Governors' Conference. The five-day event held at the Lake of the Ozarks was a grand honor for the state, but a year's planning for the First Lady. Hearnes had hoped to make it easier to fly into the remote lake area, but was unable to complete the new airport in time for the meeting. Nonetheless, seventeen governors and some one thousand guests enjoyed the First Family's lakeside hospitality that included boating excursions, pool parties, dancing, and a formal dinner of vichyssoise, beef Wellington, and strawberries Romanoff.

Three years later, the First Family entertained more governors at the lake resort when Missouri was selected as the site of the National Governors' Association. It was the first time the conference had been held in the state since Governor Park hosted the event thirty-four years earlier.

While Warren and Betty were rubbing elbows with state and national political leaders, the girls enjoyed some memorable encounters, too. They attended the governors' conferences along with their parents and made friends with the children of other chief executives. In addition, they met world leaders and celebrities, including Presidents Lyndon Johnson and Richard Nixon, as well as the Beatles.

One national figure caused a stir with his visit to the Capital City in 1968. When U.S. Senator Edward "Ted" Kennedy turned up at the Mansion during his brother Robert Kennedy's presidential campaign, rumors of a Kennedy-Hearnes ticket began to fly in the state capital. The First Lady was caught by surprise when, at the last minute, she was called on to host Kennedy for lunch at the Mansion. Though it was the cook's day off and there was little food in the

Hearnes and a group of governors just returning from Russia in 1971 confer with President Richard Nixon at the White House.

Senator Edward "Ted" Kennedy and Hearnes discuss politics over lunch at the Mansion in 1968.

Governor Hearnes on the platform with evangelist Billy Graham.

313

kitchen, Betty determined to make do. "It was summer, so we covered the dining room table with beautiful flowers from the garden and served hamburgers—lots of style, but not much food," she recalled. "I apologized, of course, for serving such everyday fare, but the Senator graciously replied that hamburger was one of his favorites."

That summer, during a year marred by tragedy, Warren and Betty attended the ill-fated Democratic National Convention. Presidential hopeful Robert Kennedy had lost his life to an assassin's bullet a month before the convention met. As Democrats gathered in Chicago to pick a candidate, demonstrators outside the convention hall staged mass protests against the war in Vietnam. From the chaotic gathering, Hubert H. Humphrey emerged as the presidential nominee of the deeply divided Democratic Party.

Betty was scheduled to sing the "Star Spangled Banner" at the closing session of the convention. The day before her appearance, she received word that her brother-in-law had died of a massive heart attack at the Mansion. He and Betty's sister had been spending the week caring for the two Hearnes girls who had remained at home. At her sister's urging, Betty stayed on and completed the performance before returning home.

Governor and Mrs. Hearnes visit with President and Mrs. Lyndon B. Johnson at the White House.

Back in Missouri the campaign season was in full swing. Taking advantage of the new state law permitting a governor two consecutive terms, Hearnes had filed for reelection. Unlike his race four years earlier, the popular Governor gained an easy primary victory. In November, Hearnes whizzed passed his Republican opponent,

St. Louis County Supervisor Lawrence Roos, racking up a 375,000 vote margin, but Humphrey was unable to wrench the presidency from Richard Nixon. With the Democratic Party in a shambles and Republicans in control in Washington, Hearnes had no hope of being appointed to national office.

On inauguration day in Missouri, Hearnes had to share his celebration with John C. Danforth, a new Republican star who claimed the office of attorney general for his party—the first such victory for the GOP since 1928.

In his inaugural address, the second-term Governor turned his attention to what he hoped to accomplish in his final four years. Making a veiled reference to a possible tax increase, he asked whether the state wanted "to keep pace or . . . to move sharply ahead."

Though he had made a campaign promise in 1964 not to raise taxes, the needs of education and mental health were too great to ignore. With a Democratic margin in the House of 109 to 54 and a favorable split of 23 to 11 in the Senate, Hearnes had more than enough votes to pass his income tax proposal. However, the measure met defeat when it was forced to a statewide referendum. Undaunted, Hearnes resubmitted the bill at the next session of the General Assembly and rounded up enough votes to get the tax hike passed into law.

In 1970 the Hearnes family took a break from politics to enjoy one of the rare privileges of living in the Mansion. Their oldest daughter, Lynn, was married in the parlor where Governor and Mrs. Park's daughter, Henrietta, had been wed nearly thirty-seven years earlier. Although the Mansion ceremony was private, nearly seven hundred people stood in line to greet the newlyweds at the reception that followed.

During his final years in office, the Governor took another look at national office. U.S. Senator Edmund Muskie was seeking the 1972 Democratic presidential nomination and Hearnes—the immediate past chairman of the National Governors' Association—was one of the first to endorse the senator. Again there was some talk of Hearnes being tapped for vice president, but the Governor later indicated he was offered the secretary of transportation post. However, when Muskie dropped out of the race, Hearnes lost the advantage his early commitment might have given him.

"The Mansion will be what you make it," Betty Hearnes counseled the new First Lady.

As the Governor's time in office drew to a close, Betty admitted to a feeling of sadness. Though she began her stay with fear that the Mansion "could never be a home," she had grown increasingly fond of the place that she now called a "little community of its own." As her final remembrance, she planned "a party for the house"—a celebration of its one hundredth birthday that she commemorated with a series of teas and historic lectures.

Though leaving the house was difficult, at least there was the anticipation of going back to Charleston where she and

The Mansion is a "little community of its own."

Warren had built a new home conveniently located next to the golf course. As usual, Betty looked on the bright side: it would be the first time in eight years they would not have to be where Warren could be reached by telephone, she told a reporter. When asked to enumerate her accomplishments, she modestly quipped, "I'm thinner." The size of the family living at home had shrunk, too. With one daughter married, another in college, only Julie B.—who had grown to be a teenager during her stay at the Mansion—would be living at home.

Neither Warren nor Betty completed all they had hoped to do. He wanted to establish a super highway to link the state with New Orleans and Chicago, but could never sell the idea of toll roads to Missourians. She did not finish the third-floor renovation, lay the gas-lighted walkway down to the river, or hold an arts festival on the Mansion lawn.

Instead, she was going home and away from the political limelight. It would be left to subsequent first ladies to carry on the work of the Mansion. Betty counseled the incoming Governor's wife, "The Mansion will be what you make it," noting that each first family puts its own stamp—for better or worse—on the home. From her own experience as Mansion hostess, she cautioned her successor, "You're just a caretaker. You can be devastated if you forget it's only temporary."

"You're just a caretaker. You can be devastated if you forget it's only temporary."

In keeping with tradition, Betty left behind a portrait of herself. It was not an oil painting like the others that lined the Mansion walls, but a handsome photographic portrait paid for by family friends. The First Lady did not need a portrait to mark her tenure at the Mansion; evidence of her devotion to the home could be seen everywhere.

In like manner, Warren left his imprint on state government. During his first term he had won approval for forty-two of his forty-five proposals; the second term brought fewer victories, but he still managed a 60 percent acceptance for his legislative package. Education was a top priority for the Governor and public schools received what was then the largest funding increase in the state's history. Missouri also gained five junior college districts, fifty-three more vocational schools, an expanded kindergarten program, and a new medical school in Kansas City.

Support for mental health care had fared well, too. According to Hearnes, the state's attitude turned from "custodial care to one of treatment and rehabilitation." Along with a 228 percent increase in funding came nine regional diagnostic clinics, the first alcoholism and drug treatment programs, and sheltered workshops throughout the state. The Governor proudly announced that Missouri had "moved from the bottom of the ladder to the top" in support of mental health.

In addition, one thousand new industries came to Missouri and twelve hundred existing businesses expanded. New commissions and departments sprang up to carry out the Governor's agenda: a Department of Community Affairs, a Clean Water Commission, a commission on the status of women and another for tourism.

Their eight years at the Mansion was the longest continuous residency in history.

In the Governor's final address to the legislature, he explained the conflict he had felt as a public servant for much of his life. "You must fight within yourself the continual contest between a normal desire for public approval and your personal sense of public duty," he told the lawmakers.

After spending the longest continuous residency at the Mansion in history, Warren Hearnes, at age forty-nine, returned to Charleston. Putting aside his twenty-two years of elective office, he became a partner in a St. Louis law firm, dividing his work between St. Louis and southeast Missouri.

However, both Warren and Betty were too young and too entrenched in public life to fade from the political scene entirely. Hearnes had his heart set on a U.S. Senate seat, but Republicans were eager to head him off. In an attempt to tarnish his image, Hearnes believed the Nixon White House targeted him for an FBI investigation. A Kansas City grand jury succeeded in putting him under a cloud for over a year, but ultimately Hearnes was cleared of any wrongdoing and won a libel suit against the *St. Louis Post-Dispatch* for the stories printed against him.

Still, the episode hurt him in 1976 when he entered a four-way primary fight for the U.S. Senate. With two well-known congressmen and a Kansas City mayor in the race, Warren and Betty knew it would be a tough battle. As usual, Mrs. Hearnes joined the fray, working full-time in her husband's St. Louis campaign office.

The winner of the hotly contested match was U.S. Representative Jerry Litton, a popular north Missouri farmer. However, in a tragic election night plane crash, Litton and his family died shortly after his victory was declared. The Democratic State Committee was left with the task of filling the ticket and chose Hearnes, the second-place contender. It was an ill-fated quest by the former Governor that ended with the victory of Republican John Danforth. An unsuccessful try for auditor two years later closed out Hearnes' attempts for state office.

In 1978 Betty entered politics in her own right. With her election as state representative, she served in the Missouri House for ten years before announcing her plan to run for governor—the first woman in Missouri history to make such a race. But then, Betty had never sought easy tasks. This time, she took on a well-financed, popular incumbent, Governor John Ashcroft, a feat that no other member of her party would attempt.

The sixty-one-year-old former First Lady conducted an active campaign, much like those that had worked for Warren Hearnes over two decade earlier. But the cost of waging a modern media contest in 1988 proved fatal to her chances. A race in 1990 to regain her seat in the House and a 1992 try for state Senate also failed.

To their credit, neither Betty nor Warren let political loss become personal defeat. They remain active contributors to their state and community. The couple still resides in Charleston, where Warren held a federal appointment as director of the Southeast Missouri Legal Services for sixteen years until his retirement in 1998. Betty chaired the state's Mental Health Commission and became a leader in helping autistic children and their families. Just as Warren was retiring, Betty, at the age of seventy-one, tossed her hat back into the political ring when she filed for the seat she had previously held in the House.

Considered one of Missouri's most dynamic and colorful political duos, Warren and Betty Hearnes have influenced Missouri politics for nearly half a century with a devotion to public service unsurpassed in the state's history.

CAMELOT REVISITED

"[The Mansion] belongs to the people of the state and should be shared with them and preserved for future generations to enjoy and admire." ~ First Lady Carolyn Bond

Nearly five inches of snow had fallen and light flurries continued as six thousand spectators gathered in the Capital City for the 1973 inauguration. Flags lining the parade route remained at half-staff in honor of former President Harry S. Truman who had died just a few weeks earlier. With a broad smile and twinkle of good humor in the corner of his eye, the new Governor doffed his top hat to cheering crowds that lined his route to the Capitol. Arriving on the inaugural platform, he shook hands with eighty-eight-year-old Forrest Donnell, the last Republican to have been sworn in as governor. At age thirty-three, Christopher "Kit" Bond would soon be the state's first Republican governor in twenty-eight years and the nation's youngest chief executive.

Missing from the festivities were the traditional lines of brightly uniformed colonels whose numbers had grown during recent administrations. Bond saw the group as a vestige of the past and vowed there would be no such display of cronyism in his administration. Instead of bestowing an honorary military rank on his supporters, the new Governor planned a luncheon for them at a local hotel.

Although Bond could control the presence of colonels at his inaugural ceremony, not everything was under his direction. Few inaugural ceremonies occur without a hitch.

Governor and Mrs. Bond greet guests at the inaugural ball.

(Facing page)
The stenciled ceiling of the Double Parlor.

319

(Above left)
In keeping with
tradition, Hearnes
rode the parade route
to the Capitol with the
Governor-elect.
(Above right)
The inaugural ball in
the Capitol rotunda.

Running ahead of schedule, or behind, becomes a problem for the Senate president pro tem who presides over the ceremony and must see to the constitutional requirement that the oath be administered at noon on inauguration day. With ten minutes to spare, the good-natured pro tem advised the shivering crowd to stomp their feet to keep warm as they awaited the sound of pealing bells from nearby St. Peter's church. Following his inaugural address, Bond went to his new office for a quiet ceremony to swear in a Springfield lawyer, John Ashcroft, as state auditor—the office Bond had given up when elected governor.

The day-long inaugural that had started with a worship service at the local Presbyterian church climaxed that evening with the traditional ball. Bond and his wife, Carolyn, joined the celebration at the Capitol rotunda, opening the dance by waltzing to the tune "Around the World in Eighty Days"—no doubt a reminder of the whirlwind campaign they had just come through so victoriously. Supporters smiled their approval as the new Governor and his thirty-one-year-old wife glided across the dance floor, displaying a charm that people had admired a decade earlier in another political couple, John and Jacqueline Kennedy.

Kit and Carolyn had met in Atlanta where she was a speech therapist and he worked as a law clerk for a year. The two literally ran into each other during a touch football scrimmage. The young attorney had already shown his prowess in academics. Graduating from Princeton with honors, he had gone on to the University of Virginia Law School, where he ranked first in the class of 1963. After completing his clerkship in Atlanta, he returned to Missouri briefly to work in the reelection campaign of Congressman Thomas Curtis. Beginning in 1964, Bond put in a three-year stint in a Washington law office before heading back to his hometown of Mexico, Missouri, intent on pursuing public office.

With him was his new bride, Carolyn Reid Bond, whom he had met so unceremoniously on the football field several years earlier and married in 1967.

Carolyn was more than a match for her handsome, politically ambitious husband. She had some impressive credentials of her own, having walked away with a Phi Beta Kappa key from the University of Kentucky and the Miss Congeniality award in a state beauty pageant.

The budding politician not only had a lovely wife to enhance his image but also had the advantage of being from an old, well-respected local family. His grandfather had founded the town's major industry, the A.P. Green refractory. Another ancestor had served in the U.S. Senate and Bond's great-grandfather, George Bond, had run for the legislature on the Republican ticket headed by Abraham Lincoln. Kit's father, Art Bond, was a Rhodes scholar and the 1925 captain of the Missouri

Carolyn asked to campaign in those area where her husband had previously lost to Democrats.

football Tigers. Despite his impressive background, Kit Bond lost his first political contest. The twenty-nine-year-old attorney was narrowly defeated in a race for congress in 1968, though he showed considerable skill in attracting votes in the predominantly Democratic ninth district.

Still intent on public service, Bond spent the next year-and-a-half as an assistant attorney general before running for state auditor in 1970. Carolyn, who had worked in political races in her home state of Kentucky, asked if she could campaign in the counties where her husband had suffered the heaviest losses during his congressional bid. She concentrated her efforts in Pike, Lincoln, and Marion counties—all traditionally Democratic. Her efforts paid off when Bond carried all three counties, leading to some amusing speculation about which of the two was the better campaigner.

Regardless, it was an upset victory for Bond over the incumbent Democratic Auditor Haskell Holman who had held the office for seventeen years and was considered by many to be unbeatable. Bond's 200,000-vote plurality was the greatest ever received by a Republican in Missouri. At age thirty-one, he held the further distinction of being the youngest auditor in the state's history. Once on the job, Bond assembled a professional staff, adding seven certified public accountants to the auditor's office where there was previously only one. He further stepped up efficiency by urging the immediate deposit of receipts.

However, by midterm the Republican auditor had something more on his mind: a race for the state's top office. Much like his predecessor Governor Warren Hearnes, Bond was not the anointed candidate of his party. Trumpeting the slogan "Leadership for a

Carolyn held some impressive credentials of her own and was more than a match for her handsome, politically ambitious husband.

Change," he took on two of the GOP's old-line vote-getters—Bus King and Gene McNary—and with it a Supreme Court lawsuit that challenged his residency as a Missourian. Though Bond was born in Missouri, he lived in the state primarily during his fifth to tenth grade school years. The legal challenge was potentially career shattering. Bond later recounted his predicament: "If I'd been thrown off the ballot, I'd been thrown out of the auditor's office, too," since the residency requirements were the same. Ultimately, Bond came out victorious both in the lawsuit and the hard-fought 1972 primary battle.

Carolyn Bond, with an undergraduate degree in speech therapy and a master's degree in counseling, was a strong advocate of special education during her husband's race for governor. On the campaign trail, she visited all 114 counties in the state and made over two hundred speeches in behalf of her husband. Reporters following the campaign took special note of the young woman, describing her as "poised, articulate, energetic. . . . cool, and perfectly coiffed."

As his party's nominee, Bond shared the general election ballot that year with a popular Republican president running for reelection—Richard M. Nixon. Many Missouri Democrats, on the other hand, having come through a divisive primary, showed little enthusiasm for their nominee, George McGovern. In the November election, Republicans made heavy gains in Missouri and nationwide. Bond defeated Democrat Edward Dowd Sr., a St. Louis attorney, to win the governorship while William Phelps, a Republican, captured the lieutenant governor's post. With Bond's appointment of John Ashcroft to fill the unexpired term as auditor, the GOP controlled half of the statewide offices—a condition that had not occurred since early in the century.

The new First Couple did not rush to move into the executive Mansion. Preferring to make the house more functional as both a private and public building, Carolyn spent two-and-a-half months rearranging the second floor living space and decorating it with their own furniture. Under the arrangement, the private quarters were confined to the upper floors and the first floor left open for public tours.

But refurbishing the Mansion proved costly both financially and politically for the Bonds. A $19,000 bathroom—much described in the press—raised eyebrows and drew adverse attention to the restoration. Carolyn dispelled the wonder by unveiling the bath area to the media. It was not the opulent display expected; one reporter

Mansion life is a lot like "living over the store." commented, "Is this all?"
Another wrote, "What began in the mind of many Missouri taxpayers as a bathroom fit for a sultan has turned into two plain, but attractive, bathrooms and a walk-through wardrobe with a storage area." Major expenses had resulted from plumbing and electrical wiring being in bad shape and from having to chip through nine inches of concrete to access the area without damaging the first-floor ceiling.

Mrs. Bond's kitchen repairs drew less attention. When a small bathroom was converted into a compact, galley-shaped kitchen, the First Lady explained that the former kitchenette with the one-burner stove needed upgrading. "My husband is afraid I'll forget how to cook," she joked to reporters. The first-floor kitchen was also improved with the addition of commercial equipment and matched dinnerware that made serving large dinner parties a lot more pleasant.

Even with the improvements, the transition to Mansion life took some personal adjustment. The division of private and public space made it a lot like "living over the store," the First Lady noted, and the

Rather than leave office at noon, Bond often worked with several aides over lunch.

trains that passed just under the bedroom window "make a lot of noise." The railroad tracks running just eighty yards from the Governor's bedroom had long been an annoyance to Mansion residents. Though the sound of jarring rail cars often rattled the windows during the middle of the night, the Bonds—like those before them—soon grew accustomed to the intrusion.

In spite of the discomforts of the old house, Kit and Carolyn each launched enthusiastically into their new roles as the state's First Couple. Kit scheduled his appointments in five-minute segments: at 10:10 a.m. a sixth-grade class might tour his office, at 10:15 a.m. there might be a legislator asking a favor for a constituent. Rather than leave his office during the noon hour, he often worked with several aides over lunch.

Docents in period costumes share the history of the Mansion during public tours.

Despite his diligence, it was a difficult first term. The Governor faced a major flood, fuel shortages, two ice storms, and several tough battles with the Democratic-dominated legislature. In addition, lawmakers and newsmen joked about the young Governor and his "Kiddie Korps"—a reference to his "Eastern-educated, mid-thirtyish, country-clubbing assistants."

Nonetheless, Bond chalked up some meaningful accomplishments. "[He] earned kudos for introducing a merit system for state employment, forging a strong open meetings law, securing the state's first campaign finance legislation, and streamlining the management of state government." He was unsuccessful, however, in passing the Equal Rights Amendment, or in resolving the location of a medium-security prison.

While her husband nudged the state forward, Carolyn worked on making the historic Mansion more meaningful to visitors. She discovered that many residents of the Capital City had never been

Mrs. Bond used her flair for design to recapture the Victorian splendor of the old house

inside the Victorian home, nor had most other Missourians. Even though the public-private aspect of living at the Mansion made it much like a "fishbowl," she felt the old home belonged to the people of the state and she wanted to share it with them.

The First Lady began regular tours of the house each Tuesday and Thursday, using twenty-five local women in period costumes as volunteer guides to assist her. The cadre of docents enjoyed telling of Governor Stewart who fed his horse oats from a sideboard in the dining room because, as he said, "[My horse is] better than a lot of people we feed around here." They told the legend of Frank James negotiating the terms of his surrender with Governor Crittenden in the Mansion library. They recounted the time when Governor and Mrs. Francis lived in the home along with their six youngsters and a menagerie of pets, including a goat. Visitors were delighted with the old stories.

Not just content to pass on the lore of the Mansion, Mrs. Bond used her flair for design to recapture the Victorian splendor of the 1871 home—a task that was more difficult and costly than she ever imagined. One writer summed up the problem: despite the work of former first ladies, the funding and decorating of the Mansion had "never really matched the splendid architecture."

The scale of the furnishings, not just their age, was an important consideration in decorating the large open spaces which had ceilings ranging from fourteen to seventeen feet high. "We think something is perfect [in size]," the First Lady said, "then, we bring it into this big house and it's lost."

"We think something is perfect then we bring it into this big house and it's lost."

Carolyn recognized, too, that a true restoration would take millions of dollars in private money, as well as extensive research.

To assure the authenticity and continuity of the renovation, Mrs. Bond announced the formation of Missouri Mansion Preservation Incorporated, (MMPI) a nonprofit, nonpartisan organization whose goal was to restore and preserve the home, to acquire period furnishings, and to provide heritage education programs. The group hoped to correct what it saw as an inclination for changing the decor at the Mansion with each administration.

Mrs. Bond looked in vain for the original plans of architect George Ingham Barnett. She talked with descendants of former first families to learn about earlier renovations. She worked with restoration architect Ted Wofford and MMPI's Fine Arts Committee to find out all she could about the era during which the house was constructed. Room by room, she raised money—nearly two million dollars in private and corporate funds—to restore the Mansion in a Renaissance Revival styling with

vibrant Victorian colors. When asked for donations of furniture, Missourians responded, making gifts to the Mansion just as the nation had made to the White House under Jacqueline Kennedy's direction. The library—the first room completed—cost nearly $75,000 to renovate, an amount equal to what it took to build and partially furnish the Mansion in 1871.

Looking to criticize the project, opponents latched on to one idea offered by the restoration architect—a dining room built into the bluffs with seating for three hundred guests. But the $1.5 million proposal found no support in the legislature or elsewhere. According to Mrs. Bond, the Mansion had more pressing needs.

The home was "the only Governor's residence in the United States that is not air conditioned in the public rooms," she said, nor was there a fire protection system. Especially annoying was the lack of temperature controls in the residence; the heat piped from the steam plant in a nearby office building was either on or off.

Carolyn adjusted her social schedule to the repair work. Once described as "a gracious antebellum hostess and horse-sense housekeeper," she refused to give in to the disruption and mockingly held an afternoon tea party on top of the

(Left)
Carolyn donned overalls and climbed the scaffolding to help with the stencil work on the ceiling.

"The Mansion has undergone more facelifts than an aging diva."

MISSOURI MANSION PRESERVATION

Before the Mansion was ever occupied in 1872, the local newspaper called for a butler to be hired to maintain and care for the home. Butlers were employed, some remaining for many years, to serve the various first families and needs of the house.

But it was not until 1974 that the task of preservation was formalized with the creation of Missouri Mansion Preservation Incorporated (MMPI). Since then, the nonpartisan, nonprofit group has received tax-deductible donations for the ongoing restoration of the Governor's Mansion and the promotion of its Missouri heritage programs.

Mary Pat Abele, the executive director of MMPI since its creation during the Bond administration, has worked with three subsequent first families in preserving and enhancing the Victorian residence. Guided tours by costumed docents and an array of special events attract more than 58,000 visitors to the home each year. Holidays such as Christmas, Easter, Halloween, and the Fourth of July offer a special opportunity to make the house festive and appealing to visitors, especially children.

325

A LIVING R

Library

Double Parlor

Ballroom

Stark Bedroom

TORATION

The Governor Edward's sideboard, the oldest piece featured in the Mansion.

The apsidal design in the carpet and table tops replicates the geometric shape of the house.

ning Room

Great Hall

THE UPPER ROOMS

Living Room

Study

Second-floor Porch

Family Dining Room

Sleigh Bedroom

D.A.R. Bedroom

scaffolding. As the restoration progressed, tourists flocked to the Mansion to view the Victorian splendor. Mrs. Bond also hosted the military ball, the traditional colonial tea for the Daughters of the American Revolution, and the Easter egg hunt started by Mrs. Dalton for disabled children. In 1973 Carolyn followed up the Easter event by sponsoring a day at the state fair for 18,000 physically handicapped persons.

In addition to celebrating the usual holidays and traditions, Carolyn commemorated one lesser-known event—the 154th birthday of women's activist Susan B. Anthony. The event gave her the chance to speak out for the passage of the Equal Rights Amendment. "We can be proud that there were women in Missouri's past who had the courage of their convictions to fight for what they thought was right," she told the 150 women gathered at a Mansion coffee. "It is time that our laws reflect the position of women in today's world," she said as she urged the ladies to make sure that Missouri joined the ranks of the thirty-eight states necessary to ratify the amendment.

The proposal failed and the First Lady drew some political criticism for her stance. But her renovation efforts brought accolades from those who recognized the importance of preserving Missouri's heritage. In 1975 the *St. Louis Globe-Democrat* picked Mrs. Bond for one of their "Women of Achievement" awards—an honor previously bestowed on two former Mansion residents, Mrs. Dalton and Mrs. Hearnes.

Though repair work caused some inconvenience, the Bonds hosted a number of special guests, among them Lady Mary Soames, Sir Winston Churchill's youngest daughter. The visit of Secretary of State Henry Kissinger and his wife, Nancy, attracted a crowd of spectators who lined up outside the fence to get a glimpse of the couple. The Kissingers breakfasted at the Mansion on French toast a la Reine, melon ring, orange juice, and sweet rolls before going to the Capitol to meet with state leaders.

The Bonds had a chance to meet more distinguished visitors in 1976 during the National Governors' Conference in Philadelphia. That year Queen Elizabeth visited the United States for the bicentennial celebration and hosted the state leaders at a tea party aboard the royal yacht.

The American bicentennial celebration also offered the First Lady an opportunity for creative expression at the Mansion. Carolyn was captivated by the idea of needlepointing a rug depicting the flowers of the fifty states. Needlepointers from

The visit of Secretary of State Henry Kissinger attracted a crowd of visitors outside the Mansion fence.

across the state submitted sample squares, competing for the chance to have their handwork included in the ten-by-eleven-foot carpet. Carolyn stitched the goldenrod, the flower of her native Kentucky, but eighty-one others—ranging in age from twelve to eighty-four years—had their work included. The carpet was finished with a floral border of the Missouri hawthorn and presented to the Mansion shortly before the Fourth of July, 1976. Although the handwork was originally intended for the floor of the Nook, concern for wear caused it to be moved to the

second-floor Stark bedroom. It was later mounted on the wall of the first-floor porch.

Carolyn took on another bicentennial project of even greater proportion. When it was learned that the Mercantile Library intended to sell their 112-piece collection of sketches by Missouri artist George Caleb Bingham, the First Lady was appalled. She was not alone. Missourians from art historians to school children felt that a part of the state's heritage was being put on the auction block.

In the heat of the controversy, the state agreed to put up a half-million dollars of the $1.8 million needed to keep the collection intact. Governor Bond immediately appointed a citizen's group to raise the remaining $1.3 million needed to purchase the collection for the state. The First Lady joined the drive, encouraging corporate donors as well as children to back the effort. During Bingham Week, groups of students all over the state washed cars, sold hand-crafted items, and held bake sales and bazaars to earn money for the project. In just over three months, 100,000 people—half of them children—contributed more than enough to reach the goal.

George Caleb Bingham satirizes a politician in one of his sketches for *Stump Speaking*.

The bicentennial needlepoint carpet depicts the flowers of the fifty states in alphabetical order with the Missouri hawthorn featured in the border.

In addition to her many projects, Mrs. Bond found time for personal pursuits. With no children in the house and the restoration in full swing, the lively First Lady often participated in tennis matches at the local country club. She was also captain of the Pachydame bowling team and once picked up a score that made her worthy of being proclaimed Bowler of the Week.

Even with the absence of children at the Mansion, the house was not without the patter of little feet—or, at least, little paws. The basset hounds, Calamity Jane (tagged with the name of Governor Francis's much maligned dog) and B. Gratz Brown (the namesake of the first governor to live in the Mansion) served as the First Pooches of Missouri. The dogs shared the annual Christmas card photo with the Bonds and Gratz stamped his paw print on the official proclamation for the Humane Society's "Be Kind to Puppy Week." While walking the bassets one evening after work, Bond told reporters, "These dogs are absolutely worthless, but we get a lot of enjoyment from them."

Bond could also take satisfaction in the national recognition he was gaining and the political prospects that came with it. *U.S. News and World Report* called him "one of the brightest stars in the state's rejuvenated Republican Party, whom many have said may be headed for the White House." In 1974, and again two years later, he was mentioned as a vice presidential possibility.

But something went wrong in 1976. To begin with, he antagonized Missouri's Republican leaders by endorsing Vice President Gerald Ford for the presidency against Ronald Reagan. Still confident he could win another term as governor, Bond let down his guard at a time when an upstart populist from Kansas City—nicknamed "Walkin' Joe" Teasdale—began speaking out against high utility bills and rousing sentiment against the Governor. The very fact that no one took the Democratic challenger seriously made Bond supporters complacent and the Governor uneasy. Four major newspapers endorsed Bond and on election night one television network even declared him the winner over Teasdale. But when the dust cleared, much to everyone's surprise, the rising star of the Republican Party had plummeted to defeat by a 13,000-vote margin.

In the wake of the loss, the Bonds—still young and ambitious—left the Mansion for Kansas

"These dogs are absolutely worthless, but we get a lot of enjoyment from them," Bond told reporters.

Something went wrong in 1976.

Bond antagonized many Republicans with his endorsement of Gerald Ford for the presidency against Ronald Reagan.

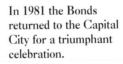
The Bonds are joined by President Ronald Reagan at a rally in Springfield in 1986.

City. Hoping to avenge the beating he had taken from Teasdale, the deposed Governor bided his time working for the Great Plains Legal Foundation, a group committed to fighting government bureaucracy and cutting red tape.

Four years later, a new, revitalized Kit Bond at forty-one years of age was ready for a rematch with his old adversary. Pledging to visit all 114 counties before election day, Kit stumped the backwaters, factory gates, and courthouses across the state. "Hi, I'm Kit Bond. 'Preciate your vote August 5," he would repeat, moving swiftly down the main streets and through the shopping malls in search of votes. "This time we're not stopping until we got all the cows in the barn," he would tell rural voters. Carolyn was less in the forefront this time. She was expecting their first child and kept a limited campaign schedule, filling in at events her husband could not attend.

Bond easily brushed passed his primary opponent, Lieutenant Governor Bill Phelps, and tackled incumbent Joe Teasdale, saying the Governor's antibusiness position had hurt the economy and run potential investors out of the state. Using a "Jobs for Missouri" theme at a time when there was a decline in the auto industry, Bond put Teasdale out of office, carrying the state by a 53 to 47 split and becoming the first Republican in Missouri to hold the office more than once. (Democratic Governors Donnelly and Hearnes had each been elected to serve two terms, but only the Hearnes years were consecutive.) In the 1980 election, President Ronald Reagan won the White House, leading a conservative stampede that placed Republicans in charge across the country.

The Bonds returned to the Capital City for a triumphant celebration. The brisk, but otherwise pleasant, day appeared to offer a good omen for Bond's second term in contrast to the frigid conditions for Teasdale four years earlier. In his ten-minute address,

In 1981 the Bonds returned to the Capital City for a triumphant celebration.

332

the returning Governor told those gathered on the Capitol lawn that he intended to offer "better government, not bigger government."

Just a few weeks after the inauguration, the Bonds had reason to celebrate once again. After thirteen years of marriage, Kit and Carolyn delighted in the birth of Samuel Reid—the red-headed youngster who marked the seventh generation of the Mexico, Missouri, family.

Bond pauses to feed his three-and-one-half-month-old son, Sam, during a proclamation signing session.

But there was little to celebrate at the Governor's office. Harsh reality awaited Bond as he took up the reins for his second term. High interest rates inflation, and a short money supply had pushed unemployment to 7.6 percent. With a slump in income caused by a declining economy, Bond was forced to spend the next few months announcing budget cuts, some of which affected him personally. Beginning with the inauguration costs, he had mailed smaller invitations to save on printing and reduced the size of the inaugural platform. Once in office, he cut staff salaries and flew on smaller state aircraft to further emphasize his economies.

In 1982 Bond proposed a standstill budget and asked the lawmakers to help him put the state's "financial house back in order." State employees received no pay raise and cabinet directors had 10 percent withheld from their operating budgets. Only education escaped the ax. "He had a lot of guts to do what he did," said Senator Edward Dirck, a Democrat and chair of the Appropriations Committee. Dirck had earlier called the Governor "politically naive," referring to Bond's inability to cope with a bickering legislature during his first term. But this time the Senator credited him with taking the unpopular steps needed to balance the budget.

During her husband's second term, Carolyn, too, tackled her job from a different perspective. With a small child to care for and more renovation underway at the Mansion, she spent much of the time in Kansas City. Still, she continued raising money to advance the restoration. At Christmas, she had the Mansion trimmed in Victorian splendor for the candlelight tours. Her holiday open house gave the public a chance to stroll through the richly decorated rooms, greet the First Family, and hear the choral music offered by local choirs. Her sharing of the Mansion ranged from hosting the wedding of a friend to entertaining such foreign dignitaries as British Prime Minister Edward Heath and the Japanese ambassador to the United States.

Both socially and politically, the Governor was more relaxed during his second term. "[His] more outgoing, informal and friendly relationship with the legislature was a major help," according to one Capitol observer. He held weekly breakfast

(Right)
The photo from the
Bonds' 1981
Christmas card.

meetings with legislative leaders, making new attempts to get involved in the law-making process. He advanced a program of home care for the elderly and an Early Childhood Development Act to identify developmental problems in preschool-aged children. His creation of the Children's Trust Fund enabled taxpayers to donate a portion of their tax refunds to child abuse prevention. Despite his good intentions, a tight budget forced one-fifth of the beds in mental hospitals to be shut down and school support slipped in national ranking.

Facing a decline in state services, Bond took a political risk. He backed off from his campaign promise not to ask for more taxes. During a special session of the General Assembly, he urged a $150 million corporate and franchise tax increase and threatened deeper budget

Sam Bond.

cuts unless it passed. The recalcitrant lawmakers refused. Fortunately, an upswing in the economy made the tax unnecessary and gave Bond a chance to leave behind a $340 million surplus.

In his attempt to cure the state's economic woes, Bond became Missouri's leading salesman. He headed a trade mission of Missouri businessmen to Japan where he urged investors to look at all the state had to offer. With the hope of promoting Missouri products at home and abroad, he established a new Department of Economic Development.

Among his victories was a $600 million bond issue designed to refurbish state properties and to generate 57,000 new jobs—a boon for the sagging construction industry in Missouri. He had promised to create 200,000 new jobs during his second term, but the nation-wide recession made it impossible. Nonetheless, evaluating his term, Bond claimed success. "I have accomplished almost all the goals I set out to accomplish," he declared.

Before leaving office, the First Lady also left an enduring legacy by compiling the book *PAST & REPAST*, a collection of favorite Mansion recipes and historical tidbits interspersed with photographs of the house and the Bond family. Over the next fifteen years, nearly 40,000 copies of the book were sold by Missouri Mansion Preservation in behalf of the Mansion's preservation.

Though Bond's term as governor was over, his interest in politics was not. In 1986 Bond used his popularity as a springboard to higher office. That year he was the only Republican to win a U.S. Senate seat previously held by a Democrat. His reelection in 1992 made him the only Republican to win statewide office in Missouri. Carolyn had earlier launched a career of her own as an interior decorator. In 1995 the couple further went their separate ways with their divorce after twenty-seven years of marriage.

On the national scene, Missouri's senior senator remains an advocate of family issues. He was a strong supporter of Head Start, Family and Medical Leave legislation, and the Parents as Teachers program. The National Journal labeled him "a conservative with a soft spot for cities and housing." Colleagues give him high marks for his gregarious manner and efforts to find solutions that work. One Democratic senator noted, "[Bond] always tries to form alliances in the sensible center"—a trait that has served him well both in the nation's capital and with his midwestern constituency.

A book of recipes and historical tidbits published in 1983 by Missouri Mansion Preservation sold nearly 40,000 copies over a fifteen-year period.

GHOST STORIES

Is the Mansion haunted? Old timers working at the 1871 Victorian home—especially those on the night shift—tell intriguing stories. They say that sometimes when it is very quiet and no one is at home, you can hear the spirits of past residents roaming the halls.

One guard working alone in the house told of hearing voices and laughter coming from the Grand Stairway as though a party was in progress. Those with a bent for the supernatural suspect it was the friendly ghost of Maggie Stephens, whose portrait hangs at the curve of the stairs. Some believe that the flamboyant, party-loving First Lady returns from time to time to host another gathering of her friends.

After hearing playful voices and random movements of the elevator between floors, one guard was convinced that intruders had somehow entered the Mansion. With gun in hand, he surveyed each floor, but found no one. Not wanting to take the chance of a reoccurring incident, he quit his job shortly thereafter.

The most spine-tingling tale, however, was told by Capitol guard Sgt. Jim Maxey. During the Bond administration, the duct work in the subattic was being repaired. As the workman left for lunch, he told Maxey, "You might want to tell the Governor that his little girl is upstairs playing in the attic."

Somewhat startled, Sergeant Maxey replied, "But the Governor doesn't have a daughter."

"Well," said the worker, "it must be a neighbor's child because I talked to an eight-or nine-year-old girl in a white dress all morning."

Sergeant Maxey lightheartedly suggested it might be the ghost of nine-year-old Carrie Crittenden, the only child to die in the Mansion. Strangely, it was exactly one hundred years since the youngster had succumbed to diphtheria shortly before Christmas 1882.

It was all too eerie for the workman, who left the Mansion quickly and never returned to complete the job.

WALKIN' JOE: IN STEP WITH MISSOURI

GOVERNOR JOSEPH PATRICK TEASDALE
MARY THERESA FERKENHOFF TEASDALE
1977-1981

"Handsome enough to be a model in a men's cologne advertisement. Serious enough to retreat to a monastery to reflect on what he is doing with his life. Unpredictable enough to come from outside the Democratic party power structure and win a governorship he was not supposed to win." ~ Fred W. Lindecke, *St. Louis Post-Dispatch*

No one thought Joe Teasdale had a chance to win the race for governor in 1976. The handsome, popular, onetime prosecuting attorney of Jackson County had never served in the legislature or held a statewide office. Furthermore, he had lost the Democratic primary for governor four years earlier in spite of a 650-mile walk across Missouri to win grassroots support. The walk was not entirely without benefit. Along the way, the thirty-five-year-old bachelor received seven or eight marriage offers and learned that Missourians had a basic distrust for the ordinary politician. But in 1976, pitted against a sitting governor seeking another term, the outcome did not look good for "Walkin' Joe" Teasdale, as he came to be known.

Nonetheless, Teasdale was a man with a mission who had friends who believed in him. He wanted to put the Department of Revenue on a merit basis, abolish cronyism in the license fee offices, close tax loopholes, and reorganize the welfare system. Whenever he spoke, he hammered away at the Public Service Commission (PSC) and excessive utility rates. Even so, as the election neared, Teasdale

(Facing page) Governor and Mrs. Joseph Teasdale descend the stairs at the inaugural ball in the Capitol rotunda.

and his close supporters felt doubtful about their chances of seizing the governor's chair from incumbent Republican Christopher "Kit" Bond. Polls taken a week before the election showed the Kansas City Democrat behind by six points.

Even though Teasdale captured an early lead on election night, NBC television declared Bond the winner at 7:02 p.m., two minutes after the polls closed in Missouri. Much to the surprise of political pundits, when all the votes were counted, Teasdale's populist message prevailed.

"I can't think of a regular Democratic organization that supported me."

The forty-year-old Democrat had pulled off one of the biggest election upsets in the state's history by a 12,500-vote margin. Teasdale's late television commercials and Bond's overconfidence had made the difference—although it did not hurt any having presidential candidate Jimmy Carter do well in the wake of the Watergate scandal. As stunned as Bond was by the upset, Teasdale was more so and refused to believe he had won until eight o'clock the next morning. When he was first addressed as "Governor," he blushed and said to just call him "Joe."

During the two months before the inauguration, Teasdale "secluded himself like a Trappist monk." Avoiding reporters, acquaintances, and favor-seekers, he turned full attention to preparing for his new job. One newspaper referred to him as the "reclusive Governor-elect." Another sent reporters dressed as joggers to photograph his early-morning run. Teasdale, admitting he was a novice to state government, said he needed the time to do a line-by-line study of the budget and to prepare his address to the General Assembly.

Though he was new to state office, Joe Teasdale was not without experience in elections and politics. As a child, he and his sister had stood on street corners and passed out sample ballots. (Later, his politically savvy sister, Maureen Galey, stood by him, organizing and running every campaign.) Teasdale's interest in government grew during his years at Rockhurst High School, a Jesuit institution in Kansas City where he competed in debate and school politics and lettered in basketball, baseball, and football. After graduating from St. Louis University School of Law in 1960, he gained his early legal experience as an assistant U.S. attorney.

In 1966 Teasdale was elected prosecutor—the youngest in Jackson County history—with the backing of the Committee for County Progress (CCP), a new group formed to oppose the old-line politicians. In spite of Joe's lifelong interest in public service, his father, a successful Kansas City attorney, always thought his son would become a priest. However, at the age of thirty-seven, Teasdale picked a bride, a shy, attractive airline secretary who was supportive of Joe's ambitions, but personally preferred homemaking to politics.

Again, with the backing of the CCP, Teasdale was reelected county prosecutor in 1968, but was defeated in his 1972 run for governor. His reappearance in 1976 against incumbent Governor Bond

HOW COLD WAS THE TEASDALE INAUGURATION?

How cold was it on January 10, 1977, the date of Joe Teasdale's outdoor inauguration? Staff writer Mark Noblin of the *Springfield Daily News* put it this way:

"It was so cold that the ink froze in reporters' pens.

It was so cold that Teasdale wore long underwear.

It was so cold that beards and mustaches were turned into icicles.

It was so cold that Walkin' Joe was given a new nickname—Gov. Freezedale—by Sen. A. Clifford Jones for his insistence on holding the ceremonies outdoors to allow more people to view them.

It was so cold that at least six National Guardsmen serving as inauguration marshals were treated for mild cases of frostbite."

Gusting wind from the river sent the chill factor plummeting to 25 to 40 degrees below zero in the Capital City. With Teasdale's decision to keep the event outdoors, two thousand shivering spectators huddled on the Capitol lawn to watch the traditional swearing-in ceremony. However, many left their seats to find shelter inside the Capitol before—and during—the Governor's six-minute inaugural address. A reporter observing the new Governor hatless and without gloves, asked if he was cold. Teasdale quipped, "I'm warm inside."

"My feet damn near fell off."
~ Senator Thomas F. Eagleton

Following the swearing-in ceremony, well-wishers gathered at the Mansion to enjoy the warm hospitality of the Governor and First Lady. One of the rosy-cheeked guests was Secretary of State Jim Kirkpatrick who labeled the day "almost as cold as Jim Blair's inauguration in 1956." Other remarks were more personal. "My feet damn near fell off," Senator Thomas F. Eagleton announced as he unbundled at the Mansion reception. "Then, realizing that he might have sounded critical of the Governor's decision to hold the ceremony outdoors, he quickly added, "It was a bold decision of the Governor and I like boldness in politics."

Among political pundits and Capitol watchers who still debate which Missouri inaugural was the coldest, Teasdale's certainly ranks near the top—and is probably the winner.

gave Democrats little cause for optimism. When forced to pick a standard-bearer, most Democratic clubs endorsed Teasdale's primary opponent William Cason. "I can't think of a regular Democratic organization that supported me," Teasdale said with some pride at having won without them.

Even when he captured the nomination, there was little financial support for his candidacy. With the big banks and other high-dollar contributors convinced of a Bond victory, Joe was forced to form a new coalition. Relying on a network of old family friends and Kansas City lawyers to buttress his campaign, he fashioned one of

A bittersweet moment as incumbent Governor Kit Bond, defeated for reelection, sits on the inaugural platform with the victorious Joe Teasdale.

the major political upsets of the era. In addition, he made history by becoming Missouri's first Irish-Catholic governor and the first Kansas Citian to hold the office.

His inauguration also proved historic. With nine inches of snow on the ground, temperatures hovered at the subzero mark, producing a chill factor of 25 to 40 degrees below zero. The traditional parade along High Street in the Capital City had already been canceled and advisors encouraged the incoming Governor to move the swearing-in ceremony to the Capitol rotunda. But because so few spectators could be accommodated indoors, Teasdale decided at the last minute to keep the event outside.

The day was further marked with the special preferences of the incoming governor. Early on inaugural morning, he attended mass at St. Peter's Church before joining state workers for coffee in the basement of the Capitol. Just before noon, the Governor-elect broke with tradition by riding in a car to the Capitol with his wife rather than the outgoing Governor.

Hatless, wind blown, and without gloves, Teasdale stood on the inaugural platform

First Lady Theresa Teasdale takes time out for a ride on her horse, Holly.

as the bells of St. Peter's church tolled the noon hour, marking the start of his swearing-in ceremony.

In his six-minute speech, he promised a more open government. However, he warned his audience of two thousand shivering Democrats not to expect him to be a traditional governor. Most of his listeners were unsure of what that meant, but they were, nonetheless, happy to have one of their own back in leadership again.

A week later, Teasdale and several hundred Missourians headed for the nation's capital for another inauguration. A Georgia peanut farmer and Washington outsider, Jimmy Carter, had captured the presidency from incumbent Republican Gerald Ford. Shortly after returning from the celebration, Teasdale gave another hint that he stepped to a different drummer when he ignored a meeting of the National Governors' Association. The traditional gathering usually topped the agenda for a new governor, but Teasdale passed up his first chance to attend the conference in favor of presiding over the opening of trout season in Missouri.

His first address to the General Assembly drew more comment. The eighty-seven-minute speech—the longest in recent memory—set forth a sixty-point legislative package ranging from higher corporate taxes to the drafting of a new state con-stitution. Theresa looked on from the upper gallery, preferring that location to the traditional seating for the First Lady next to the podium.

"Walkin' Joe" picked up the title "Joggin' Joe" because of his exercise routine.

❦

Even as Joe, Theresa, and their two-year-old son, Billy, moved from their small apartment in Kansas City to their stately new home, there were his-toric overtones. No child so young had lived in the house since the Starks occupied the residence forty years earlier.

During Teasdale's tenure, more offspring would fill the old Victorian home with the adoption of John Patrick in 1978 and the birth of Kevin in 1979. Two Shelties—Heidi and Duffy—also added to the merriment in

Teasdale told Democrats not to expect him to be a traditional governor.

Teasdale, an avid fisherman, is joined by longtime Secretary of State James P. Kirkpatrick for the opening of trout season.

the old house. Theresa had trained the pets for show and won a few trophies with Heidi. The First Lady also had a horse, but unlike earlier first families, she did not have the luxury of keeping the mare on the Mansion grounds; the convenient stable had long since been torn down with the passing of horse-drawn carriages. Holly, her horse, stayed at a nearby farm, close enough for the First Lady to take time out for an occasional ride.

While Theresa looked to stable her horse, Joe searched Jefferson City for a handball court. A physical fitness buff, the new Governor let the media know he did not expect his work schedule to keep him from sports, especially handball. When pressed for time, however, he resorted to jogging either at a nearby school track or around the Mansion's circular driveway, just as Bond had done. By rough calculation, he told reporters, twelve times around the Mansion equaled a mile.

Although the Governor showed impressive legwork on the track and playing courts, he got off on the wrong foot with the Jefferson City press corps. After winning the election, he had gone on the attack, charging Capital correspondents with being "more jaded" than any other group of reporters he had ever known. He later toned down the remark by suggesting they had "become jaded through covering too many

Everything Teasdale did evoked comment.

politicians." Nonetheless, during his first news conference, reporters showed up wearing badges that read "I'm a jaded Jefferson City reporter."

After that, the media watched his every move and reported on incidents that would have gone unnoticed in former administrations. One newscaster, after hearing Teasdale deliver a speech in Springfield urging the fifty-five-mile-an-hour speed limit, followed the Governor out of town, later reporting that the patrol-driven vehicle reached speeds of sixty-five miles an hour.

It was not unusual to see the Governor at his desk in his shirt sleeves with his stockinged feet resting upon the desk.

According to political correspondent Fred Lindecke, "Everything [Teasdale did] evoked comment: losing his voice and holding his first press conference by writing on a pad; conducting his inauguration outdoors in the frigid weather; delivering a one-

and-one-half-hour legislative message, the longest legislators could remember; and, appointing people to offices that politicians had never heard of previously." Speaker of the House Kenneth Rothman said that Teasdale endured more scrutiny than any previous governor in his memory.

One UPI correspondent called the Teasdale's press relationship the worst he had seen in twenty years of covering Missouri governors. Even so, the Governor enjoyed spirited exchanges with the media. When reporters complained that he changed his mind on major issues, Teasdale—who seldom took himself too seriously—offhandedly replied, "You'll just have to learn what I mean by taking a majority of my remarks."

Billy Teasdale gets a hug from President Jimmy Carter during a visit to Columbia.

Newsmen analyzing his early months in office complained that the Governor was not around the Capitol enough. He slipped away from his office to attend mass each day at nearby St. Peter's Church, they observed, and after church he walked to the Mansion to join his family for lunch. According to some, Teasdale devoted too much of the work week to physical fitness and fishing, and then left town, along with his family, to spend the weekend in their Kansas City apartment. Teasdale countered their charges saying he needed to get away from what he called the "pressure cooker" atmosphere, reminding reporters that he was not a typical politician and that most of his important decisions were made while jogging or fishing, not from behind a desk.

Although Teasdale had emphasized in his inaugural speech that he would not be a traditional

He was "totally unimpressed with his high office and the trappings that come with it."

chief executive, his nonconformity kept drawing criticism. He seems "to be totally unimpressed with his high office and the trappings that come with it," one reporter observed. His casual style troubled those who were accustomed to more decorum in the chief executive. It was not unusual to see the Governor at his desk in his shirt sleeves, his tie loosened at the neck, his vest unbuttoned. "When he's really comfortable . . . he removes his shoes and lounges his stockinged feet on a desk," a staffer noted.

Despite his unorthodox management style, one newsman pointed out that you "can't resist a certain fondness for a governor who not only has rejected the official limousine ('It would make me feel silly'), but who doesn't even own an automobile. Or a governor whose wife continues to rattle around in her ten-year-old car."

The Governor acknowledged the criticisms by reducing his jogging schedule from thirty to eighteen miles a week. He started putting in a sixty-hour week and kept a log to prove it. He also abandoned his weekend apartment in Kansas City. On a salary of $37,500 a year, the Governor said that giving up the $330-a-month apartment was a "financial decision, not a political one," but he admitted that stories about the amount of time he spent away from the Capitol "got my attention." Democrats also began to murmur. Party loyalists wanting more patronage jobs complained that he did not work fast enough to clear out the leftover Republican appointees.

As if it were not enough to be taunted by newsmen and nagged by Democrats, there were more concerns for the Governor at home. Living in the Mansion was unpleasant. When the family moved in, there was no furniture in the second-floor living quarters. It was a situation other first families had faced coming to the Mansion after previous residents had moved their belongings from the house. Teasdale was unclear as to whom should pay to make the place liveable—himself or the state.

For nearly three months, Joe and Theresa lived out of a suitcase and slept in twin beds in a drafty, third-floor guest room. The six-foot-two-inch Governor found that his feet dangled over the wooden foot board and let it be known that he preferred king-sized accommodations. Republicans made sport of the request before approving a $26,000 appropriation for the furnishings, paint, wallpaper, carpet, and drapes needed for the Mansion's second floor. With the new funds, the First Lady purchased several rooms of furniture with an eye toward function and the style of the house. However, when it came time to add an air-conditioning and heating system to the Mansion, the Governor balked at the $335,000 price tag and refused to make the improvements.

With small children about the home, the need was more apparent for a modern security system designed to guard both the historic building and the First Family.

"It's been the hardest year of my life."

Professional, around-the-clock protection by the Highway Patrol and Capitol security officers became a regular part of life at the Mansion. The addition of a closed-circuit television system allowed security personnel to watch the gates and grounds. Highway Patrol officers took the Teasdales' son to and from nursery school, joined the Governor on fishing trips, and followed him while he jogged.

In the interest of safety, the Governor reduced the use of prison labor at the Mansion. Teasdale feared that he or his family might be endangered because of his former role as Jackson County prosecutor. When help was needed at the Mansion, Lincoln University students waited tables, although one prison trustee was employed to take care of the laundry, sewing, and repair work.

Teasdale's "Meet with the Governor" sessions put him in touch with voters in town hall meetings across the state.

There was, however, no protecting the new Governor from political problems. As one reporter expressed it, there was not just one dragon to slay, but a whole host of such nasties, all of whom were intertwined with each other and generally untouchable because they had the force of law behind them. A case in point was the Public Service Commission, which monitored utility rates in the state. Teasdale had promised to replace four of the five PSC commissioners with those more responsive to consumers, but

he soon found that such a move was—as he put it—"a tough route to go." The Senate twice refused to confirm his appointment of consumer-advocate Alberta Slavin to the commission before narrowly granting the approval.

There were more troubles in the executive branch. His first chief of staff left after four months. When the Department of Revenue did not measure up to his expectations, Teasdale fired the director, making numerous enemies in the process. At the end of the Governor's first twenty-two months in office, only three of the nine department-level directors he had appointed remained.

Teasdale also got into a squabble with Lieutenant Governor William C. Phelps—the Republican's only statewide officeholder. The lieutenant governor, who traditionally had little to do but preside over the Senate and keep tabs

A pin featuring a well-worn shoe became a popular 1980 campaign item after this photo of Teasdale (left) appeared in the newspaper.

345

on the Governor's health, declared himself the "watchdog of state government." With Teasdale and Phelps of opposite parties, newsmen were quick to note conflict between "Missouri's political odd couple."

Fearing that Phelps might assume the Governor's powers, Teasdale refused to leave the state for over a year. He worried that in his absence Phelps—as acting governor—might replace Alberta Slavin on the Public Service Commission or cause him some other embarrassment. When in the summer of 1980, Teasdale made a trip to Washington to seek federal aid to combat a heat wave, he took the lieutenant governor with him.

The Governor showed a "genuine concern for the poor and disadvantaged."

Leery from his many encounters with politicians and newsmen, Teasdale created a so-called "Kitchen Cabinet" of friends from Kansas City and St. Louis to give him an outside perspective. Even then, battling with bureaucrats and sparring with the media took its toll on the nonconforming Governor. By the end of his first year, Teasdale had "suffered so many bloody noses" that he began to realize the difficulty in moving an entrenched bureaucracy, even with the best of intentions. At the end of his first legislative session, he had to settle for only a 40 percent acceptance of his agenda. Reflecting on the year, Teasdale acknowledged, "It's been the hardest year of my life. But I've survived. . . . It didn't get me down."

Survival, however, was not enough. Determined to give Missourians the old Joe Teasdale who had walked the state and felt their frustrations, the Governor told the 1978 General Assembly, "I'm going to be a lobbyist. And I am going to lobby for the people, for their common interest." To further emphasize the point, Teasdale officially filed as a lobbyist and established a toll-free "Action Telephone Line" to keep himself informed.

He further attempted to boost his image with his "Meet with the Governor" sessions—a political road show that put Teasdale and his cabinet face-to-face with voters in town hall meetings across the state. The Governor occasionally showed up at the forums wearing a shoe with a noticeable hole in the bottom. (During his next political campaign, a small lapel pin featuring a worn shoe sole would be distributed to the Governor's supporters.) From 250 to over 700 people attended each of the forums. Although Teasdale often answered questions in his "rambling, repetitive style" punctuated with a nervous cough, he displayed a sincerity that impressed his listeners. As one reporter commented, Teasdale conveyed to his audiences what many felt was a "genuine concern for the poor and disadvantaged."

Critics, however, fussed that the town hall meetings were nothing more than "state subsidized campaign gimmicks." Sensitive to anything that might appear to be a conflict of interest, Teasdale refused to accept even the smallest of personal gifts offered during his visits about the state; he even made his personal income tax public—the first Governor ever to do so.

While Teasdale enjoyed occasions that brought him face-to-face with "real people," he had a low tolerance for what he

Theresa Teasdale (left) meets Pope John Paul II during his 1979 visit to the United States.

considered uppity political types or fancy social events. He ignored the arrival of Britain's Prince Charles to St. Louis and attended a dinner for the royal guest only after some last-minute urging. And when Henry Ford invited members of the National Governors' Association to his estate, Teasdale skipped the swanky dinner and ate a cheeseburger at a drive-in restaurant with the head of the Highway Patrol. Theresa, however, took the opportunity for an audience with Pope John Paul II when the papal leader visited the United States.

While the Governor's nontraditional approach often raised eyebrows, it was that very quality that contributed most to his accomplishments. During his first year in office Teasdale took command of an issue that had baffled two previous governors and legislators for twelve years—the location of a new medium security prison. When the Missouri House and Senate could not agree on a site, the Governor spearheaded a drive to put the five-hundred-inmate facility near Pacific, Missouri.

The Teasdale family–Billy, Joe, John, Theresa, and Kevin.

Many felt the Governor's leadership in handling the prison site selection marked his finest hour, but he also received high marks for the quality of his appointments to boards and commissions and for naming more African-Americans to positions than his predecessors. At a time when the nation's energy supply was threatened and prices soared, he initiated the state's first comprehensive energy conservation program. Government growth and spending were curbed by his pruning of outdated programs and unnecessary jobs—a procedure that forced departments to give a detailed justification of their fiscal requests.

He further tightened the reins of state government with his zero-base budgeting. The Governor put insurance companies and nursing homes under stricter regulation and created a new agency on aging. During his term, mental health services fared well and education received the biggest increase in funding up until then. He also found the funds to replace the aging state aircraft with a new Beechcraft King Air. But he sternly refused to approve an appropriation to build the Truman office building forcing the legislature to hand out its first veto override of a governor in recent memory.

In an attempt to bring stricter ethics to government, Teasdale called for department heads to keep a log of all contacts with lobbyists—though few did. Corporate lobbyists, in turn, deflected the Governor's attempt to raise taxes on big businesses. Lawmakers rejected the Equal Rights Amendment and some of his

The Teasdales (seated on right) entertain orphans at a Christmas marionette show at the Mansion.

proposed insurance regulations. But labor unions won a victory when voters turned down a controversial right-to-work law.

The Governor kept his promise not to raise taxes; in fact, Missourians received a $53 million tax cut. This was not enough, however, to satisfy the Republican businessman Mel Hancock, an outspoken critic of state government. Largely because of his efforts, Missourians followed other states wanting to put tax and fee increases to a vote of the people. While the Hancock amendment temporarily relieved the fear of overspending by so-called big government, it would later haunt legislators and governors attempting to address the problems of cities, schools, and prisons.

In addition to his legislative woes, Teasdale had to cope with a teachers' strike and a walkout of firemen during his term. Several natural disasters also claimed his attention—the 1977 flooding in Kansas City and the 1980 tornadoes that damaged Sedalia.

In the summer of 1979, Joe and his family moved back to Kansas City in anticipation of Theresa giving birth to their third child. During their two-month absence from the Mansion, work was done on the backstairs, driveway, fence, and fire detection system. Again the Governor drew criticism from the press. Reporters chastised him because of the cost to the state for the family's temporary housing and for receiving "meals on wheels" when it was learned that on two occasions food was shuttled from the Mansion kitchen to Kansas City.

It was children, not restoration, that claimed most of her attention.

After moving back into the refurbished Mansion, the Teasdales created yet more controversy by announcing that the old structure was still unlivable. He suggested that a new home be constructed for the chief executive. The Mansion "should be a museum," he declared, "and the Governor should have a modest home."

While Mrs. Teasdale enjoyed the improvements in the old house, it was children, not restoration, that claimed most of her attention. At Christmas, she included disabled youngsters in musical performances and invited adults from the local sheltered workshop to make ornaments for the Mansion Christmas tree. Her role as honorary chair for the Year of the Child further focused her concerns on children and families. Although the First Lady shunned the spotlight and refused interviews, she was always gracious to Mansion guests, even the newsmen who assailed her husband.

Despite the hardships endured by the family during his term, Joe determined to seek another four years in office. The Governor breezed by his primary opponent, State

Treasurer James I. Spainhower, and prepared for another match with his old foe, Christopher Bond. This time Bond snatched the initiative with a campaign that flaunted his ability as a manager and his support of tax exemptions for the elderly. Teasdale was left to defend his own record.

During the summer of 1980—at the height of the campaign—Teasdale was hit with two stunning blows: the loss of a child with Theresa's miscarriage and the loss of support from his hometown newspaper. With vanishing support in the media and the legislature and a more aggressive opponent hounding his path, Teasdale faced a predictable defeat. In the hard-fought election rematch, Missourians again turned the tables on an incumbent governor. In the wake of a presidential landslide led by Ronald Reagan, Missourians set Teasdale out of office and returned Bond to the governorship by a 53 to 47 percent margin.

Defeat came hard for Joe Teasdale who had spent his political life crusading for good government; Jefferson City did not see much of him during the waning months of his administration. A Florida vacation kept him from attending the opening legislative session and he chose not to ride in the inaugural parade.

Returning to Kansas City with his wife and three sons, Teasdale resumed practicing law. He had not won the second term he desired and, like governors before him, he had not implemented all he had envisioned. Yet, "Walkin' Joe" had given Missourians reason for hope. He had listened to their concerns, fought their battles, and dared the impossible time and time again. For that, he would always be a winner.

In 1996 the Teasdales, accompanied by their three sons, returned to the Mansion for the presentation of Theresa's portrait. John Teasdale, the youngster who once played ball in the halls of the Mansion, is scheduled to play football for Notre Dame in the fall of 1998.

349

REACHING FOR THE STARS

GOVERNOR JOHN DAVID ASHCROFT
JANET ROEDE ASHCROFT
1985-1993

"No matter how many times . . . [John] was knocked down, he would get up and keep going."
~ Ashcroft's high school coach, Sheppard Woolford

Janet and John Ashcroft seemed as much a model couple of the eighties as television characters June and Ward Cleaver were of the fifties. His clean-cut, all-American image matched the style of the bustling southwest Missouri town of Springfield where he had grown up and chosen to settle. The handsome couple shared a number of interests and accomplishments: both had graduated from the University of Chicago Law School before joining the faculty of Southwest Missouri State University. They further supplemented their incomes by practicing law together and coauthoring law textbooks.

Though John was a popular professor whose classes were always filled, he missed the thrill of competition. Since his years as a star quarterback and student body president at Hillcrest High School, he had shown a strong competitive drive. His football coach recalled that "John was really aggressive. No matter how many times he was knocked down, he would get up and keep going." Ashcroft continued his sports interest, playing freshman football at Yale until a knee injury forced him to give up the sport. Completing a degree in history in 1964, he enrolled in law school and before long was back on the playing field, this time on a rugby team.

With his graduation and marriage in 1967, John put aside athletics in favor of making a living as a lawyer and teacher. However, at the age of thirty, he abandoned the safe haven of the college campus for the uncertainty of politics. In 1972 he made his first campaign for public office, running for Congress in the largely Republican seventh district of southwest Missouri. At first it seemed that John might have a home court advantage: he was from a well-respected family in the area and his father, an Assembly of God minister, had served as president of Central Bible College and Evangel College.

Ashcroft was a star player of his high school basketball, football, and track teams.

351

But as it turned out, he lost the nomination by a ratio of 50 to 45 percent to Gene Taylor, an old-line Republican. On the heels of defeat, Ashcroft was prepared to return to the classroom, that is, until he caught the eye of the newly elected Governor, Christopher "Kit" Bond—another young Republican politician. Bond, who had just vacated his position as state auditor, tapped Ashcroft to fill the unexpired term.

Ashcroft found that persistence paid off in politics as it had in sports.

In spite of his early boost into statewide office, two years later Ashcroft's political career was destined for another downhill slide. In 1974, when it was time for him to seek the auditor's office on his own, he lost his election bid to Democrat George Lehr, a certified public accountant who convinced voters that they needed his financial expertise.

Undaunted by the defeat, John recalled the lesson he had learned years earlier on the football field in his hometown: it is not the number of times you get knocked down, it is the number of times you get back up that makes the difference. Convinced that persistence pays off in politics as well as sports, Ashcroft reasoned that he had simply run for the wrong job. Voters wanted a certified public accountant rather than a lawyer to serve as auditor; there would be other opportunities to run for office where he better matched the position. During his time on the sidelines, John worked in the state attorney general's office while Janet found employment with the Department of Revenue.

On the campaign trail with John Ashcroft.

By 1976, Ashcroft was back in the Republican lineup again. This time he ran for attorney general, scoring more votes for that office than had any previous GOP candidate. Persistence had paid off, earning him a niche in state government and a forum for his ideas on law enforcement.

He toyed with the idea of running for the U.S. Senate in 1980 against the Democratic incumbent, Thomas F. Eagleton, but ultimately chose to run again for attorney general. Party leaders, as well as many GOP attorneys general nationwide, urged President-elect Ronald Reagan to cast the young Republican as the U.S. attorney general, but the effort failed. Still, Ashcroft received a measure of national attention. His tough stance on crime during his eight years as the state's leading lawyer kept him in the political forefront and made him the Republican heir apparent in the 1984 gubernatorial race.

n the campaign trail, John charmed audiences with his shirt-sleeve style oratory and boyish looks. Although he was well-versed in debate from his high school days, Ashcroft declared that most of what he knew about public speaking came from "sitting on a church bench four to five times a week" as a youngster. As much a performer as a politician, he was equally at home at a Republican gathering or a revival meeting. His gospel songs and piano melodies, many of them original compositions, delighted voters across the state.

The 1985 inaugural parade.

John also mastered the art of reducing his ideas to the
John was as much a performer as a politician.
ten-second sound bite preferred by prime time newscasters, an essential skill in a day when candidates reach voters primarily by television. He understood that voters wanted change—leaner government, budget cuts, tougher law enforcement—and articulated those concerns well.

Ashcroft shared the 1984 Republican ticket with another politician who excelled at communicating, President Ronald Reagan. Four years earlier, the nation had elected Reagan to correct what they perceived to be the excesses of government. Teamed with a popular president seeking a second term, Ashcroft held a distinct advantage over his Democratic opponent, Lieutenant Governor Kenneth J. Rothman. On election night, a strong conservative tide swept Republicans into office nationally with Ashcroft winning 108 of 114 counties in Missouri and capturing 57 percent of the

The new Governor teams up with jazz trumpeter Al Hirt and Cardinal baseball star Stan Musial at an inauguration party.

vote statewide. Coming into office on the heels of Governor Bond, his victory marked the "first back-to-back Republican administrations in Missouri since 1928."

On inaugural morning, the Ashcroft family led a sixteen-band parade from behind the wheel of their 1968

The Ashcroft
family: Janet,
Andy, Marty,
Jay, and John.

Mustang convertible. That afternoon the piano-playing Governor entertained friends at an inauguration party, teaming up with jazz trumpeter Al Hirt and former Cardinal baseball star Stan Musial on the harmonica. Later, at the inaugural ball, Ashcroft departed from the tradition of the governor and his wife having the first dance to the tune of the "Missouri Waltz." Since dancing conflicted with their religious faith, John and Janet opted to join Hirt in a piano-trumpet rendition of the state song.

There were other adjustments to be made. Moving into the Mansion meant leaving the family's two-story brick house in a Jefferson City subdivision for a spacious old Mansion that doubled as a home and public area. Janet was awestruck by the grandly restored rooms. "Sometimes I walk through this house and look up at these beautiful walls and ceilings and I still can't believe I really live here," she told reporters.

With most of the major restoration complete, the Mansion was free from many of the defects faced by former residents. The third floor—seldom used since the Hearnes era—was opened to the Ashcroft children, daughter Marty, 15, and sons Jay, 11, and Andy, 7. The ballroom once again became a playroom and the Victorian bedrooms gave way to a more practical decor. A blue pup tent frequently popped up on the Mansion lawn and a basketball goal joined the historical markers in the backyard. Also new to the house was the meeting of Janet's prayer and Bible study group—an interdenominational gathering of ladies that she hosted each week.

While Mrs. Ashcroft revamped the house to suit the family's lifestyle, the Governor was busy putting his stamp on the Capitol. During his first year in office, he made the most of a friendly legislature. Ashcroft pushed for what he called an "environment of opportunity . . . where every citizen could achieve his or her fullest God-given potential." His 1985 Excellence in Education Act outlined an ambitious agenda for carrying out his goal. The program included financial incentives to teachers and schools based on improved performance.

Mandatory seat belts and an auto insurance requirement for drivers and automobile owners also won approval from legislators. Laws to implement the state lottery and to require campaign finance disclosure passed, as did a bill making the honeybee the state insect. There was only minimal outcry when Ashcroft vetoed the $50 million appropriation for higher education, social services, and mental health in the name of keeping the budget in line. The state's economy got a boost when the

Governor went abroad in search of new business opportunities. Ashcroft made a trip to Japan and two trips to South Korea where he established an international trade office in Seoul.

Following his first legislative session, voters gave their affable chief executive a hearty 75 percent approval rating in opinion polls. (Though the next year his approval rating dropped to 59 percent, it still surpassed the 50 percent mark of former Governor Bond at midterm and Teasdale's 31 percent at the same point.)

The main criticism of Ashcroft came over his appointments to state boards, commissions, and agencies. Critics charged that about one-half of those he named had, in some way, contributed to Ashcroft's campaign. Despite these complaints, Republicans and Democrats alike credited the Governor for his good intentions and fine humor.

John found time for play, as well as for politics. An excellent water-skier and boat enthusiast, he called himself "the Will Rogers of boating." He often remarked, "I never met a boat I didn't like." However, one incident at the Lake of the Ozarks put him on crutches for a while. Ashcroft, always a bit of a daredevil, suffered a muscle tear after attempting to water-ski on a canoe paddle—a trick he had performed successfully before.

Each winter, the whole family headed West for more traditional skiing on snow-covered slopes. One such outing ended with the First Lady on crutches as a result of a broken leg. In addition to the ski vacations, Janet enjoyed trips back to

Wearing a cap with two visors, the Governor gave the St. Louis Cardinals and Kansas City Royals equal billing during the 1985 World Series.

355

their south Missouri farm "because it's one of the few times I can wear jeans anymore," she told a reporter. John, too, found the farm a pleasant retreat, calling it an "emotional backstop."

The 1985 World Series between Missouri's two major league baseball teams gave the Governor more opportunity to enjoy the friendly rivalry of sports. Ashcroft boarded a train labeled the "Governor's World Series Special" for a nine-hour trip across the state to commemorate the games. Wearing a cap with two visors, he gave the St. Louis Cardinals and Kansas City Royals equal billing. Seeing the First Couple delighted the thousands of sports fans who came out to meet the train on its whistle-stop tour.

M rs. Ashcroft, however, found that wearing two or more hats as First Lady could be frustrating. She preferred her role as parent-author to the political limelight and did all she could to maintain a normal atmosphere for the children. She wanted to be a supporter rather than a political adviser to her husband. "I don't plan to get involved running the state," she said firmly.

Mrs. Ashcroft stayed out of the news, for the most part, except for a minor tiff with the state librarian over the First Lady's request to have the library opened for

In her work on behalf of Alzheimer victims, Janet Ashcroft helped organize local support groups for families.

one of the Ashcrofts' children on a holiday weekend. Yet Janet's commitment to keep out of state affairs did not necessarily prevent her from expressing an opinion when she felt strongly on an issue. Years earlier, when her husband was attorney general, she had spoken in opposition to the controversial Equal Rights Amendment, saying "rather minor" problems of sex discrimination did not justify altering the constitution.

Like others in her position, Janet soon learned that the involvement of the Governor's wife in a situation could intimidate, or even infuriate, those affected. One such incident occurred when Janet altered the tour hours at the Mansion. In an attempt to make the residence more of a home for her family and less of a public museum, she dropped one day from the weekly tour schedule. The reduced access to the old house rankled legislators and townspeople who had come to expect the First Family to be more accommodating.

Janet found her work in behalf of Alzheimer victims less controversial. As chairman of the state's task force in the fight against the disease that had afflicted her father, she helped organize local support groups for victims and their families. She also addressed some cronic defects in the Mansion's plumbing and wiring, reglazed the porches, and restored the "dummy" windows in the Nook.

While Mrs. Ashcroft addressed her agenda, the Governor was racking up enough accomplishments to earn himself another four-year term. In 1988, during his second bid for the office, Ashcroft faced former First Lady Betty Hearnes. With little effort, the Governor cruised safely back into office with 64 percent of the vote—the largest percentage given any chief executive since the Civil War. The National Governors' Association followed by naming him to head the organization in 1991 and by asking him to chair a task force on college quality and another on adult literacy.

But Ashcroft's political charm began to thin in the final years of his second term.

The Governor took pride in keeping Missouri's low tax burden forty-ninth among the states.

By 1991 the Governor described Missouri as being in a "time of economic strain." In a difficult move, he chopped $216 million from the state's budget, handing out a six percent cut to education and twice that much to other agencies. Schools and colleges were encouraged to make do with less, to raise standards rather than salaries.

The cuts fell heavily on human services, forcing the closing of some institutions. While educators and lawmakers talked of increasing taxes to meet these needs, Ashcroft showed little interest in such an approach. As an advocate of small government and restraint in public services, the Governor took pride in keeping Missouri's low tax burden 49th among the states.

In the face of a tax-adverse governor and a sluggish economy, lawmaker proposed their own revenue package for education, a $385 million tax measure that came to be know as Proposition B. A $200 million shortfall in receipts pushed Ashcroft to endorse the proposal, but only after a number of reform measures were added. The compromise pleased neither lawmakers, educators, labor, or voters in general and the hodge-podge measure failed by a two-to-one margin.

The Governor also drew fire from advocates of social welfare, women's rights, labor, and education. "He doesn't think [government] should interfere with the lives of people, even if that means helping them," fumed the Director of the Missouri Association for Social Welfare. A Democratic legislator described him as "diligent and dependable," but not particularly "daring or in- novative." Several Republican legislators who got crossways with the Governor complained that he did not have "a philosophy that allows for dif- ferent points of view." Labor leaders stewed when Ashcroft twice vetoed the minimum wage bill before signing it into law.

Women's groups were also critical of what they called his "anti- choice" position in the abortion debate and for the small number of women he appointed to key positions. Although the Governor appointed the first African-American woman to a cabinet-level position and the first female to the state Supreme Court, Missouri still ranked near the bottom in women holding high level state appointments.

Ashcroft failed to get relief from the state's escalating desegregation payments. The court-imposed plan, which climbed from $57 million to $400 million during his term, attempted to achieve a racial balance by busing students between school districts. Heavily financed magnet schools had been set up in St. Louis and Kansas City to attract white students while schools in adjoining counties were encouraged to increase their black enrollment. The costly and controversial plan that began in the seventies continued to defy any attempt at settlement.

The Governor and legislature faced up to another reality: the state ranked near the bottom in highway improvements. In 1987 Ashcroft had joined the drive for better roads in the form of Proposition A, calling for a four-cent tax on gasoline that was subsequently approved by voters. In 1992 the plan was further expanded when the legislature passed, and Ashcroft approved, an additional six-cent gasoline tax—one of the largest tax increases in the state's history. The objective of the so-called fifteen-year plan was to bring "four-lane highways to all Missouri cities with 5,000 or more residents, roads at least twice as safe, and 40,000 new jobs." However, a decade later a reduction in federal funds and faulty financial assumptions in the original plan put its completion in question. For those who enjoyed biking and walking, the state developed the

"My philosophy is that the role of government is to provide a safe and secure environment in which people can grow. When government gets too intrusive, that's when things get fouled up—when government tells people they don't have any need for personal responsibility."

Katy Trail—two hundred miles of pathway along an abandoned railroad bed from St. Charles County to Sedalia.

(Left)
Ashcroft meets former President of the Soviet Union Mikhail Gorbachev at Westminster College.

When Ashcroft left office, one news commentator summed up his legacy. It would not be his trail or road building, budget cuts, or the creation of 338,000 new jobs, he wrote, nor would it be his appearance on the Grand Ole Opry—though it was undoubtedly a high point in his life as a vocalist. "It [would] be the entourage of young conservative judges he appointed to the Supreme Court." By the end of his second term, the Governor had picked more justices to the high court than any governor in Missouri history—a move that guaranteed a conservative court well into the twenty-first century.

Ashcroft was too young to accept the political oblivion that often came to retiring governors. He held out hope for a cabinet post in President George Bush's second administration. But when Bill Clinton won the White House in 1992, Ashcroft was temporarily sidelined again.

On the state level, Missouri Republicans, after twelve years in power, hoped to hold on to the governorship. They placed their bets on another aspiring young Republican waiting in the wings to step up from attorney general to governor. But in a scandal that rocked the state, GOP gubernatorial nominee William Webster lost the election. He later went to federal prison for twenty-one months for conspiracy and for converting state property to his own use. Ashcroft was left to turn over the reigns of office to Democratic Governor-elect Mel Carnahan.

A s the Ashcrofts prepared to move from the Mansion, Mrs. Ashcroft told reporters that she was looking forward to the family leaving public life. But Janet's yearning for "normalcy" in their lives was yet to happen. At age fifty, her husband had no thought of political retirement.

Ashcroft spent the next two years biding his time in a St. Louis law firm. Eager to get back into the political arena, John tried to win the chairmanship of the Republican National Committee in 1993. Though he made a valiant attempt to show that his views were broad enough to make him leader of his party, he bowed out of the race after receiving less than 15 percent of the committee vote.

President George Bush and Janet Ashcroft enjoy reviewing a Fourth of July parade in Marshfield.

In the wake of defeat, John turned his attention to seeking the U.S. Senate seat left vacant by retiring Republican John Danforth. He focused on congressional reform, and civic and family virtues—themes that typically sparked a responsive chord in Missouri voters. In the off-year general election, when President Bill Clinton's popularity had ebbed, Ashcroft easily beat his Democratic opponent, Kansas City Congressman Alan Wheat, by a 60 to 36 percent ratio as Republicans made huge congressional gains nationwide.

Some thought the former Governor would find it difficult in being one of a hundred senators after having held the number one spot in his home state for so long. Others felt his lack of legislative experience might be a handicap. In fact, Ashcroft adapted quickly in the nation's capital, becoming an outspoken advocate of the conservative agenda and a strong proponent of term limits, a balanced budget amendment, and his own tax plan. He wrote parts of the welfare reform bill calling for charities, churches, and com-

In Washington, Ashcroft became an outspoken advocate of the conservative agenda.

munity organizations to serve the poor, sided against funding for the arts, and lined up with tobacco companies in opposition to a higher tax on cigarettes.

His hard-line rhetoric continues to make him a favorite with the religious right

The Singing Senators, a quartet featuring baritone John Ashcroft (third from left) and three Senate colleagues, serenade guests at a Republican fund-raiser.

THE GOVERNORSHIP: A POLITICAL GRAVEYARD?

Nearly every retiring governor in reasonably good health, a supportive family, and a fair record of accomplishment has sought a political afterlife. Some put out feelers hoping for a vice presidential nod or a cabinet post. Of those who tried for another elective office, most picked the U.S. Senate. The fact that so few ever succeeded led some to call the governorship a "political graveyard."

Only two Democrats made the leap from the governor's chair to a seat in the U.S. Senate—none in recent years. Trusten Polk resigned as chief executive in 1856 to become a senator and former Governor William Stone went to the U.S. Senate in 1904. On the other hand, Governors Williams, Phelps, Folk, Stark, and Hearnes—all Democrats—tried and failed. Brown, who had earlier served in the U.S. Senate, won a vice presidential spot on the Liberal Republican ticket while serving as governor.

Joe Folk campaigned for president the entire time he was serving as governor and later made two futile bids for the Senate. David Francis, also a Democrat, had to pass up an appointment to the U.S. Senate because President Wilson refused to release him from his post as ambassador to Russia during the Bolshevik uprising.

Unlike their Democratic colleagues, former Republican governors have been more successful in securing Senate seats. Donnell, Bond, and Ashcroft all found a place in the Senate following their governorship, but Caulfield failed in trying to make the jump.

Several early governors received federal appointments, as did Dunklin and Dockery; Hyde captured a cabinet post and Francis, an ambassadorship. However, Crittenden was so scorned for his part in laying "poor Jesse [James] in his grave" that President Cleveland postponed appointing him to a diplomatic position until the matter simmered down.

The closing decade of the twentieth century found two former Missouri governors sitting in the U.S. Senate, an indicator that today the office is a better springboard to national prominence than it once was.

---

and a foe of labor and environmentalists. One newsman noted that Ashcroft's reluctance to compromise sometimes puts him at odds with leaders in his own party. Even so, he remains a forceful competitor in the Washington political arena. He runs hard and aims high just as he did on the football fields of Springfield many years earlier.

Janet, too, found her niche in the nation's capital when she returned to teaching, this time in the Howard University business school. By the summer of 1997, the couple faced more change in their lives as John entered the lineup of potential presidential candidates for the year 2000. In his quest for the Oval Office, he became a guest on national talk shows and a familiar face in the states holding early primaries. In keeping with the custom of other presidential aspirants, he authored a book, *Lessons from a Father to his Son*, that told about the impact of his father's life and teachings.

Eager to advance the conservative agenda, the freshman senator is determined to be the ball carrier for the Republican Party in the year 2000. At age fifty-five, John Ashcroft's persistent, hard-hitting approach could well make him a rising star in the GOP in the next century.

THE MISSOURI SILVER

According to naval custom, each state with a ship bearing its name provides the vessel with a set of silver for the captain's table. Missouri had two namesakes even before the practice came into vogue. The first USS *Missouri*—a side-wheel frigate equipped with backup sails—was commissioned in 1842 and was among the earliest of steam-powered vessels. It lasted only a year, however, before being demolished by fire in the harbor at Gibraltar.

During the Civil War, a Confederate iron-clad gunboat bore the state's name. The leaky, sluggish vessel, constructed quickly to meet wartime demands, was easily overcome by Union assaults.

The Navy commissioned a more substantial ship in 1903. Nicknamed the "Mizzy," the first-class battleship carried over 650 men, and was considered the most modern and powerful on the seas. On board was the first silver donated by the state. The heavy, hand-made pieces featured the state seal and a grape design. Included in the set were twenty-two cups and a 112-pint punch bowl complete with tray and ladle purchased by the state for $2,250.

Missouri—and the world—had a chance to view the 25-piece collection during the famed St. Louis World's Fair in 1904. Returned to the ship, the set remained on board until the vessel was decommissioned in 1919. But in 1929, when a sister ship needed official dinnerware, it was retrieved from storage (with two cups missing) and temporarily placed on board the USS *West Virginia*. The set was returned to storage again two months before the outbreak of World War II.

The silver was next called into service in 1947, three years after the commissioning of

The USS *Missouri* punch bowl.

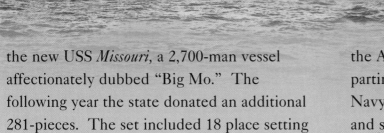

the new USS *Missouri*, a 2,700-man vessel affectionately dubbed "Big Mo." The following year the state donated an additional 281-pieces. The set included 18 place setting of dinnerware—each with 14 pieces of silver—a

Today the Missouri silver highlights small dinner parties at the Mansion.

tea and coffee service, and a pair of candelabras. Purchased with a $10,000 appropriation of the legislature, each piece bore the state seal and the words USS *Missouri*.

Before leaving for sea, the silver was displayed in the State Capitol for two days. After that, Governor Phil Donnelly and President Harry S. Truman made an official presentation of the set to the battleship that had seen action off Iwo Jima and Okinawa before serving as the location for the official signing of the World War II armistice agreement.

In 1954, after the Korean War, the USS *Missouri* was deactivated and the silver sent to Jefferson City to be stored in vaults in the Capitol basement. Later, the legislature granted a request from the Truman Library to exhibit the historic items. They remained on display from 1957 until 1982 when Governor Christopher Bond had the collection brought to the Governor's Mansion, except for one place setting left for exhibition at the library.

The dinnerware was requisitioned by the Navy during a military buildup in 1985. When

the Ashcrofts showed some reluctance in parting with the esteemed silverware, the Navy staked an undeniable claim to the set, and sent an official delegation to retrieve it.

Today the battleship is permanently moored in Hawaii and is open to the public. The silver again resides at the Governor's Mansion where its larger pieces are prominently displayed. The punch bowl is used for receptions or for large floral arrangements; the silverware often highlights small dinner parties.

FAMILIES FIRST
THE CALL TO A NEW CENTURY

*My mission as governor is to give each family in Missouri reason
to welcome the coming of the twenty-first century.*
~ Governor Mel Carnahan

Governor Melvin "Mel" Eugene Carnahan
Jean Anne Carpenter Carnahan
1993-Present

"If we are to embrace the future, we must first embrace the child." ~ Mel Carnahan

"That looks like a good one, Dad," said ten-year-old Mel Carnahan, pointing to a huge tree as they approached a curve in the road.

"You're right. Do we have any more posters left?" The back seat of their 1942 Plymouth had been full of campaign material earlier that day. Since morning they had put up dozens of the black and white posters with his father's photo and the words underneath "A. S. J. Carnahan, Democrat for Congress." The father-son team had spent the summer of 1944 covering the hillsides and main streets of south Missouri with political literature.

With the last poster under his arm and a hammer and nails in hand, Mel hopped across the ditch, under the barbed-wire fence, and headed for the "poster tree"—the type of tree he had learned to spot during their campaign swings through eighteen counties that made up the eighth congressional district.

"You've got a good eye," his father teased, flattering the youngster as he jumped back into the car. "You may grow up to be a politician yet." Mel wasn't sure. His father had lost a congressional race two years earlier and people said he would lose again. Besides that unpleasant thought, Mel could feel his sunburn beginning to smart. There would also be plenty of tick and chigger bites to remember the day. Still, he had enjoyed the visits on the town squares, the handshaking, the encouragement of supporters, and the chicken and dumplings at Mrs. uh . . . uh . . . what's-her-name's house. "I'll have to do better than that at remembering names," he thought, "if I want to keep up with Dad."

Around the table that evening Mel reviewed the day with his mother. His seventeen-year-old brother was off to war with the U.S. Navy, so there were just the three of them at home on their Carter County farm. Though his father was a rural school superintendent and his mother an

365

English teacher, a fondness for public service flowed in their bloodline. Mel's maternal grandfather, a German immigrant, was a circuit clerk; an uncle held the post of presiding judge; and, an earlier ancestor, Manasseh Cutler, served in Congress and coauthored the Northwest Ordinance. Now the call to public service welled up in his father.

Carnahan as a school boy in the Ozarks.

"At dinner each evening we talked politics and school affairs most of the time," Mel recalled. "Dad was always pushing some new idea for making schools better—a school lunch program or buses for kids living out on dirt roads who couldn't get into town. He was determined to offer a band program or a basketball team, even when it meant extra hours for him with no extra pay." Youngsters who lived in the remote Ozark hills often stayed in the Carnahan's home in order to go to school in town. Growing up in a home that placed such value on education left an imprint on young Carnahan that would direct his course in the years ahead.

Rep. A. S. J. Carnahan, Mel's father, served fourteen years in Congress.

The mild-mannered educator, A. S. J. Carnahan, defied the political pundits in 1944 and won his first public office—one that he would hold for a total of fourteen years. His election to Congress meant the family now divided its time between the nation's capital and rural Missouri. During those waning days of World War II, Congressman Carnahan won assignment to the Foreign Affairs Committee—a role that would turn the Ozark educator into an internationalist, urging a humanitarian response to the war's destruction. He visited the war-torn countries and later toured the United States, advocating the rebuilding of Europe to prevent the spread of Communism. His enthusiasm proved his downfall in the late 1950s when a backlash set in against American aid abroad. The congressman's defeat in the 1960 primary did not deter his international interests; the following year President John F. Kennedy appointed him the first U.S. ambassador to Sierra Leone, West Africa.

The earlier years that the family spent in Washington often put Mel in the company of national leaders and heightened his enthusiasm for public service. While other boys were tracking the batting averages of the Washington Senators baseball team, he was eyeing the record of another group of Senators—

the lawmakers in the nation's capital. One of the city's politicians to make an impression on him was Missouri's Republican senator, Forrest Donnell. "He always took the time to bend down to my level, look me in the eye, and talk about things of interest to a youngster," Mel recalled.

There were other inspirations, such as the time in 1948 when Mel was allowed to stand onstage while a perky, confident President Truman gave his last speech of the "Give 'em Hell" campaign at a giant rally in St. Louis. Three years later, standing in the House chamber beside his father, Mel was deeply moved by General Douglas MacArthur's retirement speech that ended with "old soldiers never die, they just fade away." Mel was especially drawn to Adlai Stevenson, the Illinois Democrat who summoned the idealism of young people, urging them to answer the "high calling" to public service—the "noble profession."

There were other influences on the teenaged Carnahan. Mel met his wife-to-be at a church youth gathering in Washington when they were both fifteen. Though she had grown up in the nation's capital, Jean Carpenter had no under-standing of the state politics that so intrigued the young man with the Missouri drawl. By their second date, Mel let it be known—to Jean's surprise—that he intended to marry her and run for public office. "I laughed," she said, "but fate kept bringing us together. My name was Carpenter and with his being Carnahan we were always seated alphabetically, side by side, in high school and college classes."

Both he and Jean completed degrees in business administration at George Washington University and were married in the church where they had met five years earlier. With a ROTC commission, Mel did a two-year stint in the Air Force before entering the University of Missouri-Columbia to earn a law degree—the customary credentials of an aspiring politician. While working in a series of part-time jobs as a church choir director, book clerk, aviation refueler, and insurance adjuster, he still earned the law school's highest honors, Law Review and Order of the Coif.

Soon after graduation, the Carnahans—by then the parents of two youngsters—settled in Rolla where he won the office of municipal judge at age twenty-six. Two years later, the voters of Phelps County elected him to the state House. By his second term, Carnahan had moved up to majority floor leader where he shepherded the state's first civil rights legislation through the General Assembly. The young legislator was inundated with honors: twice his colleagues awarded him for outstanding public service and twice the *St. Louis Globe-Democrat* recognized him with their Meritorious Service Award.

However, in 1966 when Mel tried to step up the political ladder, his career came to an abrupt halt. His defeat for the state senate at the age of thirty-two caused an early derailment of what had seemed a fast-moving political track. During the

Carnahan, a ROTC cadet, later served as a first lieutenant in the U.S. Air Force.

As Majority Floor Leader of the Missouri House, Carnahan twice received the *St. Louis Globe-Democrat*'s Meritorious Service Award.

next fourteen years, he practiced law in Rolla, raised four children, and campaigned for other candidates. Always an active community member, he headed the local school board, sang the lead in the Kiwanis quartet, and chaired his church building committee and board of deacons.

Carnahan, however, could not stay away from state politics. He waited patiently for an opening in a crowded field of aspiring Democratic candidates. In 1980 he reemerged in what turned out to be a poor year for his party. Ronald Reagan soundly defeated the sitting Democratic president, Jimmy Carter, but Missourians split their ballots. They joined much of the nation in voting for Reagan and sent Republican Christopher Bond back to the governor's office after a four-year break. On the other hand, they made Democrat Kenneth Rothman lieutenant governor while Carnahan came back with a bang, winning election as Missouri's state treasurer by more votes than any nonincumbent before him.

Once on the job, Carnahan showed a progressive bent. He began to revamp the antiquated methods in the treasurer's office, methods long since abandoned by banks and private business. In his extensive overhaul, he bid the state's account for the first time and instituted modern cash management that more fully accounted for the time value of money.

But even a successful term as treasurer was not a ticket to the governorship in 1984. Unable to raise the money needed for a full-scale campaign, Carnahan tried to win grassroots support by walking the state—a 325-mile trip from St. Louis to Kansas City that took him thirty-four days to complete. Former Governor Joseph Teasdale made a similar trek during his first, but losing, attempt for the governorship and Carnahan followed suit. Running in a three-

Carnahan completed his 325-mile walk across Missouri in thirty-four days, meeting lots of people and getting shin splints, but losing his 1984 race for governor.

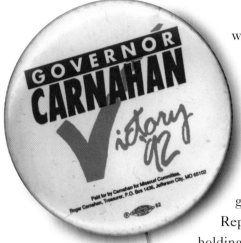

The gold-colored pin often seen on the lapel of Carnahan supporters was created after a news article during the campaign tagged him a "straight arrow."

way Democratic primary, he came in second to Lieutenant Governor Kenneth Rothman, who lost the general election to the GOP candidate, John Ashcroft. Again rejected for higher office, Carnahan returned to his Rolla law practice.

Four years later he set his sights a little lower, running for the open lieutenant governor's seat. In a year of widespread Republican victories, Ashcroft had no trouble holding on to the governorship, but Carnahan showed amazing strength, too, winning the election by almost 100,000 votes. Despite his decisive victory, partisan politics limited his role in a Republican administration. Nonetheless, as the only Democrat holding statewide office in 1988, he had a ring-side seat in the executive branch as the presiding officer of the Missouri Senate.

When he made his second run for governor in 1992 at the age of fifty-eight, Carnahan outwitted the political soothsayers and pollsters who sided with the flashier candidates. The "smart" money lined up behind the nomination of St. Louis Mayor Vincent Schomehl, making it possible for him to raise a war chest that reached $4.5 million compared to Carnahan's $2.7 million. But Carnahan carried rural Missouri and cut into his opponent's urban base, winning the nomination handily.

As the general election campaign opened, Carnahan had acquired a new luster because of his primary victory and Attorney General William Webster—long considered the inevitable winner—was beginning to stumble. During the primary campaign, serious ethical charges had been leveled at the Republican candidate. (The allegations ultimately resulted in a conviction that sent Webster to jail for twenty-one months.) The national quarrel over abortion rights also affected the race, with

The Carnahan family—along with Jean's eighty-six-year-old father—enjoying the primary night victory in 1992.

Webster taking a strong pro-life stance while Carnahan avidly supported a pro-choice position. Carnahan took an added risk by announcing that he favored a tax increase to finance improvements in education to lift Missouri from its low national ranking in support of schools.

For the first time Carnahan had the advantage of a Democratic surge at the polls; he did not have to buck the trends as he had in 1980 and 1988. Garnering 60 percent of the vote, he ran ahead of the winning Democratic presidential candidate, Bill Clinton.

As always, Jean Carnahan was in

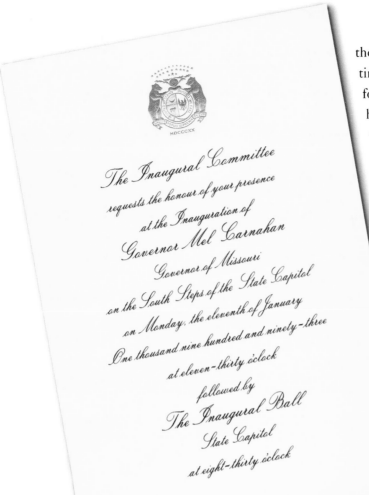

The Inaugural Committee
requests the honour of your presence
at the Inauguration of
Governor Mel Carnahan
Governor of Missouri
on the South Steps of the State Capitol
on Monday, the eleventh of January
One thousand nine hundred and ninety-three
at eleven-thirty o'clock
followed by
The Inaugural Ball
State Capitol
at eight-thirty o'clock

the middle of the campaign fight. Much of her time had been spent raising their children, caring for her father, and serving as a volunteer for a host of local activities, ranging from scout leader to Sunday school teacher to organizer of bond issue drives. She soon learned how "consuming" a statewide campaign could be. "You get up in the morning thinking about the campaign," she said, "and go to bed at night thinking about it." The come-from-behind victory was very sweet for Jean, leaving her only one regret, that her father—who lived in their home and starred in one of Mel's television commercials—died a month before the general election.

On inauguration day, snow-covered ground awaited those who arrived in the Capital City to hail the return of Democratic leadership after a twelve-year absence. As with governors of old, a horse-drawn carriage quaintly carried the new First Couple through much of the parade route until they took to the street on foot to shake hands along the way. Missing from the parade was the cadre of uniformed colonels that had gone out of vogue twenty years earlier. However, Mrs. Carnahan designed a bronze medallion suspended from a red ribbon as a keepsake for friends and supporters.

Other marks of the new administration became obvious during the swearing-in ceremony on the Capitol steps. Carnahan set the tone by selecting women and children to provide the music, pledge to the flag, and

Not since Herbert Hadley's inauguration in 1909 had a horse-drawn carriage been used to convey the Governor-elect to the Capitol for the swearing-in ceremony.

370

benediction. Following the formalities, his first official act was meeting in his office with a children's delegation from around the state.

Jean devised a Missouri Heritage Festival—an afternoon event featuring crafts, music, and entertainment for those who had hours to spend before the inaugural ball. That evening in the Capitol rotunda, the new First Couple led off the ball with the traditional "Missouri Waltz," having taken a few dance lessons in advance to insure a smooth performance.

During the next few days, Jean threw open the doors of the Mansion to thousands of visitors. "My family was from Virginia and hospitality meant no one came to our house without being invited to stay for the next meal," she recalled. It marked the beginning of her sharing her new home with tourists, children, clubs, and women's organizations as well as visiting dignitaries and legislators.

Guests to the Mansion ranged from school kids on their traditional tour of the Capital City to the vice president's wife, Tipper Gore. The First Lady, along with a cadre of costumed docents, helped tourists experience the traditional hospitality of the home. Jean would often explain that the house was designed as a "living restoration" and add with a quick smile, "That means you can sit on the furniture."

But living in an old house also meant seeing to its upkeep. Twenty years earlier the Mansion had undergone its most extensive renovation and was again needing to be refreshed. She began a series of repairs and improvements that included replacing the home's leaky roof, repainting its grillwork, and restoring its sagging ceilings. Turning her attention to the less showy area of the house, she revamped the dilapidated basement entry, staff and

As his family looks on, Carnahan takes the oath of office from Judge Don Kennedy.

The Governor's first official act was a meeting with the Children's Delegation in his new office.

Days in the Life of the Governor

A typical day for Governor Mel Carnahan began each morning at 6:15 when he put on a sweat-suit or shorts and hopped on an exercise bicycle for a forty-minute ride. The bicycle was equipped with a book rack so he could review the morning newspapers, his daily briefing book, and any speeches to be delivered that day. If the weather was right, he skipped the stationary bike and went walking or biking on the Katy Trail not far from the Capitol. After exercising, he showered, ate breakfast on the run—often just a quick banana and orange juice—and arrived at his Capitol office by 9:00 where his day began with a half-hour staff meeting.

Appointments with legislators and constituents began at 10:00 with people scheduled at fifteen minute or half-hour intervals. His lunch was cooked at the Mansion and, at noon, brought in on a tray while he continued to work, frequently using the time to

sign papers, read messages, or review problems. Office appointments resumed at about 1:30, unless his schedule took him to other areas of the state.

In the evening, there were receptions and dinners to attend, although Carnahan usually did not eat at them, preferring to dine back at the Mansion with Jean. If his timing was right—which it usually was not—he watched the news and read more newspapers. After dinner, he tackled the briefcase of work he brought home each night. During this time, he responded to mail and checked the internet for a news update. He usually finished—or gave up—by 11:00 or 12:00, taking a book or magazine to bed to help clear his mind of the day's events.

Carnahan took on additional responsibilities beyond those as the state's chief executive officer. He served as chairman of both the Southern and Democratic Governors' Associations. He also went abroad in search of new markets for Missouri-made products. Accompanied by Missouri business representatives, Carnahan led trade missions to Central and South America, southeast Europe, Korea, Israel, England, and southeast Asia to meet with business leaders and heads of state.

For relaxation, the Carnahans returned to Rolla on weekends, although the schedule seldom allowed for two full days at home. Still, Rolla was the place where they could catch up with old friends, attend their home church, go horseback riding, take long walks on country roads, or try out a new recipe (a pastime they both enjoy).

While home, Mel often drove a tractor to clean up his seventy-acre farm on which his oldest son raised cattle and horses. Carnahan also found time while governor for a quest of another sort. During his second term, he took flight instruction, earned his pilot's license, and thereby fulfilled a long-standing ambition to fly an airplane.

security offices, first-floor rest rooms, the second-floor study, and the back stairway entrance to the ballroom.

On the third floor, a fireplace mantle and mirror were installed and the area opened to musical performances and art displays. An adjacent bedroom became a Moorish-style drawing room and was named in honor of the Missouri Squires who underwrote the project. She also developed a computer inventory of all household items. The first extensive accounting of the Mansion's collection included scanned colored images and the history of each piece. The old

Victorian home took its place in cyberspace when the First Lady designed a web page of Mansion activities. For the first time, tours could be booked by computer and items purchased from the Mansion's on-line gift shop.

Weekends are a time for Mel to work on his farm and visit with neighbors.

Mrs. Carnahan sensed that the Mansion had yet a more expansive role to play in the community. In keeping with that idea, she found new ways to bring the house and its history alive, especially for children. Her creation of the Children's Hour at the Mansion brought as many as 150 youngsters to the residence each month to learn about Missouri's heritage through art, music, and dance. The annual Halloween Spooktacular sponsored by Six Flags St. Louis amusement park and the Easter Egg Hunt for children with disabilities drew throngs of visitors to the executive residence.

Carnahan earned his pilot's license during his second term as governor. Flying is a hobby also enjoyed by his son, Randy, and daughter, Robin.

Beaumont, the Carnahans' 150-pound Newfoundland, looks forward to the attention he receives from visitors to the Mansion.

On the Mansion Lawn

... the Halloween Spooktacular

... the Walt Disney Children's Arts Festival

... the Children's Hour at the Mansion

... the Easter Egg Hunt

The Carnahan family dons costumes to greet their guests at Halloween.

"I feel like my role is to manage, preserve, and share this wonderful treasure—much like a museum curator would do," Jean explained from behind the desk of her second-floor office, surrounded by computer equipment and family pictures.

One of the First Lady's most ambitious creation was the Walt Disney Children's Arts Festival, a three-day event featuring hands-on art activities and performances scattered throughout the Capitol Complex. The festival, made possible by a three-year grant secured from the Lillian B. Disney Foundation, attracted thousands of children from across the state as well as teachers, parents, and a host of volunteers.

Jean soon discovered there was more to her job as First Lady than caring for the Mansion or expanding its role. In 1993 historic floods ravaged the state, forcing the Governor to mobilize the National Guard and get federal funding to cope with the disaster. Mrs. Carnahan joined in the sandbagging and worked with the Salvation Army and the Red Cross preparing and delivering meals in an emergency response vehicle.

During one heart-wrenching moment, she remembered talking to a elderly woman made homeless by the disaster. "I'm seventy-five years old and I've lost everything," she said. "My home is gone, all my belongings are gone . . . I've even lost my cat. I can never go home again." Jean knew that the woman was probably right; she would likely be forced into some form of institutionalized care. "At that point," Mrs. Carnahan recalled, "I realized there was nothing I could say to her and we could only hug each other and cry."

Two years later saw a repeat of the high-water levels, but because Governor Carnahan had promoted a "buy-out" of those properties in the worst of the flood lands, the cost of dealing with the second disaster was far less.

From a helicopter, Jean and Mel Carnahan inspect damage inflicted by the Great Flood of '93. The Mississippi River, cresting in St. Louis at 49.58 feet, was 29.58 feet above flood stage—an all-time record.

In addition to responding to emergency problems, a governor must anticipate what is needed for the future well-being of the state. Carnahan felt that education was in deep trouble unless major support and reforms were undertaken. On the brink of a new century, Missouri schools needed to match those any place in the world; to settle for less meant economic disaster. His resolve was tested sooner than he expected. Faced with a court order only four days after his inauguration, the Governor was forced to correct the disparity

The Governor learns the art of sandbagging from several National Guardsmen fighting the 1993 floods.

between support received by urban and rural school children.

Carnahan took the occasion to call for a major overhaul in school funding. "The Outstanding Schools Act" that the Governor pushed through the first session of the legislature resulted in the most ambitious funding for public education in the state's history. With additional support for education, Missouri school children benefited from more computers, smaller classes, and better health services. The *St. Louis Post-Dispatch* heralded the Governor's success in education, as well as welfare reform and worker's compensation, "Not since the first term of Governor Warren E. Hearnes in 1965-68 have Democrats seen such a sweeping victory by a governor in the legislature."

But school reform came at a price both to the voters as well as the Governor. Opponents charged that Bill 380—"The Outstanding Schools Act"—violated a campaign pledge by Carnahan to take major tax increases to a vote of the people. Eventually, these sentiments found a spokesman in Missouri Congressman Mel Hancock. He responded by sponsoring a petition to change the state constitution with an amendment nicknamed "Hancock II" after the first tax limitation amendment he had authored in 1980.

(Upper left) Tipper Gore, wife of Vice President Albert Gore, visits the Mansion. (Center left) The Governor welcomes the Emperor and Empress of Japan to St. Louis. (Lower left) Carnahan accepts an autobiography from the Dalai Lama in St. Louis. (Above) Barbara Bush and Jean Carnahan talk with students about the importance of reading.

Mel joins workers in a Habitat for Humanity project.

Former Prime Minister Margaret Thatcher is greeted by the Carnahans, newspaper publisher Betty Weldon, and Majority Floor Leader Gracia Backer during a visit to Fulton.

Carnahan mounted a statewide campaign against the proposal. The Governor, as well as other state leaders, felt that the threatened roll back in tax increases adopted since 1980 would cause radical cuts in state services. In November 1994 a broad coalition of business, labor, agriculture, and civic groups helped to crush the measure at the polls by a better than two-to-one margin.

Despite the victory, Carnahan perceived a genuine desire for responsible tax restriction. He started work the morning after the defeat of Hancock II to craft the necessary legislation. Joining with the Missouri Farm Bureau and the Missouri State Chamber of Commerce, the Governor urged support of Amendment 4 that restricted lawmakers to raising taxes no more than $50 million a year without a vote of the people. In April 1996 Missourians gave the measure a hearty 69 percent voter approval.

The Governor faced an even more delicate political situation after his fellow Democrat, Secretary of State Judith K. Moriarity, was convicted of violating the law when she ordered the forging of an election filing document on behalf of her son. The Governor quickly called for her resignation. Her refusal forced him to call the House of Representatives into a special session for the purpose of impeachment. With Moriarity's ouster in

First Lady Hillary Clinton greets Jean Carnahan at the White House.

Jean Carnahan received the 1997 March of Dimes "Missouri Citizen of the Year" award from Anna Roosevelt (right), granddaughter of Franklin and Eleanor Roosevelt.

October 1994, Carnahan selected Democrat Rebecca "Bekki" McDowell Cook to serve as her replacement. Though Cook was unknown in political circles, the Cape Girardeau lawyer won the office in her own right at the next election.

While less controversial—and thereby less publicized—Carnahan's Commission on Management and Productivity (COMAP) may prove his most far-reaching reform. Over the years, no cliché annoyed the Governor more than the expression, "It's good enough for government work." Carnahan believed that Missourians expected excellence in government no less than they did from private business or the professions. In that spirit, Governor Carnahan in 1993 named leaders from the public and private sector to recommend improvements in operations that were gradually implemented throughout state government.

By the end of his first term, it was generally agreed that Carnahan had racked up an impressive record. Without significant primary opposition in 1996, he faced Republican candidate Margaret Kelly, the state auditor. In the election battle, Carnahan touted his progressive reforms. Since he entered office, more than 35,000 welfare recipients had been moved off the state dole and onto the payrolls. He had named more women and African-Americans to office then any previous governor. Crime had come under attack with the state doubling its prison capacity and incarcerating violent criminal on an average of ten years longer. In the flourishing economy, unemployment dropped to the lowest point in twenty years, bringing with it an influx of 300,000 new jobs.

Bill Clinton campaigning in Missouri during happier times. As President, his second term was rocked by a sex scandal involving a White House intern.

In 1997 the reenactment of the first event held at the Mansion featured old-time dances, music, and costumes.

CARNAHAN GOVERNOR 96

But Kelly poured money into television advertising, tagging the Governor "tax man Carnahan." The reference was to the legislature's passage of Carnahan's Outstanding Schools Act that carried a $315 million tax increase that opponents declared to be the largest in the state's history. (In reality a 1971 income tax hike held that dubious distinction.) Carnahan fought back the critics and on election day racked up a 57 to 40 percent victory over Kelly.

The harsh election battle was matched by equally harsh winter weather on inaugural day. Temperatures reaching into the teens caused the Carnahans to cancel the traditional parade and move the inaugural ceremony inside the Capitol rotunda. It was the first time in

DECK THE HALLS

Back: Tom, Robin, Randy, and Russ;
Front: Mel, Austin, Jean, Debra, and Andrew Carnahan.

Clockwise from top: Second-floor hall with Christmas decorations; Hanukkah candelabra from Jerusalem; the Robert Herman family of Jefferson City observe the first Hanukkah celebration at the Mansion; a guest room decorated for the holidays; and, children enjoy the reindeer on the Mansion lawn.

Clockwise from left: The library; the Mansion awaits visitors for the annual candlelight tours; camels greet the Carnahans on the lawn; a holiday buffet; and, Jean Carnahan reads to young visitors.

(Above left) A third-floor room was transformed into a Moorish-style drawing room and named in honor of the Missouri Squires. (Above right) Carnahan refurbished the governor's office that had last been decorated nearly thirty years earlier.

thirty-six years for the inaugural ceremony to be held indoors. Television monitors allowed viewing from seats placed throughout the corridors. Carnahan's speech again called for a greater commitment to education in the twenty-first century. "We must leave no child behind," he told his audience. "If we are to embrace the future, we must first embrace the child."

At the onset of his second term, Carnahan faced a legislature more divided by abortion and church-state disputes than by the usual party differences. For the first time in history, lawmakers were unable to deliver a budget to the Governor's desk in the constitutionally prescribed time. Substantive health and education bills were lost in the final days of the session. With some reluctance, legislators finally agreed on the Governor's proposal to eliminate the 3 percent sales tax on food as a way to stay within the limits of the state's revenue cap.

By contrast, during the 1998 legislative session, Carnahan saw most of his agenda put into law. Funds were appropriated for his Early Childhood Care and Education initiative designed to bring affordable, quality day-care to Missouri's children ages three to five. Another measure brought Medicaid health care coverage to 90,000 children of low- and middle-income families.

Also of profound significance was the progress made toward settling the desegregation cases and with it, the prospect of ending court control over metropolitan schools. Missourians also benefited from a tax cut, clean air legislation for St. Louis, greater funding for the arts, and targeted economic development to distressed communities. The *St. Louis Post-Dispatch* called the session "one of the most productive and progressive sessions in memory" because of the "commitment to health, education, and welfare of our children."

In 1998 the nation cheered as St. Louis Cardinal first baseman Mark McGwire set a new record when he belted his sixty-second home run of the season.

During her husband's second term, Jean continued her efforts in behalf of Missouri families. She taped public service announcements on immunization, seat belt safety, mental health, drug prevention, and breast cancer awareness. She promoted and participated in two summits on early brain development and its impact on child care and development, and testified before a House committee on behalf of Missouri's youngest citizens.

Mrs. Carnahan's focus on children unexpectedly intersected with her enthusiasm for history and writing, and led to a book about the families of the Mansion. The five-year study culminated in her authoring the book *If Walls Could Talk*—a venture that turned into the most time-consuming of her projects.

Jean continues to open the home to visitors from around the world, some 58,000 each year. When visitors suggest—as they sometimes do—that it would be more practical to sell the old home or turn it into a museum, the First Lady cringes at the thought. "The house needs to be lived in," she explains, "that's what gives meaning to the restoration and continuity to its past. It was built to be used as a residence and for public gatherings and it still serves the dual purpose today."

In 1997 the nation saw a televised tour of Missouri's historic Mansion. For three days, the producers of *America's Castles* invaded the house with cameras, lights, and wiring. The resulting film was the first documentary of the Mansion broadcast nationwide. Missouri anticipates further attention as the meeting place for the 1999 National Governors' Association when St. Louis hosts the three-day conference of state leaders. The annual event, previously held in Missouri only during the Park and the Hearnes administrations, will showcase the state to those attending from around the nation.

The Governor leads one of his Belgian horses as he talks with his grandsons, Andrew (left) and Austin.

With a little over two years remaining in his term, both Mel and Jean remain focused on education and children's issues. Their overriding concern for the well-being and future of Missouri's children stems from their own strong ties to family. Favorite moments for the Carnahans are visits and holiday reunions with the family. Their children—Randy, Russ, Robin, and Tom—live in Missouri and are all attorneys, as is their daughter-in-law, Debra. Tourists at the Mansion occasionally spot the Carnahan's two grandchildren, Austin, age nine, and Andrew, age five, making a speedy decent on the rail of the Grand Stairway or riding their bicycles about the driveway.

Fortunately, all the family enjoy politics—a condition Jean jokingly attributes to a "genetic flaw." Perhaps that is one way to explain why the topics of conversation favored when the clan gathers today are much the same as they were in Mel's childhood home years ago.

THE MISSOURI CHILDREN'S FOUNTAIN
A DREAM COME TRUE

A cast-iron fountain once adorned the Mansion lawn during the term of Governor Lon V. Stephens and his wife, Maggie. Its installation in 1900 marked the turn of the century and the hopes and optimism of a new era. The mass-produced piece was one of many cast in a popular design featuring cranes with outstretched wings beneath a basin. Another bird atop the fountain spouted water from its long, upturned beak.

Maggie Stephens, the flamboyant first lady of the day, found the Victorian fountain an ideal backdrop for her many garden parties. Old photographs, however, show that the fountain was gradually dismantled—its only remains, an ornately rimmed pool used for a flower bed.

When First Lady Jean Carnahan learned about the fountain, she decided that another one should be placed on the same site to commemorate the Mansion's 125th year. The best surviving picture of the old Stephenses' fountain was one taken about 1910 with Governor Hadley's three children playing in its waterless pool (see page 147). From that faded photo, Mrs. Carnahan conceived the idea of incorporating the sculpture of children around the base of a new fountain, which she felt would make the artwork more meaningful.

From her research, she discovered that nine-year-old Carrie Crittenden, daughter of Governor and Mrs. T. T. Crittenden (1881-1885), had died of diphtheria when the family lived at the Mansion. Her death, days before Christmas 1882, brought "desolation and great sorrow" to the house and cast a pall over the entire city. In another sad account, former First Lady Agnes Hadley made a brief reference to the "little colored boy who lives in the barn." "When I read this, I couldn't get him out of my mind," Mrs. Carnahan said. "Why was he there?

Had he run away, been orphaned, or abused?" The record only indicates that his story was one of "pathos." Mrs. Carnahan felt that these children of the Mansion had a story to tell.

With a theme for the fountain in mind, a nationwide search began for a sculptor—one with the sensitivity and talent to do a classical portrayal of children interacting with water while being sensitive to the style of the house. "I hoped for a Missouri artist," Jean recalled, "ideally, a woman, since we had the work of only one woman at the Mansion. I had nearly given up hope of finding one when Jamie Anderson, a Missouri sculptor, asked to appear before the Fine Arts Committee of Missouri Mansion Preservation. She offered a small three-dimensional wax maquette of a Victorian fountain

"I hope that each governor who lives in this house will look at the fountain and be reminded of Missouri's children."

~ Jean Carnahan

designed to complement the architecture of the Mansion. The fountain featured children who appeared to be in motion as they played against a backdrop typical of the Missouri outdoors—cattails, oak leaves, grapevines, and blue herons. The model pool also contained a free-swimming, bubbling catfish that had caught the eye of one of the children on the fountain.

"I want the viewer to feel the birds might fly away, the

Jamie Anderson,
fountain sculptor.

hair on the children move, or their clothing ruffle in the breeze," the artist explained. Movement, simplicity, discovery of youth had all been incorporated in a sensitive treatment of the forms. The committee, well-pleased with Anderson's creation, commissioned her to produce a master sculpture.

The sculptor studied bone and facial structure, visiting with doctors and dentists to learn more about the growth patterns of the full-scale children she was about to portray. She collected leaves, vines, and cattails to study, read volumes on Victorian artwork, and visited foundries in other states as she began devoting a year to creating a masterwork of art. When it came time to sculpt the last of the three children, the artist called on a live model, five-year-old Austin Carnahan, the grandson of Governor and Mrs. Carnahan. Austin, according to the artist, proved a "lively" model and undoubtedly contributed to the feeling of movement in the little boy pointing to the catfish in the water.

During a six-month process, Mrs. Anderson's sculpture was cast in bronze at the Shidony Foundry near Santa Fe, New Mexico. On Valentine's Day 1996, the 1,820-pound artwork was hoisted by crane onto its pedestal in the quatrefoil-shaped pool designed by restoration architect Ted Wofford, fitting into its surroundings as though it had been there forever. The area was enhanced by a brick plaza, benches, and a dedicatory plaque.

The Missouri Children's Fountain is more than an appealing sculpture; it is art with a message, Jean Carnahan explained. The girl atop the basin, her toes barely entering the water, is reminiscent of the shortened life of Carrie Crittenden who died at the Mansion and a vivid reminder of the health care needs of children today. The African-American boy is inspired by the youngster who once stayed in the Mansion barn. As he reaches out to grasp the flowing water, he denotes opportunity for all children. The other boy, pointing to a fish in the water below, represents today's child. Balanced against a backdrop of leaves and birds, he reminds the viewer of the need to protect the environment for future generations to enjoy. "I hope that each governor who lives in this house will look at the fountain and be reminded of Missouri's children—their health, opportunity, and environment," Mrs. Carnahan declared at the dedication of the fountain in 1996.

A Look Back
1803-1871

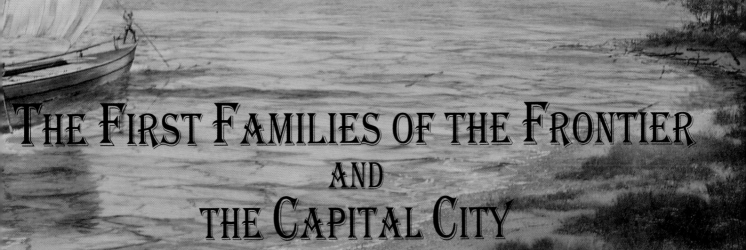

THE FIRST FAMILIES OF THE FRONTIER
AND
THE CAPITAL CITY

Each of Missouri's three Governor's Mansions sat on the majestic bluff overlooking the route once travelled by explorers Lewis and Clark.

FIRST FAMILIES OF THE FRONTIER
1803-1826

Amos Stoddard
(1804)

Missouri was once part of a much larger area known as the Louisiana Territory. The area of some 825,000 square miles was purchased by the United States from France in 1803 for $15 million. "For just three cents an acre, the President more than doubled the size of his country with the single stroke of a pen." A year after acquiring the land, Congress divided it into two parts, with a governor in New Orleans and another in St. Louis. President Thomas Jefferson named army captain **Amos Stoddard**, once a practicing attorney, to temporarily command the northern post.

The two-thousand-dollar-a-year job was hardly enough to live comfortably. One official estimated that it cost twice as much to live in St. Louis as it did in Pittsburg. To cut expenses, the bachelor Governor maintained both his home and office in rented quarters on the St. Louis riverfront at the so-called Spanish Government House. During his seven-month tenure, Stoddard attempted to muster a territorial militia, but the settlers were hard to organize and poorly armed. Reassigned to military duty, Stoddard wrote a book about the new territory he had governed and later died from wounds suffered during the War of 1812.

With Stoddard's departure, Upper Louisiana was briefly put under the jurisdiction of William Henry Harrison, the governor of the Indiana Territory. By 1805 the region had reverted to local control with the appointment of **General James Wilkinson** to command the newly designated Territory of Louisiana. To welcome his arrival, townsmen rang church bells, fired cannons, and ignited barrels of tar. In a celebration that foreshadowed later inaugurals, wine and whiskey flowed freely during a jubilant party that lasted long into the night. Accompanying the new Governor was his wife, Ann Biddle Wilkinson, a Philadelphia socialite whose struggle with tuberculosis restricted her role as a hostess.

Though in delicate health, Ann made friends easily and turned out to be better liked by the townspeople than her pompous-mannered husband. His military style of governing

James Wilkinson
Ann Biddle Wilkinson
(1805-1807)

and partiality toward wealthy French landowners irritated the frontier community and led to his transfer in less than two years. The unpopular Governor also turned out to be a traitor to his country. Known as "secret agent 13," he worked for the Spanish government even while he was serving as governor. As a chief witness at the trial of Aaron Burr, Wilkinson narrowly missed indictment for his part in the conspiracy with Burr to set up a new empire composed of western portions of the United States and land taken from Mexico.

During the unstable period that followed Wilkinson's departure, **Joseph Browne** and **Frederick Bates** temporarily became the territorial leaders until 1808 when **Meriwether Lewis** arrived in St. Louis to assume the governorship. The thirty-two-year-old bachelor had served as private secretary to Thomas Jefferson, before leading the famed Lewis and Clark expedition on its 1804-1806 exploration of the Northwest Territory. As governor, Lewis gave much of his attention to tribal and military matters. Although he had weathered the rigors of his seven-thousand-mile, twenty-eight-month expedition, he did not survive his troubled term in public office. According to historian Stephen E. Ambrose, Lewis "suffered from alcoholism, opium addiction, and probably manic depression." During his short tenure, the Governor showed signs of mental deterioration that drove him to take his own life in 1809 at the age of thirty-five.

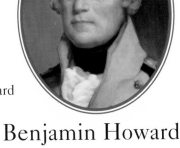

Meriwether Lewis
(1808-1809)

In spite of the changes in leadership and the harshness of frontier life, the territory grew rapidly. In 1810 as **Benjamin Howard** stepped into office, St. Louis claimed a population of 1,400. His arrival gave the community a reason to assemble for a public dinner and dance. Howard—another bachelor—had given up his job as a Kentucky congressman upon receiving President James Madison's appointment as the first governor to head the renamed Territory of Missouri. Frustrated by his assignment to such a remote area, he spent little time on the job. He went back to Kentucky, returning now and then to shore up the area's defenses against Indian raids. With the onset of the War of 1812, Governor Howard gladly gave up the job to accept a commission as general in the army.

General William Clark, the other half of the Lewis and Clark exploration team, followed him to the territorial post. Clark built a two-story brick home on Main Street in St. Louis to house his wife, five children, and vast accumulation of natural history artifacts. One wing of the house served as a display area, as well as a council chamber for official meetings. The one-hundred-foot-long room was a virtual museum filled with mementos of his trip, including piles of mastodon bones, a twelve-foot crocodile skin, and birchbark canoes that hung from the ceiling.

When he became governor, Clark continued his former

Benjamin Howard
(1810-1813)

(Left)
The Spanish
Government House
in St. Louis served
as an early executive
residence.

389

William Clark
Julia Hancock Clark
(1813-1820)

job directing territorial Indian affairs. In his dual role, he persistently worked to create friendly relations with local tribes. By 1815 Indians in the area had become more peaceable—although Clark's even-handed treatment of the tribes lessened his own popularity with the settlers.

An upward turn in the economy brought with it an increase in land prices and a brighter outlook for the pioneer community. Still, illness and death were common occurrences among frontier families and the governor proved no exception—the governor losing both his young wife and seven-year-old daughter. The tragedy was further compounded by political defeat. While Clark was out of the territory tending to family affairs, Missourians were preparing to hold their first election in anticipation of statehood. As a candidate seeking to retain his position, Clark was dependent on friends and supporters to carry on in his behalf. Such a campaign was hopeless and in the wake of his defeat, he returned to working full-time as Superintendent of Indian Affairs.

With Clark's ouster and the election of Alexander McNair, the era of territorial government ended. Optimism prevailed, but economic woes were just ahead. It took the financial Panic of 1819 a few years to reach the frontier, but its arrival brought the failure of the state's two banks, a plunge in land prices, and a decrease in immigration. The new state had some of its most troubling days yet to come.

By the time Missouri officially became a state on August 10, 1821, Alexander McNair, a successful St. Louis fur trader, had already "skinned" his political opponent in the state's first campaign for public office. The thrifty Scotsman, who vowed to reduce the salaries of the governor and judges, received 72 percent of the vote against the appointed governor, William Clark.

In addition to a penurious bent, McNair and his wife brought a degree of refinement to the office that had been missing in earlier times. He had grown up in Pennsylvania surrounded by eastern culture and manners; his wife, the daughter of a

McNair, a frugal Scotsman, vowed to reduce the governor's salary.

French nobleman, was equally well educated and polished, and could converse in both French and Spanish. Seen about St. Louis in his stylish swallow-tailed coat and tall beaver-skin hat, McNair contrasted sharply with many of the frontiersmen in their simple homespun and buckskin attire.

But neither background nor position could spare the couple the hardships of frontier life. Within a few weeks of his election, the McNairs lost two children to typhoid fever. Despite her grief, Mrs. McNair showed no inclination for self-pity. She had six remaining children to care for and another would be born before the end of her husband's term. In response to the needs of her less fortunate neighbors, the compassionate First Lady—a staunch Roman Catholic—established an interdenominational charitable society for ladies and opened her home for its meetings.

While Mrs. McNair is remembered for her benevolence, her husband left his mark as a frugal statesman who started Missouri down a conservative path that continued into the next century. As a framer of the Missouri Constitution, he had opposed setting the governor's pay at two thousand dollars a year. Later, when he was elected to office, McNair was equally harsh on the General Assembly. As governor, he refused to sign a bill giving lawmakers a four-dollars-a-day salary, with an extra dollar for presiding officers and three dollars for every twenty-five miles traveled. Using their constitutional muscle, legislators retaliated by exercising their first veto override of a Missouri governor.

There were other defeats for McNair. With the depression that followed the Panic of 1819, property values dropped, the state's two banks failed, and debtors went to prison. Farmers felt an additional curse when a plague of grasshoppers stripped their lands. Lawmakers, called into a special session by the Governor, established loan offices and authorized the issuance of a state currency—a relief measure that some thought did more harm than good.

Still, progress came in several areas during McNair's tenure: a stagecoach line was established from St. Louis to the commercial center at Franklin, the state seal was adopted, and a site was selected for the new capital and named the City of Jefferson.

But the misfortunes of the frontier continued to plague the McNair family: one child was struck by lightning, one died of yellow fever, a son was killed in battle, and another left crippled. McNair himself succumbed to the harshness of winter two years after leaving office. While serving as U.S. Agent to the Osage, he developed influenza and died shortly thereafter. Needing to support eight children—the youngest just two weeks old—Mrs. McNair placed an ad in the local newspaper offering to take in "a few gentlemen boarders." In spite of her hardships, the hearty First Lady survived to the age of seventy-six, outliving six of her children.

Alexander McNair
Marguerite de Reilhe McNair
(1820-1824)

Being governor was not new to Frederick Bates; he had already served the territory twice as its interim leader. While he brought experience to his new job, Bates offered little in the way of social skills. Friends thought him a bit eccentric—a recluse who seldom entertained at the Capitol in St. Charles. His wife was considered equally unpretentious, "retiring and quiet [with] little to say." Both preferred the solitude of "Thornhill," their thousand-acre estate overlooking the Missouri River in an area that is now the town of Chesterfield.

Bates stubbornly refused to entertain General Lafayette because of the cost.

The Governor's unsociable ways caused alarm when General Lafayette, the French military leader and American Revolutionary War hero, visited St. Louis in

Frederick Bates
Nancy Opie Ball Bates
(1824-1825)

1825. Bates stubbornly refused to entertain Lafayette in his home or elsewhere, saying the legislature had failed to appropriate money to cover the expenses.

St. Louis socialites and community leaders were appalled at the Governor's reaction, but all the more determined to make the best of the situation. Further adding to the unpleasantness of the visit, Lafayette's steamship sank on the way to St. Louis, leaving the General without most of his luggage.

Although Bates took no part in the entertainment, former Governors McNair and Clark, along with the city's mayor, properly received Lafayette. Because so many in the city were pleased to host the celebrated war hero at their own expense, the event ended up costing no more than thirty-seven dollars.

Bates's brief tenure was short on accomplishment as well as hospitality. His most memorable act as Governor was his refusal to sign a bill that called for the public flogging of anyone engaging in a duel. Although he found dueling "barbarous and . . . impious," he felt the use of a whipping post even more offensive. Credit is due him, however, for an earlier distinction. Bates compiled the first book published in the state—*The Laws of the Territory of Louisiana*, written in 1808. Less than a year into his term, Bates died of pleurisy at the age of forty-eight, leaving four children, one of whom was born six months after his death.

Abraham J. Williams
(1825-1826)

With the death of Governor Bates, the duties of office should have gone to the lieutenant governor. But Benjamin H. Reeves had resigned the post in ill health and moved to New Mexico a few months earlier. Next in the line of succession was the president pro tem of the Missouri Senate, Abraham Williams. Although the Columbia bachelor had little formal education and walked with a crutch because he was born with only one leg, he was, nonetheless, a man of many ventures. During his lifetime, he was a shoemaker, merchant, farmer, and owner of a tobacco warehouse, as well as the first state senator from Boone County.

Because the legislature did not meet during his tenure, it is unlikely Williams spent much time at the Capitol in St. Charles. However, he dutifully called the election required by law to fill the vacancy brought on by the death of Governor Bates.

Since Williams held office for only five and one-half months, he is credited with little more than appointing a Supreme Court judge. He concluded his political career in 1832 after losing the U.S. Senate nomination to Thomas Hart Benton. Overcoming his physical handicap and limited education, Williams amassed a considerable fortune during his lifetime, including over a thousand acres of land in Boone County.

THE GREAT SEAL OF THE STATE OF MISSOURI

A visitor to Missouri is unlikely to spot a grizzly bear anywhere but at a city zoo. Yet, thanks to Judge Robert Williams Wells, three grizzlies adorn the seal adopted by the legislature in 1822. Judge Wells, the designer of the emblem, felt the animals depicted the "power, courage, and hardihood" of the new state.

However, many thought the animals "looked more like toys than ferocious animals,"— some said they appeared to be monkeys. It was an observation that would later cause the original version to be referred to as the "monkey seal."

Over the years, slight modifications have altered the bears and simplified the design elements. On today's seal, the two large bears still stand on their hind legs, but are more robust in appearance and face each other rather than the viewer.

Between them is a shield divided vertically into two parts: the right hand portion, or national side, features the coat of arms of the United States. On it a bald eagle clutches a bundle of arrows in one claw and an olive branch in the other, a reminder that the power of war and peace rests with the federal government.

The state side features the grizzly bear as a symbol of strength; the crescent denotes a state that was small in population and wealth at the time, but one "which would increase like the new or crescent moon." In heraldry the crescent also stands for the "second son," meaning Missouri was the second state formed out of the Louisiana Territory.

On the belt encircling the shield is the wording, "United we stand, divided we fall," which denotes the union of states. Inscribed on a scroll at the bottom of the seal is the state motto: "Salus Populi Suprema Lex Esto." The Latin phrase taken from the writings of Cicero means "Let the welfare of the people be the supreme law." Beneath the scroll, the date 1820 is inscribed in Roman numerals to mark the year Missouri began to function as a state.

The cloud that once hovered atop the helmet— symbolic of the difficulties surrounding statehood— is no longer there. However, the stars remain: the slightly larger one in the center represents Missouri; the smaller ones, the twenty-three states that composed the Union at the time. An outer ring bears the words "The Great Seal of the State of Missouri."

While most Missourians hold the image in great esteem, humorist Mark Twain "poked fun" at the symbol of his native state. According to Twain the bears appear to be displaying the lid of a whiskey barrel from which they had drunk too freely. In his book, *Roughing It*, he describes the seal as being composed of "two dissolute bears holding up the head of a dead and gone cask between them and making the pertinent remark, United We Stand—(hic)— Divided We Fall."

Unfortunately, only a few documents remain that feature the imprint of the early seal. The original instrument was apparently lost in the fire of 1837 that destroyed the first Statehouse. The replaced seal suffered more ill treatment. When Governor Claiborne Fox Jackson hurriedly left the Capital City to take up the Confederate cause, the state seal was smuggled away in a saddle bag.

The "Monkey Seal"

The symbol of state authority was taken to Arkansas and later to Texas during the Civil War. With the end of the war, Lieutenant Governor Thomas Reynolds—who had assumed the role of Governor-in-exile upon Jackson's death—returned to Missouri, bringing the state emblem with him.

The Great Seal has remained in the Capital City since then and is housed in the office of the Secretary of State. The image is most often rendered on state documents, such as the center portion of the Missouri flag, and on the stationery of state officials.

FIRST FAMILIES OF THE CAPITAL CITY
1826-1871

John Miller
(1826-1832)

In 1831 Governor Miller opened the legislative hall of the new Capitol in Jefferson City, brought in some local fiddlers, and invited his guests to dance the cotillion and the Virginia reel. It was a special treat for the lawmakers. According to one visitor, the legislators were a "social and frolicsome set," starved for merriment in the remote river city that offered little more than a tavern and a few hotels. With only minimal accommodations in the city, the legislators housed their bachelor Governor in two rooms set aside for him on the second floor of the Statehouse that served as both Capitol and executive residence.

Miller's term was composed of a series of unique happenings. He had come into the governor's office in 1825 as the winner of the special election following the death of Governor Bates. The popular Jacksonian Democrat was the first chief executive to serve in Jefferson City and the first elected to more than one term. In his reelection bid in 1828, Miller ran for governor without opposition—a situation that has never occurred again in Missouri history.

Under the Constitution of 1820, Miller held a wide range of appointive powers. He could select the secretary of state, attorney general, supreme court and circuit judges, and all other state officers, except the lieutenant governor.

During Miller's tenure, he also enjoyed the benefits of economic prosperity. Increased revenues made it possible for him to reduce the state debt, redeem the state's paper currency, establish a state library and college, and lay the groundwork for building a penitentiary.

Legislators were a "social and frolicsome set."

Upon leaving office, Miller returned to his home in Fayette, Missouri. Lured back into politics four years later, he won a race for Congress and served three terms before retiring in St. Louis.

The bachelor governor had been quite comfortable living in two rooms above the legislative hall of the Statehouse. But the next governor, Daniel Dunklin, with six children and another on the way, needed more space for his growing family. Fortunately, the legislature concurred and, within three months of Dunklin's election, five thousand dollars was set aside for housing. Although a cholera outbreak in the city slowed construction work, by 1834 Missouri's governor had a new home—a two-story, wood and stone building that sat on the same site as the Statehouse.

Daniel Dunklin
Emily Pamelia W. Haley Dunklin
(1832-1836)

It was a strange turn of events that brought Dunklin to the Capital City. Released from the army after the War of 1812, he settled in Washington County where he served as sheriff before being admitted to the bar. Instead of practicing law, Dunklin chose to build and operate a tavern in Potosi. He might have finished out his days as a tavern keeper except for an incident that occurred in 1822. A committee that was meeting at his tavern to nominate a candidate for the legislature had balloted all day without agreement. Noting that Dunklin was a "wise man" and the owner of hundreds of the best books, the group settled on him as a suitable compromise. Six years later, the one-time tavern owner was lieutenant governor, ready to step up to the governorship.

Little is known of the First Family's personal or social life while they lived in Jefferson City. The capital newspaper noted two events: the death of the Dunklins' infant son born in 1834 and the marriage of their daughter the following year.

The local press also reported that the city's anniversary celebration of the Battle of New Orleans turned into an "explosive" affair. Five pounds of gun powder ignited in front of the Statehouse caused a blast that was heard in Fulton, thirty miles away. The General Assembly was forced to adjourn for a week until enough glass could be brought from surrounding towns to replace all of the shattered windows.

As a progressive, Dunklin ignited a few fires himself. He abolished the whipping post as punishment and approved the first prison west of the Mississippi River. The Governor also launched the state's first organized system of public education, one that established a curriculum and set the school term at six months. The groundwork he laid for tax-supported education earned him the title "Father of Missouri's School System." When the school laws passed the legislature, President Andrew Jackson wrote to Dunklin: "This is your bid for eternal fame."

Enticed by a presidential appointment, Dunklin gave up the governorship three months before the end of his term. After being named by President Jackson to be U.S. surveyor-general for Missouri and Illinois, Dunklin and his family moved back to Washington County and settled at "Maje," his estate near Pevely.

L ilburn Boggs began his adventures as a teenage boy who ran away from home to join the army. After serving in the War of 1812, he tried banking, farming, and fur trading with little success; he failed twice as a storekeeper. When his nineteen-year-old wife died, leaving him with two small children, he married Panthea Boone, granddaughter of Daniel Boone, and settled down to raise a family that grew to include ten more children. He turned to public life in 1826 with his appointment as the first clerk of Jackson County. His winning race for state senator that same year sent him to the Capital City for two terms before he was elected governor.

Lilburn W. Boggs
Panthea Grant Boone Boggs
(1836-1840)

Life was no easier for Boggs in public office than in business. During his term as governor, he faced a mountain of trouble. In 1837 the Missouri volunteers that he sent to Florida to fight in the Seminole War were faulted for their performance on the battlefield. Boggs drew more criticism when he used the state militia during the "Mormon War." Weary of repeated outbreaks of violence in and around Jackson County, Boggs issued an order calling for the religious group to be treated as enemies that "must be exterminated or driven from the state if necessary for the public peace."

As if the Governor did not have enough problems, in 1837 a fire starting in the secretary of state's office destroyed the Statehouse. For a while the fate of the nearby Governor's Mansion was in question. However, wet blankets spread on the roof and the absence of high winds saved the home from destruction.

Boggs undoubtedly had some mixed emotions about the survival of the three-year-old residence. The interior of the home was far too small for the increased social demands of the Capital City, the public room being able to accommodate only fifty to a hundred guests. In addition, Boggs was not particularly pleased with the location of the Mansion and had suggested to the legislature that it be sold and a larger site selected in a less public area.

After the fire, however, Boggs contented himself with his less-than-ideal housing and turned his attention to completing the magnificent, dome-topped Capitol already under construction on a nearby hill. The legislature had earlier appropriated $75,000 to replace the old building that was considered to be a fire hazard. By 1840 spending had spiraled to over $200,000, causing some to question the Governor's handling of the project. An investigation of the cost overrun cleared Boggs of any wrongdoing and found him "guilty of nothing more than wanting to give the state a very fine building." Before the work was completed, spending escalated to nearly four times the original estimates.

Boggs touted his building project and the strides made in education as the "fruits of his administration." To his credit, the passage of the Geyer Act in 1839 established the state's public school system and the authorization for the University of Missouri. Expansion came on other fronts as well. With congressional approval of the Platte Purchase in 1836, two million acres of land were officially added to the northwest corner of the state. Missouri endured the Panic of 1837 better than most and even reestablished two state banks while others in the nation were failing.

> "The snow was deep, the weather cold, and no one was in much of a mood for fighting."

Boggs was less successful in making the penitentiary self-supporting—a feat he tried to accomplish by leasing the institution to private contractors.

Toward the end of his term, Boggs faced more conflict. A skirmish known as the "Honey War" (1839-1840) was triggered by a border dispute between Missouri and Iowa. The narrow strip of forest land dividing the two states contained few residents, but some fine bee trees. When Iowa officials jailed a Missouri tax collector in the region, Governor Boggs sent the militia to the scene. Across the river, the governor of Iowa commanded his forces. Over one thousand troops faced each other for several weeks, although, as one observer noted, "The snow was deep, the weather cold, and no one was in much of a mood for fighting."

The standoff, immortalized in a humorous poem that "burlesqued the two governors," ended with the matter being referred to Washington. Congress established a line in 1840, but the issue was not resolved until 1851 when the U.S. Supreme Court set the boundary, dividing the disputed area almost equally. So there would be no doubt about the line, twenty-two cast-iron pillars were erected every ten miles along the border and inscribed with "Missouri" on one side and "Iowa" on the other.

An old pillar still marks the disputed Missouri-Iowa border.

Though the "war" was a minor historical incident, it was important to those living along the border. One settler noted, "I'm glad the Soopreem Court decided that I live in Ioway. I'm a farmer and I never did want a farm in Missouri. The Missouri land ain't near as good as ours."

Boggs's adversaries continued to haunt him even after he retired to his home in Independence. One evening, while sitting near his living room window reading a newspaper, he was shot in the head with seven large pieces of buckshot. Thinking the attack stemmed from Boggs's dispute with the Mormons several years earlier, Illinois authorities first jailed the religious leader, Joseph Smith. Ultimately, another suspect was arrested, but he escaped and no one was ever punished for the crime.

Boggs's brother, a physician, nursed the former Governor back to health. Undaunted by the encounter, he reentered the political arena in 1842 for a final term in the state Senate. But with the onset of the Gold Rush—his adventuresome spirit still intact—Boggs headed west and spent the remaining fourteen years of his life in California.

Thomas Reynolds
Eliza Ann Young Reynolds
(1840-1844)

Having served Illinois as attorney general, Speaker of the House, and chief justice of the supreme court, thirty-three-year-old Thomas Reynolds had already completed a successful political career. When he arrived in Fayette, Missouri, in 1829, he intended to edit the local newspaper. But three years later, he was back in politics, serving in the Missouri House. His colleagues, recognizing his ability, soon elected him to the post of Speaker.

When he later became governor, Reynolds showed his distaste for the age-old custom of imprisoning those who could not pay their debts. He considered his effort in changing this practice to be his greatest contribution. On the issue of slavery, he was less generous; an ardent states' rights advocate, he favored a life sentence for anyone who aided the escape of a slave.

During Reynolds's term, his wife Eliza transformed the Mansion, decorating their new home with mahogany furniture, coin silver, fine linen, and bric-a-brac. The elegantly furnished home was threatened by fire when a defective chimney erupted in flame. Fortunately, the quick arrival of the local bucket brigade saved the Mansion from any extensive loss.

Slander and abuse by his enemies made life unbearable.

More tragic, was the death of Governor Reynolds eight months before the end of his term. The highly sensitive Governor had recently been a target of harsh criticism for a number of his political appointments. Deeply despondent, he called for a rifle to be brought to his desk at the Mansion. Putting the weapon to his head, and using twine to discharge the trigger, the forty-eight-year-old Governor took his own life. Reynolds left a note charging that "slanders and abuse" by his enemies made life unbearable. Many at the time speculated that despondency over ill health and domestic problems had also affected his well-being.

Fate put Lieutenant Governor Meredith Miles Marmaduke in the governor's office for nine months following the suicide of incumbent Governor Reynolds, but Democrats would not give him a chance for a full term. When Marmaduke tried to gain his party's nomination, a factional dispute over monetary policy erupted at the Democratic State Convention that led to his withdrawal from the contest. Marmaduke was actually more of a merchant than a politician, anyway. He

Meredith Miles Marmaduke
Lavinia Sappington Marmaduke
(1844)

had done well in the Santa Fe trade that sent wagons of furs, salt, and other Missouri products to New Mexico in return for coffee, silver, and wool.

He had married well, too, taking as his wife the daughter of Dr. John Sappington, one of Missouri's most distinguished physicians, famed for using quinine to treat malaria. In time the Marmadukes had ten children, two of whom became high-ranking officers in the Confederate Army, despite their father's strong support for the Union. It was said that the elder Marmaduke was so highly regarded by both North and South that his property suffered little damage during the Civil War. The election of his son, General John Marmaduke, to the governorship in 1885 gave his family the distinction of having the only father and son to have both held the state's highest office.

While the governorship has never been an easy undertaking, Governor John Cummins Edwards showed utter contempt for his job by the end of his term, calling it "a despicable office for any man to be condemned to hold." He explained: "Two of my predecessors have resigned before their terms were out and a third

I have been compelled to go armed to protect myself.

committed suicide. I have been compelled to go armed to protect myself."

At the age of thirty-eight, Edwards was not without some background in the political arena. The well-educated attorney had been secretary of state, a legislator, a congressman, and, briefly, a supreme court judge.

Painting by George Caleb Bingham

John Cummins Edwards
(1844-1848)

The bachelor Governor called on his sister-in-law, who lived just blocks from the Mansion, to serve as his hostess. She brought with her a number of slaves to do the housework and cooking, and one to serve as the Governor's valet.

While Edwards was satisfied with the services provided, he was not pleased with the house. He spoke critically of the accommodations, noting the place was "destitute" of furnishings. Furthermore, he told lawmakers, the governor should not be expected to supply household necessities and entertainment expenses from his own pocket. Legislators responded with a modest appropriation to do some basic repairs, although Edwards also spent some of his own funds on improvements. He later reported that the roof had been made tight, the cellar dry, and the fireplaces abandoned in favor of stoves.

Although critical of his job and housing, Edwards won acclaim for his work as chief executive. He is remembered as Missouri's "Mexican War Governor" who sent troops to Santa Fe for the victorious encounter with Mexico. Edwards also made some advances on problems closer

Hostess: Mrs. Ivy Dixon Edwards

The Edwards
sideboard.

to home when he moved the debt-ridden state into the black and called a state convention to rewrite the constitution. In addition, he saw to the funding of schools for the deaf and blind, and the building of an "asylum for the insane" at Fulton.

In a message sounding much like those given by later governors, Edwards told lawmakers the state would prosper only if education, broader job opportunities, manufacturing, and the improvement of roads and waterways were encouraged. But economy-minded lawmakers were more interested in curbing spending—especially the Governor's—and called for an exact breakdown of his expenses. Contemptuous of the request, Edwards complied by saying that the expenses of the executive had been "various" and then gave specifics: "[The Governor's] breakfast, his dinner, or his tea, when he had time and appetite to eat it; an apple, or a sponge-cake, a piece of cheese, or a cracker, a glass of brandy or some old rye when from hard travel, much fatigue or great want of sleep, he was too unwell to take more substantial food, or else from rapid traveling had no time to stop and get it; the blacking of his boots, or the brushing of the dust out of his

The governorship is "a despicable office for any man to be condemned to hold."

coat, or hiring a servant to hasten his dinner instead of forcing him to eat through a series of courses; hack hire and omnibus fare, porterage and drayage, stage fare, railroad fare, steamboat fare on the lakes, gulfs, rivers and bays; all of these and various other items multiplied many times over, perhaps thousands, in the trips of six thousand miles, make up the items of expense to the executive—a long list hard to get and hard to give."

In spite of his lighthearted handling of criticism, the political bickering left its mark on Edwards. He told the General Assembly, "If he [the governor] stands up to his duties faithfully, the envy, and malice, and hatred, and slander, and abuse, and detraction, and calumny and vituperation heaped upon him is unbounded."

With his strenuous term behind him, Edwards joined the westward Gold Rush. At age forty-seven, he married a girl of nineteen, settled down on a California ranch, and raised eleven children. He never held public office again, except for one term—without pay—as mayor of Stockton, California. A few generations later the Governor's grandson, Ralph Edwards, also gained a degree of fame as the emcee of the radio and television show *Truth or Consequences*.

Austin Augustus King
Nancy Harris Roberts King
(1849-1853)

Austin Augustus King brought his family to Jefferson City to live in the much-maligned, poorly decorated, old Mansion that was desperate for repairs. Legislators took note and with an upswing in the economy they instructed the Kings to make needed improvements, to buy more furnishings, and to build a new outdoor kitchen.

The Mansion was not the only area that benefited from the state's surging economy. King's term also marked a period of rapid growth in Missouri, one that saw the expansion of the railroads and lead mining industries, and the development of new mail routes, roadways, and telegraph lines. A keen advocate of education, he saw to the construction of a state school for the deaf, one for the blind, and another for the mentally ill (all of which had been provided for during the Edwards administration). The First Lady shared her husband's interest in education. She had earlier built a schoolhouse on their Ray County estate to teach black children to read and write, defying the law that banned formal instruction of slaves.

In her new role as first lady, Mrs. King had the opportunity to give "splendid entertainments" at the Mansion. But life was far from idyllic for the new First Family. The community faced two outbreaks of cholera, one in 1849 and another in 1851. When a steamship docked in Jefferson City with nearly one-third of its 150 passengers ill or dying of the dread disease, churches across from the Mansion were turned into hospitals. No harm came to the King family, including their six children still living at home. However, the attorney general of the state was stricken and died during the second epidemic.

Before leaving office, King made an unsuccessful bid for Congress and two years later lost a race for the state legislature. During the Civil War, he won a congressional seat and became one of the few Democrats in Washington who supported President Lincoln. It was a costly political alliance, however, and one that led to his defeat in the proslavery congressional district he represented.

The popular Mexican War hero, Sterling Price, had no trouble winning the governorship in 1852, despite his limited campaigning due to his wife's illness. Earlier he had served as Speaker of the Missouri House and went to Congress for a term. But it was his military exploits that earned him the rank of general and enough fame to win the governorship.

After his election, the First Couple moved to Jefferson City. Later a niece joined them to help with the social duties and the care of the Prices' seven children. The young lady described the Mansion in a letter written to a relative back East. She portrayed the home as having three front rooms—an office, parlor, and sitting room—divided by folding doors that opened to make one long room for

General Sterling Price
Martha Head Price
(1853-1857)

401

entertaining. On another note, she pined, "[I would like] a good drink from the old oaken bucket that hung in the well at home. The cistern water tastes of the coal dust on the house and I can't bear to drink it."

The Governor was less concerned about the inadequacies of the old house. He busied himself with reorganizing the public school system and opening new land for settlement. After leasing the penitentiary to private contractors for the past decade, the state again took over the badly run-down facility and resumed its operation. However, Price drew the line at increasing state debt to aid the railroads—a proposal that he thought "over generous," though it passed despite his veto. The Governor was more benevolent with state officeholders. He gladly promoted an increase in their salaries while refusing to accept a raise from $2,000 to $2,500 a year for himself.

There are few records of social events during the Prices' stay at the Mansion. But one anticipated celebration in 1855 was immortalized by disaster. Much preparation had gone into planning for the arrival of the first passenger train from St. Louis over the newly completed tracks of the Pacific Railroad. Banners and bunting festooned the Capital City to mark the historic occasion.

The former Governor chose not to attack the Capital City.

Women had gathered at the Mansion to receive the six hundred guests expected that afternoon and a dinner was planned at the Capitol for the visiting dignitaries. Despite a cold, piercing wind and driving rain, townspeople gathered at the depot to greet guests.

The crowd became anxious as the time for arrival passed and the train did not appear. By nightfall, people returned to their home, fearing the worst. Without telegraph or telephones, there was no way to know what happened until a steamship arrived the next day with the news: a trestle supporting the Gasconade River bridge had collapsed, plunging the train cars onto the river bank thirty feet below. The Prices joined the relief effort as victims of the wreck were transported from the ship to hastily improvised hospitals or morgues in Jefferson City. In all, one hundred passengers were injured and thirty-four died, many of them St. Louis civic leaders.

The expected arrival of the first passenger train to the Capital City was immortalized by disaster.

Unfortunately, there was more suffering to come for the Price family and the people of Missouri. Even as the Governor left office, war clouds were gathering.

Price at first favored the Union, but later sided with the Confederacy after being appointed by Governor Claiborne Jackson to head the state militia. With the outbreak of the Civil War, General Price trained five thousand troops, marched them to southwest Missouri, and joined with the Confederates there to defeat the smaller Union Army at the Battle of Wilson's Creek.

He then proceeded to Lexington, Missouri, and captured three thousand

Federal soldiers. But there was little success after that. Price later retreated to Arkansas, was wounded at the Battle of Pea Ridge, and met several defeats in Mississippi. With his final raid into Missouri in 1864, Price brought ten thousand troops within four miles of Jefferson City. Positioned for a siege, the General chose not to attack—a tactic that some thought resulted from his warm regard for the Capital City, although Price later declared he considered taking the city too bitter and costly a struggle.

With the Southern cause going poorly, Price took refuge in Texas. At the end of the war, he moved to Mexico and established a colony for ex-Confederate soldiers. Mrs. Price arranged to take the three children who were still living at home and join her husband. Her postwar trip proved to be nearly as hazardous to the family as their wartime ordeals. She and the children were on their way to Mexico when the ship sank, and with it all the family furniture, including their beloved piano. When the family finally landed in Mexico three weeks late, General Price was so diminished by war and worry that his wife hardly recognized him.

The intended refuge for Confederates in Mexico was temporary; in 1866, seven months after Mrs. Price arrived, the family returned home with the General still sick. The following year a triple tragedy occurred with Price's death from cholera on the same day as the death of a daughter-in-law and her newborn baby Price was fifty-eight.

Trusten Polk
Elizabeth Newberry Skinner Polk
(1857)

Trusten Polk's term as Governor was "distinguished by its brevity." Inaugurated on January 5, 1857, the General Assembly elected the new Governor to the U.S. Senate a week later. Polk resigned the governorship as of February 27, making his fifty-three-day term the shortest of any Missouri governor.

Polk's tenure in the nation's capital was also abbreviated. Expelled from the Senate because of his Southern sympathies, he joined the Confederate army and served as a colonel under General Sterling Price. Even his military service was cut short when he was captured and imprisoned for several months toward the end of the war.

On his release, Polk joined General Price in Mexico to set up a colony for Confederate soldiers. Mrs. Polk, banished from St. Louis for "giving aid and encouragement to the Southern cause," suffered the additional indignity of having the family's household goods and library confiscated. After the war, however,

WHERE'S THE BIBLE?

Polk's inaugural ceremony was interrupted by an "awful and awkward pause," at least according to one St. Louis newspaper. The delay came from having no Bible on which to take the oath of office. A hasty search of the Capitol ensued, but none was found. According to the news article (disputed by local citizens), the closest Bible to be found in the Capital City was at the state penitentiary several blocks away.

Hancock Lee Jackson
Ursley Oldham Jackson
(1857)

when amnesty was granted to Confederates and their property was restored, the Polks returned to St. Louis where Trusten resumed his law practice.

Lieutenant Governor Jackson held the reins of government for only eight months after the resignation of Governor Polk. His brief tenure was marked by the Panic of 1857 and mounting political tension that would later lead to the Civil War. While Jackson's elevation to the governorship gave him the right to make the Mansion his home, it is doubtful that Mrs. Jackson and the eleven children moved to Jefferson City from their Randolph County farm.

Despite the brevity of his service, Jackson cast a historic veto, one that prevented the General Assembly from continuing its practice of granting legislative divorces. The interim Governor also took the opportunity to appoint his cousin, Claiborne Fox Jackson, as Missouri's first bank commissioner. By 1860, however, the two Democrats were adversaries, facing each other in a four-way battle for the governorship. Hancock Jackson, a proslavery advocate, was soundly trounced by his cousin who also favored slavery, but was willing to allow residents of new territories to decide the issue for themselves.

With his defeat, Hancock Jackson made no further attempts at public office. He had served as the first sheriff of Randolph County and, upon leaving the Capital City, he once again put on the badge of a lawman as a U.S. Marshall. A few years later, he moved to Oregon where he remained the rest of his life.

Robert Marcellus Stewart
Hostess: Elizabeth Westcott Severance
(1857-1861)

Robert Stewart thought he had lost his race for governor to James S. Rollins. However, when the last votes came in from the remote Ozark region of the state, Stewart had a narrow (and some thought questionable) 334-vote edge. With his victory secure, the bachelor Governor persuaded two of his nieces to leave New York and come to Missouri to oversee the social demands of his new position.

Unfortunately, the Capital City did not live up to the Governor's exaggerated claims or the young ladies' expectations. Nineteen-year-old Elizabeth Westcott wrote home, "Except for the Capitol building, executive mansion, the state penitentiary, and a few dwellings, not an imposing building met our view." The street leading to the executive home was nothing more than a "washed-out gully," she declared. "The Mansion, as they called it, was like thousands of houses in other cities, without the more modern conveniences. Hotels were not even medium," she added, although she complimented the "ranshackled" McCarty Hotel across from the Mansion for serving great "venison roasts and buffalo tongues."

Though the city was unappealing to the young lady, at least one prominent visitor was attracted to the state capital during Stewart's term. Presidential hopeful U.S. Senator Stephen A. Douglas, "the Little Giant" of the Lincoln-Douglas debates, delivered a campaign speech in Jefferson City in 1860, but there is no indication that Miss Westcott entertained him at the Mansion.

Stewart's nieces had to endure not only the disappointment of their surroundings but also the embarrassment of some of their uncle's antics. The forty-two-year-old chief executive, a lawyer and former state senator, was described by a contemporary as a "stranger to thrift, but not to alcohol." Tales of his "exuberant moods" abound. The most repeated tells of the Governor riding his horse, Dobbin, up the front steps of the Mansion and ordering the servants to feed the animal a peck of oats from the sideboard in the dining room. When asked why he did such a thing, Stewart replied that his horse was as good as he and others who ate at the house. For those who doubted the incident, it was said that hoof prints remained on the wooden front steps of the old Mansion as proof.

> Stewart was labeled "a stranger to thrift, but not to alcohol."

Another story told of how Stewart "got even" with a former crew member of a steamboat on which he once served. Stewart had signed on as a deck hand to earn his way up the Missouri River, but the young sailor's work did not suit the harsh demands of the ship's mate. To show his contempt, the old seaman booted Stewart off the gangplank. Years later, when the Governor learned that the man was in the penitentiary just blocks from the Mansion, he called for him to be brought to the warden's office. The eccentric but kindhearted Governor told the inmate point-blank that he was not good enough to stay in Missouri's penitentiary, handed him a pardon, and literally kicked him out the door.

In another show of compassion, Stewart released all the women in the prison and gave them jobs at the Mansion, where many of them—resuming their old habits—"robbed and pillaged at their heart's content."

Stewart's attempts at rehabilitation did not extend to the house. He felt the old Mansion was "uninhabitable" and a discredit "to this great and wealthy state." Twice before leaving office he pleaded with the legislature for funds to tear it down and build a new one. "The present edifice, besides being illy constructed and a very inconvenient dwelling, cannot much longer be made tenantable, even by repairs," he claimed. The General Assembly responded with a twenty-thousand-dollar appropriation for a new home, but because of the Civil War, construction was delayed for another decade.

> The old Mansion was uninhabitable and a discredit to this great and wealthy state.

In spite of his occasional improprieties, "Governor Bob," as he was known, was admired for his handling of the state's border conflicts and generally considered "a good governor, except when he was on one of his 'toots.' " He joined the Union army during the Civil War, but was relieved of his command because of his drinking problem. He later edited a newspaper in St. Joseph, but never held public office again. Stewart died at the age of fifty-six.

The curse of war and personal misfortune haunted Claiborne Jackson all his life. As a young man, he operated a general store in Old Franklin—one of the leading commercial centers in Missouri at the time. When the city was washed away by the rampaging Missouri River, Jackson moved across the river to Arrow Rock. There he met Dr. John Sappington and married the eighteen-year-old daughter of the distinguished physician. (Sappington's son-in-law, Miles Meredith Marmaduke, had earlier served as governor.)

With her death only six months after their wedding, the young widower returned to the Sappington home to ask for the hand of Louisa, another daughter of the family. This marriage produced three sons before she died in an accident five years later. Compounding the tragedy was the death of his youngest son a month later.

The tenacious young man again returned to his father-in-law's home to ask

"Don't come back for the old woman."

permission to marry the doctor's oldest daughter, Eliza, a divorcee with five children. Sappington agreed, but is said to have warned Jackson, "You can take her, but don't come back after the old woman."

Jackson and his new wife began their marriage with seven children to provide for and three more youngsters would be born to the couple during the troublesome prewar era. The pressure of domestic cares and responsibilities did not prevent Jackson from getting embroiled in the political battles of the day—struggles that would ultimately lead to more personal tragedy. He served five terms in the House—two as Speaker—and a term in the state Senate. In addition, his checkered political career featured three unsuccessful races for Congress and one for governor before he won an ill-fated term as Missouri's chief executive.

The family had hoped to move into the Mansion, but the outbreak of the Civil War and his decision to stand with the South quickly changed the course of their lives. The Governor was only six months into his term when Federal troops sailed up the Missouri River to seize the Capital City. In great haste, he gathered the state officers and fled by steamship to Boonville, leaving the city in "chaotic confusion." On the heels of Jackson's retreat, Union General Nathaniel Lyon and his 2,500 men took the Capital City without firing a shot. Townsmen received them joyously as they raised the stars and strips over the Capitol where the rattlesnake flag of

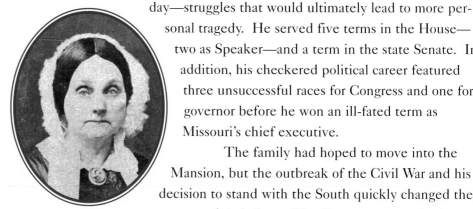

Claiborne Fox Jackson
Eliza Sappington Pierson Jackson
(1861)

the Missouri Confederacy was flying earlier. Having secured Jefferson City, Lyon proceeded to Boonville to rout the rebels before they could amass a larger force.

Jackson assembled his "government-on-the-run" in Neosho and in Cassville, but neither time did they muster a quorum of legislators. Finally, he headed for safer Confederate territory in Arkansas, setting up his headquarters in Camden near Little Rock.

Fearing for the safety of his family, he arranged for them to leave Missouri in the company of General Sterling Price's army and to relocate in Texas. Joining Mrs. Jackson on the arduous journey were her daughters, daughters-in-law, grandchildren, and twenty-some slaves. The Price family found little comfort in their new home in Red River Valley County. According to one family member, the site was "dismal . . . often invaded by Indians, and chills and fever were most prevalent." The families lived in small, closely grouped cottages and ate in a central dining area. Mrs. Jackson, a "cultured [lady] who had known nothing but the finer things of life," cared for the sick and disheartened, and oversaw the gardening and the making of clothes for the struggling little commune.

Meanwhile, back in Missouri, a state convention had installed a provisional government and named Hamilton Gamble to serve as governor until an election could be called. Jackson never reclaimed the governorship or returned to Missouri; he died in 1862 at his Arkansas headquarters. The family's tragedy continued with the loss of a son in battle in 1864 and by the death of Mrs. Jackson shortly thereafter.

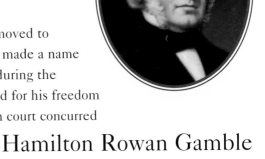

St. Louis lawyer Hamilton Gamble had retired in ill health and moved to Pennsylvania by the time the Civil War began. He had already made a name for himself as the chief justice of the Missouri Supreme Court during the famous Dred Scott case. The lawsuit centered on a slave who had sued for his freedom after being moved to a nonslave state. Two members of the three-man court concurred with the slave owner wanting to retain ownership of his "property." However, Gamble wrote a strong dissenting opinion favoring freedom for the slave.

Hamilton Rowan Gamble
Caroline Lane Coalter Gamble
(1861-1864)

Gamble gained the additional distinction of being Missouri's provisional Governor during the Civil War. After Governor Jackson fled the capital at the onset of the war, a state convention urged the sixty-two-year-old retiree to return to public service. Gamble, who had once been Missouri's secretary of state, reluctantly agreed, but did not spend much time in Jefferson City. The uncertainty of war kept the First Family in St. Louis, except when special events required their presence in the Capital City.

In 1863, still in poor health, Gamble tendered his resignation, but was convinced to remain and see the state through the conflict. Despite the Governor's heroic attempt to carry on, his condition continued to deteriorate. An accident prevented him from seeing the successful conclusion of the war. A month after he fell on the icy steps of the Mansion, the Governor died, leaving the remainder of his term to be filled by Lieutenant Governor Willard Hall.

Thomas Reynolds' feelings of duty and honor had already caused him to tangle with B. Gratz Brown, a man who would later be governor. In 1856 the two had fought one of the last duels in Missouri, a shoot-out they both managed to survive. Later, while serving as lieutenant governor, Reynolds' passion for the Southern cause led him to flee with Governor Claiborne Jackson at the onset of the Civil War. When Jackson died, Reynolds assumed the leadership of Missouri's government-in-exile, although provisional Governor Hamilton Gamble had already been installed in Jefferson City.

Thomas Chaute Reynolds
Heloise Marie Sprague Reynolds
(1862-1864)

Claiming the rebel government as the duly elected body of the state, Reynolds moved his "capital" to Marshall, Texas—a town of two thousand people, many of them wealthy Southern refugees looking for a safe haven. In attempting to simulate a capital city, Reynolds rented two houses across the street from each other—one to serve as the Capitol, the other as the Governor's Mansion. Reynolds and his wife held social events in their home in a valiant effort to re-create the life they once knew.

Missouri's Confederate Capitol (above) and Confederate Mansion (below) located in Marshall, Texas.

The self-proclaimed Governor still possessed the official state seal that had been taken from the Capitol when Governor Jackson fled from Jefferson City. Reynolds and his staff continued to use the seal as a symbol of authority to conduct what they considered to be the business of the state.

Desperately hoping to depose the provisional Governor, Reynolds joined General Sterling Price in his final invasion of the state—a venture that brought the Confederates within four miles of Jefferson City. But Price, a former governor of Missouri, changed his tactics, turning his troops toward Westport for a battle that drove the Southern forces out of the state for the last time.

When it became apparent that the Confederate cause had failed, Reynolds and his supporters joined other exiled Southerners in Mexico. Several years later, as the rebels trickled back to their homes, Reynolds and his wife resettled in St. Louis, bringing with them the state seal. As he returned the symbol of authority to the Capitol in 1869, he echoed the feelings of those who had suffered the turbulence and bloodshed of war: "May [the seal's] return be an augury of the speedy oblivion of past strife."

But life's battles were not over for Reynolds; he later lost his forty-four-year-old wife when a spark from a fire ignited her clothing as she lay sleeping by a fireplace. Reynolds remarried and spent his honeymoon in Jefferson City—the town he had once abandoned and later sought to invade. Friends remembered him kindly, however, and honored the newlyweds by standing outside their window to "serenade" them with popular songs.

Reynolds' happiness was short-lived. Eight years later, in poor health, he was killed when he jumped down the eighty-foot elevator shaft of a St. Louis building.

As a young man, Willard Hall had filed for Congress, but before the election was held, he left for Santa Fe to fight in the Mexican War. The Yale graduate and attorney quickly earned a promotion from private to lieutenant. To his surprise, he also won his congressional election, despite his absence from the state.

Released from the army to assume his new position, Hall went to Congress in 1846 for three terms, but failed in his bid for a U.S. Senate seat ten years later.

Willard Preble Hall
Olivia Oliver Hall
(1864-1865)

His move into state government came at the onset of the Civil War when a convention was called to determine if Missouri should remain in the Union. Delegates set up a provisional government, picking Hall to serve as lieutenant governor and his father-in-law to fill the office of secretary of state. With the death of Governor Gamble, Hall was positioned to move up in rank. He held the office of governor during the final year of the Civil War and then returned to St. Joseph, Missouri, to practice law and manage his farm.

"Henceforth and forever, no person within the limits of the state shall . . . know any master but God." With the signing of this declaration in 1865, Thomas Clement Fletcher put an end to slavery in Missouri.

The first chief executive whose term followed the Civil War held several distinctions: he was the state's first Republican governor; the first native-born governor; and, at the time, Missouri's youngest chief executive at the age of thirty-seven. Fletcher and his wife had the additional distinction of having been born within a few

Thomas Clement Fletcher
Mary Clarissa Honey Fletcher
(1865-1869)

weeks of each other. Because their parents were such good friends, they had betrothed their children as infants and saw to their marriage when they reached the age of twenty-four.

Nearly fourteen years later, when the Fletchers and their two children moved into the Mansion, they became the first family to inhabit the old home since before the Civil War. In spite of its shabby condition, Jefferson City socialites welcomed the chance to gather in the Governor's home for teas and receptions once again.

However, those looking for strong drink were disappointed. The First Lady, an ardent prohibitionist and a leader of the Daughters of Temperance, never served alcohol. One man—who apparently overindulged before arriving at one of her parties—came to regret it. Though it was not unusual for guests to pocket food from the Mansion table, the intoxicated visitor overtly pilfered several pieces of silverware and was later charged with grand larceny.

The intoxicated visitor overtly pilfered several pieces of silverware.

The annoyance of dealing with a silver thief did not compare with the other difficulties Fletcher faced in the postwar era. Particularly troublesome for the Governor was the so-called Drake constitution of 1865. Among its provision was the vengeful "Loyalty Act" that expelled over eight hundred public officeholders who fought for the South or showed sympathy for its cause. In the wake of the disruption in state services, Fletcher was left with the burden of filling the vacancies.

Other vocations were also purged by the act: teachers, preachers, and lawyers with Southern leanings were denied the right to vote and practice their profession. When many ministers refused to comply, Fletcher announced that "religious liberty is a political right, there is not a sentence or a word in the Constitution of the United States which gives them the right to preach at all." As it turned out, the oath was nearly impossible to enforce, was ignored in many areas of the state, and was gradually abandoned.

The new constitution also set a two-year term for governor, with the provision for reelection within a six-year period—a limitation that remained until another constitution was written in 1875, limiting a governor to one four-year term.

Upon leaving office, Fletcher returned to his St. Louis law practice, but soon opened an office in Washington, D.C. Before departing the State Capitol, however, he pointed out the shortcomings of the thirty-five-year-old Governor's Mansion. In a final speech, he told lawmakers that the home was "dilapidated in every part and cannot longer be made comfortable." Although the General Assembly had appropriated twenty thousand dollars for a new home in 1861, war and financial hardship had stalled the project. In the meantime, the rising cost of construction meant more funding would be needed from the General Assembly; the state would have to wait a few more years to have a building worthy of being called a Mansion.

When the California Gold Rush began, Joseph McClurg, a St. Louis storekeeper, gathered up his wife and children and headed west. But fortune eluded the young couple and they soon returned to Missouri. Though he had studied for the ministry, taught school, and practiced law, he chose to set up a mercantile business at Linn Creek, a leading commercial center before the war.

With the death of his wife and two of their eight children, McClurg turned his attention to politics and, in 1862, won a seat in Congress. Without a wife to fill the social requirements of his office, McClurg looked to his twenty-two-year-old daughter, Fannie, for help. During the last of her father's three terms in Washington, she attended White House parties and quickly picked up the skills of a gracious hostess.

Leaving Washington, McClurg, a Republican, returned to Missouri to run for governor. With many Democrats disenfranchised after the Civil War, he easily captured the office with a strong twenty-thousand-vote win over General John Phelps, who would have to wait for a more favorable time for his party before he would serve as governor.

Joseph Washington McClurg
Hostess: Fannie McClurg
(1869-1871)

Moving into the Mansion, the widowed Governor again turned to his daughter to act as his hostess. As firm prohibitionists, the McClurgs refrained from serving wine at the Mansion and the Governor further attempted to control alcohol by attempting to ban its sale in the state.

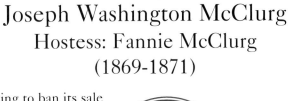

The Governor was also strict in his refusal to accept gifts. When a manufacturer delivered a piano to the house as a present for Fannie, the young lady enjoyed the instrument for only one day before her father insisted—in spite of her pleas—that it be returned.

However, her father's sternness did not prevent Fannie from having a number of beaus. Her position as the reigning hostess in Jefferson City put the young lady in touch with an array of eligible bachelors. One of her suitors, Charles Draper, was her father's private secretary. The young couple courted on horseback and on the Mansion's croquet court. At a time when croquet was gaining popularity, she and Charles played in tournaments in other cities, winning often enough to be considered champions at the game.

Some women, however, were undertaking more serious pursuits. In 1869, when the suffragettes came to Jefferson City to petition the legislature on behalf of voting rights for women, Miss McClurg and her father welcomed the ladies to the Mansion. The Governor showed his support of the cause by signing their petition. The following year, the passage of the Fifteenth Amendment gave voting rights to former male slaves and prompted a time of celebration and speech making at the Mansion, but a half century would pass before women—black and white—would be able to claim a similar victory.

In 1870 McClurg lost his bid for reelection. With a factional split in his party, McClurg, a Radical Republican, was badly beaten by Liberal Republican B. Gratz Brown. Following his defeat, he returned to his Linn Creek store and extended his business ventures into steamboating and lead mining. His daughter also returned to the family's hometown, married her croquet partner, and raised six children.

Governor	Party	Term	Age	Birth	Death
Alexander McNair	Dem. Rep.	1820-1824	45	Lancaster Co., PA; May 5, 1775	St. Louis, MO; Mar. 18, 1826, age 50
Frederick Bates	Dem. Rep.	1824-1825	47	Belmont, VA; June 23, 1777	Chesterfield, MO; Aug. 4, 1825, age 48
Abraham J. Williams (acting)	Dem. Rep.	1825-1826	44	Grant Co., WV; Feb. 26, 1781	Columbia, MO; Dec. 30, 1839, age 58
John Miller	Dem. Rep.	1826-1832	44	near Martinsburg, WV; Nov. 25, 1781	Florissant, MO; Mar. 18, 1846, age 64
Daniel Dunklin	Dem. Rep.	1832-1836	42	near Greenville, SC; Jan. 14, 1790	Potosi, MO; Aug. 25, 1844, age 54
Lilburn W. Boggs	Dem.	1836-1840	43	Lexington, KY; Dec. 14, 1792	Napa Valley, CA; Mar. 14, 1860, age 67
Thomas Reynolds	Dem.	1840-1844	44	Bracken Co., KY; Mar. 12, 1796	Jefferson City, MO; Feb. 9, 1844, age 47
Meredith Marmaduke (acting)	Dem	1844	52	Westmoreland Co., VA; Aug. 28, 1791	Arrow Rock, MO; Mar. 26, 1864, age 72
John Cummins Edwards	Dem.	1844-1848	40	Frankfort, KY; June 24, 1806	Stockton, CA; Sep. 17, 1888, age 82
Austin Augustus King	Dem.	1848-1853	46	Washington Co., TN; Sep. 21, 1802	St. Louis, MO; Apr. 22, 1870, age 67
Sterling Price	Dem.	1853-1857	43	near Farmville, VA; Sep. 11, 1809	St. Louis, MO; Sep. 29, 1867, age 58
Trusten Polk	Dem.	1857	45	near Bridgeville, DE; May 29, 1811	St. Louis, MO; Apr. 16, 1876, age 64
Hancock Lee Jackson (acting)	Dem.	1857	60	Madison Co., KY; May 12, 1796	Salem, OR; Mar. 19, 1876, age 79
Robert Marcellus Stewart	Dem.	1857-1861	42	Truxton, NY; Mar. 12, 1815	St. Joseph, MO; Sep. 21, 1871, age 56
Claiborne Fox Jackson	Dem.	1861	54	Fleming Co., KY; Apr. 4, 1806	Little Rock, AR; Dec. 6, 1862, age 56
Hamilton R. Gamble (provisional)	Unionist	1861-1864	62	Winchester, VA; Nov. 29, 1798	St. Louis, MO; Jan. 31, 1864, age 65
Thomas C. Reynolds (in exile)	Dem.	(1862-1864)	43	Charleston, SC; Oct. 11, 1821	St. Louis, MO; Mar. 31, 1887, age 65
Willard Preble Hall (provisional)	Unionist	1864-1865	43	Harpers Ferry, VA; May 9, 1820	St. Joseph, MO; Nov. 2, 1882, age 62
Thomas Clement Fletcher	Rad-Rep.	1865-1869	37	Herculaneum, MO; Jan. 21, 1827	Washington, DC; Mar. 25, 1899, age 72
Joseph Washington McClurg	Rad-Rep.	1869-1871	50	near Lebanon, MO; Feb. 22, 1818	Lebanon, MO; Dec. 2, 1900, age 82
Benjamin Gratz Brown	Lib. Rep.	1871-1873	44	Lexington, KY; May 28, 1826	Kirkwood, MO; Dec. 13, 1885, age 59
Silas Woodson	Dem.	1873-1875	53	Knox County, KY; May 18, 1819	St. Joseph, MO; Oct. 9, 1896, age 77
Charles Henry Hardin	Dem.	1875-1877	54	Trimble County, KY; July 15, 1820	Mexico, MO; July 29, 1892, age 72
John Smith Phelps	Dem.	1877-1881	62	Simsbury, CT; Dec. 22, 1814	St. Louis, MO; Nov. 20, 1886, age 71
Thomas Theodore Crittenden	Dem.	1881-1885	49	Shelby Co., KY; Jan. 1, 1832	Kansas City, MO; May 29, 1909, age 77
John Sappington Marmaduke	Dem.	1885-1887	51	Saline Co., MO; Mar. 14, 1833	Jefferson City, MO; Dec. 28, 1887, age 54
Albert Pickett Morehouse	Dem.	1887-1889	52	Delaware Co., OH; July 11, 1835	Maryville, MO; Sep. 23, 1891, age 56
David Rowland Francis	Dem.	1889-1893	38	Richmond, KY; Oct. 1, 1850	St. Louis, MO; Jan. 15, 1927, age 76
William Joel Stone	Dem.	1893-1897	44	near Richmond, KY; May 7, 1848	Washington, DC; Apr. 14, 1918, age 69
Lon Vest Stephens	Dem.	1897-1901	38	Boonville, MO; Dec. 1, 1858	St. Louis, MO; Jan. 10, 1923, age 64
Alexander Monroe Dockery	Dem.	1901-1905	55	near Gallatin, MO; Feb. 11, 1845	Gallatin, MO; Dec. 26, 1926, age 81
Joseph Wingate Folk	Dem.	1905-1909	35	Brownsville, TN; Oct. 28, 1869	Washington, DC; May 28, 1923, age 53
Herbert Spencer Hadley	Rep.	1909-1913	36	Olathe, KS; Feb. 20, 1872	St. Louis, MO; Dec. 1, 1927, age 55
Elliott Woolfolk Major	Dem.	1913-1917	48	Lincoln Co., MO; Oct. 20, 1864	Eureka, MO; July 9, 1949, age 84
Frederick Dozier Gardner	Dem.	1917-1921	47	Hickman, KY; Nov. 6, 1869	St. Louis, MO; Dec. 18, 1933, age 64
Arthur Mastick Hyde	Rep.	1921-1925	43	Princeton, MO; July 12, 1877	New York, NY; Oct. 17, 1947, age 70
Samuel Aaron Baker	Rep.	1925-1929	50	Patterson, MO; Nov. 7, 1874	Jefferson City, MO; Sep. 16, 1933, age 58
Henry Stewart Caulfield	Rep.	1929-1933	55	St Louis, MO; Dec. 9, 1873	St. Louis, MO; May 11, 1966, age 92
Guy Brasfield Park	Dem.	1933-1937	60	Platte City, MO; June 10, 1872	Jefferson City, MO; Oct. 1, 1946, age 74
Lloyd Crow Stark	Dem.	1937-1941	50	Pike Co., MO; Nov. 23, 1886	Clayton, MO; Sep. 17, 1972, age 85
Forrest C. Donnell	Rep.	1941-1945	56	Quitman, MO; Aug. 20, 1884	St. Louis, MO; Mar. 3, 1980, age 95
Philip "Phil" Matthew Donnelly	Dem.	1945-1949	53	Lebanon, MO; Mar. 6, 1891	Lebanon, MO; Sep. 12, 1961, age 70
Forrest Smith	Dem.	1949-1953	62	Ray Co., MO; Feb. 14, 1886	Gulfport, MS; Mar. 8, 1962, age 76
Philip "Phil" Matthew Donnelly	Dem.	1953-1957	61	Lebanon, MO; Mar. 6, 1891	Lebanon, MO; Sep. 12, 1961, age 70
James Thomas Blair Jr.	Dem.	1957-1961	54	Maysville, MO; Mar. 15, 1902	Jefferson City, MO; July 12, 1962, age 60
John Montgomery Dalton	Dem.	1961-1965	60	Vernon Co., MO; Nov. 9, 1900	Jefferson City, MO; July 7, 1972, age 71
Warren Eastman Hearnes	Dem.	1965-1973	41	Charleston, MO; July 24, 1923	
Christopher "Kit" Samuel Bond	Rep.	1973-1977	33	St. Louis, MO; Mar. 6, 1939	
Joseph Patrick Teasdale	Dem.	1977-1981	40	Kansas City, MO; Mar. 29, 1936	
Christopher "Kit" Samuel Bond	Rep.	1981-1985	41	St. Louis, MO; Mar. 6, 1939	
John David Ashcroft	Rep.	1985-1993	42	Chicago, IL; May 9, 1942	
Melvin "Mel" Eugene Carnahan	Dem.	1993- present	58	Birch Tree, MO; Feb. 11, 1934	

rst Lady	Married	Children	Religion	Occupation	Military
guerite Susanne de Reilhe McNair	Mar. 1805	10	Presbyterian/Catholic	Businessman, judge	Captain, War of 1812
cy Opie Ball Bates	Mar. 4, 1819	4	Quaker background	Attorney, judge	US Army
helor	Bachelor	0	unknown	Shoemaker, farmer	
helor	Bachelor	0	unknown	Businessman, journalist	Lt. Col, War of 1812
ly Pamelia Willis Haley Dunklin	Apr. 28, 1815	7	unknown	Tavern owner, attorney	War of 1812
thea Grant Boone Boggs	July 29, 1823	10	unknown	Storekeeper	War of 1812
a Ann Young Reynolds	Sep. 2, 1823	1	Methodist	Attorney, judge	
inia Sappington Marmaduke	Jan. 4, 1826	10	unknown	Engineer, farmer	Colonel, War of 1812
ma Richard Edwards (married later)	May 4, 1854	11	unknown	Attorney, judge	
cy Harris Roberts King	1827	10	unknown	Attorney, judge	Colonel, Black Hawk War
rtha Head Price	May 14, 1833	7	unknown	Attorney, farmer	Colonel, Mexican War; Gen., CSA
abeth Newberry Skinner Polk	Dec. 26, 1837	5	Methodist-Episcopal	Attorney	Colonel, Civil War
ley Oldham Jackson	Mar. 8, 1821	11	Quaker background	Farmer	Captain, Mexican War
helor	Bachelor	0	unknown	Attorney, businessman	Captain, Mexican War
za Sappington Pierson Jackson	Nov. 27, 1838	6	unknown	Storekeeper, attorney	General, CSA
oline Lane Coalter Gamble	Nov. 8, 1827	9	Presbyterian	Attorney, judge	Captain, Franklin Guards
oise Marie Sprague Reynolds	Nov. 28, 1848	0	Methodist	Attorney	
via Oliver Hall	June 22, 1864	7	unknown	Attorney	Lt., Mexican War; Gen., CSA
ry Clarissa Honey Fletcher	Apr. 16, 1851	2	Methodist	Attorney	Colonel, Union Army
lower	Oct. 18, 1841	8	Presbyterian	Attorney, businessman	Colonel, Union Army
ry Hansome Gunn Brown	Aug. 17, 1858	8	unknown	Attorney, writer	Colonel, Union Army
ginia "Jennie" Lard Woodson	Dec. 27, 1866	4	Catholic (1895)	Attorney	Colonel, Union Army
ry Barr Jenkins Hardin	May 16, 1844	0	Baptist	Attorney	
ry Whitney Phelps	Apr. 30, 1837	5	Puritan background	Attorney	General, Union Army
roline Wheeler Jackson Crittenden	Nov. 13, 1856	4	Presbyterian	Attorney	Lt. Colonel, Union Army
helor	Bachelor	0	Episcopalian	Military, editor, insurance	General, Confederate Army
rtha "Mattie" McFadden Morehouse	Jan. 10, 1865	3	unknown	Attorney, teacher	Lieutenant, Union Army
e Perry Francis	Jan. 20, 1876	6	Presbyterian	Grain business	
ah Louise "Lula" Winston Stone	Apr. 2, 1874	3	no affiliation	Attorney	
rgaret "Maggie" Nelson Stephens	Oct. 5, 1880	0	Methodist	Banker, businessman	
ry Elizabeth Bird Dockery	Apr. 14, 1869	8	Methodist-Episcopal	Physician, businessman	
rtrude Glass Folk	Nov. 10, 1896	0	Baptist	Attorney	
nes Lee Hadley	Oct. 8, 1901	3	Quaker background	Attorney	
zabeth Terrill Myers Major	June 14, 1887	3	Methodist	Attorney	
nnette Vosburgh Gardner	Oct. 10, 1896	3	Methodist	Coffin manufacturer	
rtense Cullers Hyde	Oct. 19, 1904	1	Methodist	Attorney, businessman	Capt., Mo. National Guard
lle Tuckley Baker	June 1, 1904	1	Presbyterian	Educator	
nces "Fannie" Delano Caulfield	Oct. 22, 1902	4	unknown	Attorney, judge	
anora Gabbert Park	Nov. 16, 1909	1	Disciples of Christ	Attorney, judge	
therine Lemoine Guy Perkins Stark	Nov. 23, 1931	5	Episcopalian	Military, nurseryman	Navy officer; Army Major
lda Hays Donnell	Jan. 29, 1913	2	Methodist-Episcopal	Attorney	
nita McFadden Donnelly	May 22, 1915	1	Christian Church	Attorney	
ldred Williams Smith	Oct. 12, 1915	2	Methodist	Businessman	
nita Flower McFadden Donnelly	May 22, 1915	1	Christian Church	Attorney	
nilie Garnett Chorn Blair	July 17, 1926	2	Presbyterian	Attorney	Lt. Col., Army, World War II
eraldine "Jerry" Hall Dalton	Nov. 22, 1925	2	Presbyterian	Attorney	
tty Cooper Hearnes	July 2, 1948	3	Baptist	Attorney	1st Lt., Army, Word War II
rolyn Reid Bond	May 13, 1967	1	Presbyterian	Attorney	
ary Theresa Ferkenhoff Teasdale	Oct. 13, 1973	3	Catholic	Attorney	Airman (2nd Class) Air Force Res.
rolyn Reid Bond	May 13, 1967	1	Presbyterian	Attorney	
et Roede Ashcroft	Dec. 23, 1967	3	Assembly of God	Attorney	
n Carpenter Carnahan	June 12, 1954	4	Baptist	Attorney	lst Lt., Air Force

Major Offices	Burial Site
Sheriff, St. Louis Co.; US Marshall, Missouri Territory	Calvary Cemetery, St. Louis, MO
Acting Territorial Governor, (briefly during 1807-08; 1812-13)	"Thornhill" family Cemetery, Chesterfield, MO
State Senate (1822-26); President Pro Tem Missouri Senate (1822-24)	Columbia Cemetery, Columbia, MO
US House (1837-43)	Bellefontaine Cemetery, St. Louis, MO
Sheriff, Washington Co. (1815-19); MO House (1822-23); Lt. Governor (1828-32); Surveyor-Gen. (1836)	Family Cemetery near Pevely, MO
First County Clerk, Jackson Co.; State Senate (1826-32, 1842-46); Lt. Governor (1832-36)	Napa Valley, CA
IL: Speaker; Attorney Gen; Chief Justice Sup. Ct; MO: House (1832-34); Speaker; Judge (1837-40)	Woodlawn Cemetery, Jefferson City, MO
VA: US Marshall; Circuit Clerk; MO: County Surveyor; Judge; Lt. Governor (1840-44)	Sappington Cemetery, Arrow Rock, MO
Sec.of State (1830-35, 1837); MO House (1836); US House (1841-43); Mayor, Stockton, CA (1851)	Rural Cemetery, Stockton, CA
MO House (1834-38); Circuit Judge (1837-48, 1862-63); US House (1863-65)	Richmond Cemetery, Richmond, MO
MO House (1836-38, 1840-44); House Speaker; US House (1845-46)	Bellefontaine Cemetery, St. Louis, MO
St. Louis City Counselor (1843); US Senate (1857-62)	Bellefontaine Cemetery, St. Louis, MO
Sheriff, Randolph Co.; MO Senate (1850-54); Lt. Governor (1856); U.S. Marshall	Salem, OR
MO Senate (1846-57)	Mount Mora Cemetery, St. Joseph, MO
MO House (1836-48); House Speaker (1844-46); MO Senate (1848-52)	Sappington Cemetery, Arrow Rock, MO
Circuit Attorney Howard Co; Sec.of State (1824); MO House (1846-48); Supreme Ct. (1851-54)	unknown
US District Attorney (1853-57); Lt. Governor (1861); Confederate Governor in exile (1862-64)	unknown
Circuit Attorney (1843); US House (1847-53); Lt. Governor (1861-64)	Mount Mora Cemetery, St. Joseph, MO
Deputy County Clerk (1846); Circuit Clerk	Bellefontaine Cemetery, St. Louis, MO
Circuit Clerk in Texas (1840); Deputy Sheriff, St. Louis Co. (1841-44); US Congress (1863-68)	Lebanon Cemetery, Lebanon, MO
MO House (1852-59); US Senate (1863-67)	Oak Hill Cemetery, Kirkwood, MO
KY: Legis. (1842-43, 1853-55); MO: Circuit Judge (1862-66); Criminal Judge (1885-95)	Mount Mora Cemetery, St. Joseph, MO
Circuit Attorney (1848-52); MO House (1852-56; 1858-60); MO Senate (1860-62, 1872-74)	Jewell Cemetery, Columbia, MO
MO House (1840-44); Congress (1845-63); Military Governor of Arkansas (1962)	Hazelwood Cemetery, Springfield, MO
US Congress (1872-74, 1876-78); Attorney General (1864); US Consul General Mexico (1893-97)	Forest Hill Cemetery, Kansas City, MO
none	Woodlawn Cemetery, Jefferson City, MO
Missouri House (1877-78, 1883-84); Lt. Governor (1885-87)	Oak Hill Cemetery, Maryville, MO
Mayor, St. Louis (1885-89); Sec. of the Interior (1896-97); Ambassador to Russia (1916-21)	Bellefontaine Cemetery, St. Louis, MO
Prosecuting Attorney, Vernon Co. (1872-74); US House (1885-91); US Senate (1903-18)	Deepwood Cemetery, Nevada, MO
State Treasurer (1890-97)	Walnut Grove Cemetery, Boonville, MO
Mayor, Gallatin (1881-83); US Congress (1883-99); Third Asst. Postmaster Gen. (1913-21)	Edgewood Cemetery, Chillicothe, MO
Circuit Attorney, St. Louis (1900-04); Solicitor General (1912-14)	Brownsville, TN
Pros. Attorney Jackson Co. (1901-03); Atty. Gen.(1905-09); Chancellor Washington Univ. (1923-27)	Riverview Cemetery, Jefferson City, MO
State Senate (1897-1901); Attorney General (1909-13)	Bowling Green Cemetery, Bowling Green, MO
Board of Freeholders, St. Louis	Bellefontaine Cemetery, St. Louis, MO
Mayor, Princeton, MO (1908-12); US Secretary of Agriculture (1929-33)	Trenton, MO
State Superintendent of Schools (1919-23)	Riverview Cemetery, Jefferson City, MO
US Congress (1907-09); Judge, St. Louis Court of Appeals (1910-12); City Counselor (1921-22)	Oak Grove Cemetery, St. Louis, MO
City Attorney; Platte County Prosecuting Attorney (1906-10); Circuit Judge (1923-32)	Platte City Cemetery, Platte City, MO
none	Riverview Cemetery, Louisiana, MO
Webster Groves City Attorney; US Senate (1945-51)	Bellefontaine Cemetery, St. Louis, MO
Lebanon City Atty.; Prosecuting Atty. Laclede Co.; MO House (1922-24); MO Senate (1924-44)	Lebanon City Cemetery, Lebanon, MO
County Clerk; State Tax Commissioner (1925-32); State Auditor (1933-49)	Sunny Slope Cemetery, Richmond, MO
Lebanon City Atty.; Prosecuting Atty. Laclede Co.; MO House (1922-24); MO Senate (1924-44)	Lebanon City Cemetery, Lebanon, MO
Mayor, Jefferson City (1947-48); MO House, (1929-33); Lt. Governor (1949-57)	Riverview Cemetery, Jefferson City, MO
Kennett City Attorney (1944-53); Attorney General (1953-61)	Oak Ridge Cemetery, Kennett, MO
MO House (1951-61); Secretary of State (1961-65)	
State Auditor (1971-73); US Senate (1987-present)	
Prosecuting Attorney, Jackson Co. (1967-73)	
State Auditor (1971-73); US Senate (1987-present)	
State Auditor (1973-75); Attorney General (1977-85); US Senate (1995-present)	
MO House (1965-69); State Treasurer (1981-85); Lt. Governor (1989-93)	

ILLUSTRATION CREDITS

In crediting illustrations, the following abbreviations are used to indicate the image source, location on the page, alteration, photographer, and/or artist: *t*-top, *c*-center, *b*-bottom, *r*-right, *l*-left, *frm*-frame, *bck*-background, [c]-composite, [cl]-colorized, [d]-detail, [dc]-digitally corrected, [i]-inset, [lr]-laterally reversed, [s]-screened, and [v]-vignette.

Sources:

ABC - American Book Company
ACHS - Audrain County Historical Society
AF - Abele Family
AP - Associated Press/Wide World Photos
BCHS - Boone County Historical Society
BF - Blair Family
BH - Bob Hulsey
BM - Thomas Hart Benton Mural/Vaga
BT - Bingham Trust
BWE - *Boonville Weekly Eagle*
CCHS - Cole County Historical Society
CB - Corbis-Bettmann
CF - Carnahan Family
CID - Commerce and Industrial Development Collection
CML - Winston Churchill Memorial Library
CP - Culver Pictures
DF - Donnell Family
DG - Dennis Garrels
DYF - Donnelly Family
DNR - Missouri Department of Natural Resources
EL - Dwight D. Eisenhower Library
FAAM - Friends of The Albrecht Art Museum
GC - The Granger Collection
GF - Gardner Family
GL - Gerald Lee
GMC - Governor's Mansion Collection
HC - HarperCollins Publishers
HDF - Hadley Family

HF - Hearnes Family
HHS - Hillcrest High School
HSTL - Harry S. Truman Library
JA - Jamie G. Anderson
JCNT - *Jefferson City News-Tribune*
JBS - John Bolton Stoeckley
JD - Jim Dyke
JJ - Jim Joplin
JS - John Shevlin
KCS - *Kansas City Star*
LBB - Little Bighorn Battlefield National Monument
LF - Leonard Family
MBA - Missouri Bankers Association
MC - Gerald R. Massie Collection
MDT - Missouri Department of Transportation
MDTR - Missouri Department of Tourism
MHP - Missouri State Highway Patrol
MHS - Missouri Historical Society
MMC - The MacMillan Company
MMPI - Missouri Mansion Preservation, Inc.
MSC - Missouri State Capitol
MNG - Missouri National Guard
MP - Midland Printing
MSA - Missouri State Archives
NAM - The Nelson-Atkins Museum of Art
NB - NationsBank
NCHS - Nodaway County Historical Society
PF - Park Family

PM - Pat Mantle
PPI - Penguin Putnam, Inc.
SBNO - Stark Brothers Nurseries and Orchard
SHS - The State Historical Society of Missouri
SI/REB - Smithsonian Institution/Ralph E. Becker Collection
SLAM - The Saint Louis Art Museum
SLGD - *St. Louis Globe-Democrat*
SLML - St. Louis Mercantile Library at the University of Missouri-St. Louis
SLPD - *St. Louis Post-Dispatch*
SLS - *St. Louis Star*
SLT - *St. Louis Times*
SM - *Sunday Mirror*
SUM - Joseph Summers Jr. Collection
SWB - Southwestern Bell
TF - Teasdale Family
TFH - TFH Publications
UCPO - University City Post Office
UMCA - University of Missouri Archives
USN - United States Navy
UPI - United Press International/Corbis Bettmann
VDLM - *Victorian Decorating and Lifestyle*
WF - Weil Family
WHMC - Western Historical Manuscript Collection, University of Missouri-Columbia
WU - Washington University in St. Louis

Dust Jacket, ii, iii, vi, vii[d], viii, ix[d], xi[v], xvii, xviii[v]-MMPI; xiii[d]-DG; xviii, xix-JD; Jacket Flap-CF; Signatures (Brown through Park)-WHMC; (Stark through Carnahan)-MSA.
Brown: 2 MMPI; 3 [d]-SHS; 4 [d]-CCHS; 5 *t*-*c*[d]-MMPI; 6 WF; 8 *t*-SLAM, *b*-MMPI; 9 *t*-*c*[v]-*b*-MMPI; 10 CB; 11 LBB; 12 *t*[d]-*b*-CCHS; 13 MMPI; 14 *t*-GC, *b*-CB; 15 HC; 16 MMPI; 17 *t*-CCHS, *b*-SHS; **Woodson:** 18 MMPI; 19 *t*[d]-MSC, *b*[d,lr]-SHS; 20 SHS; 21 *t*-VDLM, *b*[d]-SHS; 22 [v]-MMPI; 23 [d]-MMPI/HDF; 24 [d]-SHS; 25 MMPI; **Hardin:** 26 MMPI; 27 *t*[d]-MSC, *b*[d]-GMC; 28 ACHS; 29 WHMC; 30 [d]-SHS; 31 MMPI; 32 GC; 33 *t*-UPI/CB, *b*-CB; 34 *t*[d]-*b*-ACHS; **Phelps:** 36 MMPI; 37 [d]-MSC; 38 CB; 40 *t*-SHS, *b*[v]-MSC; 41 SHS; 42 *t*-SHS, *b*[v]-JJ; 43 *t*-SHS/BWE, *b*-JS; 44 [s]-MMPI; 45 *l*[s]-MMPI, *r*[v]-MSC; 46 [v]-SHS; 47 [d]-JS; **Crittenden:** 48 *bck*-MMPI, *tl*[v]-*tr*-CB, *cl*-SHS, *cr*-GC; 49 [d]-MSC; 50 *t*[d]-GMC, *b*[d,s]-SHS; 51 [d]-MSC; 54 *t*[v]-*b*-GC; 55 [lr,d]-PPI; 56 *tl*[d]-MMPI, *tr*-SHS *b*-MMPI; 57 PPI; **Marmaduke:** 58 *frm*-MMPI, *c*[d]-*b*-SHS; 59 [d]-SHS; 60 *c*[d]-MMPI, *b*-GC; 61 [d]-MSC; 63 [d]-SHS; 64 NB/SLAM; 66 MMPI; 67 MMPI; **Morehouse:** 68 *t*-MSA/SUM, *b*-SHS; 69 *t*[d]-MSC, *b*[d]-GMC; 70 [d,s]-SHS; 71[d]-SHS; 72 NCHS; **Francis:** 74 *tl*-*tr*[v]-*cl*[d]-*c*[v]-MHS, *bl*[lr,d]-SHS; 75 [d]-SLAM; 76 SHS; 77 [v]-SHS; 78 [d,lr]-GMC; 79 MMPI; 81 *t*-SHS, *b*-VDLM; 82 SHS; 83 *t*[d]-NB/SLAM, *b*[d]-MHS; 84 SHS; 85 SHS; 86 MHS; 87 WU; 88 *t*-UCPO, *b*-CF; 89 MHS; **Stone:** 90 MMPI; 91 [d]-MSC; 92 [d,s]-MMPI; 93 *t*[d]-GMC, *b*[lr]-SHS/SLPD; 94 [v]-SHS; 95 *t*-CCHS, *b*[v]-TFH; 98 [v]-CB/UPI; **Stephens:** 100 GMC; 101 [d]-MSC; 102 *t*[v]-*b*-MMPI/LF; 103 *t*-LF, *b*-SHS/SM; 104 *t*-LF, *b*-SHS; 105 *t*-SHS/SLS, *b*[dc]-CCHS; 106 *t*-MMPI/LF, *b*-LF; 107 *t*-*b*[v]-MMPI/LF; 108 [d,dc]-MMPI/LF; 109 SHS; 110 MSA/SUM; 111 MMPI; 112 MMPI; 113 [d,dc]-MMPI/LF; 115 MMPI/LF; 116 MMPI/LF; 117 MMPI/LF; 118 LF; 119 LF; **Dockery:** 120 MMPI; 121 *t*[d]-MSC, *b*[d]-GMC; 122 [d]-MSC/BM; 123 CF; 124 [v]-SHS; 125 [lr]-SHS; 126-127 [d]-MBA; 128 MMPI; **Folk:** 130 [dc]-MMPI; 131 *r*[d,lr]-MSC, *l*[lr]-SHS/SLPD; 132 WHMC; 133 *t*-WHMC, *b*[v]-SHS/SLPD; 134 SHS; 135 GMC; 139 *t*-WHMC, *b*[d]-WHMC; 140 *t*[dc]-*b*-SHS; 141 [v]-SHS; **Hadley:** 144 *t*[d]-CP, *bl*-*br*-WHMC; 145 [d]-MSC; 146 WHMC; 147 *t*-*br*-WHMC, *bl*-MMPI; 148 *t*-CF, *b*[v]-WHMC; 149 *t*-*b*[v]-WHMC; 150 *t*-*c*[d]-AF, *b*-MMPI/HF; 151 MMPI/HF; 152 [v]-CB; 153 *t*[v]-WHMC, *b*-MMPI; 154 [dc]-PM; 156 MSA/SUM; 157 [v]-WHMC; 158 [v]-GMC; 159 *t*[v]-WHMC, *b*-WHMC/SLT; **Major:** 160 *bck*[v]-*t*-*c*-*b*-MSA; 161 [d]-MSC; 162 CF; 163 SHS; 164 *t*-MMPI, *b*-CCHS; 165 *t*-SHS/KCS, *b*-CCHS; 166 *t*-WHMC, *b*-AF; 167 [d]-SHS; **Gardner:** 168 SHS; 169 [d]-MSC; 170 CF; 171 GMC; 172 *l*-MMPI/GF, *r*[dc]-DF; 174 *t*-WHMC, *b*[d]-

MSC; **175** *t*[d,s]-SHS, *c*-CF, *b*-SI/REB; **176** CF; **177** *r*[v]-*l*-SHS; **Hyde: 178** *tl*-GMC, *tr*-MSC, *b*[v]-SHS; **179** [v]-SHS/SLS; **181** [d]-MSC/BM; **182** *t*-CB/UPI, *b*[v]-SLML; **183** SHS; **184** [v]-MMPI; **186** [v]-SLPD; **187** SHS/SLPD; **188** *t*[d]-SHS, *b*[v]-MMPI; **189** WHMC; **Baker: 190** *c*-*b*[v]-CP; **191** *l*[v]-SHS, *r*[d,lr]-MSC; **192** CP; **194** GC; **196** MHS; **197** *t*[v]-SLML, *b*-DNR; **Caulfield: 198** MMPI; **199** [d]-MSC; **200** *r*[v]-GC, *l*[v]-CB; **202** *t*[d]-SHS, *b*-WHMC; **203** *t*[dc]-CF, *b*-WHMC; **205** [d]-WHMC; **206** MMPI/PF; **207** *c*-*b*[d]-GC; **208** JCNT; **209** GMC; **Park: 210** *t*-*l*-*r*[v,i]-CP; **211** *r*[d]-MSC, *l*-SLPD; **212** CF; **213** *t*-MMPI, *c*-SLML; **214** *t*-*b*[v,lr]-PF; **215** *t*-PF, *b*[v]-SLML; **217** PF; **218** *t*-*b*-MSA/MC; **219** *t*-*b*-PF; **220** PF; **221** PF; **222** *t*-SHS, *b*[v]-GMC; **223** MP; **224** *c*[d]-PF/SLGD, *b*-PF; **225** *t*-MMPI/PF, *b*[d,s]-PF; **Stark: 226** *t*-JBS, *l*-*r*-*b*-SBNO; **227** *r*[d]-MSC, *l*[v,lr]-SBNO; **228** SLPD; **229** *t*[lr]-SHS/SLPD, *b*-CF; **230** *l*-AP, *r*[d]-SHS; **231** SHS; **232** [dc]-MMPI; **233** GMC; **234** MSA/CID; **235** *t*[d]-MMPI, *b*-MSA; **236** SLPD; **237** *t*-*b*[d,s]-JBS; **Donnell: 238** GC; **239** *t*[d]-MSC, *b*[v]-SHS; **240** CF; **241** *t*[d]-UMCA, *b*[d]-DF; **242** DF; **243** [d]-MHP; **244** GC; **246** *t*[lr]-MMPI, *b*-GMC; **247** *t*-SLPD, *b*-SLML/AP; **Donnelly: 248** [dc]-MMPI; **249** *t*[d]-MSC, *b*-WHMC; **250** SLPD; **251** *t*-DYF, *b*-SLPD; **252** *t*-SLML, *bl*-SLPD, *br*[d]-MHP; **253** DF; **254** GMC; **255** SHS; **256** *t*[d]-WHMC, *b*-GC; **257** *t*-MDT, *bl*[dc]-SWB, *br*[v]-MMPI; **258** *t*-SLML, *b*[v]-SLPD; **259** *t*-MMPI, *b*[d]-DYF; **260** *t*[v]-EL, *b*-SLPD; **261** MHP; **Smith: 262** [dc]-MMPI; **263** *r*[d]-MSC, *l*-CF; **264** *r*-BF, *l*[v,lr]-MSA/MNG; **265** *l*[d]-MSA/MC, *r*-TL; **266** MSA; **267** SHS; **268** GMC; **270** UMCA; **271** SLPD; **Blair: 272** SWB; **273** [d]-MSC; **274** *t*-BF, *b*[v]-MSA/CID; **275** *t*-*bl*[d]-CCHS, *br*-MSA/MNG; **277** SHS/SLML/SLGB; **279** CCHS; **280** SLPD; **281** GMC; **282** SHS/KCS; **Dalton: 284** [dc]-SWB; **285** *r*[d]-MSC, *l*-HSTL/AP; **286** MMPI/BH; **287** [v]-WHMC; **288** *t*-WHMC, *l*-CF; **290** *t*-MSA/CID, *b*[dc]-SWB; **291** GMC; **292** WHMC; **293** *t*-SWB, *b*-MMPI; **294** *t*-SWB, *b*-WHMC/JCNT; **295** WHMC; **296** MSA; **297** *t*-SLML, *b*-MSA/CID; **298** MSA/CID; **299** SWB; **Hearnes: 300** HF; **301** *r*[d]-MSC, *l*-SLML; **302** *t*-CF, *b*-HF; **303** KCS; **304** *t*-SHS, *b*-MSA/MC; **305** [v]-MSA/MC; **306** *t*-*b*[lr]-HF; **307** MMPI; **308** MSA/MC; **309** MMPI/HF; **310** SLML/AP; **311** HF; **312** *t*[d]-SHS, *b*[d]-HF; **313** *t*[d]-*c*-*b*[d]-HF; **314** HF; **315** [lr]-GMC; **Bond: 318** MMPI; **319** *r*[d]-MSA, *l*-SHS/JCNT; **320** *t*-CF, *l*-*r*-SLML; **321** [v]-SLML; **323** *t*-SLML/AP, *b*[d]-MMPI; **324** MMPI; **325** *t*-MMPI, *b*[d]-AF; **326** MMPI; **327** MMPI; **328** MMPI; **329** SLML; **330** *t*-NAM/BT/FAAM, *b*[dc]-MMPI; **331** *t*-SLML, *b*-AP; **332** *t*-CB/UPI/SLML, *bl*-*br*[d]-MHP; **333** SLML/AP; **334** *t*-CF, *b*[v]-SLML; **335** MMPI; **Teasdale: 336** SLML; **337** *c*-MHP, *bl*[v,s]-KCS, *br*[v,i]-SLPD; **338** [v,lr]-TF; **339** [d]-KCS; **340** *t*[d]-KCS, *b*-TF; **341** [v]-SLPD; **342** *t*-SLML/AP, *b*[d]-TF; **343** [d]-SLML/AP; **344** [v]-TF; **345** *t*[d]-TF, *c*-CF, *bl*-SLPD/AP, *br*-CF; **346** [d]-TF; **347** TF; **348** SLML/AP; **349** MMPI; **Ashcroft: 350** MMPI; **351** HHS; **352** *t*[d]-MSA, *b*-BH; **353** *t*[d]-*b*-MHP; **354** MMPI; **355** SLML/SLGB; **356** SLPD; **357** [v]-SLML; **358** [v]-BH; **359** [d]-CML; **360** *t*-MHP, *b*-AP; **362** *t*-MSA/USN, *b*-MMPI; **363** [dc]-MMPI; **Carnahan: 364** [d]-MMPI; **365** *t*[d]-CF, *b*[d]-MMPI; **366** CF; **367** *t*[v]-CF, *b*-SLML/SLGB; **368** *t*[v]-*c*-*b*-CF; **369** *tl*-*tr*-CF, *b*-CF/KCS; **370** *t*-CF, *b*[v]-MHP; **371** *t*[v]-*b*-MHP; **372** [v]-CF/MDTR; **373** *t*-*bl*-*br*[d]-CF; **374** *t*-*tl*-*tr*[lr]-*c*-*crt*[d]-*crb*-*bl*-*br*-MMPI; **375** CF/MNG; **376** *t*[d]-MMPI, *cl*-*bl*[d]-CF, *r*[d]-MMPI; **377** *tl*-CF, *tr*-MMPI, *c*-CF, *b*[d]-MMPI; **378** *t*[v]-*c*-CF, *b*-MMPI; **379** *t*-*br*-MMPI, *bl*-CF; **380** MMPI; **381** MMPI; **382** *tl*-*tr*-MMPI, *b*[v]-SLPD; **383** [d]-CF; **384** [d]-JA; **385** MMPI; **A Look Back: 386-387** [d]-MBA; **388** *t*[d]-JD, *c*[d]-SHS, *bl*[d]-MSC, *br*[d]-SHS/MMC; **389** *t*[d]-MSC, *c*[d]-MSC, *b*[d]-SHS; **390** *l*[d,lr]-MSC, *r*[d]-SHS; **391** *l*[d]-MSC; *b*[d]-MMPI; **392** *l*[d]-MSC, *r*[d]-SHS, *b*[d]-BCHS; **393** *t*-MSA; *r*[d]-SHS; **394** *t*[d]-CCHS, *c*[d]-MSC, *b*-CF/ABC; **395** *l*[d]-MSC, *r*[d]-SHS; **396** *l*[d]-MSC, *r*[d]-SHS; **397** [d]-GL; **398** *tl*[d]-MSC, *tr*-SHS, *bl*[d]-MSC, *br*[d]-SHS; **399** *t*-SLAM, *b*[d,lr]-SHS; **400** *t*[v]-MMPI, *bl*[d]-MSC, *br*[d]-SHS; **401** *l*[d,lr]-SHS, *r*-SLML; **402** [v]-SHS; **403** *l*[d]-MSC, *r*[d]-SHS; **404** *tl*[d]-MSC, *tr*[d]-SHS, *bl*[d]-MSC, *br*[d]-SHS; **406** *l*[d]-MSC, *r*[d]-SHS; **407** *t*[d]-MSC, *b*[d]-SHS; **408** *t*[d]-MSC, *c*-*b*[d]-SHS; **409** *tl*[d]-MSC, *tr*[d]-SHS, *bl*[d]-MSC, *br*[d]-SHS; **411** *t*[d]-MSC, *b*[d]-SHS.

Photographers and Artists

Mary Pat Abele: 9-*c*, 184, 232, 246-*t*, 257-*br*, 325-*t*, 349-*b*, 364, 374-*crt*, 376-*t*, 377-*b*, 378-*b*, 379-*br*, 380-*cr*, 381-*cr-bl*, 382-*tr*, 400-*t*,

Jamie G. Anderson: 385-*sculpture* © 1994 Jamie G. Anderson. All rights reserved.

Roger Berg: xviii, 22, 40-*bl*, 45, 51, 56-*tl*, 66, 122, 188-*b*, 203-*t*, 235-*t*, 248, 293-*b*, 318, 325-*b*, 330-*b*, 362-*c*, 365-*t*

Bernstein-Rein: 374-*t*

Bob Diaz: 334-*bl*

Jim Dyke: xviii, xix, 2, 5, 9-*b*, 13, 18, 25, 31, 36, 44, 45, 58-*frm*, 60-*c*, 79, 90, 92, 120, 198, 213-*t*, 259-*t*, 388-*t*

L. Edward Fisher: 126-27, 386-87

Isabelle Francais: 95-*b*

T. Mike Fletcher: 306, 311

J. B. Forbes: 382-*b*

Dennis Garrels: xiii, 379-*bl*

Townsend Godsey: 94, 230-*r*, 231-*cr-br*

Hugo Harper and Neil Sauer: xii, 16, 56-*b*, 300(NS), 326, 327-*tl-tr-bl-br*; 328, 335, 363

Bob Hulsey: 352-*b*, 358

Clement Hurd: 15

David H. Kilper: 87

Gerald Massie: 218, 234, 235-*b*, 265-*l*, 266, 304-*b*, 305, 307, 308

Alise O'Brien: Jacket front, ii, iii, vi, vii, viii, ix, xvii, 9-*t*, 26, 130, 262, 323-*c*, 327-*cr*, 380-*tl-br*, 381-*tl-br*, 382*tl*, 385

Shanks Photography: 384

Saul Shore and Associates: 373, 383

John Bolton Stoeckley: 226-*t*, 237

Cecil W. Stoughton: 314

Lisa Heffernan Weil: Jacket back, 28, 48-*bck*, 67, 72, 88-*t*, 153-*b*, 374-*tl-tr-c-crb-bl-br*, 376-*r*, 377-*tr*, 379-*t*, 380-*tr-bl*, 381-*tr*

Official Whitehouse Photographer: 313-*t*

Wright Studio: 309, 312-*bl*

In addition to those listed above, we appreciate the efforts of everyone who helped locate the images for *If Walls Could Talk.*

SELECTED BIBLIOGRAPHY

With so few ready-made references available, most of the background material for this book was gleaned from newspapers, diaries, correspondence, scrapbooks, interviews, speeches, photographs, and manuscript collections. The resources from Missouri's statewide historical institutions, numerous local museums, and county historical societies were embellished by stories and anecdotes from first families, their decendents, former guests, friends, and staff about life at the Governor's Mansion with its many traditions. Newspapers from across the state added important information about Missouri politics, the hometown lives of first families, and the customs of the times. A day-by-day search through decades of Jefferson City newspapers gave a detailed look at life in the Capital City, as well as the many activities and events hosted by first families. The following items were particularly helpful in constructing the historical framework for Missouri's rich history and in discovering many of the Mansion's hidden stories.

Books and Articles:

Burckel, Nicholas Clare. "Progressive Governors in the Border States: Reform Governors of Missouri, Kentucky, West Virginia, and Maryland, 1900-1918." Ph.D. diss., University of Wisconsin, 1971.

Christensen, Lawrence O., and Gary R. Kremer. *A History of Missouri: Volume 4 1875 to 1919*. Columbia, Mo.: University of Missouri Press, 1997.

Coleman, Nadine Mills. *Mistress of Ravenswood*. Columbia, Mo.: Tribune Publishing, 1992.

Cooper, Martha. *The Civil War and Nodaway County, Missouri*. N.p.

Crittenden, Henry Huston. *The Crittenden Memoirs*. New York: G. P. Putnam's Sons, 1936.

Crittenden, Thomas T. "Selections from the Autobiography of Governor T. T. Crittenden." *Missouri Historical Review* 26 (1931-1932): 3-11, 142-52, and 241-55.

Dains, Mary K., ed. *Show Me Missouri Women: Selected Biographies*. Vol. 1. Kirksville, Mo.: Thomas Jefferson University Press, 1989.

Dains, Mary K., and Sue Sadler, eds. *Show Me Missouri Women: Selected Biographies*. Vol. 2. Kirksville, Mo.: Thomas Jefferson University Press, 1993.

Ferrell, Robert H. *Harry S. Truman: A Life*. Columbia, Mo.: University of Missouri Press, 1994.

Foley, William E. *The Genesis of Missouri: From Wilderness Outpost to Statehood*. Columbia, Mo.: University of Missouri Press, 1989.

Friedman, Robert Phillip. "The Public Speaking of Arthur M. Hyde." Ph.D. diss., University of Missouri-Columbia, 1954.

————. "The Candidate Speaks: Arthur M. Hyde." *Missouri Historical Review* 61 (1966-1967): 51-61.

Friends of John Ashcroft. *A Working Missouri: The Ashcroft Years, 1985-1993*. Jefferson City, Mo.: Friends of John Ashcroft, 1993.

Geiger, Louis G. "The Public Career of Joseph W. Folk." Ph.D. diss., University of Missouri-Columbia, 1948.

————. *Joseph W. Folk of Missouri*. Columbia, Mo.: Curators of the University of Missouri-Columbia, 1953.

Giffen, Jerena East. *First Ladies of Missouri: Their Homes and Their Families*. 2d ed. Jefferson City, Mo.: Giffen Enterprises, 1996.

Glashan, Roy, comp. *American Governors and Gubernatorial Elections, 1775-1975*. Stillwater, Minn.: Croixside Press, 1975.

Hahn, Harlan. "The Republican Party Conventions of 1912 and the Role of Herbert S. Hadley in National Politics." *Missouri Historical Review* 59 (1964-1965): 407-23.

Hamilton, Beryl Alex. "The Early Political Career of William Joel Stone." Master's thesis, University of Missouri-Columbia, 1950.

Hardin, Mary Barr. *Life and Writings of Governor Charles Henry Hardin*. St. Louis: Buschart Brothers Printers, 1896.

Jackson, William Rufus. *Missouri Democracy: A History of the Party and Its Representative Members--Past and Present*. 3 vols. Chicago: S. J. Clarke Publishing Co., 1935

Janke, Irene Brown. "'Regal Beyond Description': An Interpretation of the Dress of Margaret Nelson Stephens, First Lady of Missouri, 1897-1901." Master's thesis, University of Missouri-Columbia, 1991.

Kirkendall, Richard S. *A History of Missouri: Volume 5 1919 to 1953*. Columbia, Mo.: University of Missouri Press, 1986.

Lowe, James Lilburn. "The Administration of Arthur Mastick Hyde, Governor of Missouri, 1921-1925." Master's thesis, University of Missouri-Columbia, 1949.

March, David D. *The History of Missouri*. 4 vols. New York: Lewis Historical Publishing Company, 1967.

March, Julie. "Uncommon Women," *Ozarkswatch*. Forthcoming.

McCandless, Perry. *A History of Missouri: Volume 2 1820 to 1860*. Columbia, Mo.: University of Missouri Press, 1972.

McCullough, David. *Truman*. New York: Simon and Schuster, 1992.

Meyer, Duane Gilbert. *The Heritage of Missouri: A History*. Rev. ed. St. Louis: State Publishing Co., Inc., 1970.

"Missouri History Not Found in Textbooks: Are Inaugurations for the Officers or Their Wives?" *Missouri Historical Review* 43 (April 1949): 312-13.

Missouri Mansion Preservation, Inc. *Past & Repast: The History and Hospitality of the Missouri Governors Mansion*. Jefferson City, Mo.: Missouri Mansion Preservation, 1983.

Musick, John R. *Stories of Missouri*. New York: American Book Company, 1897

Nagel, Paul C. *Missouri: A Bicentennial History*. New York: W.W. Norton, 1977.

Nehring, Radine Trees. "Mary Whitney Phelps: Civil War S-Hero," *The Ozarks Mountaineer* (November/December 1993): 30-32.

Ohman, Marian M. "Missouri's Turn of the Century First Couple: Lawrence 'Lon' Vest and Margaret Nelson Stephens." *Missouri Historical Review* 91 (1996-1997): 250-73 and 406-30.

Park, Eleanora G. and Kate S. Morrow. *Women of the Mansion, 1821-1936*. Jefferson City, Mo.: Midland Printing, 1936.

Parrish, William E. *Missouri Under Radical Rule, 1865-1870*. Columbia, Mo.: University of Missouri Press, 1965.

————. *A History of Missouri: Volume 3 1860-1875*. Columbia, Mo.: University of Missouri Press, 1973.

Parrish, William E., Charles T. Jones, Jr., and Lawrence O. Christensen. *Missouri: The Heart of the Nation*. 2d ed. Wheeling, Ill.: Harlan Davidson, 1992.

Peterson, Norma L. "B. Gratz Brown: The Rise of a Radical, 1850-1863." Ph.D. diss., University of Missouri- Columbia, 1953.

————. *Freedom and Franchise: The Political Career of B. Gratz Brown.* Columbia, Mo.: University of Missouri Press, 1965.
Powell, Victor Morgan. "A Rhetorical Criticism of the Speeches of Herbert Spencer Hadley." Ph.D. diss., University of Missouri-Columbia, 1954.
Priddy, Bob. *Across Our Wide Missouri.* 3 vols. Independence, Mo.: Independence Press, 1982-1994.
Pusateri, Cosmo Joseph. "A Businessman in Politics: David R. Francis, Missouri Democrat." Ph.D. diss., St. Louis University, 1965.
Reddig, William M. *Tom's Town: Kansas City and the Pendergast Legend.* Columbia, Mo.: University of Missouri Press, 1986.
Rosenbaum, Alvin. *A White House Christmas.* Washington D.C.: The Preservation Press, 1992.
Settle, William A., Jr. *Jesse James Was His Name.* Columbia, Mo.: University of Missouri Press, 1966.
Shoemaker, Floyd Calvin, et al. *The Messages and Proclamations of the Governors of the State of Missouri.* 20 vols. Columbia, Mo.: The State Historical Society of Missouri.
Shoemaker, Floyd Calvin. *Missouri: Day by Day.* 2 vols. Columbia, Mo.: The State Historical Society of Missouri, 1942-1943.
————. *Missouri and Missourians: Land of Contrasts and People of Achievements.* 5 vols. Chicago: The Lewis Publishing Company, 1943.
Slavens, George Everett. "Lloyd C. Stark as a Political Reformer, 1936-1941." Master's thesis, University of Missouri-Columbia, 1957.
Sobel, Robert, and John Raimo. eds. *Biographical Directory of the Governors of the United States, 1789-1978*, Vol. 2. Westport, Conn.: Meckler Books, 1978.
Stevens, Walter B. *Missouri: The Center State, 1821-1915.* 4 vols. St. Louis: S. J. Clarke Publishing, 1915.
————. *Centennial History of Missouri: (The Center State) One Hundred Years in the Union, 1820-1921.* 6 vols. St. Louis: S. J. Clarke Publishing, 1921.
Stout, Laurie A. *Somewhere in Time: A 160 Year History of Missouri Corrections.* 2d ed. Missouri Department of Corrections, 1991.
Summers, Joseph S., Jr. *Pictorial Folk History of Jefferson City, Missouri, 1890-1900.* Jefferson City, Mo.: CeMoMedServ Publications, 1982.
————. *The Day the Capitol Burned, February 5, 1911: With a Brief Pictorial Review of the Development of Missouri and Its Capitols.* Jefferson City, Mo.: CeMoMedServ Publications, 1986.
Tally, Steve. *Bland Ambition: From Adams to Quayle - the Cranks, Criminals, Tax Cheats, and Golfers Who Made It to Vice President.* San Diego: Harcourt Brace Jovanevich, 1992.
Terry, Dickinson. *The Stark Story: Stark Nurseries 150th Anniversary.* St. Louis: Missouri Historical Society, 1966.
Thelen, David P. *Paths of Resistance: Tradition and Dignity in Industrializing Missouri.* New York: Oxford University Press, 1986.
Thompson, Cyrus. "Reminiscences of Official Life in Jefferson City, 1865-1875." *Missouri Historical Review* 23 (1928-1929): 550-67.
Thurman, A. L., Jr. "The Rhetorical Criticism of the Speaking of Joseph Wingate Folk." Ph.D. diss., University of Missouri-Columbia, 1953.
Towne, Ruth Warner. "The Public Career of William Joel Stone." Ph.D. diss., University of Missouri-Columbia, 1953.
Viles, Jonas. "Missouri Capitals and Capitols." *Missouri Historical Review* 13 (1918-1919) 135-56 and 232-50.
Williams, Walter. *The State of Missouri: An Autobiography.* Columbia, Mo.: Press of E. W. Stephens, 1904.
Williams, Walter and Floyd C. Shoemaker. *Missouri: Mother of the West.* 5 vols. Chicago: The American Historical Society, Inc., 1930.
Wofford, Theodore. *Missouri's Executive Mansion: A Long-range Development Study.* Missouri Mansion Preservation, Inc., 1975.
Worner, Lloyd Edson. "The Public Career of Herbert Spencer Hadley," Ph.D. diss., University of Missouri-Columbia, 1946.

Manuscript and Newspaper Collections:
Cole County Historical Society, Jefferson City, Missouri. Numerous collections and scrapbooks.
Missouri State Archives, Jefferson City, Missouri. Numerous collections including the Governors' Papers; Morning Music Club Scrapbooks, 1943-1992; and, Jane Randolph Chapter of the Daughters of the American Revolution, Scrapbooks.
Missouri State Historical Society, St. Louis, Missouri. Reference library and historical collections.
The State Historical Society of Missouri, Columbia, Missouri. Reference library, vertical files, and newspaper collections.
Western Historical Manuscript Collection, Columbia, Missouri. Numerous collections including the Benecke Family, Papers, 1816-1989; James T. Blair Jr., Papers, 1957-1961; Christopher S. Bond, Letter and Speech, SHS unp; Christopher S. Bond, Inaugural Remarks, 1973; Dutton Brookfield, Papers, 1844-1979; B. Gratz Brown, Letters, 1850; Henry S. Caulfield, Papers, 1878-1966; Henry S. Caulfield, Inaugural Ceremonies, 1929; Champ and Bennett Champ Clark Papers, 1853-1973; Thomas Theodore Crittenden Papers, 1880-1950; John M. Dalton, Papers, 1921-1965; Draper-McClurg Family, Papers, 1838-1981; Forrest Donnell, Inaugural Ceremonies, 1941; Forrest Donnell, Papers, 1941-1945; Phil M. Donnelly, Inaugural Ceremonies, 1953; Phil M. Donnelly, Papers, 1944-1957; Duncan-Jenkins-Hardin Family Papers, 1824-1904; Rory Vincent Ellinger, Papers, 1951-1973; Francis Marion Emmons, Civil War Letters, 1862-1864; Henry C. Fike, Diaries, 1851-1919; Stanley R. Fike, Papers, 1925, 1941-1985; Joseph Wingate Folk, Papers, 1902-1952; Sarah Guitar, Paper, 1931-1944; Hadley S. Hadley, Papers, 1830-1843; Charles H. and Mary J. Hardin Papers, 1828-1892; Charles M. Hay, Papers, 1919-1913; Betty Cooper Hearnes, Speech, 1971; Betty Cooper Hearnes, Tour unp; Warren E. Hearnes, Papers, 1950-1972; Arthur M. Hyde, Papers, 1919-1925; Lawrence Hyde, Papers; Kenneth C. Kaufman, story; Ben H. Lammers, Papers, n.d.; Nathaniel Leonard, Papers, 1800-1896; Edwin L. Miller Scrapbook, 1888-1897; Nadine Coleman Mills, "What Lon Stephens Said About Missouri"; Missouri Governors' Autographs, 1820-1941; Mary Phelps Montgomery, Letters, 1937-1939; Guy B. Park, Papers, 1932-1936; James S. Rollins, Papers, 1546-1968; Francis Asbury Sampson Collection, 1796-1958; Sappington Papers, 1831-1939; Forrest Smith, Papers, 1940-1953; Lloyd C. Stark, Papers, 1931-1941; Lloyd C. Stark, Papers, 1941-1972; Stephens letters unprocessed; Margaret Nelson Stephens Diary, 1897-1903; Kimbrough Stone, Papers, 1897-1958; William Joel Stone, Papers, 1878-1935; Sara Lockwood Williams, 1885-1961; and, Margaret Montgomery Zogbaum, "The Life of Mary Anne Phelps Montgomery, 1846-1942," 1967.

Family and Organization Collections:
Blair Family Photographs and Papers - Mary Margaret Blair and James Tom Blair III, St. Louis, Missouri; Donnell Family Scrapbooks - Ruth Donnell Rogers, St. Louis, Missouri; Donnelly Family Papers - David Donnelly, Lebanon, Missouri; Hearnes Family Papers - Betty Hearnes, Charleston, Missouri; Park Family Papers/Henrietta Park Krause Collection - Peggy Krause Adams; Smith Family Photographs - Forrestine Smith Lynn, Mary Joe Teterus, and Alicia Sue Hayes; Stephens Family Papers - Margaret Nelson Stephens' scrapbooks, diaries, and photographs, Charles Leonard, Ravenswood Farm, Cooper County, Missouri; Teasdale Family Photographs - Theresa Teasdale, Kansas City, Missouri; Tuesday Club Scrapbooks, Jefferson City, Missouri; and, "Governors and Governors' Wives, Nodaway County, Missouri" compiled by Martha Cooper, Maryville, Missouri.

NOTES

Abbreviations:
BWA - *Boonville Weekly Advertiser*
BWE - *Boonville Weekly Eagle*
CDT - *Columbia Daily Tribune*
CMO - *Columbia Missourian*
CMS - *Columbia Missouri Statesman*
FL - *First Ladies of Missouri*
HSTL - Harry S. Truman Library
JCDT - *Jefferson City Daily-Tribune*
JCPT - *Jefferson City Post-Tribune*

JCST - *Jefferson City State-Tribune*
KCDJ - *Kansas City Daily Journal*
KCJC - *Kansas City Daily Journal of Commerce*
KCS - *Kansas City Star*
KCT - *Kansas City Times*
MHR - *Missouri Historical Review*
MP - *Messages and Proclamations*
M&M - *Missouri and Missourians*
SDN - Springfield News

SLPD - *St. Louis Post-Dispatch*
SLGD - *St. Louis Globe-Democrat*
SLMR - *St. Louis Missouri Republican*
SLR - *St. Louis Republican*
SNL - *Springfield News-Leader*
WHMC - Western Historical Manuscript Collection, Columbia, Missouri
WM - *Women of the Mansion*

B. Gratz Brown

3 "This is the age of transition": Speech to the General Emancipation Society of the State of Missouri, St. Louis, 17 September 1862, quoted in Peterson, *Freedom and Franchise, 109.*

4 description of early St. Louis: Ibid., 13.

5 Dueling Governors: Stevens, *Missouri: The Center State,* 1: 687-99. Thomas Chaute Reynolds is sometimes confused with Governor Thomas Reynolds who served from 1840-1844.

6 "He assumes the dictator": Frank Blair to Montgomery Blair, 17 March 1859 quoted in *The Blair Family in Politics,* 1:460.

6 leniency toward rebels: Peterson, "B. Gratz Brown," 206.

7 women "did not bear arms": Peterson, *Freedom and Franchise,* 164.

7 campaign for governor: Ibid., 185.

7 "the most remarkable political revolution": Ibid., 188.

8 "dilapidated old shell": *JCPT,* 22 February 1871.

8 "You are welcome to a parlor": Governor Joseph McClurg to Governor-elect B. Gratz Brown, 30 December 1870, Missouri State Archives.

9 "unlucky mistake": Parrish, *History of Missouri,* 277.

10 "wallowing porkers": Giffen, *First Ladies of Missouri,* 95.

10 "New York society flung itself": John Burke, *Buffalo Bill: The Noblest Whiteskin* (New York: Putnam, 1973), 74.

10 "Imperial Highness": Byron Stewart, "The Meeting of Two Bears: Grand Duke Alexis at the Missouri Legislature," *MHR* 74 (1980-1981): 168-69, 177, 189.

11 "a pleasant chat": *SLR,* 24 January 1872.

11 "There is assembled here": *Missouri Democrat,* 25 January 1872.

11 "The hairdressers had their hands so full": *JCDT,* 5 December 1896.

12 "one of the most magnificent entertainments": *SLMR,* 25 January 1872.

12 "Gracious, graceful guests": *JCDT,* 5 December 1896.

12 "fearful crush. . . .ghastly" evening: Park and Morrow, *Women of the Mansion,* 158.

12 "Go on to the Senate, Henderson": Ibid., 180.

12 Klan activities: "Southeast Missouri Militia Enrolled to Fight the Ku Klux Klan," *MHR* 36 (1941-1942): 258.

13 looting of gangs: Meyer, *Heritage,* 506-7.

13 beard story: C. B. Rollins, ed., "Letters of George Caleb Bingham to James S. Rollins," *MHR* 33 (1938-1939): 68.

13 "all the advantages": Peterson, *Freedom and Franchise,* 163-64, 194.

13 "For the public good": *MP* 5:192-93.

13 "an earnest candidate": Schlesinger, *American Presidential Elections,* 1307.

14 "buttered his watermelon": Rollins, "Letters of George Caleb Bingham," 68; *BWE,* 3 April 1878.

14 "Boozy Brown": Tally, *Bland Ambition,* 150.

14 "fashionable and well-educated people": Type-written account of Colonel Anderson supporting Brown, Champ and Bennett Champ Clark Papers, WHMC.

14 "The split in the Republican ranks": William E. Parrish, review of *Freedom and Franchise: The Political Career of B. Gratz Brown,* by Norma L. Peterson, *MHR* 59 (1964-1965): 517.

14 "abundant prosperity": Shoemaker, *M&M,* 22.

15 "induct him rightly": B. Gratz Brown to James S. Rollins, 7 December 1872, James S. Rollins Papers, WHMC.

15 "political cauldron boiled": *U.S. Biographical Directory,* 200.

15 "taken so many sides": *SLMR,* 2 July 1870.

15 "Perhaps I am not the right man": Peterson, *Freedom and Franchise,* 178.

16-17 Missouri's Three Mansions: Shoemaker, *M&M,* 2:851; Park and Morrow, *WM,* 1; Summers, *The Day the Capital Burned,* 55; Marian M. Ohman, *The History of Missouri Capitols* (Columbia: University of Missouri--Columbia, Extension Division, 1982).

Silas Woodson

19 "huge rooms, magnificent furniture": Park and Morrow, *WM,* 194-97.

19 "When the party season is over": *JCDT,* 17 February 1874.

19 "Well-read, a brilliant conversationalist": Park and Morrow, *WM,* 197.

20 "elite of the state" devoured the inaugural spread: Ibid.

20 "with unflagging warmth": *JCPT,* 9 January 1873.

21 inaugural dance and attire: *St. Joseph Gazette,* 11 January 1873.

21 "greatness and grandeur": Park and Morrow, *WM,* 197.

22 The Newel Post Lady: Ibid., 198.

23 "The chandeliers, the door knobs": *JCPT,* 5 March 1873.

23 "light the gas, if": Ibid., 12 March 1873.

23 "extremely lavish": Park and Morrow, *WM,* 197.

24 "ordinary duties of life": David March, *History of Missouri,* 1:1083.

24 "with their former comrades in arms": Ibid., 1134.

24 "the beautiful belle of the state Capital": Park and Morrow, *WM,* 197.

25 "A Child's Fairyland": Ibid., 194-97.

Charles Hardin

27 "There is only one pledge": Floyd C. Shoemaker speech, 30 November 1961, Audrain County Historical Society, Mexico, Missouri.

27 "a lady of intelligence": Hardin, *Life and Writings of Governor Charles Hardin,* 205.

27 "Will our next governor permit dancing?" *JCPT,* 18 November 1874.

27 "caused many a sigh to rise": *CMS,* 15 January 1875.

28 "magnificent [and] attended by almost everyone": *JCPT,* 13 January 1875.

28 "fire of an honorable ambition. . . foundation for future respectability": Dr. Jewell to Charles Hardin quoted in Hardin, *Life and Writings,* 21-22.

28 "extraordinary ease [and] lucid diction": *Columbia Patriot,* October 1841 quoted in Park and Morrow, *WM,* 204.

28 "Delightful task!": Mary Barr Jenkins to Henry Duncan Jenkins, 13 May 1843, Duncan-Jenkins-Hardin Family Papers, WHMC.

28 "be worn out or out of fashion": Ibid.

28 "I now declare freely my love": Charles Hardin to Mary Barr Jenkins, 29 November 1842, Charles H. and Mary J. Hardin Papers, WHMC.

29 "miserable in his solitude": Hardin, *Life and Writings,* 208.

29 "lonely. . .weary. . .sad": Mary Jenkins Hardin, diary 1850s, Charles H. and Mary J. Hardin Papers.

30 "I shrink from strangers": Hardin, *Life and Writings,* 208.

30 venture "upon a stormy sea": Charles Hardin to Mary Hardin, 23 June 1874, Ibid., 210-11.

30 "bring not home": Charles Hardin to Mary Hardin, 23 August 1874 quoted in Hardin, *Life and Writings,* 209-10.

31 "great cloud of insects": *Excelsior Springs Daily Standard,* 30 April 1991.

31 "prayed the grasshoppers clear out of Missouri": "Missouriana: Plagues of the Past," *MHR* 31 (1936-1937): 62-63.

31 "come to the kingdom": *Bible,* Esther 4:14 KJV.

31 "pretend[ing] to know less": Margaret Truman, *First Ladies* (New York: Random House, 1995), 323.

31 "manna-like blessing. . . .No different from shrimp": Stevens, *Missouri: The Center State,* 573.

32 won the nomination by a "hairsbreath:" *Official Manual State of Missouri 1963-1964,* 19.

32 "the driest speaker": Ibid.

32 "loosely and carelessly": Hardin, *Life and Writings,* 43.

32 "no receptions at which people dared": *KCDJ,* 31 January 1877.

33 "that could make her pastor bat his eye": *St. Louis Times,* 1876 quoted in Hardin, *Life and Writings,* 56.

34 constantly wore black: Giffen, *FL,* 113.

34 Poem: *Land Without a Graveyard*: Hardin, *Life and Writings,* 215-16.

John Phelps

37 "Unfortunate marriage": Zogbaum, "The Life of Mary Anne Phelps Montgomery," WHMC, 3.

37 In addition to owing $500 for fabric and accessories, Mary Phelps left a $400 charge for the printing of 12,000 pamphlets with the fascinating title: "A Letter on the Subject of Matrimony." No copies of the work have been found. Julie March, "Uncommon Women" *Ozarkwatch.*

37 "that little Yankee boy": *SDN*, 8 June 1964.

38 A Run for the Money: Zogbaum, "Life of Mary Montgomery," 13-20.

39 A Frontier Bar Exam: *JCDT*, 14 March 1918.

40 Young John Phelps captured five Confederate prisoners during his first day in battle and later fought at Vicksburg. By the age of 24, he had earned the rank of general. Lockley, *Of the Journal Man*, 28 December 1926.

40 "I've come to cut": Zogbaum, "Life of Mary Montgomery," 27.

42 "to the immense task": Julie March, "Uncommon Women".

42 women "unsexed themselves": Parrish, Jones, and Christensen, *Missouri: Heart of the Nation*, 207.

42 petition was "premature" not "formally presented": Parrish, *Missouri Under Radical Rule*, 276.

42 "unwomenly women": Truman, *First Ladies*, 49.

42 the "New Woman": Betty Boyd Caroli, *First Ladies* (New York: Oxford University Press, 1987), 86.

43 "Don Juan Phelps": *BWA*, 11 August 1876.

43 "disliked the glad-hand": Zogbaum, "Life of Mary Montgomery," 57.

43 "devoid of display": *JCDT*, 13 January 1889.

44-45 Scandalous Behavior at the Mansion: *KCDJ*, 9, 30, and 31 January 1877 and 2 February 1877.

45 "But few laws are really necessary": *KCDJ*, 9 January 1877.

46 thirty-one-year-old hostess "queenly": *KCJC*, 2 February 1877.

46 first big labor revolt: David March, *History of Missouri*, 1144-45.

47 "partook of an oyster stew": *CMS*, 24 November 1886.

47 Mrs. Montgomery's final years: Julie March, "Uncommon Women"; *SNL*, 29 March 1943.

Thomas Crittenden

49 three promises: Crittenden, *Memoirs*, 57-58.

49 "big move in those days": Nagel, *Missouri*, 33.

50, 54 "Mother was never cut out for a political wife": Crittenden, *Memoirs*, 350.

50 "Am I dead, Philips?" Ibid., 495.

50 "Let's go on with the scrap": Ibid.

50 Crittenden and Cockrell held the distinction of representing the losing side in the lawsuit over the shooting of old Drum, the highly regarded foxhound eulogized by future Senator George Graham Vest in his closing argument before a Johnson County jury.

50 "a Democrat scarcely dared to live": *JCDT*, 8 June 1880.

51 "Kentucky lady": Park and Morrow, *WM*, 215.

52 How to Tell a Rebel from an Unionist: Crittenden, *Memoirs*, 69-70.

52 "first reception is always": *BWA*, 14 January 1881.

52 "should be painted inside": *MP*, 6:355-56.

52 "one of the most brilliant gatherings": *JCPT*, 9 February 1881.

54 "pet of her family": *BWA*, 22 December 1882.

54 "desolation and great sorrow": Park and Morrow, *WM*, 22.

54 bell story: Crittenden, *Memoirs*, 59.

55 Frank James surrender: *JCDT*, 6 October 1882; *JCSJ*, 6 October 1882; *SLMR*, 6 October 1882; David D. March, *Sobriquets of Missouri and Missourians*, MHR 72 (1977-1978) 258; *St. Joseph Herald*, 18 April 1882; Shoemaker, *M&M* 2:82.

56 "has been as carefully managed": Second Biennial Message, 7 January 1885 quoted in *MP* 6:427.

56 lay "poor Jesse in his grave": *CMS*, 29 January 1886.

57 "Having had long years of experience": Crittenden, *Memoirs*, 59.

57 "I Read My Obituary Four Times": Ibid., 314.

John Marmaduke

58 "Gentlemen, you see that capitol": *Columbia Herald*, 23 May 1896.

59 "He was not a lawyer": *KCS*, 20 August 1916.

59 "with plenty of servants": Ibid.

59 "John, there can be but one result": *MP*, 7:4.

60 Save Your Confederate Money: *CMS*, 16 March 1886.

61 some thought him "haughty and reticent": *SLPD*, 13 August 1884.

61 "Legislation. . . can successfully": *CMS*, 13 July 1883.

61 "political dynasty": Giffen, *FL*, 124.

62 "His first evening in office": *JCDT*, 13 January 1889.

62 "immaculately kept": Park and Morrow, *WM*, 222.

62 "We simply determined to make the best": Ibid.

63 wrestling story: Clark Papers.

63 "The walls are no longer bare": *JCDT*, 16 March 1886.

64 "dangerous to the health of a man": Shoemaker, *M&M*, 2:103.

65 "that if there was to be any drinking": *JCDT*, 7 May 1893.

65 "I will take charge of the railroad": *KCS*, 20 August 1916.

66 "entered into the spirit": *JCDT*, 10 December 1885.

66 funeral procession was the largest: *CMS*, 8 January 1888.

Albert Morehouse

69-70 war experiences: Martha Cooper, *Civil War and Nodaway County, Missouri*, part 2.

70 "dull and gloomy": *Nodaway County Democrat*, 11 January 1877.

70 "Some people are never satisfied": Cooper, *Nodaway Co. Legislators*, 13-15

70 "always attended the governor's reception en-masse": *Nodaway County Democrat*, Ibid.

71 "palace of pink": Park and Morrow, *WM*, 232.

71 "Mrs. President. . . Lovely Lady Presidentress . . . Her Serene Loveliness": Carl Sferrazza Anthony, *First Ladies: The Saga of the Presidents' Wives and their Power* (New York: W. Morrow, 1990), 84, 128.

71 "Madam Presidentress. . . Queen Dolley": Paul F. Boller, *Presidential Wives* (New York: Oxford University Press, 1988), 36.

71 "Mrs. Governor": *CMS*, 22 December 1876 and 2 February 1883; *JCDT*, 15 January 1889.

71 "Governess": Margaret Nelson Stephens diary, Charles Leonard Collection.

71 "Mistress Supreme. . . Our Lady of the Kind Heart": "The Romance of Lon and Maggie Stephens," Stephens scrapbook.

71 "first lady of the land": Caroli, *First Ladies*, 83.

72 "filling [women's] minds": Ibid., 231-32.

72 "scoundrelly liar": Clark Papers.

73 "depressed the finances of the state": Shoemaker, *M&M*, 2:107.

73 "welcomed all who. . .gathered in the City of Jefferson": Clark Papers.

73 "an ardent Prohibitionist.": *JCST*, 6 January 1888.

73 "I was offered money": *Nodaway Democrat*, 1 October 1891.

73 took his own life: *JCDT*, 24 September 1891. Missouri's fifth Governor, Thomas Reynolds, committed suicide in 1844 while living in the former executive residence.

73 Non-elected governors: "Where Missouri Governors Came From," *MHR* 43 (1948-1949): 315.

David Francis

75 "he puts off everything": *JCDT*, 27 November 1892.

75 "I was never satisfied": *Valley Magazine*, September, 1903.

76 the "New St. Louis": Ibid.

77 engaged in "grain gambling" and once voted Republican: *SLR*, 20 June 1888 quoted in Pusateri, "A Businessman in Politics: David R. Francis, Missouri Democrat," 110.

77 "the annoyances of official life": Letter of C.E. Perkins, 8 December 1888 quoted in Pusateri, "A Businessman in Politics," 128.

78 "dainty and exquisite": Park and Morrow, *WM*, 235.

78 "the bell is broken": Giffen, *FL*, 132.

79 Pet gripes: *JCDT*, 18 July 1891, 20 and 26 August 1891, and 30 March 1893.

80 "Two finely polished French-glass doors": Park and Morrow, *WM*, 248.

80 Mansion painted red: Ibid. Over the years approximately thirty more coats would be added. Not until the Hearnes administration did technology make it possible to remove the accumulation without damaging the brick.

81 "the mecca of all legislators": Park and Morrow, *WM*, 251.

81 "the most outstanding ladies": Ibid., 239.

82 "throbbing with life": Shoemaker, *M&M*, 2:120.

83 "I think it would be small compensation": Park and Morrow, *WM*, 243.

83 "engine in breeches": Shoemaker, *M&M*, 2:120.

84 The only remains of the St. Louis home located on Newstead Avenue, one block west of Lindell Boulevard, is the entry gate and stone fence. *SLGD*, 16 January 1927.

84 "Every exposition is a great international peace congress": *MP*, 7:213-14.

85 "We found tracks of Francis": *JCST*, 20 January 1902.

85 "most dangerous and undesirable": *JCDT*, 1 February 1918.

85 "moving from place to place": Walter B. Stevens, "Ambassador Francis' Book," *MHR* 15 (1920-1921): 735.

85 "stood off a mob": *JCDT*, 1 February 1918.

85 "Every one seemed to prefer": *SLPD*, 16 January 1927.

85 intrigued by Russians: Talton Ray interview with author, 20 September 1996.

86 "Mr. Ambassador, what do you think?": *MP*, 7:216.

86 The family moved to the suburbs. That final home still stands at 6464 Ellenwood Avenue in Clayton, Mo. Kevin Amsler, *Final Resting Place: The Lives and Deaths of Famous St. Louisans* (St. Louis: Virginia Publishing Co., 1997).

86 "thirty-six feet of Democrats": *Saturday Evening Post*, 12 March 1910 quoted in Pusateri, "Businessman in Politics," 26; Stephens scrapbook.

86 "If there is anything in him": *MP*, 7: 208-09.

87 his view of the future: David March, *History of Missouri*, 2:1162.

87 The Ugly Club: Ralph E. Morrow, *Washington University in St. Louis: A History* (St. Louis: Missouri Historical Society Press, 1996), 111.

88 "First in shoes,": Ernest Kirschten, *Catfish and Crystal* (Garden City, NY: Doubleday, 1965), 37.

88 "Meet me in St. Louis": Meyer, *Heritage*, 504-5; Parrish, Jones, and Christensen, *Heart of the Nation*, 275.

89 Mark Twain and the fair: *World's Fair Bulletin* 10, no. 12 (June 1995).

William Stone

91 "The greater the storm": Shoemaker, *M&M*, 2:145.

91 "tall, thin, ragged": Hamilton, "Early Political Career of William Joel Stone," 2-3.

91 "rumored in Columbia that Stone": *CDT*, 14 April 1915.

92 physical description: *SLPD*, 8 January 1893.

92 "the men one by one got up": Interview with Stone's son, Judge Kimbrough Stone quoted in Hamilton, "Early Political Career," 6.

92 "any irresistible public pressure": Ibid., 30.

93 Description of Stone's campaign and attire: Ibid., 31-32.

93 "Trial Number One": Park and Morrow, *WM*, 261.

93 "In the short intervening time": Ibid., 252-53.

93 "all the visitors in the city": *JCDT*, 10 January 1893.

94 "a dripping and disfigured ceiling": Park and Morrow, *WM*, 255-56.

95 "The money could not be spent": *JCDT*, 17 May 1893.

95 "betterment of women": *JCDT*, 9 December 1892.

95 "That is where Stone lives": Ibid.

95 "ever-changing official population": Park and Morrow, *WM*, 258.

96 "that cozy part of the large lower hall": Ibid.

97 Victorian Visitors: Ibid.; Rosenbaum, *A White House Christmas*, 65; *JCDT*, 9 December 1892.

97 "exasperating incident": Shoemaker, *M&M*, 2:152.

98 "a match for any man": Hamilton, "Early Political Career," 116.

98 Train incident: *JCDT*, 30 July 1909.

98 "pussyfoot states[man]": *BWA*, 16 March 1917 as quoted in Lawrence O. Christensen, "Prelude to World War I in Missouri," *MHR* 89 (1994-1995): 13.

99 "War will be declared": *St. Louis Star*, 8 March 1920 quoted in Jackson, *Missouri Democracy*, 1:245.

99 "I had nothing to do with this": Ibid.

99 "Gumshoe Bill": *SLGD*, 15 April 1918.

99 "stormy political career": *JCDT*, 15 April 1918.

Lon Stephens

101 "joyous social whirl": Janke, "Regal Beyond Description," 104.

101 teenage courtship: Coleman, *Mistress of Ravenswood*, 60.

102 "royal gift": Stephens scrapbook.

103 "Oh, the changes. Think of me": Coleman, *Ravenswood*, 53.

103 "I wouldn't care if he could be appointed": Stephens scrapbook.

104 "I am opposed to Mr. Stephens": Stephens scrapbook.

104 "the vexation of politics": Ohman, "Missouri's Turn-of-the-Century First Couple," *MHR* 91 (1996-1997): 270-71.

104 "Such excitement!": Coleman, *Ravenswood*, 53.

105 "We'll not send formal invitations": *JCDT*, 13 January 1898 quoted in Janke, "Regal Beyond Description," 105.

105 "scarcely habitable": *JCPT*, 27 January 1899.

106 "collision [course] between historically-minded preservationists": *CMO*, 6 November 1947.

106 her wardrobe: Coleman, *Ravenswood*, 54.

106 "that mean fox terrier": Ibid., September 23, 1897; Stephens diary.

107 mauled "by a circus wolf. . . died after swallowing": Giffen, *FL*, 145.

107 "frappe. . .in the Turkish alcove": Stephens scrapbook.

108 antics of Ruth Bryan: Coleman, *Ravenswood*, 56.

108 "I'm seeing it all, you bet!": Stephens scrapbook.

110 bicycle race: *JCDT*, 22 April 1897.

110 "the complete eclipse": Stephens scrapbook.

111 "Mansion set": Coleman, *Ravenswood*, 56.

111 "the best girl in the world": Ibid., 19.

111 "Lon ran down and brought me up ginger": Janke, "Regal Beyond Description," 58.

112 "Whiskey is the cause": Stephens diary, 3 July 1897.

112 "dance, waltz, pay court to the ladies": Stephens scrapbook.

112 her "objection to politics": Stephens diary, 9 March 1900.

112 "to rise early and attend Sunday School": Coleman, *Ravenswood*, 57.

113 "made a school yard out of the Mansion": Stephens scrapbook.

113 "penitentiary babies": Stephens diary.

113 "Our Lady of the Kind Heart": Ibid.

113 "introduced his wife as the 'Lieutenant Governor'": Ibid.

113 "If I can lighten their burdened hearts": Ibid.

114 "mingled with the male lobbyists": Stephens scrapbook.

114 Governor a victim of "petticoat rule": Ibid.

114 "I can truthfully say": Coleman, *Ravenswood*, 58.

114 "A model woman": Stephens diary.

114 "right to govern and direct public affairs abhorrent": Stephens diary, July 15, 1897.

115 Missouri's Medicine Man: Stephens scrapbook.

116 "Of course I did not sign it": Stephens diary, 12 February 1895.

116 "Oh, will I never hear. . . . laughed about it many times": Stephens scrapbook.

116 criticism "brutal" and "despicable": Ibid.

116 "lays bare the heart": Stephens scrapbook.

116 "nervous spells. . . quieting pill": Stephens diary.

117 "the most wretched prison": Ohman, "Turn-of-the-Century First Couple," 418.

117 "it's like being banished from heaven": Coleman, *Ravenswood*, 69.

117 "I am so sad tonight": Ibid., 66.

117 "I've had enough of politics": Stephens scrapbook.

117 "crying evil of the times": Shoemaker, *M&M*, 2:175.

117 "I go out from the governorship": *BWA*, February 1, 1901 quoted in Ohman, "Turn-of-the-Century First Couple."

118 "Thank God, they can no longer say": Stanley Benton Botner, "The Office of Governor of the State of Missouri" (Ph.D. diss., University of Missouri-Columbia, 1963), 68.

118 "shockingly delicate": Stephens diary.

118 a "disappointment" because he would not "speak out": Ibid.

119 "[I] put on my inauguration dress": Ibid., 73.

119 "I hardly ever go to church": Ibid., 71.

119 traveled and built home,: Janke, "Regal Beyond Description," 62; Coleman, *Ravenswood*, 73.

119 "Maggie and the Charleston": Janke, "Regal Beyond Description," 63.

119 "Queen of Missouri": *JCDT*, 27 January 1899; Coleman, *Ravenswood*, 62.

Alexander Dockery

121 "a very quiet, retiring lady": Park and Morrow, *WM*, 278.

122 Dockery's Secret Weapon: *CMO*, 18 November 1926; Stevens, *Centennial History of Missouri, 1820-1921*, 1:650.

123 "I don't know what it is": *JCST*, 20 April 1901.

123 Dockery description: "gritty". . . . aggressively economical. . . the "watchdog of the treasury": *MP*, 9:5, 13; *JCST*, 5 August 1904.

123 "Unnecessary taxation lead to surplus": *MP*, 9:7

123 supporter of the Spanish-American War: Stevens, *Center State*, 2:447.

123 "the best he could do": *JCST*, 2 October 1900.

124 "great deference:" Katherine Motley, essay about Mrs. Dockery.

124 "a delicate woman" *JCST*, 9 January 1901.

124 "plain man and he likes plain things. . . still wears boot": Ibid.

124 "bristling Van Dyke" beard: *BWA*, 28 May 1926.

124 "contribution towards advancement": *JCDT*, 27 December 1926.

124 Dockery wink: *JCST*, 9 January 1901.

125 "I had only one rule": Park and Morrow, *WM*, 291.

126 "Whenever a legislature meets": *JCST*, 2 October 1900.

127 "enthusiastic friend of education": Howard L. Conrad, ed., *Encyclopedia of the History of Missouri* (St. Louis: The Southern History Company, 1901), 2:284-87.

127 "would not be the least bit unhappy": Park and Morrow, *WM*, 289.

128 "awe and deepest responsibility": Ibid., 285.

128 "One leaves it at the close of her stewardship": Ibid.

129 "change dinner": Giffen, *FL*, 150.

129 last of the old-guard Democrats: Shoemaker, *M&M*, 2:196.

129 "best of times. . . . the worst of times": Charles Dickens, *A Tale of Two Cities* (London: Chapman and Hall, 1859).

129 "afraid my friends might try": *BWA*, 28 May 1926.

Joseph Folk

131 "No real lady": Park and Morrow, *WM*, 292.

131 "My husband. . .knew the 'game'": Ibid.

132 "another country boy": May Folk Webb, incomplete biography of Joseph W. Folk, Folk Papers, WHMC.

132 "I am neither a Democrat": Shoemaker, *M&M*, 2:221.

133 "a thin-lipped, firm mouthed". . . who "goes ahead doing": A. L. Thurman Jr., "Joseph Wingate Folk," *MHR* 17 (1922-1923): 182.

133 "limp and flabby thing": Geiger, "Joseph W. Folk of Missouri," 57.

133 "the Missouri idea": Nagel, *Missouri*, 148-50.

134 "Folk is not running": Shoemaker, *M&M*, 2:225.

134 "a touch of the old home": Park and Morrow, *WM*, 296.

134 "sermon on public morality": Shoemaker, *M&M*, 228.

135 inaugural reception: Park and Morrow, *WM*, 297-98.

135 time at the Mansion "an adventure": Ibid., 295.

135 Mrs. Folk and newsmen: Ibid., 305.

136 Toting Privileges: Ibid., 305-6.

137 "mountain of disorder": Geiger, "Joseph W. Folk," 13.

137 "boomed for the presidency": Thurman, "Rhetorical Criticism," 71, 81.

137 he "almost never" spoke: Geiger, "Joseph W. Folk," 106.

137 The First Lady. . .organized the Jefferson City Music Club": The club still remains active nearly ninety years after its first meeting at the Mansion. In remembrance of Mrs. Folk, the club continues to grant

honorary membership to each First Lady. Stephens scrapbook.

137 Christmas toys: Giffen, *FL*, 152.
138 "My first visit": Park and Morrow, *WM*, 303.
138 "fit for a king": Ibid.
138 "a hundred tubes of fire dust": *JCDT*, 24 October 1905
139 "I felt that nothing but tapestry": Park and Morrow, *WM*, 303.
140 "the man who cleaned up Missouri politics": Floyd C. Shoemaker, "Missouri's Tennessee Heritage," *MHR* 49 (1954-1955): 133.
140 "repression rather than progress": Reddig, *Tom's Town*, 62.
140 enforced blue laws: Thelen, *Paths of Resistance*, 240.
141 "master busybody": Ibid., 250.
141 "the Sunday saloon": Ibid., 240.
141 "I found out how the place": Park and Morrow, *WM*, 298.
141 "peacefully, but no joyfully": Ibid.
142 "Not even the Governor's enemies": *SLPD*, 8 January 1909 quoted in Thurman, "Rhetorical Criticism," 98.
143 "made more history": Ibid., 8
143 "Even the fireplace": Park and Morrow, *WM*, 306.
143 "Isn't this an era": Giffen, *FL*, 154.
143 "sort of a hero": Thurman, "Joseph Wingate Folk," 109.

Herbert Hadley

145 "We want Hadley": Hahn, "The Republican Party Convention of 1912," 411.
145 "one of the coldest days": Park and Morrow, *WM*, 312.
146 "Come home at once": Shoemaker, *M&M*, 2:245.
146 "most famed for his prosecution": Ibid., 242.
147 "Let the children play on the grass": Ibid., 321.
148 "You are the only man": Ibid., 241.
148 "Nineteen twelve, Oh, oh, oh": *JCDT*, 12 January 1909.
149 snow blew into the hall: Giffen, *FL*, 155.
149 "from the highest in station": *JCDT*, 12 January 1909.
149 "My dress was white satin": Park and Morrow, *WM*, 312.
149 "a grand affair that took place in another blizzard": Ibid., 317.
149 "It was essential for him": Ibid., 313.
150 looked "very handsome and comfortable": Ibid.
150 "Many a time those portraits": Ibid.
151 "Aunt Hattie. . .who couldn't either read or write": Ibid.
151 "he ate slowly and talked": Ibid., 315.
152 "May I ask you": Park and Morrow, Ibid., 320.
152 "there was a constant flow. . . Former Governor Francis once dropped by "to see it the Mansion": Ibid.
152 "All the mothers were busy": Ibid., 322, 153
152 Both of Hadley's sons followed him into law. John Hadley ran unsuccessfully for Congress and drew some attention as a possible candidate for governor in 1940. Herbert Hadley, Jr., died of appendicitis at the age of twenty-seven. Shoemaker, *M&M*, 5:6.
153 "One morning I was called": Park and Morrow, *WM*, 323.
153-54 children pleading for help: Ibid.
154 Governor vs. Artist: *JCDT*, 18 January 1912 and 2 January 1913.
155 "suspicious looking woman": *JCDT*, 27 August 1909.
155 "While economy in government": Nagel, *Missouri*, 151.
155 "the longest and one of the least productive": Burckel, "Progressive Governors in the Border States," 135.
155 "first Republican governor": *JCDT*, 16 September 1910.
155 "wanton extravagance": *JCDT*, 13 December 1909.
156 A Sudden Stroke of Lightning: *JCPT*, 5 February 1952; Stout, *Somewhere in Time*, 38; Park and Morrow, *WM*, 326.
157 "Weekends, vacations, holidays": Park and Morrow, *WM*, 316.
157 "knows almost as much about poultry": *CMO*, 11 January 1912.
158 convention: Hahn, "The Republican Party Convention of 1912," 417.
158 gave Taft a very tepid endorsement: *JCDT*, 19 June 1912.
158 "The Governor was deeply touched": Park and Morrow, *WM*, 327.
158 "I wish I could put another dress on mother": *St. Joseph News Press*, 19 February 1961.

Elliott Major

161 "Walked courageously": Park and Morrow, *WM*, 330.
162 His "four-fold aim": Shoemaker, *M&M*, 2:272.
162 "place [their] feet upon the middle path": *MP* 11:10.
162 "one of the principals in the event": Park and Morrow, *WM*, 330.
162 space "she occupied could be covered": *JCDT*, 15 January 1913.
163 "like a statue": Park and Morrow, *WM*, 331.
163 Colonels. . .will "clank their swords": *JCDT*, 28 December 1913.
163 "There is no silly froth": Park and Morrow, *WM*, 335-36.
163 superstitious: *SLR*, 12 March 1915.
164 victim of golf fever: *JCDT*, 29 November 1913.

165 "We never grew weary": Ibid., 335.
167 "touching the human side of life": *JCDT*, 6 January 1917.
167 "swept off their feet ": Park and Morrow, *WM*, 336.
167 the good roads, good schools governor: Stevens, *Center State*, 6.

Frederick Gardner

169 "A poor boy can rise": Park and Morrow, *WM*, 343.
169 "A dream come true": *Official Manual of the State of Missouri 1963-1964*, 25-26.
169 business manager of the state: Shoemaker, *M&M*, 2:280-81.
170 "She has the money to entertain": Stephens scrapbook.
170 "except that his knuckles": *JCDT*, 8 January 1917.
170 "May all your day": Park and Morrow, *WM*, 344.
170 "take hold first": Ibid., 345.
171 "This caused little comedies": Ibid., 347.
171 "Everyone would leave bedroom doors ajar": Ibid., 350.
171 a "reckless spendthrift": Shoemaker, *M&M*, 2:280.
172 Romance at the Mansion: Park and Morrow, *WM*, 348-49.
173 "It's too bad that the Governor": Ibid., 353-54.
173 "There is no time for slackers": *MP*, 11:250.
174 son goes to war: Park and Morrow, *WM*, 356-65.
175 Prohibition: Ibid., 367.
175 "could not stand the thought": Ibid.
176 women's suffrage issue: Ibid., 374-75.
176 highway program: Parrish, Jones, and Christensen, *Heart of the Nation*, 293.
177 "Jeannette wears feathers up": poem by Betty Lee Pettingill, Ibid., 370-71.
177 "A new regime": Park and Morrow, *WM*, 376.

Arthur Hyde

179 "Art Hyde gave a man more to think about": Shoemaker, *M&M*, 2:104.
180 "If I had a drop of Republican blood": Freidman, "Candidate Speaks," 52.
180 "More ambition than political judgment. . . .doomed for slaughter": Ibid.
181 "Are You Wet or Dry": Freidman, "Candidate Speaks," 59-60; *SLPD*, 29 July 1920.
182 "The crowds . . . the reception tired me": Park and Morrow, *WM*, 379.
182 "defied critics and hecklers": *Our Glorious Century*, (Pleasantville, NY: The Reader's Digest Association, Inc., 1994), 109.
183 "to legislate Democrats out": David March, *History of Missouri*, 1317.
183 "unmitigated evils": *JCDT*, 27 April 1922; Lowe, "The Administration of Arthur Mastick Hyde, Governor of Missouri," 123.
183 opposition to the governor: Lowe, "Administration of Hyde," 125-30; *JCDT*, 28 June and 3 October 1921; Freidman, "The Public Speaking of Arthur M. Hyde," 153; *Daily Capital News*, 13, 15, 27, 28 July 1921 and 4 November 1921.
183 "He is not a Republican": *St. Louis Censor* quoted in *JCDT*, 28 June 1921.
184 Mansion Casanova: Stout, *Somewhere in Time*, 55.
184 The Governor revived his programs: Freidman, "Public Speaking," 131; Meyer, *Heritage*, 589-90; Shoemaker, *M&M*, 2:306.
184 restoration work: Park and Morrow, *WM*, 379-81; Giffen, *FL*, 171 and 173.
185 daughter pleaded "more eloquently": Park and Morrow, *WM*, 391.
185 "as eager to be pleased" as she was to please them: Ibid., 382.
186 preserve "likenesses of oneself when younger": Ibid., 384.
187 lighthouse story: Friedman, "Public Speaking," 145.
187 "refusal to surrender ": *JCDT*, 13 January 1925.
187 something with "enduring practicality": Park and Morrow, *WM*, 382.
188 "The First Daughter: The Official Nuisance:" Ibid., 386-91. The so-called "Newel Post Lady," referred to by Caroline Hyde was removed in the late thirties by First Lady Katherine Stark who felt it distracted from the grandeur of the stairway.
189 the house has been "thoroughly gone over": *JCDP*, 9 January 1925.
189 "I cannot change my view": Sobel and Raimo, *Biographical Directory of the Governors of the United States*, 2:862.
189 Attitude toward Roosevelt: Caroline Hyde quoted in Friedman, "Public Speaking," 377.
189 "I love every brick in it": Park and Morrow, *WM*, 391.

Samuel Baker

191 "the greatest throng in state history": *JCPT*, 13 January 1925.
192 "We had the advantage": Park and Morrow, *WM*, 392.
193 "Common as an old shoe": *Missouri Ruralist* quoted in Baker campaign brochure, WHMC.
193 "mingled joy and reluctance": Park and Morrow, *WM*, 392.
193 bed of roses: Ibid.
193 "I'm thoroughly patriotic": *JCDP*, 19 June 1925.
193 "Fire half your employees": Ibid., 10 March 1925.
194 "climaxed a fifteen-year struggle": Shoemaker, *M&M*, 2:322.
194 "to use the Mansion if any important": *KCS*, 22 October 1933.

195 The Military Ball: *JCPT*, 24 January 1931.
195 "Flying Fool": *Our Glorious Century*, 115.
196 "I had hoped to obtain portraits": Park and Morrow, *WM*, 400.
196 effects of criticism on Baker's health: *JCPT*, 10 May 1992; Shoemaker, *Day by Day*, 341.
197 "The world does not owe you": *JCPT*, 18 June 1926 and 21 May 1927.

Henry Caulfield

199 "very strenuous and grueling experience. . . . We traveled incessantly": Frances Caulfield, "My Life at the Mansion," 2.
199 "I feel like a debutante": Francis Caulfield to her daughter Jane Caulfield, 28 November 1928, Henry S. Caulfield Papers, WHMC.
200 Republican Tide of 1928: Tally, *Bland Ambition*, 251; David March, *History*, 1:1353; Park scrapbook.
201 "true Missouri simplicity": *JCPT*, 2 January 1929.
202 "fairyland [where] things I want come so easily": Francis Caulfield diary, 8 June 1929, Caulfield Papers.
202 "It is so easy here": Ibid.
202 seemed like a "pretty big" sum: Ibid., 21 January 1929.
202 "winding floating stairway": Caulfield, "My Life at the Mansion," 4.
203 elevator signal: *JCPT*, 18 January 1929.
204 feared he was "neglecting the legislators": Caulfield diary, 19 March 1929.
204 "I spent my time shaking hands": Ibid., 26 February 1929.
204-5 ambassador's visit: Ibid., 14 May and 8 June 1929.
205 "An armed guard was always with them": Caulfield, "My Life at the Mansion," 6-7.
205 "The kitchen was in the basement": Ibid., 6.
206 "the mist rise from the willows": Caulfield diary, 29 May 1929.
206 to form "cozy corners": *JCPT*, 6 and 12 July 1929.
206 "there is always something more to do here": Caulfield diary, 30 May 1929.
206 When the Governor is trying to be very quiet": Giffen, *FL*, 185.
206 "No one but the [waste]basket and I are the wiser": Frances Caulfield, *Missouri Ruralist* 74 (April 1, 1931): 7, 11.
206 map collection: Giffen, *FL*, 184.
207 "commercialism, speed and industrialism": *JCPT*, 22 August 1929.
207 "least politically-inclined governor": Shoemaker, *M&M*, 2:340, 335, 350.
208 "the blunder of his administration": *MP*, 13:8.
209 a distant relative of FDR: Giffen, *FL*, 180.
209 "We like them [the Parks] immensely": Henry Caulfield to his daughter Jane Caulfield, 7 December 1932, Caulfield Papers.
209 The First Lady's Hemline: *SLGD Sunday Magazine*, 1 April 1962.

Guy Park

211 Description of Park home: Park scrapbook; *St. Joseph Gazette*, 13 November 1932.
211 Move to Jefferson City: *Weston Chronicle*, 23 June 1933; Park scrapbook; *KCS*, 8 January 1933; *KCDJ*, 29 December 1932.
211 "profession full of temptations": Dains, *Show Me*, 1:194.
212 "Audible weeping of older relatives": Ibid.
212 "Uncle Tom's Cabin": Reddig, *Tom's Town*, 202-03.
212 "I'll have to admit, I'm boss-ridden": *KCT*, 23 October 1932.
212 "did not consider himself a machine candidate": Ferrell, *Harry S. Truman*, 126.
212 "Boys, I'm not used to all this": *KCS*, 14 October 1932.
213 Colonels and Cannons: *Springfield Leader*, 7 January 1945; *Joplin Globe*, 21 February 1933; Park scrapbook.
214 "I consider it my duty": Park scrapbook.
214 "I have helped him read": *St. Joseph Gazette*, 13 November 1932.
215 greeted reporters in his bathrobe: Ibid., 9 November 1932.
215 "the coolest cuss I've ever seen": *KCS*, 17 October 1932.
215 Platte County swarmed to Capital City: *Platte City Landmark*, 13 January 1933.
216 "I am a Baptist": Dains, *Show Me*, 1:194.
216 An "Italian chest [sits] across the hall": *Weston Chronicle*, 23 June 1933.
218 The Beaten Biscuit: Johnston, *Harbinger Magazine*, 15-18.
219-20 Ada Boyd: Park scrapbook; Shoemaker *M&M*, 2:353; *KCS*, 28 January 1933.
220 "The people of Missouri are now my neighbors": *Weston Chronicle*, 16 June 1933.
220 "wouldn't even bite a Republican": *St. Louis Star*, 17 October 1932; Henrietta Park Krause, interview with author, Governor's Mansion, 5 January 1995.
220 "The lawn was a great source of pride to me": Park and Morrow, *WM*, 417.
221 NGA: Ibid., 415-16.
222 "Ada, why did you do this?": *KCS*, 21 May 1934.

222 "Yes, I really like to cook": *KCDJ*, 2 January 1933.
223 "I was appalled to find that no records": *St. Joseph Gazette*, 13 November 1932.
223 The last marriage of a governor's offspring while in office occurred in the previous Mansion in 1835 with the wedding of Governor Dunklin's oldest daughter, Mary.
223 "We never even mentioned politics": *KCS*, 17 November 1933.
224 Park accomplishments: *KCS*, 7 April 1933; Shoemaker, *M&M*, 2:363; Meyer, *Heritage*, 641; David March, *History*, 1366.
225 "back in old Platte": Guy Park to A. D. Gresham, 5 February 1935.
225 "He was just himself": Park scrapbook.

Lloyd Stark

227 "There are the red coats and they are ours": *Jefferson City Sunday News-Tribune*, 10 January 1937.
228 "Boys, never stop advertising": Terry, *The Stark Story*, 44-45.
229 "the most powerful boss in America": Shoemaker, *M&M*, 2:379.
229 "a severe, humorless man"; Reddig, *Tom's Town*, 280.
229 "exhuming names of [the] long-deceased": Nagel, *Missouri*, 14.
229 "In one precinct a ballotsmith erased": Ferrell, *Harry S. Truman*, 143.
230 Like his father, Lloyd Stickney Stark was a navy man. He survived the bombing of Pearl Harbor, but was later killed in World War II. *MP*, 14:6.
231 "Every time trains passed:" Ibid.
231 deficiencies in the house: *KCS*, 20 February 1938.
232 "children never knew what it was to run": Giffen, *FL*, 199.
232 plaster "hard as rocks": *KCS*, 20 February 1938.
233 "a slice of private life": Ibid.
233 "every man in his lifetime": Giffen, *FL*, 198-99.
233 pleased with the "remarkably serene results": Ibid., 200.
234-235 A Facelift for the Mansion: *KCS*, 20 February 1938; *JCPT*, 29 June 1937; Giffen, *FL*, 197-98; *JCNT*, 26 December 1937.
236 Stark and FDR: McCullough, *Truman*, 230, 240; Ferrell, *Harry S. Truman*, 150; *Cincinnati Enquirer*, 18 April 1939.
236 First Lady Talk: *KCS*, 20 February 1938.
237 "I'll beat the hell out of him." *JCNT*, 25 June 1939.
237 "The delegates ate them": Ferrell, *Harry S. Truman*, 151.

Forrest Donnell

239 "general and sweeping investigation": *JCPT*, 24 and 26 January 1941; David March, *History*, 1417; *MP*, 16:13-14.
239 "attempt to steal the governorship": Shoemaker, *M&M*, 2:400.
240 An Uncertain Victory: *KCS*, 10 November 1940.
241 "Pinpoint sharp": *Jefferson City Sunday News-Tribune*, 4 May 1941.
242 coming and going "like commuters": Ibid.
242 "Forrest Donnell—the governor down at Jefferson City": Ibid.
242 "He's enthusiastic about everything. . . . If he makes a mistake": Ibid.
242 "Father was a workaholic": Ruth Donnell Rogers, interview with author, Governor's Mansion, 25 May 1994.
242 "Departments were penniless": Shoemaker, *M&M*, 2:407.
243 her business "to welcome all who came to the door": Giffen, *FL*, 204.
243 Hilda and Jefferson City: Rogers interview; *SLPD*, March 4, 1941; Giffen, *FL*, 203-4.
244 "So, we'll have chicken:" *JCPT*, 23 November 1943.
245 "It was discussed [in 1888] when we were here": *Maryville Daily Forum*, 14 June 1943.
245 "Just the bottles, no beer in them": Virginia Henwood Gottleib, interview with author, Governor's Mansion, 20 January 1994.
245 "Mother could remember names": Rogers, interview.
246 "rare deviation from an old. . .custom": *JCPT*, 17 April 1944.
246 "Make me lovely": Rogers, interview.
247 "a needlier of Harry Truman": *SLGD*, 5 March 1980.
247 labeled Democrats "Commiecrats". . . Truman a "red sympathizer": Kirkendall, *A History of Missouri*, 350.

Phil Donnelly

249 Donnelly-Bradshaw campaign: *KCT*, 28 October 1944; *Fulton Sun*, 3 November 1944; *St. Joseph Press*, 8 November 1944; *SLGD*, 18 November 1944.
250 "It may seem strange": "Presenting State's First Lady-elect," Donnelly scrapbook, Phil M. Donnelly Papers, WHMC.
250 "the Gray Ladies do the big, little things for the soldiers": Ibid.
250-51 Donnelly's boyhood: *SLGD*, 18 November 1944.
251 "He has neither an ear or taste for music": "Who Will Reign as Missouri's First Lady," Donnelly scrapbook.
253 The "Second Lady" of the Mansion: *Lebanon Rustic Republican*, 4 May 1945; Giffen, *FL*, 209; *SLPD*, 9 November 1952. Housekeeper Barbara Pohlman's absence from the Mansion spanned all but two months of the Baker administration, all of the Caulfield years, and part of Park's term.

254 "those cows [that] keep me awake": *SLPD* article from Donnelly scrapbook.

254 "Every day some major problem presents itself": *Lebanon Rustic Republican*, 4 May 1945.

254 trouble with cooks: Giffen, *FL*, 209.

255 "in tip-top shape at all times": *Lebanon Rustic Republican*, 4 May 1945.

255-56 postwar entertaining and redecorating: Giffen, *FL*, 212.

258 "piles of rubble and unsightly excavations": Dains, *Show Me*, 1:183.

258 "very private person": Ibid.

258 "Whether or not the small restful spot": Giffen, *FL*, 213.

259 The Mystery of the Mansion Moths: Park and Morrow, *WM*, 303.

259 "Few men have walked to bat": Donnelly scrapbook.

260 the "architectural monstrosity": *KCS*, February 1955 and 9 December 1973.

261 "Anyone who's not in their cells": Roy D. Blunt and Gary R. Kremer, "The 1954 Missouri Prison Riot and the Image of the Highway Patrol," *MHR*, 87 (1992-1993): 302.

Forrest Smith

263 "Sometimes I feel like I'm confined": *Your Governor Reports*, January 4, 1950, Forrest Smith Papers, WHMC.

263 "the most visitin' man in Missouri": *MP* 17:10.

264 "More than anything else": *Your Governor Reports*, 4 January 1950.

264 family visits: Ibid., 2 August 1950, 28 March 1951, 22 August 1951; Giffen, *FL*, 217; Frank Teterus, grandson, interview with author, Governor's Mansion, 23 September 1997.

265 Mansion guests: Giffen, *FL*, 216; *Your Governor Reports*, 3 May 1950, 3 January 1951, 7 November 1951, 2 and 30 January 1952.

267 "just like a hotel": *Jefferson City Capital News*, 7 July 1951.

267 "I thought my diet was going well": *JCPT*, 17 May 1951; Giffen, *FL*, 219.

267-68 Kefauver's national crime commission: Meyer, *Heritage*, 710; *Your Governor Reports*, 4 October 1950; *JCPT*, 21 July 1950, 28 February, 7 March and 31 December 1951.

268 "freer of rackets": *Your Governor Reports*, 4 October 1950.

268 harsh feeling developed: Harry S. Truman letter to Forrest Smith, 25 February 1950, HSTL.

269 "I do not intend to let": *Your Governor Reports*, 19 September 1949.

269 "the most beneficial legislation": Ibid., 12 March 1952.

270 controversy with Blair: *JCPT*, 16 and 17 July 1951, and 1 May 1952.

270 "greatest catastrophe": *Your Governor Reports*, 26 September 1951; *JCPT*, 19 July 1951 and 13 February 1952.

270 "the worst thing I have ever seen": *SLPD*, 18 July 1951; *JCPT*, 7 September 1951.

270 wildest and most destructive raids: *Missouri Fax*, 20 May 1952.

270 "lawless uprising": *JCPT*, 23 May 1952.

271 "I have never had much desire": *JCPT*, 30 January 1952.

271 "If I had spent that much time": Ibid., 29 July 1952.

271 "more money to outfit": *Your Governor Reports*, 10 December 1952.

James Blair

275 Mother Blair: *St. Joseph News-Press*, 11 January 1957; Giffen, *FL*, 228.

276 "a lot cheaper than the uniform": Thomas Hart Benton to James Blair, 23 March 1957, James T. Blair Jr. Papers, WHMC.

276 "There is no incentive": Mildred Hunzinger, St. Louis, to Governor Blair, 17 January 1957, Blair Papers.

277 "Grand Stairway was anything but grand": *SLGD*, 4 January 1970.

277 "this old house is full of spiders": Meyer, *Heritage*, 715.

278 "no further statements": *Moberly Monitor Index*, *18* January 1957.

278 "a rat-infested fire trap": Letter of H. A. Vandercook, Dubuque, Iowa, 18 January 1957, Blair Papers.

278 "national disgrace": *KCS*, 22 May 1957.

278 half-dozen options: Ibid.; Giffen, *FL*, 227.

278 "uncomfortable and sluggish to drive": *Springfield Leader Press*, 29 April 1957.

280 "watch out for the voters": *CMO*, 23 June 1958.

280 "Missouri's number one lobbyist": *St. Joseph News-Press*, 27 February 1958.

281 "I'm not in the business": Blair Papers.

281 "two-footed whirlwind": *St. Joseph News-Press*, 27 February 1958.

281 "chewing furiously": *West Plains Daily Quill*, 6 February 1958.

281 "sitting still for two-an-a-half hours:" *KCT*, 8 January 1958.

282 "shivering in the state Mansion": *KCS*, 25 January 1959.

283 "You will have to make up your minds": *JCPT*, 27 January 1959.

283 "love the old building": *SNL*, undated clipping in Blair papers.

283 tragic accident took their lives: Chillicothe *Tribune*, 12 July 1962; Giffen, *FL*, 234.

283 Missouri Academy of Squires: *MP*, 19:6; Giffen, *FL*, 234; *Official Manual of the State of Missouri, 1993-1994*.

John Dalton

285, 287 "more tranquil pastures:" *St. Joseph Gazette*, 20 April 1963.

286 "Let's go out to eat": *KCS*, 28 January 1962.

286 "I eloped with Johnnie Dalton": *CDT*, 18 May 1962.

287 "Delivering twenty-eight speeches": *KCS*, 21 August 1960.

287 "very much put out with him": *KCS*, 21 August 1960.

287 The term "the Establishment," was not used until four years later when Democratic candidate for governor Warren E. Hearnes coined the phrase. *KCS*, 21 August 1960.

288 "pudgy face" politician with the "half-moon smile": Ibid.

288 "Governor's Secret Weapon," *Rolla Daily News*, 11 January 1961.

289 "This house makes me want to stand tall": *KCS*, 28 January 1962.

289 "Running the Mansion like running any other house": *KCT*, 14 July 1961.

289 "dour-faced" women: Ibid.

290 "a day's eating wasn't complete": Ibid.

290 not enough matching china: *KCS*, 14, 15, and 26 January 1962; *SLPD*, 15 March 1962; *SLGD Sunday Magazine*, 1 April 1962.

291 She "made friends with the old house": *SLGD Sunday Magazine*, 1 April 1962.

292 "Do you mean to tell me": Ibid.

292 The Governor's Kin Folk: *Jefferson City Times*, 15 June 1962.

292 redecorating the Mansion: *SLPD*, 20 October 1961, 20 October 1963, and 29 December 1963.

292 "I'd love to do": *SLPD*, 21 October 1961.

293 "They turned me down flat": *SLPD.*, 28 November 1976.

293 "pouring money down a rat hole": *JCPT*, 31 January 1961.

294 "Mansion has always been a stepchild": *SLPD*, 28 November 1976.

294 "Everyone feels they have to dress up": *KCT*, 7 February 1963.

295 "He does nothing but work": *KCS*, 21 August 1960.

295 Governor's Play Hardball: *KCT*, 14 July 1961.

297 has "a bird being groomed for the show": *JCNT*, 27 November 1963.

298 guests, tours, and constituent requests: Giffen, *FL*, 240-42.

298 "the housewife from Howard's Bluff": Memorandum and Speeches prepared by Tilgham R. Cloud, 29 January 1964, John Dalton Collection, WHMC.

299 "Somehow, the public's business": *St. Joseph Gazette*, 20 April 1963.

299 "Missouri has probably come farther": *MP*, 20.

299 "a controversial governor": *Jefferson City Capital News*, 5 June 1964.

Warren Hearnes

301 "I wanted to be a help": Betty Hearnes, interview with author.

301 "a small, powerful coalition": *JCPT*, 11 January 1965 and 17 February 1972.

301 knight bent on slaying the "dragon": *JCPT*, 11 January 1965.

301 "You can't beat the regular organization": *SLGD*, 13 January 1969.

302 "Are [you] going to allow": *SNL*, 10 December 1972.

302 "Mississippi county lawyer": Ibid.

302 "Betty, how am I": *Artlogue* 15, no. 5 (July-August 1994): 4.

302 "All a candidate's wife needs": *JCPT*, 11 January 1965.

303 "played at top speed": *JCPT*, 11 January 1965; *SLPD*, 1 June 1997.

303 "I made up my mind": *JCPT*, 17 February 1972.

303 "closed hunting grounds": *JCPT*, 11 January 1965.

303 "A secretary of state in Missouri": Ibid.

304 "Daddy, come back": Giffen, *FL*, 245.

304 "$164 gold-and-blue uniforms": *SLPD*, 11 January 1965.

306 pets: *JCPT*, 11 January 1965; *SLGD*, 26 December 1967; *SLGD*, 18 April 1965.

306 Leigh and Julie's school incidents: Giffen, *FL*, 255.

306 new security at mansion: Giffen, *FL*, 254.

307-309 Mansion restoration: *JCPT*, 10 October 1969; *SLGD Sunday Magazine*, 4 January 1970; Betty Hearnes, interview.

310-311 her speechmaking: Betty Hearnes, interview.

311 "I had the Governor": Betty Hearnes, speech to Missouri Mansion Preservation, 29 June 1993.

311 Shotgun Slaughter on the Mansion Lawn: *JCPT*, 22 August and 6 September 1967; Priddy, *Across Our Wide Missouri*, 105-6.

312 "Make the speech": *SLGD*, 25 May 1970.

313 "It looks like Mrs. Hearnes": Ibid.

313 Midwestern Governors' Conference: *SLGD*, 3 September 1967; *JCPT*, 30 August 1967; Giffen, *FL*, 252.

313 met world leaders: Lynn Hearnes, interview with author, June 1995.

314 "It was summer": Betty Hearnes, interview.

314 "to keep pace": *JCNT*, 26 July 1970.

315 Mansion "could never be a home": *SLPD*, 25 December 1972.

315 "I'm thinner": *SLGD*, 16 and 17 December 1972.

316 "the Mansion will be what you make it": *SNL*, 16 December 1985.

316 "You're just a care taker": Betty Hearnes, interview.

316 "custodial care to one of treatment": Ibid., 3 January 1973.
316 "You must fight within": Ibid.
317 attempt to tarnish his image: *SLPD*, 1 June 1997.

Christopher Bond

319 "[The Mansion] belongs to the people": *SLPD*, 31 October 1974.
321 which was the better campaigner: *SLGD*, 16 December 1971.
322 "If I'd been thrown": *Missouri Life*, (January-February 1981), 38.
322 "Poised, articulate, energetic": *SLPD*, 23 September 1972.
322 made the house more functional: *JCDT*, 7 January 1973; *S.NL*, 11 March 1973.
322 "Is this all?": *SDN*, 18 June 1973; *JCDT*, 4 May 1973; *SLPD*, 20 April 1973.
323 "My husband is afraid I'll forget": *CMO*, 20 April 1973.
323 "living over the store": *CDT*, 17 April 1974.
323 "Eastern-educated, mid-thirtyish": Ibid., 6 July 1980.
323 accomplishments: *SLPD*, 3 August 1980; *CMO*, 2 December 1984.
324 much like a "fishbowl": *JCDT*, 7 January and 17 April, 1973.
324 "My horse is better": *SLPD*, 22 April 1973.
324 "never really matched the splendid architecture": *SLPD*, 31 October 1974.
324 "We think something is perfect": Ibid.; *JCDT*, 23 December 1973.
325 "the only Governor's residence in the country": *JCPT*, 9 December 1975.
325 "the governor's Mansion has undergone": *SLGD*, 8 June 1975.
325 "a gracious ante-bellum hostess": *JCDT*, 20 May 1973 and 26 February 1974.
329 "We can be proud": *JCPT*, 15 February 1974.
331 "these dogs are absolutely": *CMO*, 8 September 1974.
331 "one of the brightest stars": *SLPD*, 4 November 1976; *U.S. News and World Report*, 15 November 1976.
331-32 reelection bid: *CMO*, 1 August 1980; *CDT*, 6 July 1980.
333 "better, not bigger government": *JCPT*, 12 January 1981.
333 "He had a lot of guts": *CMO*, 28 December 1984.
333 "more outgoing, informal and friendly": Ibid., 2 May 1982.
334 took a political risk: *CMO*, 2 and 28 December 1984, 13 January 1985.
334 "accomplished almost all the goals": *CMO*, 2 December 1984.
335 "a conservative with a soft spot": *National Journal* quoted in *The Almanac of American Politics 1996* (Washington DC: Baron & Co., 1996).
335 "always tries to form alliances": *SLPD*, 11 May 1997.
335 Ghost Stories: Sgt. James Maxey, capitol security guard, interview with author, Governor's Mansion.

Joseph Teasdale

337 "Handsome enough to be a model": *SLPD*, 20 March 1977.
338 "secluded himself": *SLPD*, 3 December 1976.
338 "reclusive Governor-elect": Ibid., 10 March 1977.
339 How Cold was the Teasdale Inauguration: Mark Nobles, *SDN*, undated clipping; Ibid., 16 January 1977.
339 "I can't think of a regular": *CDT*, 25 December 1977.
341 the birth of Kevin: *SLGD*, 25 September 1978 and 24 July 1979. Forty years before Mrs. Stark had given birth during her husband's term, but the child lived less than a month. The last baby actually born in the Mansion was the grandson of Governor Phelps a hundred years earlier.
342 "more jaded" than any other group: *SLPD*, 1 January 1978; *KCS*, 12 January 1977.
342 everything he did evoked comment: *SLGD*, 5 January 1978; *SLPD*, 10 and 20 March 1977.
343 seldom took "himself very seriously": *CDT*, 25 December 1977 and 9 July 1978.
343 "pressure cooker" atmosphere: *SLPD*, 10 March 1977; *SLGD*, 17 December 1977.
343 seemed "to be totally unimpressed": *CDT*, 9 July 1978.
343 "financial decision, not a political one": *SLGD*, 30 April-1 May 1977.
345 not just one dragon to slay: *SLPD*, 3 December 1976; *KCT*, 11 December 1976.
346 "Missouri's political odd couple": *SLGD*, 29 January 1977.
346 "suffered so many bloody noses": *Hannibal Courier Post*, 6 January 1978.
346 "It's been the hardest year": *SLPD*, 1 January 1978.
346 "going to be a lobbyist": State of the State address, 4 January 1978.

346 answered "questions in his rambling": *SLPD*, 18 December 1977.
346 "genuine concern for the poor": *CDT*, 9 July 1978.
346 "state subsidized campaign gimmicks." *SLPD*, 13 July 1980.
346 low tolerance for uppity events: *SLPD*, 9 and 10 November 1978; *SLGD*, 11 and 13 November 1978 and 29 August 1979.
348 Hancock amendment: Parrish, Jones, and Christensen, *Heart of the Nation*, 386.
348 the Mansion "should be a museum": *SLGD*, 20 September 1979.

John Ashcroft

351 his childhood: Shirley Shedd, "The Shaping of a Governor," *Springfield! Magazine*, (January, February, March, April 1985).
353 "first back-to-back Republican": *CDT*, 10 January 1985.
353 inauguration events: *SLPD*, 15 January 1985.
354 prayer meetings and Bible study: Giffen, *FL*, 279 and 285.
354 "environment of opportunity": *A Working Missouri: The Ashcroft Years, 1985-1993*, 31-32.
355 "Will Rogers of boating": Shedd, "The Shaping of a Governor."
356 "because it's one of the few times:" *SLPD*, 6 January 1985.
356 "I don't plan to get involved": *S.NL*, 16 December 1985.
356 "rather minor" problems: *SLPD*, 6 January 1985.
356 involvement of the governor's wife: Giffen, *FL*, 284-85.
357 "time of economic strain": *SLPD*, 30 June 1991.
357 "He doesn't think government should interfere: *Riverfront Times*, 27 January-2 February 2, 1993; *SLPD*, 22 January 1988.
357 "diligent and dependable": Ibid., 3 March 1990.
357 "a philosophy that allows": Ibid.
357 escalating desegregation payments: *A Working Missouri*.
358 "four-lane highways to all": *SLPD*, 6 August 1992 and 27 May 1991.
359 "entourage of young conservative judges: Ibid., 26 May 1991.
362-363 The Missouri Silver: "The State Presents a Silver Service to the USS Missouri," *MHR* 43 (1948-1949): 270; Francis, *The Universal Exposition of 1904*, (St. Louis: Louisana Purchase Exposition Company, 1913), 388; *KCS*, 30 June 1948.

Mel Carnahan

370 The last use of a horse-drawn carriage to transport the governor along the parade route to the Capitol was during the inauguration of Herbert Hadley in 1909. *JCPT*, 10 January 1949.
376 "Not since the first term of Governor": *SLPD*, 16 May 1996.
382 "We must leave no child behind": Inaugural address, 13 January 1997.
382 eliminate the 3 percent sales tax: *SLPD*, 7 February 1997.
382 legislators unable to deliver budget: *SLPD*, 11 May 1997.

A Look Back

388 "For just three cents:" Duncan and Burns, *Lewis and Clark*, 15.
391 "a few gentleman boarders," Dains and Sadler, *Show Me*, 2:195.
392 dueling "barbarous and impious": *MP*, 1:75.
393 State seal: publications of the Missouri Secretary of State's office.
394 "social and frolicsome set": *JCNT*, 2 January 1949, quoted in "Are Inaugurations for the Officers or Their Wives," 312.
396 enemies that "must be exterminated": McCandless, *A History of Missouri*, 1:110.
397 boundary dispute: Ibid., 114; Hake, *Iowa Inside Out*, 67.
399 "Two of my predecessors": Priddy, 1:362; *Official Manual of the State of Missouri, 1963-1964*, 8.
400 "The Governor's breakfast, his dinner": *MP*, 2:38-39.
400 "If he stands up to his duties": Shoemaker, *M&M*, 2:659.
402 "I would like a good drink": *SLPD*, 21 October 1963.
404 "Except for the Capitol building": "Are Inaugurations for the Officers or Their Wives," 312.
405 "robbed and pillaged at their heart's content": Ibid., 73.
405 "a good governor, except": Priddy, 1:154-56.
406 "You can take her": Giffen, *FL*, 79.
407 "dismal... often invaded by Indians": Ibid., 80.
410 "religious liberty is a political right": Shoemaker, *M&M*, 1:959.
410 "dilapidated in every part": McClurg, final message to General Assembly, January 1869, *MP*, 4.

INDEX

Page numbers in *italics* refer to illustrations.

and deficiencies in Mansion, 230-231; as hostess, 232; birth of child to, 233; major renovation by, 231, *234-235*

Stark, Lloyd, *227, 228, 229, 230, 231, 236*; accomplishments of 233; as nurseryman, 226-227, *228*; campaign for governor by, 228-229; criticisms of, 233, 236; Franklin Roosevelt and, 236; Harry Truman and, 229; home of, *237*; in military, *228*; inauguration of, *230*; post-Mansion years, 237; presidential aspirations of, 236-237; road construction and, 228; Tom Pendergast and, 228-*229*, 231-232; U.S. Senate race of, 237

State Capitol, 1911-fire, *156*; 1853 drawing of, *6*; 1864 view, *58*; in 1890s, *105*; current, *166, 187, 198, 217, 248*; Missouri Confederate, *408*;

Statehouse, *17*

state penitentiary, 13, 23, 46, 53, 65, 126, 138, 154, 166, *261*, 347, 394, 395, 397

Stephens, Lon Vest, *101, 102, 103, 105, 108. 109, 111, 115, 116, 117*, accomplishments of, 117; as cyclist, *108*, 109; campaign for governor by, 103-*104*; early background of, 101-102; eye trouble of, 104, 118; inauguration of, *105*; Spanish-American War and, 109; St. Louis home of, *118*

Stephens, Margaret 'Maggie', *100, 104, 106, 107, 108, 109, 111, 116, 117, 119*; as hostess, 103, 105, 107, 108, 110-112; ban on alcohol by, 111; charges against, 114, 116; death and bequests of, 119; diary of, 101, 114, 116; dress of, 105, 106, 110; education of, 101; Florida home, *119*; Ivy Terrace home of, *102;* treatment of, 111, 116, 118; parties of, *103, 107, 110, 111*, 112; pet dogs of, *106-107*; political campaigning of, 103-104; redecorating of Mansion by, 105-106; remarriage of, *119*

Stewart, Robert M., *404*-405

Stoddard, Amos, *388*

Stone, Sarah 'Lula', *93*; as hostess, 93, 96-97; improvements to Mansion by, 94-95

Stone, William Joel, *90, 91, 98*; accomplishments of, 96-97; appearance of, 92; as businessman, 92; as congressman, 92; as a speaker, 92; as U.S. Senator, 98-99; campaign for governor by, 93; Civil War and, 91; death of, 99; early background, 91; home of, *93;* inauguration of, 93; objection to World War I by, 98-99;

suicide death, of former Governor Morehouse, 73; of Thomas Reynolds, 398; of Thomas C. Reynolds, 408

summer house (gazebo), *23, 167, 206*, 234

T

Teasdale, Joseph, *336-345, 347-349;* 1976-campaign of, 338-339; 1980-campaign of, 349; accomplishments of, 346-347; attitude toward office by, 342-343; background and education of, 338; campaign walk of, *337;* defeat by Bond, 349; inauguration of, *339, 340;* media and, 342-343; post-Mansion years, 349

Teasdale, Theresa, *336, 339, 340, 343, 346-349;* additions to family of, 341, 348; major interests of, 340-341, 348; re-decorating living area by, 344

televised tours of Mansion, *298*, 383

thefts at the Mansion, at Crittenden party, 53-54; of Stephenses' silverware, 107; of Stone's wine cellar, 95

toting privileges, 136

tours of Governor's Mansion, 108, 294, 306, 323-324, 313, 357

Truman, Harry, 229, 237, 246, *247*, 255, 256, 258, 264-265, 268, 283, *285*, 319

Twain, Mark, 89, 97

U

USS Missouri silver, 246, 256, *362-363*

Walker, General Lucius Marshall, 60-61

weddings at the Mansion, Jim Tom Blair, 283; Dunklin's daughter, 395; friends of the Bakers, 194; Lynn Hearnes, 315; Lalla Nelson, *59*, 62; Henrietta Park, 223, *224, 225;* Cornelia Shannon, 24

Wilkinson, Ann Biddle, *388*

Wilkinson, James, *388*

Williams, Abraham J., *73, 392*

Wilson, Frances E., 212

Wilson, Woodrow, 142

Wofford, Ted, mansion architect, 324, 385

women's suffrage movement, 42, 114, 176, *182*, 411

Woodson, Silas, *19*; accomplishments of, 23-24; early background of, 19-20; inauguration of, 20-21

Woodson, Virginia, *19, 21*; as hostess, 21-23; live-in relatives of, *21, 24*

World War I, 98-99; 173-175

World War II, 238, 243-244